# BRIEF CONTENTS

D0163625

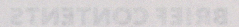

# BRIEF CONTENTS

Preface xvii

18e

# CONTEMPORARY MARKETING

## Boone & Kurtz

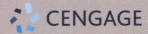

CENGAGE

Australia • Brazil • Canada • Mexico • Singapore • United Kingdom • United States

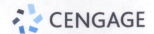

**Contemporary Marketing, 18th Edition**

Senior Vice President, Higher Ed Product, Content, and Market Development: Erin Joyner

Vice President, B&E, 4-LTR, and Support Programs: Mike Schenk

Product Director: Bryan Gambrel

Product Manager: Heather Mooney

Content Manager: John Rich

Content Developer: Megan Guiliani

Product Assistant: Tawny Schaad

Content Project Manager: D. Jean Buttrom

Digital Delivery Lead: David O'Connor

Marketing Coordinator: Audrey Jacobs

Production Service/Composition: SPi Global

Sr. Art Director: Bethany Bourgeois

Cover and Text Designer: Liz Harasymczuk/Liz Harasymczuk Design

Cover Image: cigdem/Shutterstock.com

Intellectual Property

    Analyst: Diane Garrity

    Project Manager: Sarah Shainwald

For product information and technology assistance, contact us at **Cengage Customer & Sales Support, 1-800-354-9706**

For permission to use material from this text or product, submit all requests online at **www.cengage.com/permissions**
Further permissions questions can be emailed to **permissionrequest@cengage.com**

Library of Congress Control Number: 2017960520

ISBN: 978-1-337-38689-0

**Cengage**
200 Pier 4 Boulevard
Boston, MA 02210
USA

Cengage is a leading provider of customized learning solutions with employees residing in nearly 40 different countries and sales in more than 125 countries around the world. Find your local representative at **www.cengage.com/global**

To learn more about Cengage platforms and services, register or access your online learning solution, or purchase materials for your course, visit **www.cengage.com**.

Printed at CLDPC, USA, 05-21

# CONTENTS

# PART 1
## DESIGNING CUSTOMER-ORIENTED MARKETING STRATEGIES

**CHAPTER 4    E-BUSINESS: MANAGING THE CUSTOMER
EXPERIENCE** 64

**CHAPTER 5    SOCIAL MEDIA: LIVING IN THE CONNECTED
WORLD** 86

# PART 2
## UNDERSTANDING BUYERS AND MARKETS

# PART 3
## TARGET MARKET SELECTION

# PART 4
## PRODUCT DECISIONS

CHAPTER **12**    **DEVELOPING AND MANAGING PRODUCTS** 242

# PART 5
## PRICING DECISIONS

CHAPTER **13**    **PRICING CONCEPTS** 266

**CHAPTER 14**  **PRICING STRATEGIES** 287

# PART 6
## DISTRIBUTION DECISIONS

# PART 7
## PROMOTIONAL DECISIONS

# PREFACE

# THE *CONTEMPORARY MARKETING* RESOURCE PACKAGE

Since the first edition of this book was published, *Contemporary Marketing* has continued improving on its mission of equipping students and instructors with the most comprehensive collection of learning tools, teaching materials, and innovative resources available. The upgraded 18th edition represents a new industry benchmark by delivering the most practical, technologically advanced, user-friendly resource package on the market.

## UPGRADES TO THIS EDITION

The 18th edition of *Contemporary Marketing* is more than an incremental update. It's a full-fledged reimagining of what an introduction to marketing course can be. Based on extensive industry research, student feedback, and collaboration with marketing subject matter experts nationwide, we made a number of improvements, including:

### Focus on application-based learning

Our goal is for students to "learn it today and use it tomorrow." Content is focused on practical, real-world skills that marketing professionals use on a regular basis.

### Streamlined narrative

The focus for this edition is on depth, not breadth. Rather than introduce an overly broad array of topics, we utilized industry research to choose the most relevant and current concepts—then we deep dive on those to provide students a thorough understanding of each. The result is that students learn more in less time.

### Opening and closing examples

Each section features opening and closing examples that tie directly to the learning objective and demonstrate the concepts in action. This format increases comprehension and retention of the core content.

### Chapter-ending activity

Each chapter ends with a short activity that reinforces specific learning from the chapter, further reinforcing comprehension and retention.

### Updated examples and content presentation

Examples throughout the text have been researched and refreshed to reflect current trends in marketing and business. In addition, content order was revised to better align with best practices in both the marketing field and the marketing classroom.

**MindTap integration**

This edition was created to lead with the digital product using the industry lead-ing MindTap technology platform to deliver a meaningful and effective learning experience.

## MINDTAP

MindTap is a personalized teaching experience with relevant assignments that guide students to analyze, apply, and improve thinking, allowing you to measure skills and outcomes with ease.

- *Personalize Teaching*: The content becomes yours with a Learning Path built to support your key student objectives. Control what students see and when they see it. Use it "as is" or match to your syllabus exactly—hide, rearrange, add, and create your own content.

- *Guide Students*: A unique Learning Path of relevant readings, multimedia, and activities that move students up the learning taxonomy from basic knowledge and comprehension to analysis and application.

- *Promote Better Outcomes*: Empowers instructors and motivate students with analytics and reports that provide a snapshot of class progress, time in course, engagement, and completion rates.

By combining readings, multimedia, activities, and assessments into a singular Learning Path, MindTap guides students through their course with ease and engagement. Instructors personalize the Learning Path by customizing Cengage Learning resources and adding their own content via apps that integrate into the MindTap framework seamlessly. *Contemporary Marketing* students can also find Basic PowerPoints, quizzes, animated videos, homework, and more.

## CERTIFIED TEST BANK POWERED BY COGNERO

Containing more than 2,500 questions, this Test Bank has been thoroughly ver-ified to ensure accuracy. The Test Bank includes true/false, multiple-choice, essay, and matching questions. Each question in the Test Bank is labeled with text objective, level of difficulty, and A-heads. Each question is also tagged to Interdisciplinary Learning Outcomes, Marketing Disciplinary Learning Out-comes, and Bloom's Taxonomy. The Test Bank is available via Cognero, can be loaded to your SSO account, or PDFs can be found on the product support website.

Cengage Learning Testing Powered by Cognero is a flexible, online system that allows you to:

- author, edit, and manage test bank content from multiple Cengage Learning solutions

- create multiple test versions in an instant

- deliver tests from your LMS, your classroom, or wherever you want

**Start Right Away!**

Cengage Learning Testing Powered by Cognero works on any operating system or browser.

- No special installs or downloads needed
- Create tests from school, home, the coffee shop—anywhere you have Internet access

**What Will You Find?**

- Simplicity at every step. A simple interface features drop-down menus and familiar, intuitive tools that take you through content creation and management with ease.

- Full-featured test generator. Create ideal assessments with your choice of 15 question types (including true/false, multiple choice, opinion scale/likert, and essay). Multi-language support, an equation editor, and unlimited metadata help ensure your tests are complete and compliant.

- Cross-platform capability. Import and export content into other systems.

## *CONTEMPORARY MARKETING*, 18TH EDITION WEBSITE

Our text website is filled with a whole set of useful tools. Instructors will find all the key instructor resources in electronic format: Test Bank, PowerPoint collections, and Instructor's Manual. To access these additional course materials and companion resources, please visit **www.cengagebrain.com**.

## IN CONCLUSION

We would like to thank Jeff Perlot (Green River College) for his contagious energy, innovation, and leadership of the great team of contributors involved in this re-invention: Amy Handlin (Monmouth University), Jill Attaway (Professor Emeritus at Illinois State University), R.J. Amador (Green River College), and Stephanie Hall (Cengage Learning). We are grateful to this team for their collective knowledge and creativity. Thank you to all contributors who have helped produce another *Contemporary Marketing* winner.

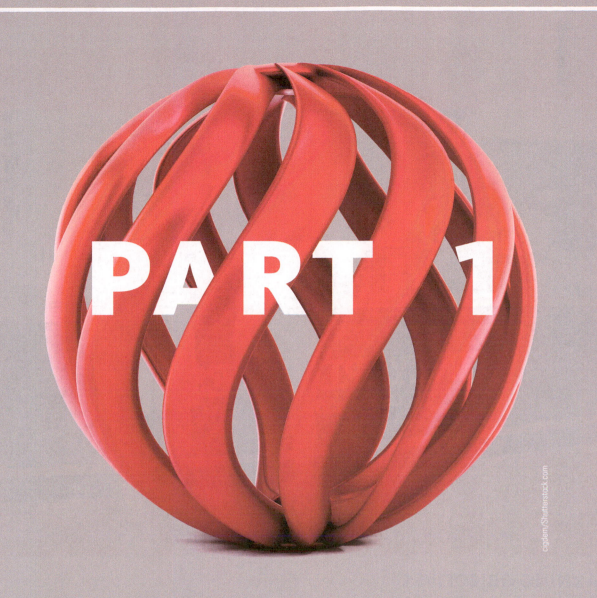

# PART 1

## DESIGNING CUSTOMER-ORIENTED MARKETING STRATEGIES

cigdem/Shutterstock.com

# 1 MARKETING: THE ART AND SCIENCE OF SATISFYING CUSTOMERS

Source: Digital Trends

## LEARNING OBJECTIVES

**1.1** Summarize how marketing creates value through the four types of utility.

**1.2** Describe the four variables of the marketing mix.

**1.3** Contrast the focus of marketing activities during the five eras of marketing history.

**1.4** Explain how relationship marketing can move customers up the loyalty ladder.

**1.5** Differentiate the six categories of marketing.

**1.6** Identify the eight functions of marketing physical goods.

**1.7** Given a description of a company's marketing mix, classify the elements of the marketing mix and the category of marketing.

# LEARN IT TODAY . . . USE IT TOMORROW

nspiration came to brothers Shep and Ian Murray, then in their 20s, when they started meeting for lunch and complaining about their desk jobs and the business attire that went with them. They decided to go into business for themselves and settled on a product they knew nothing about: neckties. If they sold enough ties, they reasoned, they could stop wearing them.

Today, more than 15 years later, Connecticut-based Vineyard Vines has grown into a multimillion-dollar business. Those familiar with the firm's success credit the Murrays' understanding of their customers' needs and their determination to make customers happy. The brothers say they're interested in dressing people not merely to go to work but rather to "take some fun to work." Their company sells clothes, but also a carefree lifestyle image many people want to adopt.

For instance, one of Shep and Ian's first decisions, when they quit their jobs and began selling ties out of their cars, was to create whimsical designs that reflected the happy summers they spent on Martha's Vineyard while growing up. Thus was born the sporty vacation theme that runs through all their bright pastel designs, featuring lobster pots, sailboats, whales, crabs, and sports paraphernalia such as tennis racquets, golf balls, and hockey sticks. Customers who would rather be sailing, swimming, golfing, or fishing are quickly drawn to the light-hearted images and the lifestyle they conjure up.

The story of Vineyard Vines reflects several foundations of contemporary marketing. Can you see how they bring the four types of utility (and value) to customers? Can you see how they utilize the four variables of the marketing mix? And can you see how their approach reflects a modern version of marketing, one that didn't always exist in past eras? If not, you'll learn all about these things in this chapter.

# 1-1  WHAT IS MARKETING?

## OPENING EXAMPLE

In 2015, Pepsi beat out Diet Coke to become the second most popular soda in the United States. While Coke remained the overall market leader, Pepsi's accomplishment startled a soda world that had believed Coca-Cola's diet beverage was invulnerable in the number-two spot. Pepsi's taste and fizz hadn't changed, and the price was the same as Diet Coke. So how did Pepsi do it? And what can this victory in the soda wars teach us about marketing?

**LO 1.1** Summarize how marketing creates value through the four types of utility.

### 1-1a
### LEARNING IT: WHAT IS MARKETING?

The goal of marketing any good or service is to boost what marketers call **utility**—the power of a good or service to satisfy the wants of consumers. The four basic kinds of utility are form, time, place, and ownership (see Exhibit 1.1).

Form utility is created when the company converts raw materials into finished goods and services. Soda makers mix just the right amounts of flavoring, sweeteners, and carbonation to deliver appealing drinks. With a ship and the ocean, a captain and staff, food and entertainment, Royal Caribbean creates a cruise. Whenever a company produces a good or service, they are offering form utility to consumers.

**utility** the power of a good or service to satisfy the wants of consumers

3

**EXHIBIT 1.1**   Four Types of Utility

| Type | Description | Examples | How this brings value |
|---|---|---|---|
| Form | Conversion of raw materials into finished goods and services | Dinner at Applebee's<br>Samsung Galaxy phone<br>Levi jeans | Satisfies hunger<br>Allows for easier communication<br>Provides clothing |
| Time | Availability of goods and services when consumers want them | Dental appointment<br>Digital photographs<br>1-800-PetMeds guarantee<br>UPS Next Day Air delivery | Allows customers to satisfy their wants and needs without waiting |
| Place | Availability of goods and services at convenient locations | Technicians available at an auto repair facility<br>Onsite day care<br>Banks in grocery stores | Provides convenience<br>Allows customers to satisfy their needs and wants without continued searching |
| Ownership (possession) | Ability to transfer title to products from marketer to buyer | Retail sales (in exchange for currency, credit, or debit card payment) | Allows customer control over their purchase<br>Provides pride of ownership |

**marketing** is the process for creating, communicating, and delivering value to customers

PepsiCo's interactive vending machine allows you to "like" their Facebook page and receive a free sample of Pepsi products.

Time and place utility occur when consumers find goods and services available *when* and *where* they want to purchase them. Redbox takes advantage of time and place utility by positioning its kiosks for renting movies and games in high-traffic spots like supermarkets and drugstores.

The transfer of title to goods or services at the time of purchase creates ownership utility. When you buy a TV and take it home, or when you buy an airline ticket and fly on a plane, you receive the value that comes from taking ownership of that good or service. This might seem obvious, but ownership utility helps to drive the emotional connection you feel with a product, which can highly influence your purchasing decisions.

Designing and marketing products that satisfy the wants and needs of consumers is the foundation for marketing. By providing these different types of utility to customers, marketers provide value. In fact, the very definition of **marketing** is the process for creating, communicating, and delivering value to customers. Ultimately, it's that value customers are paying for, whether it's a product that performs a particular function or one that provides customers a particular feeling.

## 1-1b
## CLOSING EXAMPLE

So how did Pepsi beat Diet Coke? As we've said, the product's form utility – the taste and fizz of the soda itself – never changed. Pepsi must have brought value to customers in other ways. One successful tactic was that Pepsi won fans with its innovative "Like Machines." Consumers who "liked" the PepsiCo Facebook page, either on their smartphones or on the vending machine's touch screen, received a free can of soda on the spot. This created time and place utility for the customer, while also creating word-of-mouth advertising and social media buzz. The brand also used a new advertising campaign, "Taste Life Differently," to build an emotional connection with drinkers. Remember that this emotional connection is what gives ownership utility value. Pepsi's overall approach enhanced time, place, and ownership utilities for customers, which in turn enhanced the emotional appeal and value of buying the product.

# 1-2 ELEMENTS OF MARKETING STRATEGY

## OPENING EXAMPLE

Did you know that Starbucks began as just one little store in Seattle? Today, Starbucks coffeehouses are familiar neighborhood features across America's cities and towns—as well as in airports, on highways, maybe even on your campus. In fact, the company boasts 24,000 outlets in 70 countries.

Back in Seattle, company CEO Howard Schultz sourced the world's highest-quality coffee beans to create a unique product. But developing a great beverage was just the beginning. What other marketing strategies did Schultz use to build his powerhouse brand?

**LO 1.2** Describe the four variables of the marketing mix.

### 1-2a

## LEARNING IT: ELEMENTS OF MARKETING STRATEGY

The basic elements of a marketing strategy consist of:

1. The target market.
2. The marketing mix variables of product, price, distribution, and promotion that combine to satisfy the needs of the target market.

A customer-driven organization begins its overall strategy with a detailed description of its **target market**- the group of people toward whom the firm aims its marketing efforts and ultimately its merchandise. Howard Schultz identified a target audience eager to purchase specialty coffee: relatively high-income professional men and women, living in urban or affluent suburban areas, who not only appreciated a quality beverage but also favored socially responsible, environmentally friendly businesses.[1] Some companies exclusively target household consumers; for example, Kraft Foods (now called Mondelez International) is the maker of Oreo cookies and JELL-O. Other companies, such as aircraft manufacturer Boeing, market their products primarily to business buyers like Delta Airlines and government purchasers. Still other firms provide goods and services to retailers and wholesalers. In every instance, however, marketers pinpoint their target markets as accurately as possible.

**target market** the group of people toward whom the firm aims its marketing efforts and ultimately its merchandise

### 1-2b

## MARKETING MIX VARIABLES

After marketers select a target market, they direct their company's activities toward profitably satisfying that segment. Marketing strategies are built around four variables: product, price, distribution, and promotion, as shown

**EXHIBIT 1.2**

## Four Variables of the Marketing Mix

**marketing mix** product, price, distribution, and promotion

**product** refers to a good, service, or idea

**Marketing Mix Variables**

Product

Distribution

Price

Promotion

**Target Market**

in Exhibit 1.2. Together, these variables are called the **marketing mix**. The four variables of the marketing mix are often called the 4 P's of marketing: product, price, place, and promotion. Let's look at each of the four in detail.

## PRODUCT

Fundamentally, **product** refers to a good, service, or idea. But "product" is a broader concept that also encompasses other aspects of the consumer's purchase. Product strategy may involve decisions about:

- customer service
- package design
- brand names
- trademarks, patents, and warranties

Starbucks believes in superior customer service; its "baristas" are specially trained to create a personalized buying experience. The company also pursues continuous product innovation; in addition to its popular line of espresso drinks, coffee connoisseurs will soon be able to choose from specially roasted Reserve coffees they can buy from a scoop bar.[2]

Procter and Gamble, maker of Tide laundry detergent, boosted the brand's sales when it introduced Tide Pods, an innovative single-use package that combined detergent, stain remover, and brightener.[3]

Starbucks' product encompasses not just their various drinks and food choices, but their friendly baristas, their brand name, and the design of their stores.

Sorbis/Shutterstock.com

## PRICE

**Price strategy** is the method of setting profitable and justifiable prices. One of the many factors that influence a marketer's pricing strategy is competition. While Starbucks has always charged premium prices, the company moderated its price increases after Dunkin' Donuts and McDonald's introduced cheaper brands of specialty coffee.[4] In addition to offering discounts to loyal customers who use its mobile payment app, some new Starbucks stores will also offer Reserve products at a lower price.[5]

Sometimes conditions in the external marketing environment cause difficulties in pricing strategies. Political unrest overseas, the soaring price of fuel, or a freeze that destroys crops could all affect the price of goods and services. For instance, Hershey's may need to increase the price of its popular Kisses chocolate candy if cocoa farmers have a poor harvest.

If the economy is booming, consumers generally have more confidence and are willing to shop more frequently and pay more for goods. But when the economy slows, consumers look for bargains—they want high quality at low prices. It is a challenge for marketers to strike the right balance to make enough profits to survive and grow. Currently, sales at luxury retailers such as Saks and Abercrombie & Fitch are down. But sales at local dollar stores and larger discount retailers are stronger—sometimes even luring shoppers away from traditional giants such as Target and Walmart.[6]

## DISTRIBUTION (ALSO CALLED "PLACE")

Marketers develop distribution strategies to ensure that consumers find their products in the proper quantities at the right times and places. Starbucks is building an increased number of drive-through and express stores. It also distributes bottled drinks and K-cups through grocery outlets.

**Distribution** decisions involve modes of transportation, warehousing, inventory control, order processing, and selection of marketing channels. Marketing channels are made up of institutions such as retailers and wholesalers—intermediaries that may be involved in a product's movement from producer to final consumer.

Technology continually opens new channels of distribution in many industries. For example, Amazon is experimenting with home delivery via drones.[7]

## PROMOTION

**Promotion** is broadly defined as communication to a firm's buyers about their products. Organizations use various methods for sending messages about their goods, services, and ideas. They may communicate directly through salespeople or indirectly through advertisements.

Sales promotion is a promotional tactic that entails offering incentives like a reduced price for a limited time, or a brand-consistent giveaway. During a recent promotion to celebrate National Coffee Day, Starbucks, Dunkin' Donuts, and other retailers offered free cups of coffee and deep discounts on packaged

---

**price strategy** is the method of setting profitable and justifiable prices

**distribution** decision involving modes of transportation, warehousing, inventory control, order processing, and selection of marketing channels

**promotion** is broadly defined as communication to a firm's buyers about their products

coffee and K-cups.[8] McDonald's has long utilized Happy Meals—which combine small food portions with a toy—as a promotion targeted to parents with young children.

In developing a promotional strategy, marketers blend the various elements of promotion to communicate most effectively with their target market. Many companies use an approach called integrated marketing communications (IMC) to coordinate all promotional activities so that the consumer receives a unified and consistent message. Consumers might see advertisements, receive e-mail updates, discount coupons, and any number of other types of marketing communications—all featuring the same theme and recognizable visual elements. Starbucks' famous green-and-white mermaid logo appears in its stores and ads and on all its cups, packages, loyalty rewards cards, and digital apps.

## 1-2c
## CLOSING EXAMPLE

Starbucks has come a long way from that little Seattle store. The company makes innovative use of the marketing mix to bring to life its company values, including:

- Building a culture of warmth and belonging, which effectively becomes part of their "product."
- Providing products at a variety of price points, high and low.
- Aggressively expanding worldwide so that more people have access to their products. This is an example of distribution, or "place".
- Utilizing public relations and a variety of other promotional tactics to maintain their position as one of the most valued brands in the world.

# FIVE ERAS OF MARKETING HISTORY

**LO 1.3** Contrast the focus of marketing activities during the five eras of marketing history.

## OPENING EXAMPLE

When Sue Kenworth took over her family's long-established bakery chain, Kenworth Bread and Cake (Kenworth B&C), she was open to advice from the previous CEOs—her father and grandfather. But when it came to marketing decisions, she felt like the three of them spoke different languages. Her grandfather kept urging her to hire more salespeople and run more ads. Her father questioned her emphasis on building long-term relationships. Then Sue remembered what her college marketing textbook said: the role of marketing in business has changed over time. By refreshing her memory about the five eras of marketing history, she was able to understand where her father and grandfather were coming from. At a family meeting, she explained why her path was the right one for the company's future. What did she say?

## 1-3a

# LEARNING IT: FIVE ERAS OF MARKETING HISTORY

Marketing has been viewed and practiced differently over the decades. Exhibit 1.3 identifies five eras in the history of marketing: (1) the production era, (2) the sales era, (3) the marketing era, (4) the relationship era, and (5) the social era.

## THE PRODUCTION ERA

When Sue's great-grandfather founded Kenworth B&C in 1924, he believed that high-quality baked goods would sell themselves. He developed mixing and baking techniques that turned out product faster than anyone else. With little competition and strong demand by customers tired of baking at home, Kenworth was an immediate success. Before 1925, most firms shared this **production orientation**- manufacturers stressed production of quality products and then looked for people to purchase them.

    The production era reached its peak during the early part of the twentieth century, when production shortages and intense consumer demand ruled the day. Henry Ford's mass-production line exemplified this orientation. Ford's famous statement, "They [customers] can have any color they want, as long as it's black," reflected the prevalent attitude toward marketing.

**production orientation** manufacturers stressed production of quality products and then looked for people to purchase them

## THE SALES ERA

Sue's grandfather faced new challenges when he joined the firm in the 1940s. Many competitors now baked bread and cakes as fast as Kenworth, so rapid production no longer guaranteed profitability. He hired salesmen to visit stores and restaurants—even to knock on doors in nearby communities. He also put up billboards and ran ads in the local newspapers. Like Sue's grandfather, many businesspeople from the 1920s into the early 1950s realized that increasingly sophisticated production techniques had led to more output than the market

**EXHIBIT 1.3**    Five Eras of Marketing History

| ERA | Production | Sales | Marketing | Relationship | Social |
|---|---|---|---|---|---|
| PREVAILING ATTITUDE | "A good product will sell itself." | "Creative advertising and selling will overcome consumers' resistance and persuade them to buy." | "The consumer rules! Find a need and fill it." | "Long-term relationships with customers and other partners lead to success." | "Connecting to consumers via Internet and social media sites is an effective tool." |
|  |  |  |  |  |  |
| APPROXIMATE TIME PERIOD | Prior to 1920s | Prior to 1950s | Since 1950s | Since 1990s | Since 2000s |

**sales orientation** a belief that creative advertising and personal selling will persuade consumers to buy

**seller's market** when there are more buyers for fewer products

**buyer's market** when there are more products than people willing to buy them

**consumer orientation** where the focus is on satisfying the needs and wants of consumers rather than simply producing and selling products

could readily absorb. During this more competitive era, companies adopted a **sales orientation**, a belief that creative advertising and personal selling will persuade consumers to buy.

## THE MARKETING ERA

By the time Sue's father began working for Kenworth in 1955, what was once a **seller's market** for baked goods (more buyers for fewer products) had become a **buyer's market** (more products than people willing to buy them). He had to assess the needs and wants of Kenworth's customers in order to satisfy them—finding, for example, that restaurant buyers would increase their purchases if offered single-serving rolls, which minimized waste, instead of large loaves.

The marketing concept had emerged. This meant that companies needed a **consumer orientation**- where the focus is on satisfying the needs and wants of consumers rather than simply producing and selling products . From now on, marketers would play a lead role in product planning because they had knowledge of consumer needs. Marketing and selling would no longer be regarded as a supplemental activity performed after the production process.

Today's fully developed marketing concept is a companywide consumer orientation with the objective of achieving long-term success. All facets—and all levels, from top to bottom—of the organization must contribute first to assessing and then to satisfying customer wants and needs. From marketing manager to accountant to product designer, every employee plays a role in reaching potential customers.

Companies that implement market-driven strategies are better able to understand their customers' experiences, buying habits, and needs. In talking with many restaurateurs, Sue's father learned that they worried about diners filling up on rolls and cutting back on profitable meal orders. When Kenworth introduced its line of "Lite Rolls," which were attractive and tasty but didn't make people feel full, business boomed.

## THE RELATIONSHIP ERA

Sue joined the family firm during the 1990s. Unlike her older relatives, she focused her work from the start on establishing and maintaining relationships with both buyers and vendors. For example, she developed a Kenworth newsletter and a "Baking Tips" mailer. She also created a rewards program offering discounts to repeat customers and to the stores that consistently stocked Kenworth goods.

Relationship marketing builds on the marketing era's customer orientation by developing long-term, value-added relationships over time with customers and suppliers. Like other modern marketers, Sue realized that, although it's important to attract new customers, it's even more important to encourage current customers and other partners to keep coming back. For instance, when a popular retail store always carries the Kenworth brand, consumers benefit because they know where to find their favorite Kenworth products; the retailer benefits from ongoing store traffic; and Kenworth benefits from reliable sales.

## THE SOCIAL ERA

Building on the relationship era, marketers now routinely use the Internet and social networking sites to connect with consumers. At Sue's urging, Kenworth developed an interactive website that invites visitors to take a virtual tour of the baking plant, ask questions, and share stories about how Kenworth products enhance their lives.

### 1-3b
### CLOSING EXAMPLE

Sue began the family meeting by reminding her father and grandfather about Henry Ford's experience: "Even the most innovative, highest-quality product will fail unless people understand its benefits and believe it will fill their needs!" she said. "I respect all that Kenworth accomplished in the past. But we have more competition than ever. Now, it's our relationships with loyal customers that will encourage them to trust us for quality goods, look to us for new products, and tell others why our brand is best. I'm proud to use this modern marketing philosophy to carry on our company's tradition of value and integrity!"

# 1-4 FROM TRANSACTION-BASED MARKETING TO RELATIONSHIP MARKETING

### OPENING EXAMPLE

In the past, the Weather Channel (TWC) simply delivered content whenever a viewer tuned in on TV. There was no effort to reach out to customers, anticipate their needs, or keep them coming back for more and better experiences. But as websites and apps emerged, which could also give people weather information, the cable channel needed new ways to be relevant. TWC began to replace its traditional view of marketing as a simple exchange process, or **transaction-based marketing**, with a different, longer-term approach that emphasized building relationships with one customer at a time. But how do you build stable relationships based on ever-changing weather forecasts?

**LO 1.4** Explain how relationship marketing can move customers up the loyalty ladder.

**transaction-based marketing** traditional view of marketing as a simple exchange process

### 1-4a
### LEARNING IT: FROM TRANSACTION-BASED MARKETING TO RELATIONSHIP MARKETING

Traditional marketing strategies focused on attracting customers and closing deals. Today's marketers realize that attracting new customers is no longer enough. It's even more important to establish and maintain satisfying relationships that turn one-time buyers into loyal repeat customers. Over the long term, this relationship may be translated to the lifetime value of a customer—the total revenues a customer brings to an organization, minus the investment the firm has made to attract and keep the customer.

**relationship marketing** refers to the development, growth, and maintenance of long-term, cost-effective relationships with individual customers, suppliers, employees, and other partners for mutual benefit

As defined earlier in this chapter, **relationship marketing** refers to the development, growth, and maintenance of long-term, cost-effective relationships with individual customers, suppliers, employees, and other partners for mutual benefit.

Relationship marketing gives a company new opportunities to gain a competitive edge by moving customers up a loyalty ladder—from new customers to regular purchasers, then to loyal supporters of the firm and its goods and services, and finally to advocates who not only buy its products but also recommend them to others (see Exhibit 1.4).

Relationship building begins early in marketing. It starts with determining what customers need and want, then developing high-quality products to meet those needs. This is how companies can generate new customers in the first place. But relationship building continues with excellent customer service during and after purchase. It also includes programs that encourage repeat purchases and foster customer loyalty.

Relationship marketing can be enhanced by today's technology, which enables marketers and their customers to continually stay in touch via social media, e-mail, voicemail, and other tools. It's not a one-way street: consumers may also initiate relationships after accessing positive information about brands and companies. Uses of technology in relationship marketing include:

**mobile marketing** marketing messages sent to wireless devices, such as phones and tablets

**Mobile marketing**- marketing messages sent to wireless devices, such as phones and tablets. An example is e-mail marketing, which can be used to answer frequently asked customer questions or encourage repeat purchase. Another example is apps that customers download to their phones. By providing interactivity, information, and personalization, these apps can encourage customer loyalty.

**social marketing** the use of online social media as a communications channel for marketing messages

**Social marketing**- the use of online social media as a communications channel for marketing messages. Social media platforms include Facebook, Twitter, and Pinterest. Social media platforms allow marketers to educate customers, answer questions, and gather feedback that can be used for product development or customer service. It also provides a platform for brand advocates, loyal and enthusiastic followers of a brand, to publicize their experiences with the brand.

One small business making good use of social marketing is Lolly Wolly Doodle, a children's clothing company in Lexington, North Carolina. Founder Brandi Temple started making clothes for her young daughters and realized she made more outfits than her two girls could possibly wear; so she sold the extra outfits on eBay. When her husband lost his job, they decided to move their small retail sales operation from eBay to Facebook, where they currently have almost 1.5 million likes. Temple says the company's followers have provided instant feedback about certain types of clothing and have become unofficial salespeople, posting pictures of their children wearing the company's attractive outfits.[9]

The Ford Motor Company uses social media extensively to engage with the public around the globe. The company has created *FordSocial*, which serves as a social hub for consumers, fans, and others to gather information, interact with

**EXHIBIT 1.4**

**Converting New Customers to Advocates**

Source: © 2014 Ford Motor Company

The Ford Motor Company uses social media to engage and interact with consumers.

others, share their questions and stories, and provide feedback and suggestions to the company about its various brands. Ford also hosts separate Facebook and Twitter sites in countries around the world. Its Facebook page has almost 8 million likes.[10]

When companies can convert indifferent customers into loyal ones, they generate repeat sales. The cost of maintaining existing customers is far below the cost of finding new ones, making these loyal customers extra valuable and the investment in relationship marketing worth it. Some of the best repeat customers are those who are also willing to spread the word about the product—create a buzz—among other potential purchasers, a concept known as "buzz marketing."

## 1-4b

## CLOSING EXAMPLE

As a result of its relationship marketing efforts, the Weather Channel transformed its business. The brand created a mobile app that hosts interactive conversations among users, a Twitter partnership offering real-time tweets and other customer-created content on TV, a website highlighting conditions and forecasts for 100,000 locations worldwide, a radio network with 700 affiliates, and more. It was once a cable channel that viewers watched mostly during weather disasters, but now it's a company that forecasts consumer behavior by analyzing when, where, and how often consumers check the weather. It provides people with information tailored to where they live, what they want to know, and which medium they prefer (TV, radio, mobile). Its new name, The Weather Company, reflects this change and its commitment to serve customers interactively as a lifestyle partner and a trusted friend.[11]

# 1-5   CATEGORIES OF MARKETING

**LO 1.5**   Differentiate the six categories of marketing.

**product marketing** involves efforts designed to communicate the benefits of a good or service

**person marketing** efforts designed to cultivate the attention and preference of a target market toward a person

**place marketing** efforts designed to attract visitors to a particular area; improve consumer images of a city, state, or nation; and/or attract new business

## OPENING EXAMPLE

President Barack Obama's 2012 reelection campaign broke ground in its use of promotion vehicles and relationship marketing. Instead of the TV commercials heavily relied on by past presidential candidates, Obama's team built multiple websites that gathered extensive personal data about people who contacted the campaign. This data enabled strategists to reach out to individuals one at a time, recruiting thousands of them as social media advocates who spread online buzz about Obama among their own friends and networks.[12]

Obviously, the goal of the Obama campaign wasn't to sell goods or services; it was to build support for a person. How does this approach relate to the type of marketing you know best—marketing of products?

### 1-5a
## LEARNING IT: CATEGORIES OF MARKETING

**Product marketing** involves efforts designed to communicate the benefits of a good or service. As you've learned, for-profit organizations have long used the four marketing mix variables—product, price, distribution, and promotion—to persuade target consumers to buy and to build long-term relationships.

While product marketing is the most well-known and widely used form of marketing, there are actually six categories of marketing (see Exhibit 1.5). In many cases, broader appeals focus on causes, events, individuals, organizations, and places.

**EXHIBIT 1.5**   Six Categories of Marketing

| Type | Objectives | Examples |
|---|---|---|
| **Product Marketing** | Marketing efforts designed to communicate the benefits of good or service and persuade target consumers to buy | Subaru: "Love. It's what makes a Subaru a Subaru." Geico: "15 minutes will save you 15% on car insurance." Nike: "Just do it." |
| **Person Marketing** | Marketing efforts designed to cultivate the attention and preference of a target market toward a person | Athlete Peyton Manning Denver Broncos quarterback Celebrity Blake Shelton, country singer |
| **Place Marketing** | Marketing efforts designed to attract visitors to a particular area; improve consumer images of a city, state, or nation; and/or attract new business | California: "Find Yourself Here." Tennessee: "We're Playing Your Song." West Virginia: "Wild and Wonderful." |
| **Cause Marketing** | Identification and marketing of a social issue, cause, or idea to selected target markets | "Click it or Ticket." "Refill, not landfill." |
| **Event Marketing** | Marketing of sporting, cultural, and charitable activities to selected target markets | Tokyo 2020 Summer Olympics American Diabetes Association's Tour de Cure |
| **Organization Marketing** | Marketing efforts of mutual-benefit organizations, service organizations, and government organizations that seek to influence others to accept their goals, receive their services, or contribute to them in some way | American Red Cross: "Together, we can save a life." March of Dimes: "Working together for stronger, healthier babies." St. Jude Children's Research Hospital: "Finding Cures. Saving Children." |

## OVERLAP BETWEEN MARKETING CATEGORIES

The six categories of marketing can often overlap.

*Example 1*: Avon cosmetics frequently promotes both a product and the cause of raising breast cancer awareness.

*Example 2*: Oprah Winfrey uses person marketing to promote her products, such as TV shows, magazines, and books.

*Example 3*: Office supply giant Staples (selling a product) recently partnered with the Boys & Girls Clubs of America (an organization) to sponsor its annual school supplies drive and donated supplies to more than 5,000 communities nationwide (a cause). Exhibit 1.6 illustrates the overlap between these categories of marketing.

Staples (Product)

School Supplies Drive (Cause)

Boys & Girls Club of America (Organization)

**EXHIBIT 1.6**

**Overlap Between Marketing Categories at Staples**

**cause marketing** identification and marketing of a social issue, cause, or idea to selected target markets

**event marketing** marketing of sporting, cultural, and charitable activities to selected target markets

**organization marketing** marketing efforts of mutual-benefit organizations, service organizations, and government organizations that seek to influence others to accept their goals, receive their services, or contribute to them in some way

### 1-5b
## CLOSING EXAMPLE

Barack Obama's campaign didn't just win the 2012 election; it changed the marketing of political candidates forever. Instead of passively delivering messages to television audiences, future presidential candidates would seek ways of building relationships with volunteers, donors, and, ultimately, voters. By 2016, both Hillary Clinton and Donald Trump relied heavily on social media platforms like Facebook and Twitter to identify, expand, and create loyalty among their target audiences—applying the modern practices of product marketing to the concept of person marketing in a way never seen before.

**1-6**

# EIGHT FUNCTIONS OF MARKETING PHYSICAL GOODS

### OPENING EXAMPLE

Sam's Sub Shop opened near a big university campus with great fanfair. No one in the campus community could miss the billboards and posters touting "Sam's Own Heavenly Honey-Roasted Turkey." For the first week after its grand opening, the shop did a brisk lunchtime business.

But in week two, Sam's ran out of its signature turkey. By the time a backup supply was shipped, the meat had spoiled in an overheated warehouse. Busy students and faculty who came for the product were annoyed that they'd wasted their time. Word of mouth was so negative that the shop was forced to close after just two months.

What did Sam's do wrong? And what can these mistakes teach us about the functions of marketing?

**LO 1.6** Identify the eight functions of marketing physical goods.

## 1-6a

# LEARNING IT: EIGHT FUNCTIONS OF MARKETING PHYSICAL GOODS

As a consumer, you are influenced by advertising, personal selling, and other types of promotion. You may also appreciate a seller's willingness to deliver your product. But these represent only two of the eight functions marketers perform in their efforts to build a relationship with you. Understanding these functions will make you a savvy consumer as well as an effective marketer.

On average, half of the costs involved in a tangible product—such as a Sam's Sub Shop sandwich, a pair of Gap jeans, or noise-canceling headphones—can be traced directly to marketing. Firms must spend money to create time, place, and ownership utilities. These expenditures are not associated with any of the actual production functions necessary for creating form utility; instead, they go toward the performance of eight universal marketing functions, as illustrated in Exhibit 1.7.

## 1-6b

# CLOSING EXAMPLE

You can think about marketing as a chain of connections between a firm and its customers. Each of the eight links in the chain represents a unique function. Sam's Sub Shop may have sold great turkey, but that wasn't enough to keep the store in business when it failed at buying (having enough meat on hand), transporting (shipping the perishable product quickly), and storing (using a temperature-controlled warehouse). Marketers have the best opportunity to build and maintain lasting relationships when each link in the chain is strong and fits well with the others.

**EXHIBIT 1.7**  The Eight Universal Functions of Marketing

| Function | What Is It? | Why Is It Important? | Example |
|---|---|---|---|
| **Buying** | Ensuring that product offering are available in sufficient quantities to meet customer demands. | Marketers must be able to satisfy consumers' wants and needs promptly and ahead of consumption. | A bakery must have enough flour on hand to give customers a reliable supply of bread. |
| **Selling** | Using advertising, personal selling, and sales promotion to match products to customer needs. | Marketers must communicate with consumers about how their products create value. | A consumer planning a day at the beach wants to know what sunscreens are most effective. |
| **Transporting** | Moving products from their point of production to locations convenient for purchasers. | Marketers create place utility by making goods and services available where people want to buy them. | One of Amazon's biggest competitive strengths is its ability to transport virtually any goods anywhere. |
| **Storing** | Warehousing products until needed for sale. | Marketers must have a place to keep unsold products organized, safe, and ready to be transported to store as needed. | Walmart has limited shelf space and can't stock everything they carry all at once. |

*(Continues)*

(Continued)

| Function | What Is It? | Why Is It Important? | Example |
|---|---|---|---|
| **Standardizing and Grading** | Ensuring that product offerings meet quality and quantity controls of size, weight, and other variables. | Marketers must meet consumers' expectations of product size, weight, and so on. | A tire dealer must offer tires in standard sizes that consumers know will fit their cars. |
| **Financing** | Providing credit for channel members (wholesalers and retailers) and consumers. | Wholesalers and retailers often need access to funds to finance product inventory prior to sale. Consumers often need the option of using credit cards to buy. | At holiday time when they make many purchases, consumers prefer using credit cards instead of carrying large amounts of cash. |
| **Risk Taking** | Dealing with uncertainty about future customer purchases. | When manufacturers create products based on research, they believe consumers need those products. Companies accommodate these uncertainties about future demand when they bring goods to market. | Toy makers like Mattel offers innovative toys each year based on their forecast of likely trends in children's play. |
| **Securing Marketing Information** | Collecting information about consumers, competitors, and channel members for use in decision-making. | Analysis of marketing information helps marketers understand why consumers purchase some goods and not others. This also helps determine what consumers want and need, and how to satisfy those wants and needs. | Many hotels ask customers to complete a satisfaction survey after their stays so that the hotel will know if their rooms and service meet the needs of travelers. |

 **1-7**

# ANALYZING MARKETING STRATEGY

## OPENING EXAMPLE

At the beginning of this chapter you read about Vineyard Vines, a unique—but upscale—brand of casual clothing founded by two 20-something men who initially sold ties out of their car. Today, the firm offers a full line of high-quality clothing for men, women, and children in 48 nautical-themed stores nationwide, in major retail chains, via catalog and online. They also offer their products through licensing partnerships with Major League Baseball, the National Hockey League, and the National Football League.

While Vineyard Vines does little paid advertising, it generates plenty of buzz via social media. The company also encourages positive word-of-mouth by distributing free accessories and clothing to select customer groups, sending representatives to college campuses, and training salespeople to connect with buyers one-on-one.

Let's say you were Chief Marketing Officer for Vineyard Vines. You must summarize the key elements of your marketing mix to the board of directors. What would you say?

**LO 1.7** Given a description of a company's marketing mix, classify the elements of the marketing mix and the category of marketing.

Vineyard Vines' marketing mix offers unique, premium-priced products, distributed through multiple retail channels, and a promotional strategy that relies on social media and word-of-mouth.

Source: www.jarrettbay.com

## 1-7a
# LEARNING IT: ANALYZING MARKETING STRATEGY

As discussed previously, every successful customer-driven organization begins by defining its target market. Vineyard Vines primarily targets young people, especially college students, who value a fun, sporty lifestyle and will stay loyal to the brand for decades.

As a product marketer, Vineyard Vines needs to communicate the benefits of its goods to its target market, both to persuade people to buy, and to build long-term relationships. Here's how the company is using each key variable of the marketing mix to accomplish these goals:

### PRODUCT STRATEGY

Vineyard Vines expanded its product line from menswear to clothing for women and children of all ages. The firm has also trademarked its brand name and made important decisions about design and positioning: every item is embellished with its distinctive pink whale logo, and it is positioned as a fun, outdoorsy—yet premium—lifestyle brand that competes with labels like Polo and Ralph Lauren.

### PRICING STRATEGY

Vineyard Vines is a premium-priced brand when compared to other casual clothing brands. It sometimes offers temporary, seasonal promotions to generate additional demand without undermining its premium image.

## DISTRIBUTION STRATEGY

The brand is distributed through company-owned stores, other upscale retailers, and online. Its distribution network is widened by its licensing partners and on the college campuses that host its company representatives.

## PROMOTION STRATEGY

Vineyard Vines communicates its message directly through social media and the personal selling efforts of its salespeople; and indirectly through promotions like offering free clothes to students. All of its promotional communications are integrated in style and theme—*Living the Dream*—and utilize recognizable visual elements.

# 1-8  LEARN IT TODAY . . . USE IT TOMORROW

As Vineyard Vines contemplates plans to grow the business, they want your recommendations for changes to their marketing mix that might enhance profits.

It's time to get hands-on and apply what you've learned. **See MindTap for an activity related to Vineyard Vines's marketing activities.**

## Chapter Summary

**LO 1.1  Summarize how marketing creates value through the four types of utility.**

The goal of any marketing effort is to boost utility: the power of a good or service to satisfy the needs and wants of consumers. The four types of utility include form, time, place, and ownership.

**LO 1.2  Describe the four variables of the marketing mix.**

Marketing strategy begins by identifying a target audience. Then marketers combine the marketing mix variables of product, price, distribution, and promotion to satisfy the needs of the target audience.

**LO 1.3  Contrast the focus of marketing activities during the five eras of marketing history.**

Marketing has been viewed and practiced differently over the decades. Its focus today is on building relationships.

**LO 1.4  Explain how relationship marketing can move customers up the loyalty ladder.**

Relationship marketing gives a company new opportunities to steadily increase customers' loyalty. When they start as new customers, the marketer's goal is to move them up to regular purchasers, loyal supporters, and ultimately advocates.

**LO 1.5** Differentiate the six categories of marketing.

As marketing has evolved into an organization-wide activity, its application has broadened to include product, person, place, cause, event, and organization marketing.

**LO 1.6** Identify the eight functions of marketing physical goods.

Marketers must utilize the full set of marketing functions to build and maintain lasting relationships:

buying, selling, transporting, storing, standardizing and grading, financing, risk taking, and securing marketing information.

**LO 1.7** Given a description of a company's marketing mix, classify the elements of the marketing mix and the category of marketing.

The elements of the marketing mix have distinct characteristics and uses. Marketers must decide how best to apply them to each of the six categories of marketing.

## Key Terms

utility 3
marketing 4
target market 5
marketing mix 6
product 6
price strategy 7
distribution 7
promotion 7

production orientation 9
sales orientation 10
seller's market 10
buyer's market 10
consumer orientation 10
transaction-based marketing 11
relationship marketing 12
mobile marketing 12

social marketing 12
product marketing 14
person marketing 14
place marketing 14
cause marketing 15
event marketing 15
organization marketing 15

# 2 STRATEGIC PLANNING IN CONTEMPORARY MARKETING

Sorbis/Shutterstock.com

## LEARNING OBJECTIVES

**2.1** Contrast how marketing plans differ at various levels in an organization.

**2.2** Summarize the six components of a marketing plan.

**2.3** Summarize the competitive forces of Porter's five forces model.

**2.4** Differentiate the elements of a SWOT analysis.

**2.5** Explain how the BCG matrix is used for marketing planning.

**2.6** Given an example of a strategic analysis, categorize the findings utilizing the SWOT analysis and BCG matrix.

# LEARN IT TODAY ... USE IT TOMORROW

Since its beginning in 1995, Under Armour (UA), has grown rapidly and is now poised to take on the company's #1 competitor—Nike.[1] What has led to Under Armour's success and how can the firm chip away at Nike's market leading position? It's a combination of factors, including UA's ability to find market opportunities, create compelling marketing mixes, and nurture relationships with key constituents—including customers, suppliers, and strategic retail partners. To pull this off, UA's management team across all levels of the firm engages in planning to develop its strategy and identify tactics to achieve the company's business goals. In this chapter, you'll learn about planning methods that enable firms like UA to develop a game plan to win in highly competitive markets.

# MARKETING PLANNING: THE BASIS FOR STRATEGY AND TACTICS

**LO 2.1** Contrast how marketing plans differ at various levels in an organization.

## OPENING EXAMPLE

Uber has taken the world by storm by disrupting the transportation and logistics industries. Now it is ready to tackle big issues such as city cleanliness, infrastructure, and urban crowding by partnering with urban planners and city leaders. To accomplish its goals, Uber is investing heavily in technology–including partnerships with engineering centers and automobile manufacturers Volvo and Daimler to offer self-driving cars via its network. From its humble beginnings in San Francisco as a luxury "black-car" service, Uber now operates in over 400 cities across 65 countries with approximately 4,000 of its 6,000 employed associates hired within the last year.[2]

Uber is also one of the most highly valued privately held companies in America. But how do big decisions get made at Uber? Who decides what technology investments to make or what cities are appropriate for expansion? And once those decisions are made, who oversees the daily execution of those strategies?

## 2-1a
## LEARNING IT: MARKETING PLANNING: THE BASIS FOR STRATEGY AND TACTICS

**planning** the overall process of anticipating conditions and determining the best way to achieve organizational objectives

**marketing planning** the process devoted specifically to achieving marketing objectives

**strategic planning** the process of determining an organization's long-term primary objectives and adopting courses of action that will achieve these objectives

**Planning** is the overall process of anticipating conditions and determining the best way to achieve organizational objectives. **Marketing planning** is devoted specifically to achieving marketing objectives. Product development, pricing decisions, selection of appropriate distribution channels, and decisions relating to promotional campaigns all depend on ideas formulated during marketing planning.

Planning is often classified on the basis of its scope or breadth. **Strategic planning** is the process of determining an organization's long-term primary objectives and adopting courses of action that will achieve these objectives. This process also includes the allocation of necessary resources. Strategic planning is typically the emphasis of top managers, such as the CEO and CMO.

Strategic planning lays the foundation for **tactical planning**- which defines how activities specified in the strategic plan will be implemented. Unlike strategic plans, tactical plans typically address shorter-term actions that a firm must complete to implement its larger strategies. Sometimes tactical planning requires swift decision-making and actions, and is typically the emphasis of middle-managers, such as general managers and department directors.

In turn, tactical planning is the basis for **operational planning**- where managers develop specific programs to meet goals in their area of responsibility. Exhibit 2.1 summarizes the types of planning undertaken at various levels of the organization.

Here's how the planning process at different levels might look at a company like Uber:

*Strategic planning*: The executive team, including the CEO, COO, and CMO, make long-term decisions about expansion into new markets around the globe. Let's say Indonesia was one of those markets targeted for expansion.

*Tactical planning*: Based on the strategic decision to enter Indonesia, the middle-management team in charge of Uber in Asia would set goals and milestones for having an office up-and-running in Indonesia. Tactical planning might include defining the number of drivers Uber would like to have and the total number of trips Uber would like to facilitate in the first year of operation in this new market.

*Operational planning*: Based on the tactical plan, the supervisors of the new office in Indonesia would begin advertising for drivers, advertising for riders, and setting goals and procedures for staff at the local office.

**tactical planning** defines how activities specified in the strategic plan will be implemented

**operational planning** where managers develop specific programs to meet goals in their area of responsibility

**EXHIBIT 2.1**    **Planning at Different Managerial Levels**

| Management Level | Type of Planning Emphasized at This Level | Examples |
| --- | --- | --- |
| **Top Management**<br><br>Board of directors<br>Chief executive officer<br>Chief operating officer<br>Chief financial officer<br>Chief marketing officer | Strategic planning | Organization-wide objectives<br>Fundamental strategies<br>Long-term plans<br>Total budget |
| **Middle Management**<br><br>General sales manager<br>Team leader<br>Director of marketing research | Tactical planning | Quarterly and semi-annual plans<br>Business unit budgets<br>Divisional policies and procedures |
| **Supervisory Management**<br><br>Regional sales manager<br>Supervisor—telemarketing office | Operational planning | Daily and weekly plans<br>Unit budgets<br>Departmental rules and procedures |

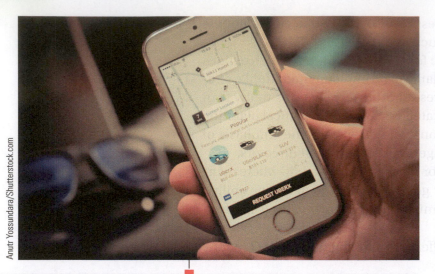

Updating Uber's riders app for use in a new market would be an example of tactical planning.

Anutr Yossundara/Shutterstock.com

## 2-1b
## CLOSING EXAMPLE

In early 2016, Uber unveiled a new brand identity–one the company hoped would resonate with customers, drivers, employees, and investors. Uber co-founder and then CEO Travis Kalanick was immersed in the process and worked with a team of colleagues for close to 36 months upgrading and rebranding Uber applications, such as Uber for drivers, riders, UberEATS and Uber Freight. The CEO-led team identified core principals they believed encompassed the type of company Uber aspired to become, which included the concepts of being grounded, populist, inspiring, highly evolved, and elevated. This is an example of strategic planning as it really happened at Uber.

However, Uber's management team understood that, while Uber is a global company, it also operates at the local level. The brand redesign team recognized the importance of providing their local teams with autonomy to create messages that reflect the local values and culture of their markets. So, the corporate rebranding team identified different color palettes for different regions around the world, but allowed local general managers to utilize tactical and operational planning to "create locally themed promotional materials, driver handbooks, and ads "for their market."[3]

## 2-2 MARKETING PLAN COMPONENTS

LO 2.2 Summarize the six components of a marketing plan.

### OPENING EXAMPLE

Large and small organizations of all types make a myriad of decisions including the allocation of resources, pursuit of new markets, introduction of new products, and the deletion of existing products. What happens behind the scenes of an organization that determines these actions? The answer most likely lies in the firm's ability to develop and implement a marketing plan.

Consider Caterpillar Inc., a manufacturer of heavy equipment machinery utilized in road construction, mining, agriculture, oil and gas, and several other industries.[4] In 2008, Caterpillar announced several plans signaling changes in its strategic direction within the U.S. truck market, including a joint venture with Navistar and the decision to stop supplying engines to U.S. truck manufacturers.[5] Did the company make the right decision to pursue these strategies, and what information would help the company's managers to determine whether any adjustment in the strategy is needed?

## LEARNING IT: MARKETING PLAN COMPONENTS

Managers involved in marketing typically create a **marketing plan** as part of their strategic planning process. A written plan is important as it enables all key employees to understand the strategic goals of the organization, their role in contributing to the organization's success, and awareness of how performance will be evaluated.

A marketing plan typically includes several sections or components (see Exhibit 2.2).

The marketing plan begins with an Executive Summary, which is a short overview of the entire marketing plan and provides key information from the major sections of the plan.

The Environmental & SWOT (Strengths, Weaknesses, Opportunities and Threats) Analysis section details the current external and internal environmental factors affecting the business as well as the company's competitive and unique capabilities. A full discussion of SWOT analysis is presented later in this chapter. A full discussion of factors in the marketing environment is presented in Chapter 3.

The Marketing Objectives section is where the plan really takes shape. This section should detail specific objectives to be achieved, which are the key drivers for what goes in the rest of the plan.

For each marketing objective, the plan will identify the marketing strategies, tactics to be implemented, and key performance benchmarks to evaluate whether the firm's activities are accomplishing the marketing objective.

For example, imagine that the general manager of the Mon Ami Gabi restaurant located in Las Vegas' Paris Hotel & Casino has completed a SWOT analysis and sees potential for strong growth in the next year.

**marketing plan** a written plan that outlines the strategic marketing goals of an organization

**EXHIBIT 2.2** Components of a Marketing Plan

| Component | Description |
|---|---|
| Executive Summary | A short overview of the entire marketing plan which provides key information from the major sections of the plan |
| Environmental & SWOT Analysis | Details the current external and internal environmental factors affecting the business as well as the company's competitive and unique capabilities |
| Marketing Objectives | Details specific objectives to be achieved by the organization |
| Marketing Strategies | Longer-term courses of action to achieve objectives |
| Marketing Tactics (Implementation) | Shorter-term actions to achieve marketing strategies |
| Key Performance Indicators | Quantifiable outcome measures to provide objective data |

**EXHIBIT 2.3**    Mon Ami Gabi Marketing Plan Elements

| Marketing Objective | Marketing Strategies | Marketing Tactics | Key Performance Indicators |
|---|---|---|---|
| Increase revenue by 50% by next year | Target local residents in addition to travelers | • Send e-mail marketing to travelers who have a reservation to stay at the Paris Hotel & Casino<br>• Promote the restaurant to local Las Vegas residents using radio & TV advertising | • Number of lunch & dinner reservations received compared to previous year<br>• Number of reservations redeemed or number of "no shows" compared to previous year |
| | Implement persuasive selling techniques to increase average sales per diner or table | • Offer drink, appetizer, and dessert specials<br>• Enhance server ability to "up-sell" customers on alcoholic beverages | • Number of drink, appetizer, and dessert specials sold per shift<br>• Average ticket sale compared to previous year<br>• Sales of "premium" brands versus "house" brands of alcohol |
| | Manage all aspects of the dining experience to improve customer satisfaction and increase positive word-of-mouth | • Decrease wait time to be seated<br>• Improve time between ordering and food delivery<br>• Ensure high quality food taste and appearance | • Average wait time for tables<br>• Average ticket times between entering into point-of-service system and food delivery<br>• Number of returns for incorrect orders and/or food quality |

As a result, one of the marketing objectives is to increase revenue by 50%. To accomplish that objective, the manager identified three strategies. For each strategy, he defined specific tactics and a measurement for the success of each one.

Exhibit 2.3 summarizes how one marketing objective translates into a number of strategies, tactics, and measurements that go in the marketing plan. This process would be repeated for any additional major marketing objectives.

The marketing plan should be flexible and allow management to re-evaluate and redirect its efforts in response to changing environmental factors or inability to achieve the objectives. By tracking the key performance indicators and comparing those outcomes to the stated objectives, managers can identify areas where they should direct their attention or shift resources in order to improve performance.

## 2-2b

## THE MARKETING PLANNING PROCESS

The process for developing a marketing plan largely mirrors the sections of a marketing plan. In a larger company, the marketing planning process consists of six steps beginning at the corporate level with the definition of a firm's mission, determination of objectives, assessment of resources, and evaluation of environmental risks and opportunities.

Guided by this information, marketers within each business unit then formulate a marketing strategy, implement the strategy through operating plans, and gather feedback to monitor and adapt strategies when necessary. Exhibit 2.4 shows the basic steps in the process.

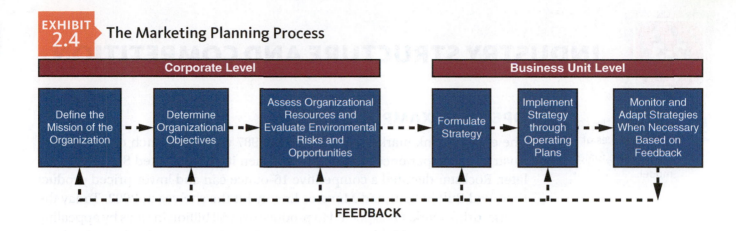

**EXHIBIT 2.4** The Marketing Planning Process

## 2-2c

# CLOSING EXAMPLE

The engine and truck team at Caterpillar likely developed a marketing plan to identify specific strategies and tactics to achieve objectives. As part of the planning process, a SWOT analysis would have been performed, and according to industry sources, Caterpillar's 40-year history of supplying on-highway diesel engines was one of its strengths and it had earned the respect of truck owners and drivers. Caterpillar's internal research indicated that "75 percent of the company's current customers use on-highway trucks in their business," which indicated an opportunity for the company to grow revenues by delivering a truck product to existing customers.[6] A likely external environmental factor impacting Caterpillar's strategy relates to the 2010 emissions standards for diesel trucks[7]–an opportunity for firms who were on target to be in compliance with the standards and a threat for those who were unable to reach the standards. In addition, the U.S. truck market was experiencing heavy consolidation and one of Caterpillar's largest customers, Paccar, was building its own plant to produce engines in Mississippi. This threatened Caterpillar's business.[8]

It seemed that Caterpillar's decision to join forces with Navistar was a good one that could lead to opportunities for the company. However, within five years of the launch of Caterpillar's CT660 vocational truck, the company decided to discontinue the truck line and exit the business.[9] What could have happened that led to a failed investment in the truck industry for Caterpillar?

Perhaps it was the decision to join forces with Navistar. While Navistar has been a long-term partner to Caterpillar it does not have the same reputation for quality products as Caterpillar and had to set aside $164 million in warranty reserves to cover repair costs associated with product claims on engines built in 2010 and 2011.[10] In addition, Navistar struggled to gain market share in the competitive truck market likely due to its failure to achieve compliance with emission standards through a redesigned engine.[11]

The lesson for Caterpillar, Navistar, and other companies is that while a SWOT analysis may highlight strengths and opportunities to leverage a firm's capabilities, the specific strategies and tactics deployed by a firm are critically important to the success of the company.

# INDUSTRY STRUCTURE AND COMPETITION

**2-3**

## OPENING EXAMPLE

The energy drink market was created in 1987 with the launch of Red Bull in Austria, and experienced major growth when it hit the United States 10 years later. Rockstar debuted a competitive 16-ounce can and lower-priced product than Red Bull in 2001, and Monster Energy hit the shelves in 2002. Today the energy drink market is expected to produce over $8 billion in sales by appealing to a target group of "older millennials."[12] Does the energy drink market have room for new entrants? What factors would be important to consider before launching a product into this industry?

## 2-3a

## LEARNING IT: INDUSTRY STRUCTURE AND COMPETITION

As part of the strategic planning process, firms should seek to understand the competitive structure of the industry. A number of years ago, renowned business strategist Michael E. Porter identified five competitive forces that influence planning strategies in a model called **Porter's Five Forces**. Porter notes that these different forces exert strong influences on an industry's profitability potential over time. Exhibit 2.5 summarizes the five competitive forces.

**Porter's five forces** five competitive forces that influence planning strategies

The *threat of new competitors* is based on the level of difficulty for entering a market or industry. For example, it's considerably more expensive to begin building automobiles like Tesla than to start a house cleaning service. As a result, car companies face a lower threat of new competitors entering the market, while house cleaning services face a constant threat. That threat might cause those services to lower their prices to remain competitive, making it hard to be profitable.

The *power of suppliers* is another threat impacting industries, as those with more powerful suppliers can charge higher prices or pass along price increases to other members in the supply chain. A chemical manufacturer selling specialized herbicides to agricultural firms like DuPont might be able to negotiate more favorable pricing because DuPont does not have an alternate supplier for this chemical. Similarly, Procter & Gamble (P&G) may possess a high degree of power when negotiating with retailers who depend on selling popular P&G brands such as Tide, Pampers, and Bounty paper towels in their stores.

*Powerful customers* are another threat because they may possess greater negotiating leverage to extract price concessions or other favorable terms. As the largest retailer in the world, Walmart has quite a reputation of squeezing its supplier partners to reduce prices in an effort to provide Walmart customers with everyday low prices. This puts pressure on profit margins for these suppliers, and even Walmart knows it. The company recently suggested its suppliers reduce their in-store and online marketing promotions as a way to reduce costs.[13]

**EXHIBIT 2.5** Competitive Forces and Profitability

| Competitive Force | Force Description | Impact on Industry Profits |
|---|---|---|
| **Threat of new competitors** | The degree to which new competitors may easily enter the industry and disrupt established firms. | If the threat is high, established firms may lower prices to fend off competition or make investments to discourage competition. This reduces industry profitability. |
| **Supplier power** | The amount of bargaining power a supplier exerts on its customers and other channel members. | If the industry structure contains suppliers with high levels of power, industry profitability will be reduced since suppliers may charge higher prices or transfer costs to other channel partners. |
| **Buyer power** | The amount of bargaining power a customer (either consumer or business-to-business buyer) exerts on its suppliers and other channel members. | If the industry contains buyers who wield power, industry profitability will suffer since buyers may demand more services, lower prices, or higher levels of quality. |
| **Threat of substitutes** | A substitute threat occurs when a product or service can be replaced with goods and services from a competing firm or industry. | If the threat of substitutes is high, industry profitability will be reduced due to increased competition. |
| **Competitive rivalry** | The intensity of competition among industry participants, usually a direct result of the four previous forces. | If competitive rivalry is high, profitability will be reduced. |

The *threat of substitutes* also is a competitive force impacting industries. If customers have the opportunity to replace a company's products with goods or services from a competing firm, the company's marketers may have to find a new market, change prices, or compete in other ways to maintain an advantage. McDonald's made what some considered a bold move when the firm announced the launch of its "McCafe"—offering upgraded coffee drinks such as lattes, cappuccinos, and mochas—in direct competition with Starbucks and Dunkin' Donuts. McDonald's recently announced an even bolder move: entering the retail grocery market by testing three new products—packages of McCafe whole beans, ground coffee, and "single-cups"—in supermarkets.[14] All of these

When McDonald's started offering high-end coffee drinks, they entered direct competition with Starbucks and Dunkin' Donuts.

Bloomberg/Getty Images

moves present a competitive threat to Starbucks because they offer a substitute for products customers might currently be purchasing from Starbucks.

The four previous forces can highly influence *rivalry among competitors*, especially if forces within that industry favor new entrants and substitutes, or provide bargaining power to suppliers and/or buyers. Industry dynamics and the economic environment can influence rivalry as well. Consider the nature of competitive rivalry in these markets:

*Soda*: Coca-Cola, Pepsi, and 7-Up
*Car Rental*: Avis, Enterprise Rent-A-Car and Hertz
*Auto*: Ford, GM, Toyota, and Honda.
*Technology*: Apple, Google, Amazon, and Microsoft

Competition between these firms and against others in their industry may lead to price discounting, aggressive product development cycles, expensive advertising campaigns, or other ways to differentiate their products. The higher the rivalry in an industry, usually the harder it is to maintain profits over time.

## 2-3b
## CLOSING EXAMPLE

Red Bull, Monster, and Rockstar are the leading brands in the energy beverage industry, with established distribution channels, customer loyalty, and deep pockets to fuel marketing campaigns. Further increasing competitive forces in this industry are the fact it has a high threat from substitutes—coffee, tea, and other products containing caffeine can easily offer many of the benefits of energy drinks, for a lower price. As a result, going head-to-head with these brands would be difficult for a new entrant to the industry.

However, given the continued growth of this segment around the globe and the ability to enter the market through contract manufacturing (which lowers the barriers to entry), new entrants are likely to emerge—especially at the local market level. Some areas where new entrants may gain ground include the "natural" and "organic" segment by capitalizing on consumers' desires for natural ingredients, zero calories, and improved flavor profiles.

# 2-4   SWOT ANALYSIS

**LO 2.4** Differentiate the elements of a SWOT analysis.

## OPENING EXAMPLE

As part of their strategic planning process, executives at Patagonia are completing a SWOT analysis to assess where its business stands in the marketplace. The review has identified a number of characteristics about Patagonia, the competitive landscape, and environmental factors influencing customers, suppliers, and the industry as a whole. The next step involves categorizing these characteristics according to the SWOT framework, with the goal of using that framework to help identify strategic objectives for the coming year.

## 2-4a
# LEARNING IT: SWOT ANALYSIS

**SWOT analysis** is an important strategic planning tool that helps managers analyze the internal and external environment to assess strengths, weaknesses, opportunities, and threats. A thorough SWOT analysis enables managers to determine how best to formulate strategic objectives that fulfill the firm's basic mission.

Strengths and weaknesses are factors internal to the firm while opportunities and threats are factors external to the firm.

Strengths represent a firm's core competencies or points of differentiation from the competition. Core competencies are capabilities that customers value and competitors find difficult to duplicate. For example, Patagonia has a strong mission to support sustainability efforts and its products are revered for their long-lasting wear and high-quality composition. In fact, Patagonia products are guaranteed for life. In addition, Patagonia encourages their customers to fix their worn garments rather than replacing them and partnered with iFixit to publish free repair guides for Patagonia products.[15] For consumers who care about sustainability and reducing their carbon footprint, Patagonia's initiatives create a strong competitive advantage and core strength.

Weaknesses are limitations that place the company at a disadvantage. Since weaknesses are factors internal to a company, the company largely controls whether those weaknesses can be overcome. Patagonia realizes that while its brand is well-recognized among outdoor enthusiasts and adventure-seeking consumers, it is not known as a fashion forward brand. In addition, the company operates a limited number of retail outlets and has a limited distribution network. Plus, Patagonia's products are expensive, especially when compared to similar items at fast fashion retail chains such as Zara and H&M, who has over 400 stores across the globe.

> **SWOT analysis** an important strategic planning tool that helps managers analyze the internal and external environment to assess strengths, weaknesses, opportunities, and threats

Patagonia's track record of supporting sustainability efforts has enhanced their brand and is a company strength.

Source: www.ecoripples.com

Opportunities are factors in the external environment that could potentially be exploited by the company. This includes opportunities to launch new products, enter new markets, or changes in the social or economic environment that might particularly benefit the firm.

Threats are factors in the external environment that could limit the company's success. Since threats are external to the company, they can't always be controlled. Examples include changing buyer tastes, government regulation, or economic turmoil.

The value of a SWOT analysis is that it can help the company formulate strategies that either create the most value or help the company avoid the biggest risks (see Exhibit 2.6).

Matching an internal strength with an external opportunity produces a situation known as *leverage*, which enables a company to seize an advantage over its competition. For example, to the extent that sustainability continues to be an issue consumers value (an external opportunity), Patagonia can continue to leverage its strength as a brand known for corporate stewardship and environmental sustainability.

On the other hand, external threats can create vulnerabilities by limiting an organization's strengths. Patagonia's sustainability culture and high-quality products with lifetime guarantees directly contrast with the fast fashion

**EXHIBIT 2.6** SWOT Analysis

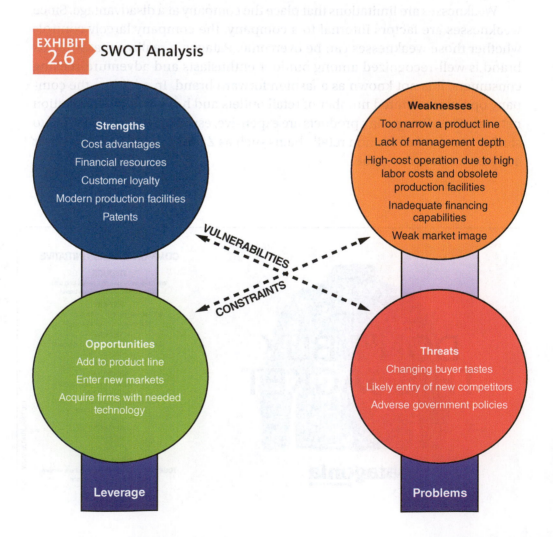

movement, which values constantly changing tastes–and in the process creates literally tons of waste. *Newsweek* reports that consumers trash about 80 pounds of clothing per year.[16]

### 2-4b

## CLOSING EXAMPLE

The Patagonia executives can now explore ways to:

- Take advantage of the company's strengths
- Address the company's weaknesses
- Exploit opportunities in the market
- Respond to threats in the environment

Perhaps they'll build upon their brand strength by emphasizing the product quality, durability, and sustainability in advertising campaigns. Maybe they'll expand the distribution network to compete better against more widely distributed brands. By understanding the threat that fast fashion poses, Patagonia can possibly formulate strategies to stay competitive while remaining true to its brand.

All of these strategic considerations were made possible by using the SWOT analysis framework.

# 2-5 PORTFOLIO ANALYSIS–A PLANNING TOOL

## OPENING EXAMPLE

Consumer snacking behavior is changing. The market for snacks has expanded from chips and crackers to fresh fruits, vegetables, yogurt, pastries, and protein bars. The change in consumer snacking behavior has big implications for Frito-Lay–a division of PepsiCo and dominant player in the salty snack segment, with a 36.6% market share[17]. How can Frito-Lay determine the appropriate allocation of resources among its various snack brands? Which ones should they aggressively market and which ones should they begin to phase out? It's not as easy as seeing which brands are making the most money now, Frito-Lay needs to determine which brands will be making the most money in the future—and which ones are past their prime.

**LO 2.5** Explain how the BCG matrix is used for marketing planning.

### 2-5a

## LEARNING IT: PORTFOLIO ANALYSIS–A PLANNING TOOL

As previously discussed, successful firms engage in marketing planning processes at the corporate and business-unit level. Small companies may offer only a few items to their customers while larger organizations frequently offer and market many products to widely diverse audiences. Citibank offers a wide range of financial and investment products to both businesses and consumers.

The BCG matrix can help companies decide which brands deserve increased investment and which ones to eventually phase out.

Barry Blackburn/Shutterstock.com

Nestlé stocks supermarkets with everything from baby food, frozen single-serve entrees, and bottled water to pet food, dietary supplements, and in-home espresso machines.

**strategic business units (SBUs)** key business units within diversified firms

This is where the concept of strategic business units comes in. **Strategic business units (SBUs)**- are key business units within diversified firms. Each SBU has its own managers, resources, objectives, and competitors. A division, product line, or single product may define the boundaries of an SBU, and each SBU typically pursues its own distinct mission and develops its own marketing plans independently of other units in the organization.

Top managers at these large firms need a method for spotting business units that deserve more investment, as well as ones that aren't living up to expectations. Portfolio analysis is a technique that enables managers to evaluate their company's business units and divisions to determine the strongest and weakest.

**Boston consulting group (BCG) matrix** a portfolio analysis framework that enables managers to plot the relative position of each business unit, brand, or product on the basis of industry growth rate and relative market share

A widely used portfolio analysis framework was developed by the Boston Consulting Group (BCG) and is known as the growth/share matrix. The **Boston Consulting Group (BCG) matrix** enables managers to plot the relative position of each business unit, brand, or product on the basis of two dimensions:

- Industry Growth Rate
- Relative Market Share

Relative market share is the percentage of a market that a firm currently controls (or company sales divided by total market sales).

After plotting all of a firm's business units, planners divide them according to the matrix's four quadrants: stars, cash cows, question marks, and dogs (see Exhibit 2.7). Each quadrant represents a unique position in the market relative to a firm's competitors and necessitates a distinct marketing strategy.

*Stars* represent units with high market shares in high-growth markets. These products or businesses are high-growth market leaders. Although they generate considerable income, they need considerable inflows of cash to finance further growth. The Apple iPhone is the top-selling smartphone in the United States, but to maintain that position, Apple continues to offer new models to demanding and tech-savvy consumers.[18]

*Cash cows* command high market shares but are in low-growth markets. Marketers for such an SBU want to maintain this status for as long as possible since the generation of cash fuels other business units that have higher growth potential. For instance, Microsoft uses the profits from sales of its Windows operating system to finance research and development for new Internet-based technologies.[19]

*Question marks* are business units with low relative market shares in high-growth markets. These SBU managers must decide whether to continue supporting these products or businesses because question marks typically require considerably more cash than they generate. If a question mark cannot become a star, the firm should pull out of the market and target other markets with greater potential. JPMorgan Chase recently stopped making student loans, saying the market isn't one that the bank can significantly grow. Industry observers point out that nationally nearly $8 billion in such loans are currently in default—a reality the bank likely took into account when making its decision.[20]

*Dogs* manage only low market shares in low-growth markets. SBUs in this category indicate a poor business position relative to competition and the BCG recommends withdrawal or divestiture as quickly as possible—unless market share position can be improved. In some cases, these SBUs can be sold to other firms where they are a better fit. Some firms build their entire business on other companies' dogs, purchasing recipes or manufacturing techniques, then reviving them into profitable SBUs. Blair Candy, an online candy retailer, specializes in hard-to-find brands like Gobstoppers, Necco Wafers, and Zagnut candy bars.[21]

**EXHIBIT 2.7** ▶ BCG Matrix

## 2-5b
# CLOSING EXAMPLE

Market share data and consumer snacking trends paint an interesting picture for Frito-Lay and its top brands. The salty snack segment sales are currently dominated by potato chips and tortilla chips, where Frito-Lay has a dominant 60% share.[22] For now, brands in that segment are cash cows, so Frito-Lay will milk profits to finance growth of other units. However, changing consumer snacking habits toward healthier options like crackers, fruit, and Greek yogurt needs to be addressed. Frito-Lay can use the BCG matrix to identify business units that represent the next stars, and even those question marks with potential. Those are the units that will receive additional investment to fuel growth.

# 2-6
# USING SWOT ANALYSIS AND BCG MATRIX

**LO 2.6**
Given an example of a strategic analysis, categorize the findings utilizing the SWOT analysis and BCG matrix

## OPENING EXAMPLE

Under Armour (UA) is an American success story. Its founder and CEO, Kevin Plank, started in his grandmother's basement in 1995 by developing a prototype "moisture wicking" shirt for football players. Now, the company operates from a former Procter & Gamble factory in Baltimore, Maryland. UA is a $4 billion a year business with over 13,000 employees.[23] While there are many factors responsible for this type of success, strategic planning is a big one. This chapter has introduced a variety of methods for strategic planning and now it's time to "get to work" actually using two of these methods: SWOT analysis and BCG matrix.

## 2-6a
## LEARNING IT: USING SWOT ANALYSIS AND BCG MATRIX

Kevin Plank, Under Armour founder and CEO, has big dreams of overcoming Nike, the market leader. UA's corporate mission is to "make all athletes better" and impact global health. These big, audacious goals are coming to fruition for Plank and UA through recent acquisitions, data mining, and new product development in several areas. For example, UA invested millions to make multiple acquisitions, including:

- MapMyFitness, a leading fitness app with over 20 million registered users was acquired for $150 million in November 2013.[24]

- MyFitnessPal, an app which enables its 80 million users to track their eating habits was acquired in February 2015 for $475 million.[25]

- Endomondo, a fitness tracking and social media app with 20 million users—80% of whom are outside of the United States—was acquired in February 2015 for $85 million.[26]

In addition, UA formed partnerships with other makers of fitness technology hardware. Investments like these can't be made randomly, they must be part of a broader plan. Let's take a look at some of the factors that UA could have considered as part of a SWOT analysis *prior* to investing so heavily in fitness-based communities and technology.

If the executive team at UA put their company and the marketing environment under a microscope, they might observe the following factors that could impact their company:

- Charismatic and empowering CEO, Kevin Plank, who is known for inspiring and motivating employees to achieve success.

- Nike is still 8 times bigger, has greater brand awareness, and bigger marketing budgets.

- Failed launch of E39 compression shirt in 2011, with heart rate monitors embedded in the fabric. Failure apparently due to lack of in-house engineering talent.
- Roster of top athletes and celebrity endorsements.
- Existence of growing fitness technology companies who have large user databases and staffs of engineers.
- Access to detailed data analytics for product sales and distribution channels (e.g. retail, online).
- Possible "substitute" products, such as Kate Hudson's *Fabletics* active wear targeted to women.
- Increasing use of athletic wear for everyday casual use.

How might UA's strategic planning team categorize these factors? There are two steps:

1. Determine whether the factors are internal to the company or part of the external environment.
2. Determine whether the factors positively or negatively impact the company.

With that information, you can categorize each factor according to the SWOT analysis framework. As a reminder:

- Positive, internal factors are *strengths*.
- Negative, internal factors are *weaknesses*.
- Positive external factors are *opportunities*.
- Negative external factors are *threats*.

Let's review the list and categorize each one.

**Charismatic and empowering CEO, Kevin Plank, who is known for inspiring and motivating employees to achieve success.** This is a clear strength. Having a strong CEO inside the company allows UA to perform at higher levels than a company without such excellent leadership.

**Nike is still 8 times bigger, has greater brand awareness, and bigger marketing budgets.** It's likely that Nike now has the brand-equity, long-term customer relationships, and systems in place to continue leading the industry. This is external to the company and could potentially have a negative impact on UA's results. This is a threat.

**Failed launch of E39 compression shirt in 2011, with heart rate monitors embedded in the fabric.** According to Plank, "this experience made (him) realize Under Armour couldn't compete with hardware companies that employ thousands of engineers and constantly turn out incremental innovations."[27] This lack of engineering expertise is internal to the company and negatively impacted their results. This is a weakness.

**Roster of top athlete and celebrity endorsements.** Securing star athletes provides brand exposure and credibility that is a hallmark of the top athletic apparel companies. These strong ties are internal and have a positive impact. This is a strength.

**Existence of growing fitness technology companies who have large user databases and staffs of engineers.** Although UA identified their lack of expertise in certain fitness technologies, companies with that expertise could help UA gain traction with new audiences. Since this is external and potentially positive, it's an opportunity.

**Access to detailed data analytics for product sales and distribution channels (e.g. retail, online).** Let's assume that UA has developed capabilities to track sales at all of their various distribution points, including their e-commerce site and through retail partners. This type of "big data" could enable UA to forecast sales and more accurately match production volumes to sales volume. Since UA has developed this capability internally, it is a strength.

**Possible "substitute" products, such as Kate Hudson's *Fabletics* active wear targeted to women.** Since the athletic apparel market has low barriers to entry, it's easy for new competitors to enter the market. If they are well-financed, they can steal market share. Since this is external to UA and could negatively impact results, it's a threat.

**Increasing use of athletic wear for everyday casual use.** A current consumer trend is the blur between athletics and leisure–sometimes called the "athleisure" market. For example, more women are wearing athletic clothes like yoga pants and leggings as clothing, which have become stylish and accepted at school, in some workplaces, and as casual wear. Since this is an external trend that could represent a new market for UA, it's an opportunity.

Exhibit 2.8 summarizes how these factors were categorized according to the SWOT framework.

**EXHIBIT 2.8**

**SWOT at Under Armour**

| Strengths | Weaknesses |
| --- | --- |
| • Charismatic & empowering CEO<br>• Athlete and celebrity endorsements<br>• Strong sales data analytics | • Failed product launch due to lack of engineering expertise in fitness technology |

| Opportunities | Threats |
| --- | --- |
| • Partnership/acquisition of fitness technology companies<br>• Athleisure trend | • Competition from Nike, the market leader<br>• Competition from new market entrants and substitute products |

## 2-6b
## CONDUCTING PORTFOLIO ANALYSIS

Under Armour has a wide range of product lines for men, women, girls, and boys. This includes athletic apparel, shoes, casual wear, and technology services. UA can utilize the BCG Matrix as a planning tool to determine the strategic value of each line or business unit. Imagine that a group of UA managers are interested in gaining a better understanding of where to invest company resources in the coming years.

Under Armor recently acquired three apps: MapMyFitness, MyFitnessPal and Endomondo. These are industry leading apps, with large user bases, in the fast-growing market of fitness tracking software and services. The high relative market share plus high growth potential means UA would classify these apps as stars according to the BCG Matrix.

UA has developed a new app called UA Record. UA Record connects several devices and is sold as the HealthBox package for $400. HealthBox includes a smart-band, which is similar to other activity trackers, and the UA Heart Band, which is a chest strap to collect heart rate data during exercise sessions. UA hopes to compete with other smart device companies such as Fitbit, Jawbone, and Garmin. Nike exited the wearables market by discontinuing the Nike FuelBand line in 2014, showing how difficult breaking into this market can be. Consumer interest in tracking activity and documenting nutrition, sleep, and exercise is high, and industry experts expect this category to experience triple digit growth over the next several years.[28] Still, HealthBox is a new product for UA and has a small market share in the wearables category. The high growth rate combined with low market share would make this business a question mark according to the BCG Matrix.

The company has also launched a technology equipped shoe called the UA SpeedForm Gemini 2 Record. This shoe "tracks and stores data such as time and date, duration, distance, and splits during workouts, runs, or walks."[29] The smart shoes from UA will compete with Nike's Nike+ line of shoes, as well as Adidas SpeedCell foot pod sensor. The Nike+ line, which launched in 2006, has the largest market share in this fast-growing category. Since the UA SpeedForm Gemini 2 is a new product it has a low market share. As a result, the shoe line would be considered a question mark according to the BCG Matrix.

Since all three of these product lines are either stars or question marks, it's likely that UA will continue investing to grow them. UA likely does not yet have product lines that would be categorized as cash cows or dogs, since they currently operate in fast growing markets.

## 2-7 LEARN IT TODAY . . . USE IT TOMORROW

UA seems well positioned to attack Nike and grab market share as the company continues to expand its product lines, make acquisitions, and capitalize on customer relationships. However, strategic planning never stops.

It's time to get hands-on and apply what you've learned. **See MindTap for an activity related to UA's marketing activities**.

# Chapter Summary

**LO 2.1  Contrast how marketing plans differ at various levels in an organization.**

Planning is often classified based on its scope or breadth where top-level managers spend more time engaged in long-range strategic planning while middle management devotes time to tactical planning. Supervisory managers such as regional sales managers engage in operational planning.

**LO 2.2  Summarize the six components of a marketing plan.**

Managers involved in marketing typically create a marketing plan as part of their strategic planning process. A marketing plan typically includes several sections or components beginning with an Executive Summary, Environmental & SWOT analysis, details regarding marketing objectives, strategies and tactics, and identification of key performance indicators.

**LO 2.3  Summarize the competitive forces of Porter's five forces model.**

Michael E. Porter identified five competitive forces that influence planning strategies in a model called Porter's Five Forces. Porter notes that these different forces exert a strong influence on an industry's profitability potential over time. The factors include the threat of new competitors, supplier power, buyer power, threat of substitutes, and competitive rivalry.

**LO 2.4  Differentiate the elements of a SWOT analysis.**

SWOT (strengths, weaknesses, opportunities, and threats) analysis helps planners compare internal organizational strengths and weaknesses with external opportunities and threats. The value of SWOT analysis is that it can help a company formulate strategies that either create the most value or help the organization avoid the biggest risks.

**LO 2.5  Explain how the BCG matrix is used for marketing planning.**

A widely-used portfolio analysis framework was developed by the Boston Consulting Group (BCG) and is known as the growth/share matrix. The BCG matrix enables managers to plot the relative position of each business unit, brand, or product based on two dimensions: industry growth rate and relative market share.

**LO 2.6  Given an example of a strategic analysis, categorize the findings utilizing the SWOT analysis and BCG matrix.**

The ability to apply the strategic planning tools of SWOT analysis and BCG Matrix are important to organizations who seek to achieve their business goals within an ever-changing marketplace and competitive environment.

# Key Terms

# 3 THE MARKETING ENVIRONMENT, ETHICS, AND SOCIAL RESPONSIBILITY

Source: www.graysonglasser.weebly.com

YOU HAVE THE RIGHT TO NAME YOUR PRICE. ONLY FROM PROGRESSIVE.

1-800-PROGRESSIVE / PROGRESSIVE CO...

## LEARNING OBJECTIVES

**3.1** Identify the five components of the marketing environment.

**3.2** Contrast the two types of competition that marketers face.

**3.3** Summarize the four major types of government regulation that affect marketing practices.

**3.4** Describe the regulatory forces that influence the marketing environment.

**3.5** Outline the economic factors that affect marketing decisions and consumer buying power.

**3.6** Describe how a change in the technological environment can impact a firm's marketing activities.

**3.7** Determine an effective marketing response to a change in the social-cultural environment.

**3.8** Given a variable of the marketing mix, describe an ethical issue related to that variable.

**3.9** Define the four dimensions of social responsibility.

# LEARN IT TODAY . . . USE IT TOMORROW

It is nearly impossible to watch an hour of television and not see Flo, the Progressive Insurance spokeswoman. She's starred in more than 100 commercials for the auto insurance company, and with nearly 5 million Facebook followers and her own Twitter handle, Flo is helping customers engage and connect with Progressive. But Flo isn't the only spokesperson pushing insurance these days—Allstate has Mayhem, Geico has a talking gecko, and The General Insurance has a cartoon general. Insurance is a highly competitive industry with numerous companies fighting for the same customers.

Progressive has lived up to its name by taking an innovative approach to auto insurance. Within its industry, Progressive was the first to provide claims service at the scene of an accident, 24 hours a day, 7 days a week. The result is that claims are settled within hours instead of days. The company was also the first to sell auto insurance online. It still does, but now the company has a mobile app, in which customers can receive insurance quotes, request roadside assistance, start a photo estimate for an insurance claim, and more.

Progressive will even show potential customers how its rates stack up against those of its competitors. Progressive believes that this "information transparency" helps to shrink the credibility gap in the insurance industry. In addition, Progressive proactively publishes monthly financial reports rather than just quarterly or annually, as other public companies do. This gives shareholders and investors access to the same information that Progressive's management uses to assess business performance.

In 2012 and 2013, Progressive was recognized by the Ethisphere Institute, an international organization for the advancement of business ethics, as one of the "world's most ethical companies." Progressive's commitment to ethical leadership, compliance practices, and corporate social responsibility landed them on the list.[1]

Together, these strategies have made Progressive a leader in the insurance industry, and their success shows the importance of being innovative and responsive in such a competitive and fast-changing environment.

# 3-1 THE MARKETING ENVIRONMENT

## OPENING EXAMPLE

Think of a brand or product you like. Maybe it's a clothing brand, an automobile maker, or fast-food restaurant. How do marketers for those brands make decisions on product features, pricing, or promotional strategy? Fundamentally, those decisions are based on consumer wants and needs, but that's not the whole story. The overall marketing environment can have a big influence on what consumers want in the first place.

For example, suppose you are a marketer for a pizza restaurant. You are faced with a seemingly simple task of figuring out how most customers will want to order their pizza—in-person at the restaurant, by phone, on the website, or through a mobile app. However, it's not so simple, as these consumer preferences are influenced by the competitive, social-cultural, and technological dimensions of the restaurant's marketing environment, all of which change over time. Understanding these dimensions is the first step in designing a successful marketing strategy.

## 3-1a

# LEARNING IT: THE MARKETING ENVIRONMENT

Marketers do not make decisions about target markets and marketing mix variables in a vacuum. As shown in Exhibit 3.1, they must take into account the dynamic nature of the five dimensions of the marketing environment:

- Competitive
- Political-legal
- Economic
- Technological
- Social-cultural

These forces provide the frame of reference for making all other marketing decisions. It's important to note that the five dimensions of the marketing environment influence one another. For example, social concerns about the natural environment have led to tighter regulations on air and water pollution, which affect the political-legal environment. Further, consumer awareness about environmental issues influences the competitive environment. Automobile makers, for instance, have turned public concerns and legal mandates about gas mileage into opportunities by developing cars that run on electricity, bio-fuel, and hydrogen. The race to develop the most fuel-efficient vehicles for the future has become extremely competitive, with car makers trying to one-up each other in the quest to transition away from fossil fuels.

## 3-1b

# CLOSING EXAMPLE

As a marketer for the pizza restaurant mentioned earlier, you might notice the social-cultural trend that customers want faster and easier ways to order just about any product they purchase. In addition, changes to the technological environment mean that almost everyone has a smartphone. And of course, the highly competitive environment in your industry means that other companies are quickly responding to these changes, meaning you should too.

Domino's Pizza responded quickly to these trends with its smartphone app. A "pizza profile" embedded in the app stores your order information, and

**EXHIBIT 3.1**

**Variables of the Marketing Mix within the Marketing Environment**

The Domino's Pizza Profile is an example of using changes in the technological environment to attract and retain customers.

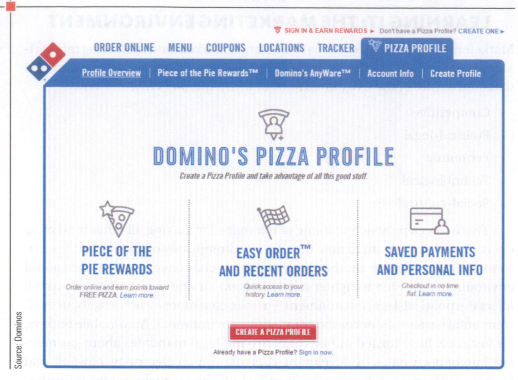

Source: Dominos

a tracker lets you know exactly how long before your pizza is delivered. If you have an "easy order" in your pizza profile, you can skip the app and order by simply texting a pizza emoji to Domino's.

As a consumer, you may not spend a lot of time thinking about the factors that affect marketers' decisions, but now you can appreciate just how many factors marketers must consider when developing a marketing mix.

## 3-2 THE COMPETITIVE ENVIRONMENT

**LO 3.2** Contrast the two types of competition that marketers face.

### OPENING EXAMPLE

McDonald's marketing executive, Jack Thompson, passes by three Starbucks stores on his drive to work. Each store is busier than the next, with a long line of cars in the drive thru and just as many customers inside ordering their morning lattes. Jack shakes his head in frustration. There is no doubt that Starbucks brews excellent coffee, but sales of McDonald's McCafé line are stagnant and Jack needs to find a way to better compete with Starbucks. McDonald's offers lattes and mochas, but Jack needs to find something that will get more customers coming in. Jack will have to come up with more than one plan to go head-to-head with Starbucks. What can Jack do to improve the McCafé line and draw more customers in?

## 3-2a

# LEARNING IT: THE COMPETITIVE ENVIRONMENT

Marketers face two types of competition. The most *direct* form occurs among marketers of similar products, such as the competition for coffee sales between McDonald's and Starbucks. Another example is when a competitive gas station such as Marathon opens across the street from a Shell retail outlet. And the cell phone market provides consumers with alternative service providers such as Verizon, AT&T, and T-Mobile.

A second type of competition is *indirect*, involving products that are easily substituted with others. For example, both McDonald's and Starbucks face the prospect that customers simply opt to make coffee at home or consume energy drinks instead of coffee or tea. In the fast-food industry, pizza competes with chicken, hamburgers, tacos, and even frozen dinners from the grocery store. In entertainment, a movie can be substituted for a concert or a night at the bowling alley. Marketers must find ways to attract consumers to their specific brand as well as to their type of product.

The **competitive environment** is where marketers of directly competitive products and marketers of substitute products compete for consumer purchases.

Marketers at every successful firm must develop an effective strategy for dealing with the competitive environment. One company may compete in a broad range of markets in many areas of the world. Another may specialize in particular market segments, such as in a specific region of the country or a particular age or income group.

Determining a **competitive strategy** involves answering the following three questions:

1. Should we compete?
2. If so, in what markets should we compete?
3. How should we compete?

The answer to the first question depends on the firm's resources, objectives, and expected profit potential. A firm may decide not to pursue or continue operating a potentially successful venture that does not mesh with its resources, objectives, or profit expectations.

Answering the second question requires marketers to acknowledge their firm's limited resources—sales personnel, advertising budgets, product development capability, and the like. They must allocate these resources to the areas of greatest opportunity. Some companies gain access to new markets or new expertise through acquisitions or mergers.

Answering the third question requires marketers to make product, distribution, promotion, and pricing decisions that give the firm a competitive advantage in the marketplace. Firms can compete on various bases, including product quality, price, and customer service.

**competitive environment** where marketers of directly competitive products and marketers of substitute products compete for consumer purchases

**competitive strategy** an effective strategy for dealing with the competitive environment

## 3-2b
# CLOSING EXAMPLE

Jack decides that in order to compete directly with Starbucks, McDonald's must present the McCafé line as a premium experience. To do this, Jack sources coffee beans from sustainable farmers and invests in expensive, new espresso machines in every McDonald's location. McDonald's even launches a mobile app with loyalty rewards and makes plans to allow mobile ordering in the near future. Jack plans to launch McCafé standalone stores, which will offer a line of new espresso drinks along with breakfast sandwiches and croissants.[2] Time will tell, but Jack feels that these changes can increase McCafé sales, and allow McDonald's to compete directly with Starbucks.

# 3-3
# THE POLITICAL-LEGAL ENVIRONMENT

<table>
<tr><td>

**LO 3.3**

Summarize the four major types of government regulation that affect marketing practices.

</td></tr>
</table>

## OPENING EXAMPLE

These days, few organizations operate as a monopoly—the sole supplier of a good or service in the marketplace. Since the late nineteenth century, the U.S. government has enacted regulations to ensure that firms have fair opportunities to compete in the market. When the government feels like the opportunities to compete have been violated, it acts to stop the violation. Can you identify a monopoly that exists in today's economy?

What is the operating system on your computer? For more than 90% of Americans, it is Microsoft Windows. In the 1990s, Microsoft was accused of operating a monopoly. The U.S. Department of Justice took Microsoft to court in 2001. So why did the government get involved, and what did Microsoft do wrong?

## 3-3a
## LEARNING IT: THE POLITICAL-LEGAL ENVIRONMENT

**political-legal environment**
the component of the marketing environment consisting of laws and regulations to maintain competitive conditions and protect consumer rights

The **political-legal environment** is the component of the marketing environment consisting of laws and regulations to maintain competitive conditions and protect consumer rights. Businesspeople must be diligent to understand the legal system's relationship to their marketing decisions.

Federal, state, and local regulations affect marketing practices, as do the actions of independent regulatory agencies. These requirements and prohibitions touch on all aspects of marketing decision making: designing, labeling, packaging, distributing, advertising, and promoting goods and services. All marketers should be aware of the major regulations that affect their activities.

The history of U.S. government regulation can be divided into four phases. The first phase was the antimonopoly period of the late nineteenth and early twentieth centuries. During this era, major laws were passed to *maintain a competitive environment* by reversing the trend toward increasing concentration of industry power in the hands of a small number of competitors. These **antitrust** laws, which were enacted more than 100 years ago, still affect business in the twenty-first century.

The second phase, aimed at *regulating competition*, emerged during the Great Depression of the 1930s, when independent merchants felt the need for legal protection against competition from larger retail store chains.

The third regulatory phase focused on *protecting consumers* by regulating how products were made and sold.

The fourth phase *deregulated specific industries*, such as telecommunications, utilities, transportation, and financial services, to increase competition.

Exhibit 3.2 lists and briefly describes the major federal laws affecting marketing.

**antitrust** laws help maintain a competitive business environment by preventing the concentration of industry power in the hands of a small number of competitors

**EXHIBIT 3.2 ▸ Major Federal Laws Affecting Marketing**

| Date | Law | Description |
|------|-----|-------------|
| **A. Laws Maintaining a Competitive Environment** | | |
| 1890 | Sherman Antitrust Act | Prohibits restraint of trade and monopolization; identifies a competitive marketing system as a national policy goal. |
| 1914 | Clayton Act | Strengthens the Sherman Act by restricting practices such as price discrimination, exclusive dealing, tying contracts, and interlocking boards of directors where the effect "may be to substantially lessen competition or tend to create a monopoly"; amended by the Celler-Kefauver Antimerger Act to prohibit major asset purchases that would decrease competition in an industry. |
| 1914 | Federal Trade Commission Act (FTC) | Prohibits unfair methods of competition; establishes the Federal Trade Commission, an administrative agency that investigates business practices and enforces the FTC Act. |
| 1938 | Wheeler-Lea Act | Amends the FTC Act to outlaw additional unfair practices; gives the FTC jurisdiction over false and misleading advertising. |
| 1998 | Digital Millennium Copyright Act | Protects intellectual property rights by prohibiting copying or downloading of digital files. |
| **B. Laws Regulating Competition** | | |
| 1936 | Robinson-Patman Act | Prohibits price discrimination in sales to wholesalers, retailers, or other producers; prohibits selling at unreasonably low prices to eliminate competition. |
| 1993 | North American Free Trade Agreement (NAFTA) | International trade agreement between Canada, Mexico, and the United States designed to facilitate trade by removing tariffs and other trade barriers among the three nations. |
| **C. Laws Protecting Consumers** | | |
| 1906 | Federal Food and Drug Act | Prohibits adulteration and misbranding of food and drugs involved in interstate commerce; strengthened by the Food, Drug, and Cosmetic Act (1938) and the Kefauver-Harris Drug Amendment (1962). |
| 1970 | National Environmental Policy Act | Establishes the Environmental Protection Agency to deal with various types of pollution and organizations that create pollution. |
| 1971 | Public Health Cigarette Smoking Act | Prohibits tobacco advertising on radio and television. |
| 1972 | Consumer Product Safety Act | Created the Consumer Product Safety Commission, which has authority to specify safety standards for most products. |

(Continues)

*(Continued)*

| Date | Law | Description |
|------|-----|-------------|
| 1998 | Children's Online Privacy Protection Act | Empowers FTC to set rules regarding how and when marketers must obtain parental permission before asking children marketing research questions. Revised in 2013 to address changes in the way children use and access the Internet and widening the definition of children's personal identification to address ways to track a child's activity online. |
| 1998 | Identity Theft and Assumption Deterrence Act | Makes it a federal crime to unlawfully use or transfer another person's identification with the intent to violate the law. |
| 1999 | Anti-Cybersquatting Consumer Protection Act | Bans the bad-faith purchase of domain names that are identical or confusingly similar to existing registered trademarks. |
| 2001 | Electronic Signature Act | Gives electronic signatures the same legal weight as handwritten signatures. |
| 2005 | Real ID Act | Sets minimum standards for state driver's licenses and ID cards and is currently being phased in. |
| 2006 | Consumer Telephone Records Act | Prohibits the sale of cell phone records. |
| 2009 | Fraud Enforcement and Recovery Act | Expands government's authority to investigate and prosecute mortgage fraud. |
| 2009 | Helping Families Save Their Homes Act | Helps homeowners avoid foreclosure and obtain affordable mortgages. |
| 2009 | Credit Card Accountability, Responsibility and Disclosure Act | Provides new rules governing credit card rate increases, fees, billing, and other practices. |
| **D. Laws Deregulating Specific Industries** | | |
| 1978 | Airline Deregulation Act | Grants considerable freedom to commercial airlines in setting fares and choosing new routes. |
| 1980 | Motor Carrier Act and Staggers Rail Act | Significantly deregulates trucking and railroad industries by permitting them to negotiate rates and services. |
| 1996 | Telecommunications Act | Significantly deregulates the telecommunications industry by removing barriers to competition in the phone and television broadcasting markets. |
| 2003 | Amendments to the Telemarketing Sales Rule | Created the National Do Not Call Registry prohibiting telemarketing calls to registered telephone numbers. Restricted the number and duration of telemarketing calls generating dead air space with use of automatic dialers; cracked down on unauthorized billing; and required telemarketers to transmit their caller ID information. |
| 2007 | Do-Not-Call Improvement Act | Extends Telemarketing Sales Rule; allows registered numbers to remain on Do Not Call list permanently. |
| 2007 | Fee Extension Act | Extends Telemarketing Sales Rule; sets annual fees for telemarketers to access the Do Not Call Registry. |

## 3-3b
# CLOSING EXAMPLE

The Microsoft case is a good example of antitrust legislation at work. The U.S. Department of Justice was successful in proving Microsoft guilty of predatory practices designed to crush competition. By bundling its own Internet Explorer browser with its Windows operating system—which runs on 90% of the world's personal computers—Microsoft grabbed the majority of the browser market from rival Netscape. It was also accused of bullying firms as large as America Online to drop Netscape Navigator in favor of its browser. Microsoft countered that consumers have clearly benefited from the integrated features in Windows and that its bundling decisions were simply efforts to offer customer satisfaction through added value. As a result of the U.S. antitrust law case, the Department of Justice required Microsoft to share its application programming interfaces with third-party companies. In addition, Microsoft was forced to make Windows compatible with non-Microsoft browser software. Without laws designed to maintain a competitive environment, we may have never seen additional choices in the browser market, such as Chrome, Firefox, and Safari.

## 3-4 TYPES OF REGULATORY FORCES

### OPENING EXAMPLE

Gerber produces several types of baby formula, including whey-based Good Start Gentle baby formula. Marketers for Gerber's baby formula know that parents want the very best for their children and often seek products from trusted brands. Gerber advertised its Good Start Gentle formula as a way to "reduce the risk of developing allergies." Advertisements for the formula read, "You want him to have your smile, not your allergies" and included "1st & only routine formula to reduce the risk of developing allergies" on the product packaging along with a gold seal that said "1st & Only Meets FDA Qualified Health Claim."[3] The U.S. Food and Drug Administration (FDA) is a regulatory agency responsible for ensuring the safety and proper labeling of foods. They monitor and determine whether health claims are qualified and then issue a regulation authorizing the claim on a food label. The gold seal and advertisements surely went a long way toward persuading parents that the Good Start Gentle formula could help prevent allergies. Unfortunately, these same labels got Gerber into some trouble. What do you think went wrong?

**LO 3.4** Describe the regulatory forces that influence the marketing environment.

#### 3-4a

### LEARNING IT: TYPES OF REGULATORY FORCES

#### GOVERNMENT REGULATORY AGENCIES

Federal, state, and local governments have established regulatory agencies to enforce laws. At the federal level, the FTC wields the broadest powers of any agency to influence marketing activities. The FTC enforces laws regulating unfair business practices and stops false and deceptive advertising. It regulates communication by radio, television, and other broadcast media. Other federal regulatory agencies include the Consumer Product Safety Commission, the Federal Power Commission, the Environmental Protection Agency (EPA), the Food and Drug Administration (FDA), and the National Highway Traffic Safety Administration (NHTSA).

## OTHER REGULATORY FORCES

Public and private consumer interest groups and self-regulatory organizations are also part of the political-legal environment. Consumer interest organizations have mushroomed since the late 1970s, and today hundreds of groups operate at national, state, and local levels. These organizations seek to protect consumers in as many areas as possible. The power of these groups has grown. For example, AARP (formerly known as the American Association of Retired Persons) wields political and economic power, particularly as more and more people reach retirement age.[4]

Self-regulatory groups represent multiple industries' attempts to set guidelines for responsible business conduct. The Council of Better Business Bureaus is a national organization devoted to consumer service and business self-regulation. The council's National Advertising Division (NAD) promotes truth and accuracy in advertising. It reviews and advocates voluntary resolution of advertising-related complaints between consumers and businesses. If NAD fails to resolve a complaint, an appeal can be made to the National Advertising Review Board, composed of advertisers, advertising agency representatives, and members of the public. In addition, many individual trade associations set business guidelines and codes of conduct, and encourage members' voluntary compliance. The Direct Marketing Association (DMA) supports consumer rights through its Commitment to Consumer Choice. Under this principle, DMA's 3,600+ organizations are required to inform consumers of their right to modify or discontinue receiving solicitations.[5]

Most marketers comply with laws and regulations. Doing so not only serves their customers but also avoids legal problems that could ultimately damage a firm's image and hurt profits. But smart marketers get ahead of the curve by providing products that will meet customers' future needs while also addressing the public good. For example, Toyota was one of the first automakers to commit to building hybrid cars. Its efforts were supported by a government tax break for purchasers of the first hybrids. Other manufacturers followed Toyota's lead in manufacturing hybrids, and government tax breaks are still available.

## 3-4b

# CLOSING EXAMPLE

Although Gerber advertised that its formula could prevent allergies, the FTC found flaws in Gerber's claims. Gerber had petitioned the FDA twice, once in 2005 and again in 2009. The first time, Gerber asked for approval in claiming that there was a relationship between whey-based baby formula and the reduced risk of children developing food allergies. The FDA denied that claim, so Gerber tried again, this time asking to add "emerging clinical research" that the whey-based formula may reduce eczema. The FDA denied Gerber again, but was willing to let the company say there was "little scientific evidence" of the relationship.[6] According to the FTC, Gerber falsely advertised that their formula was FDA approved. Further, Gerber's claims about the formula were not backed by scientific evidence. For both of these reasons, the FTC felt that consumers were not being protected.

# THE ECONOMIC ENVIRONMENT

## OPENING EXAMPLE

In December of 2007, after years of loose lending amid increasing housing prices, the real estate bubble in the United States finally burst. This ultimately caused significant decline in the stock market, and the subsequent failure of several financial institutions. Consumer confidence and spending declined, GDP began to contract, unemployment rates trended upward, and the recession reached Europe, Russia, and Japan.

Despite the grim outlook, marketers for De Beers diamonds doubled their budget in 2008, hoping that holiday shoppers would purchase pricey diamonds as gifts.[7] Because diamonds have lasting value, De Beers focused on print and television advertisements that featured the slogan, "A diamond is forever." Unfortunately, demand for diamonds fell during the recession and De Beers saw a decline in profits in 2008.[8] Where did De Beers go wrong?

**LO 3.5** Outline the economic factors that affect marketing decisions and consumer buying power.

### 3-5a

## LEARNING IT: THE ECONOMIC ENVIRONMENT

The **economic environment** consists of factors that influence consumer buying power and marketing strategies. These include: stages of the business cycle, inflation and deflation, unemployment, and income.

De Beers found that changes in the economic environment often require changes to the marketing mix.

**economic environment** consists of factors that influence consumer buying power and marketing strategies

## STAGES OF THE BUSINESS CYCLE

The overall health of the economy influences how much consumers spend and what they buy. Consumer spending accounts for about 65% of the nation's total **gross domestic product (GDP)**- the sum of all

**gross domestic product (GDP)** the sum of all goods and services produced by a nation in a year

goods and services produced by a nation in a year.[9] Because marketing activities are directed toward satisfying consumer wants and needs, marketers must first understand how economic conditions influence the purchasing decisions that consumers make.

Historically, the economy has tended to follow a cyclical pattern that alternates between longer periods of expansion and shorter periods of contraction. A period of economic contraction lasting six months or more is called a recession. Consumer buying differs in each stage of the business cycle, and marketers must adjust their strategies accordingly. In times of prosperity, consumer spending increases and buyers are willing to spend more for premium versions of well-known brands. Marketers respond by offering new products, expanding their promotional efforts, and expanding distribution. They might even raise prices to widen profit margins.

During economic slowdowns, consumers focus more on basic, functional products that carry lower price tags. Consumers limit expenditures on travel, restaurant meals, and entertainment. They skip expensive vacations and cook their own meals. During an economic contraction, marketers consider lowering prices and increasing promotions that include special offers to stimulate demand. They may also launch special value-priced products to appeal to cost-conscious buyers.

## CHANGES IN PRICES

**inflation** rising prices caused by some combination of excess demand and the increasing cost of raw materials, labor, and/or other factors of production

A major constraint on consumer spending, which can occur during any stage of the business cycle, is **inflation**—rising prices caused by some combination of excess demand and the increasing cost of raw materials, labor, and/or other factors of production.

Deflation is a general decrease in prices. While falling prices mean that products are more affordable, deflation can be a long and damaging downward spiral, causing a freefall in business profits, lower returns on most investments, and widespread job layoffs. The last time the United States experienced significant deflation was in the Great Depression of the 1930s.

## EMPLOYMENT AND INCOME

**unemployment** the proportion of people in the economy who are actively seeking work but do not have jobs

**Unemployment** is defined as the proportion of people in the economy who are actively seeking work but do not have jobs. Unemployment rises during recessions and declines during economic expansions. If more people have jobs, there is more income to be spent on goods and services.

Income is another important determinant of the economic environment because it influences consumer buying power. Many marketers are particularly interested in **discretionary income**- the amount of money people have to spend after buying necessities such as food, clothing, and housing.

**discretionary income** the amount of money people have to spend after buying necessities such as food, clothing, and housing

Historically, periods of major innovation have been accompanied by dramatic increases in living standards and rising incomes. Automobiles, televisions, telephones, computers, and the Internet are just a few of the innovations that have improved consumers' lives—and standards of living.

## 3-5b

## CLOSING EXAMPLE

De Beers may have overestimated consumer confidence or failed to recognize that consumers in its target market would delay expensive purchases during a recession. Perhaps De Beers could have lowered prices or advertised special offers for their products in order to increase demand. Regardless of its mistake, De Beers certainly learned the importance of evaluating the economic environment and adjusting the company's marketing efforts to reflect consumer behavior.

# 3-6   THE TECHNOLOGICAL ENVIRONMENT

## OPENING EXAMPLE

Marcelina Rousseau shook her head in frustration. She just finished reading another story in the newspaper about a counterfeit bust in Brooklyn that resulted in over 15,000 fake bags and wallets seized. Authorities found counterfeit products from most major luxury brands including Marcelina's MR Luxe purses and wallets. These counterfeit busts were becoming more common. There was no way for Marcelina to know how much these counterfeits were costing her in lost sales, but she was more concerned about the customers who believed that they were purchasing genuine MR Luxe bags. In the past month, MR Luxe had received multiple calls to their customer service line about a variety of craftsmanship issues—from faulty zippers to torn linings. Only one of the calls actually concerned a genuine MR Luxe product. The other five customers had unknowingly purchased counterfeit products.

Marcelina called a meeting with her executive team and said, "We must find a way to assure consumers that they have purchased a genuine MR Luxe product. What can we do?"

**LO 3.6** Describe how a change in the technological environment can impact a firm's marketing activities.

## 3-6a

## LEARNING IT: THE TECHNOLOGICAL ENVIRONMENT

The **technological environment** represents the application of knowledge based on discoveries in science, inventions, and innovations. Technology leads to new goods and services for consumers. It also improves existing products, offers better customer service, and often reduces prices through new, cost-efficient production and distribution methods. Technology can quickly make products obsolete. E-mail, for example, quickly eroded both letter writing and the market for fax machines. But technological advances can just as quickly open new marketing opportunities, sometimes in entirely new industries.

Pets have been wearing radio-frequency identification (RFID) transmitters for years, in case the pets were lost. Now RFID tags are used in many industries to

**technological environment**
the application of knowledge based on discoveries in science, inventions, and innovations

Disney's Magic band uses modern technology to both increase customer service and gather valuable data about customer behavior.

Source: WIRED.COM

locate everything from library books to laundry detergent. An RFID tag contains a computer chip with an antenna. A reader scans the tag and transmits the data from the tag to a computer. This innovation means that retailers, manufacturers, and others can locate and track inventory without opening packages. It also means that companies can track consumer behavior in greater detail. Disney unveiled a program called MyMagic+, which will allow visitors to Disney parks to preregister for wristbands embedded with RFID tags. These "MagicBands" function as room keys, park-entry tickets, Fast Passes, and credit cards. But the use of RFID to track the movement of humans is controversial because of the privacy implications.[10]

Technology can also address social concerns. In response to pressure from the World Trade Organization and the U.S. government, automakers used technology to develop more fuel-efficient vehicles and reduce dangerous emissions.

By monitoring and responding to the technological environment, marketers can gain a competitive edge with innovative products, cut costs, improve customer service, and benefit society.

## 3-6b

## CLOSING EXAMPLE

Marcelina's team deliberated on a number of options, but ultimately decided to include RFID chips in each of its products. Consumers can scan the chip through the MR Luxe app on their smartphones to authenticate the goods. Marcelina hopes that employing technology in her luxury brand will help prevent consumers from unknowingly purchasing counterfeit products, and make it more difficult for counterfeiters to reproduce luxury goods.

# THE SOCIAL-CULTURAL ENVIRONMENT

**3-7**

## OPENING EXAMPLE

Vikram Kadra, VP of marketing for Food Town supermarkets, said to his marketing team, "I've just spoken with our CFO and sales have dropped again for the third quarter in a row. We need to come up with a plan."

"There aren't any new, major competitors in any of our markets," replied Marika Harte, Marketing Manager. "I would almost feel better if there were—at least we could attribute the declining sales to that."

Brian Reid, another Marketing Manager, responded, "Well, let's look at our category sales. Sales in frozen foods, snacks, and deli are up again. The meat and seafood manager told me his crew makes pre-prepped meats twice a day now. Things like kabobs and pre-seasoned chicken quarters are selling well."

"Yes, my neighbors love the pre-prepped meats and seafood. They both work full time and their kids have soccer practice two or three nights a week; they need quick meals to fix. People are so busy these days; it seems they'd buy a peeled orange if we sold them!"

Vikram was excited now. How had he not noticed this before? Activities, meetings, and kids' practices were keeping people from spending time preparing meals. Food Town had a big opportunity to provide a solution for its busy customers and Vikram now knows just what to do.

**3-7a**

## LEARNING IT: THE SOCIAL-CULTURAL ENVIRONMENT

As a nation, the United States is becoming older, more affluent, and more culturally diverse. People express concerns about the natural environment, buying ecologically friendly products that reduce pollution. They value their time with family and friends. Marketers need to track these trends to be in tune with consumers' needs and desires. These aspects of consumer lifestyles help shape marketing's **social-cultural environment**- the relationship between marketing, society, and culture.

To remain competitive, marketers must be sensitive to society's demographic shifts and changing values. These variables affect consumers' reactions to different products and marketing practices.

*Example #1*: The baby boom generation—the 78 million Americans born between 1946 and 1964—represents a $7 trillion market. As "boomers" approach and enter retirement, marketers are scrambling to identify their needs and wants. With a longer life expectancy and the hope of more time and money to spend, boomers now view retirement much differently than earlier generations did.

*Marketer response*: Develop products related to health care, travel and leisure, and financial management that might appeal to the needs of this generation.

---

**LO 3.7** Determine an effective marketing response to a change in the social-cultural environment.

---

**social-cultural environment** the relationship between marketing, society, and culture

Another social-cultural consideration is the increasing importance of cultural diversity. The United States is a mixed society composed of various submarkets, each with its unique values, cultural characteristics, consumer preferences, and purchasing behaviors.

*Example #2*: There is a growing Hispanic market with over $1.5 trillion in purchasing power in the United States.[11]

*Marketer response*: In an effort to attract the millions of Hispanic viewers in the United States, satellite and cable TV companies now offer more Spanish-language programming. Spanish-language networks Univision and Telemundo, which once dominated the Hispanic TV market, now face competition from Comcast, Cablevision, Time Warner Cable, DISH Network, and DIRECTV.

**consumerism** a social force within the environment that aids and protects the consumer by exerting legal, moral, and economic pressures on business and government

Changing societal values have led to **consumerism**- a social force within the environment that aids and protects the consumer by exerting legal, moral, and economic pressures on business and government. Today, everyone—marketers, industry, government, and the public—is acutely aware of the impact of consumerism on the nation's economy and general well-being. Consumers today strongly believe that they should have the right to choose among various products, the right to be informed, the right to be heard, and the right to be safe.

Consumerism, along with the rest of the social-cultural environment for marketing decisions at home and abroad, is expanding in scope and importance. Today, no marketer can initiate a strategic decision without considering the society's norms, values, culture, and demographics. Understanding how these variables affect decisions is so important that some firms have created a new position—typically, manager of public policy research—to study the changing societal environment's future impact on their organizations.

DIRECTV offers a full slate of Spanish-language programming in response to changes in the social-cultural environment.

Source: channelshopping.blogspot.com

## 3-7b
## CLOSING EXAMPLE

Shifting demographics and changing lifestyles mean big changes at your neighborhood grocery store. According to a recent study by market research firm NPD Group, less than 60% of dinners eaten at home are cooked there.[12] Whether it be busy families with two working adults or young professionals, people want to eat healthy, fresh food at an affordable price. Food Town decided to focus on this social-cultural shift. Vikram hired chefs to oversee the creation of prepared meals that consumers can purchase in-store and eat at home. The meals are restaurant quality, prepared fresh daily, and are sold at a lower cost than similar meals at full-service or fast-casual restaurants.

By understanding changing demographics and other shifts in the social-cultural environment, marketers like Vikram can offer products to meet consumers' needs.

# 3-8 ETHICAL ISSUES IN MARKETING

## OPENING EXAMPLE

"Wow, Eric, the snow is really coming down out there!"

"I know. Weather report said two feet or more. JFK Airport will probably cancel most flights; let's get ready for an onslaught of calls."

Eric Detzel, Manager of the Courtyard by Marriott New York JFK Airport Hotel, knew this winter storm was good news for him. The hotel only had a handful of reservations before the storm, but with the heavy snowfalls and canceled flights, this winter storm was going to be big business for hotels in the area.

"Julie, let's change the rates in the system. Any customer calling about a room should be quoted $209 per night."

"$209? Eric, that's over $100 more than we normally charge!" exclaimed Julie, Assistant Manager. "Are you sure?"

"Absolutely! These travelers would pay twice that for a warm bed and a hot shower! I guarantee no one even flinches when you quote the price," Eric told her.

"Seems too high, Eric. I'm not sure this is a good idea," Julie told him.

"It's fine, Julie. Besides, corporate will be thrilled with the extra profit. Tell anyone who calls that the rooms are $209."

Who do you side with? Eric or Julie?

LO 3.8  Given a variable of the marketing mix, describe an ethical issue related to that variable.

## 3-8a
## LEARNING IT: ETHICAL ISSUES IN MARKETING

The five dimensions of the marketing environment described so far in this chapter do not completely capture all of the factors that influence a marketer's decisions. These environmental influences have also directed increased attention toward **marketing ethics**- defined as marketers' standards of conduct and values. As Exhibit 3.3 shows, each element of the marketing mix raises its own set of ethical issues. Before any improvements to a firm's marketing program can be made, each element must be evaluated.

**marketing ethics**  the marketer's standards of conduct and values

## 3-8b
## ETHICS IN PRODUCT STRATEGY

Ethical issues can be raised when considering decisions about product quality and lifespan. For example, planned obsolescence is intentionally designing a product to have a limited useful life. The motive of planned obsolescence is to encourage repeat purchase or faster upgrade cycles. This product strategy is sometimes seen in the mobile phone industry and video game console market.

**EXHIBIT 3.3** Ethical Issues in Marketing

**Product**
- Planned obsolescence
- Product quality and safety
- Product warranties
- Fair packaging and labeling
- Pollution

**Distribution**
- Exclusive territories
- Dumping
- Dealer rights
- Predatory competition

**Ethical Issues**

**Promotion**
- Bait-and-switch advertising
- False and deceptive advertising
- Promotional allowances
- Bribery

**Price**
- Price fixing
- Price discrimination
- Price increases
- Deceptive pricing

Product packaging and branding also raises ethical issues. Some marketers have tried packaging practices that might be considered misleading, deceptive, or unethical. Examples:

- Odd-sized packages make price comparisons difficult.
- Larger packages take up more shelf space, and consumers notice them—but the real advantage is they take away shelf space from competitors.
- Bottles with concave bottoms give the impression that they contain more liquid than they actually do.

Are these packaging practices justified in the name of competition, or are they deceptive?

### 3-8c
## ETHICS IN PRICING

Pricing is probably the most regulated aspect of a firm's marketing strategy. As a result, most unethical price behavior is also illegal. Some aspects of pricing, however, are still open to ethics abuses. For example, should some customers pay more for merchandise if distribution costs are higher in their areas? Do marketers have an obligation to warn vendors and customers of impending changes in price, discount, or return policies? And should marketers be able to change prices based entirely on supply and demand, like in the hotel example at the beginning of this section?

### 3-8d
## ETHICS IN DISTRIBUTION

Two ethical issues influence a firm's decisions regarding distribution strategy:

1. What is the appropriate degree of control over the distribution channel?

2. Should a company distribute its products in marginally profitable outlets that have no alternative source of supply?

The question of channel control typically arises in relationships between manufacturers and franchise dealers. For example, should an automobile dealership, a gas station, or a fast-food outlet be forced to purchase parts, materials, and supplementary services from the parent organization?

The second question concerns marketers' responsibility to serve unsatisfied market segments, even if the profit potential is small. For example, should marketers build retail stores in low-income areas or continue to operate in a declining rural market? This could benefit consumers, but could hurt the company. These problems are difficult to resolve.

## 3-8e

# ETHICS IN PROMOTION

Promotion raises many ethical questions because it is the most direct link between a firm and its customers. Personal selling has always been a target of criticism, and the focus of jokes about untrustworthiness. Used-car dealers, horse traders, and purveyors of unproven health remedies have been the targets of such criticisms in the past. But promotion covers many areas, ranging from advertising to direct marketing, and it is vital for marketers to monitor their ethics in all marketing communications. Truth in advertising—accurately reflecting a product's benefits and drawbacks, warranties, price, and availability—is the bedrock of ethics in promotion.

Promotion to children has been under close scrutiny for many years because children have not yet developed the skills to receive marketing messages critically. They often believe everything they see and hear. Promoting certain products to college students can raise ethical questions as well. College students are a prime market for firms that sell everything from electronics to beer. And although laws prohibit the sale of alcohol to anyone under 21, companies often advertise beer through popular items like hats, shirts, bar signs, and other collectibles. Critics have long claimed that this practice supports underage drinking.

## 3-8f

# CLOSING EXAMPLE

After 30.5 inches of snow fell in New York in January of 2016, hundreds of travelers were left stranded. Flight cancellations, mass transit shutdowns, and a local travel ban forced passengers to stay in nearby hotels for several days. The Courtyard by Marriott near JFK Airport was forced to pay restitution to customers in the amount of $48,000 and pay a civil penalty of $17,500 for price gouging.[13] New York state law forbids excessive price hikes for essential goods and services during natural disasters. In addition, Marriott hotel guidelines prohibit hotels from raising rates during times of disaster in excess of normal retail rates, even when disasters generate significant demand.

Unethical pricing not only harms customers, but ultimately harms companies as well. Understanding ethical issues as they relate to the marketing mix is important for marketers as they satisfy customer needs and wants.

# 3-9 SOCIAL RESPONSIBILITY

**LO
3.9**   Define the four dimensions of social responsibility.

## OPENING EXAMPLE

IBM is a century-old U.S. firm with more than 430,000 employees operating in almost 170 countries. It holds itself to high standards of corporate social responsibility (CSR), in part because its operations support not only companies around the world, but also cities, communities, governments, and their infrastructures. The company believes corporate citizenship "consists of far more than community service" and is constantly looking for ways to make a real difference at all levels of its large network of stakeholders.

Most of IBM's CSR efforts are international in scope, such as its Smarter Cities Challenge, which sends IBM experts to 100 cities worldwide to solve local problems in health, education, transportation, and sustainability.[14] Further, IBM focuses on using environmentally sustainable substances and materials. How do these CSR efforts relate to IBM's quest to also make a profit? Are these conflicting goals or are they directly related?

### 3-9a

## LEARNING IT: SOCIAL RESPONSIBILITY

**social responsibility** accepting an obligation to give equal weight to profits, consumer satisfaction, and social well-being in evaluating a firm's performance

Companies can do business in a way that everyone benefits—customers, the companies themselves, and society as a whole. While ethical business practices are vital to a firm's long-term survival and growth, **social responsibility** raises the bar even higher. In marketing, social responsibility involves accepting an obligation to give equal weight to profits, consumer satisfaction, and social well-being in evaluating a firm's performance. In addition to measuring sales, revenues, and profits, a firm must also consider ways in which it contributes to the overall well-being of its customers and society.

The four dimensions of social responsibility are economic, legal, ethical, and philanthropic (see Exhibit 3.4).

The first dimension of social responsibility is for companies to be *economically responsible*. Organizations have a responsibility to produce goods and services that are valued by society and to maximize profits for its owners and shareholders. Organizations must be profitable in order to pay employees and remain in business. This economic responsibility serves as the foundation for the company before it can consider any social responsibilities.

*Legal responsibility* is the organization's obligation to fulfill its economic goals by operating within the legal requirements imposed by local, state, and federal governments. Simply, the company is expected to obey the law. Illegal actions taken by organizations may include price discrimination, misleading consumers, corporate fraud, or improper labor practices.

After a company has met both economic and legal responsibilities, it can move toward *ethical responsibility*. Ethical responsibilities involve doing what is right, for example, paying fair wages, using sustainable resources, and treating

**EXHIBIT 3.4** ▶ The Four-Step Pyramid of Social Responsibility

**Philanthropic**
*Be a good corporate citizen*
▶ Contribute resources to the community; improve quality of life

**Ethical**
*Be ethical*
▶ Obligation to do what is right, just, and fair
▶ Avoid harm

**Legal**
*Obey the law*
▶ Law is society's codification of right and wrong
▶ Play by the rules of the game

**Economic**
*Be profitable*
▶ The foundation upon which all others rest

Source: The Four Step Pyramid of Corporate Social Responsibility from Business Horizons, Vol. 34, 1991, page 92, Freeman & Liedtka, "Corp. Social Responsibility."

others fairly. Companies are under no obligation to act ethically, but do so because its owners or managers believe it is the right thing to do.

The last dimension of social responsibility is *philanthropic responsibility*. Organizations operating at this level are doing so voluntarily. These responsibilities involve benefitting society and contributing resources to the community to improve quality of life. Donating money to charitable causes or participating in community outreach are examples of philanthropic responsibility.

Marketers can use several methods to help their companies behave in socially responsible ways. Socially responsible marketing involves campaigns that encourage people to adopt socially beneficial behaviors such as safe driving, eating more nutritious food, or improving the working conditions of people half a world away. And organizations that sponsor socially responsible programs not only help society but also develop goodwill for an organization, which helps the bottom line in the long run.

## 3-9b
# CLOSING EXAMPLE

IBM strives to be a good corporate citizen by supporting and improving the communities in which employees live and work. Whether through education, disaster response and recovery, or pollution prevention, IBM contributes to their social responsibility efforts in a variety of ways. While IBM is committed to being economically responsible by making a profit, it also works to be socially responsible at the legal, ethical, and philanthropic levels.

## 3-10   LEARN IT TODAY . . . USE IT TOMORROW

At the beginning of the chapter we learned about Progressive Insurance, a company that proactively responds to change instead of passively reacting to factors in its external environment. For example, more than 50 years ago, Progressive was the first auto insurance company to allow its customers to pay their premiums in installments. Due to changes in the economic environment, Progressive recognized a need and presented a solution to those customers. Today, insurance companies offer discounts to customers based on their safe driving habits. Progressive utilizes technology through their Snapshot device (which plugs into a car's on-board diagnostics port) and monitors how the customer drives. Customers then send the Snapshot device back to Progressive and, depending on their driving habits, they receive a discount on their rates. As the marketing environment continues to change, it's a safe bet that Progressive will respond quickly and creatively to remain an industry leader.

Change is a fact of life for marketers. Industry competition, legal constraints, the impact of technology, and social concerns are some of the many important factors that shape the marketing environment. All potentially have an impact on a firm's goods and services. Marketers must consider all of these factors—and seek to remain ethical and socially responsible—as they develop marketing mixes for their target customers.

It's time to get hands-on and apply what you've learned. **See MindTap for an activity related to Progressive's marketing activities.**

## Chapter Summary

**LO 3.1   Identify the five components of the marketing environment.**

The five components of the marketing environment are the competitive environment, political-legal environment, the economic environment, technological environment, and social-cultural environment.

**LO 3.2   Contrast the two types of competition that marketers face.**

The two types of competition are: (1) direct competition among marketers of similar products and (2) indirect competition among goods or services that can be substituted for one another.

**LO 3.3   Summarize the four major types of government regulation that affect marketing practices.**

The four major types of government regulation are maintaining a competitive environment, regulating competition, protecting consumers, and deregulating specific industries to increase competition.

**LO 3.4  Describe the regulatory forces that influence the marketing environment.**

Marketing activities are influenced by federal, state, and local laws that require firms to operate under competitive conditions and to protect consumer rights. Public and private consumer interest groups and industry self-regulatory groups also affect marketing activities.

**LO 3.5  Outline the economic factors that affect marketing decisions and consumer buying power.**

The primary economic factors are the stage in the business cycle, inflation and deflation, unemployment, and income. All are vitally important to marketers because of their effects on consumers' willingness to buy and consumers' perceptions regarding changes in the marketing mix variables.

**LO 3.6  Describe how a change in the technological environment can impact a firm's marketing activities.**

The technological environment consists of the application of knowledge based on discoveries in science, inventions, and innovations. By monitoring and responding to the technological environment, marketers can gain a competitive edge with innovative products, cut costs, improve customer service, and benefit society.

**LO 3.7  Determine an effective marketing response to a change in the social-cultural environment.**

The social-cultural environment is the relationship between marketing, society, and culture. To remain competitive, marketers must be sensitive to society's demographic shifts and changing values, which affect consumers' reactions to different products and marketing practices.

**LO 3.8  Given a variable of the marketing mix, describe an ethical issue related to that variable.**

Marketing ethics encompass the marketer's standards of conduct and values. Each element of the marketing mix raises its own set of ethical questions.

**LO 3.9  Define the four dimensions of social responsibility.**

The four dimensions of social responsibility are economic, legal, ethical, and philanthropic.

## Key Terms

competitive environment **45**

competitive strategy **45**

political-legal environment **46**

antitrust **47**

economic environment **51**

gross domestic product (GDP) **51**

inflation **52**

unemployment **52**

discretionary income **52**

technological environment **53**

social-cultural environment **55**

consumerism **56**

marketing ethics **57**

social responsibility **60**

# 4 E-BUSINESS: MANAGING THE CUSTOMER EXPERIENCE

Uber Images/Shutterstock.com

## LEARNING OBJECTIVES

**4.1** Summarize the five opportunities offered by digital marketing.

**4.2** List the four major forms of e-business in the business-to-business market.

**4.3** Explain three reasons consumers prefer to shop online.

**4.4** Summarize five challenges faced by online marketers and consumers.

**4.5** Summarize four factors that influence the success of an e-commerce website.

**4.6** Describe the various methods for measuring the effectiveness of an e-commerce website.

**4.7** Given an example of an online marketing activity, calculate the activity's effectiveness.

# LEARN IT TODAY . . . USE IT TOMORROW

asks once done in person, such as communicating and shopping, can now be done over the Internet. Without the Internet, *how would you go about simple activities such as:*

- Viewing a video of your favorite band
- Ordering a meal from a neighborhood restaurant
- Researching products you want to purchase
- Researching academic journals for a school project

Just a few years ago, these activities required a lot more time, effort, and cost. But now, these activities involve simply using your smartphone to open YouTube, using a restaurant's phone app, browsing Amazon.com, or remotely visiting a college's library from your laptop.

The introduction of the Internet to the public in the early 1990s started a new era in marketing communications. The tremendous increase in Internet access has brought people, businesses, and countries closer, while mobile communication has become cheaper and more accessible. Today, over 320 million people—more than 89% of the U.S. population—have access to the Internet at home, school, work, or public sites. The number of Internet users worldwide totals more than 3.6 billion.[1] Exhibit 4.1 summarizes Internet usage in countries around the world.

 **Internet Usage Around the World**

## Two-thirds worldwide use the internet, but fewer do in Africa and South Asia

*Percent of adults who use the internet at least occasionally or report owning a smartphone*

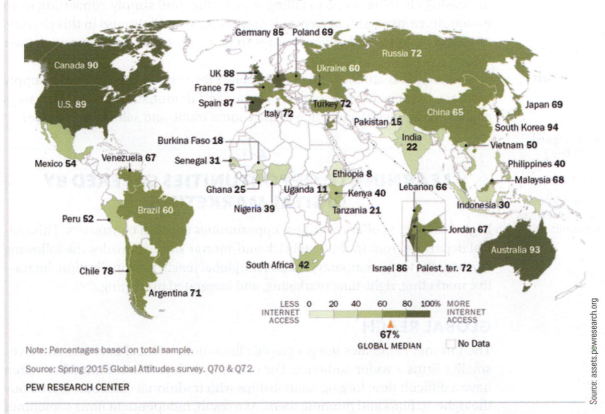

Note: Percentages based on total sample.

Source: Spring 2015 Global Attitudes survey. Q70 & Q72.

**PEW RESEARCH CENTER**

Source: assets.pewresearch.org

*(Continues)*

*(Continued)*

**E-business** is using the Internet to provide services to customers and communicate with employees and business partners. E-business includes **e-commerce**, which is the buying and selling of products online.

**Digital marketing** (also called online marketing or Internet marketing) is the process of marketing goods and services over the Internet by utilizing digital tools, such as desktop computers, mobile devices (smartphones, tablets, and laptops), websites, databases, and e-mail.

We use the Internet every day without thinking about the various aspects of online business or digital marketing. Yet, given how much these technologies have changed daily life, it's valuable to take a closer look.

# 4-1 OPPORTUNITIES OFFERED BY DIGITAL MARKETING

**LO 4.1** Summarize the five opportunities offered by digital marketing.

**e-business** using the Internet to provide services to customers and communicate with employees and business partners

**e-commerce** the buying and selling of products online

**digital marketing** the process of marketing goods and services over the Internet by utilizing digital tools

## OPENING EXAMPLE

In the past, the success of a retail store often depended on their location. The more traffic—physical foot traffic or car traffic—that passed the store, the more likely the store would get customers. However, brick-and-mortar retailers face increasing challenges due to falling store traffic. And simply converting to an e-commerce store isn't as easy as it may seem, as we'll discuss in this chapter. Retailers need to find effective ways to embrace technology to revive their sales.

Let's say you are the Marketing Manager for Sur La Table, a kitchen supply retailer who does in-store cooking classes and demonstrations. In what ways could you use digital marketing to drive more traffic and sales to your store?

### 4-1a

## LEARNING IT: OPPORTUNITIES OFFERED BY DIGITAL MARKETING

Digital marketing offers countless opportunities to reach consumers. This radical departure from traditional brick-and-mortar stores provides the following five benefits to contemporary marketers: global reach, personalization, interactive marketing, right-time marketing, and integrated marketing.

### GLOBAL REACH

The Internet eliminates the geographic limitations of local business and gives smaller firms a wider audience. For example, independent filmmakers often have a difficult time forging relationships with traditional distributors who buy the rights to films and promote them. As a result, independent films sometimes have a limited audience. But the Internet is allowing filmmakers to organize their own screenings, send messages to interested online communities, and sell films directly through their websites.[2]

## PERSONALIZATION

Web pages can be tailored for each individual customer. Netflix makes viewing recommendations by using a customer's past orders, as well as that customer's ratings, to determine what movies and TV shows a person might like.[3]

## INTERACTIVE MARKETING

Marketers use a concept called **interactive marketing** to deliver more relevant marketing messages to customers based on event triggers. McDonald's mobile app pushes notifications, like deals and coupons, at specific times—such as when customers are near a store or on certain days of the week.[4]

**interactive marketing**
delivering more relevant marketing messages to customers based on event triggers

## RIGHT-TIME MARKETING

Marketers want to reach the right person, through the right channel, at the right moment. A local hotel can run online ads targeted only to those searching for hotels within that area.

## INTEGRATED MARKETING

The Internet amplifies a company's offline promotional activities to create a consistent, customer-oriented promotional message. Red Bull's logo, colors, and the slogan "Red Bull gives you wings" are used in both online and offline promotions.

Exhibit 4.2 provides additional examples of the opportunities offered by online marketing.

**EXHIBIT 4.2** Online Marketing Capabilities

| Capability | Description | Example |
|---|---|---|
| Global reach | The ability to reach anyone connected to the Internet anywhere in the world. | A local retailer of antiques can now market and sell its goods worldwide. |
| Personalization | The ability to create products to meet customer specifications. | Walmart's website provides purchase recommendations based on your past purchases and recent searches. |
| Interactive marketing | Buyer–seller communications that are triggered based on events. | Verizon will text customers nearing their mobile phone data limit with an offer to purchase additional data. |
| Right-time marketing | The ability to provide a product at the exact time needed. | Amazon Fresh offers same-day delivery of online grocery orders. |
| Integrated marketing | Use of coordinated online promotional activities to amplify and reinforce offline promotional activities. | Coca-Cola uses the same branding (logo, slogan, tagline, colors, fonts, etc.) for a product seen on TV, online, and in stores. |

**4-1b**

## 4-1b
## CLOSING EXAMPLE

Online-only retail, dominated by U.S.-based Amazon.com and China-based Alibaba, continues to grow while brick-and-mortar retailers, such as The Limited, shut down. Fortunately, some retailers are adjusting to the shift in shoppers' habits. For example, kitchen supply retailer Sur La Table now streams in-store cooking classes and demonstrations on its website. Participants in these classes receive a 10% coupon to use in the store or on the company's website up to seven days after the class.

This shows how an effective online presence can improve the performance of traditional retail operations. Retailers taking advantage of digital marketing opportunities enhance options for their customers and increase sales for themselves.

# 4-2
# E-BUSINESS IN THE B2B MARKET

**LO 4.2**
List the four major forms of e-business in the business-to-business market.

## OPENING EXAMPLE

The website for Pepsi is all about entertainment. Recently, it focused on the Super Bowl halftime show, including interviews with the performers and videos of the performance. On the other hand, FedEx's website isn't flashy, because its main purpose isn't to entertain or sell products to household consumers. Instead, it provides practical information to help the firm's customers, most of which are businesses. The site enables customers to check rates, compare services, schedule package pickups, track shipments, and order shipping supplies. This information is vital to FedEx's customers. Those businesses access the FedEx site thousands of times a day to conduct their daily operations. While we often think of e-business as it relates to consumers, much of what happens on the Internet doesn't involve consumers at all.

## 4-2a
## LEARNING IT: E-BUSINESS IN THE B2B MARKET

**business-to-business (B2B)** transactions that happen between organizations

**Business-to-business (B2B)** transactions are those that happen between organizations, and increasingly technology is used to facilitate these transactions. Although most people are familiar with consumer-focused online firms such as Amazon and eBay, the number of consumer transactions is dwarfed by their B2B counterparts. By some estimates, B2B e-commerce revenues are more than double that of consumer transactions.[5]

In addition to generating sales revenue, B2B uses of online technology include collaborating with suppliers, communicating with employees, and facilitating orders and payments. B2B transactions, which typically involve more steps than consumer purchases, can be much more efficient when using the

Internet. There are four major forms of e-business in the B2B market: electronic data interchange, extranets, intranets, and private exchanges.

## ELECTRONIC DATA INTERCHANGE (EDI)

EDI is one of the oldest applications of technology for business transactions. It includes direct, computer-to-computer exchanges of price quotations, purchase orders, invoices, and other sales information between buyers and sellers.

Use of EDI cuts paper flow, speeds the order cycle, and reduces errors. In addition, by receiving daily inventory status reports from vendors, companies can set production schedules to match demand. A company like Boeing, who has thousands of suppliers, would use EDI to improve efficiency within their large and complex supply chain. Royal Dutch/Shell Group, a group of energy companies with operations in 140 countries, purchases millions of dollars of parts, components, supplies, and services every day. The firm replaced its network of more than 100 purchasing systems with a streamlined new system to unify procurement and reduce costs.[6]

## EXTRANETS

**Extranets** are secure networks used for e-business and accessible through the firm's website by external customers, suppliers, or other authorized users. Extranets offer an efficient way for businesses to collaborate with others by giving selected outsiders access to internal information. For example, an advertising agency might provide a client authorized access to an extranet so they can view progress on an advertising campaign and provide feedback. This type of real-time collaboration can enhance relationships with business partners.

**extranets** secure networks used for e-business and accessible through the firm's website by external customers, suppliers, or other authorized users

## INTRANET

**Intranets** are secure internal networks that help companies share information among employees, no matter the number or location. This allows employees across the globe the ability to:

**intranets** secure internal networks that help companies share information among employees, no matter the number or location

- View and share documents stored on company servers.
- Access information related to their position, including customer data, financial reports, inventory counts, and other data tracked by the company.
- Collaborate on projects using company-based applications for messaging, scheduling, file management, and data analytics.

Many companies allow employees to access the company intranet via remote access, which allows employees to log in from anywhere, including home, and do their jobs just as if they were sitting at their desk in the office. Because of this technology, more companies allow employees flexible scheduling, where they can work from home certain days per week. Some companies now have entirely distributed workforces, meaning they have no centralized offices and all employees work remotely. Automattic, the makers of Wordpress.com, the 15th most trafficked site on the Internet, has a 100%

distributed workforce of over 200 employees. They use a combination of private blogs, private chats, and messaging services to manage projects and communications.

## PRIVATE EXCHANGES

**private exchange** a secure website where a company and its suppliers share all types of data, from product design through order delivery

A **private exchange** is a secure website where a company and its suppliers share all types of data, from product design through order delivery. A private exchange integrates aspects of the company extranet and intranet, putting them together on one specialized site. The participants can use it to collaborate on product ideas, production scheduling, distribution, order tracking, and any other functions a business wants to include.

For example, Walmart has a private exchange it calls Retail Link. The system permits Walmart employees to access detailed sales and inventory information. Suppliers, such as Procter & Gamble and Nestlé, can look up Walmart sales data and forecasts to manage their own inventory and logistics, helping them better meet the needs of the world's largest retailer and its millions of customers worldwide.

### 4-2b

## CLOSING EXAMPLE

Much of the traffic that happens on the Internet is hidden to household consumers. Instead of providing news, entertainment, or retail e-commerce, that traffic is helping businesses work more efficiently and effectively with their suppliers, partners, customers, and employees. In the end, this often benefits us as consumers. When Fed Ex delivers your package from Amazon.com, it's the result of an e-business collaboration between those two companies involving ordering, tracking, and payment—all of which happens behind the scenes when you place an order.

A private exchange combines the benefits of an intranet and extranet to allow collaboration between employees, suppliers, and partners.

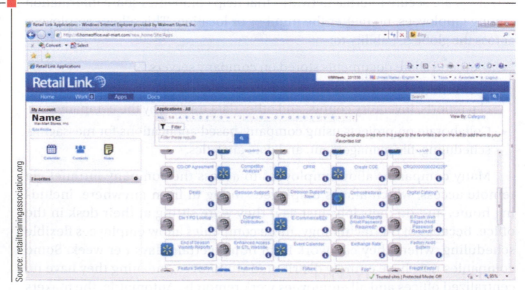

Source: retailtrainingassociation.org

# 4-3 BENEFITS OF SHOPPING ONLINE

## OPENING EXAMPLE

**LO 4.3** Explain three reasons consumers prefer to shop online.

With the Christmas holiday approaching, two consumers have decided to buy their families a new LCD TV.

Maria is looking for a 40-inch version, so she drives to the department store to see what they have. After looking at five different models and taking notes on their prices and features, she heads over to the big box electronic store. She's overwhelmed by all of the options and is now wondering if the 48-inch TV would be a better choice. So she takes notes on the brands, features, and prices for those. Unfortunately, there's no salesperson in sight who can let her know which brand might be the best choice. She asks a fellow shopper and he's convinced that LG makes the best TVs, but then another shopper overhears and says she prefers Samsung. At this point, Maria doesn't know what to do. She considers heading back to the department store to look at their selection of 48-inch TVs, since she was only looking at the 40-inch options last time she was there. But she needs to be home in 45 minutes, and won't have time. It looks like Maria won't get to purchase the TV today.

Meanwhile, Angela purchased her TV online hours ago. She didn't even leave the house and is very confident in her purchase decision.

### 4-3a
## LEARNING IT: BENEFITS OF SHOPPING ONLINE

**Business-to-consumer (B2C)** online shopping continues to grow quickly. In 2015, online sales in the United States totaled $335 billion, and that number is expected to grow to $523 billion by 2020.[7]

There are several reasons for this. First, virtually all major retailers have staked their claims in cyberspace by setting up e-commerce websites where they offer items for sale. Second, with roughly 77% of all U.S. adults owning smartphones, mobile retail is mainstream.[8] In addition, apps (application software) for phones and tablet devices can provide a direct and customized shopping experience.

Still, the biggest driver in the growth in online shopping is the shift in consumer preferences. Online shopping provides several advantages over shopping in traditional brick-and-mortar stores. Three reasons most often cited in consumer surveys: competitive pricing, access and convenience, and personalized service.

## COMPETITIVE PRICING

Many of the best deals on products, such as airfares and hotels, can be found on the Internet. The web is an ideal method for savvy shoppers to compare prices from dozens—even hundreds—of sellers. Online shoppers can compare

**business-to-consumer (B2C)** business conducted directly between a business and a consumer

Online shopping allows consumers to easily compare prices among various stores.

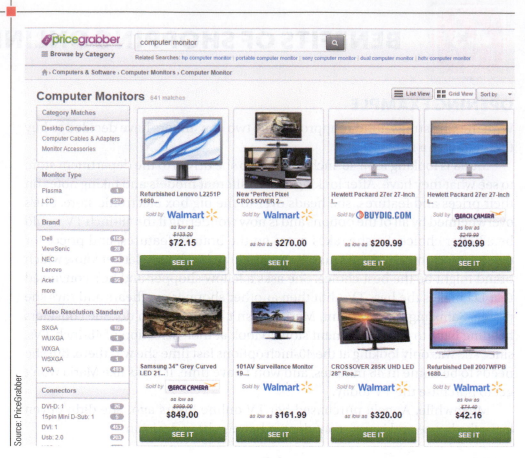

Source: PriceGrabber

features and prices at their leisure. For instance, at PriceGrabber.com, you can specify the type and size of monitor you're looking for, and the website displays a list of the highest-ranked monitors, along with the e-tailer offering the best price.

## ACCESS AND CONVENIENCE

A second important factor is shopper convenience. Cybershoppers can search for and order products from around the world at any hour of the day or night. Most digital marketers allow customers to create an account that stores their shipping and credit card information to make future purchases quicker. In addition to text search, image recognition can make locating the products you want easier. A service provided by *Elle* magazine's British website is the ability to use online photos to conduct visual matches for desired shopping items. In other words, using a digital picture of what you want—say, a pair of shoes—you can locate similar items for sale online.

Many shopping sites also feature customer reviews, where you can view ratings and comments from hundreds of actual users. This provides buyers far more information than they could gather from a brick-and-mortar store by talking to salespeople and fellow customers.

## PERSONALIZED SERVICE

Although online shopping transactions often operate with little or no human interaction, successful B2C companies know how important personalization is to a quality shopping experience. Consequently, most leading online retailers offer customized features on their websites.

Say you buy a product at Amazon and register with the site. The site welcomes you back for your next purchase by name. Using special software that analyzes your previous purchases, it also suggests several other products you might like. You even have the option of receiving periodic e-mails from Amazon.com informing you of new products. And the company offers Amazon Prime, a membership program that includes expedited free shipping for a yearly fee. Many other leading e-marketers have adopted similar types of personalized marketing.

Some websites offer customized products to match individual consumer requirements. For instance, Nike offers online shoppers the opportunity to customize a running shoe, personalizing features such as the outsole, the amount of cushioning, and the width. This type of personalized recommendation and customization is hard to replicate in a physical retail store.

### 4-3b

### CLOSING EXAMPLE

While Maria spent hours visiting brick-and-mortar stores to compare TVs, Angela simply went online. She visited a few websites, filtered for the model she wanted, and compared specs for the leading brands. The sites also showed her some personalized recommendations based on the models she had previously viewed. She was able to pore through many customer reviews, which allowed her to narrow down the list of TVs until she found the perfect one. Since she already had an account with that e-tailer, she simply signed in and checked out in just a few minutes. Seconds later she got an e-mail confirmation that the TV would ship the next day and be delivered to her front door. Angela was able to gather more information, sort through more options, and buy more confidently in much less time than it would have taken if she had shopped at a physical store.

# 4-4  CHALLENGES FACED BY ONLINE MARKETERS AND CONSUMERS

## OPENING EXAMPLE

**LO 4.4** Summarize five challenges faced by online marketers and consumers.

Every new technology used by marketers raises fresh challenges. Consumers worry that a company might capture information about them, then lose that information to hackers. The frequency and severity of information breaches within major organizations has skyrocketed, which is reflected in the many recent headlines about stolen customer data. From Target to Samsung to Blue Cross Blue Shield, the list goes on. It's likely that nearly everyone's personal information is caught up in the mix. But, there are solutions. Both businesses and consumers can help address the key challenges caused by today's technology.

## LEARNING IT: CHALLENGES FACED BY ONLINE MARKETERS AND CONSUMERS

For all its advantages, e-business poses some challenges as well. We'll discuss the five challenges here: safety of online payment, privacy issues, fraud and scams, site design and customer service, and channel conflicts.

### SAFETY OF ONLINE PAYMENT

**encryption** the process of encoding data for security purposes

In response to consumer concerns about the safety of sending credit card numbers over the Internet, companies have developed secure payment systems. Internet browsers, such as Firefox, contain sophisticated encryption systems to protect sensitive information. **Encryption** is the process of encoding data for security purposes. When such a system is active, users see a special icon that indicates they are at a protected website. In addition, the beginning of the web address will usually change from HTTP to HTTPS.

Many online shoppers are switching to payment services such as PayPal to speed checkout and make shopping more secure. A payment service ensures that fewer merchants actually see the shopper's personal information, making that information less vulnerable to hackers. These services benefit digital marketers too because they are trusted by consumers and sometimes feature lower processing fees than traditional credit card companies.[9]

### PRIVACY ISSUES

Marketing research indicates privacy as one of the top concerns of many Internet users. The European Commission adopted regulations that will require companies such as Google and Facebook to get specific consent to use consumers' personal data. The Federal Trade Commission has explored instituting a Do Not Track option, similar to the Do Not Call option to stop phone sales calls.[10]

Most consumers want assurances that any information they provide won't be sold to others without their permission. In response to these concerns, online merchants take steps to protect consumer information. For example, many Internet companies have signed on with Internet privacy organizations such as TRUSTe. By displaying the TRUSTe logo on their websites, they indicate their promise to disclose how they collect personal data and what they do with the information. Prominently displaying a privacy policy is an effective way to build customer trust.

Companies, too, are concerned about the privacy of their data, and with good reason. Hackers launched a massive cyber attack on Target, stealing login information, e-mails, and encrypted passwords for up to 110 million of its customers.

Despite repeated warnings, many Internet users often use the same password on different websites. With hackers accessing one user password, the security of that user's data will be compromised at any other sites using the same password.[11]

## FRAUD AND SCAMS

Fraud is another impediment to the growth of e-business and digital marketing. The FBI and the National White Collar Crime Center have formed a partnership called the Internet Crime Complaint Center (IC3) to receive and refer criminal complaints about cyber fraud and other Internet crimes.[12]

One type of Internet fraud is called **phishing**. It is a high-tech scam that uses e-mail or pop-up messages that claim to be from familiar businesses such as banks, Internet service providers, or even government agencies. The message usually asks the reader to "update" or "validate" account information, often stating that some dire consequence will occur if the reader doesn't respond. The purpose of phishing is to get unsuspecting victims to disclose personal information such as credit card numbers, bank account numbers, Social Security numbers, or computer passwords. Phishing is also commonly used to distribute viruses and malicious spyware programs to computer users.

Payment fraud is another problem for many digital marketers. Orders are placed online and paid for using a credit card, and the retailer ships the merchandise. Then the cardholder asks the credit card issuer for a charge-back to the e-tailer, claiming he or she never made the purchase or never received the merchandise. Some claims are legitimate, but many involve fraud. Because an online purchase doesn't require a customer's signature or credit card imprint, the merchant—not the card issuer—bears the liability in most fraud cases.

**phishing** a high-tech scam that uses e-mail or pop-up messages that claim to be from familiar businesses or even government agencies

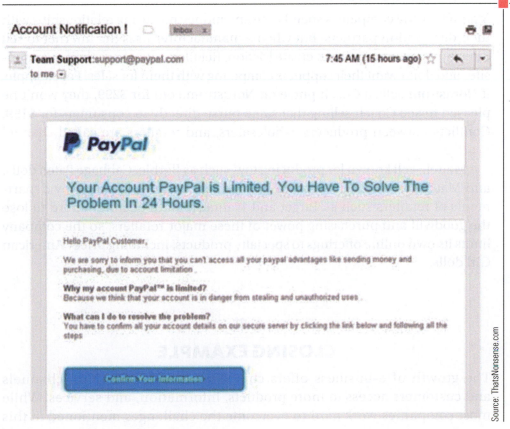

Account Notification !   Inbox

Team Support: support@paypal.com    7:45 AM (15 hours ago)
to me

**PayPal**

Your Account PayPal is Limited, You Have To Solve The Problem In 24 Hours.

Hello PayPal Customer,

We are sorry to inform you that you can't access all your paypal advantages like sending money and purchasing, due to account limitation.

**Why my account PayPal™ is limited?**
Because we think that your account is in danger from stealing and unauthorized uses.

**What can I do to resolve the problem?**
You have to confirm all your account details on our secure server by clicking the link below and following all the steps

Confirm Your Information

Source: ThatsNonsense.com

While this e-mail looks like it's from PayPal, it's actually sent by a scammer attempting to fraud recipients out of their PayPal username and password.

## SITE DESIGN AND CUSTOMER SERVICE

For firms to attract and keep customers, digital marketers must meet buyer expectations. For instance, customers want to find products easily and have questions answered quickly. However, websites are not always well designed and easy to use. Product reviews, shopping information, pop-up discount offers, and instant chats for customer questions are features that can help online retailers close sales.[13] We'll discuss factors that influence website success in the next section.

Another challenge to successful online business is merchandise delivery and returns. Behind every website that sells physical products, there must be an efficient operation for maintaining inventory, packing and tracking shipments, and handling returns. Most online retailers now have systems on their websites that allow customers to track orders from placement to delivery. Digital marketers have also worked hard on a process known as *reverse logistics*. Detailed directions on how to return merchandise, including preprinted shipping labels, are included in orders. Some, such as Nordstrom and Zappos, even pay the shipping cost for returns.

To be successful at e-business, firms must establish and maintain competitive standards for customer service. When it began offering customers the opportunity to check flight schedules and purchase tickets online, Southwest Airlines worked hard to make sure its website had the same high service standards the airline is known for. Southwest.com has proved very popular and profitable for the airline.

## CHANNEL CONFLICTS

Manufacturing companies spend time and money nurturing relationships with their distribution partners. But when a manufacturer uses the Internet to sell directly to consumers, it can create friction. Retailers often have their own websites and don't want their suppliers competing with them for sales. For example, if Nordstrom sells a Coach purse on Nordstrom.com for $299, they won't be pleased to see Coach selling that same purse directly to consumers for $199. Conflicts between producers, wholesalers, and retailers are called **channel conflicts**.

**channel conflicts** conflicts between producers, wholesalers, and retailers

Mattel, well known for producing toys such as Barbie, Cabbage Patch dolls, and Matchbox cars, sells most of its products in toy stores and toy departments of retailers such as Target and Walmart. Mattel cannot afford to lose the goodwill and purchasing power of these major retailers, so the company limits its own online offerings to specialty products, including pricey American Girl dolls.

## 4-4b

## CLOSING EXAMPLE

The growth of e-business offers companies new distribution channels and customers access to more products, information, and services. While most companies work hard to overcome the challenges mentioned in this section, you as a consumer can do your part as well. A few suggestions include the following:

- Maintain a strong password that is at least eight characters long and includes a mix of lowercase letters, uppercase letters, numbers, and/or symbols.

- Do not use the same password at multiple sites.

- Only enter your personal information, including payment information, at known sites that utilizes a secure server for checkout (web address beginning with HTTPS).

- Ignore phishing e-mails. If you receive an e-mail that asks you to log in to your account, do not click on the link in the e-mail. Rather, go directly to that site to log in and see if there are any alerts on your account.

Tips like these can help keep your private information secure and your online shopping experience stress free.

# 4-5 FACTORS THAT INFLUENCE E-COMMERCE SUCCESS

## OPENING EXAMPLE

The executive team at Pure Paleo Meals sat quietly at the conference table. The online subscription meal delivery service that launched six months ago to huge fanfare seemed in danger of failing. Yesterday's sales report told a familiar tale, only 13 new customers signed up. The day before it was only 10. The problem is Pure Paleo Meals needs to sign up at least 40 new customers per day to generate the cash needed to fund operations and keep growing.

"Didn't we get some good press coverage this week?" said one team member.

"Yes, the articles in *Bon Appetit* and *Real Simple* magazines generated a huge spike in website traffic," said the Marketing Assistant. "It's up 200% compared to last week."

"Then why haven't we seen a similar spike in new customer sign-ups?" asked the exasperated CEO. "We must be missing something, and if we don't figure it out we're going to run out of cash within months."

With that said, all eyes turned towards you. As the Director of Marketing, your job is to diagnose why Pure Paleo Meals isn't meeting growth goals, and to turn it around.

**LO 4.5** Summarize four factors that influence the success of an e-commerce website.

## 4-5a

## LEARNING IT: FACTORS THAT INFLUENCE E-COMMERCE SUCCESS

An e-business website can serve many purposes. It can provide information and news, entertain, and/or sell goods and services. When judging websites, success means different things to different businesses. Websites such as those of the *Los Angeles Times* and *USA Today* draw many visitors who want the latest news;

while YouTube and ESPN.com are successful because they attract heavy traffic from those looking for entertainment.

However, *e-commerce* websites need to attract customers who conduct business on the spot. The ability to generate revenue is driven primarily by:

- How many people visit the website (called traffic)
- How many of those visitors buy something from the website (called conversions)

An e-commerce site can get thousands, or even millions, of visitors and still fail if those visitors never become customers. To increase their chance of success, e-commerce marketers often focus on four factors that influence their ability to get conversions and grow a profitable site: user experience, product offering, checkout process, and revenue maximization.

## 4-5b
## USER EXPERIENCE

**user experience (UX)** the overall experience customers have when visiting a website

**User experience (UX)** is the overall experience customers have when visiting a website. It includes the look and feel of the site, the ease of finding what visitors want, and even the loading speed of the pages. The goal of UX is to "improve customers' satisfaction and loyalty through the utility, ease of use, and pleasure provided in the interaction" with the site.[14]

A slow-loading site will likely cause customers to leave before even viewing the homepage. If they do wait for the page to load and the website is cluttered, has an overly complex navigation menu, or is too text heavy, that also increases the chance customers will leave before seriously considering a purchase.

Designers of e-commerce sites should take great care to design pages that are clean and organized, often utilizing plenty of "white space" between objects. The navigation menu should be simple and clear, and prioritized by the links customers are most likely to click. A site with many items for sale would likely include a prominent search bar so that customers don't have to browse the entire collection of products to find what they need.

As the largest online retailer, Amazon's website demonstrates principles of good user experience, including a prominent search bar, clean and organized pages, and clear navigation menus.

Your Design/Shutterstock.com

## 4-5c
# PRODUCT OFFERING

The next factor influencing success of an e-commerce site is whether customers can buy what they want. In some cases, this means having a vast selection for customers to choose from. A general e-commerce site like Amazon.com carries millions of items and aims to be the primary destination for just about any online shopper. While a higher-end fashion site like katespade.com provides a curated selection of products that is more likely to appeal to fans of their brand. Understanding the site's target customer is the first step in deciding what products should be offered. Next, marketers can be sure to provide detailed product descriptions, attractive images, and even social proof, such as reviews. These help increase the confidence of visitors and the likelihood they'll decide to make a purchase.

## 4-5d
# CHECKOUT PROCESS

Once a customer has browsed your site and added a product to their shopping cart, the conversion process has just begun. A number of research studies indicate that 55–80% of customers abandon their shopping cart before actually checking out. Reasons include the following:

1. Checkout process was too long or complicated
2. Website required creation of an account
3. Shipping cost was too high
4. Site was not trustworthy
5. Total cost after tax and shipping was not calculated prior to checkout[15]

Strategies for increasing the number of customers who complete checkout include:

- Offering a simplified checkout process requiring as few clicks and screens as possible
- Offering guest checkout that does not require creation of a user account
- Offering free or reduced cost shipping for orders of a certain size
- Ensuring checkout is on secure server with SSL encryption
- Calculating tax and shipping earlier in the checkout process

## 4-5e
# REVENUE MAXIMIZATION

It can be hard for an e-commerce website to be profitable if most customers only purchase one item and perhaps never return to the website. **Revenue maximization** strategies are designed to:

- Increase the size of each customer transaction
- Encourage repeat visits by the customer

**revenue maximization** website strategies designed to increase the size of each customer transaction and encourage repeat visits by the customer

Amazon.com has long been a leader in revenue maximization strategies with their highly refined recommendation engine. When you are viewing any one item, they show you that item as part of a bundle that is "frequently bought together." The moment you add something to your cart, Amazon shows you a number of additional recommendations related to your purchase.

They also encourage repeat visits from customers through their Prime subscriptions, where customers pay $99 per year to receive free two-day shipping, unlimited access to Amazon video, and an assortment of other benefits. As a result, Prime members are estimated to spend over twice as much per year on Amazon.com as non-Prime members.[16]

### 4-5f
# CLOSING EXAMPLE

It's been a month since the CEO of Pure Paleo Meals asked you to improve sales before the company runs out of cash. After reviewing the website, you noticed a few troubling issues. The homepage was cluttered and confusing, leaving customers unclear on how to shop for a subscription box that fits their needs. The navigation menu had too many choices, but still didn't link to some of the meal options with the most sales potential. The checkout process required user accounts and took visitors to six different pages before they were done.

By focusing the entire web team on improving the site, you were able to complete a redesign in record time. The new site that launched a week ago provided simpler navigation, a curated selection of featured subscription boxes, faster and more secure checkout, and a recommendation engine.

Even though overall website traffic is about the same as it was last month, the number of daily customer sign-ups has tripled. This is because more of those visitors are choosing to become paying customers, which was the goal of your site redesign. The company is now profitable and poised for growth because of the changes you made to the site.

# ASSESSING THE EFFECTIVENESS OF AN E-COMMERCE SITE

**LO 4.6** Describe the various methods for measuring the effectiveness of an e-commerce website.

## OPENING EXAMPLE

The following are estimates of monthly web traffic to some popular e-commerce sites:

Target.com—136 million visitors[17]
Homedepot.com—116 million visitors[18]
Macys.com—70 million visitors[19]
Lowes.com—58 million visitors[20]

Based on this information, could you identify which site is most successful? The answer is . . . maybe. While knowing the number of visitors is certainly helpful, there are other valuable measurements that can be used as well. Picking the right ones is an important part of analyzing the success of any e-commerce site.

### 4-6a

## LEARNING IT: ASSESSING THE EFFECTIVENESS OF AN E-COMMERCE SITE

Measuring the effectiveness of an e-commerce website is tricky and requires various methods to provide a complete picture of site performance. The very definition of success for a particular online retailer will depend on their industry, target audience, company size, and a host of other factors. With that said, there are some measurements that are consistently used by online marketers across industries.

Measuring the number of **unique visitors** is an important foundation for understanding the effectiveness of a site, because each of those visitors represents a potential customer. Since each person might visit the site many times in a month, unique visitors is a more accurate measure of potential revenue than counting the total number of visits to the site. Marketers often track the volume of visitor traffic on a monthly, weekly, or even daily basis. Also, analytics software allows them to identify the source of that traffic, such as a search engine, social media post, or online ad. Doing so allows marketers to invest more time and money building the traffic sources that bring the highest-quality visitors.

**unique visitors** the number of individuals who visit a website

Once visitors are on the site, it's important to track **engagement**, or how much time users spend on a site and which pages they visit. Google Analytics is a tool for tracking these and other site usage statistics, which provide valuable information for web designers looking for opportunities to upgrade the site.[21] For example, if most users visit the home page, then immediately leave, designers will know that page needs to be improved so that visitors stay and browse the website.

**engagement** how much time users spend on the site and which pages they visit

A critical measure of success is **conversion rate**, the percentage of visitors to a website who make a purchase. *The higher the conversion rate, the better.* The formula for calculating conversion rate is:

**conversion rate** the percentage of visitors to a website who make a purchase

*Conversion rate = Number of purchases / Number of visitors to site*

E-businesses try to boost their conversion rates by ensuring that their sites have a good user experience, targeted product offering, and fast and secure checkout.

Since many online purchases are the result of an advertisement, it's important to account for those costs when measuring the success of an online store. The first important measure is **click-through rate (CTR)**, which is the percentage of users who click on an ad. *The higher the CTR, the better.* The formula for calculating click-through rate is:

**click-through rate (CTR)** the percentage of users who click on an ad

*Click-through rate = Ad clicks / Ad impressions*

An impression is any time the ad is shown to a user. Most online ad platforms, such as Google and Facebook, look closely at click-through rates before deciding which ads to show users. If users aren't clicking an ad, Google and Facebook will typically stop showing that ad and replace it with one that has higher click-through rates.

Possibly the most important measure of success for an e-commerce site is **conversion cost**, the total cost of each sale. The typical method for buying online ads is called cost-per-click (CPC), which means you pay each time a customer clicks on your ad. For example, a company running CPC ads on Facebook might pay 50 cents each time a Facebook user clicks on the company's ad. Since only a small portion of those who click on the ad will actually buy anything from the e-commerce store, measuring conversion cost is a way for marketers to analyze whether their ad campaigns are profitable. *The lower the conversion cost, the better.* The formula for calculating conversion cost is:

$$Conversion\ cost = Cost\text{-}per\text{-}click\ /\ Conversion\ rate$$

Utilizing these four measurements provides a good foundation for measuring the effectiveness of an e-commerce website.

**conversion cost** the total cost of each sale

## 4-6b
# CLOSING EXAMPLE

Knowing the number of visitors to these major retail sites was a good start, but you can now see it's only one measure of success—and possibly not the most important one. In our example, Target gets more visitors than Home Depot:

Target.com—136 million visitors[22]
Homedepot.com—116 million visitors[23]

However, what if Home Depot's engagement was higher, leading to a better conversion rate? If this were the case, it's possible that Home Depot could bring in more revenue and have a more successful e-commerce site, even though it gets fewer overall visitors.

# 4-7 OPTIMIZING THE EFFECTIVENESS OF AN E-COMMERCE SITE

**LO 4.7** Given an example of an online marketing activity, calculate the activity's effectiveness.

## OPENING EXAMPLE

It has been three months since you led the redesign of the website for Pure Paleo Meals. As a result, new customer sign-ups for the company's subscription meal delivery service have grown 400% and the company is now profitable. But there's no time to rest because two new subscription paleo meal services have popped up that are backed by large investors.

As Director of Marketing, you are responsible for growing the company's customer base even faster. Your first strategy is to drive more traffic to the site through a publicity blitz and by utilizing online pay-per-click ads. Your second strategy is to test a number of changes to your website to further increase conversion rates. You reason that if traffic can be increased by 50% and conversion rates can double, that means twice the number of new customer sign-ups.

You gather the digital marketing team and begin strategizing how to reach these goals.

## 4-7a

# LEARNING IT: OPTIMIZING THE EFFECTIVENESS OF AN E-COMMERCE SITE

In digital marketing it's often said there are no expert marketers. There are only experienced marketers and expert testers. For example, it's not unusual for a company to rotate between multiple versions of sales pages on their website to see which one generates the best conversion rate. When running Facebook or Google pay-per-click ads, a digital marketer will often test many different ads—sometimes as many as 100 different versions—to see which ones generate the most clicks at the lowest cost. With all of these tests taking place, digital marketers must closely measure the success of each one so they can allocate their time and budget to the tactics that bring the highest return.

To properly *track* results it's important to accurately *calculate* results. Measuring increases in unique visitors, time on website, and pages viewed is easy, since those are based on raw numbers. However, calculating click-through rates, conversion rates, and conversion cost require some (simple) math.

**Example—Click-through rate:** Pure Paleo Meals ran Google ads last week that received a total of 100,000 impressions and 2,000 clicks. What was their click-through rate?

**Answer:** *Click - through rate = Ad clicks / Ad impressions*
2,000/100,000 = 0.02 = 2%

This is a solid click-through rate and should mean that Google will continue to run these ads on behalf of the company.

The Facebook ads dashboard for this digital marketer shows they are testing many variations of the same basic ad to see which ones perform best.

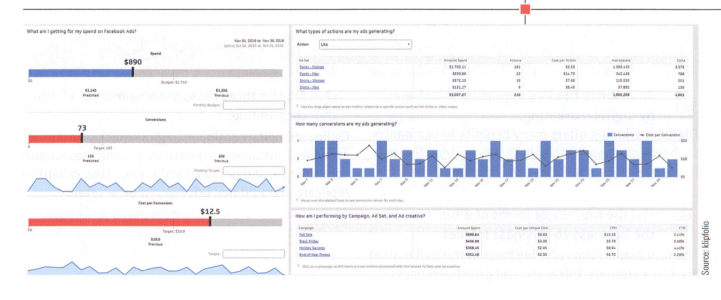

Source: klipfolio

**Example—Conversion rate:** Of the 2,000 people who visited the Pure Paleo Meals website as a result of the Google ads, 50 signed up to become customers. What was their conversion rate?

**Answer:** *Conversion rate = Number of purchases / Number of visitors to site*
50/2,000 = 0.025 = 2.5%

This is an excellent conversion rate, but you believe it can go higher.

**Example—Conversion cost:** While you're happy with the conversion rates, you want to make sure these conversions are actually profitable. On your Google ad account, you see that your average cost-per-click was $1. What is your conversion cost?

**Answer:** *Conversion cost = Cost-per-click / Conversion rate*
$1/0.025 = $40

Your conversion cost is $40 per customer. You know that each customer is worth $60 in profit in just the first month they subscribe, meaning your campaign is profitable.

# 4-8 LEARN IT TODAY . . . USE IT TOMORROW

With a firm grasp of how you plan to measure success for the Pure Paleo Meals website and ad campaigns, you ask your digital marketing team to suggest a number of sales pages and ad campaigns you can test in the coming weeks. Based on the results, you'll focus company resources on the ones that are performing best.

It's time to get hands-on and apply what you've learned. **See MindTap for an activity related to Pure Paleo's marketing activities.**

## Chapter Summary

**LO 4.1** Summarize the five opportunities offered by digital marketing.

Digital marketing offers many benefits to companies, such as global reach, personalization, interactive marketing, right-time marketing, and integrated marketing.

**LO 4.2** List the four major forms of e-business in the business-to-business market.

The four major forms of e-business in the B2B market are EDI, extranets, intranets, and private exchanges.

**LO 4.3** Explain three reasons consumers prefer to shop online.

Online shopping continues to grow quickly because it provides consumers competitive pricing, access and convenience, and personalized service that is hard to replicate in traditional brick-and-mortar retail.

**LO 4.4** Summarize five challenges faced by online marketers and consumers.

While e-business provides many advantages for companies and consumers, it does raise concerns regarding safety of online payment, privacy, fraud and scams, site design and customer service, and channel conflicts.

**LO 4.5** Summarize four factors that influence the success of an e-commerce website.

An e-commerce site must attract visitors to the website and eventually convert them to buyers. Factors that influence the success of an e-commerce site include user experience, product offering, checkout process, and revenue maximization strategies.

**LO 4.6** Describe the various methods for measuring the effectiveness of an e-commerce website.

The effectiveness of an e-commerce website and digital marketing campaigns can be measured by tracking unique visitors, engagement, conversion rate, click-through-rate, and conversion costs.

**LO 4.7** Given an example of an online marketing activity, calculate the activity's effectiveness.

The ability to properly calculate and track measurements of e-commerce website effectiveness allows digital marketers to optimize their websites and online advertising campaigns.

## ▶ Key Terms

e-business **66**
e-commerce **66**
digital marketing **66**
interactive marketing **67**
business-to-business (B2B) **68**
extranets **69**
intranets **69**

private exchange **70**
business-to-consumer (B2C) **71**
encryption **74**
phishing **75**
channel conflicts **76**
user experience (UX) **78**
revenue maximization **79**

unique visitors **81**
engagement **81**
conversion rate **81**
click-through rate (CTR) **81**
conversion cost **82**

# 5 SOCIAL MEDIA: LIVING IN THE CONNECTED WORLD

## LEARNING OBJECTIVES

**5.1** Describe the growth and use of social media.

**5.2** Contrast the three major types of social media platforms.

**5.3** Explain three ways consumers rely on social media to make buying decisions.

**5.4** Identify the types of goals marketers use for social media campaigns.

**5.5** Describe the various methods for measuring the effectiveness of social media marketing.

**5.6** Outline the seven guidelines for creating effective social media content.

**5.7** Summarize three ethical principles for social media marketers.

**5.8** Given a goal for social media marketing, determine the most effective method of measurement.

# LEARN IT TODAY ... USE IT TOMORROW

When it launched more than 10 years ago, LinkedIn was not much more than an online résumé-hosting site that struggled to amass its first million users. Today, its popularity as a professional networking and information-sharing resource is soaring.

The company now boasts more than 450 million members on its user-friendly platform, roughly $3 billion a year in revenue from subscriptions, advertising, and recruitment services[1], and a history of steady and successful innovations in building social media tools for professionals. Page views more than doubled in one recent year. LinkedIn's 10,000 employees around the world operate LinkedIn portals in 24 different languages, including Czech, Dutch, French, Italian, Malay, Russian, Spanish, Swedish, and of course English.[2]

As employers face a glut of applicants, they can be increasingly choosy about whom they hire. LinkedIn's features allow employers to rely more on personalized searches among the site's individual members. They can also use the site's vast networks of personal connections and recommendations to filter their candidate pools, advertise openings, promote their companies, and sponsor content.

Individual users benefit too. They can get insider access to job postings, read insightful posts by hundreds of industry leaders or "top influencers," and pore over company career pages and recruitment ads. While building their professional network among users of the site, they can share content with others, comment on posts, endorse others, and host video and graphics alongside their customized profiles.

What does the LinkedIn story tell us about the power of social media? How do social media platforms create value, both for marketers and for the consumers they serve?

# 5-1 WHAT IS SOCIAL MEDIA?

## OPENING EXAMPLE

Nearly a decade after launching a product called Orabrush, its inventor, Dr. Robert Wagstaff, was still selling only about 10 of the tongue cleaners per month—at $3 each. So Wagstaff hired a freelance marketing consultant to create a funny two-minute video called "How to Tell When Your Breath Stinks."

After posting the video on YouTube, the team bought YouTube's Promoted Video Ads service and also put the video on Orabrush's Facebook page. Within six weeks, about 900,000 people had seen the video, and 20% of the viewers clicked on the link to the Orabrush website. But clicks don't always mean sales. Do you think this was a good use of social media? How do you think sales were affected by this effort?

 **LO 5.1** Describe the growth and use of social media.

### 5-1a

## LEARNING IT: WHAT IS SOCIAL MEDIA?

**Social media** is defined collectively as the different forms of online communication through which users can create communities to exchange information, ideas, messages, and other content.[3] There are a variety of social media platforms to enable these communities, such as the popular blogging site WordPress, microblogging site Twitter, video-sharing site YouTube, and social networking sites Facebook and Pinterest.

**social media** different forms of online communication through which users can create communities to exchange information, ideas, messages, and other content

Despite its relatively brief existence, social media has quickly grown to be an important tool for marketers to build relationships with customers, strengthen brands, launch new products, enter new markets, and boost sales. Over 70% of adults use social media sites. This varies by age group, with 86% of 18- to 29-year-olds on social media and only 34% of those over 65. Facebook is easily the most popular social media site with visits by 68% of adults. The next closest site is Instagram (owned by Facebook), which is used by almost a third of adults.[4]

Studies show that consumers are connecting with retailers, restaurants, travel and entertainment firms, financial companies, and other businesses via social media.[5] The messages conveyed via social media wield substantial power, whether from friends and family or from organizations that users follow. The sheer number of users on social media makes it an attractive communication medium for most companies. For example, Facebook is nearing 2 billion monthly users, while several other networks have over 500 million monthly users.

With social media possessing such scale and influence among consumers, businesses are increasing their marketing efforts on these networks. By 2020, spending on social media advertising is expected to reach $50 billion; surpassing the amount of advertising dollars businesses spend on newspapers.[6]

## 5-1b
## CLOSING EXAMPLE

Thanks to its first foray into social media marketing, Orabrush sold about 10,000 tongue cleaners in less than two months. Today, Dr. Wagstaff stays in contact with his followers as "Dr. Bob" on Twitter, and Orabrush products are sold by Walgreens, CVS, Target, and other national retailers.[7] The brand is available in 30,000 stores in 25 countries, and has become the top tongue cleaner in the world.[8]

# 5-2    SOCIAL MEDIA PLATFORMS

**LO 5.2** Contrast the three major types of social media platforms.

## OPENING EXAMPLE

Starbucks launched its first social media marketing initiative in 2009, well ahead of competitors, and has continued to use this promotional approach aggressively and creatively. An especially successful example was the recent campaign for Pumpkin Spice Latte (PSL for short), one of the company's most popular seasonal products. The drink, available only during the fall, got its own Instagram, Twitter, and Tumblr accounts; eager buyers could obtain a PSL ahead of their friends by using a special link and password.[9] Suggestions for enjoying PSL appeared on Pinterest and were linked on StumbleUpon. A Facebook Messenger feature enabled fans to take a quiz or ask questions.

While the campaign was integrated around a single theme—"The Real PSL"—it actually incorporated three distinct social media platforms. Can you tell them apart? What advantages does each platform offer to marketers?

## 5-2a
# LEARNING IT: SOCIAL MEDIA PLATFORMS

**Social media platforms** act as a home base for an online community. To access the conversations held there, users must become members. Usually this is a matter of typing in a valid e-mail address and creating a password, followed by building some kind of profile. Some social media platforms require an invitation or sponsor who is already a member. Sites may also have their own rules. For example, Facebook strictly regulates where you can run a contest promotion on your timeline as well as how you may choose and contact the winner. If you violate these rules, your firm could be banned from the site.[10]

There are three basic types of social media platforms; however, many social media sites demonstrate characteristics of two and sometimes all three of these types.

## SOCIAL NETWORKING SITES

**Social networking sites** are websites or apps (such as Facebook, Pinterest, Snapchat, and LinkedIn) that provide virtual communities for people to share daily activities, send messages, post opinions, increase their circle of online friends, and more. Many companies and not-for-profit organizations, ranging

**social media platforms** the home base for an online community

**social networking sites** websites or apps that provide virtual communities for people to share daily activities, send messages, post opinions, increase their circle of online friends, and more

In addition to their regular website, American Cancer Society also manages a page on Facebook, a social networking site.

Source: Facebook

from Zappos to the American Cancer Society, use their Facebook pages to build relationships with various stakeholders.[11]

Most social networks have their own search engine, which allows users to search for topics that interest them—like "The Real PSL" on Starbucks' Facebook page. Often the keyword or phrase is preceded by a hashtag (#) to make it more easily searchable by the social network. Before launching a social media campaign, marketers may make a list of keywords that relate to the promotion, then use those keywords throughout the campaign so users land in the right place on the platform.

When they join, members of social networking sites typically create an online profile of biographical data—including photos and information such as employment, education, and relationship status. They invite friends or colleagues to join their network, and then communicate in a variety of ways— posting on their home page, sending e-mail or instant messages, or even calling or videoconferencing with chosen members. They can share their likes and dislikes about goods and services as well as links to favorite e-commerce sites.

## SOCIAL BOOKMARKING SITES

**bookmarking sites** gives users a place to save, organize, and manage links to websites and other resources on the Internet

**Bookmarking sites** give you a place to save, organize, and manage links to websites and other resources on the Internet. Usually these lists are then shared with other users. StumbleUpon is a form of search engine that directs users to web pages based on their interests, like ways to enjoy Pumpkin Spice Latte. Other examples of bookmarking sites are Digg and Reddit.

Pinterest combines social networking with bookmarking by allowing users to "pin" photos of interesting products, places, recipes, and more. Sports teams such as the NHL's Pittsburgh Penguins and football's New York Giants have hopped aboard the Pinterest bandwagon, noting that the women-dominated platform offers opportunities to engage with that demographic.[12]

## BLOGGING SITES AND FORUMS

Blogging sites and forums enable members to hold conversations by posting articles, making comments, or facilitating interactions on dedicated discussion boards.

**blogs** sites that regularly post articles and other content

**Blogs** are sites that regularly post articles and other content for readers, who can then comment on those articles and share them on other social media sites. Some blogs are created and written by single authors about single subjects, such as fitness, politics, or financial management. Other blogs function as full-fledged news or entertainment sites. WordPress is the most widely used blogging platform in the world, hosting millions of blogs and powering over a quarter of pages on the Internet. Users of the WordPress platform collectively publish over 40 million posts and receive over 60 million comments per month.[13] Major brands, such as NBC Sports, UPS, and CNN utilize WordPress to host their blogs.[14]

Tumblr is another large blogging platform, hosting over 300 million blogs.[15] Tumblr's functionality and dedicated fan base make it an attractive medium for organizations to market their brands. Starbucks' PSL campaign included a

**EXHIBIT 5.1**    Social Media Platforms

| Type | Purpose | Advantages for Marketers |
| --- | --- | --- |
| **Social Networking Sites** | Users create communities using profile pages or groups, enabling them to share content and exchange messages. | • Facilitates relationship-building with stakeholders<br>• Enables rapid dissemination of information<br>• By using keywords, can bring users directly to a company website or promotion |
| **Social Bookmarking Sites** | Users can save, organize, and manage links to Internet resources—then share those links publicly. | • Offers a way to organically distribute messages to interested and influential users |
| **Blogging Sites and Forums** | Users facilitate conversations by posting articles and messages. | • Enables sharing of content and ongoing communication with audience via organization-controlled site<br>• Can be effective for generating traffic to organization website and e-commerce store |

Tumblr game board enabling competitors to win early access to the drink. Fashion brands Calvin Klein, J.Crew, and Ann Taylor use Tumblr to post engaging images and content to draw users to their websites.[16]

Twitter began as a spin on blogging called microblogging. Twitter users send and receive "tweets," which each have a limit of 140 characters. Tweets are seen by anyone following that Twitter user. Celebrities such as Katy Perry, Taylor Swift, and Justin Bieber have over 80 million Twitter followers each. Brands also utilize Twitter to communicate with followers. Corporate sponsors of MTV's Video Music Awards use Twitter to promote their goods and services before, during, and after the program.[17] During the 2016 presidential race, Donald Trump personally tweeted regularly to motivate his 25 million Twitter followers, a first in presidential politics. While Twitter began as a microblogging site, it also demonstrates characteristics of a social network and a bookmarking site.[18]

Exhibit 5.1 summarizes the types of social media platforms and their advantages to marketers.

## 5-2b

## CLOSING EXAMPLE

"The Real PSL" campaign used social networking, bookmarking, and blogging sites in an integrated effort to turn a drink into a personality. Whether users took a quiz on Facebook, linked to content on StumbleUpon, blogged on Tumblr, tweeted on Twitter, or encountered images on Instagram or Pinterest, they "met" a Starbucks beverage cup wearing cool sunglasses and engaging in fun fall activities consistent with the brand. In just five weeks, "The Real PSL" had 107,000 Twitter followers and over 1,000 notes on its Tumblr posts.[19]

Thanks largely to its social media presence, the wildly popular drink now sells in 50 countries and brings in about $500 million a year.[20]

By integrating social media into their marketing campaign for Pumpkin Spice Latte, Starbucks increased awareness and sales for the drink.

Source: Twitter, Inc.

# 5-3 HOW CONSUMERS USE SOCIAL MEDIA

**LO 5.3** Explain three ways consumers rely on social media to make buying decisions.

## OPENING EXAMPLE

Where do you learn about cooking and eating at home? From Mom and your family traditions? From what you see in food stores or on cooking shows?

That's how it was in the past, but these days perhaps social media is one of your main sources for information about food. You might be a regular visitor to sites like Allrecipes, SparkPeople, or Tastespotting. If so, what does that tell us about the role of social media for gathering information and making purchase decisions?

### 5-3a

## LEARNING IT: HOW CONSUMERS USE SOCIAL MEDIA

Studies show an overall link between social media and trends in consumer behavior. For example, 91% of consumers have visited a brick-and-mortar store because of an online experience. Nearly 90% research a product using online search engines. And more than 60% of consumers make an in-store purchase after researching online.[21] In 2015, Facebook posts alone influenced over half of all online and offline purchases.[22]

According to a report conducted by comScore and Group M Search, roughly half of online consumers use a combination of search engines and social media in making purchase decisions. Fifty-eight percent of consumers start with search engines such as Google or Bing, while 24% go straight to social media. Here's the twist: 46% of consumers who start with social media then turn to search engines.

The impact of social media on purchasing behavior also varies by age. Global retail consultant Deloitte found that 47% of millennial shoppers are influenced by social media, compared to only 19% of other age groups. This bodes well for the future of social media marketing.[23]

Consumers rely on the communities created by social media for their buying decisions in the following ways:

1. *Discover new goods and services*: According to one recent report conducted by comScore and Group M Search, 28% of respondents said that sites like YouTube, Facebook, and Twitter helped steer them toward new brands and products.[24]

2. *To conduct research and share information*: Consumers visit blogs and social networking sites to delve further into a topic—whether it's an industry, a brand, or a specific product. Reviews or rankings by fellow consumers, along with other shared information, can carry a lot of weight in certain purchase decisions. For example, according to one survey, more than 40% of American consumers turn to social media—including YouTube, Facebook, and Twitter—for information about health care. They share opinions about everything from doctors to drugs to insurance companies.[25]

3. *To make final purchase decisions*: Another study found that 72% of consumers regard online reviews as a primary driver of their decision to buy.[26] If consumers learn about a product online, engaging with the company and other consumers via social media, they become part of the community the product's marketers want to create. Consumers may purchase the product and share their response to it through social media, widening the circle even more.

Overall, it's clear that social media are linked to trends in consumer behavior. As a result, marketers must take notice and develop strategies to address these trends.

## 5-3b

## CLOSING EXAMPLE

If you rely on social media for much or all of your information about food, you're not alone. In fact, one study found that nearly half of American consumers learn about menus, recipes, diet trends, nutritional data, and more from social media sites. Marketing research firm The Hartman Group concluded that communication via social media has altered the way American consumers eat—how they plan their meals, what they buy and where, and how they cook.[27] This doesn't mean food companies should abandon other forms of marketing in favor of social media marketing; it does suggest that, even though consumers can't smell or taste food online, they do rely on social media for a wide range of choices.

# GOALS OF A SOCIAL MEDIA MARKETING CAMPAIGN

**LO 5.4** Identify the types of goals marketers use for social media campaigns.

## OPENING EXAMPLE

PlayToday is an online service that sets up play dates for busy parents based on where they live and the ages of their children. When they founded the company, Marlene and Jim were confident that all they needed to succeed was a social media blitz. So they spent thousands of dollars publicizing their brand name and logo with "sponsored ads" on Facebook and "promoted pins" on Pinterest. They paid to boost their rankings on search engines Google and Bing. They even hired a movie production company to create a YouTube video called "The PlayToday Story."

But six months later, sales were flat. PlayToday's revenues fell short of its social media costs. Marlene and Jim couldn't understand why other start-ups had boomed after social media campaigns—while their business, so far, was a bust. What had they missed?

### 5-4a

## LEARNING IT: GOALS OF A SOCIAL MEDIA MARKETING CAMPAIGN

**social media marketing (SMM)** is developing a conversation with current and potential customers on social media platforms

Marketers generally view the overall goal of **social media marketing (SMM)** as developing a conversation with current and potential customers. However, this doesn't always mean that social media posts will be used to promote a product or publicize a sale. Any SMM plan must be built around specific goals. Marketers should ask themselves: "What do we want to accomplish through this campaign?"

Once goals are established, marketers are better able to develop strategies and choose the right platforms for their messages. Clear goals also help everyone involved in the campaign aim their efforts in the right direction. Generally, there are five types of goals marketers pursue with SMM.

## INCREASE BRAND AWARENESS AND GENERATE LEADS

The purpose of this goal is to increase the number of people who are aware of the company and its products. In addition, brands hope to increase the positive perception of the brand. Companies realize that just like with offline promotions, potential customers aren't always ready to buy upon first hearing about what a company offers. Usually the first step is to provide an introduction to the company, and then nurture that relationship until a customer is ready to buy.

**influencers** individuals with the capability of affecting the opinions and actions of others

Marketers may use social media to tap conversations with or about their intended audience—blog posts, tweets, social news, and the like. Social media also is helpful for connecting with **influencers**—individuals with the capability of affecting the opinions and actions of others. Oprah Winfrey, Lady Gaga, and Steven Spielberg made *Forbes'* recent list of the top 10 most influential celebrities.[28] You can find all of them on various forms of social media.

For example, organizations fighting amyotrophic lateral sclerosis (ALS) created the Ice Bucket Challenge, where people agreed to have a bucket of ice dumped on their heads to build awareness of the disease. The campaign went viral, attracting famous participants like Justin Bieber, Selena Gomez, and Taylor Swift, and sparking over 2.4 million tagged videos on Facebook.[29]

## INCREASE REVENUE

Typically the end goal of any promotional campaign is to increase sales. Social media marketing is no different, which is why you'll often see "Sponsored Ads" on Facebook, "Promoted Pins" on Pinterest, and "Snap Ads" on Snapchat. Still, it's important to remember that conversion rates can be quite low when advertising to new prospects. Brands have better success when first engaging with potential customers before directly pitching them. Aligning social media promotions with traditional offline promotion campaigns can also increase the return on investment for social media promotions aimed at increasing revenue.

Dollar Shave Club's #RazorBurn campaign used multiple social media channels to poke fun at old-fashioned razor products, resulting in a 31% increase in the upstart firm's Twitter engagement and helping fuel subscriber growth.[30]

## IMPROVE CUSTOMER SERVICE

Social media provides companies the ability not only to communicate directly and easily with customers, but also to detect and address the problems customers might be experiencing.

Delta Airlines has a full team dedicated to monitoring their @Delta Twitter handle and responding to customer inquiries—even about canceled flights or schedule changes. In addition, Delta can search mentions of their company across all of Twitter and directly contact unhappy customers to offer resolution. This type of real-time customer service response was not possible before social media.

## MANAGE A CRISIS

The real-time nature of social media also provides companies the ability to better manage a public relations crisis. In previous eras, providing crisis response typically had to be funneled through traditional media outlets, such as television

Dollar Shave Club ✔
@DollarShaveClub                           👤+ Follow ⌄

Your razor's so old, it brought scones to the Boston Tea Party. #RazorBurn
Write your own → dlrshv.es/Axpt93

YOUR RAZOR'S SO OLD

IT BROUGHT SCONES TO THE BOSTON TEA PARTY

HashtagRazorBurn.com

RETWEETS   LIKES
7          12

9:00 AM - 4 Sep 2015

↩ 2      ⇄ 7      ♥ 12

Source: Twitter, Inc.

Dollar Shave Club is active on multiple social media sites with the ultimate goal of increasing subscriber growth and revenue.

and newspapers. With social media, companies can respond more quickly and distribute their message more directly.

In the aftermath of the BP oil spill off the Gulf Coast, the Louisiana Tourism Coastal Coalition had one major goal: to reduce losses resulting from the spill and rebuild tourism along the Louisiana coast. Collaborating with the Internet consulting firm WSI, the coalition launched a social media campaign that included postings on Facebook, Twitter, YouTube, and Flickr. Taking its social media strategy one step further after the oil spill, the coalition hosts the Visit Louisiana Coast website that highlights the various travel opportunities along the Gulf Coast via Facebook, Twitter, Flickr, YouTube, and a travel blog.[31]

## MARKET RESEARCH AND CUSTOMER FEEDBACK

Companies now have instant access to large audiences who have shown interest in the brand by liking or following it on social media. Brands like Nike and Samsung have over 25 million people who have liked their Facebook pages. That is a potential source of feedback to guide product development, service improvements, and even international expansion plans.

Best-selling author and leading podcaster Tim Ferris often queries his loyal fans on Facebook (his page has over 750,000 likes) for ideas on podcast guests, what interview questions he should ask, and even what podcast episode formats he should experiment with. His podcast is the first business/interview podcast to pass 100 million downloads.[32]

Every strategy in an effective social media marketing campaign traces back to the campaign's goals and ultimately links to a firm's overall strategic goals. Sometimes a campaign will have more than one goal. Savored, a company that offers online reservations and discounts to restaurants in New York City, had two simple goals for its most recent social media marketing effort:

1. Collect e-mail addresses for further marketing (i.e., generate leads)

2. Sign up new members (i.e., increase revenue)

The company decided to launch a Facebook campaign with Wildfire, a web app that lets businesses create their own interactive promotions and publish them on social networks. Savored created a sweepstakes in which consumers had a chance to win $100 each week for a year at any Savored restaurant. To enter, all participants had to do was "like" Savored's Facebook page and register with their e-mail addresses. Within a couple of months, more than 12,000 people had entered the sweepstakes; 4,000 were non-members, and more than 500 of those diners signed up for Savored's service. Savored achieved its goals with targeted strategies aimed at a targeted audience.[33]

## 5-4b

## CLOSING EXAMPLE

After their disappointing start, Marlene and Jim consulted a marketing professor at the local university. When he explained the importance of setting clear goals for a social media campaign, they knew what had gone wrong. "Our original approach was scattershot," Jim admitted to investors. "But it didn't take long to fix our mistake."

The couple eliminated their sponsored ads and pins, recognizing that they needed to build brand awareness and engage with potential customers before trying to generate sales. Instead, they used Facebook and Twitter to introduce the company, post news about parenting, and invite viewers to share tips and stories. Additionally, they hired a parenting expert to encourage and answer questions on a PlayToday parenting blog.

Within six months, Facebook likes had zoomed from fewer than 50 to over 500; Twitter retweets had quadrupled; and the blog was so successful that Marlene and Jim hired a second expert to respond to the steady stream of inquiries.

"We've achieved Goal #1, building awareness and engagement," concluded Marlene. "Stay tuned for the next phase of our SMM plan: Goal #2 is to jumpstart revenue!"

# 5-5 MONITORING AND MEASURING SOCIAL MEDIA MARKETING

## OPENING EXAMPLE

You are hoping to open a small social media marketing agency for businesses in your area. While you have a lot of personal experience using social media, utilizing social media for business is fairly new to you. To gain experience, you offered to develop a full social media presence for a friend's newly opened yoga studio. It includes a Facebook page with photos and videos of the studio, Twitter posts about innovative classes, and links to other sites about the practice of yoga. But there's one big problem. When your friend asked what these activities have accomplished for her business, you realized you didn't know. You are somewhat embarrassed, even though you did this work for free. You need to get her an answer, though, because any paying clients you hope to get will ask the same questions.

> **LO 5.5** Describe the various methods for measuring the effectiveness of social media marketing.

### 5-5a

## LEARNING IT: MONITORING AND MEASURING SOCIAL MEDIA MARKETING

It's one thing to launch a social media marketing campaign, but without tracking its effectiveness you won't know whether the time and money invested is worth it. That's why it's important to know various methods for measuring the effectiveness of social media marketing.

The first step is to revisit the goals set at the beginning of the effort. Then, based on those goals, you can select the appropriate metric for measuring progress toward that goal. Measurement methods typically fall into three categories: measures of activity, measures of engagement, and measures of conversion.

## MEASURES OF ACTIVITY

Understanding the overall reach of a social media campaign can help companies understand whether they are reaching the right volume and type of customers. Measurements of activity include the following:

- *Total likes/followers/subscribers to company social media profiles*: This is the audience you can reach through your social media channels. Oftentimes, the bigger the audience, the bigger the opportunity for you to directly communicate with prospects and customers.
- *New likes/followers/subscribers to company social media profiles*: While the total activity number is important, it's also useful to know how quickly you are gaining new fans on social media.
- *Impressions for social media content*: Knowing the number of people who received your message is the foundation for most forms or promotion. Luckily, social media makes it easy to track how many people saw your blog post, watched your video, or read your tweet.

## MEASURES OF ENGAGEMENT

Having lots of likes or impressions doesn't mean that your social media activities are effective. That's why digital marketers often focus more on measure of engagement for your social audience. A more engaged audience is more likely to purchase from your company and create good word-of-mouth among their friends. This type of engagement is often what fuels growth in overall activity. Measurements of engagement include the following:

- *Likes/comments on social media content*: This could include likes and comments on Facebook posts, Pinterest pins, tweets, Snapchat stories, or blog posts. When users engage with a piece of content, it makes that content visible to their own network of friends, which in turn makes it more likely that content will go viral.
- *Re-tweets/shares/re-pins*: This type of engagement is even more powerful than likes and comments because the user is actively pushing the content to their network. This acts as a form of endorsement for your content and company, and is even more powerful when influencers, such as celebrities or leaders of a particular industry, share the content.
- *Click-through rate*: Often social media content will include links to content on the company's website, blog, or e-commerce store. This form of engagement is extremely valuable. First, it takes users off someone else's social media platform and puts them on a platform you control, which allows you to control the messaging, branding, and user experience of the pages. Second, it facilitates collection of leads, such as e-mail addresses.

## MEASURES OF CONVERSION

While activity and engagement are relevant to a number of social media marketing goals, ultimately the goal of many social media campaigns is to convert followers to customers (or repeat customers). Some social sites, such as Facebook, allow companies to conduct e-commerce right on their platform. But even when customers check out on company e-commerce sites, analytics tools allow the company to track where that traffic came from, whether it be a search engine query or a click-through from a Facebook post. This allows companies to measure their conversion rate (# of sales/# of visitors) for each of these traffic sources.

Most companies use a combination of methods to assess their SMM campaigns. This is important because no one facet of social media activity can tell the whole story. For example, a brand may gain a large number of likes or website comments for a particular piece of content, indicating increased engagement; but the brand does not benefit if a high proportion of that engagement is negative.

### 5-5b
## CLOSING EXAMPLE

To assess the value of the SMM campaign you designed for your friend, you began by asking her to specify her primary business goal. "I need to build awareness about my studio," she said. "There are lots of yoga fans in the area who don't realize they have a place so close to home to learn and practice."

Given her goal of boosting brand awareness, you looked at measurements related to activity. The number of Facebook followers for the studio had tripled since the campaign began, and over 10,000 people saw the tweets you posted in the last week. Those results should make her—and you—proud!

# 5-6 CREATING EFFECTIVE SOCIAL MEDIA CONTENT

### OPENING EXAMPLE

Over the past several years, Weight Watchers' revenues were flat and the company was looking for ways to increase sales. Because of its "community-centric" approach, Weight Watchers focused its strategies on social networking to attract new members and retain existing ones.

In 2015, the company partnered with Oprah Winfrey to launch its "Better Together" campaign, building on the star's belief that "Life is better when you share it."[34] How did Weight Watchers take advantage of this emphasis on sharing—and Oprah's celebrity—to enhance its SMM content?

**LO 5.6** Outline the seven guidelines for creating effective social media content.

### 5-6a
## LEARNING IT: CREATING EFFECTIVE SOCIAL MEDIA CONTENT

SMM content differs from traditional marketing in that it is, by definition, a two-way street. In order for SMM to succeed, the content of its messages must engage the target audience in the conversation. **Content marketing** involves creating

**content marketing** creating and distributing relevant and targeted material to attract and engage an audience, with the goal of driving them to a desired action

and distributing relevant and targeted material to attract and engage an audience, with the goal of driving them to a desired action.

Guidelines for creating effective social media content include the following:

- *A strong brand focus*: Every communication includes current messages relevant to the brand. Weight Watchers incorporates dieting tips and success stories into its website, Facebook page, Twitter feed, and YouTube videos. If Weight Watchers were to also provide pet tips and travel recommendations on social media, that would be irrelevant and off-brand.

- *A focus on the audience rather than the organization:* While it's important to maintain a strong brand identity and meet marketing goals, social media content focuses on its audience rather than promoting the company outright. Some of the most successful social media campaigns were based on stories about customers, or content generated by the customers themselves. Weight Watchers' content is about the challenges faced by dieters—like Oprah—not about the company itself.

- *Targeted keywords*: Good keywords are those the targeted audience will most likely search when looking for information about goods and services. For example, an oceanfront resort might use keywords like "beach vacation" or "hotel with watersports." They might also establish some hashtag phrases related to their campaign to make it more discoverable by other users.

- *Relevant information*: This is more than a list of product features or specifications. Content may include problem-solving tips, answers to frequently asked questions, community polls, guest writers, interviews, statistics, case studies, and so forth. Recent video content posted by Weight Watchers included "Oprah's Favorite Breakfast Meal" and "WW Presents: Recipe Ideas for Every Meal."

When Weight Watchers posted videos of Oprah discussing challenges she faced when dieting, the goal was to relate with the audience rather than focus on the company.

Source: YouTube, LLC

- *Shareworthy text and images*: Marketers can turn customers into storytellers by encouraging them to post images related to the brand. Weight Watchers' Connect app community enables and encourages customers to share stories of their dieting progress, photos, and motivational quotes.
  - In one of the most successful promotions of 2016, fast-food chain Taco Bell ran a "sponsored lens" on Snapchat. Users could take funny, memorable selfies that transformed their heads into tacos, complete with the company's Diablo sauce. In a single day, the promotion received 224 million views, more than any other sponsored lens since Snap invented this social media tool.[35]
- *Invitations to generate content via posts, shares, discussions, reviews, or other forms of dialogue with the organization as well as with fellow customers*: On its Facebook page, Weight Watchers hosts community question-and-answer sessions between customers and company leaders.
- *Promotions that offer discounts, gifts, or other special deals in exchange for participation*: To launch a gardening app called Sprout It, web developers invited their fans to snap a picture of their backyard and post it to Instagram or Twitter. The grand prize: a professional garden makeover.[36]

## 5-6b
## CLOSING EXAMPLE

Weight Watchers' partnership with Oprah demonstrated the company's savvy sense of well-focused, relevant, shareworthy content—and the celebrity's ability to deliver it. A particularly successful part of the SMM campaign was a live Facebook stream of Oprah visiting with real customers; one such video got 2 million hits.[37] The effort resulted in three straight quarters of year-over-year revenue growth for Weight Watchers. The firm's stock price got a boost, too.

# 5-7    ETHICS IN SOCIAL MEDIA

### OPENING EXAMPLE

When a photo of a 4-year-old girl wearing Crocs sandals appeared on the shoemaker's website, the girl's mother—who had posted the photo on Instagram—found out about it only when a reporter called her for comment. Without asking her permission, or even informing her of the company's intent, Crocs had simply added the image to its gallery of user-generated content.

Do you think Crocs should have contacted the mother in advance? Why or why not?

 **LO 5.7** Summarize three ethical principles for social media marketers.

5-7a

# 5-7a
# LEARNING IT: ETHICS IN SOCIAL MEDIA

Social media marketers face ethical and legal issues as part of their job. As rapidly as the various social media evolve and expand, so too will new ethical situations arise. To protect the company and its customers, it's recommended that social media marketers pay particular attention to three ethical principles: respect privacy, be honest, and be accountable.

## RESPECT PRIVACY

Although marketers try to gather as much information as possible about a target audience, they must not distribute any personal information without consent. Because social media is interactive by its nature, marketers must be vigilant about confidentiality and not letting personal information or other data accidentally slip into unauthorized hands. Violation of these practices and other privacy laws and guidelines could destroy a company's reputation and cost millions of dollars. For example, after Sony revealed a breach of its PlayStation Network customers' personal data, an investigation revealed the breach could have been avoided had Sony's software been up to date. The company was fined 250,000 British pounds (more than $415,000) and suffered serious public relations damage.[38]

## BE HONEST

Social media messages travel at lightning speed around the world; potentially millions of people may view a message in a matter of seconds or minutes. This means that postings, ads, comments, and even images come under intense scrutiny—and must be checked for accuracy, fair and realistic claims, balance and objectivity, and even (or especially) potential for misinterpretation. Sprint was forced to withdraw an online video ad featuring customers saying any word that came to mind when they heard competitor T-Mobile. A white woman said "ghetto"—prompting widespread accusations of racism and insensitivity.[39]

## BE ACCOUNTABLE

Mistakes happen. When they do, smart social media marketers take three actions to solve the problem or resolve the issue. They:

1. Acknowledge the problem and take responsibility for it
2. Communicate with the right people, via the most relevant channels, and promise to take steps necessary to correct the situation
3. Implement the agreed-upon changes and evaluate ways to avoid similar problems in the future

# 5-7b
# CLOSING EXAMPLE

While Crocs may not have broken any laws by posting the Instagram photo without permission, the company acknowledged that it had made a mistake in failing to respect the privacy of both mother and daughter. In addition to contacting the mother directly—if belatedly—Crocs reinforced its commitment to get permission before utilizing such user-generated content in the future. Instagram also chimed in, stating that it "strongly encourages brands to contact users directly."[40]

# 5-8 LAUNCHING AND MEASURING A SOCIAL MEDIA CAMPAIGN

## OPENING EXAMPLE

In 2015, LinkedIn acquired online learning company Lynda.com, a leading online learning platform offering courses in business, software, IT, and more. Many in the tech world expressed surprise, noting that the marketing task of selling subscriptions for courses and other educational content is very different from providing resources to jobseekers and those seeking to build their professional network. However, executives at LinkedIn were confident they could make the transition and effectively market Lynda.

**LO 5.8** Given a goal for social media marketing, determine the most effective method of measurement.

### 5-8a

## LEARNING IT: LAUNCHING AND MEASURING A SOCIAL MEDIA CAMPAIGN

As discussed earlier, the first step in building a social media marketing campaign is to ask what you want to accomplish from the campaign. Once you have identified the goals, you can select the appropriate measurement methods to track the success of the campaign. Exhibit 5.2 summarizes social media marketing goals and the measurements most relevant to those goals.

**EXHIBIT 5.2** Measuring Social Media Marketing Results

| Goal | Type of Measurement | Examples | Why? |
|---|---|---|---|
| **Increase brand awareness and generate leads** | Measures of Activity | • Total likes/followers/subscribers to company social media profiles<br>• New likes/followers/subscribers to company social media profiles<br>• Impressions for social media content | Measures how many users are seeing your content and indicating interest in your brand |
| **Increase revenue** | Measures of Conversion | • Conversion rate | Measures how effective each source of social media traffic is at generating revenue |
| **Increase customer service** | Measures of Engagement | • Likes/comments on social media content<br>• Retweets/shares/re-pins<br>• Click-through rate | Measures how many users are reacting to your content and/or sharing it with others |

*(Continues)*

*(Continued)*

| Goal | Type of Measurement | Examples | Why? |
|------|--------------------|----------|------|
| **Manage a crisis** | Measures of Engagement | • Likes/comments on social media content<br>• Retweets/shares/re-pins<br>• Click-through rate | Measures how many users are reacting to your content and/or sharing it with others |
| **Market research and customer feedback** | Measures of Engagement | • Likes/comments on social media content<br>• Retweets/shares/re-pins<br>• Click-through rate | Measures how many users are reacting to your content and/or sharing it with others |

## 5-9  LEARN IT TODAY . . . USE IT TOMORROW

As the Director of Social Media Management for Lynda.com, you've been tasked with building a successful social media campaign and measuring its results. But you know that the definition of success first begins with your goals for the campaign, so you schedule a meeting with your executive team to clarify.

It's time to get hands-on and apply what you've learned. **See MindTap for an activity related to Lynda's marketing activities.**

## Chapter Summary

**LO 5.1** **Describe the growth and use of social media.**

The proliferation of social media—now used by over 70% of adults—has made it an important relationship-building tool. Marketers use it to create buzz, facilitate customer engagement, and enable fans to promote their goods and services.

**LO 5.2** **Contrast the three major types of social media platforms.**

Three major types of social media platforms offer distinct opportunities for marketers: social networking sites, social bookmarking sites, and blogging sites.

**LO 5.3** **Explain three ways consumers rely on social media to make buying decisions.**

Consumers rely on social media to discover new goods and services, research and share information, and make purchase decisions.

**LO 5.4** **Identify the types of goals marketers use for social media campaigns.**

Marketers set goals at the outset of a SMM campaign to make sure it pays off in terms of what the organization needs to achieve: sales, brand awareness, crisis resolution, or other metrics.

**LO 5.5** Describe the various methods for measuring the effectiveness of social media marketing.

Marketers typically measure social media marketing in terms of activity, engagement, and/or conversion. The key is to measure progress toward achieving the campaigns' goals.

**LO 5.6** Outline the seven guidelines for creating effective social media content.

The purpose of SMM content is to engage the target audience in a two-way conversation. The most effective content has a strong brand focus; prioritizes the audience over the organization; uses targeted keywords; presents relevant information; creates shareworthy text and images; invites the audience to generate content; and offers incentives to participate.

**LO 5.7** Summarize three ethical principles for social media marketers.

Social media marketers face three key ethical considerations: privacy, honesty, and accountability.

**LO 5.8** Given a goal for social media marketing, determine the most effective method of measurement.

A SMM campaign is effective only if it achieves progress toward specific goals. Marketers must be able to match a given goal to the most relevant measurement tool or metric.

## Key Terms

social media **87**
social media platforms **89**
social networking sites **89**

bookmarking sites **90**
blogs **90**
social media marketing (SMM) **94**

influencers **94**
content marketing **99**

# PART 2

## UNDERSTANDING BUYERS AND MARKETS

# 6 CONSUMER BEHAVIOR

Source: www.skibutternut.com

## LEARNING OBJECTIVES

**6.1** Identify the three types of influences that affect the consumer decision process.

**6.2** Outline the six steps in the consumer decision process.

**6.3** Distinguish between high-involvement and low-involvement purchase decisions.

**6.4** Describe the five social factors that influence consumer behavior.

**6.5** Describe the five psychological factors that influence consumer behavior.

**6.6** Describe the four situational factors that influence consumer behavior.

**6.7** Given a consumer purchase scenario, identify the primary influences affecting the consumer decision process.

# LEARN IT TODAY . . . USE IT TOMORROW

"**S**ki Butternut is a true family mountain," says Matt Sawyer, director of marketing for the ski and snowboarding resort nestled in the Berkshire Mountains of western Massachusetts. Smaller than the peaks of Colorado or even the crags of the Green Mountains of Vermont and White Mountains of New Hampshire, Butternut is what Sawyer refers to as a "soft mountain"—one that beginners can enjoy while they grow comfortable on skis or snowboards. In fact, through extensive surveying and data collecting (as well as 50 years of experience), Ski Butternut has been able to identify exactly who its customers are—and what they want when they come to a mountain like Butternut.

The mountain's marketers, including Matt Sawyer and advertising consultant Ed Brooks, use various methods to tease out these factors in an effort to attract and keep customers. A number of factors influence consumers' decision to try Butternut, and this knowledge of consumer behavior is a critical factor for differentiating Butternut from its competition.

 **6-1** **INFLUENCES AFFECTING CONSUMER BEHAVIOR**

## OPENING EXAMPLE

Grocery shopping is where the rubber meets the road for consumer packaged goods companies. Success hinges on consumers selecting their products and placing them in the grocery cart for purchase. According to the *Food Marketing Institute*, consumers spend 4.3% of their disposable income on food to be consumed at home and make an average of 1.6 trips per week to the grocery store.[1] These trips add up to big dollars for the more than 38,000 grocery stores across the United States with $2 million or more in annual sales. The average store carries almost 40,000 items ranging from fresh produce and canned goods to cereal and beauty aids. What influences consumers to select certain products? How many "planned" versus "unplanned" purchases do shoppers make, and how can retail grocers and food marketers better understand consumer decision processes before, during, and after their trips to the store? The study of consumer behavior and the many factors that influence it provides deep insight for marketers.

**LO 6.1** Identify the three types of influences that affect the consumer decision process.

### 6-1a
## LEARNING IT: INFLUENCES AFFECTING CONSUMER BEHAVIOR

**Consumer behavior** is the process through which the ultimate buyer or household consumer makes purchase decisions. This chapter focuses on individual purchasing behavior, which applies to all consumers, while Chapter 7 is about business buying decisions. Companies who market products ranging from toothbrushes to automobiles to vacations must understand the core needs and wants of their customers, as well as the many factors that influence their purchasing behavior.

**consumer behavior** the process through which the ultimate buyer or household consumer makes purchase decisions

**social factors** external influences such as culture, social class, reference groups, family, and opinion leaders

Consumers often decide to buy goods and services based on what they believe others expect of them. **Social factors** include external influences such as culture, social class, reference groups, family, and opinion leaders. For example, a finance major may wear a dark suit, white dress shirt, and blue tie for a job interview with an investment bank because he believes conservative attire is expected in the banking industry. A high school senior might attend the college where their parents went or based on the recommendation of one of their friends.

**psychological factors** are factors internal to the individual

Consumer behavior is also influenced by factors internal to the individual, known as **psychological factors**, factors internal to the individual. Psychological factors include needs and motives, perceptions, attitudes, learning, and self-concept. For example, if a consumer is concerned about environmental issues and wants to decrease their carbon footprint, they might purchase a hybrid or electric car such as a Chevrolet Volt or Toyota Prius, use public transportation, or bike to work.

**situational factors** external factors related to the particular circumstances under which a purchase is made

Contextual or **situational factors** are external factors related to the particular circumstances under which a purchase is made. Consider how the purchase occasion might influence a consumer's choice of retail outlet or how much they might spend on clothing. A woman getting married may be willing to spend much more on a wedding dress than she'd spend on a dress for work.

## 6-1b
## CLOSING EXAMPLE

Aldi Inc. considers itself to be a leader in the grocery industry, offering "fresh, high quality groceries at everyday low prices to more than 45 million customers each month."[2] Aldi's success strategy hinges on their ability to provide the products consumers desire by understanding the decision making process and various factors that influence behavior. Aldi's store model is distinctive as they provide a no-frills shopping experience and a condensed number of items—only 2,500 compared to the 40,000 items at competing outlets.

Recently, Aldi partnered with *Cookie and Kate*, a full-time food blogger whose website has become the most visited vegetarian website in the United States to create recipes and meal plans for shoppers.[3,4] The lifestyle blog and collaboration with *Cookie and Kate* is an example of how opinion leaders, a *social factor*, can influence consumer behavior. The partnership also reflects an understanding of shopper attitudes, a *psychological factor*, as Aldi discovered that 56% of consumers make healthy eating and weight loss part of their New Year's resolutions. The recipes will enable Aldi's customers to keep their resolutions by making better food choices. In addition, Aldi's business model is heavily linked to *situational factors* and understanding how consumers are overwhelmed by the large number of choices in a traditional store. In response, they "offer only the best of customers' must-have groceries."[5] Aldi also uses branding and product packaging to influence purchase behavior around all three of these factors. For example, their *SimplyNature* line of products responds to consumer trends by eliminating over 125 artificial ingredients.

# 6-2 THE CONSUMER DECISION PROCESS

## OPENING EXAMPLE

Trevor is considering purchasing a new vehicle and has always wanted a full-size truck. He enjoys a lot of outdoor activities and believes the rugged style and capabilities of a truck mesh well with his lifestyle and occupation as a construction engineer. How will he decide which vehicle to purchase, and more importantly for marketers, how can truck brands and dealerships influence his choice? As we'll see in the next section, consumers typically complete a sequential process when making purchasing decisions and can be influenced by marketers at every step along the way.

**LO 6.2** Outline the six steps in the consumer decision process.

### 6-2a

## LEARNING IT: THE CONSUMER DECISION PROCESS

Although they might not be aware of it, consumers usually complete a step-by-step process when making purchasing decisions (see Exhibit 6.1). Marketing strategies are often designed to steer consumers through the decision process in the direction of a specific product.

**EXHIBIT 6.1**   Steps in the Consumer Decision Process

| Step | Description |
|------|-------------|
| Problem-opportunity recognition | Consumer becomes aware of a gap between an existing situation and a desired situation. |
| Information search | Consumer conducts internal or external information search to acquire information to assist in the attainment of the desired state. |
| Evaluation of alternatives | As a result of the information search, consumers identify appropriate alternatives, or their evoked set, and utilize evaluative criteria to judge the options. |
| Purchase decision | Consumers narrow choice to their top option and decide where to make the purchase. |
| Purchase behavior | Consumers actually purchase the product. |
| Post-purchase evaluation | Consumers evaluate the purchase to determine whether it helped them achieve the desired state and how satisfied or dissatisfied they are with the product. |

## PROBLEM OR OPPORTUNITY RECOGNITION

The first stage in the consumer decision process is when the consumer becomes aware of a gap between their existing situation and a desired or ideal situation. The desired situation may form as a result of unmet needs or wants. The marketer's main task during this phase of the decision making process is to help prospective buyers identify and recognize potential problems or needs. This task may take the form of advertising, promotions, or personal sales assistance.

Now, let's consider Trevor and his decision to purchase a new full-size pickup truck. Trevor is currently driving a sedan, which doesn't allow him to go off-road for hiking, hunting, or camping trips. He's traveled with friends in their trucks and likes the ability to have the cabin comfort of a car but the flexibility of cargo space for hauling equipment. Trevor's decision to purchase a truck stems from his recognition that a truck would allow him to better pursue his hobbies and would better fit his lifestyle. It's likely that Trevor's decision to purchase a truck is also influenced by truck advertisements airing on ESPN during football season, such as Ford's Future of Tough commercial showing the all-new F-150.[6]

## INFORMATION SEARCH

During the second step in the decision process, a consumer gathers information about different ways to solve a problem or achieve the desired state. The search may cover internal or external sources of information. An internal search is simply a mental review: Is there past experience with the product? Was it good or bad? An external search involves gathering information from all kinds of outside sources—for instance, family, friends, coworkers or classmates, advertisements or salespeople, online reviews, and consumer magazines. How much time and effort a consumer spends gathering information varies according to their level of experience and knowledge with the product as well as the risk involved in making a decision. Typically, consumers spend more time gathering information when purchasing expensive items, such as appliances and automobiles. In comparison, they spend less time searching for information about inexpensive grocery products like paper towels or potato chips.

The search stage enables consumers to identify alternative brands or models for consideration and possible purchase. The collection of alternatives a consumer actually considers when making a decision is known in marketing as the **evoked set**. In some cases, consumers already know which brands merit further consideration; in others, consumers make external searches to develop such information. The number of brands that are included in the evoked set may vary with the situation and the person. An immediate need, such as filling a nearly empty gas tank, might limit the evoked set. A driver with half a tank of gas, with more time to make a decision, might expand the evoked set to choose from a broader range of options that include lower prices or certain brands.

Marketers can attempt to influence the information search stage through a variety of means such as advertising, websites, publicity, and the use of personal selling. The opportunity to influence consumers during the information search stage is greater for marketers when consumers spend more time engaged in external search processes.

**evoked set** the collection of alternatives a consumer considers when making a decision

Source: Ford Motor Company

Ford makes it easier for consumers to conduct an information search by offering tools to compare different makes and models.

What about Trevor and his information search process about a new truck? Ford's research indicates that truck buyers start their search process 233 days prior to purchasing and spend 35–45% more time researching on dealer websites than car or cross-over buyers.[7] It's likely that Trevor would visit dealerships, test-drive different models, and read reviews comparing different models as part of his external information.[8] He might also talk with friends about how satisfied they are with their truck and what model they might buy in the future. As a result of the information gained from these various sources and experiences, Trevor would most likely narrow his choice to two or three models that represent his evoked set for the truck purchase.

## EVALUATION OF ALTERNATIVES

The third step in the consumer decision process is to evaluate the evoked set of options. Actually, it is difficult to completely separate the second and third steps because some evaluation takes place as the search progresses; consumers accept, distort, or reject information as they receive it. Depending upon the consumer's decision, they may identify attributes that are important to them or establish a set of criteria that will be used to compare the options. Evaluative criteria are the features a consumer considers in choosing among alternatives. These criteria can be either objective facts (a vehicle's fuel economy) or subjective impressions (a favorable view of the brand). For example, common criteria for evaluating athletic shoes may include price, construction materials, brand name, and country of origin.

Marketers attempt to influence the outcome of this stage in three ways. First, they try to educate consumers about attributes they view as important in evaluating a particular class of products. They also identify which evaluative criteria are important to an individual and attempt to show why a specific brand fulfills those criteria. Finally, they try to induce a customer to expand the evoked set to include their product.

After test driving a few vehicles, visiting websites, and reading expert reviews, Trevor narrowed his choice to three options: Ford F-150, Chevrolet Silverado, and GMC Sierra 1500. Trevor believes these three vehicles are fairly comparable on his primary criteria of performance, off-road capabilities, fuel efficiency, and towing capacity.[9]

## PURCHASE DECISION AND PURCHASE ACT

The information search and evaluation stages of the decision process result in the purchase decision and the actual purchase. At this stage, the consumer has evaluated each alternative in the evoked set based on his or her personal set of evaluative criteria and narrowed the options down to one.

The consumer then decides where—or from whom—to make the purchase. Sometimes this decision is part of the evaluation; perhaps one seller is offering a better price or better warranty than another. The purchase may be made online or in person at a retail store. The delivery options also might influence the decision of where to purchase an item.

## POST-PURCHASE EVALUATION

The final step of the consumer decision process is to evaluate the purchase, which leads to two outcomes. The buyer may feel satisfaction that their desired state has been achieved or experience dissatisfaction with the purchase. Consumers are generally satisfied if purchases meet—or exceed—their expectations. Sometimes, however, consumers experience post-purchase anxiety called cognitive dissonance. This anxiety results from an imbalance among a person's knowledge, beliefs, and attitudes. A consumer who purchased a new laptop may experience dissonance if the computer is difficult to set up, isn't as fast or lightweight as they thought it would be, or if they see an advertisement for the same model at a lower price.

Dissonance is likely to increase:

- As the dollar value of a purchase increases
- When the rejected alternatives have desirable features that the chosen alternatives do not provide
- When the purchase decision has a major effect on the buyer

If you buy a diet soda and don't like the flavor, you can toss it and buy a different one. But if you have spent more than $1,500 on a laptop computer and aren't satisfied with it, you will most likely experience dissonance. You might try to reduce the dissonance by focusing on good reviews about your choice. Or you might show a friend your new computer and how it's one of the best gaming models—without pointing out anything you find dissatisfactory such as the weight or speed.

Marketers can help buyers reduce cognitive dissonance by providing information that supports the chosen item. Automobile dealers recognize the possibility of "buyer's remorse" and often follow up purchases with letters or telephone calls offering personal attention to any customer questions or potential problems. Advertisements that stress customer satisfaction also help reduce cognitive dissonance, such as including J.D. Power ratings for new car quality.

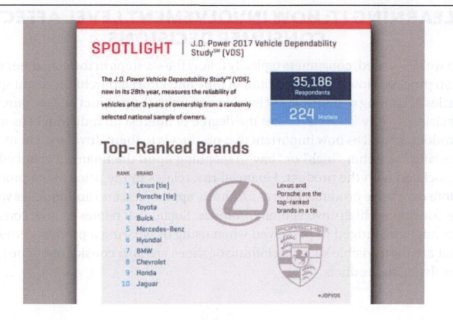

Source: J.D. Power and Associates

By reminding buyers the positive attributes of the product they just purchased, auto manufacturers and dealers hope to increase buyer satisfaction and loyalty.

## 6-2b
## CLOSING EXAMPLE

During Trevor's truck purchase process, he engaged in all aspects of the consumer decision process. Ultimately, Trevor decided to purchase the GMC Sierra from the Chevrolet dealership. The sales representative was able to obtain the color and options Trevor wanted, plus offered a great financing package. After the purchase, the sales representative sent Trevor several gift cards to use at a local car wash and reminded him that he had made a great decision. Trevor was enjoying his new truck and received lots of compliments from his friends, which further increased his satisfaction related to the purchase.

# 6-3 HOW INVOLVEMENT LEVEL AFFECTS CONSUMER DECISIONS

### OPENING EXAMPLE

Target stores wants to identify ways to better support customers by offering enhanced personal selling services for certain product categories. Most Target stores are quite large and include a range of products including grocery, clothing, electronics, and home and garden. Offering these enhanced services in every category is not economically feasible, though. What product categories would be most appropriate for Target to implement these services? The answer will depend on the level of involvement typically required for purchases in these various categories.

**LO 6.3** Distinguish between high-involvement and low-involvement purchase decisions.

6-3a

## 6-3a
## LEARNING IT: HOW INVOLVEMENT LEVEL AFFECTS CONSUMER DECISIONS

**involvement** the degree of interest an individual has in the product, as well as how important that product is to them

As we've learned, consumers typically follow the six steps in the consumer decision process. However, the amount of time and effort a purchaser might spend varies according to their level of involvement with the product and/or purchase decision. **Involvement** indicates the degree of interest an individual has in the product, as well as how important that product is to them. Involvement may be classified as either "high" or "low" depending upon the financial or social risk associated with the product. Financial risk relates to the price of the product; more expensive products such as furniture, appliances, and automobiles would be considered high-involvement products. Social risk relates to how consumers might be judged or perceived when using or wearing a product. Products that are more visible such as clothing or shoes are also considered to be high-involvement products.

## 6-3b
## CONSUMER DECISION MAKING STYLES

Another dimension of consumer decision making involves the level of problem solving required for the purchase. These styles, which correlate to the concept of high or low involvement, are termed routinized response behavior, limited problem solving, and extended problem solving (see Exhibit 6.2).

**routinized response behavior** behavior that occurs for low-involvement products that consumers purchase on a frequent basis

**Routinized response behavior** occurs for low-involvement products that consumers purchase on a frequent basis. These items are low price and often consumed in private, so both financial risk and social risk are low. Consumers generally purchase the same brand or one of a limited group of acceptable brands and spend very little time thinking about the purchase or evaluating alternatives. Examples include common household items such as toothpaste, deodorant, and dishwashing soap.

**limited problem solving** behavior that occurs for purchases that consumers make less frequently and when their knowledge or experience is limited

Consumers use **limited problem solving** for purchases that they make less frequently and when their knowledge or experience is limited. Financial and social risk may be relatively low, but the lack of knowledge leads consumers to spend more time gathering information about brands or products prior to

**EXHIBIT 6.2** Types of Consumer Decision Making

| Decision Making Style | Level of Involvement | Extent of Information Search | Length of Time to Make a Decision | Example Products |
|---|---|---|---|---|
| Routinized response behavior | Low | Little | Short | Toothpaste, detergent, deodorant |
| Limited problem solving | Low to moderate | Little to moderate | Short to medium | Clothing, cookware, personal electronics |
| Extended problem solving | High | Extensive | Long | Automobiles, furniture, college |

making a purchase decision. New products in a category may trigger a limited problem solving style, such as the introduction of a new brand of yogurt or shampoo. Alternatively, clothing purchases such as a new shirt or pair of pants may be classified as limited problem solving due to the need to try on the clothes to ensure appropriate fit.

**Extended problem solving** is the most complex decision style and occurs for high-involvement products where financial and/or social risk is high. Purchases of this type typically require an extensive information search and consumers are willing to spend considerable effort or time making the decision. Purchasing a new automobile or home, selecting furniture or appliances, or choosing a college to attend are all examples of high-involvement decisions where extended problem solving might be utilized.

**extended problem solving** the most complex decision style and occurs for high-involvement products where financial and/or social risk is high

## 6-3c
# CLOSING EXAMPLE

The Target managers set out to identify areas of the store that could benefit from increased personal selling assistance. They focus on areas where consumers are more likely to utilize extended problem solving, meaning these are high-involvement purchases that require more extensive information search and evaluation. As a result, Target decides to offer enhanced selling services in the departments selling jewelry/watches, electronics, and furniture (see Exhibit 6.3).

**EXHIBIT 6.3** Target Stores Apply Consumer Decision Making Styles

# 6-4 SOCIAL FACTORS INFLUENCING CONSUMER BEHAVIOR

**LO 6.4** Describe the five social factors that influence consumer behavior.

## OPENING EXAMPLE

Marketers understand that a variety of external factors influence consumer behavior and they're faced with increasingly difficult choices to determine how best to leverage these forces in marketing. Lilly Pulitzer is a 60-year-old women's "resort chic" lifestyle brand that started in the wealthy, high society Palm Beach, California, community and quickly became a favorite brand of stylish women such as Jackie Kennedy. The company realized they needed to attract younger customers and wouldn't survive by focusing marketing solely on their loyal, older customer base.[10,11]

What social factors might help Lilly Pulitzer attract a younger clientele, and how can they best generate awareness, sales, and loyalty?

### 6-4a

## LEARNING IT: SOCIAL FACTORS INFLUENCING CONSUMER BEHAVIOR

Social factors and group membership influence individual consumer purchase decisions in both overt and subtle ways. The five social factors include culture, social class, reference groups, family, and opinion leaders.

## CULTURAL INFLUENCES

**culture** the values, beliefs, preferences, and tastes handed down from one generation to the next

**Culture** can be defined as the values, beliefs, preferences, and tastes handed down from one generation to the next. Culture is the broadest environmental determinant of consumer behavior. Some cultural values change over time, but basic core values do not. The work ethic and the desire to accumulate wealth are two core values common in American society. Even though the typical family structure and family members' roles have shifted over the years, American culture still emphasizes the importance of family and home life. This value is strengthened during times of upheaval such as natural disasters—hurricanes, floods, wildfires, or tornadoes. Other core values include the importance of education, individualism, freedom, youth, health, volunteerism, and efficiency. Marketing strategies and business practices that work in one country may be offensive or ineffective in another. Marketers may even need to vary strategies from one area of a country to another. This is especially true in the United States, where the population continues to diversify at a rapid rate.

**subcultures** are groups with their own distinct modes of behavior

Cultures are not homogeneous groups with universal values, even though core values tend to dominate. Each culture includes numerous **subcultures**—groups with their own distinct modes of behavior. Understanding the differences among subcultures can help marketers develop more effective marketing strategies. America's population is more diverse and the three largest and fastest-growing U.S. ethnic subcultures—Hispanics, Black or African Americans, and Asians—are expected to become the majority by the year 2060. Marketers need to be sensitive to these shifts in population composition and to the differences in shopping patterns and buying habits of the members of different subcultures. Businesses must develop marketing messages that consider the needs of these different types of consumers. For example, Antonio Swad, founder of the successful franchise, *Pizza Patrón* took time to learn about Hispanic tradition and stated, "If you're trying to build rapport with the large percentage of Hispanics who are of Mexican ancestry, you'll make a better impression wishing them a happy Mother's Day on May 10 instead of the second Sunday in May. It's not that you're expressing a fundamentally different sentiment, you're just expressing it according to their traditions. And doing that tells them: "I recognize how you do this, I 'get' you."[12]

## SOCIAL CLASS

**Social class** is based upon an individual's occupation, education, income, wealth, and possessions. Social class can influence consumers' purchasing behavior due to the amount of disposable income available, as well as influence brand and store choice. Research indicates that, comparatively, consumers who shop at KMart and Walmart have lower household incomes, while Target and Kohl's attract higher-income shoppers.[13] Consumers with the highest income ranges may patronize prestige retail brands such as Nieman Marcus, Nordstrom, and specialty boutiques such as Brooks Brothers, Chanel, and Gucci. Exhibit 6.4 summarizes median household incomes by tier.

## REFERENCE GROUPS

Human beings are social creatures and may be influenced by the people or groups with whom they spend time with or identify with in some way. **Reference groups** are people or institutions whose opinions are valued and to whom a person looks for guidance in his or her own behavior, values, and conduct. Examples of reference groups include one's religious, social (e.g. fraternity, sorority, country club), leisure (e.g. golf), and occupation-related groups. The extent to which a group will exert influence on purchasing behavior varies widely but reference group influence is strongest when two conditions are met:

1. *The visibility of the product to others*: A car or workplace outfit are highly visible purchases that are more likely to be influenced by the purchaser's reference groups. While cleaning supplies or car insurance are less visible purchases that are less likely to be influenced by reference groups.

2. *The purchaser's susceptibility to influence*: Children and teens often base buying decisions on the opinion of friends or what they see in the media.

## OPINION LEADERS

In nearly every reference group, a few members act as **opinion leaders**, trendsetters who purchase new products before others in a group, and then influence others in their purchases. Opinion leaders are also likely to share their experiences and opinions via

**social class** based upon an individual's occupation, education, income, wealth, and possessions

**reference groups** people or institutions whose opinions are valued and to whom a person looks for guidance in his or her own behavior, values, and conduct

**opinion leaders** are trendsetters who purchase new products before others in a group, and then influence others in their purchases

**EXHIBIT 6.4**

### Median Household Income by Income Tier

*Median income of households, in 2013–14 dollars and scaled to reflect a three-person household*

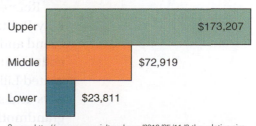

| | |
|---|---|
| All | $62,462 |

**Income tier**

| | |
|---|---|
| Upper | $173,207 |
| Middle | $72,919 |
| Lower | $23,811 |

word-of-mouth or through social media. As others in the group decide whether to try the same products, they are influenced by the reports of opinion leaders. Celebrities such as actors, musicians, and sports figures may also serve as opinion leaders through their endorsement of products or their lifestyle, which is communicated through social media platforms such as Twitter and Instagram.

## FAMILY

The family is perhaps the most important determinant of consumer behavior because of the close, continuing interactions among family members. Most people will be members of at least two families in their lifetime—those they are born into and those they eventually form later in life. The nature and structure of families has changed greatly over the last century, making it harder for marketers to base decisions on family structure alone. They often must identify who the key influencers and decision makers are in various types of households.

The increasing occurrence of the two-income family means that women have a greater role in making large family purchases, such as vacations and automobiles. Studies show that women take the lead in choosing entertainment, such as movies and restaurants. Women also now outspend men in the purchase of electronics. Conversely, as more highly educated women begin to achieve earning parity with their spouses, men are appearing more frequently at the grocery store. A research firm recently coined the term "manfluencer" to describe the growing group of men who are responsible for at least half the grocery shopping in their households.[14] Men also are taking a more active role in child care. Both of these shifts in family life mean that marketers must consider both genders as potential consumers when creating their marketing messages. Children and teenagers represent a huge market—nearly 54 million strong—and they influence what their parents buy, from cereal to automobiles. Young people now wield $1.2 trillion of their own spending power.[15]

## 6-4b

# CLOSING EXAMPLE

Which of these social factors might be ripe for Lilly Pulitzer to utilize in the quest to attract younger customers to their brand? Regarding social class, Lilly Pulitzer knew that younger customers did not have the income and discretionary purchasing power of their older, traditional clients who purchased from Lilly stores, so they collaborated with Target to create a line of 250 products that would appeal to younger buyers. The collection quickly sold out around the country and successfully introduced new customers to the Lilly Pulitzer brand.

Reference groups and opinion leaders have also been key touch points for Lilly Pulitzer, as sorority members on college campuses have embraced the brand and often are pictured in outfits they share on social media. Lilly Pulitzer collaborated with Snapchat to create branded Snapchat filters for users who visited Lilly stores. Family influences are also important for Lilly Pulitzer shoppers and some have received hand-me-down fashions from their mothers or grandmothers, or have dressed in Lilly clothing since they were children. The Lilly Pulitzer brand who seeks to dress women "from 9 to 90" seems poised for success by utilizing social factors to influence and target a younger audience.[16, 17]

# 6-5 PSYCHOLOGICAL FACTORS INFLUENCING CONSUMER BEHAVIOR

## OPENING EXAMPLE

Consumers seem fixated on health, wellness, and maintaining a youthful appearance, creating a market for products designed to help individuals achieve their goals. One company, CrossFit®, was developed by Greg Glassman, whose business now includes over 13,000 affiliates across the globe.[18] What factors drive consumers to choose CrossFit® over competing exercise facilities? In this section, we'll learn more about consumer motivations and other psychological factors that influence consumer behavior.

> **LO 6.5** Describe the five psychological factors that influence consumer behavior.

### 6-5a

## LEARNING IT: PSYCHOLOGICAL FACTORS INFLUENCING CONSUMER BEHAVIOR

Factors internal to an individual influence consumer behavior; these factors include needs and motives, perceptions, attitudes, learned responses, and self-concepts.

## NEEDS AND MOTIVES

As discussed previously, individual purchase behavior is first driven by the motivation to fill a perceived **need**, which is defined as an imbalance between the consumer's actual and desired states.

> **need** is an imbalance between the consumer's actual and desired states

Psychologist Abraham H. Maslow developed a theory that characterized needs and arranged them into a hierarchy. Maslow identified five levels of needs, beginning with physiological needs and progressing to the need for self-actualization (see Exhibit 6.5). According to Maslow, a person must at least partially satisfy lower-level needs before higher needs can affect behavior.

**Motives** are inner states that direct a person toward the goal of satisfying a need. We know that a large portion of consumers set New Year's resolutions to pursue a healthy lifestyle by eating well and exercising. Some consumers might

> **motives** inner states that direct a person toward the goal of satisfying a need

**EXHIBIT 6.5** Marketing Strategies Based on Maslow's Hierarchy of Needs

| Needs | Products | Marketing Themes |
|---|---|---|
| Physiological | Food, water, medicines, vitamins, exercise equipment and gym memberships, health care and cleaning products, sleep aids and mattresses, food for pets | Fresh Express salads: "Consistently, deliciously, fresh."<br>GNC vitamins and supplements: "Live well."<br>Colgate Total: "#1 recommended by dentists and hygienists." |
| Safety | Health and life insurance, computer antivirus software, smoke and carbon monoxide detectors, antibacterial cleaners, business protection, auto safety features | Progressive Insurance: "Helping you save money. That's Progressive."<br>Blue Cross Blue Shield Association: "The Power of Blue."<br>Better Business Bureau: "Start with trust." |

*(Continues)*

*(Continued)*

| Needs | Products | Marketing Themes |
|---|---|---|
| **Belongingness** | Cosmetics, food, entertainment, fashion, appliances and home furnishings, clubs and organizations, cars | Avon Walk for Breast Cancer: "The more of us who walk, the more of us survive." <br><br> Lowe's: "Never Stop Improving." <br><br> Lee: "Get what fits." <br><br> Payless shoes: "Save now. Feel good." <br><br> Olay: "Love the skin you're in." <br><br> Ford: "Drive one." |
| **Esteem** | Fashion, jewelry, gourmet foods, electronics, cosmetics, luxury cars, credit cards, investments, sports and hobbies, travel, spas | Rolex watches: "It Doesn't Just Tell Time. It Tells History." <br><br> Lincoln automobiles: "Travel well." <br><br> L'Oréal Paris: "Because you're worth it." |
| **Self-actualization** | Education, cultural events, sports and hobbies, motivational seminars, technology, travel, investments | University of Phoenix: "I'm a Phoenix." <br><br> Tony Robbins: "Unleash the power within." <br><br> Canyon Ranch: "The power of possibility." |

be motivated to improve their health—using diet to better control cholesterol or manage diabetes. Other consumers might be motivated to lose weight and attain a more desired physical appearance. A consumer's motivations are instrumental in guiding their behavior toward the accomplishment or fulfillment of their needs. Without motives, a consumer could have a legitimate need but never seek to satisfy that need.

Marketers attempt to arouse a consumer's sense of urgency by making a *need* "felt" and then influencing the consumer's *motivation* to satisfy that need by purchasing specific products.

## PERCEPTION

**perception** the meaning a person attributes to incoming stimuli gathered through the five senses—sight, hearing, touch, taste, and smell

**Perception** is the meaning a person attributes to incoming stimuli gathered through the five senses—sight, hearing, touch, taste, and smell. Certainly, a buyer's behavior is influenced by his or her perceptions of a good or service. Researchers now recognize that people's perceptions depend as much on what they want to perceive as on the actual stimuli because the human brain uses selective exposure to choose which inputs are processed.

Marketers use techniques such as doubling the size of a box, using certain colors or graphics, or developing unique packaging to elicit positive responses from consumers. Color is so compelling that its use on product packaging and logos often is the result of a long and careful selection process. Consider the color of packaging utilized on sour candy brands such as *Sour Patch Kids* and *Zours*. Their colorful neon packaging in bright yellow and green is a powerful signal to children who may prefer sour candy. Sometimes they can recognize the candy packaging before they can even read words.

One of the biggest challenges for marketers is getting their messages or products perceived in the first place. How can marketers break through the clutter of advertisements in the media and products that line grocery shelves? Some are utilizing multisensory marketing to gain attentions and impact purchasing behavior. For example, Showtime utilized a mobile-based advertising campaign to promote the new season of "Homeland" on the network's mobile app. The video trailer incorporated phone vibrations to coincide with a scene showing a bomb exploding to enhance the viewer's experience.[19]

## ATTITUDES

Perception of incoming stimuli is greatly affected by attitudes. In fact, a consumer's decision to purchase an item is strongly based on his or her attitudes about the product, store, or salesperson. **Attitudes** are a person's enduring favorable or unfavorable evaluations, emotions, or tendencies toward some object or idea. Attitudes are formed over time through individual experiences and group contacts and are highly resistant to change. Because favorable attitudes likely affect brand preferences, marketers are interested in determining consumer attitudes toward their offerings and identifying ways to modify or change individual's attitudes about their brand.

Consider the case of Maui Jim, maker of high-end, specialty sunglasses. Maui Jim promotes an "aloha spirit" and the brand promise to "change the way you see the world."[20] Maui Jim recently showcased its line of sunglasses during New York fashion week and at the NBA All-Star Weekend, where "over 40 A-list athletes, celebrities, stylists, and media" were wearing Maui Jim sunglasses.[21]

Maui Jim influences consumer attitudes via their connection to an "aloha spirit" and by partnering with celebrities to enhance positive feelings toward the brand.[22] The behavioral or action component of an attitude is activated at the various retail outlets that carry Maui Jim sunglasses, where representatives from Maui Jim are available to interact with customers one-on-one and influence them to purchase a pair of sunglasses.

## LEARNING

**Learning** in the marketing context, refers to immediate or expected changes in consumer behavior as a result of experience. A positive initial experience with a product is the foundation for repeat purchases and positive word-of-mouth, which provides incentive for others to experience the product. Marketers invest significant resources influencing consumers to have that first experience, and then use reinforcement to drive repeat purchases.

For example, product sampling in grocery stores and coupons are commonly used as incentives to entice consumers to try a product. Once sampled, if a consumer is positively disposed toward the product, they are more likely to purchase it and over time become a loyal consumer.

Using bright neon packaging for sour candy can affect consumer perception of the product.

**attitudes** a person's enduring favorable or unfavorable evaluations, emotions, or tendencies toward some object or idea

**learning** immediate or expected changes in consumer behavior as a result of experience

A large part of Costco's retail strategy is to offer product sampling to entice consumers to purchase items they may not have considered, as well as to enhance the shopping experience and create more loyal customers.[23] By using sampling, sales of wine increased by 300% and sales of pizza increased by 600%.

Marketers can then use reinforcement strategies to drive repeat purchases, including use of consistent branding, loyalty programs, and volume discounts.

## SELF-CONCEPT

**self-concept** a person's view of themselves

**Self-concept** is defined as a person's view of themselves and has four components, as described in Exhibit 6.6.

For example, Skip is a creative director of an advertising agency and prides himself on his artistic skills and trendsetting ability. One way he expresses this self-concept is by wearing a Shinola brand watch, which is crafted in Detroit, Michigan, to refute the notion that manufacturing in America is extinct.[24] Skip also wants others to view him as successful and talented so he can create favorable relationships with prospective clients. As part of his "looking-glass self," Skip

**EXHIBIT 6.6** Four Components of Self-Concept

| Self-Concept Components | Description |
|---|---|
| Real Self | Objective view of the total person. |
| Self-Image | An individual's view of themselves. |
| Looking-Glass Self | An individual's view of how other people perceive them. |
| Ideal Self | An individual's view of who they aspire to be. |

Consumers might express self-concept theory by wearing a certain brand of watch, such as a Shinola timepiece crafted in the city of Detroit.

Stephanie Keith/Newscom/Polaris Images/New York/NY/United States

dresses in a more fashion-forward style, prefers European designers, and drives an expensive BMW sports car. However, Skip also seeks to attain his ideal self-image of philanthropist by contributing to the community and being a mentor to others. Skip's desire to be a philanthropist may lead him to spend money in ways that allow him to contribute to worthwhile causes, such as buying season tickets to the symphony or sponsoring an underprivileged child. All of these actions demonstrate how Skip's self-concept drives a variety of his consumer purchase decisions.

## 6-5b
### CLOSING EXAMPLE

CrossFit® differentiates itself from other gyms by avoiding traditional equipment like stairclimbers, treadmills, and weight machines. You won't find any cycling or aerobics classes; and no saunas. Instead, when you walk into a "box" you'll find large squat racks with Olympic weights, kettlebells, medicine balls, jump ropes, and other functional fitness equipment. The "Workout of the Day" (WOD) is a challenging set of exercises that members complete—usually for time—while being cheered on by coaches and fellow participants. Results are posted on a whiteboard and often shared each day on Facebook. Coaches typically recommend a clean diet of mostly meat, fish, vegetables, nuts, seeds, and a little fruit. CrossFit is also a community that extends beyond any one "box" and consists of magazines, podcasts, blogs, and regional and national events.

The CrossFit environment goes beyond simply fulfilling a member's motive to get strong or lose weight, it also reinforces member perceptions and attitudes about working out in a place that promotes elite fitness. The exciting and social atmosphere of pushing through a WOD with fellow members is a learned experience that keeps members coming back again and again. And finally, the environment often aligns with the desired self-concept of its members, who sometimes say, "strong is the new skinny."

# 6-6 SITUATIONAL FACTORS INFLUENCING CONSUMER BEHAVIOR

## OPENING EXAMPLE

Stephanie is a working mom with two busy teenage daughters. She's constantly on the go to work, transporting the kids, volunteering, exercising, and shopping for the family. Stephanie visits grocery stores about twice a week and may fill in with a trip to the convenience store at least once per week. Since she's so busy, the time and days of the week she shops vary. Stephanie has noticed, though, that there are times when she's able to stick to the shopping list and other times she's more likely to make impulse purchases. She occasionally feels frustrated when shopping and is disappointed in herself for overspending. Can you relate to Stephanie? What factors are at work that alter her buying behavior? How could marketers benefit from understanding these factors? How could Stephanie benefit?

**LO 6.6** Describe the four situational factors that influence consumer behavior.

6-6a

# LEARNING IT: SITUATIONAL FACTORS INFLUENCING CONSUMER BEHAVIOR

In addition to social and psychological factors, situational factors impact behavior in known and sometimes predictable ways. Some situational elements may be controlled or created by the marketer, while others are uncontrollable elements outside of the marketer's influence. Exhibit 6.7 summarizes the four situational factors and provides examples of each.

6-6b

# CLOSING EXAMPLE

What situational factors could account for differences in Stephanie's shopping behavior at the grocery store? If Stephanie is exposed to an array of items in a large store, with many shelves of attractive products, it's more likely she'll purchase items not on her original shopping list. If she visits a smaller store with fewer options, there's less opportunity for unplanned purchases. If the store plays pleasant music and has warm lighting, perhaps Stephanie will linger longer and buy more.

The social surroundings also influence Stephanie. If she's with her husband and he doesn't enjoy shopping, she may try to reduce the time spent at the store and purchase only the necessities. If the daughters accompany her, they might add items they want to the shopping cart, increasing the amount of money spent

**EXHIBIT 6.7** ▶ Situational Factors

| Name | Definition | Examples |
|---|---|---|
| **Physical surroundings** | Store location, lighting, store size, décor, sounds, aromas, merchandise displays. Can also include factors outside the marketer's control like weather or adjacent businesses. | • Specialty clothing boutiques typically have wider aisles and sparse, uncluttered displays while discount stores have narrower aisles and shelves stocked full of goods, sometimes from floor to ceiling. |
| **Social surroundings** | The number and intent of other people around the purchaser. | • Standing in a line for concert tickets with other buyers might increase motivation to follow-through with purchase.<br>• Eating at a restaurant with friends might lead to more consumption than if dining alone. |
| **Purchase reason** | Purchasing for self versus others.<br><br>Necessary versus discretionary purchases. | • A store brand of soda may be purchased for individual consumption but name brand sodas purchased for parties or social situations.<br>• It's likely you'll stop to fill an empty gas tank regardless of how much you "want" to buy gas. |
| **Buyer's mood and condition** | The mood state (e.g. hungry, happy, sad, anxious) and condition (e.g. available spending money, illness) of the buyer. | • A hungry driver will be more likely to stop at a fast food restaurant than someone who just ate a full meal at home.<br>• A consumer who just received a bonus at work might be more likely to buy something new. |

Adapted from Belk, Russell W. (1975), "Situational Variables and Consumer Behavior," *Journal of Consumer Research*, 2 (December), 157–164.

during the shopping trip. If the store is crowded and has long checkout lines, Stephanie might try to spend less time in the store and purchase only the necessities. Or she might leave altogether without purchasing anything.

Of course, Stephanie's mood can also affect the shopping trip. If she's hungry, she might notice items that can be immediately consumed such as chips, cookies, or baked goods. If she just ate and is not hungry, she might not notice those items at all.

These situational factors are always at play when Stephanie decides to shop. While marketers can utilize knowledge of situational factors to influence purchase decisions, Stephanie's knowledge of these factors could also help her reduce the number of unplanned purchases when shopping.

# 6-7 IDENTIFYING INFLUENCES ON CONSUMER BEHAVIOR

## OPENING EXAMPLE

Through more than 1,000 surveys across ski areas in the region (and on its own mountain), Ski Butternut has amassed a comprehensive database that helps pinpoint who its customers are and what they want. "Ski Butternut believes in knowing as much as we can about our guests," explains Director of Marketing Matt Sawyer. For example, Ski Butternut collects data during the equipment rental process. When a guest rents a pair of skis or a snowboard, that person provides standard information, such as name, address, and phone number. But the guest is also asked questions about age and ability to ski or snowboard, as well as the names of other winter resorts he or she has visited. The mountain compiles both individual and family profiles. All of this information helps Matt Sawyer, Ed Brooks, and others on the marketing team devise strategies designed to compete with other ski resorts in the region.

**LO 6.7** Given a consumer purchase scenario, identify the primary influences affecting the consumer decision process.

### 6-7a

## LEARNING IT: IDENTIFYING INFLUENCES ON CONSUMER BEHAVIOR

Americans spend hundreds of billions each year on vacations and other leisure activities. Their decisions regarding how vacation or leisure dollars are spent depends on a number of social, psychological, and situational influences. By understanding each of these influences, the marketing team at Ski Butternut can build their marketing mix (product, price, place, and promotion) around those customers most likely to visit their resort. First, it focuses on families and the core value of spending time together. Matt Sawyer observes that Butternut's typical customers are families with young children, and "by capturing them early, we get to have them for a long time." Second, it reaches out to other subgroups, including senior citizens and those in the teen-to-25 age range. Senior citizens may want to perpetuate the image of themselves as physically active while enjoying membership in a group, while high school and college students want the "thrills" of skiing without the difficulty they might encounter at larger mountain resorts.

As the marketing team at Butternut contemplates future marketing decisions, they look beyond the information they have gathered about visitors to the mountain and dig deeper to identify what motivates people across the country to choose one vacation or recreational destination over another.

## EXAMPLE #1

Rob and Jonas are both affluent and married with kids. Rob sees himself as an adventure seeker and travels around the world with other hardcore skiers. Jonas sees himself as laid back and has actually never skied, instead opting to hang with fellow surfers whenever possible. Can you spot the influences on their behavior?

**Answer:**

| Description | Factor Influencing Consumer Behavior |
| --- | --- |
| Affluent (both) | Social–*Social class* |
| Married (both) | Social–*Family* |
| Sees himself as adventure seeker (Rob) | Psychological–*Self-concept* |
| Sees himself as laid back (Jonas) | Psychological–*Self-concept* |
| Travels with hardcore skiers (Rob) | Social–*Reference group* |
| Hangs with surfers (Jonas) | Social–*Reference group* |

## EXAMPLE #2

Veronica fears skiing because she broke her arm last time on the slopes. She was just a beginner then, but a friend brought her to an advanced slope and Veronica tumbled all the way to the bottom. She fears that could happen again. However, a beautiful new resort opened within an hour of her home and her bonus check at work just arrived—and it was bigger than she expected. Now she's considering whether to give skiing another try. Veronica's decision about whether to ski or not is most affected by which influences?

**Answer:**

| Description | Factor Influencing Consumer Behavior |
| --- | --- |
| Ski crash that broke arm | Psychological–*Learning* |
| Fear it could happen again | Psychological–*Perceptions* |
| Beautiful new resort nearby | Situational–*Physical surroundings* |
| Bonus check from work | Situational–*Buyer condition* |

## EXAMPLE #3

Tina and a group from her sorority are planning a three-day weekend ski vacation and want to stay at a resort that also offers spa services. There are two different ski resorts that offer spa services, but one is considered more exclusive and desirable. They are excited to take a ski vacation and view it as one last getaway before they graduate and start working. Tina received $200 from her grandmother as a birthday present and plans to use the money to cover the hotel room and ski rental fees. Tina had never skied when she was growing up but, after joining her sorority, a group of friends invited her to go with them. She fell in love with the excitement and thrill of downhill skiing and tries to go several times each season so she can progress and move to more advanced ski runs. What factors have been instrumental in developing Tina's interest in skiing and the upcoming vacation?

**Answer:**

| Description | Factor Influencing Consumer Behavior |
|---|---|
| Spa is considered more exclusive and desirable | Psychological–*Perception* |
| Last getaway before graduating and starting to work | Situational–*Purchase reason* |
| $200 birthday gift | Situational–*Buyer condition* |
| Hopes to progress and move to more advanced ski runs | Psychological–*Needs & motives* |

By looking at customer influences, the team at Ski Butternut can best identify the best new prospects for their resort, and how to persuade them to visit. At the same time, they can also identify those who might not be the best prospects, so that Butternut can avoid spending time and money promoting to people who are unlikely to become customers.

# 6-8 LEARN IT TODAY . . . USE IT TOMORROW

As a marketing intern at Ski Butternut, you've just spent the day shadowing their team to learn about consumer behavior. Later that day, your supervisor asks you some questions about what you learned. Your answers could make the difference between getting hired, or needing to find another internship.

It's time to get hands-on and apply what you've learned. **See MindTap for an activity related to Ski Butternut's marketing activities.**

# Chapter Summary

**LO 6.1 Identify the three types of influences that affect the consumer decision process.**

A variety of influences affect individuals when making purchase decisions, including social factors, psychological factors, and situational factors. It's important for marketers to understand the needs and wants of consumers as well as the factors that influence purchasing behavior.

**LO 6.2 Outline the six steps in the consumer decision process.**

Consumers complete a step-by-step process in making purchase decisions. The process begins with problem or opportunity recognition and ends with a post-purchase evaluation. Marketing strategies and tactics are often designed to steer consumers through the decision process in the direction of a specific product and attempt to influence decisions at every stage of the process.

**LO 6.3 Distinguish between high-involvement and low-involvement purchase decisions.**

Involvement indicates the degree of interest an individual may have with a product or purchase decision, and the time and level of problem solving they'll apply to the purchase process.

**LO 6.4 Describe the five social factors that influence consumer behavior.**

Five social factors influence consumer behavior and are important to marketers who design strategies to leverage these external influences. The five social factors include culture, social class, reference groups, opinion leaders, and family.

**LO 6.5 Describe the five psychological factors that influence consumer behavior.**

Personal factors internal to an individual also influence consumer behavior; these factors include needs and motives, perceptions, attitudes, learned responses, and self-concept.

**LO 6.6 Describe the four situational factors that influence consumer behavior.**

Situational influences relate to the impact of four factors unique to a time and place that affect an individual's buying behavior. The factors include physical surroundings, social surroundings, buyer intent, and a buyer's mood and condition.

**LO 6.7 Given a consumer purchase scenario, identify the primary influences affecting the consumer decision process.**

The ability to identify various influences on consumer behavior helps marketers assemble marketing mixes most likely to reach their target customers.

# Key Terms

consumer behavior **109**
social factors **110**
psychological factors **110**
situational factors **110**
evoked set **112**
involvement **116**
routinized response behavior **116**

limited problem solving **116**
extended problem solving **117**
culture **118**
subcultures **118**
social class **119**
reference groups **119**
opinion leaders **119**

need **121**
motives **121**
perception **122**
attitudes **123**
learning **123**
self-concept **124**

# 7 BUSINESS MARKETS AND BUYING BEHAVIOR

Leonard Zhukovsky/Shutterstock.com

## LEARNING OBJECTIVES

**7.1** Compare the major characteristics of the business market to the consumer market.

**7.2** Describe the four categories of business markets.

**7.3** Summarize the three major ways marketers segment business markets.

**7.4** Describe the three major factors that influence purchase decisions in the business market.

**7.5** List the seven steps in the organizational buying process.

**7.6** Outline the five roles within the buying center.

# LEARN IT TODAY . . . USE IT TOMORROW

Multiverse Incorporated is a hypothetical manufacturer of fuels and chemicals for use in industrial applications. It recently invented technology to produce an environmentally friendly biodiesel. Biodiesel technology and suppliers have been around for decades, but Multiverse's technology cuts the cost of production in half, and triples the amount of fuel produced per hour. Normally, biodiesel fuel degrades engines more quickly than petroleum-based diesel fuel, but Multiverse's technology solved this problem. In fact, Multiverse's biodiesel—branded as "Trident"—cleans engines as it burns, improving the longevity of engine parts.

As Multiverse considers how it will market Trident, it decides to focus on business market customers rather than consumer market customers. Multiverse believes that other companies, like ExxonMobil and Shell, are better suited for distributing fuel directly to consumers than it is. And selling in bulk to organizations with fleets of vehicles—such as school districts and the military—sounds more appealing to Multiverse than selling directly to individual vehicle owners.

However, before Multiverse can launch its new product, it has a number of factors to consider. Which organizations would be most interested in Trident, and why? Where are they located? How do they purchase fuel in the first place? Who are the decision makers in these organizations?

Multiverse must answer all of these questions and more before it can effectively market and sell its fuel in the business market. If it doesn't, Trident may never see the light of day.

# 7-1 NATURE OF THE BUSINESS MARKET

**LO 7.1** Compare the major characteristics of the business market to the consumer market.

## OPENING EXAMPLE

United Parcel Service (UPS) is a well-known brand and the world's largest package delivery company. It's a business that serves other businesses (B2B) and individual consumers (B2C).

UPS's consumer-oriented services include parcel pickup, delivery, and tracking services. You may have used their services yourself. UPS offers those same services to business customers, but in addition offers logistics, inventory management, and international trade services. Businesses that use UPS's Business Solutions range from aerospace and defense to government agencies and retailers.

Since the consumer and business markets are distinct in various ways, UPS looks for ways to satisfy the needs of each of these markets. For example, UPS discovered that established goods manufacturers and distributors found it difficult to create easy-to-use e-commerce sites on their own. Understanding that B2B online retail is estimated to reach $6.7 trillion in sales worldwide by 2020,[1] UPS decided to act.

UPS saw an opportunity to create an e-commerce platform that helps its business customers expand online. But to do so, UPS had a number of things to consider, as not all businesses face the same challenges, target the same markets, or offer the same products. What were some of the major characteristics that might have influenced the development and rollout of UPS's e-commerce solutions for the business market?

## LEARNING IT: NATURE OF THE BUSINESS MARKET

Several characteristics distinguish the business market (B2B) from the consumer market (B2C): product, size and number of buyers, promotion, distribution, geographic market concentration, buyer–seller relationships, and the purchase decision process.

### PRODUCT

Products purchased in the business market are typically more technical and variable in nature, while the consumer market is more standardized. A large business purchasing printers for their offices might require a number of custom specifications to be met before placing an order, while a consumer usually selects whatever options are available at the store or online. Because business purchases can be more technical and variable, accompanying services are usually more important. For instance, the business purchasing several hundred printers might also be able to negotiate free servicing of those printers.

### SIZE AND NUMBER OF BUYERS

The business market features a limited number of buyers when compared to the consumer market; however, most of those buyers purchase larger volumes than individual consumers. For example, U.S. companies pay more than $300 billion each year for office and maintenance supplies alone. That's more than the Gross Domestic Product (GDP) of most countries. In addition, government agencies contribute hundreds of billions of dollars to the business market.

Many buyers in business markets are large organizations. A few large buyers, such as McDonald's, Wendy's, and Burger King, dominate the fast-food industry. These chains have the power to name the price they will pay cattle farmers for meat, and can dictate living conditions and standards of labor on ranches.

As a buyer in the business market, McDonald's is a large customer for sellers of meat and other food products.

### PROMOTION

Because business customers require more customization and service, and because business customers usually purchase in larger quantities, promotion in the business market emphasizes personal selling. In the consumer markets, personal selling is typically reserved for larger, more complex purchases like houses and cars.

For most consumer purchases though, such as items you might purchase at the grocery store, advertising is a more cost-effective form of promotion.

## DISTRIBUTION

Business market distribution channels are typically shorter and more direct, with products passing through fewer intermediaries than they do for consumer markets.

## GEOGRAPHIC MARKET CONCENTRATION

The U.S. business market is more geographically concentrated than the consumer market. Manufacturers often converge in certain regions of the country, making these areas prime targets for business marketers. For example, the Midwestern states of Indiana, Wisconsin, Iowa, Michigan, and Ohio lead the nation in manufacturing, which is a significant driver of the business market.

In the automobile industry, suppliers build plants close to their customers. Volkswagen's supplier park near its Chattanooga assembly plant is home to more than 17 different vendors. The campus allows suppliers to produce or assemble products close to the plant, reducing costs, controlling parts inventory, and increasing flexibility.

## BUYER–SELLER RELATIONSHIPS

An especially important characteristic of business markets is the relationship between buyers and sellers. These relationships often are more enduring and complex than consumer–market relationships. In the business market, a single transaction may generate millions of dollars for a company.

## PURCHASE DECISION PROCESS

Suppliers who serve business markets must work with multiple decision makers, especially when selling to larger organizations. Managers at several levels may influence final orders, and the overall process is more formal and professional than the consumer purchasing process. As a result, business purchases typically require longer time frames.

Exhibit 7.1 compares the business and consumer markets. Based on these differences, Exhibit 7.2 describes how the differences might play out in the real world.

## 7-1b
# CLOSING EXAMPLE

Through market research, UPS learned that companies were looking to offer the following elements in their online customer experience: full product descriptions, mobile-friendly websites, in-stock inventory, and negotiable terms of sale. UPS discovered that they had core competencies in all of these areas and were able to help businesses provide the same to their customers. The result was UPS Ready® Program, a turnkey—but customizable—solution for businesses to create an e-commerce presence.[2] With a new product to sell, UPS was then able to use its salesforce to contact businesses, explain the service, and customize it for clients as needed.

**EXHIBIT 7.1**   Comparing Business and Consumer Markets

|  | Business-to-Business Markets | Consumer Markets |
|---|---|---|
| **Products** | More technical and variable; accompanying services more important | More standardized; service important, but less than for business markets |
| **Size and Number of Buyers** | Fewer buyers, but each is larger | More buyers because it mainly consists of individuals and households |
| **Promotion** | Emphasis on personal selling | Emphasis on advertising |
| **Distribution** | Relatively short, direct channels to market | Product passes through a number of intermediaries en route to customer |
| **Geographic Market Concentration** | More geographically concentrated because business industries often cluster | Less geographically concentrated because consumers are dispersed throughout the market |
| **Buyer–Seller Relationships** | More enduring, complex relationships | Infrequent direct contact; relationships of relatively short duration |
| **Purchase Decision Process** | Diverse group of organization members make decision | Individual or household unit makes decision |

**EXHIBIT 7.2**   Example of Comparison Between Business and Consumer Markets

|  | Business-to-Business Markets | Consumer Markets |
|---|---|---|
| **Scenario** | **Boeing selling planes to major airlines around the world** | **Kellogg's selling cereals to consumers** |
| **Products** | Planes are customized to fit the needs of each customer | Same cereal product sold in all stores across the country |
| **Size and Number of Buyers** | Less than 100 potential customers, but a single purchase can be billions of dollars | Over 100 million potential customers, but each purchase is less than $10 |
| **Promotion** | Mainly promoted through direct sales force | Mainly promoted through advertising and sales promotion |
| **Distribution** | Boeing sells directly to the airlines | Kellogg's may sell to a wholesaler, who sells to the retailer, who then sells to the end consumer |
| **Geographic Market Concentration** | While Boeing's customers are located all over the world, many of Boeing's suppliers locate around their major factories | Consumers dispersed all across the country |
| **Buyer–Seller Relationships** | Most airlines have purchased from Boeing for decades | Consumer may buy Kellogg's cereal this month and switch to another brand next month |
| **Purchase Decision Process** | Airlines have teams of buyers overseeing purchase decisions, most of which must be approved by executives at the company. Decision process sometimes takes years. | Individual consumer can make purchase decision in seconds while shopping at grocery store |

## 7-2    CATEGORIES OF BUSINESS MARKETS

**LO
7.2**    Describe the four categories of business markets.

### OPENING EXAMPLE

General Electric (GE) knows that more than 90% of business market buyers report using social media in their decision processes. In fact, the company has developed an enviable reputation in its industry for forward-thinking and successful use of social media and mobile apps to find and generate new business market customers.

GE wants to deliver content it considers "micro-relevant," which means targeting just the right customers rather than the biggest audiences, and it delivers content specific to industry needs. For example, one mobile app allows restaurants to estimate the energy savings they can reap with more energy-efficient lighting. Another app facilitates railroads' ability to monitor their tracks and gather diagnostics on their locomotives. Yet another helps manage gas turbines and electric transformers, while others allow health care professionals to review x-ray images using Wi-Fi technology.

The company reaches the many industries it serves by focusing on specific markets and providing them with specific content. But how are these major markets fundamentally different from each other? Understanding their differences is the foundation for knowing how to best serve them.

### 7-2a

## LEARNING IT: CATEGORIES OF BUSINESS MARKETS

Four major categories define the business market: commercial, reseller, government, and institutional. Each is defined by market size, participants, and specific products sold.

### COMMERCIAL

**commercial market** individuals and firms that acquire products to support, directly or indirectly, production of other goods and services

The **commercial market** is the largest segment of the business market. It includes all individuals and firms that acquire products to support, directly or indirectly, production of other goods and services. When Dell buys computer chips from Intel for their computers, that transaction takes place in the commercial market. Likewise, when Pepperidge Farm purchases wheat to mill into flour for one of its cookies, this takes place in the commercial market.

Some products transacted in the commercial market become components in other finished goods, such as RFID chips for credit cards. Other products are simply used in the production of a good or service, such as electricity used to operate machinery at an auto manufacturing plant. And still others contribute to a firm's day-to-day operations, such as custodial supplies. The commercial market includes manufacturers, farmers, and other members of resource-producing industries; construction contractors; and providers of services such as transportation, public utilities, financing, insurance, and real-estate brokerages.

## RESELLER

The second category includes retailers and wholesalers, known as **resellers**. Most resale products—such as clothing, appliances, sports equipment, and automobile parts—are finished goods that buyers sell to final consumers. ACCO Brands supplies paper clips, ring binders, sheet protectors, and fasteners to Office Depot, which in turn sells them to consumers.[3]

**resellers** a business market comprised of retailers and wholesalers

In other cases, buyers may further process or repackage a product before reselling. For example, a retail meat market may purchase a side of beef and then cut and wrap individual pieces before selling to its customers.

## GOVERNMENT

The government category of the business market includes domestic institutions of government—federal, state, and local—as well as foreign governments. This vital business market segment makes a wide variety of purchases, ranging from cement for making highways to military uniforms to Internet services. The primary motivator behind government purchasing is to provide some form of public benefit, such as infrastructure or national defense.

## INSTITUTIONAL

Institutions, both public and private, include a wide range of organizations, such as hospitals, churches, skilled care and rehabilitation centers, colleges and universities, museums, and not-for-profit agencies. Some institutions, such as public higher education, must rigidly follow standardized purchasing procedures, but others have less formal buying practices. Business marketers often benefit by setting up separate divisions to sell to institutional buyers.

### 7-2b
## CLOSING EXAMPLE

GE offers a wide array of goods and services, and markets its products in all four categories of the business market. In order to target businesses within each category, GE must focus its efforts on differentiating its message across a wide variety of platforms, without confusing its audience. On its corporate website, GE has implemented an easy-to-use search tool. Targeted search proactively funnels visitors to the appropriate page, based on their stated interest. This simple tool allows GE to produce and disseminate targeted information to its business market customers.

Office Depot is a reseller because it purchases office supplies for resale to customers rather than for internal use at the company or as part of a production process.

shutter_o/Shutterstock.com

# 7-3

# SEGMENTING B2B MARKETS

**LO 7.3** Summarize the three major ways marketers segment business markets.

## OPENING EXAMPLE

Fikes Products sells janitorial supplies and services to restaurants, retailers, and other businesses in the Pacific Northwest. As stated on their website, the Kent, Washington-based company is "proudly obsessed with the dirty details," and offers a wide array of goods and services, to include air fresheners, foam soap dispensers, dumpster deodorizers, and sanitization programs.[4] It's safe to say that if you want a clean business environment, Fikes can make that happen.

As it expands beyond its roots in the Pacific Northwest, Fikes has been encountering a challenge that other companies face as they scale: the marketplace has too many potential customers. Why would companies be daunted by too many potential customers?

The key to understanding this dilemma has to do with scarcity of resources. Even for a company where resources seem to be flowing into company coffers faster than number crunchers can count, there is always a limited supply of resources available to market goods and services. And, since competition is steep in the business market, understanding which slice of the market to go after is a difficult task to undertake.

What are some considerations that management and marketing teams at Fikes must consider to compete effectively?

## 7-3a

## LEARNING IT: SEGMENTING B2B MARKETS

Business marketers service a wide variety of customers, so marketers must identify the different market segments they serve. Different market segments can be identified by demographic characteristics, customer type, or end-use application.

### DEMOGRAPHIC CHARACTERISTICS

As in consumer markets, demographic characteristics provide useful segmentation criteria for business markets. For example, firms can be grouped by size, based on sales revenues, or by number of employees. Likewise, firms can be grouped by their geographic location or the number of products they offer. For example, Fikes could decide to target businesses that are under $1 billion in revenue, or only business locations on the West Coast.

### CUSTOMER TYPE

Customers can be grouped by type or industry. This is more specific than the four business market categories mentioned in the previous section. For example, within the commercial market alone, customers could be grouped by manufacturers, restaurants, grocery stores, and many other groupings.

**Customer-based segmentation** is often used in business markets and flows from the understanding that different types of business market customers often require a more precise or complex level of product customization, especially when compared to consumer market customers. For example, Fikes could use this type of segmentation to initially target manufacturers and retailers, but wait until those market segments are established before targeting restaurants and local governments.

**customer-based segmentation** grouping customers by type or industry

## END-USE APPLICATION

**End-use application** segments the business market based on the ultimate way in which a buyer uses a product. For example, Xerox's business market customers for its printers may range from a local bicycle repair shop to the U.S. Department of Defense. The local repair shop likely requires low-volume use while the Department of Defense requires high-volume use. Since printers capable of high-volume use command higher prices, Xerox might prioritize selling to those customers before allocating resources to the businesses who don't print as much.

**end-use application** segmenting the business market based on the ultimate way in which a buyer uses a product

## 7-3b
## CLOSING EXAMPLE

As Fikes Products expands into new business markets, it segments the marketplace based on customer type and end-use application. The restaurant industry, for example, has different sanitization requirements than the retail industry, and Fikes must develop and market its products differently to satisfy different industries. Further, within the restaurant industry, certain restaurants will use paper towels differently than others, so the end-use application becomes an important method used to further segment this market. With a greater understanding of potential clients in new business markets, Fikes Products will continue to beat back unwanted grease and grime in an ever-expanding marketplace.

# 7-4   THE BUSINESS BUYING PROCESS

## OPENING EXAMPLE

You are the purchasing manager for MyMap Inc., a manufacturer of GPS devices for automakers. The company has decided to upgrade its manufacturing facility with $5 million in automated assembly equipment. Before approaching equipment suppliers, you must analyze your needs, define the project's goals, develop technical specifications for the equipment, and establish a budget.

At the same time, those equipment suppliers should understand what might influence MyMap's purchase. Are you looking for the lowest price, fastest

**LO 7.4** Describe the three major factors that influence purchase decisions in the business market.

delivery, highest quality, or some other combination of factors? And are you the primary decision maker, or are you part of a purchasing team with various opinions about the company's equipment needs?

**7-4a**

## LEARNING IT: THE BUSINESS BUYING PROCESS

The purchasing process in the business market is more complex than in the consumer market. Business purchasing—otherwise known as "buying" or "procurement"—takes place within a formalized framework consisting of budgets, cost projections, and profit considerations. Furthermore, B2B buying decisions usually involve many people representing a variety of individual and organizational goals. To understand organizational buying behavior, business marketers require knowledge of influences on the purchase decision process such as environmental factors, organizational factors, and interpersonal influences.

### ENVIRONMENTAL FACTORS

**environmental factors** economic, political, regulatory, competitive, and technological considerations

**Environmental factors** include economic, political, regulatory, competitive, and technological considerations. All of these influence business market purchasing decisions.

### ORGANIZATIONAL FACTORS

Purchasing methods differ among firms, and successful B2B marketers must understand their clients' organizational structures, policies, and purchasing processes. A company with a centralized purchasing process operates differently from one that delegates purchasing decisions to divisional or geographic units. An equipment supplier hoping to sell to MyMap would want to know these policies before approaching them with a proposal.

### INTERPERSONAL INFLUENCES

Economic factors, such as a growing or shrinking economy, influence purchase decisions in the business market.

Many people may influence business market purchases, and considerable time may be spent obtaining the input and approval of various members of a firm. Both group and individual forces are at work here, as decisions made by committee come about differently than those made by individuals. Business marketers should know who in an organization will influence buying decisions for their products, and should know each of their priorities.

To effectively address the concerns of all people involved in the buying decision, marketers must also be well versed in the technical features of their products. They must also interact well with employees of various departments involved in the purchasing decision. For example, representatives for medical products frequently visit hospitals and doctors' offices to discuss the advantages of their products and build a rapport with clinical staff.

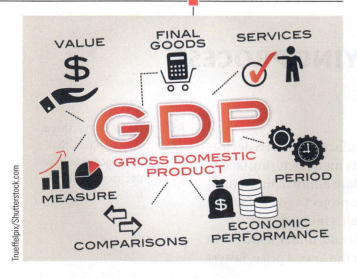
Trueffelpix/Shutterstock.com

### 7-4b
## CLOSING EXAMPLE

Multiple considerations influence MyMap's purchasing decisions in the business market.

For example, in the event of a downturn in the economic environment, MyMap may decide to defer purchases of new equipment, as sales of its GPS systems to automobile companies might decline. On the other hand, if a new regulation is approved in California mandating that all new vehicles come equipped with a GPS system, MyMap will likely upgrade their factory quickly to satisfy the emerging demand. Even something as simple as a conflict between managers at MyMap about purchasing priorities could delay the buying decision. Factors like these should be taken into consideration by any equipment supplier hoping to get an order from MyMap.

# 7-5 THE ORGANIZATIONAL BUYING PROCESS

## OPENING EXAMPLE

King's Hawaiian, a Southern California-based maker of authentic Hawaiian sweet breads has a problem. Though it recently expanded into a new facility, significantly increasing its manufacturing capacity,[5] King's Hawaiian must plan for an unknown future. Mark Taira, their CEO, is obviously excited about the continuing success of his family business, but must respond to increasingly rapid changes in consumer demand. These changes have a direct impact on how King's Hawaiian manages its buying process.

**LO 7.5** List the seven steps in the organizational buying process.

King's Hawaiian follows a structured buying process to meet current and future production needs.

### 7-5a
## LEARNING IT: THE ORGANIZATIONAL BUYING PROCESS

The organizational buying process follows a sequence of activities. Although not every buying situation requires every one of these steps, marketers to business customers must familiarize themselves with the entire process in order to be most effective.

The steps in the organizational buying process are summarized in Exhibit 7.3.

### STEP 1: ANTICIPATE OR RECOGNIZE A PROBLEM, NEED, OR OPPORTUNITY

Both consumer and business purchase decisions spawn from an existing or anticipated problem, need, or opportunity. Perhaps a firm's computer system will soon become

Source: cookingcontestcentral.com

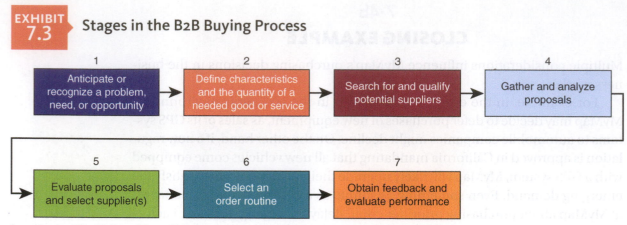

**EXHIBIT 7.3** Stages in the B2B Buying Process

Source: Based on Michael D. Hutt and Thomas W. Speh, Business Marketing Management: B2B, 11th ed. (Mason, OH: South-Western, 2013).

outdated, or a sales representative demonstrates a new inventory tracking system that corrects a long-standing bottleneck in a firm's supply chain. These issues must be solved, and the solution often involves purchasing a good or service. At King's Hawaiian, for example, the gluten-free lifestyle embraced by many Americans today may impact sales of their sweet breads moving forward. As a result, they may consider new suppliers of ingredients for their bread dough.

## STEP 2: DEFINE CHARACTERISTICS AND THE QUANTITY OF A NEEDED GOOD OR SERVICE

Buyers must translate these needs into detailed specifications for the product they want to purchase. Following with the King's Hawaiian example, Mark Taira and his team may decide to purchase flour that is both organic and gluten-free, satisfying anticipated demand from their customers.

## STEP 3: SEARCH FOR AND QUALIFY POTENTIAL SUPPLIERS

The choice of a supplier may be relatively straightforward if there are limited options within that market or industry. For example, a company needing to source a specialized product that is patented by a particular supplier has only one company to choose from. Other searches for suppliers may involve more complex decision-making practices. A company that wants to buy a group life insurance policy, for example, must weigh the various provisions and programs among different vendors. At King's Hawaiian, there are multiple suppliers of organic, gluten-free flour. Each supplier follows different procedures and quality standards in their production. Mark Taira and his team will need to evaluate each supplier and select the one to move forward with.

## STEP 4: GATHER AND ANALYZE PROPOSALS

Suppliers often submit written proposals to compete for business market opportunities, which are then gathered together and analyzed by the purchasing firm. If the buyer is a government or public agency, this stage of the purchase process may involve a competitive bidding process. During such a process, each supplier develops a bid, including a price that aims to satisfy the criteria determined by the purchasing firm. While competitive bidding is less common in the private sector, a company may follow a similar practice to purchase nonstandard materials, complex products, or custom products. The purchasing team at King's Hawaiian received bids from a number of suppliers, each with a different price, production time, and quality guarantee. Now they must evaluate each proposal and select one or more suppliers.

## STEP 5: EVALUATE PROPOSALS AND SELECT SUPPLIER(S)

After gathering and analyzing supplier proposals, a firm must evaluate and judge each proposal, attempting to select the one that is most likely to satisfy its needs. Proposals for sophisticated equipment, such as a large computer networking system, may propose wildly different strategies, or offer distinct product offerings, and the final selection may involve a number of trade-offs.

There are many criteria to evaluate beyond price. Relationship factors—such as communication and trust—may also be important to the buyer. Other criteria include reliability, delivery record, time from order to delivery, quality, and order accuracy. The King's Hawaiian purchasing team decided to evaluate potential suppliers based on quality, delivery times, and price, in descending order.

## STEP 6: SELECT AN ORDER ROUTINE

Once a supplier has been chosen, buyer and vendor must work out the best way to process future purchases. Ordering procedures can vary considerably. However, most orders will include product descriptions, quantities, prices, delivery terms, and payment terms. And companies today have a variety of options for submitting orders: written documents, phone calls, or online. The purchasing team at King's Hawaiian chose a single supplier for its organic, gluten-free flour and sent a purchase order to the supplier via e-mail.

## STEP 7: OBTAIN FEEDBACK AND EVALUATE PERFORMANCE

During the last step, buyers measure each vendor's performance. Sometimes this evaluation involves a formal assessment of product quality, delivery performance, prices, technical knowledge, and overall responsiveness to customer needs. Additionally, vendors may be measured according to whether or not they have lowered the purchasing firm's costs or reduced its employees' workloads. In general, larger firms are more likely to use formal evaluation procedures, while smaller companies tend toward informal evaluations. After King's Hawaiian receives the first shipment of organic, gluten-free flour from its new supplier, it bakes multiple sample batches of sweet bread, and evaluates their consistency. It also reviews whether the flour was delivered on time and in the right quantity.

## CLOSING EXAMPLE

Business is sweet at King's Hawaiian. Its problems are nice problems to have, as they came about by ongoing demand for their sweet breads. But, as consumer tastes and buying habits change, King's Hawaiian must anticipate the need for new and different suppliers for its raw materials. By doing so, it anticipates an even sweeter future.

# 7-6    BUYING CENTER ROLES

**LO 7.6** Outline the five roles within the buying center.

## OPENING EXAMPLE

Toysmith, a Sumner, Washington-based manufacturer and distributor of children's toys was recently considering a novel toy concept, the melting snowman.[6]

"The melting what?!" said Martin Crowley, Toysmith's VP of product development. As an otherwise innovative and forward-thinking member of the executive team, Martin did not initially see the potential for such a product. But Martin's team shared what they saw at a recent toy factory tradeshow.

"It works like this," one of the product developers said. "The kit uses soft putty to shape and decorate a snowman. At room temperature, the snowman slowly melts into a puddle, without leaving a mess behind."

It took Martin some time to get on board with selling a puddle of snowman parts, but he trusted his team and Toysmith decided to bring this toy to market.

As Toysmith began reaching out to its partner retailers, including small, independent stores and big box stores like Target and Walmart, they had to consider a number of factors. In particular, Toysmith had to consider which employees at these retailers needed the most convincing. At Walmart in particular, Toysmith needed to identify the right decision makers if their melting snowman would ever see the light of day on store shelves. How did Toysmith determine this?

### 7-6a
## LEARNING IT: BUYING CENTER ROLES

As discussed earlier, business market purchasing behavior responds to many influences, such as environmental, organizational, and interpersonal factors. Purchasing decisions also involve a number of people along the way, each with a different role.

A company's **buying center** encompasses everyone involved in any aspect of its buying activity. It is an informal group whose composition and size vary among purchase situations and firms. To be clear, a buying center is not part of a firm's formal organizational structure. For example, the buying center of

**buying center** encompasses everyone involved in any aspect of a company's buying activity

equipment for a medical research laboratory may include the architect who designed the lab, the scientists who work there, the purchasing manager who screens contractor proposals, the chief executive officer who makes the final decision, and the vice president of research who signs the formal contracts for the project. There are typically five main roles in a buying center: users, influencers, gatekeepers, buyers, and deciders.

## USERS

**Users** are the people who will actually use a good or service. Their influence on the purchase decision will vary, depending on the situation. Users sometimes initiate purchase actions by requesting products, and they may also help develop product specifications, especially for custom designs. Users often influence the purchase of office equipment, for example. Toysmith's melting snowman is ultimately used by consumers. Though not part of the buying center at Walmart, Toysmith must have a complete understanding of what drives consumers to purchase the melting snowman, in order to convince the team at Walmart to stock their shelves with it.

**users** people who actually use a good or service

## INFLUENCERS

**Influencers** affect the buying decision by supplying information to guide the evaluation of alternatives, or by establishing buying specifications. Influencers are typically technical staff, such as engineers or quality-control specialists. Toysmith has positioned the melting snowman toy as an impulse buy for consumers at the check-out counter. But even though Walmart's "impulse" buying team will be making the decision about whether or not to try out the melting snowman, the buying teams from other departments—such as the toy buying team—may influence the purchasing decision.

**influencers** people who affect the buying decision by supplying information to guide the evaluation of alternatives, or by establishing buying specifications

## GATEKEEPERS

**Gatekeepers** control the information that all buying center members ultimately review. They may exert this control by distributing printed product data or advertisements, or by deciding which salespeople may speak to certain individuals in the buying center. A purchasing agent might allow some salespeople to speak with the engineers responsible for developing specifications, but deny others the same privilege. For example, the office manager for a medical group may decide whether or not to accept and ultimately pass along sales literature from a pharmaceutical detailer to other members of the buying center. At Walmart, buyers' assistants are very important gatekeepers, as they control the flow of potential vendors to their respective buyers. Toysmith has cultivated relationships with buyers' assistants that will help get this new product in front of the actual buyers.

**gatekeepers** people who control the information that all buying center members ultimately review

## BUYERS

**Buyers** have the formal authority to select a supplier and begin securing the good or service. Toysmith has positioned its melting snowman as an "impulse" purchase, so Walmart's impulse buying team will be making the decision about whether or not to bring on the melting snowman.

**buyers** people who have the formal authority to select a supplier and begin securing the good or service

## DECIDERS

**deciders** people who actually select a good or service

**Deciders** actually select a good or service. In many cases, the buyer and the decider are the same person—but not always. For example, a firm's buyer may have the formal authority to select a supplier, but the firm's chief executive officer may want to provide final sign-off on the purchase, making them the true decider. Another example of a decider might be a design engineer who develops specifications intended specifically for a single vendor. While the buyer might have the formal authority to select a supplier, the design engineer effectively decided who that supplier would be through the design specs. For this reason, the identity of the decider is the most difficult role for a salesperson to uncover. In the case of Toysmith at Walmart, the decider is the lead buyer of the impulse purchasing team, she is empowered to make the final decision.

B2B marketers face the task of determining the specific role and the relative decision-making influence of each buying center member. Business marketers sometimes find that their contacts with a firm's purchasing department often fail to reach the buying center members who have the greatest influence, because often these individuals may not work in the purchasing department at all.

### 7-6b
## CLOSING EXAMPLE

A product like the melting snowman could have been viewed as suspect. But Toysmith's retail partners trusted in their industry knowledge and gave it a chance. At Walmart, Toysmith navigated and pitched to the right members of the buying center. Toysmith knew from previous experience who the gatekeepers and deciders were on that team. With that knowledge in hand, Toysmith sold the Walmart buying center on the melting snowman, which now sells in their stores and online. Today, kids and parents around the country delight in watching that little puddle of putty snow form on their coffee tables.

**7-7**

# LEARN IT TODAY . . . USE IT TOMORROW

Multiverse carefully planned its strategy for launching Trident biodiesel fuel. It had already decided to pursue the business market. Although this market would have fewer buyers and the sales process would take longer, any single purchase could total millions of dollars.

Next, they focused on buyers in the government and institutional categories. Since these categories are huge, they further segmented these markets by organizations exceeding $1 million in fuel purchases per year and organizations that manage fleets of at least 50 vehicles.

Multiverse is aware that a focus on renewable fuel sources is driving purchase decisions in these types of organizations, but they also realize the complexity of selling to these customers. Often the buying teams exceed 10 people, purchase decisions take many months, and the process involves detailed proposals and competitive bidding. Multiverse knew that the hardest part of the selling process would be to identify who plays the key roles in the buying center at each organization. They didn't want to spend six months negotiating with one team, only to find out that team doesn't have any authority to decide on the supplier or formally initiate the purchase.

The good news for Multiverse is that Trident is just one of the products it offers to the business market. With its extensive understanding of the business market landscape, Multiverse has strong prospects for growth.

It's time to get hands-on and apply what you've learned. **See MindTap for an activity related to Multiverse's marketing activities.**

## ▶ Chapter Summary

**LO 7.1 Compare the major characteristics of the business market to the consumer market.**

Several characteristics distinguish the business market (B2B) from the consumer market (B2C), including products, size and number of buyers, promotion, distribution, geographic market concentration, buyer–seller relationships, and purchase decision process.

**LO 7.2 Describe the four categories of business markets.**

Four major categories define the business market: commercial, reseller, government, and institutional. Each is defined by market size, participants, and specific goods and services transacted.

**LO 7.3 Summarize the three major ways marketers segment business markets.**

Business marketers service a wide variety of customers, so marketers must identify the different market segments they serve. The overall process of segmenting business markets divides markets based on organizational characteristics and product applications. The three major ways to segment business markets are by demographics, customer type, and end-use application.

**LO 7.4 Describe the three major factors that influence purchase decisions in the business market.**

To understand organizational buying behavior, business marketers require knowledge of influences on the purchase decision process. These influences are environmental factors, organizational factors, and interpersonal factors.

**LO 7.5 List the seven steps in the organizational buying process.**

The organizational buying process follows a sequence of activities. Although not every buying situation requires every one of these steps, marketers to business customers must familiarize themselves with the entire process in order to be most effective.

**LO 7.6 Outline the five roles within the buying center.**

A company's buying center encompasses everyone involved in any aspect of its buying activity. It is an informal group whose composition and size vary among purchase situations and firms. There are typically five main roles in a buying center: users, influencers, gatekeepers, buyers, and deciders.

# Key Terms

kpzfoto/Alamy Stock Photo

## LEARNING OBJECTIVES

**8.1** Describe the global business landscape in terms of U.S. imports, U.S. exports, and major industries.

**8.2** Differentiate between WTO, NAFTA, and EU in terms of basic functions and member countries.

**8.3** Summarize the five major factors that influence the global marketing environment.

**8.4** Summarize the six alternative strategies for entering global markets.

**8.5** Describe the five alternative marketing mix strategies used in global marketing.

**8.6** Given an example of a company's goals for expanding globally, determine the most appropriate market entry strategy.

# LEARN IT TODAY . . . USE IT TOMORROW

Many people would assert that New York's Broadway is the hub of the musical theater universe. Some would argue that the West End in London holds that title. Nederlander Producing Company has a firm foothold in both cities. Founded in Detroit in 1912 by David T. Nederlander, the company is in its third generation as a family-owned, family-run company that produces shows and owns theaters here and abroad.

Along with nine theaters in New York, Nederlander owns three prestigious locations in London. According to Nick Scandalios, executive vice president of the Nederlander Organization, Nederlander is one of the few successful American theater production companies in the United Kingdom. But, just because a show works in one country doesn't mean it will work in another. The audiences might prefer different types of shows, performers speak different languages, and the availability of talent for cast and crew can differ. Producers must consider even the smallest differences. For example, when moving a show from England to New York, slight variations in word use or interpretation could make a joke that soars in one place flop in another. For this and other reasons, it took Nederlander and Co-Lead Producer Scott Sanders

about six years and $10 million to bring a new production of the hit musical *Evita* from London back to New York. This process included everything from discussions with creators Andrew Lloyd Webber and Tim Rice to the hiring of new performers.

Nederlander has also set its sights on locations in countries like China and Turkey. Because of the complexities of expanding globally, Nederlander Worldwide Entertainment signed a global strategic partnership agreement with the China Arts and Entertainment Group (CAEG). Nederlander will help CAEG get its productions into overseas markets, while CAEG will help Nederlander enter the Chinese market.

Nederlander's experience reinforces that to succeed in global marketing, today's marketers answer questions such as:

- How do our products fit into a foreign market?
- How can we turn potential threats into opportunities?
- Which strategic alternatives will work in global markets?

Many of the answers to these questions can be found by studying techniques used by successful global marketers, as we'll do in this chapter.

# 8-1 GLOBAL MARKETING

**LO 8.1** Describe the global business landscape in terms of U.S. imports, U.S. exports, and major industries.

## OPENING EXAMPLE

Can you imagine if you could only purchase products and services produced in the United States? Which products do you use on a daily basis that you would no longer have? Do you use an iPhone or a Samsung phone? Do you wear Nike or Adidas shoes? Do you drink coffee? All of these products are produced outside of the United States and are imported for your consumption. Does the location of where products are produced influence your purchasing decisions? What would life be like without these products?

### 8-1a

### LEARNING IT: GLOBAL MARKETING

As the list of the world's 10 largest public corporations reveals, less than half of these companies are headquartered in the United States (see Exhibit 8.1). For most companies—large and small—global marketing is rapidly becoming

**EXHIBIT 8.1** World's 10 Largest Public Companies (Ranked by Annual Sales)

| Rank | Company | Country | Industry | Sales (US $ billion) |
|---|---|---|---|---|
| 1 | Wal-Mart Stores | United States | Discount stores | 482.1 |
| 2 | Sinopec | China | Oil and gas operations | 283.6 |
| 3 | PetroChina | China | Oil and gas operations | 274.6 |
| 4 | Royal Dutch Shell | Netherlands | Oil and gas operations | 264.9 |
| 5 | Volkswagen Group | Germany | Auto and truck manufacturers | 246.2 |
| 6 | ExxonMobil | United States | Oil and gas operations | 236.8 |
| 7 | Toyota Motor | Japan | Auto and truck manufacturers | 235.8 |
| 8 | Apple | United States | Computer hardware | 233.3 |
| 9 | BP | United Kingdom | Oil and gas operations | 218.7 |
| 10 | Berkshire Hathaway | United States | Investment services | 210.8 |

Source: Data from "The Global 2000," Forbes, accessed March 6, 2017, www.forbes.com.

a necessity. The demand for foreign products is increasing, both for U.S. products abroad and foreign products in the United States. The rapid globalization of business and the boundless nature of the Internet have made it possible for every marketer to become an international marketer.

Global trade can be divided into two categories: **exporting**- marketing domestically produced goods and services abroad, and **importing**- purchasing foreign goods and services. Global trade is vital to a country for several reasons. It expands markets, makes production and distribution economies possible, allows companies to explore growth opportunities in other nations, and makes them less dependent on economic conditions in their home nations.

For North American marketers, trade with foreign markets is especially important because the U.S. and Canadian economies represent a mature market for many products. This makes revenue growth at home more difficult. Outside North America it is a different story. Economies in many parts of sub-Saharan Africa, Asia, Latin America, Central Europe, and the Middle East are growing rapidly. This opens up new markets for U.S. products as consumers in these areas have more money to spend and demand for American goods continues to grow.

Exhibit 8.2 summarizes the top export and import partners for the United States.

**exporting** the marketing of domestically produced goods and services abroad

**importing** the purchasing of foreign goods and services

## EXPORTS

The United States used to export mainly physical goods and agricultural products, but this has changed for a number of reasons. In the 1800s, more than 90% of Americans worked in farming; today, less than 1.5% do. Likewise, manufactured goods no longer account for the lion's share of U.S. production output; today, only about 10% of the workforce is employed in manufacturing. Despite these shifts, the United States continues to produce record volumes

**EXHIBIT 8.2** Top U.S. Trading Partners—Exports and Imports

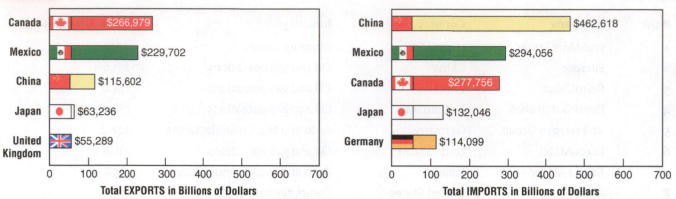

Source: http://trade.gov/mas/ian/build/groups/public/@tg_ian/documents/webcontent/tg_ian_003364.pdf

of agricultural and manufactured goods. However, the share of U.S. exports from service industries continues to increase. This is because nearly four of every five dollars in the nation's gross domestic product comes from services such as banking, entertainment, business and technical services, retailing, and communications.[1]

The financial services industry, already a major presence outside North America, is expanding globally even faster via the Internet. Today, even the most novice web users visit finance websites to pay bills, do their banking, or trade stocks online. According to a recent Pew Research Center study, 51% of American adults use online banking services (and 32% do their banking by mobile phone).[2]

The entertainment industry is another major service exporter. Movies, TV shows, and music groups often travel to the ends of the earth to entertain their audiences. Almost a century of exposure to U.S.-made films, TV programs, and, more recently, music video clips has made international viewers more familiar with American culture and geography than of any other nation on earth. The most recent installments of the Avengers, Transformers, and Star Wars movie series grossed considerably more in foreign markets than in the United States.

## IMPORTS

Importing goods and services from other countries provides several benefits such as increased access to resources, lower prices, and expanded choices for consumers. Some firms rely on purchasing raw materials abroad as input for their domestic manufacturing operations. A North Carolina furniture manufacturer may depend on purchases of South American teak, while a shoe manufacturer may import leather from Italy.

Because manufacturing and labor costs are lower in countries like Mexico and China, many firms choose to manufacture products and services there in order to reduce total costs and offer lower prices to consumers. Experts estimate that an iPhone produced solely in the United States would cost approximately $600 more than current models produced in China.[3]

Importing goods and services also provides consumers with myriad choices on everything from clothing to computers to fresh produce. Among the top U.S. imports are crude oil, machines, engines and pumps, consumer electronics, and passenger cars.[4]

## 8-1b
## CLOSING EXAMPLE

Without imports, a country would be limited to providing consumers with only the goods and services produced within its own borders. Instead of choosing among 20 different types of athletic shoes, you may have only two or three choices. And they would likely cost you much more. The produce section at the grocery store would look a lot different, too. Bananas, mangoes, tomatoes, and avocados are imported from other countries and would be available in limited supply. Even though you may not realize it, global trade impacts consumers as well as marketers on a daily basis. The importing and exporting of so many products plays an important role in the U.S. economy, and your future job might very well involve global marketing, either here in the United States or overseas.

# 8-2 MULTINATIONAL ECONOMIC INTEGRATION

## OPENING EXAMPLE

Selling products to another country can be complicated for any business, especially since each country might have its own tax policies, trade restrictions, and currency. It gets even more complicated if two countries have disagreements about trade, leading to increased **tariffs**, which are taxes levied against imported goods. These complications show up in the news regularly. Recently, the United Kingdom began the process of leaving the European Union, creating angst among global businesses large and small. And the United States has submitted formal complaints to the World Trade Organization regarding China's tariff on imported chicken. What do these things even mean? How would they impact you as a global marketer? And how might they impact you as a consumer?

**LO 8.2** Differentiate between WTO, NAFTA, and EU in terms of basic functions and member countries.

**tariffs** taxes levied against imported goods

## 8-2a
## LEARNING IT: MULTINATIONAL ECONOMIC INTEGRATION

To address the complications related to international trade, a noticeable trend toward multinational economic integration has developed since the end of World War II. Multinational economic integration can be set up in several ways. The simplest approach is to establish a **free-trade area** in which participating

**free-trade area** where participating nations agree to the free trade of goods among themselves, abolishing tariffs and trade restrictions

nations agree to the free trade of goods among themselves, abolishing tariffs and trade restrictions.

Despite the many factors in its favor, not everyone is enthusiastic about free trade. For more than a decade, Americans have lost jobs when employers outsourced their work to countries like Mexico, where wages are lower. Now, workers in Mexico face the same outsourcing threat as their employers begin outsourcing work to China, where wages are even lower. And even workers in China face this outsourcing threat as production moves to countries such as Bangladesh and Philippines, where wages are lower still.

Although productivity and innovation are said to grow more quickly with free trade, workers often find themselves working longer and for reduced pay as operations move overseas. At the same time, these shifts in global production and trade have lowered consumer costs, improved company profits, and increased product choice. Whether these tradeoffs are a net benefit to Americans continues to be debated. To understand the global marketing environment, it's useful to know the basics of WTO, EU, and NAFTA—three important examples of multinational economic integration.

## THE WORLD TRADE ORGANIZATION

**World Trade Organization (WTO)** a 164-member organization that oversees trade agreements among its members, serves as a forum for trade negotiations, mediates trade disputes, monitors national trade policies, and works to reduce trade barriers throughout the world

The **World Trade Organization (WTO)** is a 164-member organization that

- oversees trade agreements among its members,
- serves as a forum for trade negotiations,
- mediates trade disputes,
- monitors national trade policies, and
- works to reduce trade barriers throughout the world.

In cases of trade disputes, WTO decisions are binding on member countries. Countries that seek to become members of the WTO must participate in rigorous rounds of negotiations that can last several years. Russia holds the record for waiting the longest: Having applied for membership in 1993, its application was approved in 2011.[5]

To date, the WTO has made slow progress toward its major policy initiatives: liberalizing world financial services, telecommunications, and maritime markets. Trade officials have not agreed on the direction for the WTO. Big differences between developed and developing nations create a major roadblock to its progress, and its activities thus far have focused more on dispute resolution than on reducing trade barriers. But the WTO also provides important technical assistance and training for the governments of developing countries.[6]

## THE EUROPEAN UNION

**European Union (EU)** 28 countries make up the EU, which works to remove trade restrictions, permit the free flow of goods and workers throughout member nations, and promote human rights

The best-known example of a multinational economic community is the **European Union (EU)**. The EU

- has adopted a common currency,
- works to remove trade restrictions,

- permits the free flow of goods and workers throughout member nations, and

- promotes human rights within member countries and around the world.

As Exhibit 8.3 shows, 28 countries make up the EU. Currently six countries—Albania, Iceland, Macedonia, Montenegro, Serbia, and Turkey—are candidates for membership. With a total population of more than 510 million people, the EU forms a huge common market.[7] In addition to simplifying transactions among members, the EU looks to strengthen its position in the world as a political and economic power. Its recently ratified Treaty of Lisbon is designed to further streamline operations and enables the EU to enter into international agreements as a political entity. However, the recent vote by Britain to leave the EU has some economists wondering about the union's viability for the long term.

## THE NAFTA ACCORD

More than two decades after the passage of the **North American Free Trade Agreement (NAFTA)**—an agreement between the United States, Canada, and Mexico that removes trade restrictions among the three nations—negotiations among the nations continue. The three countries insist that they will not create a trade bloc similar to the European Union; that is, they will not focus on political

**North American Free Trade Agreement (NAFTA)** an agreement between the United States, Canada, and Mexico that removes trade restrictions among the three nations

---

**EXHIBIT 8.3**    The 28 Members of the European Union

integration but instead on economic cooperation. NAFTA is particularly important to U.S. marketers because Canada and Mexico are two of its largest trading partners.

NAFTA is a complex issue, and from time to time groups in one or more of the three countries chafe under the agreement. In Mexico, farm workers have charged that NAFTA puts their industry at a disadvantage. In Canada, some observers claim NAFTA has compromised their country's oil reserves. In the United States, critics argue that U.S. workers lose jobs to cheap labor south of the border. Yet since NAFTA's passage, these three countries daily conduct more than $2.5 billion in trade with one another and have experienced GDP growth as a result.[8]

## 8-2b
## CLOSING EXAMPLE

Globalization affects almost every industry and individual throughout the world, at least in some way. Trade agreements generally make importing and exporting goods between countries easier, however changes in agreements or policies can have a tremendous impact on how companies participate in global business. The United Kingdom's exit from the EU concerns U.S. companies because it could lead to lower U.S. exports. Additionally, companies like BorgWarner, which produces automotive parts for Volkswagen, Peugeot, and Renault, may see huge financial losses as automakers building in the United Kingdom lose the benefit of tariff-free access to Europe.[9]

When member nations of the WTO fail to comply with trade agreements, the WTO can act as a mediator. For example, the United States has filed multiple complaints to the WTO regarding tariffs China has implemented on chicken products imported into the country. These tariffs resulted in an 80% drop in U.S. chicken exports to China.[10] This is important because poultry suppliers such as Tyson and Pilgrim's Pride are impacted and face financial losses if trade disputes between the countries are not resolved.

# 8-3 THE INTERNATIONAL MARKETING ENVIRONMENT

**LO 8.3** Summarize the five major factors that influence the global marketing environment.

## OPENING EXAMPLE

Unilever, producer of food, beverages, cleaning agents, and personal care products, outperforms competitors Proctor & Gamble and L'Oréal in emerging markets. Countries such as Pakistan, Indonesia, and Egypt have a large population living in poverty, yet Unilever was able to make significant gains in these countries. In 2015, emerging markets accounted for 57% of Unilever's sales compared to just 20% in 1990.[11] So how did Unilever utilize information from its external environment to adjust its global strategy?

## 8-3a

# LEARNING IT: THE INTERNATIONAL MARKETING ENVIRONMENT

As in domestic markets, the environmental factors discussed in Chapter 3 have a powerful influence on the development of a firm's global marketing strategy. Marketers must pay close attention to changing demand patterns as well as economic, social-cultural, political-legal, technological, and competitive influences when they venture abroad.

## INTERNATIONAL ECONOMIC ENVIRONMENT

A nation's size, per-capita income, and stage of economic development determine what types of products will be successful there. Nations with low per-capita incomes may be poor markets for expensive industrial machinery but good ones for agricultural hand tools. These nations cannot afford the technical equipment that powers an industrialized society. Wealthier countries may offer prime markets for many U.S. industries, particularly those producing consumer goods and services and advanced industrial products.

Infrastructure—the underlying foundation for modern life that includes transportation, communications, banking, utilities, and public services—is another important economic factor to consider when planning to enter a foreign market. An inadequate infrastructure may constrain marketers' plans to manufacture, promote, and distribute goods and services in a particular country. Recognizing that distribution could impact business in the Philippines, Unilever recruited larger retail stores to serve as sub-distributers to small, independently owned stores in the country. Owners from the larger stores receive discounts on Unilever products while the smaller stores benefit by getting access to more Unilever brands.[12]

Changes in exchange rates can also complicate international marketing. An exchange rate is the price of one nation's currency in terms of another country's currency. Fluctuations in exchange rates can make a nation's currency more or less valuable compared with those of other nations, which affects the prices of goods imported into the country. For example, an unfavorable exchange rate can make it hard for a U.S. exporter to China to compete on price with goods produced in China.

**infrastructure** the underlying foundation for modern life that includes transportation, communications, banking, utilities, and public services

**exchange rate** the price of one nation's currency in terms of another country's currency

## INTERNATIONAL SOCIAL-CULTURAL ENVIRONMENT

Before entering a foreign country, marketers should study all aspects of its culture, including language, education, religious attitudes, and social values. As generalized examples, the French love to debate and are comfortable with frequent eye contact; in China, humility is a prized virtue, colors have special significance, and it is insulting to be late; while Swedes value consensus and do not use humor in negotiations. Navigating social norms that are commonly understood among the citizens of a foreign country takes time, patience, and a willingness to learn about other cultures.

Language plays an important role in global marketing. Marketers must make sure not only to use the appropriate language for a country but also to ensure that the message is correctly translated and conveys the intended meaning. Marketers for Mercedes Benz suggested that the company enter the Chinese market under the name "Bensi." Unfortunately, this translated to "rush to die."[13] Mercedes quickly changed their name in China to "Ben Chi" which translates to "dashing speed."

## INTERNATIONAL POLITICAL-LEGAL ENVIRONMENT

Global marketers must continually stay abreast of laws and trade regulations in each country in which they compete. Legal requirements of host nations affect foreign marketers. Despite China's many advances in recent years—and even as it attempts to build a modern economy—the Chinese government continues to censor the Internet. More than 731 million Chinese currently use the Internet—more than the entire population of the United States.[14] In 2010, Google removed its search engine from mainland China over the country's strict censorship rules, but is currently in talks with China's government to return to the Chinese market.[15]

Political conditions often influence international marketing as well. Political unrest in places such as the Middle East, Africa, Eastern Europe, Spain, Greece, and South America sometimes results in acts of violence, such as destruction of a firm's property or even deaths from bombings or other violent acts. As a result, many Western firms utilize **political risk assessment (PRA)** units to evaluate the political risks of the marketplaces in which they operate.

**political risk assessment (PRA)** when a company or business unit evaluates the political risks of the market-places in which they operate

The political environment also involves labor conditions in different countries. For decades, Chinese laborers have suffered workplace abuses, including forced labor, withholding of pay, and other unfair practices. While recently enacted labor laws give workers more rights, violations still exist.[16]

Assorted trade barriers also affect global marketing. These barriers fall into two major categories: tariffs—taxes levied on imported products—and administrative, or nontariff, barriers. Some tariffs impose set taxes per pound, gallon, or unit; others are calculated according to the value of the imported item. Administrative barriers are more subtle than tariffs and take a variety of forms, such as customs barriers, quotas on imports, unnecessarily restrictive standards for imports, and export subsidies. Because the GATT and WTO agreements eliminated tariffs on many products, countries frequently use nontariff barriers to boost exports and control the flow of imported products.

## INTERNATIONAL TECHNOLOGICAL ENVIRONMENT

More than any innovation since the telephone, Internet technology has made it possible for both large and small firms to connect to the entire world. The Internet transcends political, economic, and cultural barriers, reaching every corner of the globe. It has made it possible for marketers to add new business channels. It also helps developing nations compete with industrialized nations. However, a huge gap still exists between the regions with the greatest Internet usage and those with the least. Asia, Europe, and North America together account for about 76% of the world's total Internet usage while Africa accounts for only 9%.[17]

## INTERNATIONAL COMPETITIVE ENVIRONMENT

Due to technological advancements, many shoppers are now global consumers, having become more comfortable with domestic and international online retail. In fact, 66% of consumers now shop across borders.[18] This creates more competition within any given country because consumers have more choice. It is important that marketers are mindful of the competitive forces in the countries they target and the interdependence of the other environmental forces. A major key to achieving success in foreign markets is the ability to adapt products to local preferences and culture, because competitors from those countries likely already understand these local preferences. Restaurants like McDonald's succeed outside the United States by paying attention to local tastes and modifying their menu. Similarly, Yum! Brands has seen success in India by catering to local tastes. The company's aggressive overseas expansion strategy includes operating nearly 300 KFC stores in India, along with its other leading brands Pizza Hut and Taco Bell.[19]

### 8-3b

## CLOSING EXAMPLE

Unilever was able to identify an expanding middle class within certain emerging markets and capitalized on this opportunity with several initiatives. In India, Hindustan Unilever Limited (HUL) trained local women to be rural sales agents, selling Unilever products within their communities. This initiative aims to financially empower rural women and create opportunities for them to provide income for their families.[20] Similar programs have been launched in Egypt, Vietnam, Bangladesh, Pakistan, and Sri Lanka. Unilever also recognized that lower-income consumers may not be able to afford Unilever products. As a result, Unilever offers single-use packets of soap and shampoo as well as small bars of soap at a

REUTERS/Alamy Stock Photo

Unilever's introduction of single-use packets of shampoo was a response to social-cultural differences in certain global markets.

lower price than traditional sizes.[21] Unilever was able to recognize factors in its external environment that affected the company's global business. By making small adjustments, Unilever was able to make a big impact in its foreign markets.

# STRATEGIES FOR ENTERING FOREIGN MARKETS

**LO 8.4** Summarize the six alternative strategies for entering global markets.

## OPENING EXAMPLE

"It's time to expand our business, Tony. We've been shipping our Cioccolato chocolates to 20 different countries for the last four years," Rosa told her brother. "We could do so much more."

"It seems risky," Tony replied. "Our parents poured their life into this little store and I don't want to mess it up!"

"We weren't meant to stay a tiny store in Little Italy forever! People outside of New York City deserve to taste our chocolate."

"They can, they just order on our website," Tony told her.

"Exactly! Thirty-five percent of our sales come from online orders. Taking the brand global will work. Our chocolates are amazing and customers love our flavor combinations."

"OK, you've convinced me," Tony relented. "There's one big problem though. How do we even start?"

Choosing the appropriate strategy for entering foreign markets depends on the industry, company size, and goals for global expansion. What global entry strategy is right for Cioccolato?

## 8-4a

## LEARNING IT: STRATEGIES FOR ENTERING FOREIGN MARKETS

Besides generating additional revenue, firms can benefit from international distribution for many other reasons. For example, marketers may encounter new ideas for product development, new approaches to distribution, or clever new promotional tactics that they may apply successfully in their domestic market or in other international markets.

Organizations may choose six strategies for entering foreign markets: exporting, franchising and foreign licensing, subcontracting, international divisions, acquisitions, and joint ventures (see Exhibit 8.4). In general, the greater degree of control offered by a strategy, the greater level of risk required to pursue that strategy. Firms often use more than one of these entry strategies.

### EXPORTING

Exporting, another basic form of global marketing, allows companies to distribute their goods globally without setting up formal operations in those markets. Many firms export their products as the first step in international business. But

**EXHIBIT 8.4** Strategies for Entering Foreign Markets

**Degree of Control**

Low · · · · · · · · · · · · · · · · · · · Moderate · · · · · · · · · · · · · · · · · · · High

| Exporting | Contractual Agreements<br>Franchising<br>Foreign Licensing<br>Subcontracting | International Direct Investment<br>Acquisitions<br>Joint Ventures<br>International Divisions |
|---|---|---|

Low · · · · · · · · · · · · · · · · · · · Moderate · · · · · · · · · · · · · · · · · · · High

**Degree of Risk**

even large businesses use it for global expansion. Furniture manufacturer IKEA has built an entire exporting strategy around its modular furniture. Because IKEA's furniture is lightweight, packs flat, and comes in components that customers can assemble, the firm can ship its goods almost anywhere in the world at a lower cost than manufacturers of traditional furniture.[22]

There are companies that specialize in assisting businesses wanting to export. An export trading company (ETC) buys products from domestic producers and resells them abroad. While manufacturers lose control over marketing and distribution to an ETC, it helps them export through a relatively simple and inexpensive channel, in the process providing feedback about the overseas market potential of their products.

An export-management company (EMC), provides the first-time exporter with expertise in locating foreign buyers, handling necessary paperwork, and ensuring that its goods meet local labeling and testing laws. However, the manufacturer retains more control over the export process when it deals with an EMC than if it were to sell the goods outright to an export-trading company.

## FRANCHISING AND FOREIGN LICENSING

A **franchise** is a contractual arrangement where the franchisee agrees to meet the operating requirements of a manufacturer or a franchiser. The franchisee receives the right to sell the products and use the franchiser's name as well as a variety of marketing, management, and other services. One advantage of franchising is risk reduction by offering a proven concept. Standardized operations typically reduce costs, increase operating efficiencies, and provide greater international brand recognition. However, the success of an international franchise depends on its willingness to balance standard practices with local customer preferences. Fast-food companies like McDonald's have been successful franchisers around the world because the company has menu offerings that cater to local tastes.

**Foreign licensing** grants foreign marketers the right to distribute a firm's merchandise or to use its trademark, patent, or process in a specified geographic area. These arrangements usually set certain time limits, after which agreements are revised or renewed. Polo Ralph Lauren, an American clothing and home goods brand, has foreign licensing partners that distribute its clothing. Polo

**franchise** is a contractual arrangement where the franchisee agrees to meet the operating requirements of a manufacturer or a franchiser

**foreign licensing** grants foreign marketers the right to distribute a firm's merchandise or to use its trademark, patent, or process in a specified geographic area

Ralph Lauren says these licensing relationships allow the companies to take advantage of each other's strengths—Polo Ralph Lauren's creativity and design expertise and the licensing partners' ability to consistently manufacture and distribute within their home markets.[23]

Franchising and foreign licensing offer several advantages over exporting, including access to local partners' marketing information and distribution channels, and protection from various legal barriers. Compared to exporting, manufacturers and brand owners also retain much more control over how their products are marketed and sold. Because this strategy often requires limited capital outlays, many firms, both small and large, regard it as an attractive entry strategy.

## SUBCONTRACTING

**subcontracting** when the production of goods or services is assigned to local companies

When **subcontracting**- the production of goods or services is assigned to local companies. Using local subcontractors can prevent mistakes involving local culture and regulations. Manufacturers might subcontract with a local company to produce their goods or use a foreign distributor to handle their products abroad or provide customer service.

Manufacturing within the country can provide protection from import duties and may be a lower-cost alternative that makes it possible for the product to compete with local offerings. It can also have a downside if local suppliers don't make the grade or if a manufacturer imposes an unrealistically tight timeframe on a supplier to deliver the product, leading to long hours or sweatshop conditions in the factory. Nike has long subcontracted factories in south Asian countries to manufacture the company's products. While Nike was able to take advantage of lower manufacturing costs, the company faced criticism for working conditions in the factories. After backlash and protests tarnished the company's image and financial performance, Nike created the Fair Labor Association (FLA). The FLA is a non profit group which works to improve the lives of millions of workers around the world.[24] Today Nike continues to publish corporate social responsibility reports detailing their standards and commitments.

### 8-4b

# INTERNATIONAL DIRECT INVESTMENT

**international direct investment** financial investment in foreign firms or facilities

Another strategy for entering global markets is **international direct investment** in foreign firms or facilities. Although high levels of involvement and high risk potential are characteristics of investments in foreign countries, firms choosing this method often have a competitive advantage. Direct investment can take several forms.

## INTERNATIONAL DIVISIONS

A company with the resources and commitment to enter a foreign market can invest in building or creating a wholly owned facility there. Most large companies, such as GE, Microsoft, and Boeing, have offices and/or factories in countries around the world. In fact, more than half of all Ford personnel are located outside the United States.[25] While setting up international divisions requires significant resources and planning, once the office is running, the company retains complete control over its operations.

## ACQUISITIONS

A company can buy an existing firm in a country where it wants to do business. Asian firms, particularly Chinese, have been seeking to purchase U.S. businesses, mostly in industries involving natural resources, such as oil, natural gas, metals, and coal. However, they have been making inroads in industrial, technology, and finance companies as well. China's Meidu Holding Company recently acquired U.S.-based Woodbine Acquisition, an oil and gas development company.[26] Acquiring a foreign company gives the buyer a fully functioning operation in a new country, but this strategy usually requires significant investment.

## JOINT VENTURES

Companies may also engage in international marketing by forming **joint ventures** in which they share the risks, costs, and management of the foreign operation with one or more partners. Because India puts limits on foreign direct investment, Gap recently announced that it has signed a letter of intent to form a partnership with Indian conglomerate Arvind Brands to open retail stores in India.[27]

Jaguar Land Rover (JLR), a brand that struggled in China under Ford's ownership, was sold to India's Tata Motors in 2008. In 2012, Jaguar Land Rover and China's Chery Automotive formed a joint venture. JLR hoped that the partnership would help increase sales in one of its fastest-growing markets. China has now become Jaguar Land Rover's biggest market.[28]

Although joint ventures offer many advantages, foreign investors may encounter problems due to language, culture, and operational differences that can exist between the partnering companies.

**joint ventures** when companies share the risks, costs, and management of the foreign operation with one or more partners

### 8-4c
## CLOSING EXAMPLE

Which market entry strategy is right for Cioccolato? Although Tony has several options for expanding, he is a conservative businessman who likely prefers a low level of risk. An international direct investment such as a joint venture has high risk potential and is not a fit for Cioccolato. It's probably too expensive as well. While contractual agreements have a lower level of risk than international direct investments, franchising and foreign licensing may be better suited for companies with strong brand recognition. Cioccolato has one location in New York City and probably does not have enough brand recognition to go this route. Tony's best bet for Cioccolato is to export utilizing an export trading company or export management company. These options are low risk, lower cost, and are a good starting point for Tony. If Cioccolato is successful in foreign markets, Tony may consider contractual agreements or a direct investment in the future.

# 8-5 MARKETING MIX STRATEGIES

**LO 8.5** Describe the five alternative marketing mix strategies used in global marketing.

## OPENING EXAMPLE

One of the most popular cookies in the United States is the Oreo. Whether you dunk them in milk and take a bite, or twist off the top wafer and eat the filling, just about everyone has an emotional attachment to the chocolate wafer cookie. In the mid-nineties, Kraft foods launched Oreos in China. Unfortunately, sales were just mediocre in China with Kraft holding only 3% of the Chinese market.[29] Nearly a decade after it was first launched, Kraft decided to research why the cookie wasn't selling well. What do you think Kraft did wrong?

## 8-5a
## LEARNING IT: MARKETING MIX STRATEGIES

In developing a marketing mix, global marketers first concentrate on two basic decisions:

- Do we change our product for the international market?
- Do we change our promotional strategy for the international market?

As described in Exhibit 8.5, the answers to those questions will result in marketers pursuing one of the following five strategies:

1. Straight extension
2. Promotion adaptation
3. Product adaptation
4. Dual adaptation
5. Product invention

A firm may choose to follow a one-product, one-message straight extension strategy. This strategy permits economies of scale in production and marketing.

**EXHIBIT 8.5** International Marketing Mix Strategies

|  |  | Product Strategy | | |
|---|---|---|---|---|
|  |  | **Same Product** | **Product Adaptation** | **New Product** |
| **Promotion Strategy** | **Same Promotion** | **Straight Extension**<br>General Mills Cheerios<br>Coca-Cola<br>Mars Snickers candy bar | **Product Adaptation**<br>Campbell's soup<br>Exxon gasoline | **Product Invention**<br>Nonelectric sewing machines<br>Manually operated washing machines |
|  | **Different Promotion** | **Promotion Adaptation**<br>Bicycles/motorcycles<br>Outboard motors | **Dual Adaptation**<br>Coffee<br>Some clothing |  |

Also, successful implementation creates universal recognition of a product for consumers from country to country.

Other strategies call for product adaptation, promotion adaptation, or both. Marketers in the greeting-card industry adapt their product and messaging to cultural differences. For example, Russians are unlikely to send a card to a man on his 40th birthday. The reason: A common superstition in Russia that says big parties for a man celebrating that particular milestone attract "the Death."

Finally, a firm may select product invention to take advantage of unique foreign market opportunities. To match user needs in developing nations, an appliance manufacturer might introduce a hand-powered washing machine, even though such products became obsolete in industrialized countries years ago.

Once one of those five product and promotional strategies is chosen, marketers must also implement pricing and distribution strategies to support them.

## 8-5b
## CLOSING EXAMPLE

After a decade on the market in China, Kraft decided to research why Oreos weren't selling well. Chinese consumers said the Oreo was, "a little bit too sweet and a little bit too bitter."[30] This information led Kraft to ask more questions about the Oreo and how the company could alter the Oreo to better appeal to the Chinese audience. Kraft realized that the straight extension strategy was not working. Kraft struggled in China because the Chinese consumers historically did not eat a lot of cookies, but also because they did not find the taste appealing. In addition, the Chinese consumers felt that Oreos were too expensive.[31] As a result, Kraft moved to a dual adaptation strategy. The company adapted the recipe to appeal to Chinese palates. Over time, Kraft introduced a green tea flavored filling and Oreo wafers. In addition, Kraft offered Oreos in smaller packages at a lower price. Promotions for Oreos were changed, as well. Traditional

Kraft used a dual adaptation strategy for selling Oreos in China by altering both their product and promotion.

Source: simconblog.wordpress.com

advertisements in the United States featured parents showing the practice of the "Twist, Lick, Dunk" method of eating Oreos. New advertisements in China needed to show the ritual of pairing cookies and milk as well as the "Twist, Lick, Dunk" method. Kraft flipped their traditional advertisements to have young children show their parents or older adults how to eat the cookies. Kraft's adjustments were successful—Oreos are now the best-selling cookie in China.

# 8-6 DETERMINING A MARKET ENTRY STRATEGY

**LO 8.6** Given an example of a company's goals for expanding globally, determine the most appropriate market entry strategy.

## OPENING EXAMPLE

With 26 theaters across the United States, three in London, and a strategic partnership with the China Arts and Entertainment Group (CAEG), Nederlander has been successful in global expansion and now has plans to expand even further. Turkey has a long history with theater dating back to the Ottoman Empire. Since the 1990s, there have been new theater openings and the foundation of several theater groups. The International Istanbul Theater Festival is held every two years and features national, international, classical, and contemporary renditions for audiences to enjoy. Nederlander has set its sights on Istanbul and needs to determine the most appropriate market entry strategy.

### 8-6a
## LEARNING IT: DETERMINING A MARKET ENTRY STRATEGY

When the Nederlander Group decided to expand, executives researched and identified several markets as possibilities. Nederlander's previous expansion to London was a relatively easy decision as London's West End had a similar theater scene to Broadway in New York City as well as English-speaking theater patrons.

Now, its executives aim to open two theaters in Istanbul which will host concerts, dance performances, and Broadway musicals. Jimmy and James Nederlander are open to taking risks when it comes to global expansion. Having been in business for 100 years, the Nederlander family have a keen sense for what works and doesn't work in the theater business.

While the Nederlanders feel confident in the demand for additional theater venues in Turkey, given the country's rich history with performing arts, the Nederlanders recognize that they will likely employ a product adaptation strategy when bringing Broadway shows to Istanbul. Turkish is the main language in Istanbul and the Nederlanders must be sure that language and meaning are not lost in translation. Typically, the company will work with an experienced industry professional and local professional to adjust shows appropriately for the foreign audience. This allows the Nederlanders to maintain a great deal of control over the production, while adapting it for local needs. But, while they'd love to retain total control over production at the new venues, the level of adaptation needed for this market requires expertise and local talent the Nederlanders don't currently possess.

For these reasons, the Nederlanders have decided to partner with a company in Istanbul to develop the performing arts center. This joint venture presents the possibility for a high level of risk, but also allows the Nederlander Group a high degree of control. The partnership also provides shared responsibility of management, ensuring that productions are culturally appropriate for Turkish audiences. With the addition of the center in Istanbul—and the marketing clout of Nederlander—they hope to put Istanbul on the global theater map.

Like the Nederlanders, any company choosing a global entry strategy should carefully consider its primary goals before choosing how to enter a new market.

Exhibit 8.6 summarizes the advantages and disadvantages of each entry strategy.

**EXHIBIT 8.6** ▶ Comparison of Market Entry Strategies

| Strategy | Advantages | Disadvantages | Appropriate for . . . |
|---|---|---|---|
| Exporting | • Low cost<br>• Easiest way to sell in foreign markets | • Lack of control over how products are marketed and sold<br>• Company may not acquire knowledge about foreign markets that would help build a competitive advantage | Companies looking for the lowest cost and lowest risk way to sell in new markets |
| Franchising and licensing | • More control over how products are marketed and sold<br>• Allows company to acquire knowledge about new markets that could be applied to product development and promotion strategies | • Poor quality or service from international partners could damage brand | Companies wanting increased control over sales and marketing of their products, while limiting capital outlays |
| Subcontracting | • Lower cost alternative, allows company to compete with local offerings<br>• Protection from import duties | • Lack of control over factory or working conditions<br>• Lack of control over lead times or quality | Companies looking for cost advantages or local expertise in marketing or distribution |
| International divisions | • Company retains complete control over operations<br>• Allows for easy customization to local market preferences | • Requires significant resources and planning | Large corporations with significant sales or operations in foreign markets |
| Acquisitions | • Fully functioning organization in new country | • Requires a significant investment | Companies looking to quickly and firmly establish a presence in new markets |
| Joint ventures | • Shared risks and costs<br>• Access to partner's knowledge and expertise of foreign market | • May encounter problems due to language, culture, or operational efficiencies | Companies that may lack the full resources necessary to expand globally, but who want a strong presence in new markets |

**8-7**

# LEARN IT TODAY . . . USE IT TOMORROW

You were just hired as a marketing assistant at Nederlander. As part of your training process, they have asked you to watch a video about the company's marketing activities, then report to your manager what you have learned. You hope to make a good first impression, promotions at this company mean opportunities for travel around the world.

It's time to get hands-on and apply what you've learned. **See MindTap for an activity related to Nederlander's marketing activities.**

## Chapter Summary

**LO 8.1** Describe the global business landscape in terms of U.S. imports, U.S. exports, and major industries.

Global marketing expands a company's market, allows firms to grow, and makes them less dependent on their own country's economy for success.

**LO 8.2** Differentiate between WTO, NAFTA, and EU in terms of basic functions and member countries.

The World Trade Organization oversees GATT agreements, mediates disputes, and tries to reduce trade barriers throughout the world. The European Union is a customs union whose goal is to remove all barriers to free trade among its members. The North American Free Trade Agreement removes trade restrictions among Canada, Mexico, and the United States.

**LO 8.3** Summarize the five major factors that influence the global marketing environment.

The five major factors that influence the global marketing environment are the economic, social-cultural, technological, political-legal, and competitive environments.

**LO 8.4** Summarize the six alternative strategies for entering global markets.

The six alternative strategies for entering global markets are exporting, franchising and foreign licensing, subcontracting, international divisions, acquisitions, and joint ventures.

**LO 8.5** Describe the five alternative marketing mix strategies used in global marketing.

The five alternative marketing mix strategies used in global marketing include straight extension, promotion adaptation, product adaptation, dual adaptation, and product invention.

**LO 8.6** Given an example of a company's goals for expanding globally, determine the most appropriate market entry strategy.

Marketers must consider factors such as risk propensity, local demand for the product, degree of control, and knowledge of the foreign market when considering which market entry strategy is most appropriate.

## Key Terms

exporting **151**
importing **151**
tariffs **153**
free-trade area **153**
World Trade Organization (WTO) **154**
European Union (EU) **154**

North American Free Trade Agreement (NAFTA) **155**
infrastructure **157**
exchange rate **157**
political risk assessment (PRA) **158**
franchise **161**

foreign licensing **161**
subcontracting **162**
international direct investment **162**
joint ventures **163**

# PART 3

# TARGET MARKET SELECTION

# 9 MARKET SEGMENTATION, TARGETING, AND POSITIONING

Source: www.chabel-view.com

**REI**
www.rei.com

## LEARNING OBJECTIVES

**9.1** Describe the two primary market classifications.

**9.2** Summarize the three components necessary for effective market segmentation.

**9.3** Describe four types of geographic segmentation.

**9.4** Summarize the five most commonly used demographic variables.

**9.5** Contrast psychographic segmentation with other segmentation variables.

**9.6** Describe the three forms of behavioral segmentation.

**9.7** Distinguish between the three basic strategies for reaching target markets.

**9.8** Explain how marketers build value propositions utilizing positioning strategies.

**9.9** Given a target market profile, classify each variable according to its base of segmentation.

# LEARN IT TODAY . . . USE IT TOMORROW

REI is an outdoor and sporting goods retail cooperative with 80 stores in the United States, more than 3.5 million members, and 1.7 million Facebook followers. In addition to providing apparel and equipment for a variety of outdoor activities, REI is in the adventure travel business and offers 150 worldwide destinations with expert guides to engage travelers in immersive outdoor experiences. REI Adventures is interested in promoting its tours more widely and attracting additional customers to its service. It believes this may also boost customer purchases of apparel and equipment from REI.

But obviously not everyone is a good target audience for REI Adventures. It's likely that customers will share some particular characteristics, but which ones? And how can REI precisely identify its target audience so they don't waste promotional dollars pitching people who are unlikely to buy?

## 9-1    TYPES OF MARKETS

### OPENING EXAMPLE

PepsiCo has a strong lead over Coca-Cola in bottled water, juices, and sports drinks—which are some of the fastest growing beverage categories. PepsiCo, like other beverage companies, uses a dual marketing approach to promote its products—one approach for consumers and another approach for businesses, such as restaurants and grocery stores. How does the type of market influence a company's strategies, and why should marketers understand the differences between the two markets?

### 9-1a

### LEARNING IT: TYPES OF MARKETS

A **market** is a group of people with sufficient purchasing power, authority, and willingness to buy. Marketers must use their expertise to understand the market for a good or service, whether it's a new athletic shoe for marathon runners or a new accounting software program for large corporations.

Products usually are classified as either consumer products or business products. **Consumer products** are bought by ultimate consumers for personal use for example, cell phones, sports tickets, or fashion magazines. **Business products** are purchased for use either directly or indirectly in the production of other goods and services for resale.

Most products purchased by individual consumers, such as grocery store items and restaurant meals, are considered consumer products. On the other hand, steel and bulk cotton are examples of items generally purchased by manufacturers and therefore classified as business products. For example, Ford purchases steel to manufacture automobiles, and textile manufacturers such as Burlington Industries convert raw cotton into cloth.

**market** a group of people with sufficient purchasing power, authority, and willingness to buy

**consumer products** products bought by ultimate consumers for personal use

**business products** products purchased for use either directly or indirectly in the production of other goods and services for resale

However, in many cases, a single product can serve different uses. Tires purchased for the family car constitute consumer products, but tires purchased by Ford Motor Company to be mounted on its Ford Fusion during production are business products because they become part of another product destined for resale. To determine the classification of an item, consider two elements:

- Who will buy the product
- How or why the product will be used

The bottle of shampoo you buy at the supermarket is a consumer product, but if the Hyatt hotel chain purchases large quantities of the same shampoo in individual-sized bottles from the manufacturer or wholesaler, it becomes a business product.

As discussed in the chapter on business markets, companies must approach marketing differently depending on whether they are selling to consumer or business markets. Each market is unique in terms of how products are sold, promotional tactics, number of customers, and more. The remainder of this chapter will focus on marketing of consumer products.

### 9-1b

## CLOSING EXAMPLE

Pepsi utilizes different strategies and tactics depending upon whether it is marketing to businesses or consumers. The consumer market is typically reached through advertising, such as 30-second television commercials and sponsorship during the Super Bowl game. The 2017 Super Bowl commercials featured Pepsi's Zero Sugar and LIFEWTR products, which appeal to health-conscious consumers.[1]

However, sales representatives are typically used to serve business customers, such as restaurants and retail outlets. They interact with store managers to discuss end-of-aisle displays or other in-store promotions which could boost sales.

# 9-2  CRITERIA FOR EFFECTIVE MARKET SEGMENTATION

**LO 9.2**
Summarize the three components necessary for effective market segmentation.

### OPENING EXAMPLE

The Nebraska-based Design Basics company, one of the largest home plan design companies in the country, is trying to determine which market segments to pursue. It knows that it can't market to everyone—and not even everyone in the market for a home plan is its ideal customer. The problem is it doesn't even know where to begin its segmentation efforts. Poor segmentation could lead to ineffective marketing mixes—and a lot of wasted money.

## 9-2a

# LEARNING IT: CRITERIA FOR EFFECTIVE MARKET SEGMENTATION

Many markets include consumers with different lifestyles, backgrounds, and income levels. Nearly everyone buys toothpaste, but that does not mean every consumer is looking for the same thing in the brand of toothpaste he or she buys. So, it is unusual for a single marketing mix strategy to attract all sectors of a market.

The **target market** for a product is the segment of consumers most likely to purchase a particular item. By identifying, evaluating, and selecting a target market to pursue, such as consumers who prefer toothpaste made with all-natural ingredients or those who want an extra-whitening formula—marketers develop more efficient and effective marketing strategies. Marketing now takes place on a global basis more than ever, incorporating many target markets. To identify those markets, marketers must determine useful ways for segmenting different populations and communicating with them successfully.

The division of the total market into smaller, relatively homogeneous groups is called **market segmentation**. Both profit-oriented and not-for-profit organizations practice market segmentation but it doesn't automatically guarantee success in the marketing arena. However, segmentation can be an effective tool when three requirements are met. The segment must be significant in size and purchasing power, profitable, and consistent with the firm's marketing capabilities.

**target market** the segment of consumers most likely to purchase a particular item

**market segmentation** the division of the total market into smaller, relatively homogeneous groups

## SIGNIFICANT IN SIZE AND PURCHASING POWER

*Example*: With jobs, incomes, and decision-making power, female consumers represent a hefty amount of purchasing power, over $7 trillion, or more than 60% of the nation's wealth.[2] Women control or influence the purchase of more than 85% of all consumer goods, including items such as stocks and bonds for investment, personal computers, and family vehicles.[3] With this information in mind, car manufacturers and dealers now market directly to women.

## PROFITABLE

*Example:* A segment could be very large, with high aggregate purchasing power, but still be unprofitable for certain companies and products. For example, India's market of vehicle owners is growing fast, with over 50,000 new vehicles being registered every day.[4] However, because of low average incomes, the India market wouldn't necessarily be profitable for Ferrari or BMW.

## CONSISTENT WITH THE FIRM'S MARKETING CAPABILITIES

*Example:* Harley-Davidson, whose motorcycles were thought to be the exclusive domain of men, are now purchased by women who represent a growing segment of their business. Female consumers have increased discretionary income due to their working status and represent a sizeable market opportunity.

**EXHIBIT 9.1**    Segmentation Analysis for Design Basics

| Segment | Size & Purchasing Power | Profitable | Consistent with Firm's Capabilities |
|---|---|---|---|
| Women homeowners and/or women researching new home construction | Female consumers represent more than 60% of the nation's wealth with over $7 trillion in purchasing power.[6] | Women significantly influence 80–90% of consumer purchases.[7] | Based on market feedback, Design Basics changed product design to offer improved storage options with space for muddy boots, backpacks, car keys, mail, and cell phone chargers. Publishes *Her Home* digital magazine twice a year focusing on women's perspectives on design, construction, and products for the home.[8] |

As a result, Harley-Davidson utilizes targeted ads in women's magazines, hosts annual "garage party" events throughout the United States geared specifically to women, and supports a website for women motorcyclists.[5] In addition, they offer riding gear and apparel for women. If Harley-Davidson was unable or unwilling to adjust its marketing mix to appeal to women, then it would not represent an effective segment for them.

*Example:* In several countries, cars are driven on the left side of the road, instead of the right side like they are in the United States. While many of these countries offer large, potentially profitable markets, an automaker unwilling to modify its cars to put the steering wheel on the other side of the car could not successfully pursue these markets.

Market segmentation attempts to isolate the traits that distinguish a certain group of consumers from the overall market. An understanding of the group's characteristics–such as age, gender, geographic location, income, and buying patterns—plays a vital role in developing a successful marketing strategy. For best results, marketers often seek to pinpoint a number of factors affecting buying behavior in the target segment.

## 9-2b

## CLOSING EXAMPLE

Design Basics decided to pursue women as a target market for its home plan designs. Exhibit 9.1 evaluates how well a female segment addresses the criteria for effective market segmentation.

Because this segment satisfies all three criteria, it's an effective market segment for Design Basics to pursue.

Design Basics publishes *Her Home* digital magazine, which targets content to women about home design, construction ideas, and other products.

Source: www.Designbasics.com

# 9-3
# GEOGRAPHIC SEGMENTATION

## OPENING EXAMPLE

How do companies decide where to locate their businesses or what products to offer in various areas? Let's say you were in charge of choosing new store locations for Walgreens, which already has over 8,000 stores throughout the United States. It's likely that you'd use geographic segmentation to determine potentially profitable locations, as well as guide decisions on which products might sell best in those locations.

## 9-3a
## LEARNING IT: GEOGRAPHIC SEGMENTATION

In the following sections, we discuss the four common bases for segmenting consumer markets: geographic segmentation, demographic segmentation, psychographic segmentation, and behavioral segmentation. These segmentation approaches offer important guidance for marketing strategies, provided they identify significant differences in buying behavior.

Marketers have long practiced **geographic segmentation**—dividing an overall market into homogeneous groups based on their locations. Geographic location does not ensure that all consumers in a location will make the same buying decisions, but this segmentation approach helps identify some general patterns.

Four geographic variables, including market size, market density, climate, and region, may influence a consumer's needs and the profit potential for a company.

**geographic segmentation** dividing an overall market into homogeneous groups based on their locations

## MARKET SIZE

**Market size** may be defined as the number of individuals residing in a particular geographic market area. Exhibit 9.2 shows populations of the 10 largest cities in the United States and the 10 states with the largest populations. California tops the list with more than 38 million residents and three of the top 10 cities. Wyoming is the least-populous state, with less than 600,000 residents.

While population numbers indicate the overall size of a market, other geographic indicators such as job growth give useful guidance to marketers, depending on the type of products they sell. Automobile manufacturers might rank geographic areas by household income, because it is an important factor in the purchase of a new car.

**market size** the number of individuals residing in a particular geographic market area

*Using Market Size—Example #1:* When selecting store locations for Walgreens, it's likely that far more stores would be located in California than in North Dakota because of the overall size of the market. However, this measure alone doesn't tell the whole story, because California covers a larger geographic area than North Dakota. Additional types of geographic segmentation may be needed to guide decisions about new store locations.

**EXHIBIT 9.2** **The 10 Largest Cities and the 10 Most Populous States in the United States**

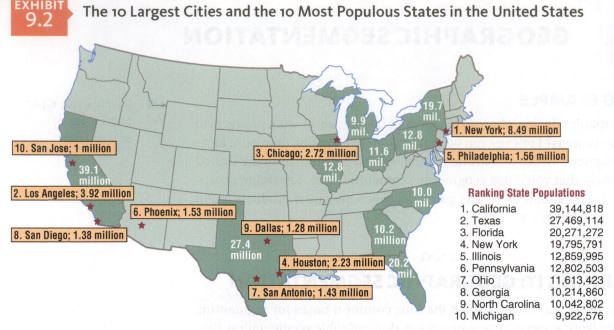

Sources: "Top 50 Cities in the U.S. by Population and Rank," *Info Please*, accessed September 20, 2017, www.infoplease.com; U.S. Census Bureau, "National and State Population Estimates: July 2015," accessed September 20, 2017, www.census.gov.

*Using Market Size—Example #2:* Companies that sell online nationwide often find that a majority of their orders come from large states like California, Texas, and New York. This information can help companies allocate their promotional spending to the largest markets, where it will likely have the highest return.

## MARKET DENSITY

**market density** the number of residents within a specific geographic area, such as a square mile

**Market density** is the number of residents within a specific geographic area, such as a square mile. Urban areas have the greatest population density, with large numbers of individuals residing within a small geographic area. Rural areas have the lowest population density. Consumer lifestyles can differ dramatically between these areas. City dwellers often rely on public transportation and may get along fine without automobiles, whereas those who live in the suburbs or rural areas depend on their own cars and trucks. Also, those who live in the suburbs spend more on lawn and garden care products than city dwellers. Marketers can use this type of information to determine where their products are most likely to be successful.

*Using Market Density—Example #1:* Understanding market density would help you pinpoint locations for new Walgreens stores. While you might only have one store every 15 miles in rural areas, it's possible you could have multiple stores within 15 blocks in a high-density urban area.

*Using Market Density—Example #2:* Dollar General stores found success by entering rural areas that had few alternatives for grocery and consumer packaged products. However, now Dollar General is developing smaller footprint stores in urban areas to produce growth and appeal to value-conscious consumers. They have plans to open 1,000 new stores of various sizes according to the market density of the area.[9]

## CLIMATE

Climate is also a useful geographic segmentation approach since weather patterns and temperature ranges likely affect consumer needs. Snow blowers and winter coats would be considered necessities in most of the Midwest and Northeast areas of the United States, while a customer living in the South would have little need for a snow blower or even a snow shovel.

*Using Climate—Example:* Walgreens stores in warmer, sunnier climates might dedicate more shelf space to sunscreen, while stores in colder climates might dedicate space to gloves and hats.

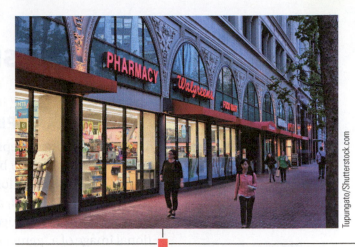

While Walgreens stores in rural areas might be large and far apart, stores in urban areas are often smaller and located close together.

## REGION

The region of the country can also be a useful segmentation approach. Demand for some categories of products can vary according to region, and marketers must be aware of how these regions differ. The most obvious differences can be driven by climate, which is discussed above, but regional differences go beyond weather. They can be driven by differences in culture, recreational opportunities, incomes, and other reasons. For example, a recent survey found that Seattle and Portland, Oregon, top the list in coffee consumption. On the other hand, those in the Mountain states like Nevada and Colorado are most likely to drink tea.[10] Marketers can use this type information to determine where their products will most likely be successful.[11]

*Using Region—Example:* REI likely determines the mix of products within a particular store based on the region of the country. For example, in the Mountain states, including Colorado and Wyoming, stores might carry more products for snow skiing and snowboarding. Stores near the coast in Florida and South Carolina might stock items for customers vacationing at the beach. Examples would be swimsuits or salt-water fishing equipment. It's important to note these distinctions aren't simply due to climate, but the particular geography and recreational opportunities that are available in these regions.

### 9-3b

## CLOSING EXAMPLE

Walgreens uses geographic segmentation to help make decisions about store locations and what to carry in those stores. For example, Florida, California, and Texas have the highest number of stores, while Vermont, Wyoming, and Alaska have the lowest number of stores.[12] About 76% of all Americans live within a 5-mile radius of a Walgreens store and over 10 million customers visit daily.[13] Walgreens utilizes marketing research to identify the best products for its stores and recently announced an initiative to focus on the top 10 grocery items consumers desire.[14] It's possible that the top 10 grocery items in one market could be entirely different from another. These differences could particularly be driven by market density, climate, and region.

# 9-4

# DEMOGRAPHIC SEGMENTATION

LO
9.4     Summarize the five most commonly used demographic variables.

## OPENING EXAMPLE

The gaming industry represents a sizeable market opportunity, with industry predictions expecting $35 billion in revenues for mobile games, $32 billion for PC games, and $28 billion for console games.[15] How can video game companies such as Nintendo, Microsoft, and smaller developers capture a profitable share of the market? With such a huge market, game developers can't be limited by the traditional image of a "gamer"—a white male in his teens or twenties. Gamers actually come from all demographic segments, as you'll learn about in this section.

## 9-4a

## LEARNING IT: DEMOGRAPHIC SEGMENTATION

**demographic segmentation** defines consumer groups according to demographic variables such as gender, age, ethnic group, family life cycle stage and household type, and income

The most common method of market segmentation—**demographic segmentation**—defines consumer groups according to demographic variables such as gender, age, ethnic group, family life cycle stage and household type, and income. Marketers review vast quantities of available data to complete a plan for demographic segmentation, one of the primary sources for demographic data in the United States is the Census Bureau.

The following discussion considers five of the most commonly used demographic variables, which are also called bases of segmentation (see Exhibit 9.3). Keep in mind that, while demographic segmentation is helpful, it can also lead to stereotyping—a preconception about a group of people—which can alienate a potential market or cause marketers to miss a potential market altogether. The idea is to use segmentation as a starting point, not an endpoint. Demographic segmentation can help marketers communicate effectively with their target markets.

Exhibit 9.4 provides examples of how marketers might use these bases of segmentation.

**EXHIBIT 9.3** Five Bases of Demographic Segmentation

| Demographic Variable | Explanation | Segment Examples |
|---|---|---|
| Gender | Gender can be an important segmentation base with some products used exclusively by men or women while others are used by both genders. | Male<br>Female |
| Age | Segmentation based on age may also be effective and can be easily employed. Different ages and generations typically have different income levels and consumer preferences. | School-age children<br>Preteens (also called tweens) and teens<br>Millennials<br>Generation X<br>Baby Boomers<br>Seniors |

*(Continues)*

*(Continued)*

| Demographic Variable | Explanation | Segment Examples |
|---|---|---|
| **Ethnicity** | America's racial and ethnic composition is constantly changing. The three largest and fastest growing are Hispanics, African Americans, and Asian Americans. | White<br>Hispanic<br>African American<br>Asian American<br>Native American<br>Mixed Race |
| **Family lifecycle stages and household type** | The process of family formation and dissolution, as well as the number of people or composition of a household. Consumer preferences can change—even for the same person—as they travel through family lifecycle stages or shift the composition of their household. | Singles<br>Couples with no children<br>Couples with young children<br>Single parents<br>Empty nesters (couples with grown children)<br>Same-sex couples and LGBT households |
| **Income and expenditure** | In general, as household income increases, a smaller percentage of expenditures goes for food and a larger percentage goes to recreation, education, and other items. | High income<br>Middle income<br>Low income |

**EXHIBIT 9.4**    Using Demographic Segmentation for Marketing

| Segmentation Base | Marketing Data | Marketing Application |
|---|---|---|
| **Gender** | Female consumers often control purchasing in their households and for others (e.g., aging parents, adult children), and their spending influence is expected to grow.[16] | Dove's Real Beauty Sketches uses an empowering message aimed toward a female demographic to create favorable impressions and more positive perceptions of the brand[17] |
| **Age** | Children 12 and under exert considerable influence over family purchases. | Food industry spends $10 billion each year marketing to children and Target, the Minneapolis-based retailer spent $118 million in a back-to-school campaign in 2015. In 2016, they enlisted kids to design, direct, and perform in a series of seven TV ads.[18] |
| **Ethnicity** | The Hispanic population in the United States is growing faster than the African American population with 54 million consumers, and Hispanic buying power is growing nearly three times the national average | Clorox Company utilized an integrated marketing campaign, including spots on Telemundo and Univision, as well as radio, digital, and direct mail—all in Spanish—to market Clorox cleaning products as a way to prevent germs.[19] |
| **Family lifecycle stage and household type** | According to the U.S. Census Bureau, one birth occurs every 8 seconds. | There will be continuing demand for cribs, changing tables, baby clothes, diapers, and car seats. Changes in this birth rate would signal the need for companies in this category to respond accordingly. |
| **Income and expenditure patterns** | The median household income is $56,000. | Various automobiles are marketed to middle-income consumers; examples are Ford's Fiesta and Fusion which can be purchased for $14,000 and up. |

9-4b

### 9-4b
## CLOSING EXAMPLE

The majority of people—even females—believe that most video game players are men. However, you might be surprised to learn that equal numbers of men and women play video games. However, more men identify themselves as "gamers" (15% of men and 6% of women). This is likely due to the types of games they play and the amount of time spent playing them.[20] This marketing data is important for any video game developer.

A visit to the app store or your local GameStop underscores the likely influence of demographics on video game purchases.[21] For example, the popular *Call of Duty* franchise is rated "M" for mature and likely appeals to a predominantly male audience, while *Bubble Guppies* for the Nintendo DS is rated "EC" for early childhood. Recognizing the significance of the adult female gaming audience, game makers such as Nintendo are including more women on its development teams. Recently, it has found success in attracting women to its popular *Animal Crossing: New Leaf game*.[22] These are examples of how demographic segmentation can affect everything from product development to promotion.

# 9-5    PSYCHOGRAPHIC SEGMENTATION

**LO 9.5** Contrast psychographic segmentation with other segmentation variables.

## OPENING EXAMPLE

In today's fragmented media market, consumers have a range of options for programming, from traditional network television, cable, satellite, and streaming services such as Netflix. Many programs rely on advertising revenue to fund the development and ongoing cost of production. For example, an advertiser pays $485,000 for a 30-second spot during Thursday night football and $272,000 for a 30-second ad on NBCs break-out drama *This Is Us*.[23] Who's watching these shows and how can producers convince companies to advertise to their viewers? While demographic segmentation is an important tool for targeting customers, marketers increasingly use psychographic segmentation to make these decisions.

### 9-5a
## LEARNING IT: PSYCHOGRAPHIC SEGMENTATION

Marketers traditionally referred to geographic and demographic characteristics as the primary bases for dividing consumers into market segments. Still, they have long recognized the need for fuller, more lifelike portraits of consumers in developing their marketing programs. As a result, psychographic segmentation became a useful tool for gaining sharper insight into consumer purchasing behavior. **Psychographic segmentation** is defined as differentiating population groups according to values and lifestyle factors which are common to the group. Consumer lifestyles include attitudes, values, social activities, media usage habits, and more.

The most common method for developing psychographic profiles of a population is to conduct a large-scale survey asking consumers to agree or disagree with a collection of statements describing various activities, interests, and opinions. The resulting data allow researchers to develop lifestyle profiles that help guide all aspects of the marketing mix. Based upon the survey responses, marketers can then develop a separate marketing strategy that closely fits the psychographic makeup of particular lifestyle segments.

For example, researchers from the *Pew Research Center* utilized a telephone survey of adults across the United States to obtain information about their book reading habits.[24] Respondents were asked about their frequency of reading books as well as the medium—print, digital, or audio. Interestingly, the research found that 73% of respondents had read a book in the last 12 months with the following breakdown by book format:

- 38% read only print books.
- 28% read both print and digital books.
- 6% read only digital books.

The research also noted some changes in consumer habits regarding devices used to read digital books, with 15% using a tablet computer, 13% accessing a book with their smartphone, and 11% using a desktop or laptop computer. In addition, 8% used a dedicated e-reader device such as a Kindle or Nook when reading books. This insight is helpful to companies such as Amazon and Barnes & Noble, as well as publishing companies who seek to generate revenue through sales of books. Understanding consumer habits and preferences enables marketers to make good decisions regarding book formats, pricing, and promotion activities.

Psychographic segmentation is a good supplement to demographic and geographic segmentation.

**psychographic segmentation** differentiating population groups according to values and lifestyle factors which are common to the group

Two of the 66 market segments defined by PRIZM that segments households by demographics, consumer lifestyle behavior, media usage, and more.

Source: segmentationsolutions.nielsen.com

*Using Psychographics—Example:* If BMW had data indicating that households with incomes over $200,000 were most likely to buy, this would represent a demographic variable. As a result, they could layer on geographic segmentation by identifying the zip codes in the United States with the highest concentration of these households. This doesn't necessarily help BMW design a promotional campaign. However, a psychographic profile might indicate that these households more likely subscribe to *Wall Street Journal*, shop at Whole Foods, and watch *The Voice*. This additional psychographic information would help BMW know where to run ads and what to say in those ads.

Marketers may also utilize PRIZM, an industry-leading segmentation service that blends research on demographics, consumer lifestyle behavior, media usage, and shopping habits to divide every U.S. household in terms of 66 segments.[25] PRIZM data can help marketers plan new products, select distribution channels, and create advertising campaigns targeted to the segments most likely to purchase their product.

### 9-5b
## CLOSING EXAMPLE

Activities, such as the shows people watch and their social media habits, provide insight that helps advertisers make spending decisions. Advertisers pay approximately $470,000 for a 30-second spot during *The Walking Dead*[26] and, according to Nielsen data, close to 17 million tuned into the 7th season opener. During the show's airing, sponsors included Emirates airlines featuring Jennifer Aniston, Lincoln Motor Company featuring Matthew McConaughey, T-Mobile, and Verizon.[27] The decisions to run ads during this particular show, with these particular celebrities, is a direct result of research into the psychographics of these viewers.

# 9-6
# BEHAVIORAL SEGMENTATION

**LO 9.6** Describe the three forms of behavioral segmentation.

### OPENING EXAMPLE

The beverage industry is highly competitive, giving consumers the ability to choose from many brands offering a variety of products. This includes bottled water, sports and energy drinks, and carbonated beverages. The range of choices available can make market segmentation difficult because these drinks can appeal to such a wide range of consumers. You might be just as likely to see someone drinking a Coke in the city as in the country. While it's not uncommon to see a college student drinking a Monster Energy Drink, it's also not surprising to see a middle-aged construction worker drinking one too. And bottled water seems to be enjoyed by people with just about any psychographic profile. Should beverage makers then abandon the idea of segmenting their markets when building marketing mixes?

## 9-6a

# LEARNING IT: BEHAVIORAL SEGMENTATION

The methods for market segmentation discussed previously—geographic, demographic, and psychographic—form an important basis for identifying target customers who will be the focus of a marketing mix. However, as critical as these methods are, they are somewhat indirect. For instance, just because someone has a higher income doesn't necessarily mean they will be interested in luxury clothing. Or just because someone lives in rural America doesn't mean they enjoy hunting. Fortunately, there is another method for market segmentation that is more direct and based on actual consumer behavior.

**Behavior segmentation** is beneficial to marketers because:

- They can focus marketing efforts based on demonstrated behavior of actual users
- They can use those behaviors to group or classify individuals who may exhibit similar behavior

Exhibit 9.5 summarizes the three primary forms of behavioral segmentation.

**behavior segmentation** groups individuals who exhibit similar behaviors, such as benefits sought, usage rates, and level of brand loyalty

**EXHIBIT 9.5**  Forms of Behavioral Segmentation

| Forms of Behavioral Segmentation | Description | Examples |
|---|---|---|
| Benefits sought | Focuses on the attributes consumers seek and benefits they expect to receive from a good or service.<br><br>This knowledge allows marketers to focus on reinforcing those core benefits in new and existing products, and communicating those benefits in their promotional campaigns. | • Starbucks customers are willing to pay extra to savor a pleasant experience and feel pampered and appreciated.<br>• Women who prefer working out at Curves may prefer a female-only environment that eliminates unwanted male attention. |
| Usage rates | Segments can be classified based upon the amount of product purchased.<br><br>Segments might be classified as heavy, moderate, and light users.<br><br>Often, a small group of heavy users can account for a large portion of consumption for a product. | • Those who use Facebook can be classified as heavy, medium, and light users. Heavy users spend an average of 44 minutes per day compared to 17 minutes for medium users and 5 minutes for light users.[28] |
| Brand loyalty | Segments can be classified according to the strength of brand loyalty a consumer feels toward a product.<br><br>Companies can target brand loyal customers when launching new products or entering new categories, since those customers may represent the most likely early adopters of those new products. | • American Airlines offers a frequent flyer program to encourage loyalty and reward those who accrue miles with free or discounted travel.<br>• Disney utilized brand loyalty when branching into new markets, such as Adventures by Disney, Disney Cruise Lines, and even a Disney hotel in Hawaii called Aulani. |

## 9-6b
## CLOSING EXAMPLE

Market segmentation will always be important for beverage manufacturers, even though ready-to-drink beverages are consumed by such a wide and varied cross section of consumers. Brands are able to use behavioral-based segmentation to guide their marketing decisions.

The functional beverage market, which includes energy and sports beverages, continues to grow as consumers seek healthier drink options. Skinnygirl now offers Protein Tasty Nutrition Shakes targeted to women who want to maintain a healthy weight and reduce calorie consumption by feeling full. By knowing the benefits consumers seek from its products, Skinnygirl can promote how consumption of the 80 calorie, zero sugar product helps customers achieve their nutrition goals.

Traditional soft drink companies such as Coca-Cola and PepsiCo might utilize usage rates to promote their brands since it's likely that consumption can be differentiated among light and heavy users. For example, a recent study conducted in Colorado found that 7.5% of high school students consumed no "sugary drinks"—defined as soda, sports and energy drinks, and other sugar-sweetened drinks—compared to 11% who drank them four times daily and 30% who consumed at least one per day.[29]

These behavioral market segmentation tactics are a valuable addition to geographic, demographic, and psychographic methods when designing marketing mixes.

# 9-7 STRATEGIES FOR REACHING TARGET MARKETS

**LO 9.7** Distinguish between the three basic strategies for reaching target markets.

## OPENING EXAMPLE

The travel industry has changed significantly due to the Internet. Now, consumers can access information, compare prices, and purchase airfares, hotel rooms, and cruises without using a travel agent. However, this change has created additional challenges for travel and leisure providers who wish to attract customers. Without travel agents as their primary conduit to target customers, these companies must reach the desired markets directly. But not every company will choose the same strategy for doing so, nor should they.

## 9-7a
## LEARNING IT: STRATEGIES FOR REACHING TARGET MARKETS

Marketers spend a lot of time and effort developing strategies that best match their firm's product offerings to the needs of particular target markets. An appropriate match is vital to success. Marketers typically choose among three basic strategies to effectively reach target markets (see Exhibit 9.6).

**EXHIBIT 9.6**    Three Strategies for Reaching Target Markets

| Strategy | Description | Example | Advantages | Disadvantages |
|---|---|---|---|---|
| **Undifferentiated marketing** | All customers are targeted using a single marketing mix; also called **mass marketing**. | Red Bull is sold in the same format, with the same branding, worldwide. | • Provides production efficiencies<br>• Focuses on similarities in needs or desired benefits versus dissimilarities | • Vulnerable to competitors who offer specialized alternatives to targeted segments |
| **Differentiated marketing** | Several different market segments are targeted using a different marketing mix for each segment. | Nike offers specialized shoes for athletes pursuing various sports (e.g., basketball, running, tennis, golf, soccer). | • Increased customer satisfaction<br>• Potentially higher overall revenue | • Higher production and promotion costs<br>• Inventory costs may increase |
| **Concentrated marketing** | A single market segment is selected and the firm concentrates its efforts on profitably satisfying that segment; also called **niche marketing**.<br><br>Potential customers may be targeted at very narrow, basic levels such as by ZIP code, specific occupation, lifestyle, or behavior. | Tesla's Model S sport sedan offers high performance and energy efficiency to an upscale target market.<br><br>Amazon makes product recommendations to shoppers based on past purchase history and/or the products they are viewing. | • Potential competitive advantage over firms trying to reach multiple markets<br>• Increases efficiency of marketing mix, especially promotion | • Chosen segments may not produce sufficient revenue to be profitable<br>• New competition within targeted segment can greatly impact revenue |

## 9-7b
# CLOSING EXAMPLE

Travel and leisure service providers may utilize different strategies to reach their desired target markets depending on their business goals and characteristics of the market. Southwest Airlines might implement a mass marketing approach to capture the broader market for air travelers. An upscale airline, such as Emirates, may utilize a differentiated marketing approach to target discriminating travelers who appreciate enhanced luxury. This could include traveling business executives or high-income recreational travelers. Emirates offers business and first-class customers services such as limo rides to the airport, spa and beauty treatments in its signature lounges, and gourmet meals on flights. A company such as NetJets utilizes concentrated marketing by targeting a small, specialized segment of high-income travelers who want to avoid traditional airline flights altogether. Flyers on NetJets can arrive at a special tarmac and walk right on to their private jet.

**undifferentiated marketing (mass marketing)** when all customers are targeted using a single marketing mix

**differentiated marketing** targeting several different market segments using a different marketing mix for each segment

**concentrated marketing (niche marketing)** selecting a single market segment and concentrating efforts on profitably satisfying that segment

# 9-8 POSITIONING STRATEGIES AND VALUE PROPOSITIONS

**LO 9.8** Explain how marketers build value propositions utilizing positioning strategies.

## OPENING EXAMPLE

Core Natural Water was recently developed by producer and songwriter Dr. Luke (Lukasz Gottwald) in partnership with Lance Collins, creator of Fuze and NOS Energy Drink. Core Natural Water is a new entrant in the functional water category which provides vitamins and minerals to help consumers stay hydrated. Core Natural Water has signed Katy Perry, Diplo, and Becky G as music brand ambassadors and investors. But in this crowded market, Core Natural Water must be crystal clear about its value proposition, or they risk getting lost in a sea of competitors.[30]

### 9-8a

## LEARNING IT: POSITIONING STRATEGIES AND VALUE PROPOSITIONS

Once firms have selected their target markets, they must decide how best to position the product. The concept of **positioning** seeks to put a product in a certain position, or place, in the minds of prospective buyers. Marketers use a positioning strategy to distinguish their firm's offerings from those of competitors, and to develop communications that create the desired position within the customer's mind. This can create a stronger relationship with the target audience, which should result in improved sales, customer satisfaction, and loyalty.

To position a product, firms must clearly articulate their **value proposition**, an explanation of how consumers will benefit from the product and why the company is uniquely qualified to provide those benefits.[31]

Marketers utilize a number of strategies to define their value proposition and position themselves in the market (see Exhibit 9.7).

A value proposition can represent one or a combination of the above positioning strategies. Regardless of the chosen positioning strategy, marketers want to emphasize a product's unique advantages and differentiate it from competitors. A **positioning map** provides a valuable tool for helping managers position products by graphically illustrating consumers' perceptions of competing products within an industry. Marketers can create a competitive positioning map from information solicited from consumers or from their accumulated knowledge about a market. A positioning map usually presents two different characteristics important for a product category and shows how consumers view a product and its major competitors based on these characteristics. Exhibit 9.8 shows how a positioning map might look for selected retailers using the characteristics of price and perceived quality.

A positioning map can help companies identify market positions that are crowded with competitors and should be avoided. They can also help identify market positions that are relatively unchallenged. Upstart search engine

**positioning** seeks to put a product in a certain position, or place, in the minds of prospective buyers

**value proposition** an explanation of how consumers will benefit from the product and why the company is uniquely qualified to provide those benefits

**positioning map** a graphical illustration of consumers' perceptions of competing products within an industry

**EXHIBIT 9.7**    Four Positioning Strategies

| Positioning Strategy | Description | Example |
|---|---|---|
| **Value** | Value represents what the customer receives in exchange for the costs of the product. Value positioning does not require the lowest price, but rather that customers believe the purchase was "worth it." | • Nordstrom's offers top brands, specialized shopping services, and an upscale store ambiance, all at higher prices.<br>• TJ Maxx promotes lesser-known brands in a self-service, no-frills store atmosphere, all at lower prices. |
| **Product attributes** | Specific product attributes or features are highlighted to create the desired perception of the brand or consistency with the buyer's self-concept. | • Cutco emphasizes its lifetime guarantee, riveted construction, double-D blade design, and dishwasher safe attributes to market their premium knives, with an average price of $100 each. |
| **Competitive** | Focus on product or company attribute, but specifically in relation to the competition. | • Verizon commercials present direct comparisons of their data speed and coverage compared to AT&T Wireless and T-Mobile. |
| **Product use or application** | Specifically associate a product with a particular use or application. | • Benadryl is positioned as an anti-allergy medicine, but Unisom—which typically utilizes the same primary ingredient as Benadryl—is positioned as a sleep aid. |

DuckDuckGo surpassed 10 billion searches in 2016. Their value proposition revolves around privacy, with the tagline "smarter search without tracking." Due to increasing concerns about how Google, Yahoo, and Bing collect and use customer data, DuckDuckGo was able to stake out a relatively untouched position in the search engine market.[32]

## 9-8b
## CLOSING EXAMPLE

Dr. Luke believes Core Natural Water is superior to competing brands due to its ability to "help health conscious consumers discover a better way to hydrate through Core's 'Perfect PH' water." Core might direct attention to the specific attributes of the product and how the pH level provides benefits to consumers. According to Lance Collins, "The optimal pH range for our bodies is between 7.35 and 7.45. Only when our body's pH level is within this range can we effectively absorb the vitamins and minerals we need to survive. Since water accounts for up to 75% of the body, it's easy to see why the water we drink greatly impacts the pH of the body."[33] Dr. Luke could also employ a competitive positioning strategy to differentiate Core from Aquafina and Vitamin Water, who don't actively target the PH levels of their product.

**EXHIBIT 9.8**

**Hypothetical Positioning Map for Selected Retailers**

# 9-9 CLASSIFYING SEGMENTATION VARIABLES

**LO 9.9** Given a target market profile, classify each variable according to its base of segmentation.

## OPENING EXAMPLE

REI Adventures is interested in promoting their tours more widely and attracting additional customers to its travel services. Since not everyone is a good target audience, it must precisely target the most receptive audience so money isn't wasted on ads that don't convert. Luckily REI Adventures has a secret weapon, an existing database of customers who have shopped at REI stores and provided their e-mail address. REI can first promote to this list, but that might not yield enough potential customers. REI needs a way to find customers just like the ones who shop at their stores. How can they efficiently find these potential customers?

## 9-9a
## LEARNING IT: CLASSIFYING SEGMENTATION VARIABLES

By using market segmentation, REI is able to run sponsored posts to a highly targeted "lookalike audience" of prospects who share several commonalities with REI's existing customers.

Marketers have lots of choices for segmenting markets to identify a target audience. The four primary segmentation bases are geographic, demographic, psychographic, and behavioral. All four bases can be utilized in combination to create a more complete customer profile and enable marketers to effectively communicate their value proposition.

With advances in technology and increased use of social media, the ability for companies to use market segmentation variables to reach new customers is easier than ever. Advertisers who have an e-mail list or Facebook business page can utilize information about their existing customers to pursue new "lookalike audiences" just like them. Facebook scans the user profiles of a company's existing customers or fans to find commonalities in their geography, age, gender, education, interests, behaviors, and more. This analysis is based on information users have put in their profile, pages they have liked, and the types of content they interact with the most.

Once Facebook has determined the commonalities among the existing customers and fans of the advertiser, a "lookalike audience" can be created to match the profile of that audience. This provides the advertiser with a potentially huge list of highly targeted prospects who match the most important characteristics of their existing audience.

**REI** ✔
September 22, 2015

Autumn officially begins tomorrow but it's not too early to plan for a winter getaway! Let REI Adventures help you ring in the New Year outside at Zion National Park and Bryce Canyon National Park: http://bit.ly/1FdxanL

👍 1.3K                    37 Comments  66 Shares

👍 Like        💬 Comment        ➤ Share

Source: Facebook

**EXHIBIT 9.9** Example Information from Facebook Profiles of REI Customers

| Jane | Sarah | Tiffany |
| --- | --- | --- |
| • 33 years old (demographic) | • 60 years old (demographic) | • 48 years old (demographic) |
| • Graduated from UCLA (demographic) | • Graduated from Baylor University (demographic) | • Graduated from New York University (demographic) |
| • Lives in Los Angeles area (geographic) | • Lives in Dallas area (geography) | • Lives in Connecticut (geography) |
| • Likes hiking groups on Facebook (psychographic) | • Posts biking and running workouts (psychographic) | • Likes yoga studios on Facebook (psychographic) |
| • Clicks on sponsored advertisements from outdoor sporting goods/apparel retailers (behavioral) | • Clicks on sponsored advertisements from outdoor sporting goods/apparel retailers (behavioral) | • Clicks on sponsored advertisements from outdoor sporting goods/apparel retailers (behavioral) |

For instance, assume that REI Adventures is interested in promoting its five-day Zion and Bryce Canyon women's hiking trip, which includes the scenic trails of Angels Landing and the Navajo Loop. Spacious tents, cots, nutritious meals, guided yoga sessions, and private transportation are all included in the tour price. Since the adventure is for women only, REI's first step is to upload their e-mail list of several hundred thousand women customers so that Facebook can identify the user profiles. The Facebook algorithm would search for commonalities among the users. Exhibit 9.9 provides an example of three such user profiles. Notice that although the age, occupation, and location of these three profiles are different, they share some commonalities such as college degree, active lifestyle, and interest in purchasing outdoor sporting goods/apparel from retailers.

Facebook then searches for other users that share these common segmentation variables. In our example, they find a lookalike audience of an additional 300,000 women. This provides a robust sample of brand new, prospective customers who will likely be interested in a sponsored post from REI about the adventure vacation to Zion and Bryce Canyon. By running sponsored posts only to this lookalike audience, REI Adventures is able to execute a highly targeted and efficient ad campaign, and sell out their trip.

## 9-10   LEARN IT TODAY . . . USE IT TOMORROW

REI would like your help identifying the segmentation bases of its typical online shopper based on user profiles of those who "like" it on Facebook. REI is interested in increasing the number of customers who purchase products from REI's website by running ads to a "lookalike audience" that has similar characteristics to REI's existing Facebook followers. The first step in finding commonalities among existing followers is to categorize their traits by various bases of segmentation.

It's time to get hands-on and apply what you've learned. **See MindTap for an activity related to REI's marketing activities.**

# Chapter Summary

**LO 9.1 Describe the two primary market classifications.**

Consumer products are bought by ultimate consumers for personal use. Business products are purchased for use either directly or indirectly in the production of other goods and services for resale.

**LO 9.2 Summarize the three components necessary for effective market segmentation.**

The three criteria for effective segmentation are that the segment should be significant in size and purchasing power, profitable, and consistent with the firm's marketing capabilities.

**LO 9.3 Describe four types of geographic segmentation.**

Marketers have long practiced geographic segmentation—dividing an overall market into homogeneous groups based on their locations. Four types of geographic segmentation are market size, market density, climate, and region.

**LO 9.4 Summarize the five most commonly used demographic variables.**

The most common method of market segmentation—demographic segmentation—defines consumer groups according to demographic variables such as gender, age, ethnic group, family lifecycle stage and household type, and income.

**LO 9.5 Contrast psychographic segmentation with other segmentation variables.**

Psychographic segmentation is defined as differentiating population groups according to values and lifestyle factors which are common to the group.

**LO 9.6 Describe the three forms of behavioral segmentation.**

Segmentation based upon how consumers behave with respect to a product may also enable marketers to group or classify individuals who exhibit similar behavior. Three forms of behavioral segmentation are segmentation by benefits sought, usage rates, and brand loyalty.

**LO 9.7 Distinguish between the three basic strategies for reaching target markets.**

Marketers spend a lot of time and effort developing strategies that best match their firm's product offerings to the needs of particular target markets. An appropriate match is vital to the firm's marketing success. Marketers have identified three basic strategies to effectively reach target markets: undifferentiated marketing, differentiated marketing, and concentrated marketing.

**LO 9.8 Explain how marketers build value propositions utilizing positioning strategies.**

Once firms have selected a target market, marketers must then decide how best to position the product. The concept of positioning seeks to put a product in a certain position, or place, in the minds of prospective buyers.

**LO 9.9 Given a target market profile, classify each variable according to its base of segmentation.**

The four primary segmentation bases are geographic, demographic, psychographic, and behavioral. All four bases can be utilized in combination to create a more complete customer profile and enable marketers to effectively communicate their value proposition.

# Key Terms

market **173**
consumer products **173**
business products **173**
target market **175**
market segmentation **175**
geographic segmentation **177**
market size **177**

market density **178**
demographic segmentation **180**
psychographic segmentation **183**
behavioral segmentation **185**
undifferentiated marketing
  (mass marketing) **187**
differentiated marketing **187**

concentrated marketing (niche
  marketing) **187**
positioning **188**
value proposition **188**
positioning map **188**

# 10 MARKETING RESEARCH

Kaspars Grinvalds/Shutterstock.com

## LEARNING OBJECTIVES

**10.1** Describe the six steps in the marketing research process.

**10.2** Summarize the four sources of secondary marketing research data.

**10.3** Compare the three principal methods of collecting primary marketing research data.

**10.4** Outline four considerations for conducting marketing research in global markets.

**10.5** Summarize how technology is used to assist collection and analysis of marketing research data.

**10.6** Given a list of marketing research data from various sources, classify as either primary or secondary data.

# LEARN IT TODAY . . . USE IT TOMORROW

Netflix used to be the company that mailed you DVDs of movies in little red envelopes. Now it's a streaming entertainment company that's earned multiple Emmy nominations for three original series that never aired on broadcast television.

With a $6 billion budget for content,[1] 10% of which is reserved for original programming, Netflix has the potential to transform the way consumers view entertainment—and the way companies produce and provide it. The proof? The company knew "House of Cards," its streamed political drama, would be a hit even before audiences had seen it.

Netflix has inked profitable new deals with television networks that let subscribers stream broadcast favorites such as "Breaking Bad" one season after broadcast, instead of the traditional four years. Its enthusiastic plunge into original programming has brought the company's masterful command of big data the most attention. Netflix has made expert use of its huge and complex database, which steadily captures the likes, dislikes, habits, searches, and preferences of its more than 80 million streaming customers worldwide.[2] It then translates that data into closely guarded algorithms. That's how the company knew political dramas such as "House of Cards" would be successful.

U.S. viewers now watch more movies online than on Blu-Ray discs or DVDs. This format shift seems likely to give Netflix more market power and strengthen the reliability of its unparalleled database and algorithms. Some worry that traditional TV ratings have become irrelevant. Netflix can already claim that its recommendations make up 60% of what streaming subscribers opt to watch, and that this kind of influence will allow it to greatly reduce its marketing costs and develop better-targeted programming.[3]

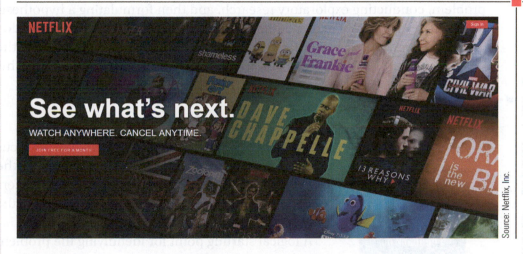

American entertainment company Netflix streams thousands of movies and shows on demand to subscribers. Netflix's ability to analyze viewing habits of subscribers gives them a competitive advantage in the industry.

Source: Netflix, Inc.

## 10-1  THE MARKETING RESEARCH PROCESS

### OPENING EXAMPLE

In 2007, Lego embarked on a four-year global market research effort. The company had bounced back from near bankruptcy just a few years earlier and was now looking to refocus on the core business of creating Lego construction sets.

Conducting market research would provide the company with the information needed to influence future product decisions. Let's take a look at the marketing research process and see how Lego utilized the steps.

## 10-1a

# LEARNING IT: THE MARKETING RESEARCH PROCESS

Collecting and managing information about what customers need and want is a challenging task for any marketer. **Marketing research** is the process of collecting and using information for marketing decision making. Research data comes from a variety of sources, such as:

- Well-planned studies designed to elicit specific information
- Sales force reports, accounting records, and published reports
- Controlled experiments and computer simulations

Businesses rely on marketing research to provide the information they need to make effective decisions. The chances of making good decisions improve when the right information is provided at the right time during decision making. Marketing researchers follow a six-step process. They begin by defining the problem, conducting exploratory research, and then formulating a hypothesis to be tested. Next, they create a design for the research study and collect needed data. Finally, researchers interpret and present the research information. Exhibit 10.1 summarizes this process.

## DEFINE THE PROBLEM

A well-defined problem permits researchers to focus on securing the exact information needed for the solution. Clearly defining the question that researchers need to answer increases the speed and accuracy of the research process.

A logical starting point for identifying the problem might be to evaluate the firm's target market and marketing mix elements. Suppose, for example, a firm has recently changed its promotional strategies. Research might then seek to answer the question, "Is our new promotional campaign more or less effective than previous campaigns?" The firm's marketers might also look at possible environmental changes. Perhaps a new competitor entered the firm's market. Decision makers will need information to help answer the question, "What must we do to distinguish our company from the new competitor?"

Researchers at Lego started their marketing research process with the question, "Who buys Legos?"

**marketing research** the process of collecting and using information for marketing and decision making

**EXHIBIT 10.1**

**The Marketing Research Process**

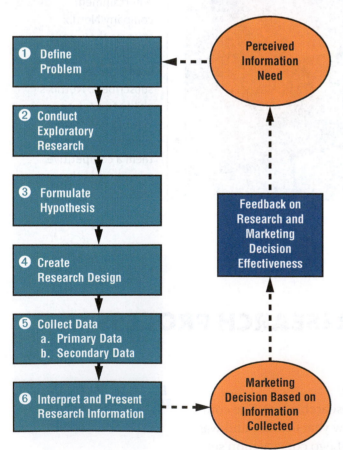

They discovered that, in the United States, around 90% of Legos were purchased for boys.[4] Lego previously tried marketing products to girls, but found little success. Recognizing that there was a huge market of young girls who were not playing with Legos, researchers refined their research question to, "Why aren't girls playing with Legos?"

## CONDUCT EXPLORATORY RESEARCH

Once a firm has defined the question it wants to answer, researchers can begin **exploratory research**. Exploratory research seeks to discover the cause of a specific problem by discussing the problem with informed sources both inside and outside the firm, and by examining data from other information sources. Marketers at Lego may choose to talk with customers and retailers to gather some preliminary information. Researchers may also seek information from overall market data, as Lego did. Exploratory research can include an evaluation of company records, such as sales and profit analyses, and available competitive data. This initial research is the basis for the next step in the process.

**exploratory research** seeks to discover the cause of a specific problem by discussing the problem with informed sources both inside and outside the firm, and by examining data from other information sources

## FORMULATE A HYPOTHESIS

After defining the problem and conducting exploratory research, the marketer needs to formulate a **hypothesis**—a tentative explanation for some specific event. A hypothesis is a testable statement about the relationship among variables. It sets the stage for more in-depth research by further clarifying what researchers need to test. For example, Lego may notice that a larger percentage of Lego "Classic" sets were purchased for girls than the percentage of Lego Star Wars™ or Lego NINJAGO™ sets. Lego might hypothesize that this is due to Lego Classic sets being more gender-neutral. To test its hypothesis, Lego may interview girls on the types of Lego sets they would like to play with and why.

**hypothesis** a testable statement about the relationship among variables

Not all studies test specific hypotheses. However, a carefully designed study can benefit from the rigor introduced by developing a hypothesis before beginning data collection and analysis.

## CREATE A RESEARCH DESIGN

To test hypotheses and find solutions to marketing problems, a marketer creates a **research design**- a master plan for conducting marketing research. This includes defining the types of research to be utilized and the selection of respondents. The goal of this step is to ensure the research will measure what it's intended to measure. Poorly designed research plans can yield misleading or inaccurate results, and waste valuable resources.

**research design** a master plan for conducting marketing research

The Lego Foundation is the largest global sponsor of play research and helps Lego gather accurate, first-hand data about its customers.[5] In this anthropology-like research approach, Lego observes children playing in their natural habitat. Beyond playing with Legos, researchers can see how children play with a variety of toys, which can give researchers better insight into their overall play patterns. The decision to use direct observation, in addition to other types of data collection, is one of the decisions Lego made during the research design portion of its marketing research process.

## COLLECT DATA

**secondary data** information from previously published or compiled sources

**primary data** information collected for the first time specifically for a marketing research study

Marketing researchers gather data that can be classified as secondary or primary. **Secondary data** is information from previously published or compiled sources. Census data is an example. **Primary data** refers to the information collected for the first time specifically for a marketing research study. An example of primary data is statistics collected from a survey that asks current customers about their preferences for product improvements.

Secondary data offers two important advantages:

- It's almost always less expensive to gather than primary data
- Researchers usually spend less time to locate and use secondary data

A research study that requires primary data may take several months to complete, while a researcher often can gather secondary data in a matter of days, or even hours.

However, secondary data has limitations that primary data does not. First, unless updated regularly, published information becomes obsolete. A marketer analyzing the population of various areas may discover that even the most recent census figures are already out of date because of rapid growth and changing demographics. Second, published data collected for an unrelated purpose may not be completely relevant to the marketer's specific needs. For example, census data does not reveal the brand preferences of consumers.

Although research to gather primary data can cost more and take longer, the results can provide richer, more detailed information than secondary data offers. The choice between secondary and primary data is tied to cost, applicability, and effectiveness. Many marketing research projects combine secondary and primary data to fully answer marketing questions. This chapter examines specific methods for collecting both secondary and primary data in later sections.

Initially, Lego was able to collect secondary data through sales information which led to the discovery of the gender gap in Lego purchases. Lego then set out to gather primary data through observation, focus groups, and interviews with 4,500 girls and their mothers.[6]

## INTERPRET AND PRESENT RESEARCH DATA

The final step in the marketing research process is to interpret the findings and present them to decision makers in a format that allows them to make effective judgments. Possible differences in interpretations of research results may occur between marketing researchers and their audiences due to differing backgrounds, levels of knowledge, and experience. Both oral and written reports should be presented in a manner designed to minimize such misinterpretations.

Through the market research process, Lego was able to gather data that, when analyzed, revealed some interesting findings. Lego discovered that while girls liked to build Lego sets, they didn't build them the same way that boys did. Girls preferred to build in smaller chunks, tell stories, and rearrange along the way.[7] Girls also responded to Lego minifigures much differently than boys. Boys often played with minifigures in the third person, while girls played with minifigures as avatars—as a representation of themselves in the Lego set. After interpreting and analyzing the data, Lego was able to use it to update its product development plans and its promotional messaging.

## 10-1b
## CLOSING EXAMPLE

In 2012, Lego introduced Lego Friends, a new product line designed just for girls. The Friends line features five main characters, each with their own name and backstory. The mini doll figures are more detailed than the traditional Lego minifigures. Lego Friends feature pastel bricks and building sets include a hair salon, puppy daycare, and party shop. Lego has grown an average of 15% annually since launching the Friends line and the "Girls Building Sets" category experienced double-digit growth.[8]

By following the marketing research process, Lego was able to conduct effective research which influenced product decisions. Understanding how girls play led to the development of Lego Friends brick sets, which has expanded to include online games and activities, and a Netflix original cartoon series.

After several failed attempts to produce brick sets targeted directly to girls, Lego finally found success with Lego Friends.

defotoberg/Shutterstock.com

# 10-2

# SECONDARY DATA COLLECTION

**LO
10.2**   Summarize the four sources of secondary marketing research data.

## OPENING EXAMPLE

Sean Morgan, owner of Fit Body Gym, meets with his director of marketing to discuss two new locations that he wants to open.

"Jen, I have a few specific cities in mind for the new gyms," Sean says. "But we need to make sure the right demographic lives there—a young, active population with disposable income. We have a limited budget to work with, can we afford surveys or focus groups?"

"We don't need to do surveys," Jen replies. "The information we need is already available."

"What do you mean?" Sean asks.

"We can use secondary data. It's information that is previously published from other sources. The best part is it won't cost as much as focus groups or surveys. And I can get started right away!"

What type of secondary data do you think Jen should use?

## 10-2a

## LEARNING IT: SECONDARY DATA COLLECTION

Secondary data is the information from previously published or compiled sources, and comes from many sources. The overwhelming quantity of secondary data available at little or no cost challenges researchers to select only data relevant to the question being researched. There are four main sources of secondary data, the first is internal to the company while the others are external.

## INTERNAL DATA

Internal data includes sales records, product performance reviews, website analytics, and marketing reports. Marketers can find valuable data in their firm's own internal records. Marketers analyze sales performance records to gain an overall view of company efficiency and to find clues to potential problems. Sales analysis is one of the least expensive and most important sources of marketing information available to a firm. Accounting data—information from a firm's financial statements—and marketing cost analysis are also good sources of internal information.

While internal data is valuable, it's usually too limited in scope to provide a full picture of most research questions. For marketers at Fit Body Gym, the company's internal data about membership totals and profitability of existing gyms won't help them answer their key research question, "where should we open our next locations?" Fortunately, vast amount of data are available outside the company from three main sources.

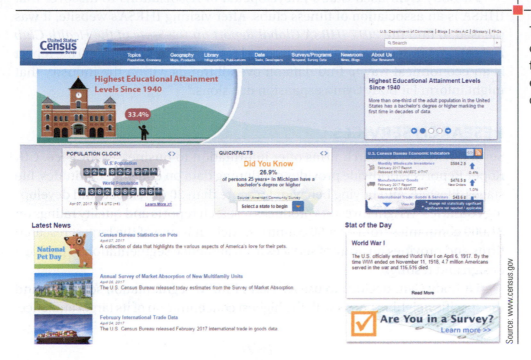

The census.gov website can be a valuable resource for marketers searching for economic and demographic data.

Source: www.census.gov

## GOVERNMENT DATA

The U.S. government is a leading source of marketing data. Conducting a periodic census of housing, population, business, manufacturing, agriculture, minerals, and governments, the U.S. Census Bureau provides the most frequently used government statistics. The Census Bureau also conducts a census of population every 10 years, which contains a wealth of valuable information for marketers. It breaks down the U.S. population of more than 320 million people by very small geographic areas, making it possible to determine population traits by city block or census tract in large cities. It also divides the populations of nonmetropolitan areas into census tracts, which are important for marketing analysis because they highlight small groups of about 1,500 to 8,000 people with similar traits.

Marketers, such as local retailers and shopping center developers, can readily access census data to gather vital information about customers in an immediate neighborhood without spending time or money to conduct comprehensive surveys.

Fit Body Gym was able to visit census.gov to research the possible expansion cities for data on population size, age, incomes, and more.

## INDUSTRY PUBLICATIONS

A trade association, an organization of businesses who operate within an industry, may be an excellent source of data. Gale's Encyclopedia of Associations, available online and in many libraries, can help marketers track down trade associations specific to the industry they are researching. Business and trade magazines often publish a wide range of valuable data. For example, the advertising industry continuously collects data on audiences reached by various media.

Fit Body Gym used Gale's Encyclopedia of Associations to discover that IHRSA is an association of fitness clubs. After visiting IHRSA's website, it was pleased to find the *2017 IHRSA Global Report on the State of the Health Club Industry*. While it doesn't provide city-level research, at less than $200 the report is an economical way to find data on overall trends within the industry that might inform Fit Body Gym's expansion decisions.[9]

### RESEARCH SERVICES

Several national research firms offer information to businesses for a fee. GfK Roper Reports Worldwide provides continuing data on consumer attitudes, life stages, lifestyle, and buying behavior for more than 30 developed and developing countries. Wright Investors produces research reports and quality ratings on 31,000 companies from over 60 countries. Nielsen is one of the largest research firms and provides an array of services from audience segmentation to package design and testing.

Fit Body Gym decided to use Nielsen's PRIZM segmentation service to find the specific neighborhoods with the highest concentration of its target audience.

## 10-2b
## CLOSING EXAMPLE

Marketers, such as Jen at Fit Body Gym, can utilize secondary data to gather information quickly and inexpensively. The information that Fit Body Gym is looking for can be easily obtained from census data, industry publications, or a research service. While the census data can provide marketers information such as population, age, and income, a research service can provide information on lifestyle and buying behavior. Using the PRIZM segmentation data, Jen made an important find; the two cities Fit Body Gym was targeting for expansion didn't actually have a high concentration of their target audience. Fortunately, the company found two other cities that are an even better fit and began making plans to open at least three new gyms in each city. Gathering this data using primary research methods would have taken months and cost tens of thousands of dollars. But using secondary data took only a few days and cost a small fraction of that.

# PRIMARY RESEARCH METHODS

**LO 10.3** Compare the three principal methods of collecting primary marketing research data.

### OPENING EXAMPLE

For many new parents, sleep is a precious commodity—for baby and themselves. Johnson & Johnson, a trusted provider of baby-related products, conducted research to determine if it could identify patterns that led to better sleep. Researchers recognized that secondary data would not provide the information needed, so they set out to collect primary data. Over 400 mothers and young children, who had been identified as having sleep problems ranging from small to severe, participated in the study, which included a survey and completion of a daily sleep diary.[10] Data collected from the primary research indicated that babies did, in fact, benefit from a nightly bedtime routine.

How do you think Johnson & Johnson could use this information in its marketing efforts and product decisions?

## 10-3a
# LEARNING IT: PRIMARY RESEARCH METHODS

Primary data refers to information collected for the first time specifically for a marketing research study. Marketers use a variety of methods to conduct primary research, such as observation, survey, and test marketing. The choice of methods depends on the issues under study and the decisions marketers need to make. In some cases, researchers use a combination of methods.

## OBSERVATION

Marketers trying to understand how consumers behave in certain situations find observation a useful technique. In observational studies, researchers view the overt actions of the subjects they're studying. Examples of observation include:

- Counting the number of cars passing by a potential site for a restaurant
- Tracking foot traffic patterns within a grocery store
- Observing customers unpacking and using a product for the first time

Sometimes observation takes place in a public setting and sometimes it's part of a controlled experience in which consumers agree to participate, such as when cookware manufacturers video consumers in their own kitchens to evaluate how they use their pots and pans.

Another type of observation method is **interpretive research**- a method in which a researcher observes a customer or group of customers in their natural setting and interprets their behavior based on an understanding of the social and cultural characteristics of that setting. In interpretive research, the researcher first spends an extensive amount of time studying the culture, and for that reason, the studies are often called *ethnographic studies*. The word ethnographic means that a researcher takes a cultural perspective of the population being studied. For that reason, interpretive research is often used to examine consumer behavior within a foreign culture where language, values, and expectations are subject to different cultural influences. After experiencing a number of product failures in low-income markets in Latin America, Procter & Gamble began an "immersion research" program called "Living It," in which the company's managers and executives spent time with low-income families around the world, living in their homes to develop a better understanding of their needs and desires. P&G's subsequent sales suggest that the effort was worthwhile. Among the mistakes the firm addressed was a low-sudsing detergent it had previously introduced in Mexico, unaware that most of its customers there were manual laborers who associated suds with cleaning power.

**interpretive research** a method in which a researcher observes a customer or group of customers in their natural setting and interprets their behavior based on an understanding of the social and cultural characteristics of that setting

## SURVEY

Observation alone cannot supply all of the information researchers desire. They must ask questions to get information on demographics, attitudes, motives, and opinions. There are several methods for collecting survey data.

*Telephone Interviews*: Telephone interviews are a quick and inexpensive method for obtaining a small quantity of relatively impersonal information. Simple, clearly worded questions are easy for interviewers to pose over the phone and are effective at drawing appropriate responses.

*Personal Interviews*: One way of obtaining detailed information about consumers is the personal interview, because the interviewer can establish rapport with respondents and explain confusing or vague questions. In addition to contacting respondents at their homes or workplaces, marketing research firms can conduct interviews in shopping centers, airports, and other public places where they gain wide access to a diverse range of consumers.

**focus group** a small group of individuals in one location to discuss a subject of interest

*Focus Groups*: A **focus group** brings together a small group of individuals in one location to discuss a subject of interest. Unlike other interview techniques that elicit information through a question-and-answer format, focus groups usually encourage a general discussion of a predetermined topic. Focus groups are a particularly valuable tool for exploratory research, developing new product ideas, and preliminary testing of alternative marketing strategies.

*Online or Mail Surveys*: Although personal interviews can provide very detailed information, cost considerations usually prevent their use in a large-scale study. An efficient, cost-effective alternative to one-on-one interviews is a survey. Delivered to many individuals online or by mail, surveys can provide anonymity that may encourage respondents to give candid answers. The U.S. Census is an example of a mail survey.

The growing number of Internet users has spurred the growth of online surveys. Armed with a user-friendly tool such as Survey Monkey, even a novice can build, deliver, and analyze a survey. Using a service such as Google Surveys, a researcher can build a survey and have it deployed to a demographically targeted audience for as little as 10 cents per respondent.

## TEST MARKETING

**test marketing** a marketing research technique that involves introducing a new product in a specific geographic area and then observing its degree of success

**Test marketing** is a marketing research technique that involves introducing a new product in a specific geographic area and then observing its degree of success. Up to this point, a product development team may have gathered feedback from focus groups or surveys, but test marketing is the first stage where the product performs in a real-life environment. Some firms omit test marketing and move directly from product development to full-scale production, citing three problems with test marketing: (1) It is expensive; (2) competitors quickly learn about the new product and may develop competing products; and (3) some products are not well suited to test marketing. On the other hand, test marketing a product on a small scale can ultimately save companies

**EXHIBIT 10.2**    Comparison of Primary Research Methods

| Methodology | Type of Data Collected | Time | Relative Cost |
|---|---|---|---|
| **Observation** | Observation of consumer behaviors and habits that can inform marketing decisions | Medium (weeks to months) | Moderate |
| **Survey** | Collection of consumer opinions and attitudes that can inform marketing decisions | Short (days to weeks) | Low |
| **Test marketing** | Measurement of actual product performance in the marketplace | Long (months to years) | High |

money, because it gives them the ability to identify problems within their marketing mix—and fix them—before rolling the product out nationwide.

Exhibit 10.2 compares primary research methods in terms of types of data collected, time required, and relative cost.

## 10-3b
## CLOSING EXAMPLE

From its primary research, Johnson & Johnson was able to prove that a bedtime routine has a positive impact on a baby's sleep habits. The company developed a three-step routine which it advertises as clinically proven to help babies sleep better and longer.[11] Marketers tell parents that a warm bath using Johnson's baby shampoo, followed by a soothing massage with Johnson's baby oil, and quiet time with free lullabies from Johnson's BEDTIME® App will help baby sleep better. Not only does Johnson & Johnson help babies and parents get better sleep, the company also benefits from parents purchasing more Johnson's baby products.

The company's BEDTIME® App also allows parents to log and track their baby's sleep. The app in turn helps Johnson & Johnson collect sleep data for analysis–providing them additional primary research. The company now reports the success of the three-step routine, based on data from more than 300,000 babies.[12]

Source: dealseekingmom.com

The BEDTIME® app continually collects data from users to help Johnson & Johnson conduct further research.

# 10-4  CONDUCTING INTERNATIONAL MARKET RESEARCH

### OPENING EXAMPLE

While some companies may struggle to conduct international market research, Estée Lauder has found effective methods to do so—especially in the Asia-Pacific market. The company sold almost half of its existing cosmetics brands in China,

**LO 10.4**    Outline four considerations for conducting marketing research in global markets.

Osiao is a luxury skincare line developed for the unique needs of Asian skin.

Source: thebeautygypsy.com

but wanted to do a better job of catering to Chinese tastes. In 2012, Estée Lauder launched a luxury beauty brand specific to the Chinese market: Osiao. Containing plant extracts, such as ginseng and Asiatic pennywort, the brand is backed by years of research with women in China, Korea, and Japan.

What do you think is different about international market research? How do you think Estée Lauder did it effectively?

### 10-4a

## LEARNING IT: CONDUCTING INTERNATIONAL MARKET RESEARCH

As companies expand globally, they need to gather more knowledge about consumers in other countries. Although marketing researchers follow the same basic steps for international studies as for domestic ones, they often face some very different challenges. There are four considerations for conducting marketing research in global markets: access to secondary data, language differences, the global business environment, and data collection methods.

### ACCESS TO SECONDARY DATA

Not every country's government collects reliable census data like the United States, however organizations can tap many secondary resources as they research global markets. One major information source is the U.S. government, which offers a wealth of information through its dedicated website, Export.gov. Here, marketers can find marketing research, business leads, and other data on international trade and intellectual property protection drawn from sources across the U.S. government. The site's treasure-trove of international marketing research is organized by country (more than 130 nations) and by industry. Personalized counseling and customized research are available (the latter for a fee), as well as guidance on improving international business strategy, targeting markets overseas, evaluating international business partners, and increasing brand awareness around the world. Another resource is the World Bank website. The World Bank collects data including population, education levels, and employment information for each country through its website, worldbank.org.

## LANGUAGE DIFFERENCES

When conducting international studies, companies must be prepared to deal with both language and cultural differences, even when conducting simple surveys. Poorly translated research questions can result in misleading data. One method to prevent language issues is to employ back translation. In this method, professional translators interpret a previously translated document back to the original language. Marketers then compare the translation to the original document, hoping to eliminate any errors or questionable translation.

## GLOBAL BUSINESS ENVIRONMENT

Companies also need to take a good look at a country's business environment, including political and economic conditions, trade regulations affecting research studies, and the potential for short- and long-term growth. For example, a company might learn that its product category is expected to grow 30% per year in China for the next 10 years; however, this information might be meaningless if political or trade conditions would prevent the company from expanding to China in the first place. Many marketers recommend tapping local researchers to accurately assess the potential of foreign markets.

## DATA COLLECTION METHODS

Businesses may need to adjust their data collection methods for primary research in other countries, because some methods do not easily transfer across national frontiers. Face-to-face interviewing, for instance, remains the most common method for conducting primary research outside the United States.

While mail surveys are a common data collection method in developed countries, they are useless in many other nations because of low literacy rates, unreliable mail service, and a lack of address lists. Telephone interviews also may not be suitable in other countries, especially those where many people do not have phones. Focus groups can be difficult to arrange because of cultural and social factors. To help with such challenges, a growing number of international research firms offer experience in conducting global studies.

## 10-4b
## CLOSING EXAMPLE

While Estée Lauder was performing well in Asian markets, the company wanted to increase its efforts in China and did so by opening the Estée Lauder Companies Innovation Institute. The research center has laboratories for biology research, but also focuses on consumer and market research. While not all companies can open a research center in a foreign location, they can implement some of Estée Lauder's best practices. Employing local researchers, as Estée Lauder has, can help eliminate any language and culture errors. Personal interviews and focus groups were conducted by local employees. As Fabrizio Freda, president and CEO of Estée Lauder says, "If you do [research] from the U.S. with people that are not local, that would be a risk."[13]

Understanding the global business environment has also been necessary for the beauty brand. Recent restrictions on luxury gifting by China's government have threatened the luxury goods market. Osiao is positioned as a luxury brand, with facial serums that cost around $210.[14] As a result, the company is rolling out the Osiao brand slowly. Though international market research poses challenges, understanding the language, culture, and business environment of your target market can ensure your research is completed smoothly and accurately.

# 10-5 TECHNOLOGY IN MARKETING RESEARCH

**LO 10.5** Summarize how technology is used to assist collection and analysis of marketing research data.

## OPENING EXAMPLE

The number of babies born in the United States is around 4 million per year.[15] This statistic makes expectant moms an attractive segment for retailers. Stores, such as Target, recognize the importance of reaching moms-to-be as soon as possible. Traditionally, Target would send offers and advertisements for all things baby related after an expectant mother created a baby shower registry with the store. The company realized, however, that the expectant mother may also be simultaneously receiving advertisements from other retailers. Marketers at Target wondered if there was a way to reach these moms-to-be earlier—before other retailers could.

A Target statistician began to analyze purchasing habits of pregnant women leading up to their due date. By analyzing the products that women with baby registries were buying in the months leading up to giving birth, the statistician was able to identify about 25 products that, when analyzed together, created a "pregnancy prediction" score.[16] With this information, Target was able to send advertisements to expectant customers as early as the second trimester of their pregnancy. Marketers at Target believed that this gave them an advantage over competitors—securing brand loyalty before other retailers had a chance. Not only would an expectant mother purchase more baby items from the store, but she was also likely to buy other items that she might normally purchase somewhere else.

Target was incredibly successful in predicting customers who were pregnant and then advertising to fit their specific needs. Initially, this seemed like exactly what Target was shooting for, and the algorithm was performing flawlessly. In fact, the only thing the algorithm couldn't seem to predict was something everyone else already knew—people don't always like a know-it-all.

## 10-5a

# LEARNING IT: TECHNOLOGY IN MARKETING RESEARCH

In past eras, marketing researchers gathered little more than written testimonials from purchasers of their firm's products. Research methods became more sophisticated during the 1930s as the development of statistical techniques led to refinements in sampling procedures and greater accuracy in research findings. Now, computer technology has significantly changed the complexion of marketing research in three key ways.

## DATA COLLECTION

In the past, all market research had to be conducted and tabulated manually, but no longer. As mentioned earlier, the growing number of Internet users has spurred the growth of online surveys. Using the web speeds up the survey process, increases sample sizes, ignores geographic boundaries, and dramatically reduces costs. Researchers have also devised ways to cultivate the focus-group environment on the Internet. Online focus groups can be both cost- and time-efficient, with immediate results in the form of discussion transcripts. Technology also offers increasingly sophisticated ways for observing consumer behavior. For example, the television industry relies on data from people meters, electronic remote control devices that record the TV viewing habits of individual household members to measure the popularity of TV shows. And the nature of Netflix's streaming technology allows it to automatically collect every interaction that customers have with its service.

## DATA REPORTING AND ACCESS

In the past, research organizations often compiled reports and sold them to marketers at very high prices. Now, market research can be acquired more quickly and less expensively than ever. The Internet has spurred the growth of research aggregators—companies that acquire, reformat, and then resell premium research reports that have already been published. Aggregators put valuable data within reach of marketers who lack the time or the budget to commission customized research. Because web technology makes their databases easy to search, aggregators such as Datamonitor and eMarketer can compile detailed, specialized reports quickly and cost-effectively.[17]

The technological advances of the last two decades—the Internet, smartphones, social media, and more—have given rise to what's called **big data**—data that originates in unprecedented volume and at unprecedented speed from the world around us. These advances make it possible for anyone—from a student entrepreneur who is running a fledgling business from his or her dorm room to the global marketing department of a Fortune 500 firm—to gather and analyze data from customers, prospects, visitors to a website or Facebook page, and many other sources. The volume, speed, and sheer variety of big data are bringing about great changes in the way organizations learn about their customers. And while the purpose and principles of marketing research have not changed, the speed and volume—and the possibilities—are greatly increased.

**big data** the data that originates in unprecedented volume and at unprecedented speed from the world around us

eMarketer allows users to search hundreds of digital topics to find reports and charts to aid their research.

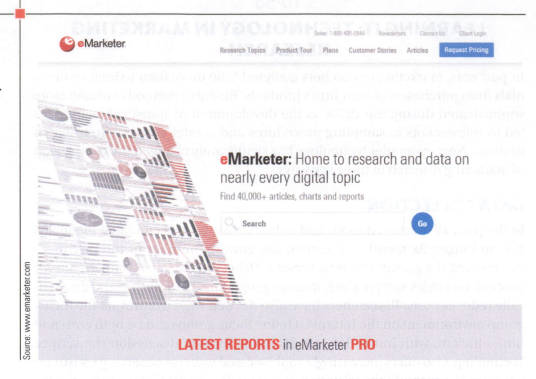

Source: www.emarketer.com

Big data has the potential to help companies increase revenue, improve return on investment, and build market share. The greatest challenge for marketers is being able to manage and analyze all of this data—more than 2.5 quintillion bytes of data created every day.[18]

## DATA ANALYSIS

In the past, marketers had to manually interpret data to make marketing decisions, now technology allows marketers to quickly process massive amounts of complex data that would be impossible to interpret manually.

**data mining** a technique in which a user employs special software to search through computerized data files to detect patterns

**Data mining** is a technique in which a user employs special software to search through computerized data files to detect patterns. It focuses on identifying relationships not obvious to marketers—in a sense, answering questions that marketing researchers may not even have thought to ask. Data mining is an efficient way to sort through huge amounts of data and to make sense of that data. It helps marketers create customer profiles, pinpoint reasons for customer loyalty, analyze potential returns on changes in pricing or promotion, and forecast sales. Data mining offers considerable advantages in retailing, the hotel industry, banking, utilities, and many other areas, and it holds the promise of providing answers to many specific strategic questions.

**predictive analytics** the use of marketing intelligence data and model scenarios to create forecasts

**Predictive analytics** refers to the use of marketing intelligence data and model scenarios to create forecasts. Marketers in many industries use predictive analytics to set strategy and direction. Using data captured through data mining, predictive analytics allows marketers to focus their efforts on customer targets with the greatest likelihood of purchasing the company's product. Again, these types of insights would be nearly impossible without the computing power available today.

The power of companies such as Amazon and Netflix to mine and analyze vast amounts of customer data serves as a competitive advantage because they can optimize their product offerings and pricing to maximize profitability.

## 10-5b
## CLOSING EXAMPLE

Target's use of data mining allowed the company to effectively market to expectant mothers much earlier than other retailers could. Marketers at Target were confident that the pregnancy prediction model would increase sales in baby related items and solidify brand loyalty with a valuable target market. However, Target's pregnancy prediction model worked so well that the company predicted a teen's pregnancy before she had told her father that she was expecting.[19] Based on the teen's purchases at the store, Target predicted the teen was pregnant and began to send her coupons for items such as cribs and diapers. When her father complained to the manager of the local Target store, Target realized its marketing efforts to expectant mothers needed to change.

Target recognized that while the accuracy of the prediction model was an advantage, sending a catalog full of baby items might be considered overly invasive to a woman who had yet to announce her pregnancy. While Target continued to direct advertisements to pregnant women, marketers began to include items in the advertisements such as patio furniture, vacuums, or pet items to make the advertisements appear random.[20] Although Target does not report earnings on specific divisions, overall Target revenues have increased from $44 billion in 2002, when the company began using the pregnancy prediction algorithm, to $73 billion in 2016.[21] Company President Gregg Steinhafel told a room of investors that Target had a "heightened focus on items and categories that appeal to specific guest segments such as mom and baby."[22]

## 10-6 CLASSIFYING DATA AS PRIMARY OR SECONDARY

### OPENING EXAMPLE

Technological advances enabled Netflix to take the old principle "Know your audience" to new heights—almost overnight. For marketers, understanding the customer mindset is a critical and ongoing task: What are their buying preferences and what factors influence those preferences? What's behind customer loyalty?

The ever-growing power and capabilities of technology have made it possible for companies such as Netflix to quickly collect mountains of data about their customers (seemingly with minimal effort). However, not all the information can be learned from Netflix's internal data. For example, internal data does not give Netflix information about people who are not Netflix subscribers. What shows do they watch, and why don't they subscribe to Netflix? These questions need to be answered using primary data.

**LO 10.6** Given a list of marketing research data from various sources, classify as either primary or secondary data.

## EXHIBIT 10.3  Examples of Marketing Research

| Type of Data | Examples |
|---|---|
| Primary | • Observation<br>• Surveys, including personal interviews and focus groups<br>• Test marketing |
| Secondary | • Internal data such as sales reports, marketing cost reports, product reviews<br>• Government data including census information<br>• Industry publications<br>• Research services |

### 10-6a

## LEARNING IT: CLASSIFYING DATA AS PRIMARY OR SECONDARY

Marketers must understand the difference between primary and secondary data, and when to use each type of data in a marketing research project (see Exhibit 10.3).

Suppose that Netflix was hoping to conduct research to discover if subscribers would be interested in paying an extra fee to watch pay-per-view sporting events such as wrestling, boxing matches, or exhibition basketball games. Researchers could access secondary data such as industry reports that show purchase rates for these types of shows. Netflix researchers could also collect primary data by surveying current subscribers to find out their interest level in pay-per-view programming. But for other types of research questions, secondary data might not suffice.

## 10-7   LEARN IT TODAY . . . USE IT TOMORROW

As Netflix looks to expand its offerings and grow to new markets, the company would like to conduct market research to help guide decisions in these areas. To ensure the validity of its research results, Netflix would like to use a broad mix of secondary and primary data sources. Help Netflix categorize the data it has collected or plans to collect.

It's time to get hands-on and apply what you've learned. **See MindTap for an activity related to Netflix's marketing activities.**

# Chapter Summary

**LO 10.1** Describe the six steps in the marketing research process.

The six steps in the marketing research process are define problem, conduct exploratory research, formulate hypothesis, create research design, collect data, and interpret and present research information.

**LO 10.2** Summarize the four sources of secondary marketing research data.

Secondary data is information from previously published or compiled sources and comes from many sources. The four sources of secondary marketing research data are internal, government, industry, and research services.

**LO 10.3** Compare the three principal methods of collecting primary marketing research data.

Primary data refers to information collected for the first time specifically for a marketing research study. The three principal methods of collecting primary marketing research data are observation, survey, and experimental.

**LO 10.4** Outline four considerations for conducting marketing research in global markets.

The four considerations for conducting marketing research in global markets include access to secondary data, language differences, the global business environment, and data collection methods.

**LO 10.5** Summarize how technology is used to assist collection and analysis of marketing research data.

Technology has changed how marketing research is collected, reported, and analyzed. Marketers can now analyze volumes of data and find insights within that data that would have been nearly impossible using manual analysis techniques of the past.

**LO 10.6** Given a list of marketing research data from various sources, classify as either primary or secondary data.

It is important for marketers to understand the difference between primary and secondary sources of data so they can design marketing research projects that accurately answer the right questions within the time and budget required by the company.

# Key Terms

marketing research **196**
exploratory research **197**
hypothesis **197**
research design **197**

secondary data **198**
primary data **198**
interpretive research **203**
focus group **204**

test marketing **204**
big data **209**
data mining **210**
predictive analytics **210**

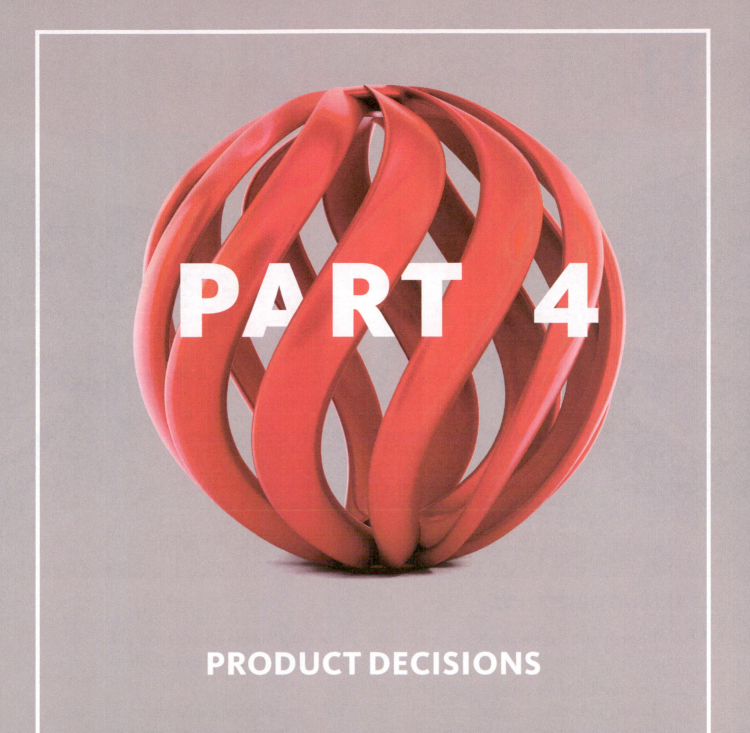

# PART 4

## PRODUCT DECISIONS

# 11 PRODUCT AND BRANDING CONCEPTS

Sorbis/Shutterstock.com

## LEARNING OBJECTIVES

**11.1** Distinguish between goods and services.

**11.2** Contrast the three classifications of consumer products in terms of consumer factors and marketing mix factors.

**11.3** Identify the six types of business products.

**11.4** Summarize the major elements of brand equity.

**11.5** Differentiate the methods used to develop and protect brand identity.

**11.6** Outline the various types of brand strategies used by marketers.

**11.7** Explain how companies organize to manage brands and products.

**11.8** Summarize the three major objectives of packaging.

# LEARN IT TODAY ... USE IT TOMORROW

In Chapter 2, we introduced you to the story of Under Armour. It might seem unlikely that a college athlete's efforts to overcome being "short and slow" could grow into a multi-billion-dollar sports apparel company, but that's the story behind Under Armour. Founder Kevin Plank was a college football player who believed that the sweat-collecting properties of cotton gear slowed him down on the field. Soon he was spending most of his spare time and meager savings testing fabrics to find a material that would carry moisture away from the body.

These days, Under Armour generates more than $2 billion in annual revenue and is expanding its retail distribution around the world. Under Armour has built a brand image around professional quality products at affordable prices, so it has added other athletic gear to its line. Mouth guards, sports bras, basketball shoes, running shoes, and football cleats now complement Under Armour's original moisture-wicking apparel. But as it continues to expand, Under Armour must maintain its brand image, or risk losing market share to competitors.

# 11-1 WHAT ARE GOODS AND SERVICES?

### OPENING EXAMPLE

A -1 Contruction Rentals rents and sells equipment used for building projects in Los Angeles, California.[1] Ranging from air compressors for nail guns, to moving vans with powerful lift gates, to concrete mixers, A-1 is in business to help companies build. In addition to their equipment rentals and sales, A-1 provides temporary services for construction sites, including portable toilets and power poles. It's safe to say that without A-1's service offerings, construction sites would be stopped up and powered down.

As A-1's product offerings include both goods and services, its marketers must remain flexible. For example, when the construction industry is slow, A-1 focuses on marketing and selling discounted equipment, rather than marketing their construction services. When the industry is booming and services are in high demand, A-1 chooses to focus on marketing their equipment rentals for job-site shortages. As A-1 continues to expand and optimize their marketing strategy, it must consider how to define and market its goods and services most effectively.

**LO 11.1** Distinguish between goods and services.

## 11-1a
### LEARNING IT: WHAT ARE GOODS AND SERVICES?

The term product refers to both goods and services. **Goods** are tangible products that customers can see, hear, smell, taste, and/or touch. Televisions, shovels, and cereal are examples of goods. In contrast, **services** are intangible products. You can't hold a service in your hand. Haircuts, car repairs, and dental work are examples of services.

Services can be distinguished from goods in several ways:

1. *Services are intangible*: Services do not have physical features buyers can see, hear, smell, taste, or touch prior to purchase.

**goods** tangible products that customers can see, hear, smell, taste, and/or touch

**services** intangible products

Beyla Balla/Shutterstock.com

**Good**

Jacob Lund/Shutterstock.com

**Service**

A good is a tangible product that customers can see and touch, while a service is an intangible task that satisfies the needs of a customer.

2. *Services are inseparable from the service providers*: The names of doctors, lawyers, or hair stylists are synonymous with the service they provide. A house-cleaning service like Merry Maids depends on its workers to leave each house spotless, because its reputation is built on this service.

3. *Services are perishable*: Providers cannot maintain inventories of their services. A day spa can't stockpile facials or pedicures. A travel agent can't keep quantities of their product on a shelf. For this reason, some service providers, such as airlines and hotels, may raise their prices during times of peak demand—during spring break from school, for example—and reduce them when demand declines.

4. *Companies cannot easily standardize services*: For example, a physical therapist will provide a similar service to her clients, but every client will have a slightly different experience. Likewise, a hair coloring from a salon stylist will be slightly different for each customer. Many service-based firms attempt to change this, however. Most fast-food chains promise that your food will be ready within a certain number of minutes, and it will taste the way you expect it to, no matter which location you visit. A hotel chain may provide the same amenities at every location—a pool, fitness room, free breakfast, and cable movies.

## 11-1b

### GOODS–SERVICES CONTINUUM

Sometimes it is difficult to determine whether or not a product is a good, a service, or a mix of both. One tool that marketers use to distinguish services from goods is the goods–services continuum (see Exhibit 11.1).

A car, for example, is a *pure good*. It's a physical product that customers can see, hear, and touch.

Dinner at an exclusive restaurant, however, is a mix of goods and services. It combines the physical goods of gourmet food with the intangible services of an attentive wait staff and elegant surroundings.

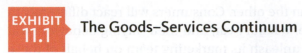

**The Goods–Services Continuum**

Pure good                    Mixture of good and service                    Pure service

On the other side of the continuum, a dentist provides a *pure service*—cleaning teeth, filling cavities, offering whitening treatments.

## 11-1c

## CLOSING EXAMPLE

Learning through experience and customer interactions, A-1 observed that most contractors need both equipment *and* jobsite services, even though most contractors initially come to A-1 needing one or the other. Now, when branch managers are talking to clients about specific equipment, they know to inquire about whether the client also needs training, maintenance, or delivery services for that equipment. And when a client is asking about a particular jobsite service, the branch manager knows to learn as much about the project as possible so they can assess whether A-1 carries any equipment that might help the client complete the job more efficiently and safely. A comprehensive marketing strategy, focusing on both goods and services from the outset, will help A-1 become the go-to resource for contractors in Los Angeles.

# 11-2    TYPES OF CONSUMER PRODUCTS

## OPENING EXAMPLE

Oxford Road, a marketing consulting firm, has clients that span many different industries.[2] Dan Granger, Oxford Road's CEO and founder, is results-driven and focused on bringing clients, "more customers... over and over again." Its clients include well-established and startup companies, most of which offer products to the consumer market.

Suppose that Oxford Road has taken on three new clients: a gum producer, a TV manufacturer, and a niche luxury car company. The firm knows that each of these company's products is classified differently, and each requires a wholly

**LO 11.2** Contrast the three classifications of consumer products in terms of consumer factors and marketing mix factors.

different marketing strategy than the other. Consumers will react differently to a pack of gum than a new TV or a luxury car, and their buying behaviors will follow suit. When preparing to unleash its marketing team on behalf of these new clients, Oxford Road must determine how to effectively build a marketing mix for each client.

## 11-2a

# LEARNING IT: TYPES OF CONSUMER PRODUCTS

Not all consumer products are the same, so they can't be marketed the same way. A good starting point for building a marketing mix is to first understand the type of product you are selling. Buying behavior for various types of products is different, and knowing these differences will influence a number of marketing decisions.

The most common classification scheme for products divides them into three groups: convenience products, shopping products, and specialty products. Exhibit 11.2 summarizes these three categories and provides some examples of products in each of them.

Think of the categorization process as a continuum representing degrees of effort expended by consumers. At one end of the continuum, consumers casually pick up convenience items. At the other end, consumers search extensively for specialty products. Shopping products fall between these extremes.

## CONVENIENCE PRODUCTS

**convenience products**  goods and services consumers want to purchase frequently, immediately, and with minimal effort

**impulse goods and services**  products purchased on the spur of the moment

**staples**  convenience products that consumers frequently purchase to maintain a ready inventory

**Convenience products** are goods and services consumers want to purchase frequently, immediately, and with minimal effort. Milk, bread, and toothpaste are convenience goods. Convenience services include 24-hour roadside assistance, walk-in nail salons, copy shops, and dry cleaners.

Marketers further subdivide the convenience category into impulse items and staples. **Impulse goods and services** are purchased on the spur of the moment—for example, picking up a pack of gum at the supermarket register.

**Staples** are convenience products that consumers frequently purchase to maintain a ready inventory—gasoline, shampoo, and milk, for example.

**EXHIBIT 11.2**  **Classification of Consumer Products**

| Consumer Products | | |
|---|---|---|
| **Convenience Products** | **Shopping Products** | **Specialty Products** |
| *Impulse Items:* Magazines, gum, candy  *Staples:* Gasoline, dry cleaning, milk | *Homogeneous:* Airplane flights, computers  *Heterogeneous:* Child care, furniture, Zumba, yoga instruction, Caribbean cruise | Lexus and Mercedes luxury cars, tax attorney, Tory Burch designer clothes and accessories, Botox injections |

Marketers spend many hours and resources creating messages for consumers about these products, partly because there are so many competitors.

Because convenience products are usually low cost, advertising is typically the most cost-effective form of promotion.

## SHOPPING PRODUCTS

In contrast to convenience products, consumers purchase **shopping products** only after comparing competing products' price, quality, style, and color. Shopping products typically cost more than convenience purchases. This category includes goods such as automobiles, furniture, electronics, and appliances, as well as services like child care, auto repairs, insurance, and hotel stays. The purchaser of a shopping product lacks complete information prior to the buying trip, and gathers information during the buying process.

Because shopping products have higher prices and require more planning before purchase, advertising can be used to raise brand awareness, though personal selling is often involved during the purchase process. For example, consumers might visit an electronics store based on an advertisement they saw for a television, but they'll likely want to speak with a sales associate before making the purchase.

## SPECIALTY PRODUCTS

**Specialty products** offer unique characteristics that compel buyers to purchase particular brands. Examples of specialty goods include Hermès scarves, Kate Spade handbags, Ritz-Carlton resorts, Tiffany jewelry, and Ducati motorcycles. Specialty services include professional services such as financial advice, legal counsel, and cosmetic surgery.

Purchasers of specialty products typically undergo an extensive search for their first purchase of a particular product or brand. But once loyal to that brand, buyers making future purchases know exactly what they want—and they are willing to pay accordingly. These buyers begin shopping with complete information, and they often refuse to accept substitutes. Because consumers are willing to exert considerable effort to obtain specialty products, producers can promote

> **shopping products** products more expensive than convenience items and ones where the shopper lacks complete information prior to the buying process

> **specialty products** higher-end products offering unique characteristics that compel buyers to purchase particular brands

**High-end clothing is a specialty good**

**Tax services are a specialty service**

**EXHIBIT 11.3**    Marketing Impact of the Consumer Products Classification System

| | Convenience Product | Shopping Product | Specialty Product |
|---|---|---|---|
| **Consumer Factors** | | | |
| Planning time involved in purchase | Very little | Considerable | Extensive |
| Purchase frequency | Frequent | Less frequent | Infrequent |
| Importance of convenient location | Critical | Important | Unimportant |
| Comparison of price and quality | Very little | Considerable | Very little |
| **Marketing Mix Factors** | | | |
| Price | Low | Medium to High | High |
| Importance of seller's image | Unimportant | Very important | Important |
| Distribution channel length | Long | Relatively short | Short |
| Number of sales outlets | Many | Few | Very few |
| Promotion | Advertising and promotion by producer | Combination of personal selling and advertising | Emphasis on personal selling, supported by image advertising |

them through relatively few retail locations. In fact, some firms intentionally limit the range of retailers carrying their products to bolster their brand image. Both highly personalized service by sales associates and image advertising help marketers promote specialty items.

## 11-2b
# HOW THE MARKETING MIX APPLIES

While not all products can be easily classified into one of these three categories, this classification system helps guide marketers in developing a successful marketing strategy. Buyer behavior patterns differ for the three types of purchases. Exhibit 11.3 summarizes the differences in consumer buying behavior across the three categories and how that impacts the marketing mix for each.

## 11-2c
# CLOSING EXAMPLE

Through its research, Oxford Road learns that customers for its gum producer are shopping in convenience stores, and aren't comparing prices against other gums. Its advertising strategy, therefore, will focus on the gum's low price. For the TV manufacturer, Oxford Road found that consumers are comparing price, quality, and reputation among competing brands, so it plans to promote the unique attributes and overall value of its client's products. Lastly, for the luxury car company, Oxford Road knows that its consumers will spend a considerable amount of time evaluating the purchase decision, and that a sustained personal selling campaign will pay off in the end. With an effective application of the marketing mix for each of its clients, Oxford Road will deliver on its client promise, and bring in "more customers" into the future.

# TYPES OF BUSINESS PRODUCTS

## OPENING EXAMPLE

**LO 11.3** Identify the six types of business products.

Spoke-N-Wheel is a hypothetical custom dirt bike manufacturer. They saw demand for customization in the dirt bike industry, fueled by professionals and amateur enthusiasts, and started a business building dirt bikes from the ground up. Business has been good and their operations run like the well-oiled machines they build.

In order for Spoke-N-Wheel to produce its custom dirt bikes, it must purchase a number of business products. Some of these products—such as timing belts—are purchased on a regular basis. Other products—such as a fume hood for the factory floor—are purchased occasionally, or only once. Some business products will become a part of Spoke-N-Wheel's finished dirt bikes, while others will only be used in the manufacturing process. The purchasing needs of a business are complex, as different purchases are used for entirely different purposes. Understanding these differences helps Spoke-N-Wheel decide when these purchases should be made, and who at the company should be making them.

### 11-3a

## LEARNING IT: TYPES OF BUSINESS PRODUCTS

The classification system for business products emphasizes product uses rather than customer buying behavior. Business market products generally fall into one of six categories for product uses: installations, accessory equipment, component parts and materials, raw materials, supplies, and business services. Exhibit 11.4 illustrates the six types of business products, with examples of each.

### INSTALLATIONS

The specialty products of the business market are called **installations**. This classification includes major capital investments for new factories, heavy machinery, customized software, and major telecommunications systems. Purchases of

**installations** major capital investments in the B2B market

**EXHIBIT 11.4**    **Classification of Business Products**

**Installations**
Airbus 380
Toyota truck plant,
Starwood Hotels,
natural gas pipeline

**Components**
Intel chips,
Cummins
diesel engines,
Spandex fabric

**Business Services**
CSX (railroad),
ServiceMaster
(janitorial services),
Ryder (trucking),
Pinkerton (security
services)

**Business Products**

**Accessory Equipment**
Microsoft Surface tablet,
Apple iPad,
Herman Miller office
chairs, Samsung
Galaxy
smartphone

**MRO Supplies**
Bosch staplers,
Weyerhaeuser paper,
Gorilla duct tape
3M scotch tape

**Raw Materials**
sugar, crude oil, silk,
titanium, iron ore

Boeing's 787 Dreamliner airplanes by Qantas and Kenya Airways are considered installations for those airlines.

As installations often have a long product life and are very expensive, they represent major purchasing decisions for organizations. A purchasing firm often buys such a product for its efficiency and performance over its useful life. Negotiations often extend over several months and involve numerous decision makers. Price typically does not dominate purchase decisions for installations.

## ACCESSORY EQUIPMENT

**accessory equipment** products such as power tools, computers, and office furniture that typically cost less and last for shorter periods than installations

**Accessory equipment** includes products such as power tools, computers, smartphones, and office furniture. This category costs less and has a shorter product life than installations. Although quality and service are influential over purchases of accessory equipment, price is often the biggest driver of purchasing decisions. Marketing accessory equipment requires continuous representation and dealing with the widespread geographic distribution of purchasers.

## COMPONENT PARTS AND MATERIALS

Whereas business buyers use installations and accessory equipment in the process of producing their own final products, **component parts and materials** represent finished business products of one producer that become part of the final products of another producer. Processing chips and glass screens for iPhones are examples.

Purchasers of component parts and materials need regular, continuous supplies of standardized products. They generally contract to purchase these items for set periods of time. Marketers commonly emphasize direct sales, and satisfied customers often become regular buyers.

Oleksandr Lysenko/Shutterstock.com

Component parts and materials, such as processing chips and glass screens, are finished products that are used in the production of another final product.

## RAW MATERIALS

Natural resources like coal, copper, and lumber, and farm products, such as beef, eggs, and soybeans, are considered **raw materials**. These products resemble component parts and materials because they become part of the buyers' final products; however, they typically represent an underlying natural resource that requires minimal processing and packaging. Cargill supplies many of the raw materials for finished food products—corn, flour, food starch, and sweeteners. Food manufacturers then turn these materials into finished products, including cake and bread.[3]

**component parts and materials** finished business products of one producer that become part of the final products of another producer

**raw materials** natural resources that become part of a final product

## SUPPLIES

If installations represent the specialty products of the business market, supplies represent the business market's convenience products. **Supplies** constitute the regular products a firm uses in daily operations, such as paper, pens, and tape. These items do not become part of the products buyers offers to their customers.

A purchasing manager buys supplies as a routine job duty. Wholesalers often facilitate sales of supplies because of the low unit prices, the small order size, and the large number of potential buyers. Because supplies are relatively standardized, heavy price competition frequently keeps costs under control.

**supplies** the regular products a firm uses in daily operations

## BUSINESS SERVICES

**Business services** includes the intangible products firms buy to facilitate their production and operations. Examples of business services are financial services, insurance, security, legal advice, and consulting. Many service providers sell the same services to both consumers and organizational buyers—telephone,

**business services** intangible products firms buy to facilitate their production and operations

gas, and electricity, for example—although service firms may maintain separate marketing groups for the two customer segments.

## CLOSING EXAMPLE

Spoke-N-Wheel's custom dirt bikes use raw materials such as steel on a regular basis. They buy shocks and tires to use as components on their bikes. It's important that team members in charge of product design and production are involved in these purchases. However, a purchasing manager for their administrative offices is usually in charge of purchasing services, such as legal advice, or supplies, such as paper. With an understanding of how and where to purchase business products, Spoke-N-Wheel will be able to maximize profits and accelerate into the future.

# 11-4 MANAGING BRANDS FOR COMPETITIVE ADVANTAGE

**LO 11.4**  Summarize the major elements of brand equity.

## OPENING EXAMPLE

Nike has one of the most well-defined brand names in the world, represented by one of the most recognized brand marks: the Swoosh. Consumers know the Swoosh represents a diverse athletics business, not just another shoe company. Since its founding in 1964, Nike has spent billions of dollars to create, protect, and maintain their brand. But Nike's brand has some work to do, especially in the women's fitness industry.

Nike is the largest women's fitness brand in the world, says Jeanne Jackson, Nike's president of product and merchandising. But it does not rule the market in the same way it dominates men's fitness. Competitors like Lululemon and Athleta, for example, have re-defined the industry with trend-setting active and athleisure apparel, while Nike's focus on women's apparel lagged behind. Now, as Nike looks to dedicate even more time and resources to the women's market, it must consider how its brand is perceived, and what needs to change.[4]

### 11-4a

## LEARNING IT: MANAGING BRANDS FOR COMPETITIVE ADVANTAGE

Think of the last time you went shopping for groceries. As you moved through the store, chances are your recognition of various brand names influenced many of your purchasing decisions. Perhaps you chose Colgate toothpaste over Crest, or loaded Heinz ketchup into your cart instead of the generic brand.

A **brand** is a name, term, sign, symbol, design, or some combination that identifies the products of one firm while differentiating these products from competitors.

**brand** a name, term, sign, symbol, design, or some combination that identifies the products of one firm while differentiating these products from competitors

Marketers recognize the powerful influence products have on customer behavior, and they work to create strong identities for their products and to protect them. Branding is the process of creating that identity. Satisfied buyers respond to branding by making repeat purchases of the same product because they identify the item with the name of its producer.

## 11-4b
## BRAND LOYALTY

Brands experience widely varying consumer familiarity and acceptance. A snowboarder might insist on a Burton snowboard, but the same consumer might show little loyalty to brands in another product category, such as bath soap. Marketers measure brand loyalty in three stages: brand recognition, brand preference, and brand insistence.

**Brand recognition** refers to consumer awareness and identification of a brand. It is often a company's first objective for newly introduced products. Marketers begin the promotion of new items by trying to make them familiar to the public. Advertising offers one effective way for increasing consumer awareness of a brand. Once consumers have used a product, seen it advertised, or noticed it in stores, it moves from the unknown to the known category, increasing the probability that some of those consumers will purchase it.

**brand recognition** consumer awareness and identification of a brand

McDonald's, Apple, and Disney are among the most valuable brands in the world.[5]

Faiz Zaki/Shutterstock.com

r.classen/Shutterstock.com

chrisdorney/Shutterstock.com

At the second level of brand loyalty, **brand preference**- buyers rely on previous experiences with a product when choosing it over competitors' products. Brand preference is common in clothing, electronics, and restaurants.

**Brand insistence**- the ultimate stage in brand loyalty, leads consumers to refuse alternatives and to search extensively for the desired product. A product at this stage has achieved a monopoly position within the minds of its consumers. Although many firms try to establish brand insistence with all consumers, few achieve this ambitious goal. Companies that offer specialty or luxury goods and services, such as Rolex watches or Lexus automobiles, are more likely to achieve this status than those offering mass-marketed goods and services.

## 11-4c
# BRAND EQUITY AND PERSONALITY

A brand can go a long way toward making or breaking a company's reputation. A strong brand identity backed by superior quality offers important strategic advantages for a firm. First, it increases the likelihood that consumers will recognize the firm's products when they make purchase decisions. Second, a strong brand identity can contribute to buyer perceptions of product quality. Branding can also reinforce customer loyalty and encourage repeat purchases. A consumer who tries a brand and likes it will probably look for that brand on future store visits. All of these benefits contribute to a valuable form of competitive advantage called *brand equity*.

**Brand equity** refers to the added value the brand gives to a product in the marketplace. Brands with high brand equity often command comparatively large market shares and higher prices.

Global advertising agency Young & Rubicam developed a brand equity system called the BrandAsset Valuator.[6] According to Y&R, a firm builds brand equity sequentially on four dimensions of brand personality. These four dimensions are as follows:

- *Differentiation* refers to a brand's ability to stand apart from competitors. Brands such as Tesla and Victoria's Secret stand out in consumers' minds as symbols of unique product characteristics. Nike's brand represents technical know-how and validation by professional athletes.

- *Relevance* refers to the real and perceived pertinence of the brand to a consumer segment. A large number of consumers must feel a need for the benefits offered by the brand in order for the brand to have relevance in the marketplace. Nike's customers are men, women, old, young, competitive athletes, and recreational athletes, all of who relate in some way to the benefits offered by Nike's products.

- *Esteem* is a combination of perceived quality and consumer perceptions about a brand. A rise in perceived quality or in public opinion about a brand enhances a brand's esteem. But negative impressions reduce esteem. Nike was one of the brands most damaged from the FIFA bribery scandal in 2015, as it is one of the largest supporters of the FIFA organization.[7]

- *Knowledge* refers to the extent of customer awareness of the brand and understanding of what it stands for. Knowledge implies that customers feel an intimate relationship with a specific brand. Nike's customers have a well-established understanding of its brand as an athlete-approved, premium provider of shoes and apparel.

## 11-4d
## CLOSING EXAMPLE

As Nike continues competing in the women's market for athletic apparel, it is building upon the technical expertise that its brand has long represented. For example, it has recently developed a sports bra that uses "Flywire" technology, originally developed for supportive shoes. Its plus-size line is the first of its kind, and offers more than 200 products for that market. Further, Nike has recently launched its Nike+ Training Club app, an experience developed with women in mind. With its history of focusing on premium design and technical product offerings, Nike hopes to leverage its existing brand equity to dominate the women's market.[8]

# 11-5   PROTECTING BRAND IDENTITY

### OPENING EXAMPLE

Philips & Co. was founded in 1891 in the Netherlands to "manufacture incandescent lamps and other electrical products." From those functional beginnings, the Philips brand name is now synonymous with innovation, quality, and efficient solutions.[9] Today, Philips provides technologies to improve everything from healthcare to everyday living.

But these associations with the Philips name are no accident. They were created over time through a consistent and sustained effort that incorporates legal, creative, and operational strategies. Philips' strong brand identity is the result.

**LO 11.5** Differentiate the methods used to develop and protect brand identity.

## 11-5a
## LEARNING IT: PROTECTING BRAND IDENTITY

Organizations identify their products in the marketplace in a variety of ways. Sunkist Growers stamps its oranges with the name Sunkist. Iams stamps a paw print on all of its pet food packages. For well over a century, Prudential Financial has used the Rock of Gibraltar as its symbol. While providing a sought-after product is the foundation for any successful brand, another important step is deciding how to identify a firm's products in the marketplace.

Keith Homan/Shutterstock.com

Green Giant is the brand name. The distinctive green lettering along with the green giant character is the brand mark.

**brand name**  the part of a brand that can be spoken and distinguishes a firm's offerings from those of its competitors

**brand mark**  is a symbol or pictorial design that distinguishes a product

**trademark**  a brand for which the owner claims exclusive legal protection

**trade dress**  the visual cues used in branding that create an overall look differentiating a brand or product from competitors

## BRAND NAMES AND BRAND MARKS

A name plays a central role in establishing brand and product identity. The American Marketing Association defines a **brand name** as the part of a brand that can be spoken. It can consist of letters, numbers, or words and forms a name that identifies and distinguishes the firm's offerings from those of its competitors. The brand name itself is not associated with any design elements. However, firms can also identify their brands by using brand marks, which do incorporate elements of design. A **brand mark**, or logo is a symbol or pictorial design that distinguishes a product, such as the Jolly Green Giant for Green Giant vegetables.

Effective brand names convey brand image, and are easy to pronounce, recognize, and remember. Marketers try to overcome problems with easily mispronounced brand names by teaching consumers the correct pronunciations. For example, early advertisements for the Korean carmaker Hyundai explained that the name rhymes with *Sunday*.

When a class of products becomes generally known by the original brand name of a specific offering, the brand name may become a descriptive generic name. If this occurs, the original owner loses exclusive claim to the brand name. Generic names such as nylon, aspirin, escalator, kerosene, and zipper started as brand names.

## TRADEMARKS

The high value of brand equity encourages firms to take steps to protect what they invest in their brands. A **trademark** is a brand for which the owner claims exclusive legal protection. To receive trademark protection, companies file an application with the U.S. Patent and Trademarking Office. Trademark protection confers the exclusive legal right to use a brand name, brand mark, and any slogan or product name abbreviation. Trademark protection can even be applied to words or phrases, such as Bud for Budweiser or the Met for the Metropolitan Opera in New York City.

A trademark should not be confused with a trade name, which identifies a company. The Coca-Cola Company is a trade name, but Coke is a trademark of the company's product. Some trade names mirror the companies' brand names. For example, Johnson & Johnson is both the company name and a trademarked brand name.

## TRADE DRESS

While brand names and brand marks mainly involve wording or a logo, trade dress is a broader category of brand identity. **Trade dress** is the visual cues used in branding that create an overall look differentiating a brand or product from competitors. These visual components may be related to color, size, package shapes, graphics, and similar design factors. Often it's the combination of visual cues creating a "total image" of the product or company that constitutes trade dress.

The look and feel of a Chipotle restaurant, of a Home Depot store, or a McDonald's Happy Meal box are examples. Trade dress can be protected by applying to the U.S. Patent and Trademarking Office.

It's important to differentiate between the methods used to develop and protect a brand. Referring to the picture above, the name Starbucks is the brand name. The distinctive lettering and the mermaid logo are the brand mark. Since Starbucks has filed for trademark protection, their brand name and brand mark are legally protected. The combination of visual cues at a Starbucks, including their brand mark, cup design, use of green, and store layout represent their trade dress.

Amazon is the brand name. That name in the distinctive lettering with the smile is the brand mark.

## 11-5b
## CLOSING EXAMPLE

Philips associates its brand with a push "to make the world healthier and more sustainable through innovation." Their integrated lighting solutions can more efficiently light a home in the U.S., while their ultrasound technology can reduce infant mortality in Uganda.[10] But all of this work to offer innovative solutions would be compromised if customers couldn't differentiate Philips from its competitors. So, on top of its drive to offer quality products, Phillips maintains its brand identity by protecting their distinctive brand name, brand marks, and sleek trade dress.

Starbucks has developed one of the strongest brands in the world.

# 11-6

# TYPES OF BRAND STRATEGIES

**LO 11.6** Outline the various types of brand strategies used by marketers.

## OPENING EXAMPLE

American Pet Nutrition (APN) is a pet food manufacturer based in Ogden, Utah. It has a number of product lines for both dogs and cats, and prides itself in "following the strictest standards of safety and quality."[11] One of APN's top sellers is its line of no-frills dog food called Atta Boy!, and it churns out batch after batch for its furry clientele.

Suppose you are the new Director of Marketing at APN. The product design team comes to you and proposes expanding the Atta Boy! brand into dog treats. In addition, the Vice President of Marketing (i.e. your boss) tells you there is a lot of opportunity for extending the Atta Boy! line into cat food. You can only choose to move forward with one of these brand strategies. How will you decide which one?

## 11-6a

## LEARNING IT: TYPES OF BRAND STRATEGIES

Brands are typically classified in three distinct ways: generic, private, and manufacturer. Each has a different set of characteristics that defines it. In making branding decisions, firms weigh the benefits and drawbacks of each type of brand.

Some firms sell their products without any efforts at branding. These items are called **generic products**. They are characterized by plain labels, little or no advertising, and no brand names. Common categories of generic

**generic products** products sold without any efforts at branding

Johnson & Johnson markets a whole family of products under their brand.

Raihana Asral/Shutterstock.com

products include food and household staples. The market share for generic products increases during economic downturns but subsides when the economy improves. However, many consumers request generic substitutions for brand-name prescriptions at the pharmacy whenever they are available.

**Manufacturer brands**- also called *national brands*, refer to a brand name owned by a manufacturer or other producer. These are what most people think of when they think of a brand. Examples include Kellogg's, Dole, Sony, and Chevrolet. These brands can consist of an individual product or a family of products that are labeled under the same brand. For example, Johnson & Johnson offers a line of baby powder, lotions, and baby shampoo under its name, and Pepperidge Farm products, including bread, rolls, and cookies, carry the Pepperidge Farm brand. It's important to note that brands aren't always named after their parent company. Unilever, for example, markets Ben & Jerry's, Bertolli, Lipton, and Promise food products, while PepsiCo markets SoBe drinks and Quaker Oats oatmeal.

> **manufacturer brands** a brand name owned by a manufacturer or other producer

In contrast to manufacturer brands, many large wholesalers and retailers place their own brands on the merchandise they market. The brands offered by wholesalers and retailers are called **private brands** (or *private labels*). Although some manufacturers refuse to produce private-label goods, most regard such production as a way to reach additional market segments. Kroger offers their brand of Simple Truth products in many categories within their QFC and Fred Meyer grocery stores. Kroger contracts with a variety of manufacturers to make these products, which are all labeled with the Simple Truth private brand that is owned by Kroger. However, a manufacturer of a major brand, such as Crest toothpaste, would be unlikely to offer their product under the Simple Truth label because it could erode the equity of the Crest brand. The growth of private brands has increased over the years. A recent survey found that "Eighty-three percent of consumers indicated that they sometimes buy private label brands if the product is better or it offers a higher value than the national brand."[12]

> **private brands** brands offered by wholesalers and retailers

## 11-6b
# BRAND EXTENSION VS. LINE EXTENSION

Some brands become so popular that marketers look for ways to leverage their brand equity with new products. The first strategy is **line extension**, which refers to the development and implementation of new sizes, styles, or related product offerings. For example, when Cheerios is offered in different sizes and flavors on the cereal aisle, this is line extension.

> **line extension** the development and implementation of new sizes, styles, or related product offerings

A more complex strategy is **brand extension**, which is attaching a popular brand name to a new product in an unrelated product category. An example would be a brand of Cheerios bread or cake mix. By establishing brand extensions, marketers hope to gain access to new customers and markets by building on the equity already established by their existing brands.

> **brand extension** implies attaching a popular brand name to a new product in an unrelated product category

## 11-6c
# CLOSING EXAMPLE

Faced with a difficult choice as the new Director of Marketing at APN, you have decided to expand the Atta Boy! brand into dog treats. After conducting research with your team, you uncover pent-up demand for dog treats from existing Atta

Boy! customers. This represents a line extension because it's a related product offering in the existing dog food category. Though there might be opportunity for brand extension into the cat food market, the Atta Boy! brand name isn't well-recognized there, and intense competition from larger competitors like Purina would require significant advertising expenditures. Based on your recommendation, the VP of Marketing moves forward with the line extension to Atta Boy! dog treats, to the delight of dogs everywhere.

# 11-7  ORGANIZING BRANDS AND PRODUCTS

**LO 11.7** Explain how companies organize to manage brands and products.

## OPENING EXAMPLE

Angela Winstone, Hasbro's VP of Global Brand Strategy and Marketing, has called a meeting with her brand managers to brainstorm a new marketing strategy.

"Our toys are offline, our toys are online," Angela says to her team. "But we need to make sure our brands work together across all formats. We don't want to create isolation between app-based products and physical products."

She cites a recent study conducted by Juniper Research stating that such "smart toys" will be an $11 billion industry by 2020.

Before concluding the meeting, Angela asks her brand managers to generate ideas for ensuring there are synergies across different product formats. In a company with so many brands and products, this type of coordination takes a team.

### 11-7a

## LEARNING IT: ORGANIZING BRANDS AND PRODUCTS

Because of the value associated with strong brand equity, firms expend considerable resources and assign specific staff with the development and maintenance of their brands. This is especially important when a company has multiple brands and product lines, each with their own target markets and marketing mixes. In these cases, there are too many variables to consider and decisions to make for any one person.

**brand manager (product manager)** marketer responsible for a single brand or product

Traditionally, companies have assigned the task of managing a brand's marketing strategies to a **brand manager (product manager)**. The precise title and responsibilities for these positions vary by company and industry. In general, brand and product managers support the marketing strategies of an individual brand or product line, set prices, develop advertising and sales promotion programs, and work with sales representatives in the field. They also support and coordinate efforts of the firm's sales force, marketing researchers, and advertising department. Brand and product managers often lead new product development programs, including creation of new product ideas and recommendations for improving existing products.

*Example*: Apple would have a manager overseeing their iPhone line, a separate manager overseeing their iPad line, and another manager overseeing their line of Macbooks.

The traditional model of having brand and/or product managers is not always the best fit for a company. For example, major consumer goods manufacturers, like Unilever and Procter & Gamble, sell about 80 percent of their products to national retail chains. In this case, **category management** might be used, in which a manager oversees a number of product lines and brands within a single category.

*Example*: Procter & Gamble might have one category manager who oversees the dental care category for Walmart. This manager would try to maximize profitability of all of Procter & Gamble's toothpaste, mouthwash, and floss brands on that aisle.

Some manufacturers that are too small to dedicate a category manager to each retail chain assign a category manager to each major channel, such as convenience stores, drugstores, grocery stores, and so on.[13]

Large, diversified companies might use a mix of brand managers, product managers, and/or category managers.

Patti McConville/Alamy Stock Photo

A category manager may oversee multiple product lines or brands within a particular retail chain or industry category.

**category management** product management system in which a manager oversees a number of product lines and brands within a single category

## 11-7b

# ORGANIZING FOR NEW PRODUCT DEVELOPMENT

A firm needs to be organized in such a way that its personnel can stimulate and coordinate new product development. Most companies assign product-innovation functions to one or more of the following three entities: new product committees, new product departments, or product managers.

### NEW PRODUCT COMMITTEES

The most common organizational arrangement for developing a new product is to center these functions in a new product committee (sometimes called a venture team). This group typically brings together experts in areas such as marketing, finance, manufacturing, engineering, and research.

### NEW PRODUCT DEPARTMENTS

Many companies establish separate, formally organized departments to generate and refine new product ideas. The departmental structure overcomes the temporary nature of new product committees and encourages innovation as a permanent full-time activity. The new product department is responsible for all phases of a development project within the firm, including screening decisions, developing product specifications, and coordinating product testing.

### PRODUCT MANAGERS

As mentioned earlier, the product or brand manager often leads new product development programs, including creation of new product ideas and recommendations for improving existing products.

### 11-7c
# CLOSING EXAMPLE

At the next meeting, Angela Winstone listens to ideas from her brand managers.

"Why don't we integrate a chip in our stuffed Elmo toys that tracks how often a child laughs with Elmo?," says the Elmo brand manager.

"Great idea! I think that we could integrate that data into an enjoyable, laugh-based game," says the brand manager for Sesame Street–themed apps.

Angela is responsible for maintaining a clear and consistent vision across brands so that each individual brand manager knows what to focus on. As a result of this structure, Hasbro will continue to drive new product development and satisfy its mission to assist children "in triumphing over their critical life obstacles and to bring the joy of play into their lives."[14]

# 11-8    THREE MAJOR OBJECTIVES OF PACKAGING

**LO 11.8**  Summarize the three major objectives of packaging.

## OPENING EXAMPLE

H.J. Heinz Co. hadn't redesigned its ketchup bottle since 1983. Customers looked for its iconic look on store shelves, and data validated this fact. But with the arrival of flexible food pouches in recent years—which are less expensive to manufacture and easier to use than plastic bottles—Heinz considered making a change.

Heinz's strategic product design and marketing teams developed a flexible, 10-ounce ketchup pouch with pouring spout for half the price of its traditional 20-ounce bottle. And for its restaurant customers, the unique "Dip and Squeeze" design of its pouches holds three times as much ketchup as traditional restaurant packets, so fewer are needed per order. Heinz invested significant time and resources developing this new product, but will it appeal to its consumers while also maintaining the Heinz brand image?

### 11-8a
## LEARNING IT: THREE MAJOR OBJECTIVES OF PACKAGING

Like its brand name, a product's package can powerfully influence buyer purchase decisions. A package serves three major objectives: protection against damage, spoilage, and pilferage; assistance in marketing the product; and cost-effectiveness.

kenary820/Shutterstock.com

Source: heinzfoodservice.com

What does Heinz hope to accomplish with the new packaging?

## PROTECTION AGAINST DAMAGE, SPOILAGE, AND PILFERAGE

The first objective of packaging is to offer physical protection for the merchandise. Products typically pass through several stages of handling between manufacturing and customer purchase, and a package must protect its contents from damage. In addition, packages of perishable products, such as food, must protect the contents against spoilage. Product tampering is also a concern for many firms. For example, over-the-counter medicines are sold in tamper-resistant packages covered with warnings informing consumers not to purchase merchandise without protective seals intact. All of the packaging formats that Heinz developed served this objective because they offer airtight seals that keep the product fresh and secure. This packaging objective is more important for some categories than others. For example, packaging for eggs or delicate electronics usually emphasizes protection, while packaging for sporting goods and tools does not.

## ASSISTANCE IN MARKETING THE PRODUCT

The proliferation of new products, changes in consumer lifestyles and buying habits, and marketers' emphasis on targeting smaller market segments have increased the importance of packaging as a promotional tool. Marketers combine colors, sizes, shapes, graphics, and typefaces to establish distinctive trade dress that sets their products apart from the competition. For example, many firms address consumer concerns about protecting the environment by designing packages made of biodegradable and recyclable materials. Like the brand name, a package should evoke the product's image and communicate its value.

When it introduced the "dip and squeeze" pouches, Heinz was responding to consumer feedback about having to open and dispose of multiple small packets of ketchup when at fast food restaurants.

## COST-EFFECTIVENESS

Although packaging must perform a number of functions, it must do so at a reasonable cost. Sometimes changes in the packaging can make packages both cheaper and better for the environment. A redesign of the standard gallon milk jug, for example, could cut shipping costs and lessen its environmental impact. By redesigning their bottles, Heinz was able to cut costs and maximize profits.

## 11-8b

# LABELS

Labels were once a separate element applied to a package. Today, they are an integral part of packaging strategy. Labels perform both promotional and informational functions. A **label** carries an item's brand name or symbol, the name and address of the manufacturer or distributor, information about the product's composition and size, and recommended uses. Labels also contain UPC and other stock-keeping codes that allow retailers to organize products and track inventory. The right label can play an important role in attracting consumer attention and encouraging purchases.

Key pieces of legislation regulate labeling and its fair use. Some of the most influential of these are as follows:

**label** a branding component that carries an item's brand name or symbol, the name and address of the manufacturer or distributor, information about the product's composition and size, and recommended uses

- *The Fair Packaging and Labeling Act of 1966* requires that labels provide adequate information concerning the package contents and that a package design facilitate value comparisons among competing products.

- *The Nutrition Labeling and Education Act of 1990* imposes a uniform format in which food manufacturers must disclose nutritional information about their products.

- *The Food Allergen Labeling and Consumer Protection Act of 2004* requires that food labeling disclose all major food allergens in terms the average consumer can understand. According to the FDA, eight allergens account for most documented allergic reactions to food, and all must be identified. They are milk, eggs, peanuts, tree nuts, fish, shellfish, soy, and wheat.[15]

In addition, the Food and Drug Administration (FDA) has mandated design standards for nutritional labels that provide clear guidelines to consumers about food products. The FDA has also tightened definitions for loosely used terms such as *light, fat free, lean,* and *extra lean,* and it mandates that labels list the amounts of fat, sodium, dietary fiber, calcium, vitamins, and other components in typical servings.

## 11-8c

# CLOSING EXAMPLE

Heinz hoped that its innovative pouch design and convenience would appeal to younger consumers, both in grocery stores and in food-service outlets. It trusted in the strength of its brand to convince customers to buy. The company advertised the fact that it kept the same, respected ketchup formula, but improved upon the product delivery. And customers responded. The food-service pouch has already sold over a billion units, including to Wendy's and Chick-fil-A.[16]

Sheila Fitzgerald/Shutterstock.com

While labels serve an important marketing function, certain laws regulate what can be printed on them.

## 11-9　LEARN IT TODAY . . . USE IT TOMORROW

One of Under Armour's core marketing strategies has been "patient" sponsorship: signing on professional athletes before they hit superstar status.[17] Sid Jatia, Under Armour's VP of direct-to-consumer media, explains that there is "a ton of scientific research over how an athlete can perform over the next five to 10 years, there's a team dedicated to it." And as sponsored athletes and teams move up the ranks, so does Under Armour's brand.

Beyond professional sponsorship, Under Armour is dedicated to building a global community of fitness enthusiasts, which further boosts Under Armour's brand image. With recent acquisitions of fitness apps like MapMyFitness and MyFitnessPal, Under Armour has more than 180 million fitness community members on its rolls. Jatia says that the community is a "social channel" in itself, which the brand will continue to make use of, and tie into its core marketing strategies. As it does, Under Armour will continue to innovate and market new products that push technical and physical boundaries for its consumers.

It's time to get hands-on and apply what you've learned. **See MindTap for an activity related to Under Armour's marketing activities.**

# Chapter Summary

**LO 11.1     Distinguish between goods and services.**

Services are intangible products. You can't hold a service in your hand. By contrast, goods are tangible products that customers can see, hear, smell, taste, and/or touch.

**LO 11.2     Contrast the three classifications of consumer products in terms of consumer factors and marketing mix factors.**

A firm's choices for marketing a good or service depend largely on the products themselves and the characteristics and behavior of the target market. Products sold in the consumer market are marketed differently than products marketed in the business market. Some products fall into both categories.

**LO 11.3     Identify the six types of business products.**

The classification system for business products emphasizes product uses rather than customer buying behavior. Business market products generally fall into one of six categories for product uses: installations, accessory equipment, component parts and materials, raw materials, supplies, and business services.

**LO 11.4     Summarize the major elements of brand equity.**

Brand equity refers to the added value a brand name gives to a product in the marketplace. Brands with high brand equity often command comparatively large market shares, and consumers may pay little attention to differences in prices.

**LO 11.5     Differentiate the methods used to develop and protect brand identity.**

Brands are classified in three distinct ways: generic, private, and manufacturer. Each has a different set of characteristics that defines it. In making branding decisions, firms weigh the benefits and drawbacks of each type of brand.

**LO 11.6     Outline the various types of brand strategies used by marketers.**

Because of the value associated with strong brand equity, firms expend considerable resources and task-specific staff with the development and maintenance of their brands. Brand managers, category manager, and product managers are common roles used in organizations today.

**LO 11.7     Explain how companies organize to manage brands and products.**

Organizations identify their products in the marketplace with brand names, brand marks, and distinctive packaging, and protect these brand elements with trademarks.

**LO 11.8     Summarize the three major objectives of packaging.**

Like its brand name, a product's package can powerfully influence buyers' purchase decisions. A package serves three major objectives: protection against damage, spoilage, and pilferage; assistance in marketing the product; and cost-effectiveness.

# Key Terms

goods **217**

services **217**

convenience products **220**

impulse goods and services **220**

staples **220**

shopping products **221**

specialty products **221**

installations **223**

accessory equipment **224**

component parts and
   materials **225**

raw materials **225**

supplies **225**

business services **225**

brand **226**

brand recognition **227**

brand preference **228**

brand insistence **228**

brand equity **228**

brand name **230**

brand mark **230**

trademark **230**

trade dress **230**

generic products **232**

manufacturer brands **233**

private brands **233**

line extension **233**

brand extension **233**

brand manager (product
   manager) **234**

category management **235**

label **238**

# 12 DEVELOPING AND MANAGING PRODUCTS

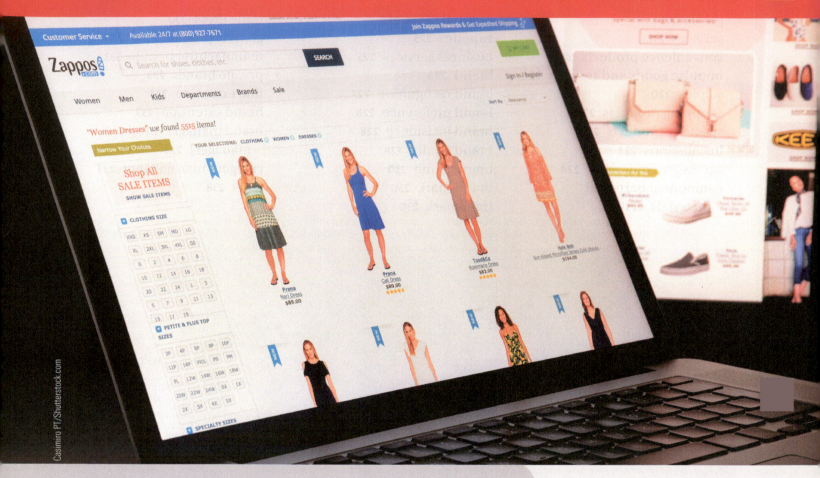

Casimiro PT/Shutterstock.com

## LEARNING OBJECTIVES

**12.1** Summarize the four strategies for new product development.

**12.2** Describe the six steps in the product development process.

**12.3** Describe the five categories of purchasers based on relative time to adoption.

**12.4** Differentiate the four stages of the product lifecycle in terms of industry sales and profits.

**12.5** Given an example of a product, identify marketing strategies for that product's stage of the product lifecycle.

**12.6** Distinguish product mix breadth from product line depth.

**12.7** Summarize methods commonly used for measuring and managing product quality.

# LEARN IT TODAY . . . USE IT TOMORROW

From its humble beginnings as the first online shoe store, Zappos has grown to nearly gargantuan proportions. Now owned by Amazon, the online retailer carries most of the top footwear and apparel brands, along with handbags and luggage, and last but not least, home furnishings and beauty products. In other words, if Zappos were a brick-and-mortar store, you could live there.

The merchandising team, which includes lead buyers, assistant buyers, and merchandising assistants, scours the earth for the best brands in any product category—then meets with vendors and decides which will sell best at Zappos. The company's buyers concentrate entirely on a single category of products. "Our buyers are aligned around lifestyles—so our hiking buyer will buy only hiking products and our running buyer will buy only running products." But specialization doesn't stop there. "Our buyers buy stuff that they're passionate about," explains Hill. "For example, our running buyers are running marathons and half-marathons and 5Ks."

This makes them virtual experts in the category of goods they buy for Zappos to sell online to consumers.

Zappos prefers to hire its buyers based on their passion for a specific activity or product category. "If we can hire them for their passion for the category, we can teach them all the skills of buying," says Hill. In fact, the buyers themselves have created categories at Zappos, based on their own interests. That's how Zappos began selling outdoor apparel and footwear, as well as designer fashions. The other avenue that Zappos takes for developing categories is through customer feedback—if enough customers request a new category or specific brand, Zappos will work hard to bring it to them.

Zappos has so masterfully built its brand that its leaders are viewed as online product management gurus. But as you'll learn in this chapter, much of its success stems from faithfully executing core strategies that can work in virtually any product category or type of business. What are these strategies? What gives Zappos this competitive edge?

# STRATEGIES FOR NEW PRODUCT DEVELOPMENT

## OPENING EXAMPLE

Harley Davidson has been selling motorcycles for more than 100 years. Its bikes have consistently been positioned as masculine and individualistic, enabling riders to live life on their own terms by taking to the open road. While some fans have gone so far as to get tattooed with the Harley Davidson name and logo, most have been content with buying branded T-shirts, ornaments, and socks.

In the 1990s, the company ventured far afield from its traditional offerings, launching a group of new products including Harley Davidson aftershave, perfume, and even wine coolers. All of the items were marketplace duds. So what were Harley Davidson's marketers thinking? And what do you think they did wrong?

 **LO 12.1** Summarize the four strategies for new product development.

### 12-1a

## LEARNING IT: STRATEGIES FOR NEW PRODUCT DEVELOPMENT

As markets evolve and consumer needs change, firms must add new items to continue to prosper. Some new products may offer major technological breakthroughs. Other new products simply extend existing product lines.

**EXHIBIT 12.1**

## Product Development Strategies

|  | Old Product | New Product |
|---|---|---|
| **Old Market** | Market Penetration | Product Development |
| **New Market** | Market Development | Product Diversification |

**market penetration strategy**  seeks to increase sales of existing products in existing markets

**market development strategy**  concentrates on finding new markets for existing products

Ritz crackers offers variations of its core product as a way to further penetrate the snack food market.

**product development**  the introduction of new products into established markets

Source: helpfulhomemade.com

Exhibit 12.1 identifies four alternative product development strategies: **market penetration, market development, product development**, and **product diversification**.

A firm's strategy choice depends on:

- Its existing **product mix** (discussed later in this chapter)
- The match between current offerings and the firm's overall marketing objectives
- The current market positions of its products

A **market penetration strategy** seeks to increase sales of existing products in existing markets. Firms can attempt to extend their penetration of markets in several ways. They may modify products, improve product quality, or promote new and different ways to use products. Packaged-goods marketers often pursue this strategy to boost market share for products in mature categories. For example, Mondelez introduced miniature and low-salt versions of its popular Ritz crackers to deepen its penetration of the snack food market.

A **market development strategy** concentrates on finding new markets for existing products. Market segmentation is often utilized for finding these new markets. New Jersey-based supermarket chain Asian Food Markets once targeted chiefly Asian shoppers. Today, however, the family-owned enterprise has expanded its reach beyond Asian customers by more widely promoting their selection of fresh produce, meat and poultry, and Chinese-inspired dishes for takeout.[1] Besides finding new demographic markets for an existing product, a market development strategy might involve finding new geographic markets, such as expanding internationally. While movie ticket sales in the United States have been relatively flat in the last decade, movie studios are more aggressively promoting in other countries. As a result, global movie ticket sales have doubled over that same time period.[2]

The strategy of **product development** refers to the introduction of new products into established markets. For example, the television market is well-established, with almost every home in the United States having at least one TV. Now, 4K technology, also called ultra-high definition, is the latest product development in this market, promising brighter and crisper images than those on 3-D TVs. The introduction of 4K has spurred development of new products for streaming content, cable boxes, and Blu-ray converters compatible with 4K TVs.[3]

Finally, a **product diversification strategy** focuses on developing entirely new products for new markets. Some firms look for new target markets that complement their existing markets, like a maker of baby food introducing infant clothes. Others look in completely new directions. Several years ago, PepsiCo began diversifying its product lines beyond items that are "fun for you" to items that are "good for you"—including juices, nuts, and oatmeal.[4]

> **product diversification strategy** focuses on developing entirely new products for new markets

## 12-1b
## CLOSING EXAMPLE

Harley Davidson's foray into cosmetics and wine was an attempt at product diversification. But its marketers erred by introducing offerings incompatible with its tough, independent, and powerful brand identity.

The company quickly shifted back to its original focus on product development—creating bike parts, equipment, clothing, and other accessories for avid motorcycle fans. Sales bounced back. In 2016, over half of all new heavyweight registered motorcycles in the United States were Harley Davidsons.[5]

# 12-2   THE NEW PRODUCT DEVELOPMENT PROCESS

## OPENING EXAMPLE

Can a company insulate itself against new product failure? The global beauty giant L'Oreal has certainly tried. With the goal of winning 1 billion new customers over the next decade, the firm opened a global research center in Paris for the sole purpose of developing new hair-coloring, hair-care, and hair-styling products.[6] But just because an organization commits significant resources to new product development doesn't mean its new creations will survive. For example, poor sales forced L'Oreal to withdraw Inneov, a line of nutritional supplements introduced into the European market.[7]

There is no guarantee against new product failure. So firms try to minimize their risk by following a step-by-step development process. Where do you think the process begins—and how does it end? Once you understand these steps,

> **LO 12.2** Describe the six steps in the product development process.

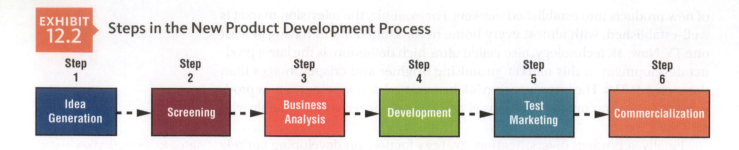

EXHIBIT 12.2  Steps in the New Product Development Process

you'll see where new products come from—and you'll appreciate what it takes to make them successful.

## 12-2a

# LEARNING IT: THE NEW PRODUCT DEVELOPMENT PROCESS

Developing a new product is often time-consuming, risky, and expensive. Usually, firms must generate dozens of new product ideas to produce even one successful product. In fact, the failure rate of new products averages 80%. Products fail for a number of reasons, including inadequate market assessments, poor screening and project evaluation, product defects, and inadequate launch efforts. And these blunders cost a bundle: Firms invest nearly half of the total resources devoted to product innovation on products that become commercial failures.

A new product is more likely to become successful if the firm follows the six-step development process shown in Exhibit 12.2: (1) idea generation, (2) screening, (3) business analysis, (4) development, (5) test marketing, and (6) **commercialization**. Of course, each step requires decisions about whether to proceed further or abandon the project. And each step involves a greater financial investment.

Traditionally, most companies develop new products through phased development, which follows the six steps in an orderly sequence. Responsibility for each phase passes first from product planners to designers and engineers, then to manufacturers, and finally to marketers. The phased development method can work well for firms that dominate mature markets and can develop variations on existing products. But with rapid changes in technology and markets, companies often feel pressured to speed up the development process, which sometimes blurs the lines between the six steps.

### IDEA GENERATION

New product development begins with ideas from many sources: suggestions from customers, the sales force, research and development specialists, competing products, suppliers, retailers, and independent inventors. L'Oreal gets most of its ideas from its Paris-based beauty product experts. In contrast, Bose

**commercialization** when a new product idea is ready for full-scale manufacturing and marketing

L'Oreal screens new product ideas by assessing product uniqueness, estimating availability and cost of raw materials, and evaluating compatibility with current product lines.

REUTERS/Alamy Stock Photo

Corporation has built its brand by staying at the forefront of technology. Spending over $100 million a year on research, the company leads the market for advanced audio products, like noise-cancelling headphones and TV sound systems.[8]

## SCREENING

Screening separates ideas with commercial potential from those that cannot meet company objectives. Some organizations maintain checklists of development standards in determining whether a project should be considered further. These checklists typically include factors such as product uniqueness, availability of raw materials, and the proposed product's compatibility with current product offerings, facilities, and capabilities. L'Oreal would likely abandon a new product idea if a key ingredient is too costly or in short supply.

## BUSINESS ANALYSIS

A product idea that survives the initial screening must then pass through business analysis. This stage consists of assessing the new product's potential market, growth rate, and likely competitive strengths. Before L'Oreal chose to introduce an anti-frizz hair agent, for instance, its marketers would determine how the product could improve on the effectiveness of other brands. Marketers must also evaluate the compatibility of the proposed product with organizational resources, like manufacturing capacity or warehouse space.

L'Oreal might contact industry influencers and loyal customers to discuss new product concepts, get input, and utilize that input to further refine the products.

## DEVELOPMENT

Development refers to the conversion of a new product idea, like an anti-frizz product, into a visible product, like a hair cream or spray. At this stage, the company develops a prototype version of the product or initiates smaller, test production runs of the product. Financial outlays increase substantially at this stage. The conversion process is the joint responsibility of the firm's development engineers, who turn the original concept into a real product, and its marketers, who provide feedback on consumer reactions to the product design, package, and other physical features.

## TEST MARKETING

After a company develops a prototype or early production version of the product, it may decide to test market it to gauge consumer reactions and verify that the product will perform well in a real-life environment. For example, L'Oreal could pick two or three major cities in which to release the new product and gauge results. If the product does well, the company can proceed to commercialization. If it flops, the company can fine-tune certain features and reintroduce it, or pull the plug on the project altogether. Industries that rely heavily on test marketing are snack foods, automobiles, and movies. Of course, even if a product tests well and reaches the commercialization stage, it may still take a while to catch on with the general public.

## COMMERCIALIZATION

When a new product idea is ready for full-scale manufacturing and marketing, it reaches the commercialization stage. For L'Oreal, an example might be the introduction of their new anti-fizz hair spray worldwide. Commercialization of a major new product can expose the firm to substantial expenses. It must establish marketing strategies; fund outlays for production facilities; and acquaint the sales force, marketing partners, and potential customers with the new product.

### 12-2b

# CLOSING EXAMPLE

While L'Oreal was unable to find success with Inneov, new product failures are less common for this cosmetics powerhouse than for many other companies. In large part, that's because its new product development process is one of the most rigorous in the industry—and can serve as a model for other industries.

# 12-3 NEW PRODUCT ADOPTION

## OPENING EXAMPLE

The Rogers family reunion is an annual event. From 85-year-old Grandma Sue to 6-year-old Frankie, all crowd around the buffet table to enjoy the traditional spread of fried chicken, potato salad, and Grandma's fudge brownies. When it comes to communication devices, however, everyone goes their own way.

Grandma stays close to the kitchen so she can get calls on her landline phone. She's had it for 40 years and can't be convinced she needs a cellphone.

Sixty-year-old Uncle Bill pulls out a flip phone when it rings. After replacing it in his pocket, however, he admits to his younger siblings that he's finally shopping for an iPhone. "I'm the last guy at work without one," he admits. "I guess it's time."

Frankie's mom, Barbara, carries an iPhone and take photos of her niece and nephew. She smiles fondly as the young professionals proudly describe the newest addition to their home: a virtual voice-controlled personal assistant. "Sounds interesting," Barbara comments. "I might buy one down the road, but not until I research the brands and read product reviews."

The last family member to arrive is 20-year-old Harris. While apologizing for being late, he's thrilled to show off the virtual reality headset he just bought. "I wanted to be the first in my fraternity house to have one! Isn't it cool?"

And 6-year-old Frankie? For now, he's just enjoying the TV show live-streaming on a laptop tablet.

There are generally five categories of purchaser. Can you categorize the members of the Rogers family based on the types of communication devices they favor? Why are these preferences important to marketers?

### 12-3a

## LEARNING IT: NEW PRODUCT ADOPTION

When a new product is introduced, all consumers move through the **adoption process** a series of stages from first learning about the new product to trying it and deciding whether to purchase it regularly or reject it. These stages in the consumer adoption process can be classified as follows:

1. *Awareness*: Individuals first learn of the new product, but they lack full information about it.
2. *Interest*: Potential buyers begin to seek information about it.
3. *Evaluation*: They consider the likely benefits of the product.
4. *Trial*: They make trial purchases to determine its usefulness.
5. *Adoption/Rejection*: If the trial purchase produces satisfactory results, they decide to use the product regularly.

**LO 12.3** Describe the five categories of purchasers based on relative time to adoption.

**adoption process** a series of stages from first learning about the new product to trying it and deciding whether to purchase.

Marketers must understand the adoption process to move potential consumers to the adoption stage. Once marketers recognize a large number of consumers at the interest stage, they can take steps to stimulate sales by moving these buyers through the evaluation and trial stages.

## 12-3b
# THE DIFFUSION PROCESS

Not all consumers move through the adoption process at the same pace, though. The process by which new products are accepted into the marketplace is called the **diffusion process**. Obviously, companies want their new products to move through this process fast and become immediate hits. However, while some groups of consumers jump at the chance to buy new, innovative products, some groups of consumers are much slower than others to try something unfamiliar. Because of this diversity of consumer adoption, the vast majority of new products take time to win acceptance by the overall market.

Exhibit 12.3 shows the different categories of consumers and how they proceed through the diffusion process.

A few people, known as **innovators**, are first to make trial purchases; typically, they make up the first 2.5% of buyers. Then the number of adopters increases rapidly as the value of the product becomes apparent. The adoption rate finally diminishes as the number of potential consumers who have not adopted, or purchased, the product diminishes. The laggards, at 6%, are the last holdouts. This chart, of course, excludes those who never adopt the product.

Innovators tend to be the most highly educated of the consumer groups. They are younger than the others and more willing to take risks on daring new technologies like driverless cars. They are also more mobile than later adopters and more open to changing both their jobs and addresses.

**Early adopters** care more than innovators about what other people think. They hope others will see them as leading the way in purchase trends. In fact,

---

**diffusion process** the process by which new products are accepted into the marketplace

**innovators** people who are first to make trial purchases

**early adopters** people who are quick to purchase the latest product once it is somewhat established

---

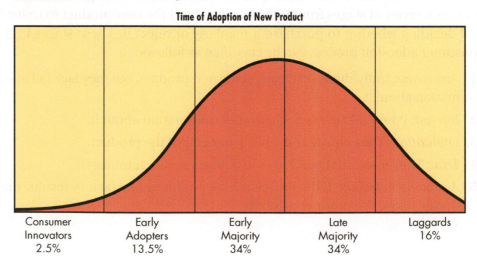

**EXHIBIT 12.3    Categories of Consumer Adopters Based on Relative Times to Adoption**

**Time of Adoption of New Product**

| Consumer Innovators 2.5% | Early Adopters 13.5% | Early Majority 34% | Late Majority 34% | Laggards 16% |

they are often opinion leaders who effectively create buzz about new products. While early adopters might not rush to buy driverless cars quite yet, they are quick to purchase the latest hybrids as that category is better established.

Members of the early majority tend to be mainstream in outlook and middle class in income and education. They are careful and pragmatic in their adoption decisions, typically waiting to buy a new product until its benefits have been clearly demonstrated in the marketplace.

Members of the late majority are generally older and more risk-averse than other groups. In general, these consumers only buy a new product when its diffusion in the marketplace is nearly complete; at this point, they face peer pressure or job requirements to adopt it. The late majority has finally come aboard with iPhones and laptops, for instance.

Laggards are fearful of change and bound by tradition in outlook and behavior. They tend to be older and lower in social class than other groups. By the time laggards finally adopt new products, like DVDs, the products have largely been overtaken by far newer formats, like digital downloads.[9]

While the basic differences among consumer adoption categories are apparent across all kinds of new products, these differences become especially clear when it comes to new technologies.[10,11] Innovators seek out new technologies and enjoy experimenting with them. Early adopters keep an eye on what the innovators are doing, and are eager to get onboard with a new technology when they see how it could help enhance their lives or improve their social or professional standing.

Members of the mainstream, or early majority, won't take the initiative in seeking out new technologies. However, these consumers are not averse to new technologies, and will readily adopt them when they are surrounded by other adopters.

The late majority will typically wait for significant price reductions or other marketing incentives before they adopt a new technology. Laggards will try to avoid purchasing a new technology at all—and will sometimes succeed. For example, a small number of telecommunications customers still insist on using landlines instead of cellphones.

## 12-3c
# FACTORS AFFECTING RATES OF ADOPTION

To some extent, marketers can influence the speed of the consumer adoption process by manipulating five characteristics of a product innovation:

1. *Relative advantage*: An innovation that appears far superior to previous ideas offers a greater relative advantage—reflected in terms of lower price, physical improvements, or ease of use—and increases the product's adoption rate. Uber quickly demonstrated that its car service was usually cheaper and more reliable than traditional taxis.

2. *Compatibility*: An innovation consistent with the values and experiences of potential adopters attracts new buyers at a relatively rapid rate. Consumers comfortable with the miniaturization of computing technology are attracted to smartphones, for instance, and the size of their display screens.

Uber encouraged quicker market adoption by making it easy to hail a ride, offering an app that could easily be downloaded to almost any phone, and by simplifying the user experience. One click of a button hails your ride and payment happens automatically when you arrive at your destination.

Richard Levine/Alamy Stock Photo

3. *Complexity*: The relative difficulty of understanding how innovation influences the speed of acceptance. In most cases, consumers move slowly in adopting new products they find difficult to understand or use. Farmers took 13 years to accept hybrid seed corn, despite its potential to double crop yields.

4. *Possibility of trial use*: An initial free or discounted trial of a good or service means adopters can reduce their risk of financial loss when they try the product. A coupon for a free item or a free night's stay at a hotel can accelerate the rate of adoption.

5. *Observability*: If potential buyers can observe an innovation's superiority in a tangible form, the adoption rate increases. In-store demonstrations or even advertisements that focus on the superiority of a product can encourage buyers to adopt a product.

## 12-3d
## CLOSING EXAMPLE

When it comes to communication devices, the Rogers family spans every category of consumer adoption. Harris is an innovator, while the young professionals are early adopters. Barbara belongs to the early majority, Uncle Bill to the late majority, and Grandma Sue to the group known as laggards. (Frankie may be a budding innovator—but at the moment, he's focused on the benefits of the product at hand.)

Understanding these stages of consumer adoption is important for marketers. Whatever good or service they're offering, finding traction with early purchasers and using them to build momentum can mean the difference between a new product that's a hit and one that's a flop.

# 12-4  THE PRODUCT LIFECYCLE

## OPENING EXAMPLE

If you own a DVD player, can you remember the last time you bought new DVDs for it? If not, you're hardly alone. While they successfully pushed VHS cartridges off store shelves in the 1990s, sales of DVDs have been plummeting since 2006. First the players were replaced by Blu-ray devices and gaming consoles; then streaming services like Netflix replaced the discs themselves.[12]

Like people, home entertainment technologies—and other products and services—pass through stages as they age. The stages of people's lives are called infancy, youth, adulthood, and old age. What do you think marketers call the equivalent stages in the product lifecycle? And what do those stages mean in terms of industry sales and profits?

**LO 12.4** Differentiate the four stages of the product lifecycle in terms of industry sales and profits.

## 12-4a

### LEARNING IT: THE PRODUCT LIFECYCLE

The **product lifecycle** is the progression of a product through four basic stages: introduction, growth, maturity, and decline (see Exhibit 12.4).

The product lifecycle concept applies to products or product categories within an industry, not to individual brands. There is no set schedule or time frame for a particular stage of the lifecycle.

**product lifecycle** the progression of a product through four basic stages: introduction, growth, maturity, and decline

### INTRODUCTORY STAGE

During the **introductory stage** of the product lifecycle, a firm works to stimulate demand for the new-market entry. Merchandise in this stage might bring new technology to a product category. In this phase, the public becomes acquainted

**introductory stage** first stage of the product lifecycle, in which a firm works to stimulate sales of a new product

---

**EXHIBIT 12.4** ▶ Stages in the Product Lifecycle

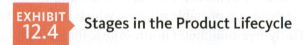

with the item's merits and begins to accept it. Industry sales volume begins to grow, however profits don't immediately follow. Technical problems and financial losses are common during the introductory stage as companies fine-tune product design and spend money on advertising.

A product category currently in the introductory stage is driverless cars. GM, Ford, and BMW have all expressed their intent to put driverless cars on the road within the next decade. Initially, costs will be high and profits minimal. However, these companies hope market growth in the category will eventually produce big profits.[13]

## GROWTH STAGE

**growth stage** second stage of the product lifecycle that begins when a firm starts to realize substantial profits from its investment

Sales volume rises rapidly during the growth stage as new customers make initial purchases and early buyers repurchase the product. In the **growth stage**, a firm starts to realize substantial profits from its investment. However, as sales volume rises and the product category becomes more attractive, competitors enter the marketplace, creating new challenges for marketers. For example, after early years of strong growth and profitability in the cell phone market, competition has turned fierce among Apple, Samsung, and LG Electronics.[14] As a result, industry profits often peak and begin to decline during the growth stage.

## MATURITY STAGE

**maturity stage** third stage of product lifecycle, in which industry sales reach a plateau

Sales of a product category continue to grow during the early part of the **maturity stage**, but they eventually reach a plateau as the backlog of potential customers dwindles. By this time, many competitors have entered the market, and industry profits continue to decline as competition intensifies. Digital cameras are in the maturity stage.

## DECLINE STAGE

**decline stage** final stage of the product lifecycle, in which innovations or shifts in consumer preferences bring about a steady decline in industry sales

In the **decline stage** of a product's life, innovations or shifts in consumer preferences bring about a steady decline in industry sales. Dial telephones became touch-tone phones, which evolved into portable phones, which have now been replaced with cell phones. Thirty-five-millimeter home-movie film was replaced with videotape, which was in turn replaced by DVD. Now DVD sales are declining quickly as movie viewing shifts to streaming services such as Netflix and Amazon Video.

## 12-4b
### CLOSING EXAMPLE

DVDs are far from obsolete, but they're taking a beating in the marketplace. In 2015, sales of the discs plunged by 12%—while revenues from digital streaming rose 18%.[15] In 2016, disc purchases still generated $5.4 billion, but subscriptions to streaming services like Netflix produced nearly a billion dollars more ($6.2 billion).[16]

Despite their current success, however, marketers of streaming technologies shouldn't get complacent. While we can't foresee how soon, many of today's innovations will, in their turn, become tomorrow's white elephants. The challenge for companies is to invest in products that will have the longest, most productive life spans.

# MARKETING ACROSS THE PRODUCT LIFECYCLE

**12-5**

## OPENING EXAMPLE

Are you a fan of onion dip made by mixing dried soup mix with sour cream? If so, you enjoy one of the most popular treats in America—but you may not know where it came from.

When dried soup mixes were introduced by Lipton in the mid-twentieth century, most American homemakers welcomed the product to help speed up the daily chore of cooking for their families. But as time went on, women prepared fewer and fewer meals from scratch. Lipton needed a way to shore up demand for what was clearly a mature product.

Enter onion soup dip, first featured on Lipton packages as a recipe suggestion in 1958. Almost immediately, the idea for this simple snack and party food took off like a rocket. Today, an estimated 220,000 Lipton Onion Soup packets are used every day.[17]

In marketing terms, Lipton was tremendously successful in extending the lifecycle of dried onion soup. How did the company do it? Can others do the same?

**LO 12.5** Given an example of a product, identify marketing strategies for that product's stage of the product lifecycle.

## 12-5a

## LEARNING IT: MARKETING ACROSS THE PRODUCT LIFECYCLE

Companies don't market all products in their portfolio the same. Instead, they tailor their marketing decisions based on the stage of any particular product in the product lifecycle (see Exhibit 12.5).

During the introductory stage, when the product is unknown to the public, promotional campaigns are needed to raise awareness about the product. Additional promotions try to induce distribution partners, like wholesalers and retailers, to carry the product. In 2015, General Mills mounted a heavy TV advertising campaign to inform buyers about its new gluten-free Cheerios.

During the growth stage, marketers must encourage hesitant consumers to make trial purchases. Word-of-mouth reports, mass advertising, and lowered prices or other sales promotion incentives all can be effective in stimulating trial. Cheerios offered coupons and special discounts to encourage trial of the gluten-free product.

**EXHIBIT 12.5**

## Marketing Challenges Across the Product Lifecycle

| Stage in Product Lifecycle | Key Marketing Challenge | Key Marketing Approaches |
|---|---|---|
| **Introductory** | Need to stimulate initial demand | • Communicate information to consumers about product features through advertising<br>• Induce distribution channel members to carry the product, sometimes through discounting |
| **Growth** | Need to encourage trial purchases | • Use promotional tools and price discounts to motivate hesitant buyers |
| **Maturity** | Need to counter intense competition | • Shift focus of promotions to emphasize competitive differences<br>• Differentiate product through focus on attributes like quality, reliability, service, redesign<br>• Possibly redesign product or offer additional colors, styles, features |
| **Decline** | Maximize remaining profits | • Prune product lines to streamline production and lower costs<br>• Cut back on advertising and other promotional expenses<br>• Evaluate product for deletion |

At the maturity stage, differences between competing products often diminish as competitors discover the characteristics most desired by customers. Heavy promotional outlays are needed to emphasize any differences still separating competing products. Some firms try to differentiate their products by focusing on attributes like quality, reliability, and service. Others focus on product redesign or seek ways to expand their target audience.

In the tablet market, for example, Microsoft ran a hard-hitting advertising campaign to convince buyers that its Surface Pro was a more powerful desktop substitute than the Apple iPad. Mocking the iPad's inability to run desktop apps like Windows Office, the campaign also faulted the Apple product for lacking a keyboard and USB port—and for charging a higher price.

After a period of significant growth, the tablet market in the United States may be entering the maturity stage, where competitors often shift promotional campaigns to focus on competitive differences.

Source: YouTube, LLC

For products and product categories in the decline stage, marketers must carefully evaluate the best strategy. If overall sales volume remains strong, then the company might choose to streamline production costs by offering fewer models and features. They will also typically scale back promotional expenses. The cost savings of these decisions may allow marketers to cut prices to stay competitive, while maintaining reasonable margins. The goal during this stage is to maximize profits and market share while the product remains viable.

Despite their best efforts at extending the product lifecycle, marketers must sometimes prune product lines and eliminate unpromising products to avoid wasting resources. After battling it out with Sony in the DVD player arena, Toshiba finally conceded defeat and announced it would stop making its HD DVD player. That left Sony the winner in the marketplace with its Blu-ray format.

## 12-5b
# EXTENDING THE PRODUCT LIFECYCLE

Marketers usually try to extend each stage of the lifecycle for their products as long as possible. Product lifecycles can stretch indefinitely as a result of decisions designed to increase the frequency of use by current customers; increase the number of users for the product; find new uses; or change package sizes, labels, or product quality.

### INCREASING FREQUENCY OF USE

During the maturity stage, total sales can still rise—even though no new buyers enter the market—if current customers buy more frequently than they formerly did. For instance, consumers buy some products during certain seasons of the year.

Marketers can boost purchase frequency by persuading these people to try the product year-round. For decades, most people used sunscreen only during warm and sunny seasons of the year. With greater warnings about the risks of sun damage and skin cancer, companies now advertise the benefits of using sunscreen year-round.

### INCREASING THE NUMBER OF USERS

A second strategy for extending the product lifecycle is to increase the overall market size by attracting new customers who previously have not used the product. By offering a gluten-free version, General Mills made Cheerios a safe breakfast option for parents of children with gluten allergies.

### FINDING NEW USES

New applications for mature products include oatmeal as a cholesterol reducer, antacids as a calcium supplement, and aspirin for promoting heart health. The Clorox Company promotes its Hidden Valley Ranch salad dressing as a dip for any food ranging from crab to pretzels and pizza.

Arm & Hammer's website lists dozens of alternative uses throughout the house for its baking soda. Consumers can use baking soda to clean crayon off walls, to fuel an "erupting volcano" science experiment, or as an agent to balance the pH in swimming pool water.[18]

### 12-5c
## CLOSING EXAMPLE

Lipton found a new use for a mature product by promoting dried onion soup as the key ingredient in onion dip. Without this initiative, the familiar soup packets might well have gone the way of film cameras. Instead, Lipton was able to extend the lifecycle of the product, making it a staple of Super Bowl parties and campus get-togethers throughout America.

## 12-6

# THE PRODUCT MIX

**LO 12.6** Distinguish product mix breadth from product line depth.

## OPENING EXAMPLE

Johnson & Johnson offers a broad line of retail consumer products in the U.S. market as well as business-to-business products to the medical community. Consumers can purchase over-the-counter medications, nutritional products, and first-aid products, among others. Health-care professionals can prescribe medicines and obtain medical and diagnostic devices. LifeScan, one of the firm's subsidiaries, offers an entire suite of products designed to help diabetes patients manage their condition. DePuy, another subsidiary, manufactures orthopedic implants and joint replacement products.[19]

Does this sound like a random assortment of health care goods? It's not. In fact, these products clearly relate to each other. Do you know how?

### 12-6a
## LEARNING IT: THE PRODUCT MIX

**product line** a group of related products sold under the same brand

**product mix** an assortment of product lines and individual product offerings

**product mix breadth** the number of different product lines a firm offers

A **product line** is a group of related products sold under the same brand. A company's **product mix** is its assortment of product lines and individual product offerings. The right blend of products allows a firm to maximize sales opportunities within the limitations of its resources. Marketers typically measure product mixes according to product mix breadth and product line depth.

**Product mix breadth** refers to the number of different product lines the firm offers.

*Example #1*: Apple offers iPhones, iMacs, iPads, and a number of different product lines. All of those lines together represent Apple's product mix breadth.

*Example #2*: Toyota offers the Camry, Corolla, 4Runner, and a number of different models. Each of those types of vehicles represents a product line. All of the lines together represent Toyota's product mix breadth.

**Product line depth** refers to the number of variations in each product line. Variations may be in size, flavor, color, or another relevant difference.

*Example #1*: Within the iPhone product line, Apple offers multiple screen sizes and different amounts of memory. The number of major variations among the iPhone models offered represents their product line depth.

*Example #2*: Within the Toyota Camry product line you can choose from several different models, including the LE, SE, Hybrid LE, and more. These major variations represent product line depth.

**product line depth** the number of variations in each product line

## 12-6b

## MANAGING THE PRODUCT MIX

Adding breadth and depth to the product mix requires careful thinking and planning; otherwise, a firm can end up with too many products, including some that don't sell well. Marketers may ask two questions to assess the need for changes:

1. Has the firm ignored a viable consumer segment? If so, that segment may be served by increasing product line depth to offer a new product variation.

2. Does the firm gain equal contributions from all items in its portfolio? If not, the product mix may be overly broad and discontinuing some product lines–or reducing product mix breadth—could cut costs and possibly increase revenues.

Sometimes a firm may benefit from increasing both breadth and depth. Italian shoe manufacturer Geox is known for its patented breathable fabric that keeps feet cool and comfortable. With annual sales near $1 billion, Geox is adding depth to its women's shoe line in the form of trendy styles, like strappy sandals. The firm is also broadening its product mix breadth with apparel and shoe lines for men and children, made of similar breathable fabrics that help keep consumers cool and dry.[20]

## 12-6c

## CLOSING EXAMPLE

An important element in Johnson and Johnson's success is the breadth of its health care product mix. The firm is able to satisfy different sectors of the market (consumers, caregivers, health care businesses and institutions) as well as a range of needs within each sector. Additionally, Johnson and Johnson products are medicine chest staples largely because of the depth of its product lines (see Exhibit 12.6). For example, first aid kits are rarely without Band-Aid brand bandages in various shapes, sizes, and materials. Over the course of your life, you may have used Finger-Care Tough Strips, Comfort-Flex, Activ-Flex, or Advance Healing Blister bandages—possibly all of them.

EXHIBIT
12.6 Johnson and Johnson Product Mix

**Product Mix Breadth**

**Product Line Depth**

| Over-the-Counter Medicines | Nutritionals | Skin and Hair Care | Oral Care | Medical Devices and Diagnostics |
|---|---|---|---|---|
| Motrin pain reliever | Lactaid digestive aid | Aveeno lotions | Listerine oral rinse | Ethicon surgical instruments and systems |
| Tylenol pain reliever | Splenda artificial sweetener | Clean & Clear facial cleansers and toners | REACH dental floss | LifeScan diabetes management products |
| Benadryl antihistamine | | Johnson's baby shampoo | Rembrandt whitening toothpaste | Orthopedic joint replacement products |
| Mylanta antacid | | Neutrogena soaps and shampoos | Listerine whitening strips | |

Source: Company website, www.jnj.com, accessed March 13, 2014.

## 12-7  QUALITY AS A PRODUCT STRATEGY

LO
12.7

Summarize methods commonly used for measuring and managing product quality.

### OPENING EXAMPLE

In the casual-dining segment of the restaurant industry, Cheesecake Factory "takes the cake" in terms of customer satisfaction. In a survey of more than 6,000 restaurant patrons, the California-based chain outranked competitors in customers' overall satisfaction and likelihood they'd recommend the brand to others.[21]

Importantly, it was more than the food that drove those rankings. Of course, the quality of a restaurant meal matters to people—but so does the quality of the service they receive, from the time they arrive to when their checks are paid.

The quality of a tangible good is usually apparent in how the product functions or how long it lasts. These characteristics are important to customers and measurable by marketers. The quality of a service, however, is trickier to assess. Think of your favorite restaurant. What does that restaurant do to earn your high marks? How can marketers pursue quality as a product strategy—for both goods and services?

### 12-7a

## LEARNING IT: QUALITY AS A PRODUCT STRATEGY

Quality is a key component to a firm's success in a competitive marketplace. The goal of quality as a product strategy first developed in the United States in the 1920s, but the quality campaign did not pick up speed until the 1980s. Initially, its focus was on improving manufacturing processes to stem the market share losses of Ford, Xerox, Motorola, and other large firms to Japanese competitors. Today, commitment to quality has spread to service industries, not-for-profit organizations, government agencies, and educational institutions.

The quality movement is also strong in European countries. The European Union's ISO 9001 standards define international, generic criteria for quality management and quality assurance. ISO 9001 apply to any organization, regardless of the goods or services it produces. Many European companies require suppliers to achieve ISO certification, a rigorous process that takes several months to complete, as a condition of doing business with them.[22]

There are several methods of ensuring product quality.

## BENCHMARKING

Firms often rely on an important tool called benchmarking to set performance standards. A typical **benchmarking** process involves three main activities:

- Identifying manufacturing or business processes that need improvement.
- Comparing internal processes to those of industry leaders.
- Implementing changes for quality improvement.

**benchmarking** a method of measuring quality by comparing performance against industry standards

Benchmarking requires two types of analyses: internal and external. Before a company can compare itself with another, it must first analyze its own activities to determine strengths and weaknesses. For example, a restaurant might scrutinize its falloff of diners on weekday nights. This assessment establishes a baseline for comparison. External analysis involves gathering information about the benchmark partner to find out why the partner is perceived as the industry's best—perhaps a larger restaurant draws crowds by offering discounted weekday specials. A comparison of the results provides an objective basis for making improvements. From time to time, firms of all sizes—particularly large firms—benchmark their practices against their competitors and other players in their industry. Often, organizations follow a formal, complex program, but benchmarking can also take a simpler, more informal approach as well.

## LEAN AND SIX SIGMA

Two other quality-improvement tools are common in today's marketplace: Lean and Six Sigma. While both seek to boost the efficiency of production and marketing processes, they differ in emphasis. Lean is focused on identifying and eliminating waste in production systems; Six Sigma targets defects and unnecessary variations. For example, a Lean initiative might find that the company is paying to warehouse more inventory than necessary to fulfill orders on time. The solution: improving communication with customers about when they actually need new shipments. A Six Sigma project might seek to address variations in customer satisfaction ratings from store to store. Its recommendations could include standardizing customer-service training and improving supervision of salespeople across stores.

# QUALITY OF SERVICES

**service encounter** the point at which the customer and service provider interact

As a consumer, your perception of the quality of a service is usually determined during the **service encounter**-the point at which the customer and service provider interact. Employees such as bank tellers, cashiers, and customer service representatives have a powerful impact on their customers' decisions to return or not. You might pass the word to your friends about the friendly staff at your local car wash, the slow cashiers at a local supermarket, or the huge scoops of ice cream you got at the nearby ice cream stand. Those words form powerful marketing messages about the services you received.

Online retailer Zappos.com (now part of Amazon) built its business on delivering exceptional customer service by, among other things, providing free shipping, maintaining a 365-day return policy, and paying rigorous attention to hiring only those whose passion for customer service matched the company's high standards. The decision to focus on customer service rather than on marketing enabled Zappos to grow to a billion-dollar company. In fact, consumers regularly name Zappos number one in customer service.[23]

Poor service can cut into a firm's competitiveness. When server problems hit an Amazon data center recently, its cloud computing platform shut down. The outage also brought down several major websites that rent cloud space from Amazon: Instagram, Vine, and others. In all, the sites were out of commission, or at least partly disabled, for about an hour. Although Amazon issued an apology and explanation, this latest outage and other past events underscored the unreliability of cloud computing.[24] Deserved or not, consumers often perceive such technology glitches as customer-service problems and, dissatisfied, they may begin to seek alternatives.

**service quality** the perceived level of service a customer receives

**Service quality** is determined by five variables. In the case of a highly rated restaurant like Cheesecake Factory, these variables include:

1. *Tangibles*, or physical evidence. For example, the restaurant is clean and comfortable; staff are neatly dressed and groomed.

2. *Reliability*, or consistency of performance and dependability. Whenever you visit the restaurant, you can count on getting prompt, courteous service.

3. *Responsiveness*, or the readiness to serve. You never need to wait for attention at the restaurant: the menu is presented right away, dishes are cleared as soon as they're empty, and the check is ready when you are.

4. *Assurances*, or the confidence communicated by the service provider. The manager who takes your reservation might say, "No worries–we'll have your table ready as soon as you arrive."

5. *Empathy*, which shows the service provider understands customers' needs and is ready to fulfill them. Your waiter may ask, "May I refill your water glass or bring you more bread?"

A gap that exists between the level of service customers expect and the level they received can be favorable or unfavorable. If you get a larger steak than you expected, or your plane arrives ahead of schedule, the gap is favorable, and you are likely to try that service again. If your steak is tiny and cold, or your plane is two hours late, the gap is unfavorable, and you may seek out another restaurant or decide to drive the next time.

### 12-7c
### CLOSING EXAMPLE

In addition to the quality and healthiness of its food, Cheesecake Factory won accolades from customers for the atmosphere of its restaurants. In highly competitive markets like casual dining, such intangible quality attributes can hold the key to a company's success.

Cheesecake Factory isn't resting on its laurels. In an innovative partnership with IBM and N2N Global, the chain is collecting and analyzing reams of data to understand every aspect of the customer experience and rapidly respond to any problem spots.[25] This ever-increasing emphasis on quality means good news for Cheesecake Factory fans—and good opportunities for its marketers.

 **12-8**

# LEARN IT TODAY . . . USE IT TOMORROW

Online shoe retailer Zappos has built its success by developing and managing a unique selection of products. Another key strength: while many brands offered on the site are available elsewhere, customers buy from Zappos because they know they'll get unparalleled customer service.

It's time to get hands-on and apply what you've learned. **See MindTap for an activity related to Zappos's marketing activities.**

## Chapter Summary

**LO 12.1 Summarize the four strategies for new product development.**

The most effective strategy for new product development depends on a firm's current product mix and market conditions. Companies may choose to develop new offerings through market penetration, market development, product development, or product diversification.

**LO 12.2 Describe the six steps in the product development process.**

To minimize the risks of new product development, firms follow a disciplined step-by-step development process. The steps include idea generation, screening, business analysis, development, test marketing, and commercialization.

**LO 12.3** Describe the five categories of purchasers based on relative time to adoption.

Consumers differ significantly in how rapidly they adopt new products. The fastest group is known as innovators; other categories iwnclude early adopters, early majority, late majority, and laggards.

**LO 12.4** Differentiate the four stages of the product lifecycle in terms of industry sales and profits.

Like people, products progress through lifecycle stages: introductory, growth, maturity, and decline. Each of these stages is associated with distinctive fluctuations in overall industry sales and profits.

**LO 12.5** Given an example of a product, identify marketing strategies for that product's stage of the product lifecycle.

Marketers face different challenges as their products move through the product lifecycle. They may need to stimulate demand, encourage trial, counter intense competition, or make deletion decisions.

**LO 12.6** Distinguish product mix breadth from product line depth.

The breadth of a product mix refers to the number of different products a firm sells. Product line depth refers to variations in each product the firm markets in its mix.

**LO 12.7** Summarize methods commonly used for measuring and managing product quality.

Product quality as a marketing strategy may be pursued for both tangible goods and intangible services. Methods such as quality programs, benchmarking, and implementation of Lean or Six Sigma methods can help firms make objective, actionable quality assessments.

# Key Terms

# PART 5

## PRICING DECISIONS

# 13 PRICING CONCEPTS

Rawpixel.com/Shutterstock.com

## LEARNING OBJECTIVES

**13.1** Describe the three foundations of pricing strategy.

**13.2** Summarize the three pricing objectives.

**13.3** Calculate pricing using the markup and margin methods.

**13.4** Differentiate between fixed and variable costs.

**13.5** Calculate breakeven point.

**13.6** Describe how the cost-volume-profit relationship affects pricing strategy.

**13.7** Given cost information and pricing objectives, calculate the breakeven point for a product.

# LEARN IT TODAY ... USE IT TOMORROW

Americans love their pizza and, according to a recent report, 3 billion pizzas are sold annually—totaling almost $39 billion. This translates to 46 slices of pizza per person per year.[1] The pizza market is highly competitive with chains such as Pizza Hut and Dominos accounting for 61% of the market and independent pizzerias making up the rest. However, chain stores are seeing sales increase while independent pizzerias are seeing business decline.[2] Like most businesses, pizza restaurants must control costs and implement pricing strategies that enable them to earn a reasonable profit, while still attracting customers in this competitive industry. Even the best pizza company can fail if the product is priced improperly. Fortunately for restaurant managers and owners, there are core pricing concepts that explain the relationship between costs, demand, and profitability. These concepts help marketers determine what to offer and how much to charge.

# 13-1 FOUNDATIONS OF PRICING STRATEGY

## OPENING EXAMPLE

Travis previously worked as a barista at a major coffee retailer, then started his own mobile coffee business where he sets up shop at multiple locations throughout the city. He uses Facebook and Instagram to alert customers to his weekly schedule and notify them of new flavors and bakery items. When starting the business, Travis wasn't sure how to price his products. But he knew his business success and personal income depended on the ability to set prices that covered his costs, were in-line with the competition, and took into account consumer demand for specialty coffee drinks. How should Travis determine the "best" price for his products?

### 13-1a

## LEARNING IT: FOUNDATIONS OF PRICING STRATEGY

In most economies, **price** refers to the amount of funds required to purchase a product. This chapter discusses the process for determining a profitable but justifiable price. Marketers must understand the critical role price plays in the consumer decision making process and adjust multiple aspects of the marketing mix accordingly. While there are a number of factors to consider when building a pricing strategy, the three foundations are costs, potential demand, and competition. This chapter and the next will build upon these three concepts.

**price** the amount of funds required to purchase a product

### THE INFLUENCE OF COSTS ON PRICING DECISIONS

Marketers must calculate the costs associated with making their products and set a price that, at a minimum, covers those costs. Consider the company LG, which sells a number of electronics and household appliances. When they produce an OLED television, there are material and labors costs directly attributed to the production of that TV. Those costs constitute a floor for the price of the televisions, because selling below those costs would mean LG is losing money on the sale of each TV. Ideally, the selling price of each TV brings in enough to cover the direct costs of production and helps contribute to the regular fixed costs (or operating costs) of the company, such as rent, utilities, and salaries of non-production staff. But at the very least, production costs should be covered for each unit. While some companies might sell a product below the production costs for short-term promotional purposes, this is not a sustainable strategy over the long term.

## POTENTIAL DEMAND AND PRICING DECISIONS

Marketers should also understand how price might affect a consumer's willingness to buy the product. For most products, as the price increases fewer consumers are willing to buy the product. Out of a group of 100 college students, most might be willing to buy a mobile phone at $200, but a smaller group would be willing to buy one at $600 if it had better features and was higher quality. However, very few—if any—would be willing to buy a phone at $10,000 no matter what features it had. If costs represent the price floor, the price point at which no more customers are willing to buy represents the price ceiling.

The relationship between price and potential demand can be driven by many factors and varies over time. For example, consider the savvy umbrella salespeople who appear seemingly out of nowhere on the streets of New York when a rain storm hits. How much would you be willing to pay for an umbrella during a rain storm? Probably a lot more than on a sunny day, when it's hard to sell an umbrella at any price. When gas is less expensive, sales of hybrid cars usually slow down because they cost more than conventional gas-fueled cars. However, when gas prices spike, more consumers are willing to pay the higher price for hybrid cars because the increased fuel efficiency saves them money overall.

## COMPETITION AND PRICING DECISIONS

Competition also affects a firm's pricing strategy, perhaps even more than cost. Suppose LG can produce a TV for $500, which normally would represent the price floor for a product. If all of LG's competitors can offer a similar TV for $300, LG would have a tough time selling any of their TV's for $500 or more. In this case, LG would need to either cut costs so they could price competitively, or enhance features to differentiate their product and justify the higher price. Frequently, companies do both.

In the wireless phone industry, the three major carriers have fairly similar pricing and data plans. However, they differentiate themselves in other ways, such as by the conditions they put on data use, charges for additional lines, and network speed. Exhibit 13.1 summarizes the price differences and details recently offered by various cell phone providers.[3]

Some companies may seek to match or beat competitor prices to remain attractive to consumers. Consider the competitive landscape of the fast-food market, where McDonald's, Burger King, and Taco Bell constantly battle it out for market share. While each maintains a full menu of items at "regular prices" they also offer value menus to attract price conscious customers. The use of

**EXHIBIT 13.1**    **Competitive Pricing of Carriers**

| Features | Verizon | AT&T | T-Mobile |
|---|---|---|---|
| Price | $80/month plus taxes and fees | $100/month plus taxes and fees | $70/month including taxes and fees |
| 2nd line charge | $60/month | $55/month | $30/month |
| Average download speed mbps[4] | 30 mbps | 16 mbps | 12 mbps |
| Average upload speed mbps[5] | 18 mbps | 5 mbps | 16 mbps |
| Data plan | Unlimited | Unlimited | Unlimited |
| Other | Must use auto-pay.<br><br>If using a hotspot, Verizon may limit speeds after 10GB per month is reached | Applies only to DirecTV subscribers (minimum of $50 per month).<br><br>May reduce data speeds after 22GB per month is reached. | Must use auto-pay.<br><br>Speed may be reduced for those who are the top levels of data usage. |

Source: Company website. http://www.pcmag.com/article/345123/fastest-mobile-networks-2016/34. Accessed April 14, 2017.

value menus has increased over the years as these companies seek to remain competitive. However, value pricing sometimes creates other difficulties in that restaurant chains can struggle to remain profitable when prices are barely above production costs.[6] In response, some of these restaurants have actually launched

Many fast-food restaurants utilize value menus to stimulate consumer demand and remain competitive, but they should at least cover production costs when pricing these items.

premium products to differentiate themselves and command higher prices. The launch of the artisan grilled chicken sandwich at McDonald's is an example of this strategy.

## 13-1b
## CLOSING EXAMPLE

Pricing decisions are complex and Travis should consider all three foundations of pricing strategy—costs, demand, and competition. For example, Travis pays for beans, milk, cups, and labor to provide product to customers; but he also pays for operating expenses associated with running his business. Travis must consider these costs when setting prices in order to ensure he can, at a minimum, cover them. He should also understand how pricing affects demand and consider ways to maximize profit while still making sure enough customers remain willing to buy. He can't sell at $1 per cup because that wouldn't cover his costs. He also can't sell at $20 per cup because nobody would buy at such a high price. Travis looks for the perfect price where he can attract the maximum number of customers at the highest reasonable price per unit. This perfect price is highly influenced by the prices offered at various specialty coffee retailers and chain stores like McDonald's and Dunkin' Donuts. After researching what these companies charge, Travis prices his regular coffees and baked goods at or below his competitors. But then he charges higher prices for his specialized drinks that nobody else in town offers. This helps Travis maximize pricing while addressing each of the three foundations of pricing strategy.

# 13-2     PRICING OBJECTIVES

**LO 13.2** Summarize the three pricing objectives.

### OPENING EXAMPLE

Many consumers today are price conscious and seek to make good use of their hard-earned money at the grocery store. While consumers may have brand preferences, it's likely that some decisions will occur at the point-of-sale when price could play a key role in determining which brand makes it into the shopping cart. Yusef is planning a trip to the grocery store and wants to spend a little extra time comparing products to decide which ones he should really buy. Sometimes he's driven by price alone, but sometimes he carefully considers quality. In the process, this careful price comparison may also reveal the underlying pricing objectives of the companies offering these products.

## 13-2a
## LEARNING IT: PRICING OBJECTIVES

While costs, potential demand, and competition are the foundations of pricing strategy, they feed into more specific pricing objectives that align with a company's overall goals. A firm might, for instance, set an objective of becoming the dominant producer in its market. This would likely lead to the adoption of a low-price policy that involves offering substantial price discounts to its retail partners. Alternatively, a company might seek to be perceived as the highest quality producer of products in their category. As a result, they might utilize higher levels of pricing to signal the prestige value of its product. For example, The Caldrea Company offers Mrs. Meyer's Clean Day, a line of environmentally friendly household cleaning products that are priced at least 30% higher than ordinary brands it competes with at the grocery store.[7]

Pricing objectives vary from firm to firm, and can be classified into three major groups: (1) volume or sales, (2) competition, and (3) prestige (see Exhibit 13.2)

## VOLUME OR SALES OBJECTIVES

Companies may price to drive a particular amount of sales volume. This volume could relate to production capacity, distribution opportunities, profit requirements, or comparisons with previous year sales. Consider the prices charged for various makes and models of automobiles. Ford may have utilized volume or sales objectives when pricing its popular Fiesta model at $13,500, which created a 20% increase in sales compared to the previous year.[8] Presumably, the list price is sufficient to cover the costs of production, marketing, and distribution—plus provides an acceptable level of profitability to both Ford and the dealership who sells the car.

Another volume-related pricing objective relates to market share—specifically the practice of reducing prices, at least temporarily, to gain market share. Gaining market share is often pursued as a goal since research supports a positive relationship between a firm's market share and profitability. Using price cuts alone to gain market share can be risky though, because customers can become dependent on them. Procter & Gamble experienced poor sales growth in some markets after increasing prices on some products to better cover their costs. In the hope of winning back some of the market share it lost, the company announced it would roll back those price increases.[9]

**volume or sales objectives**
pricing practices aimed at achieving a particular sales volume or market share

**EXHIBIT 13.2** Pricing Objectives

| Objective | Purpose | Example |
|---|---|---|
| **Volume or sales objectives** | Sales maximization | A car manufacturer pricing to ensure they sell through their production capacity for the year |
| | Market share | Vita Coco temporarily cutting prices on coconut water to gain market share in the category |
| **Competition objectives** | Competitive parity | Airlines and neighboring gas stations often match each other's prices |
| | Value pricing | Apple adds new features to the iPhone to justify its higher price compared to Samsung's Galaxy. |
| **Prestige objectives** | Lifestyle | High-priced luxury apparel and accessories |
| | Image | Premium-price free trade coffee |

Often companies are better off utilizing all aspects of the marketing mix to maximize market share, with temporary price cuts being just one tactic for winning more customers.

## COMPETITION OBJECTIVES

**competition objectives** pricing practices intended to maintain pricing parity or emphasize overall product value to avoid direct price comparison

A second set of pricing objectives is driven mainly by competition. The first type of competitive objective is to maintain pricing parity. Pricing is a highly visible component of a firm's marketing mix and an easy tool for obtaining a differential advantage over competitors. However, when competitors continually undercut each other to gain that advantage, it can lead to a price war that damages all companies involved. Many firms attempt to promote stable prices by meeting competitors' prices, but not drastically undercutting them. This objective is commonly seen in the airline industry, where one airline will put a particular flight route on sale, only to have their price immediately matched by competitors who fly that same route. It's also commonly seen in fiercely competitive categories dominated by two market leaders whose strategy has shifted from gaining market share to maintaining market share. Examples are Coca-Cola and Pepsi in the soda category, and McDonald's and Burger King in the fast-food category.

Value pricing is another competitive pricing objective that incorporates other elements of the marketing mix. In value pricing, a firm emphasizes the benefits a product provides in comparison to the price and quality levels of competing offerings. By emphasizing overall product value, firms can avoid direct price comparisons and even increase profits. Trader Joe's—a rapidly growing grocery chain that began in the Los Angeles area and has since expanded nationwide—uses value pricing for the more than 2,000 upscale food products

Trader Joe's uses value pricing to sell upscale food products and avoid direct price comparisons with competitors.

Edelheit/ZUMA Press, Inc./Alamy Stock Photo

it develops or imports. It sells wines, cheeses, meats, fish, and other unique gourmet items at slightly higher prices than you might find for similar items at a regular grocery store, but can do so by emphasizing quality and sustainability. For example, Trader Joe's tuna is caught without environmentally dangerous nets, its dried apricots contain no sulfur preservatives, and its peanut butter is organic.[10]

## PRESTIGE OBJECTIVES

**Prestige pricing** establishes a relatively high price to develop and maintain an image of quality and exclusiveness. Such objectives reflect marketers' recognition of the role of price in creating an overall image of the firm and its product offerings. Prestige objectives affect the price tags of such products as David Yurman jewelry, Tag Heuer watches, Baccarat crystal, and Lenox china. When a perfume marketer sets a price of $400 or more per ounce, this choice reflects an emphasis on image far more than the cost of ingredients. Analyses have shown that ingredients account for less than 5% of a perfume's cost. Thus, advertisements for Clive Christian's No. 1 that promote the fragrance as "the world's most expensive perfume" use price to promote product prestige. Diamond jewelry also uses prestige pricing to convey an image of quality and timelessness.

Prestige pricing can be seen in just about any category. While the majority of pens cost $3 or less, Mont Blanc pens can sell for $300 or more. While the majority of bottled waters cost $3 or less per liter, Veen bottled water can cost over $15 per liter.

**prestige pricing** establishing a relatively high price to develop and maintain an image of quality and exclusiveness

## 13-2b
## CLOSING EXAMPLE

Yousef visited his local grocery store and decided to compare prices of products that he typically purchased. Can you determine the pricing strategies used by the various brand managers?

| Product/Brand | Retail Price | Price per ounce or use |
|---|---|---|
| **Protein Shake** | | |
| Muscle Milk (4–11 ounce cartons) | $6.15 | **$0.14 per ounce** |
| Special K (4–10 ounce cartons) | $6.00 | **$0.15 per ounce** |
| **Peanut Butter** | | |
| Skippy creamy (16.3 ounce) | $2.77 | **$0.17 per ounce** |
| Jif creamy (16 ounce) | $2.56 | **$0.16 per ounce** |
| **Lunchmeat** | | |
| Applegate Farms sliced Black Forest Ham (7 ounce) | $5.32 | **$0.76 per ounce** |
| Hillshire Farm sliced ham (9 ounce) | $3.24 | **$0.36 per ounce** |
| **Tortilla Chips** | | |
| Tostito's Original Restaurant Style (13 ounce) | $4.94 | **$0.38 per ounce** |
| Great Value Restaurant Style (13 ounce) | $1.95 | **$0.15 per ounce** |

In examining the prices charged for protein shakes and peanut butter, Yousef believes these companies are implementing a competitive pricing strategy since the unit prices are within one penny. It appears the companies are seeking to establish competitive parity by pricing the items in line with the competition.

However, the lunchmeat examples show wide price differences between the two brands with Applegate charging 111% more than Hillshire Farms. Applegate Farms, a brand who is committed to all natural and organic farming practices is implementing a prestige pricing approach to appeal to consumers who value healthier food options.

The tortilla chips category shows the price of a popular brand, Tostito's, compared to a private label brand, Great Value. The significant discount for Great Value likely indicates a volume or sales objective intended to increase market share by winning over customers who otherwise would have purchased Tostito's.

# 13-3  CALCULATING MARKUP AND MARGIN

**LO 13.3** Calculate pricing using the markup and margin methods.

## OPENING EXAMPLE

Spin is a specialty bicycle shop that offers high-end road and mountain bikes to cycling enthusiasts in the area. When the store first opened, owners Jamal and Kiran wanted a simple approach for pricing their products—including bicycles, apparel, and accessories. Based on their research of the industry, they learned the average markups and margins used by other successful bicycle shops. Problem is, Jamal and Kiran didn't know how to calculate prices based on this information.

## 13-3a

## LEARNING IT: CALCULATING MARKUP AND MARGIN

Once managers have established pricing objectives, they can turn their attention to pricing calculations. Markup and margin are two straightforward methods for calculating sales prices.

### PRICING USING MARKUP

**cost-based pricing** using the product cost plus a target markup percentage to calculate the sales price

**Cost-based pricing** is using the product cost plus a target markup percentage to calculate the sales price. Because the markup percentage is related to cost, this is called cost-based pricing. For cost, a manufacturer would use their production cost, which is materials plus production labor. A retailer would use their wholesale cost of purchasing from a manufacturer or distributor.

The desired markup percentage is often based on industry norms, historical markup percentages used by the business, or certain profitability objectives. To calculate the sales price using **markup**, multiply the cost by one plus the target markup percentage.

**markup** the cost multiplied by one plus the target markup percentage

A California winery may determine that the cost associated with one bottle of merlot wine is $10 and the target markup for this type of product is 40%. The sales price would be calculated as follows:

$$Sales\ Price\ =\ Cost \times One\ plus\ target\ markup\ percentage$$
$$Sales\ Price\ =\ \$10 \times (1 + .40)$$
$$Sales\ Price\ =\ \$10 \times 1.4$$
$$Sales\ Price\ =\ \$14$$

If the California winery wishes to apply this same markup to all wines in their merlot line, they can easily calculate the sales price of any other product using the same calculation. Suppose a different merlot wine had a cost of $20. Assuming the winery was using the same 40% markup target, the sales price would be calculated as follows:

$$Sales\ Price\ =\ Cost \times One\ plus\ target\ markup\ percentage$$
$$Sales\ Price\ =\ \$20 \times (1 + .40)$$
$$Sales\ Price\ =\ \$20 \times 1.4$$
$$Sales\ Price\ =\ \$28$$

Businesses that use markup sometimes apply the same markup percentage across all products, but more often have a target markup for different types of products. An electronics store might use one markup target for TVs, another for computers, and another for video consoles.

## PRICING USING MARGIN

A second pricing method is **margin** or gross margin percentage, which is the portion of sales revenue left over after paying product costs. Margin is also called gross profit.

**margin** the portion of sales revenue left over after paying product costs

Utilizing the margin approach enables firms to price their products to realize a desired percentage of profit. Like markup percentages, target margins are often based on industry norms, historical markup percentages used by the business, or certain profitability objectives. To calculate the sales price using margin, divide the cost by one minus the target margin percentage.

Suppose a shoe retailer wants to make 35% margin, or gross profit, on all pairs they sell. One pair of women's dress shoes costs them $100. They could calculate their sales price as follows:

$$Sales\ Price\ =\ Cost\ /\ One\ minus\ target\ margin\ percentage$$
$$Sales\ Price\ =\ \$100 / (1 - .35)$$
$$Sales\ Price\ =\ \$100 / .65$$
$$Sales\ Price\ =\ \$153.80$$

If the firm determined that a 35% profit margin was not sufficient to achieve its objectives, it could identify the new selling price by applying the desired gross margin percentage. Let's suppose the store wants work boots with an $80 cost to earn a 55% margin. They would calculate sales price as follows:

$$Sales\ Price = Cost/One\ minus\ target\ margin\ percentage$$
$$Sales\ Price = \$80/(1-.55)$$
$$Sales\ Price = \$80/.45$$
$$Sales\ Price = \$177.78$$

These pricing approaches are easy to use and apply, assuming that the costs associated with the product can be accurately identified. While some incorrectly use the terms markup and margin interchangeably, it's clear they are different and should not be confused. Markup is a percentage added to the cost of the product and margin is a percentage of the sales price left over after paying for the cost of the product. The markup percentage is anchored to the cost and the margin percentage is anchored to the selling price.

For example, let's compare a 60% markup and a 60% margin on a television that a retailer buys from the manufacturer for $500. Using this cost, they calculate sales price as follows:

$$Sales\ Price\ Using\ 60\%\ Markup = \$500 \times 1.6 = \$800$$
$$Sales\ Price\ Using\ 60\%\ Margin = \$500/(1-.6) = \$500/.4 = \$1,250$$

Mathematically speaking, the sales price using a margin percentage will always be higher than the sales price using the same markup percentage. For example, if a t-shirt store buys shirts at $10 each and sells them at $20, that is a 100% markup but a 50% margin.

## 13-3b

# CLOSING EXAMPLE

Jamal and Kiran now have a better understanding of markup and margin. They researched industry publications and surveyed some other bike shops. The most reliable data they could find was that bikes often sell at a 40% margin and accessories sell at 60% margins. Target markup percentages were harder to find for their industry, so they decided to set retail prices using these margin targets, as summarized in the table below.

| Product | Wholesale Cost | Desired Margin | Price Calculation | Retail Sales Price |
|---|---|---|---|---|
| Trek Top Fuel 9.8 Mountain Bike | $3,120 | 40% | 3,120 / (1-.40) | $5,200 |
| Bontrager Lithos Mountain Bike Helmet | $70 | 60% | 70 / (1-.60) | $175 |

Jamal and Kiran were pleased to find that these prices were comparable to what other bike shops in town were using. This allowed them to remain competitive, while still making a solid profit.

# 13-4   FIXED AND VARIABLE COSTS

## OPENING EXAMPLE

Assume you are opening a fitness center in your local area. You'll offer regular monthly memberships that give access to gym equipment and standard fitness classes. But you'll also sell premium fitness classes, where members will pay an extra fee each time they attend. You'll also sell supplements and accessories, like boxing gloves and jump ropes, which members bring to classes. You have a good handle on your cost to run the basic operation, including rent, utilities, marketing, and basic staffing. But each time you hire a trainer to run a premium class, or sell a supplement, that adds additional costs to the business. You must be sure to account for those costs too or you'll lose money.

**LO 13.4** Differentiate between fixed and variable costs.

### 13-4a

## LEARNING IT: FIXED AND VARIABLE COSTS

A product's total cost is composed of total **variable costs** and total **fixed costs**. Variable costs, such as raw materials and labor costs, change with the level of production, and fixed costs, such as lease payments, administrative staffing, and insurance costs, remain stable at any production level within a certain range. Marketers typically seek pricing that covers the total costs, not just variable costs alone.

**variable costs** costs that change with the level of production

**fixed costs** costs that remain stable at any production level within a certain range

Let's first examine the possible fixed costs associated with running a fitness facility. First, you would likely pay a monthly lease. You would need insurance coverage to protect against damage from a storm or fire, plus liability insurance to cover any claims associated with members getting hurt. You decided not to purchase equipment outright, so you leased weights and cardio equipment, and will have a monthly payment for that. You would pay for electricity, telephone, Internet, and other utilities on a monthly basis. You will also have salaries for the staff who run the facility, no matter how many members come in each day. These are all fixed or operating costs, because they are necessary for the daily functioning of the business and aren't directly related to the number of customers you have. In fact, these expenses have to be paid even if you have no members at all.

Variable costs, on the other hand, are those which change as levels of sales or production increase or decrease. In manufacturing, these costs typically relate to raw materials used in the product and direct labor costs for production. For businesses that purchase from manufacturers or wholesalers, variable costs are the per unit costs for the items they buy. At your fitness facility, if there is no demand for you to sell protein powder, then you won't have any expenses associated with it. But if 100 members per month want to buy protein powder, you'll need to purchase 100 bottles from your wholesaler. If 200 members want to buy, then you'll need to purchase 200 bottles. There is a direct link between your sales levels and the expenses related to those sales. Your premium classes are another variable expense. The instructor for your premium bootcamp class charges $50 per class. If you don't have any members who want that class, you won't need to pay that $50 instructor charge. But if you have enough members to put that class on 10 times each week, you'll need to pay the instructor $500 ($50 x 10) per week to run the class.

However, it's important to note that while variable costs may rise as production or sales increase, it's possible that the per unit costs associated with the variable costs could decline due to production efficiencies. For the bootcamp example, the $500 you are paying for the instructor each week might initially serve 100 total members. This equates to a cost of $5 per member each week. However, if the popularity of the class grows to 200 members (which is your maximum weekly capacity for these classes), this drops your cost per member to $2.50.

Cost efficiencies like this are common in manufacturing, especially printing. Due to costs associated with setting up a production run, printing 500 brochures might cost $500, resulting in a per unit cost of $1. However, running 1,000 brochures might cost $600—just $100 more—resulting in a per unit cost of 60 cents.

## 13-4b
## CLOSING EXAMPLE

You now have a better grasp of the difference between fixed and variable costs, and how the number of members you attract will affect pricing. After accounting for all your monthly fixed or operating costs, you calculate that a $50 per month membership fee is just right. If you hit your membership goals, you'll cover your fixed costs and make a decent profit. If you exceed those membership goals, you'll make even more profit because your fixed expenses won't increase as a result.

You then calculate the variable costs of adding premium classes and selling supplements. You know that, unlike your fixed expenses, as the number of premium classes offered or supplements sold goes up, so do your variable expenses. Knowing this helps you price everything to ensure that all costs are covered and you can make a good profit, regardless of how fast the business grows.

# 13-5    BREAKEVEN ANALYSIS

**LO 13.5**    Calculate breakeven point.

## OPENING EXAMPLE

Your new FitBracelet factory just opened and is ready to produce the best wearable fitness trackers on the market. You are now meeting with your national sales team to set goals for the upcoming year. Since your product is well differentiated from competitors, you're confident there will be enough potential customers. However, you know that as price goes up fewer customers will be willing and able to buy the product. As a result, the team agrees that a price of $200 is competitive and provides the best chance of gaining some market share in the wearable category. With a variable cost (including materials and production labor) of $100 per bracelet, you make a good gross margin per unit. But the fixed costs of running the factory, including the lease, utilities, office salaries, and marketing, will total $5 million this year. While you'd love the team to sell hundreds of thousands of bracelets this first year, you know that at a minimum the company needs to breakeven in order to remain viable. How many bracelets do you need to sell this year?

## 13-5a
# LEARNING IT: BREAKEVEN ANALYSIS

**Breakeven analysis** is the method for determining the amount of product that must be sold at a given price to generate sufficient revenue to cover total costs—both fixed and variable. At the breakeven point, profits are zero since all revenues generated are used to cover costs.

The breakeven point in terms of units is found by using the following formula:

$$\text{Breakeven point (in units)} = \text{Total Fixed costs/Gross Margin}$$
$$\text{(or Contribution Margin)}$$

Exhibit 13.3 graphically depicts the breakeven point. In this example, the selling price is $10 and the variable cost is $5, providing a gross margin per unit of $5. This gross margin is also called contribution margin, because that is how much a sale of each unit "contributes" to covering fixed costs. In the chart, fixed costs of $40,000 are represented by the horizontal line, which doesn't change as the quantity produced goes up.

The total cost line includes both fixed costs and the $5 variable cost for each unit produced. This is why the total cost line begins at $40,000 and increases as quantity increases. If the volume is zero and no units are produced or sold, the fixed costs of operating the business still must be paid. The total costs increase, however, as more units of product are produced or sold. For example, the total costs for different quantities are as follows:

| | | | | |
|---|---|---|---|---|
| 0 units produced | = | $40,000 fixed costs + $0 variable cost | = | $40,000 total cost |
| 1,000 units produced | = | $40,000 fixed costs + $5,000 variable costs | = | $45,000 total cost |
| 5,000 units produced | = | $40,000 fixed costs + $25,000 variable costs | = | $65,000 total cost |

The total revenue curve begins at zero when no units are sold and no revenue is realized. As units are sold, total revenue increases by the sales price of each unit sold. The breakeven point is the point at which total revenue equals total cost. Returning to our formula, we can calculate the breakeven point in this example as follows:

| | | |
|---|---|---|
| Breakeven point (in units) | = | Total Fixed cost/Gross Margin |
| Breakeven point (in units) | = | $40,000/($10 − $5) |
| Breakeven point (in units) | = | $40,000/$5 = 8,000 units |

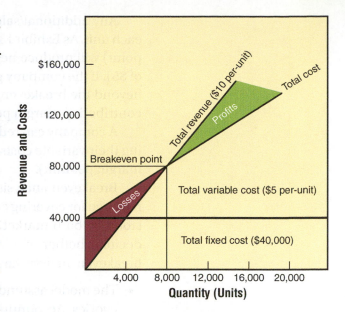

**EXHIBIT 13.3**

**Breakeven Chart**

**breakeven analysis** the method for determining the amount of product that must be sold at a given price to generate sufficient revenue to cover total costs—both fixed and variable

Any additional sales will generate per-unit profits equal to the margin for each unit. As Exhibit 13.3 reveals, sales of 8,001 units (1 unit above the breakeven point) will produce net profits of $5 ($10 sales price less per-unit variable cost of $5). If the company generated sales of 10,000 units, that would be 2,000 units beyond the breakeven point and its profit would be $10,000 (2,000 units × $5 contribution margin per unit).

A company can reduce breakeven point by reducing their fixed costs, reducing their variable costs, or increasing sales price (which increases contribution margin per unit).

Breakeven analysis is an effective tool for marketers in assessing the sales required for covering costs and achieving specific profit levels. It is easily understood by both marketing and non-marketing executives and may help them decide whether required sales levels at a certain price are realistic. However, breakeven analysis has some shortcomings.

- The model assumes costs can be clearly divided into fixed and variable categories. Accounting methods at various companies sometimes differ as to how certain expenses should be categorized.

- The model assumes per-unit variable costs do not change at different levels of operation. In reality, per-unit variable costs often go down as production quantities increase (due to purchasing and production efficiencies).

- Breakeven is a cost-based model and does not directly address the crucial question of whether consumers will purchase the product at the specified price. While a marketer can utilize a number of price assumptions when calculating breakeven points, further research is needed to validate whether those pricing and sales volume assumptions are realistic.

## 13-5b
## CLOSING EXAMPLE

To calculate the breakeven point for FitBracelet, divide your fixed costs of $5 million by your margin per unit.

Breakeven point   =   $5,000,000/$200 sales price − $100 production cost

Breakeven point   =   $5,000,000/$100 margin per unit

Breakeven point   =   50,000 units

Your sales team is confident they can sell at least 75,000 units, which would yield the company a tidy profit in its first year of business.

# 13-6   THE COST-VOLUME-PROFIT RELATIONSHIP

**LO 13.6**  Describe how the cost-volume-profit relationship affects pricing strategy.

### OPENING EXAMPLE

Mobility Transport Systems is the manufacturer of the SafetySure gait belt, a secure way for caregivers and medical staff to move patients a short distance, such as from a wheelchair to a bed. Use of a gait belt can reduce back strain for caregivers and reduce the risk of injury. The current costs to produce the belt are $4 per unit and the annual sales volume is 100,000 units. Mobility Transport Systems markets the gait belt to hospitals and nursing homes, and to individuals who provide family care at home.

There are several competitors offering products with the same basic function, but most differ slightly in terms of handles, buckle closures, and construction. Mobility Transport Systems retails the 54-inch model for $10 while North Coast Medical retails a similar model for $9. Mobility Transport Systems is evaluating their pricing strategy and considering a lower price to achieve greater parity with North Coast Medical. However, they're unsure how this might affect overall profits, because a lower price also means lower margins. And they aren't sure whether sales volume will increase enough to make up the difference. They have hired you as a pricing consultant to assist their analysis.

### 13-6a

## LEARNING IT: THE COST-VOLUME-PROFIT RELATIONSHIP

As previously discussed, costs establish the floor for setting prices. And breakeven point helps ensure that pricing covers both fixed and variable costs. Beyond that, competition and consumer demand at various price levels, and the firm's objectives will drive the ultimate pricing decision. Marketers usually seek to identify the price that optimizes overall profits while maintaining a competitive advantage. They know that a higher price results in better margins, but likely decreases sales volume, which affects profits. Lower prices might boost sales volume, but the smaller gross margin must be taken into account. This interplay between prices, demand, and overall profitability is called the **cost-volume-profit (CVP)** relationship.

Just Desserts, a commercial bakery, was interested in evaluating their pricing structure for the cheesecakes they sell to local restaurants. The whole cheesecakes cost $6 to produce with a wholesale price to restaurants of $10. Right now, Just Desserts sells 800 cheesecakes per week, which is 80% of their weekly capacity of 1,000 cheesecakes. To boost sales volume, they are considering cutting prices. They are fairly certain that the increase in volume would make up for the decrease in per unit margin. But another option is to increase prices and see if the extra margin makes up for any decrease in sales volume. To analyze these options, the sales and marketing team created the following three scenarios (see Exhibit 13.4).

Just Desserts was surprised by the results of their analysis. Although cutting prices would significantly increase the number of cheesecakes sold from 800 to 1,000, their gross margin would drop from $3,200 per week to $2,000. On the other hand, while raising prices would cut sales volume considerably, Just Desserts would realize higher overall profits. Seeing this cost-volume-profit relationship gave the company new insights about pricing strategy. Where previously they considered cutting prices to increase volume, they now realize it would be more profitable to increase prices and invest the additional gross margin into another sales rep. By doing so, they hope to maintain the higher margins while boosting sales back up to 800 cheesecakes per week.

**cost-volume-profit (CVP)** the relationship between prices, demand, and overall profitability

**EXHIBIT 13.4**    Pricing and Volume Scenarios for Just Desserts

| Scenario | Projected Sales Volume | Total revenue | Total variable cost | Total gross margin |
|---|---|---|---|---|
| Keep price at $10 | 800 cheesecakes per week | 800 × $10 = $8,000 | 800 × $6 = $4,800 | $8,000 − $4,800 = $3,200 |
| Cut price to $8 | 1,000 cheesecakes per week | 1,000 × $8 = $8,000 | 1,000 × $6 = $6,000 | $8,000 − $6,000 = $2,000 |
| Increase price to $12 | 600 cheesecakes per week | 600 × $12 = $7,200 | 600 × $6 = $3,600 | $7,200 − $3,600 = $3,600 |

The CVP relationship affects pricing strategy by showing marketers how changes in price and sales volume will affect overall profitability. The results of any CVP analysis will depend on variables such as existing profit margins and price sensitivity of customers. While cutting prices would result in less gross margin for Just Desserts, for another company or product it might result in a profit increase due to a sharp boost in sales volume. While increasing pricing would result in more gross margin for Just Desserts, for another company or product it might result in a drastic cut in profits if that price increase caused demand to crash. Marketers must examine each pricing scenario by carefully estimating how changes in price might change demand, then calculating the overall effect on profits of making that price change.

## 13-6b
## CLOSING EXAMPLE

Mobility Transport Systems is prepared to analyze their pricing strategy with the goal of maximizing profitability. As their consultant, you asked the company to not only analyze the effect of cutting prices, but to analyze the effect of raising them. Below are the scenarios you calculated for a cost-volume-profit analysis.

| Description | Sales Price | Cost | Projected Sales | Total Revenue | Total Variable Costs | Total Gross Profit | Change in gross profit from current price |
|---|---|---|---|---|---|---|---|
| Current price | $10 | $4 | 100,000 | $1,000,000 ($10 x 100,000) | $400,000 ($4 x 100,000) | $600,000 | – |
| Decrease sales price to match North Coast Medical | $9 | $4 | 150,000 | $1,350,000 ($9 x 150,000) | $600,000 ($4 x 150,000) | $750,000 | $150,000 |
| Increase sales price | $12 | $4 | 60,000 | $720,000 ($12 x 60,000) | $240,000 ($40 x 60,000) | $480,000 | ($120,000) |

Mobility Transport Systems now sees that cutting prices to match North Coast Medical should result in significantly higher sales volumes and higher gross profits. While they did evaluate the idea of increasing prices to increase margins per unit, they learned through research that customers in this market are price sensitive and a price increase would dramatically cut sales volume. Increasing prices would actually decrease their total gross profit by $120,000. The results of this CVP analysis helped Mobility Transport Systems make an informed decision to seek price parity with a competitor, and perhaps increase market share in the process.

# 13-7 APPLYING BREAKEVEN ANALYSIS

## OPENING EXAMPLE

Jane Dough Pizza is an independent pizza restaurant with one location in a town of 20,000 residents. The restaurant has found success with its fast casual format, where customers can choose from a wide array of pizza toppings, crust flavors, and sauces when customizing their pizza. While the restaurant offers delivery and carry out, many customers enjoy dining in because of the upscale ambiance, where they receive free drinks with the order of a pizza. Over the last two years, Jane Dough has grown and their annual revenue is currently $480,000.

Jane Dough's biggest competitor is Domino's, which is the second-largest pizza chain nationwide with over 5,000 locations. Domino's franchise owners benefit from nationwide advertising, smartphone apps, online ordering, and integration with various social media sites. According to industry reports, the local Domino's store generates sales of $814,000.

Jane Dough hopes to continue growing their business and look for ways to compete more effectively against Domino's. The owner is considering a variety of changes, such as adding delivery services, investing in technology to provide online ordering, and has even contemplated creating a smartphone app. Jane Dough has hired a consultant to help the business analyze their current situation and offer recommendations.

> **LO 13.7** Given cost information and pricing objectives, calculate the breakeven point for a product.

## 13-7a
## LEARNING IT: APPLYING BREAKEVEN ANALYSIS

Jane Dough hires Pinnacle Consultants to analyze their current situation. Pinnacle Consultants conducts some secondary research on the pizza restaurant industry and learns that there are several issues impacting businesses across the United States:[11]

- Independent pizza restaurant store sales are down while pizza chain restaurant store sales are increasing
- The millennial generation is technology savvy and likes to use their smartphone to shop, place orders, and take photos of their purchases—even pizza
- Delivery services are a source of competitive advantage
- Consumers desire natural ingredients with no additives or hormones

An upscale pizza restaurant might set higher prices to achieve their prestige pricing objectives, but must also generate enough demand to cover their total costs.

Angela Aladro mella/Shutterstock.com

After reviewing the market, Pinnacle Consultants confirmed that Jane Dough Pizza should continue pursuing prestige pricing objectives by focusing on target customers who value a nice dining atmosphere and the fresh, natural, high quality food. In comparison, Domino's is pursuing a volume or sales objective to maximize market share by offering a more limited menu and low-priced pizzas.

Using data provided by Jane Dough and gathered from industry sources, Pinnacle Consultants prepared a chart to compare the business to the local Domino's franchise (see Exhibit 13.5).

This information helped Jane Dough understand their position relative to Domino's. Even though they originally intended to pursue a prestige pricing objective, their current price was similar to Domino's. Even worse, their margins were lower than Domino's at 77% versus 63%.

Given their objective of prestige pricing to differentiate from chain competitors, Jane Dough decided that 75% margins would be reasonable. Using the margin calculations, they arrived at a new average price for their pizzas.

**EXHIBIT 13.5**    **Selected Financial Information for Jane Dough and Domino's**

| Description | Jane Dough | Local Domino's Franchise |
| --- | --- | --- |
| Annual pizza sales | $480,000 | $814,000 |
| Total fixed costs (rent, equipment, fixtures, utilities, insurance, salaries) | $190,000 | $125,000 |
| Average price of a large, 2-topping pizza | $11.00 | $9.00 |
| Variable costs per pizza (ingredients, labor) | $4.00 | $2.00 |

$$\text{Sales price using margin calculation} = \$4 \text{ cost}/(1 - 75\% \text{ target margin})$$
$$= 4/.25$$
$$= \$16 \text{ sales price}$$

While this price would cut sales volumes a little, Jane Dough's target audience tends to be less price sensitive to a quality product like this. A CVP analysis showed that even with the slight drop in volume, overall gross profits would increase.

Jane Dough next considered the effect of investing in delivery drivers and a programmer to create and manage their online store and smartphone app. This would add $100,000 to total fixed costs, bringing them to $290,000. With pizzas now priced at $16 and the higher fixed costs, Jane Dough Pizza set out to calculate their new breakeven point.

$$\text{Breakeven point} = \$290,000/\$16 \text{ sales price} - \$4 \text{ cost}$$
$$= \$290,000/\$12$$
$$= 24,167 \text{ pizzas}$$

Since this breakeven point was far below their order volume last year, and well below the revised sales projections, Jane Dough felt confident revising their average pizza price to $16. This would improve differentiation from Domino's, provide more convenient ordering options, and increase profits overall.

# 13-8    LEARN IT TODAY. . .USE IT TOMORROW

Jane Dough Pizza now better understands how to use pricing to achieve their marketing objectives, fund improvements to their business, and realize a target profit for each pizza sold. As they continue seeking competitive advantage, Jane Dough is analyzing these suggested changes to the business and would like your help.

It's time to get hands-on and apply what you've learned. **See MindTap for an activity related to Jane Dough Pizza's marketing activities.**

## Chapter Summary

**LO 13.1 Describe the three foundations of pricing strategy.**

Marketers consider three factors when establishing the price for a product: costs, potential demand, and competition.

**LO 13.2 Summarize the three pricing objectives.**

Pricing objectives vary from firm to firm and can be classified into three major categories: volume or sales, competition, and prestige.

**LO 13.3** Calculate pricing using the markup and margin methods.

There are two common methods of pricing: markup and margin. Markup is calculated by targeting a certain percentage over cost and margin is calculated by targeting a certain gross profit from the sale.

**LO 13.4** Differentiate between fixed and variable costs.

A product's total cost is composed of variable costs and fixed costs. Variable cost, such as raw materials and labor costs, change with the level of production while fixed or operating costs, such as insurance and lease payments, remain stable at any production level within a certain range.

**LO 13.5** Calculate breakeven point.

Breakeven analysis is the method for determining the amount of product that must be sold at a given price to generate sufficient revenue to cover total costs—both fixed and variable.

**LO 13.6** Describe how the cost-volume-profit relationship affects pricing strategy.

When setting prices, marketers will often evaluate different price and sales volume assumptions to estimate how they affect the overall profits of the company. This interplay between prices, demand, and profitability is called the cost-volume-profit (CVP) relationship.

**LO 13.7** Given cost information and pricing objectives, calculate the breakeven point for a product.

To accurately assess the effect of pricing decisions on a company, a marketer must be able to understand different pricing objectives, calculate prices using markup or margin goals, categorize and calculate fixed and variable expenses, and determine breakeven points.

# Key Terms

# 14 PRICING STRATEGIES

Jonathan Weiss/Shutterstock.com

## LEARNING OBJECTIVES

**14.1** Explain how price elasticity affects potential demand for a product.

**14.2** Compare the primary types of forecasting methods used to determine demand.

**14.3** Contrast the three primary competitive pricing strategies.

**14.4** Outline three types of pricing tactics used by marketers.

**14.5** Explain how price affects consumer perceptions of quality.

**14.6** Describe the legal constraints on pricing.

# LEARN IT TODAY . . . USE IT TOMORROW

Dollar General, the Tennessee-based chain of discount retailers, has more than 13,000 U.S. stores and recently announced record high sales of $22 billion. Like other "extreme value" chains, the fast-growing retailer is drawing many more customers than before, and these shoppers are spending more per visit than in the past. Low-income families as well as middle-class consumers are shopping at Dollar General, which recently opened, remodeled, or relocated 1,806 stores.

Dollar General expects sales to continue to increase as it opens another 1,000 new stores and invests approximately $70 million in compensation and training for store managers. With success based on low-priced items and convenient locations, Dollar General is beginning to encroach on the market segment traditionally held by chains like Walmart, Target, and Costco. Operating 14 distribution centers and stores in 43 states, Dollar General is also taking share from grocery stores and drug chains.[1]

How does Dollar General earn so much with low prices on brand names like Kimberly Clark, Procter & Gamble, Kellogg, Hanes, Nabisco, and General Mills? The answer is that the company doesn't really offer "low prices." Instead, by selling products in smaller sizes than other discount chains like Walmart, it actually offers low price *points*, which yield higher profit margins. In other words, although the items in the store carry nominally low prices, their smaller sizes mean customers are paying more per ounce than they might pay for the same item at Walmart. Because Dollar General shoppers may have low purchasing power at any given time, they can only afford to buy small amounts at a time and must also shop more frequently. Dollar General caters to their buying habits and financial constraints.

Dollar General is demonstrating advanced use of pricing strategies, which we'll learn more about in this chapter.

# 14-1 HOW PRICE AFFECTS DEMAND

**LO 14.1** Explain how price elasticity affects potential demand for a product.

## OPENING EXAMPLE

Both Brown Town and Yellowville have popular downtown shopping districts with nearby parking. But Brown Town has five parking facilities within the district, while Yellowville has only one. You are the owner of one of Brown Town's five garages. Recently, you also purchased the single facility in Yellowville.

Costs are increasing across the parking industry, so you decide to boost prices in both your garages by the same amount. You know that customers won't be happy, and you're bracing for a downturn in business. All else being equal, are you more likely to lose customers in Brown Town or in Yellowville? Why?

### 14-1a

## LEARNING IT: HOW PRICE AFFECTS DEMAND

In Chapter 13, you learned about several essential pricing concepts, including the foundations for pricing, core pricing objectives, the cost-volume-profit relationship, and how to calculate breakeven point. These concepts influence how marketers approach the process of setting prices. But because pricing is such a dynamic and impactful component of the marketing mix, there are a number of other influences and strategies that marketers must consider when making pricing decisions. We'll discuss those in this chapter, starting with a more thorough discussion of the relationship between supply and demand.

**Supply** refers to the amounts of a product that will be offered for sale at different prices during a specified period. For example, if most people will pay $20 for a pair of shoes there might be only one supplier willing to manufacture and sell shoes at that price. However, if most people will pay $100 for a pair of shoes, there are likely many more manufacturers willing to jump into the market. Generally, the higher the price, the more supply.

On the other hand, **demand** refers to the amounts of a product that consumers will purchase at different prices during a specified time period. There will be fewer consumers willing to buy shoes at $200 a pair than there will be at $20 a pair. As price goes down, demand goes up.

In the ideal situation, suppliers will make just enough product and price it in such a way that consumers buy it all. When this happens, it's called market equilibrium. In the real world, market equilibrium is often temporary—if it even happens at all. What more likely happens is that when a product is selling well, the supplier will ramp up production. Plus, other suppliers will enter the market, creating even more supply. When the market gets oversupplied like this, prices often drop because sellers must cut prices to compete for customers. The opposite happens as well, such as when demand for a product outstrips supply and customers bid up the price of the product. This pattern is seen in the housing market, such as in the recession of 2008 when there was a much larger supply of houses than there were purchasers. As a result, prices dropped as much as 40% in some markets. By 2017, the opposite was true. There were many buyers, but not as much inventory of houses, causing buyers to bid against each other and drive prices higher. Many homeowners were able to sell for more than their original asking price.

Marketers must be sensitive to the state of supply and demand in a market when making pricing decisions. Even more importantly, marketers must be aware of how any changes in pricing will affect potential demand for their product in the future.

**supply** the amounts of a product that will be offered for sale at different prices during a specified period

**demand** the amounts of a product that consumers will purchase at different prices during a specified time period

When there is high demand for a product, suppliers can often sell at a higher price.

# 14-1b
# PRICE ELASTICITY

**elasticity** the measure of the responsiveness of purchasers and suppliers to price changes

**elasticity of demand** the percentage change in the quantity of a product demanded divided by the percentage change in its price

**Elasticity** is the measure of the responsiveness of purchasers and suppliers to price changes. The price **elasticity of demand** is the percentage change in the quantity of a product demanded divided by the percentage change in its price. A 10% increase in the price of eggs that results in a 5% decrease in the quantity of eggs demanded yields a price elasticity of demand for eggs of 0.5.

Consider a case in which a 1% change in price causes more than a 1% change in the quantity demanded. Numerically, that means an elasticity measurement greater than 1.0. When the elasticity of demand is greater than 1.0, that demand is said to be elastic. In other words, the customers for that product are very sensitive to price changes, and even small increases in price can lead to big decreases in demand.

If a 1% change in price results in less than a 1% change in quantity, a product's elasticity of demand will be less than 1.0. In that case, the demand is called *inelastic*. This means that customers for that product are not as sensitive to price changes. For example, the demand for cigarettes is relatively inelastic; research studies have shown that a 10% increase in cigarette prices results in only a 4% sales decline.

Before a marketer makes any decisions about pricing products, they should have an understanding of the elasticity—or sensitivity to price changes—of their target market.

## DETERMINANTS OF ELASTICITY

Why is the elasticity of demand high for some products and low for others? One major influence is the availability of substitutes or complements. If consumers can easily find close substitutes for a product, they are more sensitive to price changes, meaning demand is more elastic. Highly competitive industries tend to have elastic demand because competitors aggressively promote their products as substitutes for other brands. This helps explain the increase in value menus at fast food restaurants like McDonald's, Burger King, and Taco Bell.

In competitive markets with more competitors, customers are more sensitive to price changes.

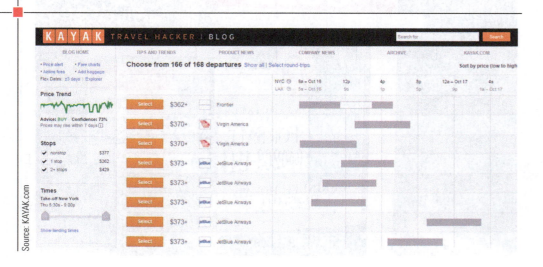

Source: KAYAK.com

As increasing numbers of buyers complete their transactions online, the elasticity of a product's demand is increased. Today the Internet lets consumers contact many more providers directly, often giving them better selections and prices through service sites such as Shopzilla.com for electronics, Net-à-Porter. com for high-fashion clothing, and Kayak.com for travel bargains. This increased competition makes it harder for any one brand to unilaterally raise prices without risking a drop in demand.

In general, demand for luxury goods is more elastic than demand for products perceived as necessities. For example, few vacation travelers will buy first class airplane seats unless offered a substantial discount, but a fairly large increase in the price of milk will typically have a small effect on demand.

Elasticity also depends on the portion of a person's budget spent on a product. Demand for matches is very inelastic despite the ease of finding substitutes, because people spend so little on them that they hardly notice a price change. In contrast, the demand for housing or transportation is more sensitive to price changes, even though they are necessities, because both consume large parts of a purchaser's budget.

## 14-1c
## CLOSING EXAMPLE

A price increase at your Brown Town parking garage is more likely to hurt business than the same increase at your Yellowville facility. That's because a key influence on elasticity of demand is the availability of substitutes. In Brown Town, four other garages compete for your customers' patronage. In Yellowville, the only alternative to paying your price is to park far away from the shopping district. In other words, demand in Brown Town is more elastic than in Yellowville; when shoppers realize there's a cheaper garage nearby, they'll try to save money on parking so they can spend more in the stores.

# 14-2 FORECASTING DEMAND

## OPENING EXAMPLE

A biotech firm is poised to make a major push into cutting-edge diagnostic technology. But before signing off on the new direction, the Director of Marketing asks his marketing team to forecast demand for products based on the new technology. While he trusts the judgment of his team members, the director of marketing wants to be on the safe side. He reaches out to experts at top biomedical research institutions like Johns Hopkins and Duke, soliciting their opinions of how this breakthrough could affect the market.

What are the advantages of this forecasting approach? What are its downsides?

**LO 14.2** Compare the primary types of forecasting methods used to determine demand.

## 14-2a
# LEARNING IT: FORECASTING DEMAND

Forecasts of future demand play major roles in new product decisions, production scheduling, financial planning, inventory planning, and other business considerations. It also impacts pricing decisions for reasons discussed in the previous section. Although sales forecasters use an array of techniques to predict the future—ranging from computer simulations to studying trends identified by futurists—their methods fall into two broad categories: qualitative and quantitative forecasting.

**Qualitative forecasting** techniques rely on subjective data that reports opinions rather than using statistical data. **Quantitative forecasting** is based on statistical data, such as using past sales results to estimate future demand, or conducting small tests that can be extrapolated to estimate demand in the larger market. As Exhibit 14.1 shows, each method has benefits

**qualitative forecasting**
techniques that rely on subjective data that reports opinions rather than using statistical data

**quantitative forecasting**
techniques that rely on statistical data, such as past sales or results from small tests

**EXHIBIT 14.1**    Benefits and Limitations of Various Forecasting Techniques

| Techniques | Benefits | Limitations |
|---|---|---|
| **Qualitative Methods** | | |
| Jury of executive opinion | Opinions come from executives in many different departments <br><br> Quick <br><br> Inexpensive | Managers may lack background knowledge and experience to make meaningful predictions |
| Delphi technique | Group of experts may predict long-term events such as technological breakthroughs | Time-consuming <br><br> Expensive |
| Sales force composite | Salespeople have expert customer, product, and competitor knowledge <br><br> Quick <br><br> Inexpensive | Inaccurate forecasts may result from low estimates of salespeople concerned about their influence on quotas |
| Survey of buyer intentions | Useful in predicting short-term and intermediate sales for firms that serve selected customers | Intentions to buy may not result in actual purchases <br><br> Time-consuming <br><br> Expensive |
| **Quantitative Methods** | | |
| Test market | Provides realistic information on actual purchases rather than on intent to buy | Alerts competition to new product plans <br><br> Time-consuming <br><br> Expensive |
| Trend analysis | Quick <br><br> Inexpensive <br><br> Effective with stable customer demand and environment | Assumes the future will continue the past <br><br> Ignores possible changes in marketing environment |

and limitations. Because of this, most organizations use a combination of both techniques.

## QUALITATIVE FORECASTING TECHNIQUES

### Jury of Executive Opinion

The technique called the **jury of executive opinion** combines and averages the outlooks of top executives from such areas as marketing, finance, and production. For example, department stores routinely ask top buyers for different product lines—like women's apparel or home furnishings—for their opinions about how consumer tastes are changing and whether the store should stock new brands. This quick and inexpensive method generates good forecasts for sales and new product development. It works best for short-run forecasting.

**jury of executive opinion** qualitative forecasting method that assesses the sales expectations of various executives

### Delphi Technique

Like the jury of executive opinion, the **Delphi technique** solicits opinions from several people, but it also gathers input from experts outside the firm, such as academic researchers, rather than relying completely on company executives. It is most appropriately used to predict long-run possibilities, such as technological breakthroughs, that could affect future sales and the market potential for new products.

Here's how the Delphi technique might work. If Mattel were working on a new artificial intelligence-enabled Barbie doll, they might seek feedback from a panel of AI experts from leading universities and child psychologists who specialize in studying patterns of play. They would combine this input with opinions solicited internally to create a forecast. Although firms have successfully used Delphi to predict future technological breakthroughs, the method is both expensive and time-consuming.

**Delphi technique** qualitative forecasting method that gathers several rounds of feedback from experts inside and outside the firm

### Sales Force Composite

The **sales force composite** technique develops forecasts based on the belief that organization members closest to the marketplace—those with specialized product, customer, and competitive knowledge—offer the best insights concerning short-term future sales. It typically works from the bottom up. Management consolidates salespeople's estimates first at the district level, then at the regional level, and finally nationwide to obtain an aggregate forecast of sales that reflects all three levels. The toymaker described above might solicit opinions first from salespeople who sell dolls to major retailers, then from sales managers who supervise all girls' toys accounts in select regions, and finally from the company's national sales directors.

**sales force composite** qualitative forecasting method based on the combined sales estimates of the firm's salespeople

The sales force composite approach has some weaknesses, however. Because salespeople recognize the role of their sales forecasts in determining sales quotas for their territories, they are likely to make conservative estimates. Moreover, their narrow perspectives from within their limited geographic territories may prevent them from considering the impact on sales of trends developing in other territories, forthcoming technological innovations, or the major changes in marketing strategies. Consequently, the sales force composite is best used in combination with other techniques.

## Survey of Buyer Intentions

A **survey of buyer intentions** gathers input through mail-in questionnaires, online feedback, telephone polls, and personal interviews to determine the purchasing intentions of a representative group of current and potential customers. This method suits firms that serve limited numbers of customers but often proves impractical for those with millions of customers, such as Mattel and other mass market toymakers. Also, buyer intentions do not necessarily translate into actual purchases. These surveys may help a firm predict short-run or intermediate sales, but they employ time-consuming and expensive methods.

# QUANTITATIVE FORECASTING TECHNIQUES

## Test Marketing

Test marketing frequently helps planners assess consumer responses to new-product offerings. The procedure typically begins by establishing one or more test markets to gauge consumer responses to a new product under actual marketplace conditions. Cities like Nashville, Cincinnati, and Indianapolis are among the top ten metropolitan areas chosen as test markets in the United States because they are seen as microcosms of the country on key measures like income, age, and gender distribution.[2]

These tests also permit experimenters to evaluate the effects of different prices, alternative promotional strategies, and other marketing mix variations by comparing results among different test markets. The primary advantage of test markets is the realism they provide for the marketer. On the other hand, these expensive and time-consuming experiments may also reveal marketing plans to competitors.

## Trend Analysis

**Trend analysis** develops forecasts for future sales by analyzing historical sales. It implicitly assumes the collective causes of past sales will continue into the future. When historical sales data is available, planners can quickly and inexpensively complete trend analysis.

Of course, trend analysis cannot be used if historical data is not available, as in new-product forecasting. Also, trend analysis makes the dangerous assumption that future events will continue in the same manner as the past. Any variations in the determinants of future sales, like demographic changes or the entry of new competitors, will cause deviations from the forecast. In other words, this method gives reliable forecasts during periods of steady growth and stable demand. If conditions change, predictions based on trend analysis may become worthless.

### 14-2b

## CLOSING EXAMPLE

The biotech firm used the Delphi technique to forecast demand for products incorporating a new diagnostic technology. Because this approach is costly and time-consuming, marketers generally limit Delphi forecasts to situations where they must predict long-run prospects for new, potentially breakthrough, products.

## 14-3 PRICING STRATEGIES

### OPENING EXAMPLE

In the crowded mid-priced restaurant market, Sizzler is known for its afford-able steak platters, like a $16.99 sirloin and lobster special. Outback Steakhouse meets or beats its rival's basic steak prices, but also offers an enhanced product for $24.99: a filet instead of sirloin, with two sides instead of one.[3]

What's the logic in Outback's pricing strategy? Does it apply in other markets?

#### 14-3a

## LEARNING IT: PRICING STRATEGIES

The specific strategies firms use to price products grow from their overall pric-ing objectives (discussed in Chapter 13). Pricing objectives represent the firm's priorities when setting prices, such as reaching a certain sales volume, directly addressing competition, or communicating prestige. Once *objectives* are set, pricing *strategies* can more specifically guide marketers toward the selection of a price. In general, firms can choose from three pricing strategies: skimming, penetration, and competitive pricing.

### SKIMMING PRICING STRATEGY

Derived from the expression "skimming the cream," **skimming pricing strategies** are also known as market-plus pricing. They involve intentionally setting a rel-atively high price compared with the prices of competing products. Although some firms continue to use a skimming strategy throughout most stages of the product lifecycle, it is more commonly used as a market-entry price for distinc-tive goods or services with little or no initial competition. When the supply begins to exceed demand, or when competition catches up, the initial high price is dropped.

When Nissan launched its all-electric car, the Leaf, the com-pany priced the vehicle at more than $35,000. Tesla Motors's high-end electric car's starting price in the United States is more than $69,000.[4]

The jewelry category is a good example of price skimming. Although discounters, such as Costco and Home Shopping Net-work (HSN), offer gold pieces for a few hundred dollars, firms such as

---

**LO 14.3** Contrast the three primary competitive pricing strategies.

**skimming pricing strategies** intentionally setting a relatively high price compared with the prices of competing products

Tesla uses a skimming *strategy* by pricing their cars relatively high. For now, this is necessary to cover their high costs, but even when costs drop it's likely Tesla will continue utilizing premium prices to support their overall prestige pricing *objectives.*

Sergey Kohl/Shutterstock.com

Tiffany and Cartier command prices ten times that amount just for their brand names. Their exclusivity justifies the pricing—and the price, once set, rarely falls.

Skimming allows a manufacturer to quickly recover its research and development (R&D) costs. Pharmaceutical companies, fiercely protective of their patents on new drugs, justify high prices because of astronomical research and development (R&D) costs: an average of 16 cents of every sales dollar, compared with 8 cents for computer makers and 4 cents in the aerospace industry.

## PENETRATION PRICING STRATEGY

A **penetration pricing strategy** sets a low price as a major marketing weapon. Marketers often price products noticeably lower than competing offerings when they enter new markets that have dozens of competing brands. Once the product achieves some degree of recognition through consumer trial purchases stimulated by its low price, marketers may increase the price to the level of competing products.

A penetration pricing strategy is sometimes called market-minus pricing, with the premise that a lower-than-market price will attract buyers and move a brand from an unknown newcomer to at least the brand-recognition stage or even the brand-preference stage. Penetration pricing is common among cable and Internet providers, which typically offer low rates for a specified introductory period, then raise the rates. If competitors view the new product as a threat, marketers attempting to use a penetration strategy often discover that rivals will simply match their prices.

Retailers may use penetration pricing to lure shoppers to new stores. Strategies might take forms such as zero interest charges for credit purchases at a new furniture store, two-for-one offers for dinner at a new restaurant, or an extremely low price for first-time customers.

Some auto manufacturers have been using penetration pricing for some new models to attract customers who might not otherwise consider purchasing a vehicle. India's Tata Motors launched the world's cheapest car—the Nano, which carries a price tag of $2,500 in India. Currently, the lowest-priced car in the United States is the Nissan Versa, with a sticker price of $12,800.[5]

**penetration pricing strategy** setting a lower price than competitive offerings in order to stimulate demand and market acceptance

Cable and Internet providers often use a low, penetration pricing *strategy* for a specified period as a way to pursue their overall *objective* of gaining market share.

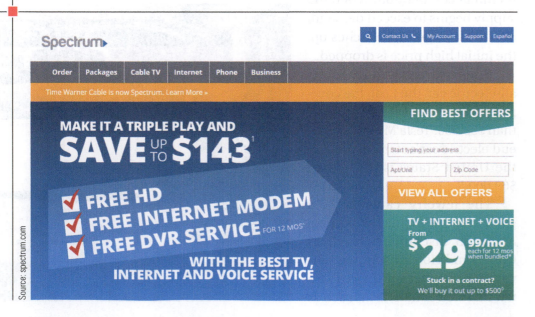

Source: spectrum.com

One popular pricing myth is that a low price is a sure sell. Low prices are an easy means of distinguishing the offerings of one marketer from other sellers, but such moves are easy to counter by competitors. Unless overall demand increases when prices drop, overall price cuts will mean less revenue for all firms in the industry. In addition, low prices may generate an image of questionable quality.

## COMPETITIVE PRICING STRATEGY

Although many organizations rely heavily on low price as a competitive weapon, research shows that nearly two-thirds of all firms use **competitive pricing** as their primary pricing strategy. These organizations know that a price war can hurt everyone in the industry, so their overall objective is to maintain competitive parity. Based on that objective, their specific pricing strategy is to reduce the emphasis on price competition by matching other firms' prices and concentrating their own marketing efforts on the product, distribution, and promotion elements of the marketing mix.

Retailers such as Home Depot and Lowe's both use price-matching strategies, assuring consumers that they will meet competitors' prices. Grocery chains, such as Kroger and Stop & Shop, may compete with seasonal items: soft drinks and hot dogs in the summer, hot chocolate and turkeys in the winter. As soon as one store lowers the price of these items, the rest follow suit.

Once competitors routinely match each other on price, marketers must turn away from price as a marketing strategy, emphasizing other variables to develop areas of distinctive competence and attract customers. For a clothing store, for example, that might mean offering personalized services such as gift wrapping or custom tailoring.

**competitive pricing** pricing strategy designed to reduce emphasis on price as a competitive variable by matching competitors' prices and focusing on other ways to differentiate products

### 14-3b
### CLOSING EXAMPLE

Outback Steakhouse uses competitive pricing, where organizations try to de-emphasize price by matching rivals' prices and then concentrating their marketing efforts on other parts of the marketing mix. You might see Outback and Sizzler as equivalent if all you want is a cheap steak; but Outback hopes to impress you with its higher quality—though still affordable—alternatives. That higher-quality steak can serve as a tie-breaker that attracts customers to Outback instead of Sizzler, all while avoiding a price war that could hurt both companies.

 **14-4**     # PRICING TACTICS

## OPENING EXAMPLE

Procter and Gamble (P&G) is one of the world's most successful marketers of cleaning and personal care products. In particular, the firm is known for premium brands like Tide laundry detergent, Bounty paper towels, and Charmin

**LO 14.4** Outline three types of pricing tactics used by marketers.

toilet tissue. While these products carry higher prices than several competitors, they enjoy strong market share and generate big revenues for the company. So why do you think P&G also sells significantly cheaper alternatives, like Cheer detergent, Bounty Basic, and Charmin Basic? Don't these products compete with P&G's other products for the same buyers?

## 14-4a

# LEARNING IT: PRICING TACTICS

Once a firm has established its overall pricing strategy, it can support that strategy by utilizing specific pricing tactics such as psychological pricing, product-line pricing, and promotional pricing.

## PSYCHOLOGICAL PRICING

**psychological pricing** pricing tactic based on the belief that certain prices or price ranges make products more appealing to buyers

**Psychological pricing** applies the belief that certain prices or price ranges make products more appealing to buyers. While no research offers a consistent foundation for such thinking, marketers practice several forms of psychological pricing.

For example, prestige pricing sets a relatively high price to convey an image of quality and exclusiveness that appeals to status-conscious consumers. This technique is used by such brands as David Yurman jewelry, Baccarat crystal, and Lenox china. Advertisements for Clive Christian's No. 1 that promote the fragrance as "the world's most expensive perfume" explicitly use price to promote product prestige.

Another psychological pricing technique that can be used for any product is odd pricing. In odd pricing, marketers set prices at odd numbers just under

As "the world's most expensive perfume," Clive Christian's use of psychological pricing *tactic* aligns with their overall prestige pricing *objective*.

PA Images/Alamy Stock Photo

round numbers. Many people assume that a price of $9.95 is more appealing to consumers than $10, supposedly because buyers interpret it as $9 plus change.

## PRODUCT-LINE PRICING

**Product-line pricing** is the practice of setting a limited number of prices for a selection of merchandise. This approach considers the relationships among all of the items the firm sells, instead of viewing each in isolation. For example, one well-known clothier might offer three lines of men's suits: one priced at $250, a second at $495, and the most expensive at $799. These price points help the retailer define important product characteristics that differentiate the three product lines and help the customer decide on whether to trade up or down.

Retailers practice product-line pricing to satisfy shoppers desiring different price ranges, while maintaining simplicity. Within their preferred range, shoppers can concentrate on other product variables, such as colors, styles, and materials. For example, Lord and Taylor's carries affordable women's lingerie brands like Adore Me, priced between $11–49, as well as Italian luxury imports like La Perla, priced at $110 and up. Once a customer has identified which line better fits their needs, they'll know they can evaluate the products within that line knowing the general price range for any of those products.

A potential problem with product-line pricing is that once marketers decide on a predictable price range for a product line, they may have difficulty making price changes in the future or adding products to the line that fall outside the

**product-line pricing** pricing tactic where the firm sets a limited number of prices for a selection of merchandise

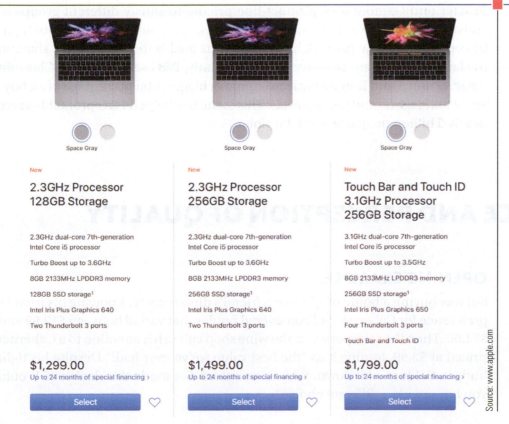

| New | New | New |
|---|---|---|
| 2.3GHz Processor 128GB Storage | 2.3GHz Processor 256GB Storage | Touch Bar and Touch ID 3.1GHz Processor 256GB Storage |
| 2.3GHz dual-core 7th-generation Intel Core i5 processor | 2.3GHz dual-core 7th-generation Intel Core i5 processor | 3.1GHz dual-core 7th-generation Intel Core i5 processor |
| Turbo Boost up to 3.6GHz | Turbo Boost up to 3.6GHz | Turbo Boost up to 3.5GHz |
| 8GB 2133MHz LPDDR3 memory | 8GB 2133MHz LPDDR3 memory | 8GB 2133MHz LPDDR3 memory |
| 128GB SSD storage[1] | 256GB SSD storage[1] | 256GB SSD storage[1] |
| Intel Iris Plus Graphics 640 | Intel Iris Plus Graphics 640 | Intel Iris Plus Graphics 650 |
| Two Thunderbolt 3 ports | Two Thunderbolt 3 ports | Four Thunderbolt 3 ports |
| | | Touch Bar and Touch ID |
| **$1,299.00** | **$1,499.00** | **$1,799.00** |
| Up to 24 months of special financing › | Up to 24 months of special financing › | Up to 24 months of special financing › |
| Select | Select | Select |

Apple frequently uses product-line pricing by uniformly pricing their low, middle, and high-end versions of any product line.

Source: www.apple.com

traditional range. Rising costs, therefore, force sellers to either change the entire price line structure, which results in confusion, or cut costs through production adjustments. The second option opens the firm to customer complaints that its merchandise is not what it used to be.

## PROMOTIONAL PRICING

**promotional pricing** pricing tactic in which a lower-than-normal price is used as a *temporary* ingredient in a firm's marketing strategy

In **promotional pricing**, a lower-than-normal price is used as a *temporary* ingredient in a firm's marketing strategy. In other words, it's a short-term version of penetration pricing.

Managing promotional pricing efforts requires marketing skill. Customers may get hooked on sales and other promotional pricing events. If they know their favorite department store has a one-day sale every month, they will likely wait to make their purchases on that day. When J.C. Penney nixed its longtime policy of offering weekly sales, coupons, and other discounts, customers abandoned the store in droves; the retailer was forced by angry shoppers to restore its traditional price cuts.[6]

**loss leaders** pricing tactic where goods are priced below cost to attract customers to stores in hopes they will buy other merchandise at regular prices

Retailers rely most heavily on promotional pricing. In one type of technique, stores offer **loss leaders**- goods priced below cost to attract customers who, the retailer hopes, will also buy regularly priced merchandise. The milk at your grocery store is likely a loss leader. Around Thanksgiving, many grocers offer the traditional turkey as a loss leader in the hope that customers will buy the other dinner ingredients there as well.[7]

### 14-4b

## CLOSING EXAMPLE

Procter and Gamble uses product-line pricing to satisfy different groups of consumers who prefer particular price ranges. The company offers both high-priced Tide and low-priced Cheer because its goal is to boost market share in the laundry detergent category overall. Similarly, P&G sells Charmin, Charmin Basic, Bounty, and Bounty Basic to capture a bigger total percentage of all buyers of toilet tissue and paper towels. This tactic has helped P&G profitably serve nearly 5 billion people around the globe.

## 14-5    PRICE AND PERCEPTION OF QUALITY

**LO 14.5** Explain how price affects consumer perceptions of quality.

### OPENING EXAMPLE

Sol was buying a bottle of wine for a friend's dinner party. Knowing his friend's preference for Cabernet, Sol considered bottles that varied between $12.99 and $24.50. Then the salesperson at the wine shop called his attention to a Cabernet priced at $3.99, touting it as "the best value we've ever had!" Despite his tight budget, Sol turned it down. Why do you think Sol made this decision? Would you have made a different choice?

## 14-5a

# LEARNING IT: PRICE AND PERCEPTION OF QUALITY

Price is often an important indicator of a product's quality to prospective purchasers. Many buyers interpret expensive products as high-quality products. Because prestige is often associated with high price tags, manufacturers of some status brands go to great lengths to prevent discounting. For example, Movado watches can be purchased only at official Movado-approved jewelry stores, and the brand never goes on sale. Even a more mainstream, non-luxury brand like Apple avoids discounting to maintain the integrity of their premium brand image.

Science has confirmed just how impactful these perceptions can be. A study by California Institute of Technology and Stanford had 20 subjects taste five wines ranging in price from $5 to $90. As you might predict, the subjects preferred the more expensive wines over the cheaper ones. Beyond these subjective reports, brain scans showed increased activity when subjects drank the wines they preferred more. Could this simply confirm that more expensive wines actually do taste better? Not in this case, because there were actually only two wines, and they were each labeled with both high and low prices. The preference the test subjects showed for the more expensive wines was influenced by their perceptions of quality—which was entirely influenced by the prices of each wine.[8]

Perceptions of quality can go beyond high-priced prestige products and extend to any product where consumers feel the value they received was more than the price paid. In a study by Dan Ariely from Duke University, a table was set up on campus offering two types of chocolates: Lindt truffles for 26 cents and Hershey's Kisses for 1 cent. Since the truffles would normally cost much more, about half the students selected the truffles, even though they cost 26 times as much as the Hershey's Kisses, showing how much perceived value is a driver of consumer behavior.[9]

A new type of prestige surrounds eco-friendly products. Many consumers are willing to pay more for green products—those made with environmentally sustainable materials and processes. These purchases make consumers feel good about what they are doing to help the environment, which can support their self-concept.

This perception of value even works at the other end of the pricing scale, where low-priced brands may differentiate themselves by promising—and delivering—a relatively high level of quality for the money. Target regularly introduces product lines created by famous designers or celebrities, such as Victoria Beckham, but offers them at competitive prices. The Dollar General approach, described at the start of this chapter, is to charge reliably low prices for trusted brands—though in small sizes that actually cost more per ounce than customers might pay at other stores.

While there is a link between price and perception of quality, supply and demand still play a role in purchasing patterns. As prices go up there will be fewer consumers willing to buy. Marketers of prestige products willingly make this supply and demand trade-off because their products usually command higher gross profit margins.

Consumers often define certain limits within which their quality perceptions vary directly with price. A potential buyer regards a price below the lower limit as too cheap and a price above the higher limit as too expensive. This perception holds true for both national brands and private-label products.

## 14-5b
## CLOSING EXAMPLE

Sol's decision illustrates how consumers connect quality perceptions to price. While he didn't have money to spare, he saw the cheap bottle of Cabernet as beneath the caliber of wine he wanted to give his friend. It's possible that a $10.99 or $11.99 choice would have been acceptable, but the $3.99 wine was perceived by Sol to be low quality. Because Sol had not actually tried any of these wines, it shows how price alone was the key driver of his perceptions of quality.

# 14-6
# PRICING AND THE LAW

**LO 14.6**  Describe the legal constraints on pricing.

## OPENING EXAMPLE

In 2014, Midwest grocery chain Woodman's filed suit against Clorox Company. According to the complaint, Clorox had previously sold brands like Glad bags and Clorox bleach to the 15-store retailer at the same discounted prices offered to giants Sam's Club and Costco, then had suddenly revoked the discounts based on Woodman's small account size.[10]

Arguing that the case was moot because it would no longer sell to Woodman's on any terms, Clorox asked a judge to dismiss the suit. What do you think the judge decided?

## 14-6a
## LEARNING IT: PRICING AND THE LAW

Pricing decisions are influenced by a variety of legal constraints imposed by federal, state, and local governments. Included in the price of products are not only the costs of raw materials, processing and packaging, and profit for the business, but also various taxes. For instance, excise taxes are levied on a variety of products, including real-estate transfers, alcoholic beverages, and motor fuels. Sales taxes can be charged on clothing, furniture, restaurant meals, and many other purchases.

While the free market and laws of supply and demand are typically the main drivers of pricing decisions, there is a role for regulation to ensure that pricing is conducted in a fair, transparent, and competitive manner. For example, many people looking for tickets to a high-demand sporting event or concert have encountered an expensive, sometimes illegal, form of pricing called "ticket scalping." Scalpers purchase tickets they expect to resell at a higher price. Although some cities and states have enacted laws prohibiting the practice, it continues to occur in many locations.

The ticket reselling market is both highly fragmented and susceptible to fraud and distorted pricing. In response, buyers and sellers are finding that the

NetPhotos/Alamy Stock photo.

StubHub offers a transparent and competitive market for reselling event tickets, which in the past was often limited to scalpers who bought tickets and sold them at highly inflated prices outside the event venue. Scalping is prohibited in many states and cities.

Internet is helping create a market in which both buyers and sellers can compare prices and seat locations. Web firms like StubHub.com and TicketsNow.com are ticket clearinghouses for this secondary market. These firms have signed deals with several professional sports teams that allow season ticket holders to sell unwanted tickets and buyers to purchase them with a guarantee. NHL and NBA fans have saved up to 30% by buying playoff tickets from StubHub at the last minute.[11]

The following section reviews some of the most important legal constraints on pricing.

## ROBINSON-PATMAN ACT

The **Robinson-Patman Act** (1936) was inspired by price competition triggered by the rise of grocery store chains. This Depression-era law prohibits **price discrimination** when selling the same product in the same amount to two different customers. It rules that differences in price must reflect actual cost differentials, such as additional transportation costs for customers located in remote locations. This law also prohibits selling at unreasonably low prices to drive competitors out of business. Supporters justified Robinson-Patman by arguing that the rapidly expanding chain stores of that era might be able to attract substantial discounts from suppliers anxious to secure their business, while small, independent stores would pay suppliers higher prices. As long as companies can demonstrate that their price discounts and promotional allowances do not restrict competition, they avoid penalties under the Robinson-Patman Act. For example, a manufacturer could offer lower prices to major retail chains by offering volume discounts for large orders. If these volume discounts are offered to all customers, regardless of their company size, it's typically not price discrimination.

**Robinson-Patman Act** a Depression-era law that prohibits price discrimination when selling the same product in the same amount to two different customers

**price discrimination** when a supplier offers the same product to two buyers at two different prices

## UNFAIR-TRADE LAWS

**unfair-trade laws** laws which require sellers to maintain minimum prices for comparable merchandise

Most states supplement federal legislation with their own **unfair-trade laws**, which require sellers to maintain minimum prices for comparable merchandise. Enacted in the 1930s, these laws were intended to protect small specialty shops from loss-leader pricing tactics in which chain stores might sell certain products below cost to attract customers. While these laws can sometimes be hard to enforce, their goal is to deter intentional predatory pricing by larger companies.

## FEDERAL TRADE COMMISSION

The U.S. Federal Trade Commission (FTC) was created "To prevent business practices that are anticompetitive or deceptive or unfair to consumers." With the slogan "Protecting America's Consumers," the FTC oversees enforcement of over 70 laws. While most of these laws don't relate specifically to pricing, they influence pricing in a number of ways. For example, the Fair Packaging and Labeling Act can prevent a manufacturer from overpricing a product by misrepresenting the quantity or identity of what's being sold.

### 14-6b
## CLOSING EXAMPLE

The judge in the case of Woodman's vs. Clorox refused to dismiss the retailer's complaint, meaning the lawsuit would continue and Woodman's case would be heard. He cited the Robinson-Patman Act, which requires equal treatment by sellers of all customers, regardless of size. So, despite many changes in the business world since 1936, when Robinson-Patman was enacted, fairness in pricing remains a core principle of marketing.

# 14-7  LEARN IT TODAY ... USE IT TOMORROW

Dollar General's success is based on low prices for major national brands, a strategy well suited to categories with highly elastic demand and standardized products. For less price-sensitive consumers, however, a marketer must carefully weigh other factors before choosing a pricing approach. Apply what you've learned to a business where brand image and the nature of competition are critical pieces in the pricing puzzle.

Only Organics is a Massachusetts-based startup chain of cafes serving healthy salads and sandwiches, with ingredients sourced from farms that use environmentally sensitive cultivation techniques. Founder Robin Jenkins is excited about her early success, and is ready to expand to the rest of New England. However, her investors want to know her pricing strategy before sinking money into new sites. They're concerned about the chain's ability to compete with the many local eateries in states like New Hampshire and Vermont.

Fortunately, one investor offered to pay for a survey of buyer intentions, which Robin commissioned from a market research firm. The good news:

among 500 potential customers who responded to mail and online question-naires, a big majority claimed they were likely to try Only Organics. But comments from personal interviews were mixed. While most interviewees strongly preferred responsibly cultivated food and were willing to pay premium prices for it, many expressed skepticism. They wouldn't commit to trying Only Organics unless they could be convinced that its suppliers actually used environmentally sensitive practices.

It's time to get hands-on and apply what you've learned. **See MindTap for an activity related to Only Organic's marketing activities.**

## Chapter Summary

**LO 14.1  Explain how price elasticity affects potential demand for a product.**

The concept of elasticity explains why consumer purchasing patterns vary for certain products, but not for others, when price goes up or down.

**LO 14.2  Compare the primary types of forecasting methods used to determine demand.**

Several qualitative and quantitative techniques are available to help marketers forecast future demand for a product or service.

**LO 14.3  Contrast the three primary competitive pricing strategies.**

Firms choose among skimming, penetration, and competitive pricing strategies based on their overall marketing strategies and organizational objectives.

**LO 14.4  Outline three types of pricing tactics used by marketers.**

To execute an overall pricing strategy, marketers may utilize psychological pricing, product-line pricing, and promotional pricing.

**LO 14.5  Explain how price affects consumer perceptions of quality.**

To many consumers, price signals the quality of a prospective purchase. Often, high prices are associated with high quality, while low prices are indicators of low quality.

**LO 14.6  Describe the legal constraints on pricing.**

Pricing decisions in the United States must conform with various laws and regulations imposed by federal, state, and local governments.

## Key Terms

supply  289
demand  289
elasticity  290
elasticity of demand  290
qualitative forecasting  292
quantitative forecasting  292
jury of executive opinion  293

Delphi technique  293
sales force composite  293
survey of buyer intentions  294
trend analysis  294
skimming pricing strategies  295
penetration pricing strategy  296
competitive pricing  297

psychological pricing  298
product-line pricing  299
promotional pricing  300
loss leaders  300
Robinson-Patman Act  303
price discrimination  303
unfair-trade laws  304

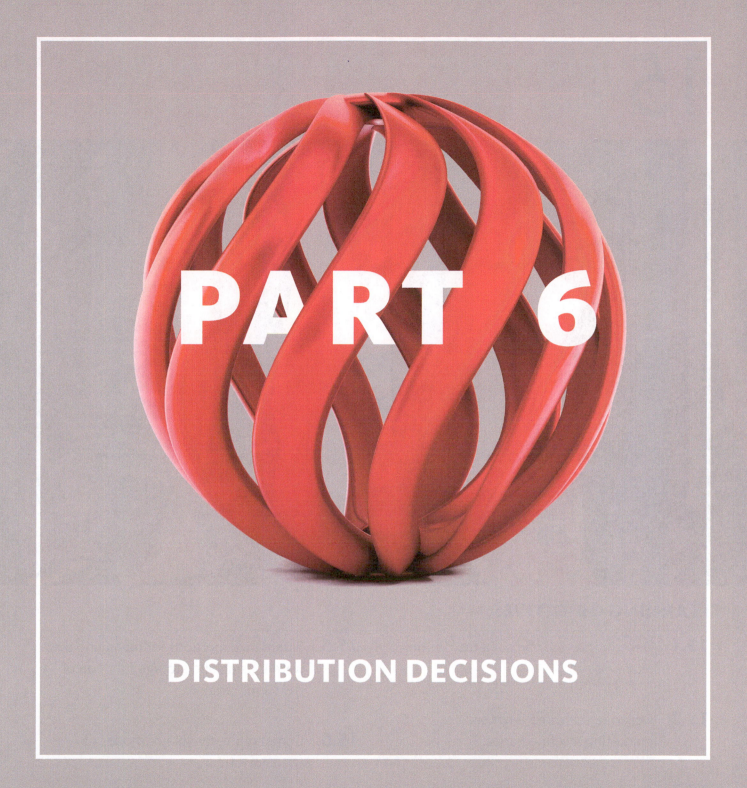

# PART 6

## DISTRIBUTION DECISIONS

# 15 DISTRIBUTION CHANNELS AND SUPPLY CHAIN MANAGEMENT

Iulian Valentin/Shutterstock.com

## LEARNING OBJECTIVES

**15.1** Describe the four types of distribution channels.

**15.2** Describe the three functions of marketing intermediaries.

**15.3** Outline the five factors that influence selection of distribution channels.

**15.4** List the key priorities for each function of the manufacturing supply chain.

**15.5** Summarize methods for managing the warehousing and storage function of the supply chain.

**15.6** Compare the five major modes of transportation.

**15.7** Given an example of a supply chain, identify methods for accomplishing the priorities of that supply chain.

# LEARN IT TODAY ... USE IT TOMORROW

Miniboss is a hypothetical manufacturer of custom tailored clothes for toddlers. The Miniboss business model is high-end and operates like custom suit suppliers for adults, such as Ascot Chang and William Fioravanti.[1,2] Miniboss is a vertically integrated business, meaning it controls all elements of production, from design, to ordering raw materials, to manufacturing, to sales and delivery.

Affluent parents place custom orders for their toddlers, Miniboss produces the custom clothes via a just-in-time manufacturing model, and ships within seven days via express air delivery. As a result, Miniboss's flagship clothing line, TopToddler, is winning awards and social media buzz for its child-friendly materials and designs. New client orders have doubled in the last three months alone.

As it continues to expand, Miniboss has a number of things to consider regarding its distribution channels and supply chain. So far, Miniboss has not partnered with other companies that specialize in distribution. Should they consider using these types of companies? Further, Miniboss has fulfilled all orders directly, shipping at retail prices through UPS. Should Miniboss contract with a dedicated carrier? And what about other delivery methods besides express air?

Miniboss must answer questions like these in order to maximize efficiency along its distribution channels and supply chain. If it doesn't, Miniboss will stay "mini" in more ways than one.

# 15-1 WHAT ARE THE FOUR DISTRIBUTION CHANNELS?

## OPENING EXAMPLE

LO 15.1   Describe the four types of distribution channels.

Procter & Gamble produces hundreds of products across multiple product categories. Its many billion dollar brands—like Bounty paper towels and Crest toothpaste—are well known in the industry and by millions of consumers around the world.[3] P&G's marketing departments have millions of dollars at their disposal to market P&G products across different channels, and reach consumers where they live, work, and shop.

Assume that you are one of the marketing managers for P&G's hair care category, including products such as Head & Shoulders and Pantene. You and your team have been tasked with allocating $20 million to different distribution channels to connect P&G's hair care brands with consumers. Which distribution channels are available to you, and which would prove most effective?

### 15-1a
### LEARNING IT: WHAT ARE THE FOUR DISTRIBUTION CHANNELS?

**Distribution channels**–also called marketing channels bring buyers and sellers together to complete transactions. These channels consist of the individuals and organizations who manage the flow of product from producers to consumers. Even the best product would never see the light of day without a plan for making that product available at the right time in the right place to the right customers. No single channel best serves the needs of every company. Instead of searching

**distribution channels** the individuals and organizations who manage the flow of product from producers to consumers

for the best channel for all products, a firm must analyze channels in light of consumer needs to determine the most appropriate channel or channels for the firm's goods and services.

## 15-1b
# TYPES OF DISTRIBUTION CHANNELS

The first step in selecting a distribution channel is determining which type of channel will best meet both the seller's objectives and the distribution needs of customers. There are four distribution channels to choose from: direct channel, channels using marketing intermediaries, dual distribution, and reverse channels.

## DIRECT CHANNEL

**direct channel** carries goods directly from a producer to the ultimate user

**direct selling** a marketing tactic in which a producer establishes direct sales contact with its product's final users

The simplest and shortest distribution channel is a direct channel. A **direct channel** carries goods directly from a producer to the ultimate user (see Exhibit 15.1). This channel is often supplemented with **direct selling**, a marketing tactic in which a producer establishes direct sales contact with its product's final users. Direct selling is an important option for goods requiring extensive demonstrations for persuading customers to buy.

A company can utilize more than one direct channel. For example, Bose sells audio equipment directly to consumers online and through its own physical retail stores. In both cases, they bypass the use of other distribution partners to sell their products.

## CHANNELS USING MARKETING INTERMEDIARIES

Although direct channels allow simple and straightforward marketing, they are not practical in every case. Some products serve markets in different areas of the country or world, or have large numbers of potential end users. Other categories of products rely heavily on repeat purchases. The producers of these products may find more efficient, less expensive, and less time-consuming alternatives to

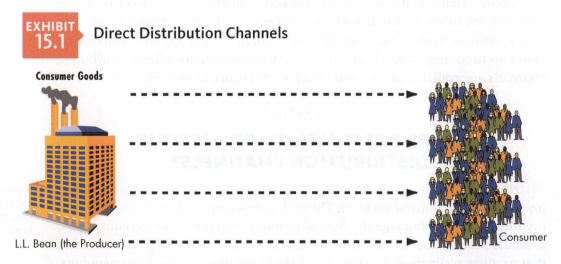

**EXHIBIT 15.1** Direct Distribution Channels

**Consumer Goods**

L.L. Bean (the Producer)

Consumer

L.L. Bean (the producer) uses direct channels by selling straight to consumers without its products passing through other distributors or retailers.

direct channels by using marketing intermediaries. A **marketing intermediary** (or middleman) is an organization that operates between producers and consumers to help bring the product to market. There are three primary types of marketing intermediaries: retailers, wholesalers, and agents.

Retailers specialize in selling product to consumers by opening stores, hiring sales staff, marketing to generate consumer traffic, and displaying merchandise in ways that encourage purchasing.

**Wholesalers** (or distributors) take title to the goods, store them in warehouses, and distribute them to retailers, other distributors, and sometimes end consumers.

A **sales agent** is a third-party person or company who represents the producer to wholesalers and retailers. Sales agents are essentially a contracted sales force with expertise in a particular market or geography. They are particularly important for smaller firms which might not be able to afford a full-time sales staff, or for firms going into new markets. Sales agents don't buy or take title to the product, but serve as go-betweens for producers and their distribution partners.

There are several configurations of distribution channels using intermediaries, including:

- Producer to retailer to consumer
- Producer to wholesaler to retailer to consumer
- Producer to sales agent to wholesaler to retailer to consumer

Exhibit 15.2 shows the flow of goods through a channel using various types of intermediaries. These different configurations are sometimes considered distinct distribution channels as well.

**Vertical integration** is when a producer assumes control over functions that were previously handled by an intermediary. For example, Apple used to only distribute its products through other retailers, but practiced vertical integration when deciding to open its own retail stores.

**marketing intermediary** an organization that operates between producers and consumers to help bring the product to market

**wholesalers** marketing intermediary who takes title to the goods, stores them in warehouses, and distributes them to retailers, other distributors, and sometimes end consumers

**sales agent** a third-party person or company who represents the producer to wholesalers and retailers

**vertical integration** when a producer assumes control over functions that were previously handled by an intermediary

**EXHIBIT 15.2** **Distribution Channels Using Marketing Intermediaries**

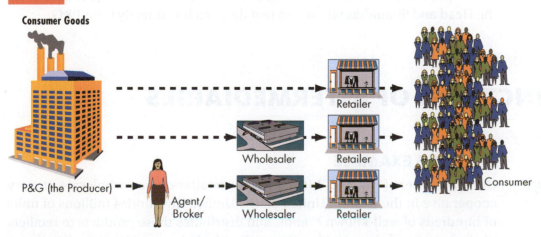

Procter & Gamble (the producer) partners with a number of agents, wholesalers, and retailers to distribute its products to consumers all over the world.

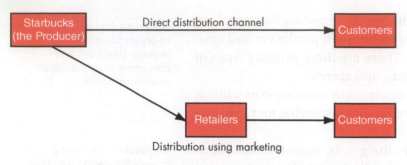

Starbucks (the producer) distributes its bottled Frappuccino drinks using direct channels by selling to consumers in its own stores. They also utilize intermediaries, such as distributors and retailers, to offer these products at grocery stores and convenience stores.

**EXHIBIT 15.3**

**Dual Distribution**

**dual distribution** the movement of products through two or more channels to reach the firm's target market

**reverse channels** channels designed to return goods to their producers

## DUAL DISTRIBUTION

**Dual distribution** refers to the movement of products through two or more channels to reach the firm's target market (see Exhibit 15.3). Nordstrom, for instance, has a three-pronged distribution system, selling through stores, catalogs, and online. Marketers usually adopt a dual distribution strategy either to maximize their firm's coverage in the marketplace or to increase the cost-effectiveness of the firm's marketing effort.

## REVERSE CHANNELS

While the traditional concept of distribution channels involves the movement of goods and services from producer to consumer, firms should not ignore **reverse channels**—channels designed to return goods to their producers. Purchase a new set of tires, and you'll find a recycling charge for disposing of the old tires. Reverse channels have gained increased importance with rising prices for raw materials, increasing availability of recycling facilities, and a move toward increased environmental sustainability.

Reverse channels also handle product recalls and repairs. An appliance manufacturer might send recall notices to the buyers of a washing machine. An auto manufacturer might send notices to car owners advising them of a potential problem and offering to repair the problem at no cost through local dealerships.

### 15-1c

## CLOSING EXAMPLE

Hair care products have traditionally reached consumers through brick-and-mortar retailers, though online sales are increasing. As marketing manager for P&G's hair care products, you and your team see an opportunity to utilize a dual distribution strategy for your shampoos and conditioners. You decide to allocate additional marketing dollars to sponsor sales promotions with your retail distribution partners, plus you fund a YouTube ad campaign that drives customers to the Head and Shoulders website so that they can buy directly from P&G.

## 15-2    FUNCTIONS OF INTERMEDIARIES

**LO 15.2** Describe the three functions of marketing intermediaries.

### OPENING EXAMPLE

Unified Grocers ("Unified") is the largest retailer-owned wholesale grocery cooperative in the western United States. Unified inventories millions of units of hundreds of well-known brands, and distributes these products to retailers of all shapes and sizes. Golden Creme, Special Value, and Western Family are familiar names to consumers throughout the West.[4]

Recently, Unified has unveiled a new addition to its private label offerings "designed to appeal to the growing consumer preference for natural and organic products." Unified will inventory natural and organic products, and market them to retailers under the Natural Directions brand. As it does so, it will work with multiple intermediaries in a number of distribution channels, coordinating with suppliers and retailers to inventory and sell products like fair trade coffee, organic applesauce, and acai aronia juice to consumers. But, if Unified can source the products and sell them under its own private label brand, why not sell directly to consumers and cut out additional intermediaries? Learn about which intermediaries are most important to Unified and its Natural Directions brand.

## 15-2a

# LEARNING IT: FUNCTIONS OF INTERMEDIARIES

The producer of a product might be tempted to believe they should always sell directly to consumers. After all, it cuts out any middlemen and allows the company to keep all of the profit. However, intermediaries can often perform these distribution functions more effectively and less expensively than the producer. In the end, partnering with the right intermediaries can often result in more sales volume and profit for the producer. Intermediaries perform three important functions, including facilitating the exchange process, lowering the cost of logistics, and increasing a company's sales and marketing infrastructure.

### FACILITATE THE EXCHANGE PROCESS

A producer can cut the costs of buying and selling to multiple customers by using an intermediary. For example, if Unified chose to develop, facilitate, and maintain direct contacts for its Golden Creme branded products—with all of its millions of customers around the country—it would likely go out of business due to the cost required to cultivate and maintain those contacts. Instead, Unified partners with retailers to act as intermediaries, reducing the number of contacts that Unified needs to make in order to reach the same number of customers. See Exhibit 15.4 for a visual representation.

### LOWER COST OF LOGISTICS

By using intermediaries, a manufacturer does not need to incur the cost of buying or leasing a network of its own warehouses to inventory product, or operate its own fleet of vehicles to deliver product. Instead, it can partner with a logistics company to ship product or a wholesaler who can inventory and deliver product to retailers or end-users. If Unified wanted to bring its Western Family branded dairy products to market internationally, for example, it could rely on established logistics providers like Maersk

**EXHIBIT 15.4**

**Intermediaries Facilitate the Exchange Process**

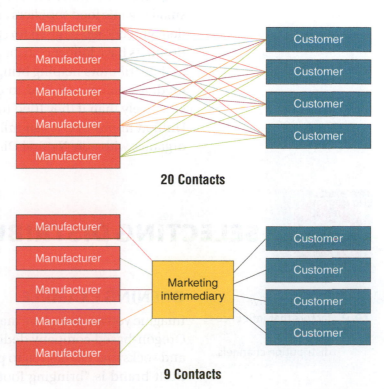

20 Contacts

9 Contacts

and Hapag-Lloyd, rather than building and maintaining its own fleet of expensive container ships.

### INCREASE SALES AND MARKETING INFRASTRUCTURE

Intermediaries provide cost effective sales and marketing services to manufacturers as well. Consider how many thousands of sales representatives Unified would need to hire to reach retailers and consumers across the United States—and how expensive that would be. Instead, Unified works with large sales and marketing firms that have an existing sales force, or partners with large retailers like Walmart who have thousands of locations and service millions of existing customers on a daily basis.

## 15-2b
## SHORT AND LONG DISTRIBUTION CHANNELS

A short distribution channel involves few intermediaries. By contrast, a long distribution channel involves several intermediaries working in succession to move goods from producers to consumers. Business market products usually move through short channels due to geographic concentrations and comparatively fewer business purchasers. Service firms market primarily through short channels, because they sell intangible products and need to maintain personal relationships within their channels. Haircuts, manicures, and dental cleanings all operate through short channels.

## 15-2c
## CLOSING EXAMPLE

Regarding its Natural Directions brand, Unified sources product using agents for small organic food suppliers and then distributes through hundreds of independent grocers and large chain stores. A number of its Natural Directions-branded products have longer distribution channels than others, with additional agents and distributors helping bring these products to customers. Using these intermediaries allows Unified to expand its reach and do so more efficiently and effectively than if they tried to manage all of these functions alone. As a result, Unified hopes that it can influence more customers to "explore the world of organics with new Natural Directions!"

# 15-3
# SELECTING DISTRIBUTION CHANNELS

**LO 15.3** Outline the five factors that influence selection of distribution channels.

### OPENING EXAMPLE

Imagine you are one of the marketing managers at Keen Footwear, the Portland, Oregon-based company dedicated to designing high-quality "footwear, bags, and socks that enable you to play anyplace without a ceiling." Keen's American Built brand is "bringing footwear manufacturing back to the USA," and its products are all assembled in the United States.[5] You have been assigned the task of effectively marketing the American Built line of products across different distribution channels. In order to do so, you and your team must consider a number of factors that influence the final selection of distribution channels. Which factors would be most influential in your decision-making?

### 15-3a

# LEARNING IT: SELECTING DISTRIBUTION CHANNELS

Firms face several strategic decisions when choosing distribution channels for their products.

Consider the following questions: What characteristics of a retailer make it the best channel option for a company? How many intermediaries should be utilized? Why would a firm market a single product through multiple channels?

A variety of factors affect the selection of a distribution channel. These include market, product, organizational, competitive, and intensity factors.

## MARKET FACTORS

As discussed previously, products are intended for either consumer or business market end-users. Business market purchasers usually prefer to deal directly with manufacturers (except for routine supplies or small accessory items), but most consumers make their purchases from retailers. Marketers often sell products that serve both business users and consumers through more than one channel.

Other market factors also affect channel choice, including the market's needs, its geographic location, and its average order size. To serve a concentrated market with a small number of buyers, a direct channel offers a feasible alternative. In serving a geographically scattered area, distribution through intermediaries makes sense.

*Example*: A farm equipment manufacturer is targeting a defined, but relatively small number of buyers. They are more likely to utilize direct channels or choose intermediaries who specialize in selling to farms. Choosing channels that offer wider distribution, but don't sell to farms, would be a poor choice.

## PRODUCT FACTORS

Product characteristics also guide the selection of the optimal distribution channel strategy. For example, perishable goods, such as fresh fruit and vegetables, milk, and fruit juice move through short distribution channels to reduce storage time. Products with low unit costs—such as cans of dog food, bars of soap, and packages of gum—typically travel through long channels so that they can gain the widest distribution possible.

*Example*: While far more people visit Walmart stores than car dealerships in any given week, it's unlikely that car manufacturers would try to sell through Walmart, as it's not the right venue for a product of that size and price.

## ORGANIZATIONAL FACTORS

Companies with strong financial, management, and marketing resources feel less need for help from intermediaries. This affects distribution channel selection. A large, financially strong manufacturer can hire its own sales force, warehouse its own goods, and extend credit to retailers or consumers. A firm with a broad product line can usually market its products directly to retailers or business users, because its own sales force can offer a variety of products. High sales volume spreads selling costs over a large number of items, generating adequate returns from direct sales.

By contrast, a small firm with fewer resources may do better with the aid of intermediaries. Single-product firms often view direct selling as unaffordable.

*Example*: Apple has the resources to sell directly through its own stores, which requires leasing of space, hiring of staff, and stocking of inventory. A small manufacturer of iPhone accessories likely does not have the resources to sell through its own stores and is better off partnering with retail intermediaries like Apple and Best Buy.

## COMPETITIVE FACTORS

Marketers sometimes choose distribution channels to either avoid competitors or compete with them head-to-head. Sometimes businesses will only work with distributors who offer exclusivity, meaning they will not carry a competitor's line. In many categories, this is not possible, as wholesalers often carry most major brands so that they can provide the best assortment to their retail customers.

Businesses that explore new distribution channels must be careful to avoid upsetting their channel intermediaries. Distribution channels work smoothly only when members cooperate in well-organized efforts to achieve maximum operating efficiencies. Two types of conflict—horizontal and vertical—can hinder the normal functioning of a distribution channel.

**horizontal conflict**
disagreements among channel members at the same level, such as two or more wholesalers or retailers

**Horizontal Conflict** results from disagreements among channel members at the same level, such as two or more wholesalers or retailers. For example, a retailer that was previously the exclusive seller of a manufacturer's product might be upset if the manufacturer begins selling that product through other retailers. This could lead to price competition among the retailers, which could undermine the manufacturer's marketing strategy.

**vertical conflict** disagreements among channel members at different levels

**Vertical Conflict** results from disagreements among channel members at different levels. For example, retailers may develop private brands to compete with producers' brands or producers may establish their own retail stores or create mail-order operations that compete with retailers.

The basic antidote to channel conflict is effective cooperation among channel members. Cooperation is best achieved when all channel members regard themselves as equal components of the same organization. Today firms look for new ways to handle both online and offline channels without damaging relationships.

*Example*: Costco often sells products from major brands at discount prices. To avoid upsetting its other retail partners (a vertical conflict), these brands often sell product to Costco in exclusive bundles or sizes not available anywhere else. This helps avoid direct price comparison.

Mira/Alamy Stock Photo

Brands will sometimes offer custom versions of a product to different channel partners in order to avoid vertical conflict.

## INTENSITY FACTORS

Another key channel strategy decision is the intensity of distribution. **Distribution intensity** refers to the number or percentage of intermediaries (usually retailers) through which a manufacturer distributes its goods in a particular market. Optimal distribution intensity should ensure adequate market coverage for a product. Adequate market coverage varies depending on the goals of the individual firm, the type of product, and the consumer segments in its target market. In general, distribution intensity varies along a continuum with three general categories: intensive distribution, selective distribution, and exclusive distribution.

- *Intensive Distribution*: An **intensive distribution** strategy seeks to distribute a product through all available retailers in a trade area. Because Dove practices intensive distribution for many of its products, you can pick up one of its chocolate bars or ice cream products just about anywhere—the supermarket, the convenience store, and even the drugstore. Usually, an intensive distribution strategy suits items with wide appeal across broad groups of consumers.

- *Selective Distribution*: In **selective distribution**, a firm chooses only a limited number of retailers in a market area to handle its line. By limiting the number of retailers, marketers can reduce total marketing costs while establishing strong working relationships within the channel. Moreover, selected retailers often agree to comply with the company's strict rules for advertising, pricing, and displaying its products. This helps protect the company's brand.

**distribution intensity** the number or percentage of intermediaries (usually retailers) through which a manufacturer distributes its goods in a particular market

**intensive distribution** seeks to distribute a product through all available retailers in a trade area

**selective distribution** when a firm chooses only a limited number of retailers in a market area to handle its line

exclusive distribution when a producer sells to only a small number of retailers or grants exclusive rights to a wholesaler or retailer to sell its products in a specific geographic region

- *Exclusive Distribution*: When a producer sells to only a small number of retailers or grants exclusive rights to a wholesaler or retailer to sell its products in a specific geographic region, it practices **exclusive distribution**. The automobile industry provides a good example of exclusive distribution. A city with a population of 100,000 probably does not need more than a single Jaguar car dealer, for example. Exclusive distribution agreements also govern marketing for some major appliance and apparel brands.

Marketers may sacrifice some market coverage by implementing exclusive distribution. However, they often develop and maintain an image of quality and prestige for the product. If it is harder to find a Free People silk dress, for example, the product seems more valuable. In addition, exclusive distribution limits marketing costs because the firm deals with a smaller number of accounts. In exclusive distribution, producers and retailers cooperate closely in decisions concerning advertising and promotion, inventory carried by the retailers, and prices.

*Example 1*: The objective for a brand like Red Bull is to gain market share and maximize sales volume. Its distribution strategy is to seek intensive distribution, such as through convenience stores and grocery stores.

*Example 2*: On the other hand, a high-end shoe company like Kenneth Cole wants to maintain its brand by only working with retailers that can agree to the company's rules for pricing and product display. While Kenneth Cole could pursue a distribution partner with more intensive market coverage, like Target, that would not be a strategic fit for its brand.

A brand like Red Bull seeks intensive distribution, so it partners with retailers that have thousands of stores. A brand like Kenneth Cole is more selective and partners with retailers that have fewer outlets. These distribution decisions meet each company's strategic objectives.

A fundamental marketing principle governs channel decisions: A member of the channel must perform certain central functions that your firm couldn't do more efficiently or less expensively on its own. A manufacturer might bypass its wholesalers by establishing regional warehouses, maintaining field sales forces, serving as sources of information for retail customers, or arranging details of financing. But this requires managing a number of business functions that the company might rather outsource to those who specialize in them.

Sheila Fitzgerald/Shutterstock.com

RosaBetancourt 00 people images/Alamy Stock Photo

## 15-3b
# CLOSING EXAMPLE

You and your marketing team at Keen Footwear have considered a number of factors that will determine which distribution channels to use.

**Market factors:** Your target audience is diverse and geographically dispersed. You'll choose distribution partners who can reach this audience.

**Product factors:** Your product is relatively small and durable. You could choose either short or long channels, and the product is appropriate for any number of wholesalers and retailers that carry similar products.

**Organizational factors:** Your company is growing, but still has limited resources. While the company can utilize direct channels to sell online, it's best to utilize intermediaries to distribute product in physical retailers.

**Competitive factors:** Since your products are well differentiated from the competition, you are not bothered by partnering with intermediaries who also carry your competition's products. However, you will avoid vertical channel conflicts by assuring your retail partners that Keen will never undercut its prices in the company's e-commerce store.

**Intensity factors:** While you would like wide distribution, Keen makes premium products. You will choose selective distribution by finding distribution partners who have a fairly large number of outlets, but where you can still control how your product is priced, displayed, and sold.

# 15-4  COMPONENTS OF THE SUPPLY CHAIN

## OPENING EXAMPLE

Pier 1 Imports buys its eclectic mix of items from vendors in more than 50 countries, most representing small companies. If high-demand items or seasonal products arrive late to its six North American distribution centers, or are shipped in insufficient quantities, Pier 1 may miss opportunities to deliver popular shopping choices to its more than 1,000 retail stores. In turn, it could lose ground to competitors like Pottery Barn and Crate & Barrel.

An efficient supply chain is critical to Pier 1's ultimate success or failure. What are some of the components that Pier 1 needs to consider along its supply chain?

**LO 15.4** List the key priorities for each function of the manufacturing supply chain.

## 15-4a

# LEARNING IT: COMPONENTS OF THE SUPPLY CHAIN

As discussed earlier, a distribution channel is made up of the individuals and organizations that manage the flow of product from producers to consumers. If Oberto, which manufactures beef jerky, partners with a wholesaler, who then sells to QFC grocery stores, these are the members of the distribution channel.

**supply chain** the complete sequence of suppliers and activities that contribute to the creation and delivery of goods and services

The **supply chain**, also known as the *value chain*, is the complete sequence of suppliers *and activities* that contribute to the creation and delivery of goods and services. The supply chain begins with the raw material inputs for manufacturing a product then proceeds to actual production activities. The final link in the supply chain is the movement of finished products through the distribution channel to customers. Activities specifically related to the physical movement and management of raw materials or products are called logistics. This is most commonly associated with trucking and other modes of transportation, but can also include warehousing and storage.

Exhibit 15.5 illustrates some of the priorities that firms need to consider for each activity along the supply chain—whether they are in charge of that activity or utilize a supply chain partner.

Not all members of the supply chain are considered members of the distribution channel. For example, if Oberto sold directly to customers via its website, this is a direct distribution channel with no marketing intermediaries. However, Oberto might use UPS to actually deliver customer orders, making UPS a member of the supply chain in charge of the outbound logistics function.

To manage the supply chain, businesses must look for ways to optimize the function of each activity.

*Example 1*: Sara Lee might have market tested an idea for a delicious new cake, and have multiple retailers ready to carry the product. However, if Sara Lee can't acquire the raw materials to make the product, or partners with a logistics company that always delivers late, then Sara Lee will have trouble fulfilling retailer demand on time, if at all.

**EXHIBIT 15.5**  **The Supply Chain of a Manufacturing Company**

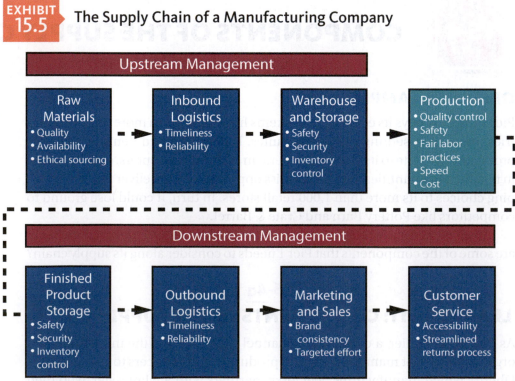

Source: Adapted from Figure 2.2, Ralph Stair and George Reynolds, Principles of Information Systems, 10th ed., Cengage Learning, © 2012. Reproduced by permission.

*Example 2*: If LG has retailer orders for 250,000 OLED televisions for the Christmas season, but half of those TVs get damaged in the warehouse when a storm hits, LG will lose ground to its competitors.

*Example 3*: Suppose FitBit hired a third-party sales firm to represent its products to electronics retailers. If that firm misrepresents the product or spends time visiting the wrong types of stores, FitBit sales will likely suffer.

From the perspective of a producer, supply chain management takes place in two directions: upstream and downstream. **Upstream management** involves managing raw materials, inbound logistics, and warehouse and storage facilities. **Downstream management** involves managing finished product storage, outbound logistics, marketing and sales, and customer service.

## 15-4b

# MANAGING THE SUPPLY CHAIN

Companies choose a variety of methods for managing the supply chain. They can include high-tech systems like radio frequency identification and regular person-to-person meetings. The following sections examine common methods for streamlining and managing logistics and the supply chain as part of an overall distribution strategy.

*Radio Frequency Identification*:  One tool marketers use to help manage logistics is **radio frequency identification (RFID)** technology. With RFID, a tiny chip with identification information is placed on an item. That chip can then be read by a radio frequency scanner from a distance, making tracking easier. These chips are already widely used in tollway pass transmitters, allowing drivers to zip through tollbooths without stopping or rolling down their windows to toss change into baskets. They are also embedded in employee ID cards that workers use to open office doors without keys.

*Enterprise Resource Planning*:  Software is an important aspect of logistics management and the supply chain. An **enterprise resource planning (ERP) system** is an integrated software package that consolidates data from among the firm's units. Roughly two-thirds of ERP system users are manufacturers concerned with production issues such as sequencing and scheduling.

*Logistical Cost Control*:  To reduce logistical costs, businesses are reexamining each link in their supply chains to identify activities that do not add value for customers. By eliminating, reducing, or redesigning these activities, they can often cut costs and boost efficiency. Some companies try to cut costs and offer value-added services by outsourcing some or all of their logistics functions to specialist firms.

## 15-4c

# CLOSING EXAMPLE

Pier 1 meticulously organizes its supply chain to lower costs and save time. Careful coordination of Pier 1's supplier network, logistics processes, and inventory control is the key to its continuing success. Its growing online presence has

**upstream management** the management of raw materials, inbound logistics, and warehouse and storage facilities

**downstream management** the management of finished product storage, outbound logistics, marketing and sales, and customer service

**radio frequency identification (RFID)** a tiny chip with identification information is placed on an item That chip can then be read by a radio frequency scanner from a distance, making tracking easier

**enterprise resource planning (ERP) system** an integrated software package that consolidates data from among the firm's units

spurred upgrades to its warehousing strategy and shipping partnerships. As a result, Pier 1 continues to generate strong profits, with thousands of products available to customers in the right time at the right place.[6,7]

# 15-5

# KEY PRIORITIES OF WAREHOUSING AND STORAGE

**LO 15.5** Summarize methods for managing the warehousing and storage function of the supply chain.

## OPENING EXAMPLE

Lenka's Fresh Snacks (LFS), the producer of the Lenka Bar, is a granola bar manufacturer based in Yoe, Pennsylvania. LFS produces a number of granola bars for its 450 retail partners across the eastern seaboard, manufacturing them in its 4,000-square-foot facility. According to Steve Rasovsky, CEO, the best-selling flavors for Lenka Bar are peanut butter, and nuts and berries.[8]

As LFS continues to expand, it has decided to add a new flavor to its product line: chia seeds and almonds. These ingredients have different order quantities and storage requirements than other ingredients already used in manufacturing. As it considers how to move forward, LFS must consider a number of issues regarding warehousing and storage. What are some of the key priorities that it must consider?

Every new ingredient for Lenka Bar must be ordered and stored before it can be used in production. With hundreds of potential ingredients, LFS must carefully manage its warehousing and storage needs.

## 15-5a

## LEARNING IT: KEY PRIORITIES OF WAREHOUSING AND STORAGE

A firm's warehousing and storage function contains the following elements:

1. *Inventory control*: quantity of inventory the firm maintains at each location

Source: www.Lenkabar.com

Source: www.Lenkabar.com

2. *Protective packaging and materials handling*: how the firm packages and efficiently handles goods in the factory, warehouse, and transport terminals

3. *Warehousing*: the distribution system's location of stock and the number of warehouses the firm maintains

## INVENTORY CONTROL

Inventory control is critical, as companies need to maintain enough inventory to meet customer demand without incurring costs for carrying excess inventory. Some firms attempt to keep inventory levels under control by implementing just-in-time (JIT) production, where companies keep low inventory and rely on suppliers to quickly deliver parts just when they are needed. This requires precise demand forecasting that must be shared up the supply chain. As discussed earlier in this chapter, companies are beginning to use RFID technology to more precisely track the quantity and whereabouts of their inventory.

> *Example 1*: THE DOWNSIDE OF TOO MUCH INVENTORY: LFS could stock 10,000 boxes of each product to ensure that inventory is always available for retailers to order. However, producing and holding that inventory requires a lot of money that could be put to other uses, such as sales and marketing.
>
> *Example 2*: THE DOWNSIDE OF TOO LITTLE INVENTORY: LFS could decide to carry very little inventory in order to conserve cash until a product is ordered. But suppose they receive a large order for a product, only to find out that its raw material supplier is out of stock for the next eight weeks. LFS's customers might not be willing to wait and could cancel their order and buy from a competitor.

## PROTECTIVE PACKAGING AND MATERIALS HANDLING

Logistics managers arrange and control activities for moving products within plants, warehouses, and transportation terminals. These activities compose the materials handling system. Two important concepts influence many materials handling choices: unitizing and containerization.

**Unitizing**, or palletizing, combines as many packages as possible into each load that moves within or outside a facility. Logistics managers prefer to handle materials on pallets (platforms, generally made of wood, on which

**unitizing** or palletizing, combining as many packages as possible into each load that moves within or outside a facility

Consolidating products onto a pallet makes them easier to transport and minimizes damage.

Dmitry Kalinovsky/Shutterstock.com

goods are transported). Unitizing systems often lash materials in place with steel bands or shrink packaging. Unitizing promotes efficient materials handling because each package requires minimal labor to move. Securing the materials together also minimizes damage and pilferage.

Logistics managers extend the same concept through **containerization**—combining several unitized loads into a single, well-protected load. A container of oil rig parts, for example, can be loaded in Topeka and trucked to Kansas City, where rail facilities place the shipment on a high-speed run-through train to New York City. There, the parts are loaded onto a ship headed to Saudi Arabia. Containerization markedly reduces the time required to load and unload ships, and limits in-transit damage to freight because individual packages pass through fewer handling systems en route to purchasers.

**containerization** the process of combining several unitized loads into a single, well-protected load

## WAREHOUSING

Products flow through two types of warehouses: storage and distribution. A *storage warehouse* holds goods for moderate to long periods in an attempt to balance supply and demand for producers and purchasers. By contrast, a *distribution warehouse* assembles and redistributes goods, keeping them moving as much as possible. Many distribution warehouses or centers physically store goods for less than 24 hours before shipping them to customers.

Logistics managers have attempted to save on transportation costs by developing central distribution centers. A manufacturer might send a single, large, consolidated shipment to a break-bulk center—a central distribution center that breaks down large shipments into several smaller ones and delivers them to individual customers in the area. Many Internet retailers use break-bulk distribution centers.

Logistics managers can cut distribution costs and improve customer service dramatically by automating their warehouse systems. Although automation

Containerization can reduce costs and ease handling for large quantities of a product—or for large products that would otherwise be difficult to transport.

elbud/Shutterstock.com

technology represents an expensive investment, it can provide major labor savings for high-volume distributors like grocery chains.

Every company must make a major logistics decision when it determines the number and location of its storage facilities. Two categories of costs influence this choice:

- Warehousing and materials handling costs
- Delivery costs from warehouses to customers.

Large facilities offer economies of scale in facilities and materials handling systems; per-unit costs for these systems decrease as volume increases. Delivery costs, on the other hand, rise as the distance from warehouse to customer increases.

## 15-5b
## CLOSING EXAMPLE

Adding a new flavor to the Lenka Bar product line requires that LFS takes a new look at its warehousing and storage functions.

To minimize the costs and space required to carry inventory of this expanded line of products, LFS researched demand from its 450 retail partners and will institute a JIT manufacturing system. LFS will share the demand forecast with its suppliers to ensure that everyone has the right materials available at the right time.

LFS will begin unitizing its cases of finished goods onto pallets to simplify inventory handling. Before they were using cases stacked on racks. This made orders easier to fulfill, because retailers order by the case, but made all other aspects of the warehousing operation less efficient.

Now that LFS is moving to JIT manufacturing, it can continuing growing using its existing storage warehouse. This is because the space that was previously dedicated to storing stockpiles of raw ingredients can now be used to store inventory of finished product. Not only does LFS save money by not having to store as much inventory, it can avoid having to build or buy a larger warehouse.

 **15-6**   # MODES OF TRANSPORTATION

### OPENING EXAMPLE

Susan M. Brownell is the VP of supply management at the U.S. Postal Service (USPS). She is responsible for managing supplier relationships with over $12 billion in expenditures and $6 billion of inventory.[9] Many of these suppliers provide transportation and delivery services for USPS and its customers.

In order to save taxpayer dollars, Brownell has been tasked with optimizing transportation costs for mail and package deliveries. At the same time, in order to compete with private competitors like FedEx, Brownell is expected to maintain, if not increase the quality of USPS delivery services. What are some of the transportation options available to Browning, and how should she evaluate which ones to use?

**LO 15.6**   Compare the five major modes of transportation.

# LEARNING IT: MODES OF TRANSPORTATION

Whether moving product around the block or around the world, logistics managers choose from five major modes of transportation. Each mode has its own unique characteristics.

## RAILROADS

Railroads continue to control the largest share of the freight business as measured by ton-miles. The term *ton-mile* refers to shipping activity required to move one ton of freight one mile. Rail shipments quickly rack up ton-miles because this mode provides the most efficient way for moving bulky commodities over long distances. Rail carriers generally transport huge quantities of coal, chemicals, grain, non-metallic minerals, wood products, and automobiles.

## MOTOR CARRIERS

The trucking industry is also an important factor in the freight industry—the American Trucking Association reports that trucks haul more than 10.5 billion tons of freight each year, making deliveries to areas railroads simply can't reach.[10] Trucking offers important advantages over the other transportation modes, including relatively fast and consistent service for both large and small shipments.

Technology has also improved the efficiency of trucking. Many trucking firms now track their fleets via satellite communications systems. In-truck computer systems allow drivers and dispatchers to make last-minute changes in scheduling and delivery.

## WATER CARRIERS

Two basic types of transport methods move products over water: inland or barge lines, and oceangoing deepwater ships.

Barge lines efficiently transport bulky, low-unit-value commodities such as grain, gravel, lumber, sand, and steel. A typical lower Mississippi River barge line may stretch more than a quarter mile across. Large ships also operate on the Great Lakes, transporting materials like iron ore from Minnesota and harvested grain for market. These lake carrier ships range in size from roughly 400 feet to more than 1,000 feet in length.

Oceangoing supertankers from global companies like the Maersk Line are the size of three football fields and almost double the capacity of other vessels. At full capacity, the ships can cut one-fifth of the cost of shipping a container across the Pacific Ocean. Shippers that transport goods via water carriers incur low costs compared with the rates for other transportation modes. However, transit time is often longer than other options.

## PIPELINES

Although the pipeline industry ranks third after railroads and motor carriers in ton-miles transported, many people are unaware that it even exists. More than 2.5 million miles of pipelines crisscross the United States transporting energy products—enough to circle the planet 100 times. The pipelines are operated by

Ocean tankers can carry thousands of containers, each loaded with raw materials or finished goods, such as toys or electronics. When the ship arrives in port, the containers can be easily unloaded and transported by truck or rail to their inland destinations.

Aun Photographer/Shutterstock.com

about 3,000 large and small firms.[11] Oil pipelines carry two types of commodities: crude (unprocessed) oil and refined products, such as gasoline, jet fuel, and kerosene.

Although pipelines offer low maintenance and dependable methods of transportation, a number of characteristics limit their applications. They have fewer locations than water carriers, and they can accommodate shipments of only a small number of products. Finally, pipelines represent a relatively slow method of transportation; liquids travel through pipelines at an average speed of only three to four miles per hour.

## AIR FREIGHT

Air freight is defined as the shipment and transfer of goods through an air carrier. Though air freight doesn't haul anywhere near the amount of ton-miles as other modes of transportation, it provides a number of benefits to shippers. For example, products can be delivered to remote or hard-to-reach locations more easily via air; an airport at the destination is all that is required. Further, time sensitive material can more easily be shipped "express" via air, anywhere in the world. Smaller and mid-sized companies take advantage of express shipping, as it allows them to participate in international trade more easily than via other modes of transportation. Shipping by air freight also provides a higher level of security than many alternatives, as airport controls over cargo are strictly managed.

### 15-6b

## COMPARING THE FIVE MODES OF TRANSPORT

Exhibit 15.6 compares several characteristics of the five modes of transportation. Although all shippers consider reliability, speed, and cost when choosing the most appropriate transportation methods, they assign varying levels of importance to

**EXHIBIT 15.6**    Comparing Modes of Transportation

| Mode | Speed | Dependability in Meeting Schedules | Frequency of Shipments | Availability in Different Locations | Flexibility in Handling | Cost |
|------|-------|-----------------------------------|------------------------|------------------------------------|------------------------|------|
| Rail | Average | Average | Low | Low | High | Average |
| Water | Very slow | Average | Very low | Limited | Very high | Very low |
| Truck | Fast | High | High | Very extensive | Average | High |
| Pipeline | Slow | High | High | Very limited | Very low | Low |
| Air | Very fast | High | Average | Average | Low | Very high |

each criterion based on their situation. Examples of types of goods most often handled by the different modes of transport include:

- *Railroads*: lumber, iron, steel, coal, automobiles, grain, and chemicals, plus containerized loads of finished products such as electronics, clothing, and furniture.
- *Motor carriers*: clothing, furniture, fixtures, lumber, plastic, food, leather, and machinery
- *Water carriers*: fuel, oil, coal, chemicals, minerals, and petroleum products; automobiles, electronics, clothing, and toys from foreign manufacturers
- *Pipelines*: oil, diesel fuel, jet fuel, kerosene, and natural gas
- *Air freight*: flowers, medical testing kits, and gourmet food products sent directly to consumers

## INTERMODAL OPERATIONS

**intermodal operations**
utilizing a combination of transport modes to improve customer service and achieve cost advantages

**Intermodal operations** include a combination of transport modes, such as rail and highway carriers (piggyback), air and highway carriers (birdyback), and water and air carriers (fishyback), to improve customer service and achieve cost advantages. Different combinations provide advantages to firms, depending on the scenario. Managers seek to maximize efficiency across available options, to save both cost and time.

### 15-6c

## CLOSING EXAMPLE

As the USPS already uses a sophisticated combination of intermodal transportation, Susan Brownell has a number of options available to optimize the supply chain. She may decide, for example, that motor carriers should be relied upon to transport the bulk of domestic first-class mail until fuel prices increase to a certain level, at which point an automated system would begin to route more mail via rail to save money. Packages above a certain price point, or with a certain value, might always be shipped by air, increasing security and satisfying customer demand for fast delivery. As the USPS continues to cut costs to improve finances,[12] the modes of transportation it decides to utilize will become more important than ever before.

# 15-7 ACCOMPLISHING THE PRIORITIES OF A SUPPLY CHAIN

Miniboss has a strategic plan in place for growth, and has prepped its supply chain for expansion of the TopToddler line of clothing products. It had already identified a number of fabric suppliers that could handle projected sales volumes. Further, the Miniboss manufacturing facility can take on up to five times the current demand. However, there are additional opportunities that Miniboss has identified to make manufacturing, distribution, and transportation more efficient and less expensive. Its top priorities are to always have the right product at the right time for customers, while also cutting logistics costs that have eaten into margins in the past.

**LO 15.7** Given an example of a supply chain, identify methods for accomplishing the priorities of that supply chain.

## 15-7a
### LEARNING IT: ACCOMPLISHING THE PRIORITIES OF A SUPPLY CHAIN

Firms that tightly manage their supply chain can lower costs and improve customer satisfaction. Through in-house research, Miniboss identified three items in its Top-Toddler line that account for nearly 70% of total purchases across the country. Based on this information, Miniboss plans to anticipate demand and manufacture these items *before* they are ordered, ship them via truck to warehouses operated by intermediaries around the country, and let those intermediaries fulfill orders locally.

A number of benefits are provided to Miniboss and its customers through this updated supply chain. First, Miniboss's supply chain will be more predictable, limiting the chances of being out of stock and missing out on customer orders. At the same time, shipping costs will be reduced, as it uses motor carriers instead of more expensive air freight, saving Miniboss money. This savings will allow it to pay intermediaries to warehouse, store, and fulfill orders for its products. Because of the long-term contracts Miniboss negotiated with these intermediaries, its warehousing and storage costs will actually be lower than when they were storing inventory at the manufacturing facility. And further, as delivery times for the final product are reduced from seven days to two, Miniboss's reputation among its customers will become that much stronger.

Even better news for Miniboss is that TopToddler is only one of its product lines. With an improved understanding of and experience with its supply chain, Miniboss will continue to be a "boss" in custom manufacturing for years to come.

# 15-8 LEARN IT TODAY . . . USE IT TOMORROW

As Miniboss continues to expand, it must maintain efficient and conflict free distribution channels and supply chains. Help Miniboss develop and implement its distribution and supply chain strategy.

It's time to get hands-on and apply what you've learned. **See MindTap for an activity related to Miniboss's marketing activities.**

## Chapter Summary

**LO 15.1  Describe the four types of distribution channels.**

Distribution channels bring buyers and sellers together to complete transactions. There are four types: direct, channels using marketing intermediaries, dual distribution, and reverse channels.

**LO 15.2  Describe the three functions of marketing intermediaries.**

Partnering with the right intermediaries can often result in more sales volume and profit for the producer. Intermediaries facilitate the exchange process, lower the cost of logistics, and increase sales and marketing infrastructure.

**LO 15.3  Outline the five factors that influence selection of distribution channels.**

A variety of factors affect the selection of a distribution channel. These include market, product, organizational, competitive, and intensity factors.

**LO 15.4  List the key priorities for each function of the manufacturing supply chain.**

The supply chain, also known as the *value chain*, is the complete sequence of suppliers and activities that contribute to the creation and delivery of goods and services. Managers of each function in the supply chain seek to accomplish priorities specific to that function.

**LO 15.5  Summarize methods for managing the warehousing and storage function of the supply chain.**

A firm's warehousing and storage system includes inventory control, protective packaging and materials handling, and warehousing.

**LO 15.6  Compare the five major modes of transportation.**

Whether moving products around the block or around the world, logistics managers choose from five major modes of transportation: railroads, motor carriers, water carriers, pipelines, and air freight. Each mode has its own unique characteristics.

**LO 15.7  Given an example of a supply chain, identify methods for accomplishing the priorities of that supply chain.**

Accomplishing the distribution priorities of a firm involves careful selection of intermediaries and careful management of each function of the supply chain.

## Key Terms

| | | |
|---|---|---|
| distribution channels **309** | horizontal conflict **316** | radio frequency identification (RFID) **321** |
| direct channel **310** | vertical conflict **316** | |
| direct selling **310** | distribution intensity **317** | enterprise resource planning (ERP) system **321** |
| marketing intermediary **311** | intensive distribution **317** | |
| wholesalers **311** | selective distribution **317** | unitizing **323** |
| sales agent **311** | exclusive distribution **318** | containerization **324** |
| vertical integration **311** | supply chain **320** | intermodal operations **328** |
| dual distribution **312** | upstream management **321** | |
| reverse channels **312** | downstream management **321** | |

# 16 RETAILING AND DIRECT MARKETING

ehrif/Shutterstock.com

## LEARNING OBJECTIVES

**16.1** Describe the retailing sector in the United States in terms of size, major companies, and marketing channels.

**16.2** Describe the six components of retail strategy.

**16.3** Given a component of retail strategy, summarize the key strategic considerations for that component.

**16.4** Outline the four bases for categorizing retailers.

**16.5** Describe the five basic types of direct marketing and nonstore retailing.

**16.6** Given a manufacturer's goals for retailing their products, determine the most effective retail strategy.

# LEARN IT TODAY . . . USE IT TOMORROW

Everyone likes ice cream—or sherbet. But suppose you could have the best of both, in one cup or cone? And what if you could buy your favorite treat at your local market? Jim King, founder and CEO of GaGa, is doing his best to see that your frozen dessert wishes come true. Nearly 10 years ago, King—a former TV news anchor—began experimenting with his grandmother GaGa's recipe for lemon sherbet. He made a few batches and peddled them to retailers in his home state of Rhode Island before visiting Munroe Dairy, a home-delivery dairy farm. The owner ordered 500 pints on the spot—and GaGa was in business.

Once the Munroe Dairy order was filled, the Kings had to decide where and how to sell their product—directly to consumers, via wholesalers, or to retailers. Early on, they tried selling through an ice cream company. "We sold zero," recalls Michelle. Consumers would have to pay about $100 for a six-pint order instead of $4.99 for a pint at the grocery market. The reason was the astronomical cost of shipping—SherBetter had to be shipped overnight in a heavy box with dry ice. The television shopping networks HSN and QVC also invited the Kings to sell their product on television; as a former news anchor, Jim would be a natural on camera. But the Kings declined—again because of the high cost of shipping directly to consumers.

Where do you think the Kings should sell their SherBetter pints? What are their options? Which one will work best?

# 16-1 RETAILING IN THE UNITED STATES

**LO 16.1** Describe the retailing sector in the United States in terms of size, major companies, and marketing channels.

## OPENING EXAMPLE

Specialty retailers, which carry a specific line of merchandise, have recently faced challenges as consumer shopping habits have changed. Tractor Supply Co. (TSC), which sells products to support a rural lifestyle—everything from live chickens to electric fencing accessories—must adjust to those changing customer habits. Imagine that two TSC marketers are deciding how to respond to market changes.

One marketer thinks the company should focus on expanding by way of additional brick-and-mortar locations. She identifies several regions where TSC could build new stores. Although TSC has a website where customers can place orders, only 30% of the company's products are available to purchase online. She doesn't think TSC should invest any additional time or resources into developing the website because the company's target market, owners of small farms, hunters, and equestrians, are unlikely to purchase online. While building physical locations is a costlier investment, the company has enough cash from operations to expand without adding long-term debt.

The second marketer sees that online purchasing has increased not only at TSC, but also at other retailers such as department stores and general merchandise retailers. He reasons that while owners of small farms, hunters, and equestrians are not typical online shoppers, some of them live a significant distance from the closest TSC store. Although he agrees that expanding brick-and-mortar locations is still important to company growth, focusing on TSC's e-commerce will have the biggest impact.

Which marketer do you agree with? What do you think is the right decision for TSC's growth?

## 16-1a

# LEARNING IT: RETAILING IN THE UNITED STATES

Retailers are the marketing intermediaries in direct contact with ultimate consumers. **Retailing** describes the activities involved in selling merchandise to these consumers. Retailers represent the distribution channel to most consumers, because a typical shopper has little contact with manufacturers and virtually no contact with wholesaling intermediaries. Retailers determine locations, store hours, number of sales personnel, store layouts, merchandise selections, and return policies—factors that often influence consumers' images of the offerings more strongly than consumers' images of the products themselves.

**retailing** the activities involved in selling merchandise to consumers

Consumers rely on retailers for everything from shoes and clothes to hardware supplies. In the United States, retail sales in 2016 were $5.5 trillion and the retail industry accounted for 16% of the U.S. GDP.[1] Retail is the largest private-sector employer in the United States, providing 29 million Americans with jobs.[2] The largest retailers in the United States are significant in both revenue and number of stores (see Exhibit 16.1). But while Walmart, Kroger, and Costco continue to build new locations each year, other retailers are forced to close stores due to lagging sales and changing consumer shopping habits. JCPenney, Macy's, The Limited, and RadioShack are just a few of the retailers that have recently announced store closings.

Historically, shoppers have utilized brick-and-mortar locations to browse and compare products and make purchases, but technology is changing the way consumers shop. In the past decade, conventional retailers have recognized the increasing power of the Internet, and have responded by adding e-commerce sites to complement their brick-and-mortar stores. A survey by UPS found that shoppers now make 51% of their purchases online.[3] E-commerce retailers

**EXHIBIT 16.1** Largest Retailers in the United States (Ranked by Annual Sales)

| Rank | Company | 2015 Sales (bill.) | Number of Stores |
|------|---------|--------------------|------------------|
| 1 | Walmart | $353.1 | 5,182 |
| 2 | The Kroger Co. | $103.9 | 3,747 |
| 3 | Costco | $83.5 | 476 |
| 4 | The Home Depot | $79.3 | 1,965 |
| 5 | Walgreens | $76.6 | 8,052 |
| 6 | Target | $73.2 | 1,774 |
| 7 | CVS Health | $72.2 | 9,659 |
| 8 | Amazon.com | $61.6 | n/a |
| 9 | Albertsons | $58.4 | 2,311 |
| 10 | Lowe's | $57.5 | 1,805 |

Source: Data from "Top Retailers 2016," National Retail Federation, accessed April 5, 2017, www.nrf.com.

like Amazon.com dominate online retail sales in comparison to the other top 10 retailers. Even though Walmart is six times larger overall than Amazon, Walmart's online sales are just a small piece of its overall sales, at less than 3% of total revenue.[4] But Walmart's online presence is growing. The company reported 29% growth in U.S. e-commerce sales for the last quarter of 2016 and plans to slow store openings in order to invest in digital growth.[5]

## 16-1b
## CLOSING EXAMPLE

Although it is a long way from being one of the top ten retailers in the United States, Tractor Supply Co. has experienced increasing profits for the last 20 years. In 2016, the specialty retailer earned $437 million in net profit and opened its 1,500th store.[6] Many retailers today fear Amazon because of its vast selection and convenient ordering, but TSC isn't worried. While Amazon does carry some of Tractor Supply's merchandise, TSC feels the knowledge of its store associates combined with the high cost of shipping bulky items will keep customers coming to the brick-and-mortar locations to make purchases.

However, TSC is taking steps to improve its e-commerce shopping experience. Currently, TSC's online sales are less than 1% of its revenue.[7] TSC Chief Information Officer Rob Mills led an effort to improve the company's e-commerce website allowing for a simpler customer experience through easier navigation and increased speed.[8] In addition, TSC added a "buy online, pick up in store" feature to further enhance the customer experience.

It isn't always necessary for a marketer to choose between expanding physical locations or enhancing their online presence. As illustrated by Tractor Supply Co., marketers can focus on both. It is important, however, for companies to understand the shifting dynamics of how—and where—consumers want to make purchases. TSC's decision to enhance its e-commerce site was wise, as an estimated 190 million U.S. consumers shopped online in 2016 and that number is expected to grow each year.[9]

# 16-2

# RETAILING STRATEGY

**LO 16.2** Describe the six components of retail strategy.

## OPENING EXAMPLE

Although Ulta is a 27-year-old brand, CEO Mary Dillon feels like the company is just getting started. In the United States, Ulta is the biggest specialty beauty retailer by sales, and yet many women have never heard of it.[10] The company boasts 20,000 products in over 900 stores, but only has a 4% market share of a $127 billion beauty market.[11] Mary Dillon has plans for Ulta, however, and with experience marketing Gatorade, McDonald's, and U.S. Cellular, she understands retail strategy. What elements do you think make up a company's retail strategy? What can Ulta do to increase its brand awareness?

## 16-2a
# LEARNING IT: RETAILING STRATEGY

A retailer develops a marketing strategy based on the firm's goals and strategic plans. Part of this strategy includes developing a retailing mix to satisfy the chosen market. The retailing mix specifies merchandise strategy, customer service standards, pricing guidelines, promotion goals, location/ distribution decisions, and store atmosphere choices (see Exhibit 16.2). The combination of these elements projects a desired retail image and attracts the company's target market. The components of retailing strategy must work together to create a consistent image that appeals to the store's target market.

## MERCHANDISING STRATEGY

A retailer's merchandising strategy guides decisions regarding the items it will offer. A retailer must decide on general merchandise categories, product lines, specific items within lines, and the depth and width of its assortments. One retailer might sell only one category of merchandise, while others might sell in a variety of categories.

In its effort to sell "all things beauty," Ulta sells well-known brands like Maybelline and Cover Girl as well as high-end cosmetics and professional hair care products. Store associates are knowledgeable about the products Ulta sells and can answer questions and make suggestions to customers. In contrast, Target also carries well-known cosmetic brands, but sells clothing, electronics, groceries, and other items as well.

## CUSTOMER SERVICE STRATEGY

While some stores offer a no-frills shopping experience, others build their retailing strategy around heightened customer services for shoppers. Gift wrapping, alterations, return privileges, bridal registries, consultants, delivery and installation, and online shopping via store websites are all examples of services that add value to the shopping experience. A retailer's customer service strategy must specify which services the firm will offer and whether it will charge customers for these services.

Unlike other beauty retailers, Ulta allows customers to try products before they buy. In-store samples and hair dryers that are plugged in encourage customers to see and feel the products. Ulta stores also boast full-service salons offering haircuts, facials, and manicures. These simple touches allow Ulta to attract and retain target customers while increasing sales and profits. Walgreens, which operates over 8,000 pharmacies, has plans to upgrade its beauty offerings. While it has traditionally been a self-serve

EXHIBIT
16.2

Components of Retail Strategy

shopping experience, about one-quarter of its stores now have beauty-trained associates that provide product demonstrations and consultations. Walgreens' website offers hair-styling tutorials with links to purchase products used to create the styles.

## PRICING STRATEGY

Prices reflect a retailer's marketing objectives and policies. They also play a major role in consumer perceptions of a retailer. Consumers realize, for example, that when they enter an Hermès boutique, they will find expensive merchandise such as leather handbags priced at $3,800 and up, along with men's belts at $720 and up. In contrast, customers of Tuesday Morning or Big Lots expect totally different merchandise and much lower prices.

Ulta accommodates a wide audience by offering both high-end brands and affordably priced products. Nordstrom department stores target a smaller audience by selling mainly high-end makeup brands such as Laura Mercier, Yves Saint Laurent, and Bobbi Brown.

## LOCATION/DISTRIBUTION STRATEGY

Retail experts often cite location as a potential determining factor in the success or failure of a retail business. A retailer may locate at an isolated site, in a central business district, or in a planned shopping center. The location decision depends on many factors, including the type of merchandise, the retailer's financial resources, characteristics of the target market, and site availability.

Within the last few years, Ulta stores made a move from strip malls to locations near urban centers, changing the perception of the store from discount shopping to an "oasis for women."[12] Additionally, Dillon recognized the importance of the company's e-commerce efforts. Ulta built two distribution centers to improve the delivery times for online purchases.[13] In contrast, Avon, a direct-selling beauty company, distributes its products online and through independent representatives.

## PROMOTIONAL STRATEGY

To establish store images that entice more shoppers, retailers use various promotional techniques. Through its promotional strategy, a retailer seeks to communicate information about its stores—locations, merchandise selections, hours of operation, and prices. If merchandise selection changes frequently to follow fashion trends, advertising is typically used to promote current styles effectively. Promotions, such as frequent buyer rewards programs, help retailers attract shoppers and build customer loyalty.

Ulta utilizes advertisements during prime-time television shows as well as direct mail and print advertisements in fashion magazines to promote the store. General merchandiser Walmart features makeup and beauty items in its weekly circular and places advertisements in magazines. Starbucks, on the other hand, does very little paid advertising, instead opting to generate traffic via word of mouth and by strategically locating their stores (which is part of their location/distribution strategy).

## STORE ATMOSPHERICS

While store location, merchandise selection, customer service, pricing, and promotional activities all contribute to a retailer's brand identity, stores also project their personalities through **atmospherics**- physical characteristics and amenities that attract customers and satisfy their shopping needs. Atmospherics include both a store's exterior and interior décor.

**atmospherics** the physical characteristics and amenities that attract customers and satisfy their shopping needs

Ulta has created store interiors that are bright and clean with an open layout and wide aisles. The company believes this allows for a fashionable and calming shopping experience.[14] In sharp contrast, another specialty beauty retailer, Sephora, has stores that feature sleek, black features and loud, thumping music—targeting a younger demographic.

### 16-2b
## CLOSING EXAMPLE

The retail strategy under Mary Dillon's guidance is working. In 2016, Ulta landed on the National Retailer Federation's Hot 100 Retailers list, which recognizes the fastest-growing retailers by sales growth.[15] Ulta ranked 21st on the list with 24% net sales growth over the previous year. Ulta increased online sales by 56% and opened over 100 stores in 2016.[16] Paying attention to store atmospherics, customer service strategy, and other elements of retail strategy can help retailers, like Ulta, provide customers with a unique and appealing shopping experience.

# 16-3 STRATEGIC CONSIDERATIONS FOR RETAIL STRATEGY

### OPENING EXAMPLE

If you've ever been in the market for a new television, laptop, or video game, chances are you've been to a Best Buy store. With more than 1,900 locations, Best Buy is the largest consumer-electronics retailer in the world. The company's future looks promising as it has experienced recent online growth and h. h. gregg's closure means Best Buy could experience market-share gains.[17]

But just a few years ago, Best Buy's outlook was not so positive. After several years of declining sales and profits, financial experts weren't convinced there was anything the retailer could do to turn its performance around. Competitor Circuit City had closed and the threat of Amazon loomed. So, what considerations did Best Buy make to its retail strategy to turn its performance around?

**LO 16.3** Given a component of retail strategy, summarize the key strategic considerations for that component.

## 16-3a

# LEARNING IT: STRATEGIC CONSIDERATIONS FOR RETAIL STRATEGY

A retailer starts to define its strategy by selecting a target market. Factors that influence the retailer's selection are the size and profit potential of the market and the level of competition for its business. Retailers pore over demographic, geographic, and psychographic profiles to segment markets. In the end, most retailers identify their target markets in terms of certain demographics.

Best Buy has identified a number of target markets which likely include small business owners, affluent professionals, adopters of new technology, and sub-urban families. Once a retailer has identified its target market, it must develop a retailing mix to satisfy the chosen market. You have already been introduced to the components of retail strategy; let's now focus on the strategic considerations for each component.

## MERCHANDISING STRATEGY

To develop a successful merchandise mix, a retailer must weigh several priorities. First, it must consider the preferences and needs of its previously defined target market, keeping in mind that the competitive environment influences these choices. Would the target market rather buy products from a retailer that specializes in one category or are they looking for a one-stop shop where they can buy just about anything? The retailer must also consider the overall profitability of each product line and product category, as managing multiple categories requires working with more vendors, monitoring more competitors, and coordinating logistics for more items.

Best Buy offers a complete range of electronic product categories and multiple brands within each category. Several popular brands have a

The Samsung Experience Shop within Best Buy stores sells selected merchandise in an intimate setting, providing a welcoming environment that attracts shoppers to their "store within a store."

Neilson Barnard/Getty Images

store-within-a-store inside Best Buy locations. Samsung, Sony, Microsoft, Magnolia, and Pacific Home Kitchen each have large product displays and, in some cases, separate checkout areas. Associates in these areas are employed by the manufacturer, reducing Best Buy's labor expenses.[18] By offering a complete range of electronic products, Best Buy becomes a trusted source for consumers' electronic needs. And employing the store-within-a-store format with knowledgeable associates from the manufacturer provides another layer of product expertise. Walmart, on the other hand, sells various types of electronics alongside groceries, sporting goods, and hardware items, making it a one-stop shop for consumers.

## CUSTOMER SERVICE STRATEGY

Choosing which services to offer and how much to charge customers for these services depends on several conditions: store size, type, and location; merchandise assortment; services offered by competitors; customer expectations; and financial resources.

The basic objective of all customer services focuses on attracting and retaining target customers, thus increasing sales and profits. Some services enhance shopper comfort while other services are intended to attract customers by making shopping easier and faster than it would be without the services. However, offering higher levels of customer service comes with a cost that might not be compatible with a retail strategy focused on a no frills, low-price shopping experience.

Electronics are made up of many complex components, most of which the average consumer is unfamiliar with. With services like Geek Squad at Best Buy, customers can utilize home installation, set up, support, and repair for thousands of products. Of course, customers must pay for these services. If Best Buy were to offer these services for free, the retailer would likely have to increase prices on the items it sells.

## PRICING STRATEGY

Retailers determine a pricing strategy based on several key factors: type of product, company objectives, competitor pricing, and customer perceptions. The amount a retailer adds to a product's cost to set the final selling price is the markup. The amount of the markup typically results from two marketing decisions:

1. *Services performed by the retailer*: Other things being equal, stores that offer more services charge larger markups to cover their costs.

2. *Inventory turnover rate*: Other things being equal, stores with a higher turnover rate can cover their costs and earn a profit while charging a smaller markup.

A retailer's pricing strategy exerts an important influence on its image among present and potential customers. In addition, the markup affects the retailer's ability to attract shoppers. An excessive markup may drive away customers; an inadequate markup may not generate sufficient revenue to cover costs and return a profit.

Best Buy found that many consumers would visit Best Buy brick-and-mortar locations to examine and compare products and then purchase the product online for a lower price through another retailer. This is a process known as **showrooming**. While Best Buy's prices are comparable to its competitors', the company introduced price matching to reduce lost sales through showrooming. The company's Price Match Guarantee includes price matching products sold by Amazon and other online retailers. Best Buy's current pricing strategy makes its products accessible to a wide range of consumers. If Best Buy were to increase prices and eliminate its price matching promise, it might alienate a portion of its target market.

**showrooming** when a customer examines and compares products at a store, then buys the product through an online retailer

## LOCATION/DISTRIBUTION STRATEGY

Location and number of stores is an important consideration for every retailer. Companies must consider the cost to rent or build a location, convenience for customers, proximity to competitors, and the type of products sold. Best Buy locations are almost all exclusively located in **planned shopping centers**. A planned shopping center is a group of retail stores designed, coordinated, and marketed to shoppers in a geographic trade area. A community shopping center is often positioned next to other big box retailers and specialty stores, and offers convenience for customers.

**planned shopping centers** a group of retail stores designed, coordinated, and marketed to shoppers in a geographic trade area

In 2012, Best Buy opted to close about 50 of its large stores and opened smaller format Best Buy Mobile stores.[19] These smaller locations carry cell phones and are located inside shopping malls. Although Best Buy's larger stores are profitable, operating smaller format stores allowed the retailer to reduce costs.

Distribution impacts how efficiently a retailer gets its products to customers. In order to better compete with Amazon, Best Buy offers same day in-store pickup on many items purchased online. If an item is not available for same day pickup, customers may opt to have the item shipped to their local Best Buy store for free. These options are convenient and easy for customers. A customer looking for a specific product no longer has to call or drive to several locations to find it. Instead, they just order the product online and choose a location to pick up their purchase.

## PROMOTIONAL STRATEGY

National retail chains often purchase advertising space in newspapers, on radio, and on television. Other retailers promote their goods over the Internet or use wireless technology to send marketing messages to customers' cell phones. Consumers are increasingly using their smartphones and tablet devices to surf the web. Decisions about the amount and type of promotion are influenced by the target market and other components of the retailer's strategy. For example, a retailer with many strategically placed locations might be able to limit advertising and still generate the traffic needed for growth and profitability. As mentioned earlier, Starbucks is an example. A discounter like Dollar General, which sells at lower prices and operates on tighter margins, might concentrate on weekly newspaper circulars rather than expensive television advertising.

Best Buy employs many different promotional techniques including weekly circulars, commercials, banner ads on websites, and in store promotions. Although advertising can be expensive, Best Buy is willing to spend millions to help grow its business and gain market share. Promotions also help Best Buy remain at the top of consumers' minds when they are in need of a new camera, printer, or cell phone.

## STORE ATMOSPHERICS

A store's exterior appearance, including architectural design, window displays, signs, and entryways, helps identify the retailer and attract its target market shoppers. The interior décor of a store should also complement the retailer's image, respond to customers' interests, and, most importantly, induce shoppers to buy. Interior atmospheric elements include store layout, merchandise presentation, lighting, color, sounds, scents, and cleanliness. Some retailers invest minimal time and energy considering store atmospherics, instead focusing on merchandise variety, efficiency, and low prices.

However, when designing the interior and exterior of a store, marketers must remember that many people shop for reasons other than just purchasing needed products. Other common reasons for shopping include escaping the routine of daily life, avoiding weather extremes, fulfilling fantasies, and socializing with family and friends. As a result, many retailers spend more time and money designing store environments that will emotionally appeal to their target audience. Retailers must evaluate how important this additional investment of resources is to their overall success and competitiveness.

Products at Best Buy are displayed to encourage trial by customers. Televisions are tuned to the same stations so customers can compare size, color, and definition. Laptops are turned on so shoppers can explore their features. Video game consoles are available for consumers to try out the latest game. In addition, products are grouped together with clear signage to help customers easily navigate the large stores.

### 16-3b

## CLOSING EXAMPLE

In late 2012, Best Buy CEO Hubert Joly initiated a "Renew Blue" campaign to revive the retailer. Key points of this movement were to "reinvigorate and rejuvenate the customer experience" and "work with vendor partners to innovate and drive value."[20] This included enhancing in-stock performance for physical locations, implementing price matching, enhancing in-store pickup, creating store-within-a-store formats, and training employees.[21] The retailer also enhanced some of its physical locations and closed large stores opting for small-store formats. These changes to Best Buy's retail strategy have helped to turn around the company's bleak outlook. Recently, the electronics retailer reported net earnings of $198 million in the third quarter of 2016—beating Wall Street expectations of $150 million.[22]

# 16-4   CATEGORIZING RETAILERS

**LO 16.4**   Outline the four bases for categorizing retailers.

## OPENING EXAMPLE

Retailers that sell similar items may approach retail strategies in entirely different ways. The number of product lines sold, services provided to customers, and how products are sold can differ greatly between competing retailers.

Stitch Fix is a clothing retailer that sells its "fixes" through its website and mobile app. Customers receive five clothing and accessory items through the mail about a week after scheduling their fix. Customers try on the items at home, keep what they like, and mail back the rest in a prepaid envelope. Prior to ordering, customers fill out a style questionnaire online and a personal stylist—with the help of some computer algorithms—picks out tops, dresses, accessories, or shoes to mail to the customer. Stitch Fix recently expanded its fixes to include men and plus-size women.

Nordstrom is a department store that sells clothing, shoes, and accessories as well as home goods and beauty items in 122 stores across the United States and Canada. Customers can purchase women's, men's, plus-size, and maternity items in stores or online and through its mobile app. Nordstrom also has personal stylists, alterations and tailoring, and a store credit card.

Although both retailers sell similar items, they have unique approaches to reaching customers. As a result, each of these retailers are categorized differently.

## 16-4a
## LEARNING IT: CATEGORIZING RETAILERS

Because new types of retailers continue to evolve in response to changes in consumer demand, a universal classification system for retailers has yet to be devised. Certain differences do, however, define several categories of retailers: forms of ownership, shopping effort expended by customers, services provided to customers, and product lines carried. These categories are not mutually exclusive, meaning you could categorize all retailers in a city by form of ownership or categorize them by product lines carried–or another method. It's the same group of retailers, they are just being categorized using different methods.

### CLASSIFICATION BY FORM OF OWNERSHIP

Perhaps the easiest method for categorizing retailers is by ownership structure, distinguishing between chain stores and independent retailers. Chain stores are groups of retail outlets that operate under central ownership and management, while an independent retailer is someone who is responsible for their own business. Chain stores can utilize economies of scale by purchasing large volumes of products for a lower price than independent retailers pay. Because a chain may have hundreds of retail stores, it can afford extensive advertising, sales training, and computerized systems for merchandise ordering, inventory management, forecasting, and accounting. Target, Sephora, and Safeway are all chain stores.

## CLASSIFICATION BY SHOPPING EFFORT

Another classification system is based on the reasons consumers shop at particular retail outlets. This approach categorizes stores as convenience, shopping, or specialty retailers.

**Convenience retailers** focus their marketing appeals on accessible locations, extended store hours, rapid checkout service, and adequate parking facilities. Local food stores, gasoline stations, and dry cleaners fit this category. Pennsylvania-based Wawa convenience stores offer customers various items, including gasoline and private-label breakfast treats, ready-to-eat salads, and seasonal fresh fruit.

Shopping stores typically include furniture stores such as Ethan Allen, appliance retailers, clothing outlets, and sporting goods stores. Consumers usually compare prices, assortments, and quality levels at competing outlets before making purchase decisions. Consequently, managers of shopping stores attempt to differentiate their outlets through advertising, in-store displays, well-trained and knowledgeable salespeople, and appropriate merchandise assortments.

**Specialty retailers** combine carefully defined product lines, services, and reputations in attempts to persuade consumers to expend considerable effort to shop at their stores. Examples include Macy's, Sephora, and Footlocker.

**convenience retailers** stores that appeal to customers by having accessible locations, extended store hours, rapid checkout service, and adequate parking

**specialty retailers** stores that combine carefully defined product lines, services, and reputations in attempts to persuade consumers to expend considerable effort to shop at their stores

## CLASSIFICATION BY SERVICES PROVIDED

Another category differentiates retailers by the services they provide to customers. This classification system is essentially a continuum between self-service and full-service retailers. The middle of that continuum is often called self-selection.

A gas station is a self-service retailer because you can fill your car and pay without any assistance. On the other hand, LensCrafters is a full-service eyeglass retailer. Associates help customers choose frames and coordinate lens orders with the in-store lab.

Most retailers fall somewhere in between, so they are considered self-selection. At Albertsons and Kroger grocery stores, you can usually purchase what you need with little assistance, but help is there if you need it. At Best Buy, you can choose to consult with a store associate, but you can also select products on your own. However, you will still need assistance for checkout.

## CLASSIFICATION BY PRODUCT LINES

Grouping retailers by product lines produces three major categories: specialty stores, general-merchandise retailers, and food retailers.

A specialty store typically focuses on a single product category. However, it stocks this category in considerable depth or variety. Specialty stores include a wide range of retail outlets, including fish markets, health food stores, shoe stores, and bakeries. Although some specialty stores are chain outlets, many are independent, small-scale operations. They represent perhaps the greatest concentration of independent retailers who develop expertise in one product area and provide narrow lines of products for their local markets.

Specialty stores should not be confused with specialty products. Specialty stores often carry convenience and shopping goods. The label specialty reflects the practice of handling a specific, narrow category of merchandise, whether it be low-priced goods or luxury items. For example, Office Depot is a specialty store that offers a wide selection of office-related needs such as copy paper, printer ink, writing utensils, and office furniture. Gloria Jean's Coffees sells whole-bean coffees, beverages, and gifts.[23] IKEA sells an extensive variety of home furnishings and housewares.

**General merchandise retailers** carry a wide variety of product lines stocked in some depth, distinguish themselves from specialty retailers by the large number of product lines they carry. Target and Walmart are examples of general merchandise retailers. This category also includes variety stores, department stores, and mass merchandisers, such as discount houses, and off-price retailers.

Food retailers and **supermarkets** are a unique category of retailer that represents a mix between specialty and general merchandise. While they mainly sell a wide variety of items in the grocery category, many food retailers also sell merchandise in other categories, such as floral, office supplies, and medicine. This category is differentiated by size, variety, assortment, service levels, and other characteristics. Whole Foods is a higher-end food retailer selling a variety of natural and organic items, while Fred Meyer is a supermarket focused on groceries, but also selling electronics, and even hardware. Conventional supermarkets, limited assortment supermarkets, and warehouse clubs, like Costco, are included in this category.

## 16-4b

## CLOSING EXAMPLE

In considering the bases for categorizing retailers, Stitch Fix and Nordstrom share some similarities and differences. Stitch Fix is an independently owned retailer while Nordstrom is considered a chain store. When categorizing retailers based on shopping effort, we would see that both retailers are considered specialty stores.

Each of the retailers offer some services. Stitch Fix offers personal styling services as part of each customer order, so it would be considered a full-service retailer. Nordstrom customers may select items on their own or through a personal stylist, categorizing the retailer as both self-selection and full-service.

In classifying by product lines, Stitch Fix is considered a specialty store. It focuses on a particular product category, but at considerable depth. Nordstrom, however, carries more than just clothing, shoes, and accessories. The retailer also sells home goods, such as towels, bedding, dinnerware, and bakeware. It is considered a **department store**, which is a series of specialty stores under one roof.

---

**general merchandise retailers** stores that carry a wide variety of product lines stocked in some depth and distinguish themselves from specialty retailers by the large number of product lines they carry

**supermarkets** stores that sell mainly groceries, but also a wide selection of items in other categories

**department store** a series of specialty stores under one roof

# 16-5 DIRECT MARKETING AND NONSTORE RETAILING

## OPENING EXAMPLE

"Alright, Griffin, let's get started on the project for our Entrepreneurship class. Professor Hall suggested thinking about either a product we need that isn't currently offered or a current product we could market and sell in a new and innovative way."

"Yeah, I've been thinking about this. I had to go to the store yesterday to buy razors. Why are they so expensive? $12 for a razor and $33 for replacement blades! Maybe we could think of a new way to sell razors."

"Really? This seems kind of silly. Are you going to sell them out of a vending machine?"

"No, Alex. I'm thinking we could do some sort of mail order club and sell the razors for $1. We could call it Dollar Shave Club."

If you overheard this conversation, would you think this is a good idea? The vast majority of all shaving razors are sold in grocery and drug stores, along with many other items that shoppers buy at the same time. Is it realistic to create a specialty business that sells only razors—and only online?

### 16-5a

## LEARNING IT: DIRECT MARKETING AND NONSTORE RETAILING

Although the majority of retail transactions still occur in physical stores, direct marketing and nonstore retailing are an important component of the distribution and promotion strategies of many companies. **Direct marketing** and nonstore retail are broad concepts that include direct mail, direct selling, online retailing, direct-response retailing, and automatic merchandising. Some companies use these tactics as their sole method for distributing and promoting products, while others use them to complement their physical stores and traditional promotional methods. Direct and interactive marketing expenditures are responsible for hundreds of billions of dollars in yearly purchases.

### DIRECT MAIL

Direct mail is a form of direct marketing that comes in many forms: sales letters, postcards, brochures, booklets, catalogs, and DVDs. Both not-for-profit and profit-seeking organizations make extensive use of this distribution channel.

Direct mail offers several advantages, such as the ability to select a narrow target market, achieve intensive coverage, send messages quickly, choose from various formats, provide complete information, and personalize each mailing piece. Response rates are measurable and higher than other types of advertising. In addition, direct mailings stand alone and do not compete for attention with magazine articles and television programs. On the other hand, the per-reader

---

**LO 16.5** Describe the five basic types of direct marketing and nonstore retailing.

**direct marketing** a broad concept that includes direct mail, direct selling, online retailing, direct-response retailing, and automatic merchandising

cost of direct mail is high, effectiveness depends on the quality of the mailing list, and some consumers object to direct mail, considering it "junk mail."

Marketers are making a shift from direct mail to digital advertisements. In 2015, direct mail volume fell with marketers spending $47 billion. Overall digital ad spending jumped 19% to $59 billion and, in 2016, passed television ad spending with over $75 billion.[24]

## DIRECT SELLING

Through direct selling, manufacturers completely bypass retailers and wholesalers. Instead, they set up their own channels to sell their products directly to consumers. Avon, Pampered Chef, LuLaRoe, and Tupperware are all direct sellers.

## ONLINE RETAILING

As discussed in Chapter 4, online retailers sell directly to customers via e-commerce stores. Amazon is the largest online retailer, selling everything from books to electronics to fresh groceries. While this type of nonstore retailing is only about two decades old, even the largest physical retailers, like Walmart, are aggressively investing in their online retailing operation in order to compete.

## DIRECT-RESPONSE RETAILING

Direct-response retailing is often a hybrid of physical retail, online retail, and direct mail promotion. Customers of a direct-response retailer can order merchandise by mail or telephone, by visiting a mail-order desk in a retail store, or online. The retailer then ships the merchandise to the customer's home or to a local retail store for pickup.

Many direct-response retailers rely on direct mail, such as catalogs, to create telephone and mail-order sales and to promote online purchases of products featured in the catalogs. Some firms, such as Lillian Vernon, make almost all their sales through catalog orders. Mail-order sales have grown at about twice the rate of retail store sales in recent years.

Direct-response retailers are increasingly interacting with customers online. With no retail locations, L.L. Bean was historically a direct mail company that relied entirely on their mailed catalogs to generate phone and mail-in sales. Now the catalog is more likely to drive sales at their e-commerce site.

## AUTOMATIC MERCHANDISING

Today, nearly 26,000 vending machine operators sell about $7 billion in convenience goods annually in the United States alone.[25] Although U.S. vending machines primarily sell items such as snacks, soft drinks, or lottery tickets, Japanese consumers use automatic merchandising for everything, including fresh sushi and new underwear. Recently, U.S. marketers have begun to realize the potential of this underused marketing tool. Several vending-machine companies, such as the California-based Fresh Healthy Vending and HUMAN

Healthy Vending, with offices on both coasts, work with schools to replace traditional vending-machine offerings with fresh, healthy snacks.[26]

## 16-5b
## CLOSING EXAMPLE

Although Dollar Shave Club didn't actually start from an entrepreneurship class project, Founder and CEO Michael Durbin did want to solve a problem that many men deal with—purchasing razors in a store can be expensive.[27] Additionally, driving to the store and finding the store associate with the key to unlock the razors provided an extra layer of inconvenience. Durbin knew that if he could mail customers a razor and replacement blades on a monthly basis—and do so inexpensively—he could have a great product. Durbin's use of nonstore retailing and direct marketing allowed greater control over the product and company. His strategy worked—in its third year, Dollar Shave Club brought in $65 million in revenue and in 2016, Durbin sold Dollar Shave Club to Unilever for a cool $1 billion.[28]

# 16-6 DETERMINING AN EFFECTIVE RETAIL STRATEGY FOR MANUFACTURERS

### OPENING EXAMPLE

Implementing the retail strategy for GaGa SherBetter has not always been easy. Grocery stores seem like an obvious choice for the SherBetter product, but the Kings can't afford the huge slotting allowances charged by larger supermarkets. A slotting fee in the frozen section of a large supermarket chain could run as much as $35,000 to $40,000 just to place one product on the shelf at 600 to 800 stores.

Jim also researched the possibility of becoming a retailer himself—opening a scoop shop. But he quickly realized that the business model just wouldn't work for his company. Jim determined that the projected expense of purchasing and maintaining a building and property was too high for GaGa. In addition, ice cream shops generally offer a wide variety of products, including ice cream, sherbet, frozen yogurt, smoothies, shakes, and more. GaGa only had SherBetter to offer—albeit in a growing array of flavors.

There are many elements that influence a manufacturer's retail strategy. What elements should Jim consider when determining the best strategy for SherBetter?

**LO 16.6** Given a manufacturer's goals for retailing their products, determine the most effective retail strategy.

## 16-6a
## LEARNING IT: DETERMINING AN EFFECTIVE RETAIL STRATEGY FOR MANUFACTURERS

When considering their retail strategy, manufacturers must consider their goals for retailing their products. In turn, they will look for retailers most compatible with those goals. As always, the basis for selecting retail partners is whether they reach and serve the company's target market in a way that is consistent with the company's objectives and brand. A company like GaGa would want to ask questions such as the following:

- What types of retailers would attract our target audience?
- What types of retailers already—or would be willing to—carry a product like ours?
- Should our product be sold in a retailer that specializes in our category or in a general merchandise retailer?
- What types of retailers would help us accomplish our distribution intensity goals?
- What types of retailers offer pricing objectives that are a good fit for our brand?
- What types of retailers would offer the customer service and store atmospherics we hope to associate with our brand?

Since GaGa produces frozen dessert products, this limits the retail locations where GaGa can sell its product. A store that doesn't have any frozen products would probably not be a good fit, but a retailer with a large frozen food section might be. In addition, GaGa needs to consider where customers would expect to buy a pint of SherBetter. While a butcher shop most likely has freezers, it's likely not a good retail partner for GaGa since most customers do not visit a butcher looking for frozen desserts.

The Kings identify SherBetter as a super-premium dessert product. As a result, a prestige price will help to maintain this image among customers. This also impacts the retail locations where the SherBetter product should be sold, because a price discounter would not be a good fit for a brand like this.

GaGa will also need to consider how to best promote the SherBetter product given their goals. If GaGa were to select children as part of their target market, then they would want to select retail partners who advertise in parenting magazines and run commercials during children's cartoons. Partnering with a wine store would likely not be a good fit given these goals.

All of these elements must be considered to find retail partners who represent the best fit with the goals of GaGa's marketing mix.

# 16-7  LEARN IT TODAY . . . USE IT TOMORROW

Let's learn more about GaGa and see how they navigated decisions about selecting retail distribution for SherBetter.

It's time to get hands-on and apply what you've learned. **See MindTap for an activity related to GaGa's marketing activities.**

# Chapter Summary

**LO 16.1** Describe the retailing sector in the United States in terms of size, major companies, and marketing channels.

Retail is the largest private-sector employer in the United States. In 2016, retail sales were $5.5 trillion. Major retailers include Walmart, Kroger, Costco, The Home Depot, and others. Consumers purchase retail products through brick-and-mortar locations as well as through the Internet and mobile applications.

**LO 16.2** Describe the six components of retail strategy.

The six components of retail strategy include: merchandise strategy, customer service standards, pricing guidelines, promotion goals, location/distribution decisions, and store atmosphere choices.

**LO 16.3** Given a component of retail strategy, summarize the key strategic considerations for that component.

Every component of retail strategy presents a unique set of strategic considerations. Retailers must consider their target market, the products they will sell, what services to offer customers, an appropriate pricing strategy, and more.

**LO 16.4** Outline the four bases for categorizing retailers.

The four bases for categorizing retailers are: forms of ownership, shopping effort expended by customers, services provided to customers, and product lines carried.

**LO 16.5** Describe the five basic types of direct marketing and nonstore retailing.

The five basic types of direct marketing and nonstore retailing include: direct mail, direct selling, online retailing, direct-response retailing, and automatic merchandising.

**LO 16.6** Given a manufacturer's goals for retailing their products, determine the most effective retail strategy.

When selecting retail partners for distribution of their products, manufacturers should select partners with a retail strategy that's compatible with the manufacturer's brand and marketing objectives.

# Key Terms

retailing **333**
atmospherics **337**
showrooming **340**
planned shopping centers **340**

convenience retailers **343**
specialty retailers **343**
general merchandise
  retailers **344**

supermarkets **344**
department store **344**
direct marketing **345**

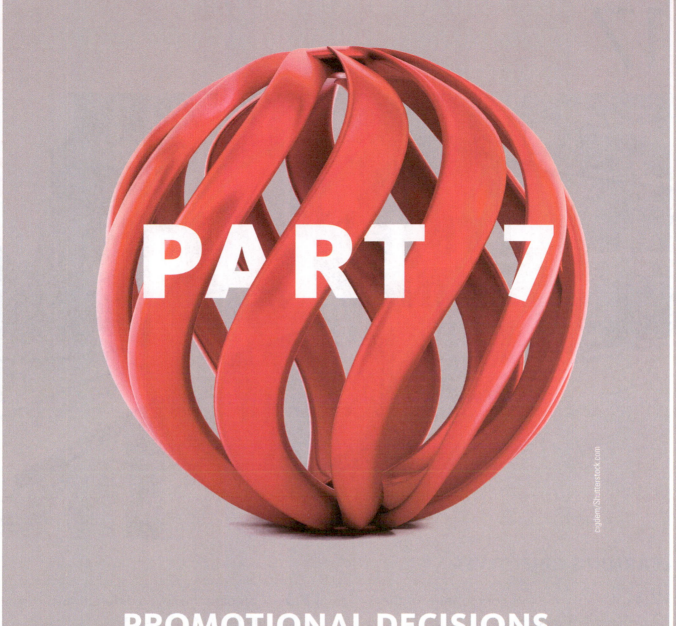

# PART 7

## PROMOTIONAL DECISIONS

crgidem/Shutterstock.com

# 17 INTEGRATED MARKETING COMMUNICATIONS, ADVERTISING, AND PUBLIC RELATIONS

Luckies/Shutterstock.com

## LEARNING OBJECTIVES

**17.1** Identify the five components of the promotional mix.

**17.2** Explain how the communications process relates to the AIDA concept.

**17.3** Describe the various objectives of promotion.

**17.4** Describe the types of appeals used by advertisers.

**17.5** Compare the seven different advertising media.

**17.6** Describe the roles of public relations, publicity, and cross-promotion in an organization's promotional strategy.

**17.7** Critique a promotional mix based on the five factors that influence the effectiveness of a promotional mix.

# LEARN IT TODAY . . . USE IT TOMORROW

If you live in southern New England—and are a pizza lover—you'd probably assume that everyone knows about Pepe's Pizzeria. But Ken Berry, CEO of Pepe's, understands the importance of spreading the word about his company's pizza.

Pepe's has built a loyal following through the years, and this word-of-mouth advertising is impossible to buy or replicate. Pepe's value proposition is pretty straightforward. The pizza sells itself—one bite, and pizza lovers are hooked. So, the main objective is to make consumers aware of the restaurant, which now has several locations in the tri-state area surrounding New York City. As the new Fairfield location neared its opening date, Pepe's alerted current customers with a simple message printed on top of each pizza box (coincidentally, many of Pepe's regular New Haven diners actually lived in Fairfield). The company also published press releases and advertised the grand opening of the new restaurant.

Billboards along the interstate highway proved to be effective with travelers, as did some direct-mail efforts. Pepe's also focused on social media, which Berry refers to as "the new word of mouth."

Pepe's also enjoys positive public relations surrounding its charitable giving. The company website has a tab allowing customers to request donations for its particular charities, and the restaurant conducts regular "Good Neighbors Nights," from which it donates 15% of its proceeds to a designated not-for-profit group. All of these efforts roll together into cohesive marketing communications with one major goal. "Our challenge is to build our brand and protect it," says Berry, "and to make sure we deliver every day."

The success of Pepe's promotional efforts shows how using advertising, sales promotion, and public relations together can make each tool more powerful than if used alone.

# 17-1 INTEGRATED MARKETING COMMUNICATIONS

## OPENING EXAMPLE

As director of advertising for a cereal company, you're excited to report to the CEO about a great new deal you've struck: For the same money you've been spending on TV commercials, boxes of your cereal will be prominently displayed in the kitchen set of a popular new Netflix comedy. But the boss isn't impressed. "I don't understand," he says. "That sounds like a lot of money for an untried advertising substitute." How do you respond?

**LO 17.1** Identify the five components of the promotional mix.

### 17-1a

## LEARNING IT: INTEGRATED MARKETING COMMUNICATIONS

Stop and think for a moment about all the marketing messages you receive in a day. While watching TV, when streaming music, while driving in a car, and when surfing online. Knowing that all of these promotional communications—and

**integrated marketing communications (IMC)** the coordination of all promotional activities to produce a unified, customer-focused promotional message

**promotional mix** advertising, personal selling, sales promotion, direct marketing, and public relations

many more—compete for your attention, marketers use **integrated marketing communications (IMC)** to reach you in a coordinated, consistent manner that will make their messages stand out from the rest.

Instead of viewing each part of the **promotional mix** as isolated components, an IMC strategy looks at these elements together. With an IMC strategy, marketers can create a unified personality for the product or brand because all of their various marketing communications align with one another. For example, in order to reach the young male consumers who are its prime recruits, the U.S. Navy sponsored the Winter X Games, a favorite of men 13–17 years of age. As part of that campaign, the Navy communicated a consistent and unified message across ESPN's TV, digital, print, and radio platforms.[1]

## 17-1b
# ELEMENTS OF THE PROMOTIONAL MIX

Like the marketing mix, with its product, pricing, distribution, and promotion elements, the promotional mix is a blend of variables carefully designed to satisfy the needs of a company's customers and achieve organizational objectives. The major components of the promotional mix are advertising, personal selling, sales promotion, direct marketing, and public relations—with new variants like buzz and viral marketing developing all the time (see Exhibit 17.1).

## ADVERTISING

**advertising** paid, nonpersonal communication through various mass media channels

**Advertising** is paid, nonpersonal communication through various mass media, such as television, radio, magazines, or online. It is a major promotional mix component for thousands of organizations—total ad spending in the United States is estimated at more than $200 billion;[2] digital ad spending alone is estimated at more than $72 billion.[3] Mass consumption and geographically dispersed markets make advertising particularly appropriate for marketing goods and services aimed at large audiences likely to respond to the same promotional messages.

**EXHIBIT 17.1**

**Integrated Marketing Communications (IMC)**

Personal selling

Sales promotion

IMC—a unified, customer-focused promotional message

Advertising

Public relations

Direct marketing

Advertising campaigns are increasingly augmented by two related practices: product placement and sponsorship. In product placement, marketers pay a fee to display a product prominently in a film or TV show. Today, hundreds of products appear in movies and on television shows, and the fees charged for these placements have soared. Recently, product placement even became the reason for making a movie—as in the case of *The LEGO Movie*.[4]

In sponsorship, an organization supports an event or activity with money or in-kind resources in exchange for a direct association with that event or activity. The sponsor purchases access to the activity's audience and the image associated with the activity. Today's sponsorships are most prevalent in sports—LPGA events, NASCAR, the World Cup, the Super Bowl, NCAA basketball, and more. Companies may also sponsor reading and child-care programs, concerts, art exhibits, and humanitarian programs.

In the case of naming rights of venues like sports arenas, the name serves as a perpetual advertisement. For example, Dallas Cowboys fans stream into AT&T Stadium. In some cities, sponsors are now getting access to public facilities; Los Angeles County offers naming rights to its rail, bus, and transit stations,[5] while New Orleans courts sponsors for its city parks.[6]

## PERSONAL SELLING

**Personal selling** is a seller's promotional presentation conducted person-to-person with the buyer. It may take place face-to-face, over the telephone, or by online video. It may involve one salesperson and one buyer, or a team of salespeople pitching a group of buyers.

Personal selling is the oldest form of promotion, dating back to the beginnings of commerce. It remains critical today: More than 14 million people in the United States have careers in sales and related occupations.[7] They may sell real estate, insurance, and financial investments or tractors, automobiles, and vacuum cleaners; they may work in retail or wholesaling; they may be regional managers or in the field. In other words, the range of selling jobs, as well as the products they represent, is huge.[8]

> **personal selling** a seller's promotional presentation conducted person-to-person with a buyer

## SALES PROMOTION

**Sales promotion** consists of marketing activities that provide a short-term incentive, usually in combination with other forms of promotion, to supplement or otherwise support the objectives of the promotional program. This broad category includes displays, trade shows, coupons, contests, samples, premiums, and product demonstrations. Restaurants, including those serving fast food, often place certain items on the menu at a lower price "for a limited time only." Advertisements may contain coupons for free or discounted items for a specified period of time. Or companies may conduct sweepstakes for prizes, such as new cars or vacations, which may even be completely unrelated to the products the companies are selling.

> **sales promotion** marketing activities that provide a short-term incentive to make a purchase

## DIRECT MARKETING

Another element in a firm's integrated promotional mix is **direct marketing**, the use of direct communication to generate a response in the form of an order, a request for further information (lead generation), or a visit to a place

> **direct marketing** the use of direct communications to generate a response in the form of an order, a request for further communication, or a visit to a place of business

of business to purchase specific goods or services (traffic generation). While many people equate direct marketing with direct mail, this important promotional category also includes direct-response advertising and infomercials on television, direct-response print advertising, and direct-response online advertising.

## PUBLIC RELATIONS

**public relations** a firm's communications and relationships with its various stakeholders, including customers, suppliers, stockholders, employees, the government, and the general public

**Public relations** refers to a firm's communications and relationships with its various stakeholders, including customers, suppliers, stockholders, employees, the government, and the general public.

**publicity** an aspect of public relations where marketers seek unpaid placement of news about the company or a product in mass media or on social media

**Publicity** is the marketing-oriented aspect of public relations where marketers seek unpaid placement of news about the company or a product in mass media or on social media. Compared with personal selling, advertising, and sales promotion, expenditures for public relations are usually low in most firms. Because companies do not pay for publicity, they have less control over whether the press or electronic media publish good or bad news. This often means consumers find this type of news source more believable than company-disseminated information.

### 17-1c

## VARIANTS OF THE PROMOTION MIX

**guerrilla marketing** using unconventional, innovative, and low-cost techniques to attract consumers' attention

While not necessarily categories of the promotion mix themselves, some additional promotional approaches are worth mentioning. **Guerrilla marketing** is using unconventional, innovative, and low-cost techniques to attract consumers' attention. Firms—especially those that can't afford the huge costs of print and broadcasting—often look for an innovative, low-cost way to reach their market. For example, some guerrilla marketers stencil their company and product names anywhere graffiti might appear. Street artists are hired to plaster company and product logos on blank walls or billboards.

Buzz marketing can be part of guerrilla marketing. This type of marketing works well to reach college students and other young adults. Marketing firms may hire students to mingle among their own classmates and friends, creating buzz about products ranging from Redbull energy drinks to CBS Sports Network.[9] Often called "campus ambassadors," they may wear logo-bearing T-shirts or caps, leave Post-it notes with marketing messages around campus, or chat about the good or service with friends during class breaks or over meals.

Viral marketing is another form of guerrilla marketing that has rapidly caught on with large and small firms. In Dove's "Real Beauty Sketches" ad video, an FBI-trained artist sits behind a screen and sketches faces of women, first based on their self-description, then on the description by a stranger. The strangers' descriptions often were uncannily close to the subject's appearance—underscoring the marketer's point that most women are their own worst beauty critic. The video's message struck an emotional chord with consumers, with more than 163 million views across more than 110 countries.[10]

## 17-1d
## CLOSING EXAMPLE

The deal you've struck is for product placement. Your boss is misinformed; this technique is not a substitute for advertising, but rather is a form of advertising that supplements traditional campaigns. He's correct in pointing out that its cost is high but that's because marketers have found it highly effective for more than 20 years in boosting brand recognition and loyalty.

# 17-2    THE COMMUNICATION PROCESS

### OPENING EXAMPLE

Jeans By Jeremy is a denim clothing chain that has achieved great success by marketing to young professional women in their 20s and 30s. When the owner decided to target teens, he placed ads featuring teenage models in the same high profile fashion magazines that had worked so well at building sales in the past: Glamour, Allure, and Cosmopolitan. The ads were hip and eye-catching. But the response from teens was poor—in fact, it was close to nonexistent. What went wrong?

LO 17.2  Explain how the communications process relates to the AIDA concept.

## 17-2a
## LEARNING IT: THE COMMUNICATION PROCESS

When you have a conversation with someone, do you wonder whether the person understood your message? Do you worry that you might not have heard the person correctly? Marketers have the same concerns: When they send a message to an intended audience or market, they want to make sure it gets through clearly and persuasively. That is why the communication process is so important to marketing.

The **sender** acts as the source in the communication system as they seek to convey a **message** (a communication of information) to a receiver. An effective message accomplishes three tasks:

1. It gains the receiver's attention.
2. It achieves understanding by both receiver and sender.
3. It stimulates the receiver's needs and suggests an appropriate method of satisfying them.

**sender**  source of the message communicated to the receiver

**message**  a communication of information

## 17-2b
## THE AIDA CONCEPT

The three tasks just listed are related to the **AIDA concept** (**a**ttention, **i**nterest, **d**esire, **a**ction), the steps consumers take in reaching a purchase decision. First, the promotional message must gain the potential consumer's attention. It then seeks

**AIDA concept**  the steps consumers take in reaching a purchase decision

to arouse interest in the good or service. Next, it stimulates desire by convincing the would-be buyer of the product's ability to satisfy his or her needs. Finally, the sales presentation, advertisement, or sales promotion technique attempts to produce action in the form of a purchase now or in the future. This process is demonstrated in Exhibit 17.2 for three different components of the promotional mix.

The message begins with **encoding**—that is, translating it into understandable terms and transmitting it through a communications channel. **Decoding** is the receiver's interpretation of the message. The receiver's response, known as **feedback**, completes the system. Throughout the process, **noise** (in such forms as ineffective promotional appeals, inappropriate advertising media, or poor radio or television reception) can interfere with the transmission of the message and reduce its effectiveness.

The marketer is the message sender in Exhibit 17.2. He or she encodes the message in the form of sales presentations, advertising, displays, or publicity releases. The **channel** for delivering the message may be a salesperson, a PR outlet, a website, or an advertising medium. Decoding is often the toughest step in marketing communications because consumers do not always interpret messages the same way as senders do. Because receivers usually decode messages according to their own frame of reference or experience, a sender must carefully encode a message to match the target's frame of reference. Consumers are exposed daily to thousands of messages through many media channels. Because the typical person will choose to process only a few messages, poorly encoded messages are wasted communications expenditures.

That's why feedback is important to marketers: It enables them to evaluate the effectiveness of their marketing communications process and tailor their future messages accordingly.

**encoding** translating a message into understandable terms and transmitting it through a communications channel

**decoding** the receiver's interpretation of the message

**feedback** the receiver's response to a message

**noise** forms of interference with the transmission of a message that reduce its effectiveness

**channel** the medium for delivering a message, such as a salesperson, a PR outlet, a website, or an advertising medium

**EXHIBIT 17.2** Relating Promotion to the Communication Process

| Type of Promotion | Message Sender | Encoding by Sender | Channel | Decoding by Receiver | Response | Feedback |
|---|---|---|---|---|---|---|
| **Personal selling** | SAP system (an enterprise software company) | Sales presentation on new applications of system | SAP sales representative | Office manager and employees discuss sales presentation and those of competing suppliers. | Customer places order for SAP system. | Customer asks about a second system for a subsidiary company. |
| **Dollar-off coupon (sales promotion)** | SC Johnson | Coupon for Pledge Duster Plus | Coupon insert in Sunday newspaper | Newspaper reader sees coupon for Pledge Duster Plus. | Shopper buys product using the coupon. | SC Johnson researchers see increase in market share. |
| **Television advertising** | Capital One | Advertisement featuring "What's in Your Wallet" slogan | Network television ads during program with high percentages of adult viewers | Adults see an ad and decide to try out the card. | Customer applies for Capital One card. | Customer makes purchases with Capital One card. |

Noise represents interference at some stage in the communication process. It may result from disruptions such as transmissions of competing promotional messages over the same communications channel, misinterpretation of a sales presentation or advertising message, receipt of the promotional message by the wrong person, or random events like people conversing or leaving the room during a television commercial. Noise can also result from distractions within an advertising message itself, like buzzwords and jargon that few consumers understand.

### 17-2c
## CLOSING EXAMPLE

While the teen-oriented ads for Jeans By Jeremy may have been visually appealing to its audience, it was a mistake to place them in magazines targeted to a different demographic group. Inappropriate media placement is an example of noise in marketing communications, which may be caused by any type of interference with the processes of encoding, decoding, or feedback. Publications like *Teen Vogue* and *Seventeen* might have been more appropriate channels and achieved better results.

# 17-3   THE OBJECTIVES OF PROMOTION

### OPENING EXAMPLE

Congratulations! You just cut the ribbon on Special Sweets, your new organic chocolate store. You plan to splash your store's name all over local billboards, confident that customers will soon be lining up at the door. But your marketing professor dampens your spirits when she cautions that creating awareness of your store, while critical, won't be enough to build sufficient traffic.

"I recommend following up those billboards with ads that stimulate demand," she says. "Then you'll need sales promotions to encourage trial and retain loyal customers."

Now your head is spinning. Pulling out the notes you took in class, you realize what she's talking about: Different promotions may be necessary to achieve different objectives, even for the same company or product. So what's the best way to promote Special Sweets?

**LO 17.3** Describe the various objectives of promotion.

### 17-3a
## LEARNING IT: THE OBJECTIVES OF PROMOTION

As a variable in the marketing mix, the overall function of promotion is to inform, persuade, and influence the consumer's purchase decision. However, the objective of a specific promotion may vary depending on the organization's needs and challenges at a given point in time. Among the most common promotional objectives are to create awareness, stimulate demand, encourage product trial, and retain loyal customers.

## CREATE AWARENESS

New product marketers must clear a significant hurdle before anyone will buy what they're selling: Potential customers need to know the product exists. That's why the objective of advertising and other promotion at the introductory stage of the product lifecycle is to create awareness. For many organizations, rapid accomplishment of this objective is critical to recoup the costs of product development and fund additional promotional efforts.

But the importance of creating awareness isn't limited to new products. Growing or mature products may design promotions to raise the profile of a brand image, make untapped target audiences aware of the brand, or call attention to product features. For example, in light of recent concerns about childhood obesity, McDonald's promotes the inclusion of fruit in its kids meals.

Billboards will surely help create awareness of Special Sweets. A new store could also benefit from simple repetition of its name in other promotional venues, like posters or streaming radio ads.

## STIMULATE DEMAND

Consumers may be aware of a product but uninterested in buying it until they know how it stacks up against competition. In this situation, the objective of promotion is to stimulate demand by differentiating the product from alternatives. For Special Sweets, advertising or other promotional efforts would highlight the high quality and great taste of the products. This approach is known as building **selective demand**- demand for a specific brand based on attributes important to potential purchasers.

Promotion may also seek to build demand for a product category, not for a particular brand within that category. Known as **primary demand** stimulation, this approach is used when a category is new and unfamiliar to prospective buyers. For example, instead of concentrating on its brand, Special Sweets could emphasize the health and environmental sustainability of organic chocolate as compared to mass produced chocolates.

**selective demand** demand for a specific brand based on attributes important to potential purchasers

**primary demand** seeks to build demand for a product category, not for a particular brand within that category

## ENCOURAGE PRODUCT TRIAL

Let's say prospective customers are aware of a product and favorably impressed by what it offers compared to the competition, but they're still not buying. What's wrong? Often the problem is inertia: Without an incentive to change their routines, consumers won't take the time or risk involved in trying something different.

The objective of promotion in these situations is to encourage product trial by making it easy and reducing risk. For example, to attract new readers, newspapers like the *New York Times* and *Wall Street Journal* offer weekly or monthly access to their websites on a trial basis. The trial costs nothing and is not intrusive; dissatisfied readers can simply ignore the publications.

For Special Sweets, giving away free samples outside the store or offering half-price coupons on your website may be effective ways to achieve this objective. You might also run an online contest: anyone who posts a funny

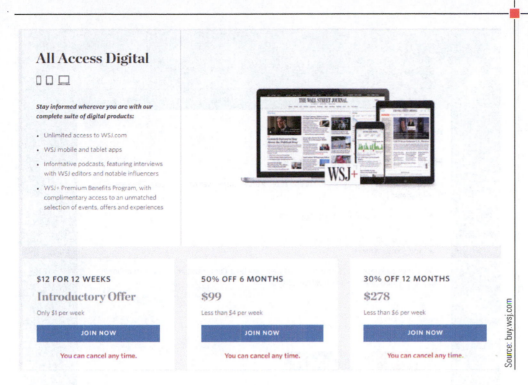

*Wall Street Journal* offers discounted trials to attract new readers.

Source: buy.wsj.com

chocolate-eating photo on the store's Facebook page gets the chance to win a year's supply.

## RETAIN LOYAL CUSTOMERS

Over time, successful businesses must do more than close one-time sales. It's far more expensive to find new buyers than to keep current ones, so marketers also use promotion to maintain and strengthen relationships with loyal customers. This is the promotional objective of frequent-buyer or reward programs, popularized by airlines and hotels but also widely used in other categories. For example, home goods retailer Big Lots offers a Buzz Club to frequent shoppers, who can earn 20% discount coupons, access to VIP events, and advance notice of special deals.

Advertisements, too, play a role in customer retention. Persuasive ads for Special Sweets will not only attract new buyers, but also reassure existing purchasers about the choice they made, and encourage them to recommend the brand to others.

## 17-3b
## CLOSING EXAMPLE

Now you get it: Special Sweets needs a multifaceted promotion plan. You decide to stick with simple billboards to create awareness, then switch to radio ads that will explain all the ways organic chocolate is superior to supermarket brands. You strike a deal with neighboring restaurants to encourage trial; they'll give out free samples of your candy in return for placing their flyers in

Rewards programs encourage loyalty by providing incentives to repeat buyers.

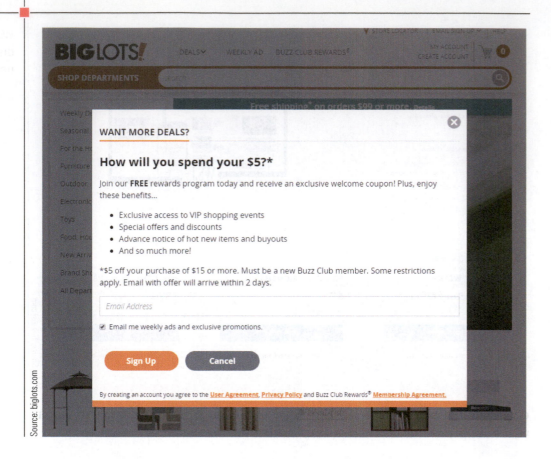

Source: biglots.com

your store. To retain loyal customers, you plan to enroll them in a Celebrations Club that will send members half price coupons on their birthdays and anniversaries.

Finally, you send a big box of chocolates to your marketing professor to say thanks for her help.

# ADVERTISING APPEALS

 **LO 17.4** Describe the types of appeals used by advertisers.

## OPENING EXAMPLE

In the hit TV series *Mad Men*, a dramatization of the ad industry in the 1960s, lead adman Don Draper told his clients: "Advertising is based on one thing: happiness. And do you know what happiness is? It's freedom from fear."

Based on that rationale, a 2015 TV commercial for Nationwide Insurance featured a young boy talking wistfully about everything he missed in life after dying from an accident. The company hoped its ad would sell insurance to people who feared accidents, especially those involving children.

However, the ad was widely panned and quickly taken off the air. If Don Draper was right, why do you think this happened?

## 17-4a

# LEARNING IT: ADVERTISING APPEALS

Marketers work to create an ad with meaningful, believable, and distinctive appeals—one that stands out from the clutter and is more likely to escape being skipped over by consumers.

Ads usually are created not individually, but as part of specific campaigns. An **advertising campaign** is a series of different but related ads that use a single theme and appear in different media within a specified time period. In developing a creative strategy, advertisers must balance message characteristics—the tone of the appeal, the information provided, and the conclusion to which it leads the consumer—with the story the ad tells, and its emphasis on verbal or visual elements.

Should the tone of the advertisement focus on a practical appeal such as price or gas mileage, or evoke an emotional response by appealing to, say, fear, humor, or sex? Would a celebrity endorsement make the ad more memorable? Should it compare the brand to a competitor? These are critical decisions in ad creation.

**advertising campaign** a series of different but related ads that use a single theme and appear in different media within a specified time period

## FEAR APPEALS

In recent years, marketers have relied increasingly on fear appeals. Ads for insurance, autos, and even batteries, imply that the wrong buying decision could lead to property loss, injury, or other bad outcomes. Recent Allstate commercials feature "Mayhem," a wild-eyed character who describes the adverse consequences of being uninsured.[11]

Fear appeals can backfire when viewers practice selective perception and tune out statements they perceive as too strong, implausible, tasteless, or simply overdone. For example, prescription drug advertising based on people's fear of illness has become so pervasive that some consumer researchers predict a consumer backlash.

## HUMOR IN ADVERTISING MESSAGES

A humorous ad seeks to create a positive mood related to a firm's goods or services, but advertising professionals differ in their opinions of the effectiveness. Some believe humor distracts attention from brand and product features; consumers remember the humor but not the product. Humorous ads, because they are so memorable, may lose their effectiveness sooner than ads with other kinds of appeals.

In addition, humor can be tricky because what one group of consumers finds funny may not be funny at all

Allstate combines fear and humor with its use of "Mayhem"

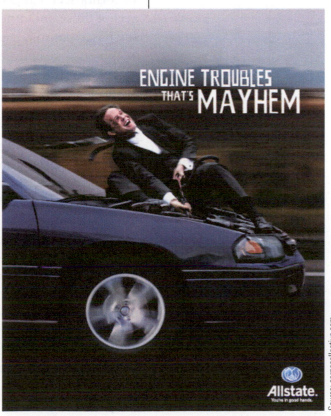

ENGINE TROUBLES THAT'S MAYHEM

Allstate.
You're in good hands.

Source: cargocollective.com

Humorous ads, like the hamsters in this Kia TV ad, seek to create a positive mood related to a company or product. Often though, consumers will remember the ad but not remember the company or product it was for.

Source: www.autoevolution.com

to another group. For example, Mountain Dew's "PuppyMonkeyBaby" Super Bowl TV spot won raves among millennial males but elicited confusion and disgust from older viewers.[12]

## ADS BASED ON SEX

Ads with sex-based appeals immediately attract attention. Advertisements for Victoria's Secret lingerie and clothing are designed this way. While many people accept these and other ads, they do not appeal to everyone. In other cultures, sex-based ads may cause offense. Marketers using sex-based appeals know they walk a fine line between what is acceptable to the consumers they want to reach and what is not.

## CELEBRITY TESTIMONIALS

Using celebrity spokespeople in ads can improve product recognition in a promotional environment filled with hundreds of competing 15- and 30-second commercials and online promotions. Advertisers use the term "cutting through clutter" to describe this advantage. Celebrity endorsements are also popular in foreign countries.

Both the number of celebrity ads and the dollars spent on them have risen in recent years. Professional athletes like NBA star LeBron James are among the highest-paid product endorsers. In a recent year, James reportedly earned $42 million from endorsement deals with such firms as The Coca-Cola Company, McDonald's, Nike, Samsung, and State Farm.[13]

Studies of consumer behavior show that celebrities improve the product's believability, product recall, and brand recognition. However, celebrity endorsements can also go awry. A personality who endorses too many products may create marketplace confusion. Customers may remember the celebrity but not the product or brand; worse, they might connect the celebrity to a competing brand. Another problem arises if a celebrity isn't credible; for example, celebrities who endorse political candidates may lack credibility unless they're perceived as knowledgeable about the issues.[14]

Some advertisers try to avoid problems with celebrity endorsers by using cartoon characters as endorsers, like the GEICO gecko, the Kia Hamsters, or the Keebler elves. Some advertisers may actually prefer cartoon characters because the characters never say anything negative about the product, they do exactly what the marketers want them to do, and they cannot get involved in scandals.

## COMPARATIVE ADVERTISING

Firms whose products are not the leaders in their markets often favor **comparative advertising**- an approach that emphasizes advertising messages with direct or indirect comparisons to dominant brands in the industry. For example, wireless telecommunications carriers Sprint and T-Mobile have invited comparison to market leader Verizon in a series of ads touting the strength of their networks and the speed of their services.[15] By contrast, advertising by market leaders seldom acknowledges that competing products even exist, and when they do, they do not point out any benefits of the competing brands.

**comparative advertising** an approach that emphasizes advertising messages with direct or indirect comparisons to dominant brands in the industry

### 17-4b
## CLOSING EXAMPLE

The Nationwide ad was generally judged insensitive and depressing. In fact, it generated such intense criticism that the firm's CEO resigned several months later. While Draper was right in touting the power of fear appeals, this fiasco illustrates the kind of backlash such appeals may provoke if audiences perceive them as over the top or inappropriate. The various types of appeal can be extremely effective—or they can backfire. Marketers must carefully weigh the pros and cons of each.

### 17-5
# MEDIA SELECTION AND SCHEDULING

### OPENING EXAMPLE

In the aftermath of a massive oil spill caused by its rigs in the Gulf of Mexico, petroleum firm BP faced a major public relations crisis. The company was blamed by the press and by much of the public for poor safety procedures and a lack of concern for the environment.

BP decided to respond on television. The firm aired multiple TV commercials that stressed its commitment to repairing the environmental damage and rebuilding the local economy. Why did BP choose television to communicate its message, despite the high costs of this medium?

**LO 17.5** Compare the seven different advertising media.

**17-5a**

# LEARNING IT: MEDIA SELECTION AND SCHEDULING

One of the most important decisions in developing an advertising strategy is the selection of appropriate media to carry a firm's message to its audience. The media selected must be capable of accomplishing the communications objectives of informing, persuading, and reminding potential customers of the good, service, person, or idea advertised.

Research identifies the ad's target market to determine the market's size and characteristics. Advertisers then match the target characteristics with the media best able to reach that particular audience, while weighing the advantages and drawbacks of each option. For example, radio is highly effective at reaching local markets, though it lacks the "show and tell" capability that may be important for products with striking design or other distinctive visual features. Newspapers are also a good choice when the audience is localized, but ads in this medium may be forgotten with the day's headlines.

**media selection** choosing a form of media for advertising

The objective of **media selection** is to achieve adequate media coverage without advertising beyond the identifiable limits of the potential market. Television offers the most extensive reach, though its high upfront cost may make it unaffordable for small businesses. Finally, cost comparisons between alternatives should determine the best possible media purchase. Exhibit 17.3 summarizes the advantages and disadvantages of each form of media.

**EXHIBIT 17.3** Comparison of Major Forms of Media

| Medium | Advantages | Disadvantages |
|---|---|---|
| Television | Largest reach | Very expensive |
| | Audio visual presentation has a high impact | Message can be quickly forgotten |
| | Ads can be run frequently | Increasingly ignored by users of digital video recorders (DVR) |
| Radio | Can target local audiences | Lacks visual imagery |
| | Low relative cost | Listener's attention is limited |
| | Short lead times for placing ads | Difficult for driving listeners to follow the ad's "call to action" |
| Newspapers | Can reach large, local audiences | Short life, especially for daily publications |
| | Short lead times for placing ads | High volume of ads limits exposure |
| | Ads can be run frequently | Hard to target specific market segments |
| Magazines | Selective targeting | High cost |
| | Long life | Long lead times (30–90 days) |
| | Good reproduction of visuals | Infrequent publication |
| Direct mail | Highly selective and personal targeting | Very expensive on a per-piece basis |
| | Easy to measure performance | Often thrown away as "junk mail" |
| | Hidden from competitors | |

*(Continues)*

*(Continued)*

| Medium | Advantages | Disadvantages |
| --- | --- | --- |
| Outdoor | Geographic selectivity | Allows only very short messages |
|  | Can be placed close to point of sale | Seldom attracts reader's attention |
|  | Allows for frequent repetition | Criticized as blight on landscape |
| Digital media | Highly selective targeting | Cost per click can be high. |
|  | Available for almost any ad budget | Concerns about security and privacy. |
|  | Real-time, measurable feedback | Uncertainty about how to evaluate return on investment |

## TELEVISION

Television—network and cable combined—accounts for just over 40 cents of every advertising dollar spent in the world.[16] Television advertising is attractive because it allows marketers to reach local and national markets. Whereas most newspaper advertising revenues come from local advertisers, the greatest share of television advertising revenues comes from organizations that advertise nationally. In the past decade, cable television's share of ad spending and revenues has grown tremendously in tandem with the booming size of its audience. Cable advertising offers marketers access to more narrowly defined target audiences than other broadcast media can provide—a characteristic referred to as "narrowcasting." The great variety of special-interest channels devoted to subjects like cooking, golf, history, home and garden, health, fitness, and shopping attract specialized audiences and permit niche marketing.

Television advertising offers the advantages of mass coverage, powerful impact on viewers, repetition of messages, flexibility, and prestige. It's disadvantages include high costs and it's easily forgettable. Also, due to DVR, many viewers are able to skip through advertisements.

## RADIO

Radio advertising has always been a popular media choice for targeting advertising messages to local audiences. Most radio listening was traditionally done in cars. But podcast radio now allows customers to widen their listening times and choices through computers and mobile devices. With an estimated monthly audience of 155 million people—over half the U.S. adult population—online radio listenership continues to grow.[17]

Marketers frequently use traditional radio advertising to reach local audiences. Advertisers like radio for its ability to reach people while they drive because they are a captive audience. Other benefits include low cost, flexibility, and mobility. The variety of stations allows advertisers to easily target audiences and tailor their messages to those listeners. Disadvantages to radio advertising include distracted listeners and lack of visual imagery (unlike print, online, and TV ads).

## NEWSPAPER

Newspaper advertising as a whole is losing ground to alternative media vehicles. However, it continues to be strong in local markets and is estimated to account for $16.2 billion in annual advertising expenditures.[18] Despite the downward trend, newspaper innovations like interactive websites, virtual reality reporting, (which enables readers to "experience" the news) and "chatbots," (which provide personalized headlines) hold promise for the industry and are likely to create new promotional opportunities.[19]

The primary advantage of newspaper advertising is the flexibility it offers, because the ads can vary from one locality to the next. Unlike television or radio advertising messages, newspaper readers can keep printed advertising messages and refer back to them. Newspaper advertising does have some disadvantages. One of these is relatively poor reproduction quality, although that is changing as technology improves. Newspapers also struggle to "get through the noise" of other advertisers. To retain big advertisers like trendy designers and national retailers, some newspapers like *The New York Times* and *Wall Street Journal* have launched their own annual or semiannual fashion magazines, taking advantage of their finely tuned distribution capabilities.

## MAGAZINES

The primary advantages of magazine advertising include the ability to reach precise target markets, quality reproduction of images, long life, and the prestige associated with some magazines known for visual artistry, such as *National Geographic* and *Architectural Digest*. The primary disadvantage is that magazines have high costs and require long lead times for marketers who want to place ads.

Media buyers study circulation numbers and demographic information for various publications before choosing optimal placement opportunities and negotiating rates. The top magazine by circulation is *AARP The Magazine*, which reaches over 37 million readers.[20] However, circulation isn't the only criteria important to marketers: an advertiser of specialized products like sports equipment or craft supplies might choose a magazine read by an audience that is not huge in numbers but is highly involved with such products.

## DIRECT MAIL

Direct-mail advertising includes sales letters, postcards, leaflets, folders, booklets, and catalogs. This medium accounted for nearly $50 billion of spending in a recent year.[21] Its advantages come from direct mail's ability to segment large numbers of prospective customers into narrow market niches. In addition, it offers speed, flexibility, detailed information, and personalization. Disadvantages of direct mail include high production costs, reliance on the quality of mailing lists, and some consumers' resistance to it.

A particular downside to direct mail is clutter, which explains why it is commonly derided as "junk mail." So much advertising material is stuffed into people's mailboxes every day that the task of grabbing consumers' attention and evoking interest can be daunting to direct-mail advertisers.

## OUTDOOR ADVERTISING

Outdoor advertising is one of the oldest and simplest media businesses. Advertisers in the United States spent over $9 billion on outdoor advertising in a recent year.[22] Traditional outdoor advertising takes the form of billboards, painted displays on the walls of buildings, and electronic displays. Transit advertising includes ads placed inside and outside buses, commuter trains, and stations.

Outdoor advertising quickly communicates simple ideas. It also offers repeated exposure to a message and strong promotion for locally available products. But like every other type of ad, outdoor advertising produces clutter. It also suffers from the brevity of exposure to its messages by passing motorists. As a result, most of these ads use striking, simple illustrations, short selling points, and humor to attract people interested in products, such as beverages, vacations, local entertainment, and lodging.

Another problem relates to public concerns over aesthetics. Legislation regulates the placement of outdoor advertising near interstate highways. Also, local ordinances in many cities regulate the size and placement of outdoor messages. Hawaii prohibits them altogether.

## DIGITAL MEDIA

Digital media—especially websites and social media sites—are being used more and more by advertisers. Keyword ads dominate spending on online advertising. In a recent year, Google's ad revenues totaled nearly $80 billion, and many firms are increasing their interactive advertising budgets.[23] In a recent year, mobile advertising revenues in the United States exceeded $20 billion and are expected to continue their explosive growth.[24]

Technology is helping revive outdoor advertising with digital billboards that use animation and video.

Robert Landau/Alamy Stock Photo

Through emerging technology known as augmented reality, virtual imaging can be incorporated into real-time video on a mobile phone, creating an exciting new experience for cell phone users.[25] Pokemon Go is an example of augmented reality, and this technology may offer benefits to local advertisers, such as restaurants and retail stores.

While advertising on digital media can be highly targeted, costs-per-click can be high and it can sometimes be difficult to measure return on investment.

## 17-5b
## CLOSING EXAMPLE

While BP's television advertising was costly, the company chose this medium because it needed to reach a mass audience in an impactful, memorable way. Fortunately, its budget was large enough to cover substantial message repetition over several months. Thanks to the campaign, BP largely succeeded in restoring its corporate reputation, muting its critics, and recapturing customer loyalty.

# 17-6    PUBLIC RELATIONS

**LO 17.6** Describe the roles of public relations, publicity, and cross-promotion in an organization's promotional strategy.

### OPENING EXAMPLE

Childhood obesity is a growing problem. Many doctors blame increased consumption of fast food—which, they believe, is driven by the industry's promotion to kids.

In a series of press conferences and guest editorials in newspapers around the United States, the American Academy of Pediatrics (AAP) has called for a ban on fast food advertising during children's TV programming. In response, fast food marketers like McDonald's use similar publicity tools to point out that they offer healthier choices than ever, like fruit and low-fat milk—and that advertising to children is perfectly legal. However, the fast food companies are at a disadvantage in their public relations campaigns. Why?

## 17-6a
## LEARNING IT: PUBLIC RELATIONS

Public relations (PR) is the firm's communications with various stakeholders, including customers, employees, stockholders, suppliers, government agencies, and the society in which it operates. It is concerned with building a positive image for all parts of the organization. In addition to its traditional activities, such as persuading public attitudes and creating a good corporate image, PR also supports advertising in promoting the organization's goods and services.

Public relations has grown in importance as a result of increased public pressure on industries regarding corporate ethical conduct and environmental issues. Many top executives have become more involved in public relations as the public expects top managers to take greater responsibility for company actions. Some CEOs have been proactive in public relations, becoming the "face" of their companies in ways that enhance brand reputation. For example, Zappos CEO Tony Hsieh wrote a book about his company's values that put him—and Zappos—on the map as corporate culture innovators.[26]

The PR department is the link between the firm and the media. It provides press releases and holds news conferences to announce new products, the formation of strategic alliances, management changes, financial results, or similar developments. The PR department may also issue publications and documents such as newsletters, brochures, and reports.

## PUBLICITY

The aspect of public relations most directly related to promoting a firm's products is publicity, which focuses on unpaid placement of news regarding the product in a print, social, or broadcast medium. Firms generate publicity by creating special events, holding press conferences, and preparing news releases and media kits. Many businesses, like Starbucks and Sam's Club, built their brands with virtually no advertising.

While publicity benefits from minimal costs compared with other forms of promotion, it does not deliver its message entirely for free. Publicity-related expenses include the costs of employing staff assigned to create and submit publicity releases, the costs of events, and other related expenses. Firms often pursue publicity to promote their images or viewpoints. Other publicity topics involve organizational activities such as plant expansions, mergers and acquisitions, management changes, and research breakthroughs. A significant amount of publicity provides information about goods and services, particularly new products.

Because many consumers consider news stories to be more credible than advertisements, publicity releases are often sent to media editors for possible inclusion in news stories. The media audiences perceive the news as coming from the communications media, not the marketers.

A key disadvantage of publicity is that the firm has little control over when a media outlet might run a story about its company or product, if they even run a story at all. In addition, the firm has little control over what that story might say. Sometimes, a press conference or publicity event can backfire by getting very little coverage, or generating media coverage that portrays the company in a negative light.

## CROSS-PROMOTION

In recent years, marketers have begun to combine their promotions with other companies using a technique called **cross-promotion**, in which marketing partners share the cost of a promotional campaign that meets their mutual needs. Often cross-promotion is utilized for similar

**cross-promotion** when marketing partners share the cost of a promotional campaign that meets their mutual needs

Source: www.medium.com

Nestle and Google utilized cross-promotion using a mix of advertising, public relations, and sales promotion.

or complementary products, but not always. For example, in a partnership between Nestle's Kit Kat and Google's Android, 50 million Kit Kat bars were created with Android's branding; candy buyers got a chance to win a Nexus Tablet or Google Play gift cards. Marketers realize these joint efforts between established brands provide greater benefits in return for both organizations; investments of time and money on such promotions will become increasingly important to many partners' growth prospects.

## 17-6b
## ETHICS AND PR

Promotion is the element in the marketing mix that raises the most ethical questions. One issue is the insertion of product messages in media programs without full disclosure to audiences of the marketing nature of the messages. To woo younger consumers, especially teens and those in their 20s, advertisers attempt to make these messages appear as different from advertisements as possible; they design ads that seem more like entertainment.

In online ads, it is often difficult to separate advertising from editorial content, because many sites resemble magazine and newspaper ads or television infomercials. Another ethical issue surrounding online advertising is the use of "cookies," small text files automatically downloaded to a user's computer or mobile device whenever a site is visited. Each time the user returns to that site, the site's server accesses the cookie and gathers information: What site was visited last? How long did the user stay? What was the next site visited? Marketers claim that cookies help them determine consumer preferences and tailor offerings specific to them. The problem is that cookies can and do collect personal information without the user's knowledge.

## 17-6c
## CLOSING EXAMPLE

Because many journalists lean toward the AAP's position, the doctors' group receives a great deal of supportive media coverage in addition to the publicity it generates on its own. Conversely, fast food companies have fewer friends in the media and must work hard to overcome this disadvantage and get their message across.

Recognizing that the controversy won't go away, some leading marketers like McDonald's and Disney, frequently issue press releases focused on their health education initiatives and improvements in the nutritional profile of their menus. In other efforts to offset the bad publicity, they frequently sponsor philanthropic events and organizations in local communities to demonstrate their concern for the families they serve.

# 17-7 PROMOTIONAL MIX EFFECTIVENESS

## OPENING EXAMPLE

Paula runs an advertising specialty firm that sells pens and keychains imprinted with her customers' brand names. She asked two promotion consultants for advice—but got conflicting recommendations.

Consultant #1 advised Paula to launch a nationwide ad campaign. "Your products will look great in big print ads, in TV commercials, and on highway billboards," he argued. "Advertising is the right promotion tool for you because pens and keychains are simple, low priced, and purchased by many different customers."

But Consultant #2 urged her to rely on personal selling. "You need personal salespeople to explain why customers should buy from you. Your products are simple, but customizing them is a complex process. While you have a large number of prospects, they are all business customers who buy in big quantities and spend a lot of money at a time; they don't want single pens or keychains."

Which consultant is right?

> **LO 17.7** Critique a promotional mix based on the five factors that influence the effectiveness of a promotional mix.

## 17-7a

## LEARNING IT: PROMOTIONAL MIX EFFECTIVENESS

Marketers strive to develop an effective promotional mix by evaluating various factors.

## NATURE OF THE MARKET

The number of buyers and the type of customer in a marketer's target audience should affect the promotional mix. Advertising is most often appropriate to reach large numbers of consumers scattered across geographic areas. Personal selling works better for business customers, wholesale buyers, and consumers making high-priced and/or high-involvement purchases. Sometimes firms switch between advertising and personal selling to target different markets for their goods: Pharmaceutical companies, for example, send salespeople to hospitals but run TV commercials to promote their drugs to consumers.

## NATURE OF THE PRODUCT

Personal selling is generally best for custom or complex products requiring frequent maintenance, like enterprise hardware and software systems. Advertising works better for standardized products, like soft drinks. In general, consumer goods, especially convenience products, lend themselves more readily to advertising than business goods. Within the B2B market, installations like machinery require more personal selling effort than operating supplies, such as printing paper and toner cartridges.

## PRICE

Low-unit-price products are usually advertised in mass media, where the marketer's cost per contact is low. In contrast, high-priced goods like boats or luxury condos can rarely be sold without well-presented information from qualified salespeople. Increasingly, such pitches include high-tech elements such as video presentations on a tablet or augmented reality features embedded in a display.[27]

Exhibit 17.4 summarizes how these factors affect choice of promotional method.

## STAGE IN THE PRODUCT LIFECYCLE

The promotional mix also must be tailored to the product lifecycle. In the introductory stage, both personal selling and nonpersonal promotion (advertising, sales promotion) are used in the following ways:

- *Personal selling*: Contact marketing intermediaries (wholesalers, retailers) to secure interest in and commitment to handling the new item.

- *Trade shows*: Inform and educate prospective dealers and ultimate consumers about the new item's competitive advantages.

- *Advertising and sales promotion*: Create awareness, provide information, and stimulate initial purchases.

As the product moves into the growth and maturity stages, the promotional mix should change. Advertising gains more relative importance in persuading and reminding consumers to make purchases. Salespeople attempt to convince marketing intermediaries to expand distribution.

**EXHIBIT 17.4**   Factors Affecting Promotional Mix

---

**Conditions Favoring Advertising**

- Many buyers dispersed across geographic areas
- Highly standardized products, especially convenience goods
- Consumer markets
- Low-unit-value products

**Conditions Favoring Personal Selling**

- Limited number of buyers
- Custom or complex products requiring frequent maintenance
- Business or wholesale markets
- High-priced, high-involvement purchases

In maturity and early decline, firms frequently reduce advertising and sales promotion expenditures as market saturation is reached and new competition appears.

## FUNDS AVAILABLE FOR PROMOTION

The cost of some promotional options may put them out of reach. For example, CBS charged $5 million for a single 30-second slot during a recent Super Bowl telecast[28]–a price far too steep for many firms, despite the relatively low cost per each of the millions of viewers. If a company wants to hire a celebrity to promote its brand, the fee can also run into six or seven figures. Firms with smaller budgets might opt for online advertising, sales promotion, or publicity as their primary promotional types.

### 17-7b
## CLOSING EXAMPLE

Fortunately, Paula chose the recommendation of Consultant #2. Instead of spending a lot of money in ads, she invested in a cutting-edge sales training program. Her sales team improved its skills enough to close new accounts with a soda company and a fast food chain, business accounts she'd never cracked before. She keeps a careful eye on the television and billboard ads run by her clients–because she knows that the more customers they attract, the more of her pens and keychains they'll buy.

# 17-8  LEARN IT TODAY . . . USE IT TOMORROW

Congratulations! You've been hired as the new director of promotion for Pepe's Pizza. Your task is to guide the company's expansion into two new products.

**Pizza sauce for restaurants:** The target customer is major chains throughout the nation. Since businesses order in larger volume than individual consumers, it's cost-effective for Pepe's to offer customized flavoring and spiciness of the pizza sauces based on customer needs.

**Frozen pizza for consumers:** You will work with a manufacturer to mass produce value-priced pizzas that are the closest thing to eating at Pepe's. You hope to gain distribution in grocery stores throughout the country, but also want to generate awareness and demand among consumers who have never heard of Pepe's Pizza.

Knowing that this expansion requires significant changes to Pepe's traditional promotional mix, you sit down to figure out the best approach.

It's time to get hands-on and apply what you've learned. **See MindTap for an activity related to Pepe's promotional activities**.

# Chapter Summary

**LO 17.1** Identify the five components of the promotional mix.

To make their messages stand out from competition, marketers seek to integrate advertising, personal selling, sales promotion, direct marketing, and public relations in a consistent, coordinated way.

**LO 17.2** Explain how the communications process relates to the AIDA concept.

Effective promotional messages must gain attention, arouse interest, and stimulate desire. These tasks relate to the AIDA concept (attention, interest, desire, action), the steps consumers take in reaching a purchase decision.

**LO 17.3** Describe the various objectives of promotion.

Promotions are designed to achieve specific objectives important to the firm. Among the most common promotion objectives are to create awareness, stimulate demand, encourage product trial, and retain loyal customers.

**LO 17.4** Describe the types of appeals used by advertisers.

An effective appeal can help an ad break through the clutter. Among the most common advertising appeals are fear, humor, sex, celebrity testimonial, and comparison to competitors.

**LO 17.5** Compare the seven different advertising media.

Distinctive strengths and weaknesses are associated with each of the seven major advertising media: television, radio, newspapers, magazines, direct mail, outdoor, and digital media.

**LO 17.6** Describe the roles of public relations, publicity, and cross-promotion in an organization's promotional strategy.

The importance of public relations is growing as organizations become increasingly aware that they need a favorable public image and can gain additional media exposure through publicity.

**LO 17.7** Critique a promotional mix based on the five factors that influence the effectiveness of a promotional mix.

Organizations evaluate various market and product factors to help them select the best promotional mix. These include nature of the market, nature of the product, price, stage in the product lifecycle, and funds available for promotion.

# Key Terms

integrated marketing communications (IMC) 354
promotional mix 354
advertising 354
personal selling 355
sales promotion 355
direct marketing 355
public relations 356

publicity 356
guerrilla marketing 356
sender 357
message 357
AIDA concept 357
encoding 358
decoding 358
feedback 358

noise 358
channel 358
selective demand 360
primary demand 360
advertising campaign 363
comparative advertising 365
media selection 366
cross-promotion 371

# 18 PERSONAL SELLING AND SALES PROMOTION

DayOwl/Shutterstock.com

## LEARNING OBJECTIVES

**18.1** Contrast the factors that favor use of personal selling versus advertising.

**18.2** Describe the four sales channels.

**18.3** Explain how each step in the sales process relates to the AIDA concept.

**18.4** Summarize the seven steps of the sales process.

**18.5** Describe the seven key functions of a sales manager.

**18.6** Summarize eight types of sales promotion.

**18.7** Given an example of market conditions and promotional objectives, identify the most effective promotional tactic.

Hormel Foods based in Austin, Minnesota, is known for its pork products including the iconic Spam canned meat. But Hormel also offers a wide-range of meal solutions to the consumer and business markets. Its diversified portfolio of consumer brands includes Skippy peanut butter, Chi Chi's tortilla chips, Wholly Guacamole, and Muscle Milk. The company sells to consumers through the retail grocery market, but also serves the restaurant and hospitality industry. While Hormel utilizes advertising and public relations to raise awareness and create positive sentiment around their brand, these aren't their only promotional tactics. In fact, their multi-channel sales force is a critical piece of Hormel's strategy to maximize distribution in both consumer and business markets. In addition, Hormel utilizes a variety of sales promotion techniques to stimulate purchases and encourage loyalty. The challenge for Hormel is finding the right promotional tactic for the right situation so they can leverage their marketing dollars and grow their brand.

## 18-1

# PERSONAL SELLING

**LO 18.1** Contrast the factors that favor use of personal selling versus advertising.

## OPENING EXAMPLE

Paul Joffre owns a remodeling company, Windows & More, which specializes in replacement windows, siding, and awnings for residential customers. He is a member of the local building contractors' association and typically has a display at the home show every spring. He's been contacted by several media outlets in the area and is considering making some changes to his promotional mix. Paul has never advertised on the radio or television and has primarily relied on personal selling activities to gain customers. How can Paul determine whether or not he should use advertising as part of his promotional mix?

### 18-1a

## LEARNING IT: PERSONAL SELLING

As discussed in Chapter 17, marketers attempt to create an optimal blend of promotional mix elements (advertising, personal selling, sales promotion, direct marketing, and public relations) to achieve their objectives. This chapter will focus on the personal selling and sales promotion aspects of the promotional mix.

**personal selling** person-to-person promotional presentation to a buyer

**Personal selling** is person-to-person promotional presentation to a buyer. The sales process is essentially interpersonal, and it is basic to any enterprise. Accounting, engineering, human resource management, production, and other organizational activities produce no benefits unless a seller matches the needs of a customer. The more than 14 million people employed in sales occupations in the United States testify to the importance of selling.[1] Personal selling is much costlier and time consuming than other types of promotion because of its direct contact with customers. This makes personal selling the single largest marketing expense in many firms.

Since both advertising and personal selling represent large expense categories for firms, it's important to identify factors that may favor greater use of advertising or personal selling. Exhibit 18.1 provides a review of these factors (several of which were discussed in Chapter 17).

Let's examine each of these factors in the context of Paul Joffre's Windows & More remodeling business.

- *Consumer Location*: Windows & More typically works with customers who live within a 60-mile radius of their showroom, as Paul has determined that most customers are willing to drive an hour or less to shop for home remodeling needs. In addition, Paul wants to focus on a smaller geographic market to manage his transportation expenses. A geographically concentrated customer base favors the use of personal selling.

- *Number of Consumers*: Any home or apartment building that is 10 or more years old could be part of the target market for window and siding replacement. If Windows & More were a national company, this might favor advertising because there are a high number of potential customers. But since Windows & More only services a fairly small area, advertising might not be economically feasible. Instead, personal selling would be favored for a market with such a relatively small number of customers.

- *Product Features–Complexity & Customization*: Home remodeling or window replacement can be a complex process where customers select from many options to fit their needs. Therefore, personal selling would be most appropriate.

- *Channels*: Windows & More sells direct to customer, with no distributor, retailers, or other marketing intermediaries in between. This would also favor personal selling.

None of these factors would entirely exclude the use of advertising as a promotional option, but any advertising campaigns would need to utilize media that are highly targeted and can efficiently reach potential customers.

**EXHIBIT 18.1** Factors Affecting the Importance of Personal Selling in the Promotional Mix

| Variable | Conditions That Favor Personal Selling | Conditions That Favor Advertising |
|---|---|---|
| **Consumer** | Geographically concentrated | Geographically dispersed |
| | Relatively low numbers | Relatively high numbers |
| **Product** | Expensive | Inexpensive |
| | Technically complex | Simple to understand |
| | Custom made | Standardized |
| | Special handling requirements | No special handling requirements |
| | Transactions frequently involve trade-ins | Transactions seldom involve trade-ins |
| **Price** | Relatively high | Relatively low |
| **Channels** | Relatively short | Relatively long |

Personal selling is a vibrant, dynamic process. As competition increases, personal selling takes on a more prominent role in the marketing mix. Salespeople must communicate the advantages of their firms' goods and services over those of competitors. They must be able to:

- Focus on a customer's needs and create solutions that meet those needs.
- Follow through before, during, and after a sale.
- Know the industry and have a firm grasp not only of their own firm's capabilities but also of their competitors' abilities.
- Work hard to exceed their customers' expectations.

Relationship marketing affects all aspects of an organization's marketing function, including personal selling. Instead of working alone, many salespeople now operate in sales teams. The customer-focused firm wants its salespeople to form long-lasting relationships with buyers by providing high levels of customer service, since this is more likely to drive repeat sales and referrals.

Personal selling is an attractive career choice for today's college students. According to the Bureau of Labor Statistics, jobs in sales and related fields are expected to grow by about 5% over the next decade.[2] Company executives usually recognize a good salesperson as a hard worker who can solve problems, communicate clearly, and be consistent. In fact, many companies are headed by executives who began their careers in sales.

### 18-1b
## CLOSING EXAMPLE

Paul Joffre of Windows & More now has a much better sense of why personal selling is most appropriate for his business. He will concentrate his efforts on utilizing this element of the promotion mix to attract new customers for his business. He also feels more confident in discussing his needs with media representatives from local radio or television stations who contact him to discuss advertising, since he now understands the rationale for concentrating his promotional expenses on personal selling efforts.

# 18-2  THE FOUR SALES CHANNELS

**LO 18.2** Describe the four sales channels

## OPENING EXAMPLE

Grainger, a publicly traded industrial supplier (NYSE:GWW), was recently named one of *Fortune's Most Admired Companies*[3] and provides over 1.5 million products to maintain, repair, or operate facilities. Grainger achieves over $10 billion in annual sales by serving approximately 3 million businesses across the globe through a variety of sales channels. How are these sales channels classified and what differentiates one channel from another? Why should companies utilize multiple sales channels to serve their customers?

## 18-2a

# LEARNING IT: THE FOUR SALES CHANNELS

Personal selling occurs through several types of communication channels: over-the-counter selling (including online selling), field selling, telemarketing, and inside selling. Each of these channels can be used for business-to-business and business-to-consumer selling. Many organizations use a number of different channels.

## OVER-THE-COUNTER SELLING

**Over-the-counter selling** typically describes selling in retail or wholesale locations in which customers come to the seller's place of business. It is the most frequently used personal selling channel. Customers typically visit the seller's location on their own initiative to purchase desired items. Some visit their favorite stores because they enjoy shopping. Others respond to appeals, such as personal letters of invitation from store personnel and advertisements for sales, special events, and new-product introductions.

A key differentiator for the over-the-counter-selling channel is the level of knowledge of the sales representatives. Business-to-business firms such as Enterprise Rent-A-Car and Grainger conduct training programs for their associates so they are better equipped to address customer needs. In contrast, retail operations such as Walmart and Kohl's utilize over-the-counter-selling but may not need to provide the same level of training to their associates.

Grainger operates over 668 branch locations across the globe with about half in the United States, one third in Canada, and the remaining branches in Latin America and Europe. Customers may visit a local branch or have Grainger deliver in-stock products within two business days. This makes it easy for customers to obtain their desired items.[4]

**over-the-counter selling**
selling in retail or wholesale locations in which customers come to the seller's place of business

Source: www.achrnews.com

Over-the-counter selling is common for business-to-business transactions where customers visit the warehouse or sales facility to order in-person. Customer service and salesperson expertise is a key differentiator in this type of environment.

## FIELD SELLING

**field selling** sales calls made at the prospective customer's location on a face-to-face basis

**Field selling** involves making sales calls on prospective and existing customers at their businesses or homes. Field sales of large software installations or large industrial installations, such as Airbus's A380 double-deck airliner, often require considerable effort and technical expertise. Largely because it involves travel, field selling is typically more expensive than other selling options.

In fairly routine field selling situations, such as calling on established customers, the salesperson basically acts as an order-taker. Consider the PepsiCo route delivery salesperson who ensures that convenience stores, groceries, and large box stores have Pepsi products. They deliver product, install point-of-sale materials, and ensure the retailer has appropriate inventory. But more complex situations may involve weeks or months of preparation, formal presentations, and many hours of post-sales call work.

According to its *Fact Book*,[5] Grainger uses multiple channels, including dedicated sales account executives to serve customers. The field sales representatives typically interact with larger customers who are relationship driven, have more complex needs, operate multiple locations, and are interested in working with fewer suppliers. Grainger believes their multi-pronged approach enables them to effectively and efficiently reach a broad group of customers from small accounts to large, multi-national companies.

## TELEMARKETING

**telemarketing** when the selling process is conducted by phone

**Telemarketing** is when the selling process is conducted by phone. It functions to provide sales and service to customers, and is used for both business-to-business and direct-to-customer markets. Both inbound and outbound telemarketing are forms of direct marketing.

**outbound telemarketing** sales method in which sales personnel contact potential buyers by phone

For **outbound telemarketing**, or phone sales, sales personnel contact potential buyers by phone, reducing the substantial costs of personal visits to customers' homes or businesses. A major drawback of consumer-oriented telemarketing is that most consumers dislike the practice, and more than 220 million have signed up for the national Do Not Call Registry.[6] If an unauthorized telemarketer does call any of these numbers, the marketer is subject to a fine of up to $16,000.[7] Phone sales is still very common, and somewhat more accepted, in the B2B markets though.

**inbound telemarketing** sales method in which prospects call a seller to obtain information, make reservations, or purchase products

**Inbound telemarketing** typically involves a toll-free number that customers can call to obtain information, make reservations, and purchase goods and services. Inbound reps are mainly order takers who handle straightforward questions or purchases. This form of selling provides maximum convenience for customers who initiate the sales process. Many large catalog merchants, such as Pottery Barn, L.L.Bean, Lands' End, and Performance Bike, keep their inbound telemarketing lines open 24/7.

## INSIDE SELLING

**inside selling** the process of inbound sales management utilizing phone, mail, and the Internet

**Inside selling** is a more advanced version of inbound telemarketing that requires more experienced sales reps. While accepting an order for products at Pottery Barn is a somewhat simple transaction, discussing technical specs for a custom

ESB Professional/Shutterstock.com

Some firms use telemarketing because the average call cost is low and companies point to a high rate of success.

piece of manufacturing equipment requires an inside sales rep with specialized expertise. Inside sales reps perform two primary jobs: They turn opportunities into actual sales, and they support technicians and purchasers with current solutions. A successful inside sales force relies on close working relationships with field representatives to solidify customer relationships.

Grainger utilizes inside sales representatives who assist customers and provide "the support they need to solve problems."[8] Further, these representatives utilize consultative selling techniques to establish rapport, ask questions to identify needs, recommend products to address needs, and effectively close the sale.

## 18-2b
## CLOSING EXAMPLE

Grainger, like many firms, finds value in blending sales channels to create a successful, cost-effective sales organization. Existing customers whose business problems require complex solutions are likely best served by the traditional field sales force. Other current customers who need answers, but not the same attention as the first group, can be served by inside sales reps as needed. Over-the-counter sales reps serve existing customers who are located near the branch locations by supplying information and completing sales transactions. Telemarketers may be used to strengthen communication with customers or to reestablish relationships with customers that may have lapsed over a few months.

# 18-3  THE SALES PROCESS AND AIDA CONCEPT

**LO 18.3**  Explain how each step in the sales process relates to the AIDA concept.

## OPENING EXAMPLE

Brittany is the sales manager for a medical staffing recruiting firm and conducts weekly sales meetings with her team members. In the recruiting industry, a successful "sale" is when a qualified job candidate is hired by one of the clients of Brittany's firm. All sales representatives have been trained on the selling process but Brittany thinks the staff could benefit from learning more about how the sales process aligns with the AIDA concept. Which steps in the sales process provide the representatives with the opportunity to create attention, interest, desire, and action?

## 18-3a
## LEARNING IT: THE SALES PROCESS AND AIDA CONCEPT

As discussed in Chapter 17, the AIDA concept (attention, interest, desire, action) describes the steps consumers pass through when reaching a purchase decision. Marketers must first ensure the promotional message gains the potential consumer's attention. They then seek to stimulate interest in the good or service. Next, marketers must spark desire by convincing the would-be buyer of the product's ability to satisfy his or her needs. Finally, marketing communication—whether a sales presentation, advertisement, or sales promotion technique—attempts to produce action in the form of a purchase.

In personal selling, the sales process typically follows a sequence of activities:

1. Prospecting and qualifying
2. Approach
3. Presentation
4. Demonstration
5. Handling objections
6. Closing
7. Follow-up

These steps in the selling process can and should be aligned with the AIDA concept to be in sync with the consumer's decision process (see Exhibit 18.2). Once a sales prospect has been qualified, an attempt is made to secure his or her attention. The presentation and demonstration steps are designed to generate interest and desire. Successful handling of buyer objections should prompt further desire. Action occurs at the close of the sale.

Salespeople modify the steps in the sales process to match their customers' buying processes. A consumer who eagerly looks forward to the local baseball team's new season each year needs no presentation except for details about scheduled games, special events, and pricing. But the same consumer might expect to test drive new cars and receive a demonstration from an auto dealer when looking for a new car, or might appreciate a presentation that compares different models when evaluating the purchase of a new television.

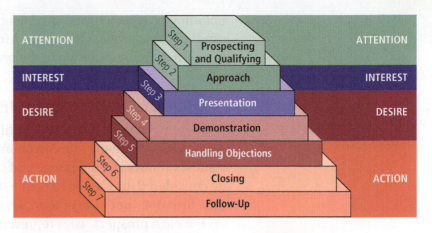

EXHIBIT
18.2

The AIDA Concept
and the Personal
Selling Process

### 18-3b
## CLOSING EXAMPLE

Brittany is excited to share the AIDA concept with her team and encourage them to be more creative as they utilize the sales process to create attention, interest, desire, and action among prospective customers. For example, as the representatives are qualifying leads and planning their approach, what information or details about positions would best stimulate the attention of these prospects? During the presentation about possible career opportunities, which details could heighten a prospect's interest? How could the sales representative demonstrate the opportunity in a tangible way to create desire, as well as manage any resistance the prospect might have about the position? What type of closing methods would be most successful in creating action? Lastly, how can representatives be more intentional in following up with clients to gauge their satisfaction and continue to develop a relationship? If Brittany can successfully hone these skills among her team members, she believes they will achieve their sales goals.

# 18-4    THE SALES PROCESS

## OPENING EXAMPLE

Derek Hernandez is a field sales representative with Sherwin-Williams and works from a branch retail store location in a city of about 200,000 people. He typically begins his morning at the store to pick-up orders and check-in with colleagues, then spends most of the day making calls with customers–facility managers, paint contractors, and other business accounts who have needs for paint and related supplies. Sherwin-Williams invests heavily in technology and has equipped their sales team with tablets and smart phones, which enable them to be more efficient and consistently reach monthly sales quotas. How does Derek utilize the sales process and why is it important to follow a sequential and deliberate process as a representative?

**LO
18.4** Summarize the seven steps of the sales process.

### 18-4a
## LEARNING IT: THE SALES PROCESS

Professional sales representatives utilize a sequential process designed to create attention, interest, desire, and action by the prospect. The process can be flexible to accommodate different situations but typically includes seven steps, including prospecting and qualifying, approach, presentation, demonstration, handling objections, closing, and follow-up. The following sections provide greater details for each step in the process.

## PROSPECTING AND QUALIFYING

**prospecting** the process of identifying potential customers

**Prospecting** is the process of identifying potential customers. Leads for prospects come from many sources: online, trade show exhibits, previous customers, friends, vendors and suppliers, and social and professional contacts. Prospects are considered the life-blood of sales representatives since no sales can be made if the firm does not have potential customers.

**qualifying** determining whether the prospect meets certain criteria for making a purchase

For each prospect, sales representatives must attempt to qualify whether or not the prospect is a suitable potential customer. **Qualifying** involves determining that the prospect meets certain criteria using the acronym NAME.

- Do prospects possess the appropriate **N**eed for the product?
- Do prospects have the **A**uthority to make the purchase decision?
- Do prospects have the **M**onetary resources to make the purchase?
- Are prospects **E**ligible to purchase?

Even though an employee in a firm might like your products, he or she might not be authorized or eligible to make the purchase, or have the financial means to purchase the product. This is why qualifying is such an important step in the sales process.

As a sales representative with Sherwin-Williams, Derek Hernandez uses a proprietary customer relationship management system to keep track of prospects and customers and monitor his progress toward goals. The company routinely adds prospect names to the database and Derek sets aside time each week to review new leads and gather information about them. Once a lead is qualified, Derek is ready to invest more time to pursue the business opportunity.

## APPROACH

**approach** the initial contact with the prospective customer

Once sales representatives have identified a qualified prospect, the next step involves gathering relevant information and planning an **approach**—the initial contact with the prospective customer. Before contacting the customer, it's important to gather information to develop an understanding of his or her business, current suppliers, and other pertinent details.

**precall planning** the process of conducting research and gathering information before a sales call

The process of conducting research and gathering information is known as **precall planning** and the information obtained is utilized to tailor the approach and presentation to the prospective customer's needs and situation. Derek Hernandez with Sherwin-Williams finds it easy to obtain information as part of his precall planning process. He may use the Internet to find the company's website. However, many of Sherwin William's customers are small, independent businesses who often do not have their own website. In those cases, Derek checks LinkedIn to obtain information about key decision makers, or views sites such

Dean Drobot/Shutterstock.com

The research conducted during precall planning can help sales reps understand the needs of key decision makers, making it more likely they'll address these needs and gain a sale. While it can be a time-consuming step, it's critical to the sales process—especially in competitive industries.

as Yelp to read reviews. He might also talk with other customers or those in the industry who may know the business or prospect to obtain greater insight. Derek strives to answer the following questions:

- Who am I contacting and what are their responsibilities within the company?
- What is their knowledge level? How much information do they already have about my products, services, or competition?
- What are their needs and objectives? Do they appreciate detailed technical information or prefer more general information?
- What type of information is most important to them and what are the issues that are driving the purchase? Are they looking to save time? Save money? Something else?

Derek may not be able to gather information about all of these areas, but if he can obtain more insight about the prospect prior to contacting them, he's likely to be more successful in getting their attention and establishing rapport.

## PRESENTATION

Next in the process is the **presentation**- where sales representatives convey the marketing message to the potential customer. During the presentation, sellers typically connect a buyer's needs to the benefits of the product. They describe the product's major features, point out its strengths, and for additional support may mention how other customers have experienced success with the product. One popular form of presentation is a "features–benefits" framework, where sellers talk about the good or service in terms meaningful to the buyer.

**presentation** describing a product's benefits and relating them to the customer's problems or needs

Sherwin-Williams sales representatives, such as Derek, customize their presentation according to the customer's situation. For example, Sherwin-Williams has developed coating products tailored to healthcare settings. These coating products are fast-drying and low-odor, which are important features to these clients. Hospitals, nursing homes, and physician offices are constantly in use and facility managers wish to minimize downtime and disruption. If Derek is meeting with a hospital facility manager, he can review product brochures, share customer testimonials, and discuss why the product line is best suited to the client's situation and needs.

## DEMONSTRATION

**demonstration** when the buyer has the opportunity to try out or otherwise see how a product works before purchasing

One of the most important advantages of personal selling is the opportunity to demonstrate a product. During a **demonstration**, the buyer gets a chance to try the product or physically see how it works. A demonstration might involve a test drive of the latest hybrid car or an in-store cooking class using pots and pans that are for sale.

A tangible product such as paint, brushes, and other paint-related products are easily demonstrated by Sherwin-Williams representatives. Derek enjoys the opportunity to allow prospective buyers to use the product on a sample wall or test area so they can visualize how the product looks, smells, and covers the surface area. If Derek is meeting with a facility manager whose company maintains their own staff of painters, the paint contractors may participate in the discussion as well so they can ask questions, express their concerns, and use the product prior to purchase.

## HANDLING OBJECTIONS

**objections** expressions of resistance by the prospect

Potential customers often have legitimate questions and concerns about a good or service they are considering. **Objections** are expressions of resistance by the prospect, and it is reasonable to expect them. Objections might appear in the form of stalling or indecisiveness. "Let me call you back," your prospect might say, or "I just don't know about this." Or your buyer might focus on something negative, such as high price.

Sales representatives should address objections without being aggressive or rude. Objections should be welcomed and treated as an opportunity to reassure the buyer about features, durability, availability, and the like.

When Derek was new to his position as sales representative with Sherwin-Williams, he was somewhat afraid of objections. After being in the field for several years, he knows to expect a common set of objectives and he's prepared to respond. Over the years, he and other sales representatives at Sherwin-Williams have developed their top 10 objection list and give each other tips on how best to handle each one. Derek knows that customers who give objections are demonstrating interest in the product but need to be reassured that the product truly meets their needs. He also understands that they are business professionals and must justify their purchase decision. He looks forward to this stage in the process as it's one step closer to securing the business and getting an order for products.

## CLOSING

The moment of truth in selling is the **closing**- the point at which the salesperson asks the prospect for an order. If a presentation has been effective and the sales representative has handled all objections, a closing would be the natural conclusion to the meeting. But sellers may still find it difficult to close the sale. Closing does not have to be thought of in terms of a "hard sell." Instead, customers can be asked, "Would you like to give this a try?" or "Do I have your approval to proceed?"

**closing** the point at which the salesperson asks the prospect for an order

Other methods of closing Derek might use include the following:

1. Addressing the prospect's major concern about a purchase and then offering a convincing argument. *"If I can show you how our new fast-drying paint product will reduce the facility downtime by 40%, would you be willing to give it a try for this project?"*

2. Posing choices for the prospect in which either alternative represents a sale. *"Would you prefer to order the paint and primer combination or purchase the items separately?"*

3. Advising the buyer that a product is about to be discontinued or will go up in price soon (but be completely honest about this—you don't want a customer to learn later that this was not true).

4. Remaining silent so the buyer can make a decision on his or her own.

5. Offering an extra inducement designed to motivate a favorable buyer response, such as a quantity discount, an extended service contract, or a low-interest payment plan.

Even if the meeting or phone call ends without a sale, the effort is not over. Sales representatives can follow-up by e-mail or send a written note to keep communication open, letting the buyer know the seller is ready and waiting to be of service.

## FOLLOW-UP

The word *close* can be misleading because the point at which the prospect accepts the seller's offer is where much of the real work of selling begins. It is not enough to close the sale and move on. Relationship selling involves reinforcing the purchase decision and ensuring the company delivers the highest-quality goods and services. Salespeople must also ensure that customer service needs are met and that satisfaction results from all of a customer's dealings with the supplier firm. Otherwise, some other supplier may get the next order.

Follow-up activities are key for account representatives like Derek at Sherwin-Williams. Most customer orders are fulfilled at the local branch and delivered to the job site. This provides an opportunity to ensure the correct products were delivered as ordered. Derek often contacts his buyers by phone or e-mail to see if the customer is experiencing any issues. If there are problems with paint coverage or technical issues such as peeling, Derek or others at Sherwin-Williams can assist the customer and work to correct any problems. Derek hopes to provide a level of service where customers will continue to use Sherwin-Williams products and works hard to create loyal customers.

## 18-4b
## CLOSING EXAMPLE

The seven-step sales process is alive and well for representatives like Derek Hernandez at Sherwin-Williams. The representatives receive training, encouragement, and appropriate tools to professionally meet buyer's needs from prospecting and qualifying to closing and follow-up.

# 18-5    SALES MANAGEMENT FUNCTIONS

**LO 18.5** Describe the seven key functions of a sales manager.

## OPENING EXAMPLE

Stacey Williams is a district manager with Federated Insurance and currently manages a sales team of eight representatives in the southeastern district. She often participates in job fairs at local colleges and tries to stay involved with recruitment activities so she can ensure coverage in her markets. She enjoys her position as a district manager but sometimes feels overwhelmed since the job requires so many different functions. What would happen if Stacey decided to ignore some of these functions?

## 18-5a
## LEARNING IT: SALES MANAGEMENT FUNCTIONS

The overall direction and control of personal selling efforts are in the hands of a firm's sales managers. In a typical geographic sales structure, a district or divisional sales manager might report to a regional manager. This manager in turn reports to a national sales manager or vice president of sales. Exhibit 18.3 provides an example organizational chart for a company that divides its sales force by region.

Currently, there are more than 365,000 sales managers in the United States.[9] The sales manager's job requires a unique blend of administrative and sales skills, depending on their level in the sales hierarchy. Sales skills are particularly important for first-level sales managers, because they are involved daily in the continuing process of training and directly leading the sales force. But as people rise in the sales management hierarchy, they require more managerial skills and fewer sales skills to perform well.

**EXHIBIT 18.3**    **Example of Sales Organizational Chart**

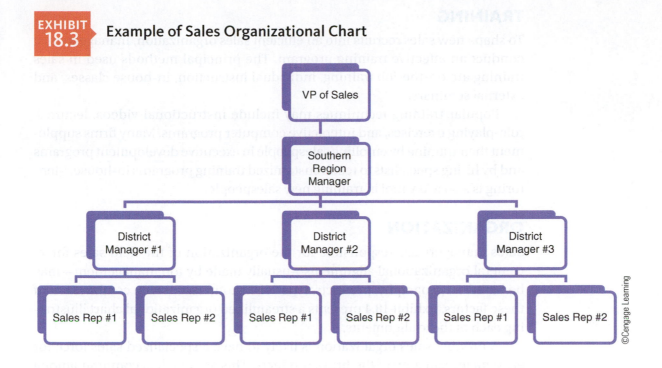

©Cengage Learning

The sales manager performs seven basic managerial functions:

1. Recruitment and selection
2. Training
3. Organization
4. Supervision
5. Motivation
6. Compensation
7. Evaluation and control

## RECRUITMENT AND SELECTION

Recruiting and selecting successful salespeople are among the sales manager's greatest challenges. After all, these workers will collectively determine how successful the sales manager is and are directly responsible for achieving sales goals. New salespeople might be recruited from colleges, trade schools, the military, other companies, and even the firm's current nonsales staff. Careful selection of salespeople is important for two reasons. First, a company invests a substantial amount of time and money in the selection process. Second, hiring mistakes can damage relationships with customers and are costly to correct.

Many companies offer screening tests such as Gallup's Analytics-Based Hiring program, which can be utilized to identify potential high performing candidates who possess the right set of qualities—personality, drive, and determination—to successfully contribute to the firm.

## TRAINING

To shape new sales recruits into an efficient sales organization, managers must conduct an effective training program. The principal methods used in sales training are on-the-job training, individual instruction, in-house classes, and external seminars.

Popular training techniques may include instructional videos, lectures, role-playing exercises, and interactive computer programs. Many firms supplement their training by enrolling salespeople in executive development programs and by hiring specialists to teach customized training programs in-house. Mentoring is also a key tool in training new salespeople.

## ORGANIZATION

Sales managers are responsible for the organization of the field sales force. General organizational alignments—usually made by top management—may be based on geography, products, types of customers, or some combination of these factors. Exhibit 18.4 presents a streamlined organizational chart illustrating each of these alignments.

A product sales organization is likely to have a specialized sales force for each major category of the firm's products. This approach is common among B2B companies that market large numbers of highly technical, complex products sold through different channels.

Firms that market similar products throughout large territories often use geographic specialization. Multinational corporations may have different sales divisions on different continents and in different countries. A geographic organization may also be combined with one of the other organizational methods.

The individual sales manager also must organize the sales territories within his or her area of responsibility. Factors such as sales potential, strengths and weaknesses of available personnel, and workloads are often considered in territory allocation decisions.

**EXHIBIT 18.4**  **Basic Approaches to Organizing the Sales Force**

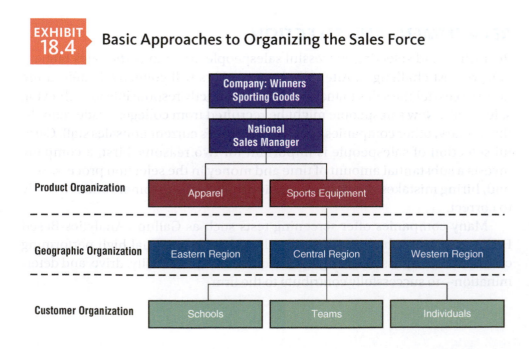

## SUPERVISION

Sales managers have differing opinions about the optimal level of supervision for the sales force. A concept known as **span of control** helps provide some general guidelines. Span of control refers to the number of sales representatives who report to first-level sales managers. The most effective span of control is affected by factors such as complexity of work activities, ability of the individual sales manager, degree of interdependence among individual salespeople, and the extent of training each salesperson receives. A 6-to-1 ratio has been suggested as the optimal span of control for first-level sales managers supervising technical or industrial salespeople. In contrast, a 10-to-1 ratio is recommended if sales representatives are calling on wholesale and retail accounts.

**span of control** the number of sales representatives who report to first-level sales managers

## MOTIVATION

What motivates salespeople to perform their best? The sales manager is responsible for finding the answer to this question. The sales process involves problem solving, which sometimes includes frustration—particularly when a sale is delayed or falls through. Information sharing, recognition, bonuses, incentives, and benefits can all be used to help defray frustration and motivate a sales staff. Creating a positive, motivating environment doesn't necessarily mean instituting complex or expensive incentive programs. Monetary reward is often considered king. But sometimes simple recognition—a thank-you, a dinner, a year-end award—can go a long way. It is important for the sales manager to figure out what types of incentives will be most effective with his or her particular group of employees.

## COMPENSATION

Money is an important part of any person's job, and the salesperson is no exception. Sales compensation can be based on a commission, a straight salary, or a combination of both. Bonuses based on end-of-year results are another popular form of compensation. The increasing popularity of team selling has also forced companies to set up reward programs to recognize performance of business units and teams. Today, about 25% of firms reward business-unit performance.

A **commission** is a payment tied directly to the sales or profits a salesperson achieves. For example, a salesperson might receive a 5% commission on all sales. But while commissions reinforce selling incentives, they may cause some sales force members to overlook nonselling activities such as completing sales reports, delivering promotion materials, and servicing existing accounts. In addition, salespeople who operate entirely on commission may become too aggressive in their approach to potential customers, which could backfire.

**commission** a payment tied directly to the sales or profits a salesperson achieves

A **salary** is a fixed payment made periodically to an employee. A straight salary plan gives management more control over how sales personnel allocate their efforts, but it may reduce the incentive to find new markets and land new accounts.

**salary** a fixed payment made periodically to an employee

## EVALUATION AND CONTROL

Perhaps the most difficult tasks required of sales managers are evaluation and control. Sales managers are responsible for setting standards and choosing the best methods for measuring sales performance. Sales volume, profitability, and changes in market share are the usual means of evaluating sales effectiveness. They typically involve the use of **sales quotas**- specified sales or profit targets that

**sales quotas** specified sales or profit targets that the firm expects salespeople to achieve

the firm expects salespeople to achieve. A particular sales representative might be expected to generate sales of $2.25 million in his or her territory during a given year. In many cases, the quota is tied to the compensation system. Technology has greatly improved the ability of sales managers to monitor the effectiveness of their sales staffs. In today's marketing environment, other measures, such as customer satisfaction, profit contribution, share of product–category sales, and customer retention, also come into play.

## 18-5b
## ETHICAL AND LEGAL ISSUES IN SALES

Today's experienced, highly professional salespeople know long-term success requires a strong code of ethics. They also know a single breach of ethics could have a devastating effect on their careers. A difficult economy or highly competitive environment may tempt some salespeople—particularly those new to the business—to behave in ways they might later regret. Companies must be sure to create and enforce corporate cultures that reduce the opportunity to engage in unethical behavior and encourage appropriate, professional behavior. At a minimum, today's companies should have a written code of conduct, foster open communication, and ensure all employees are upholding the company values and leading by example.

## 18-5c
## CLOSING EXAMPLE

At Federated Insurance, district managers like Stacey Williams perform many of the seven functions identified in this section. As previously discussed, Stacey attends college job fairs and, if she meets someone whom she believes is a good fit for her team, she schedules a 30-minute personal interview. If the candidate meets the company's criteria, Stacey will refer the candidate to be screened using an objective sales profile test. If the screening tool indicates the candidate has the requisite characteristics, they are moved forward and additional interviews and background checks are performed. It's an extensive process but Stacey believes this is key to securing candidates who will be successful on the job.

Once hired, candidates are placed at the home office and receive a one-year training program that includes both product and sales training. However, sometimes candidates are needed in the field and may be moved to field positions before the one-year training program is complete. When this occurs, Stacey spends more one-on-one time providing mentoring to the new representative.

In Stacey's district, account representatives are organized by geographic territory and exclusively work within their defined areas. They are free to contact a wide variety of customer types across different industries and size of accounts.

Stacey's team includes eight sales representatives with varying levels of experience, which is slightly higher than recommended. However, since some representatives have been working with Federated Insurance for a longer period of time, they do not require as much oversight as less senior representatives.

To motivate her team, Stacey utilizes a variety of techniques such as gift cards, monthly recognition lunches, and inspiring e-mail messages. Account representatives are paid a base salary plus commission. Sales is performance driven and those who perform well typically have greater opportunities to advance within the company. Stacey enjoys the time to review performance and tries to address any performance issues as directly as possible. Federated Insurance also uses a database system so Stacey can track her reps and see whether or not they're on track to reach their quotas.

# 18-6 SALES PROMOTION

## OPENING EXAMPLE

Paisley Lane Soaps is a family-owned natural products manufacturer who is starting to establish distribution accounts with grocery stores. The company is considering offering both consumer-oriented and trade-oriented sales promotions to increase the number of units sold. What methods might be most successful for the firm and how should they spend their limited promotional dollars?

**LO 18.6** Summarize eight types of sales promotion.

### 18-6a

## LEARNING IT: SALES PROMOTION

**Sales promotion** includes marketing activities other than personal selling, advertising, and publicity designed to enhance consumer purchasing and dealer effectiveness. Sales promotion techniques were originally intended as short-term incentives aimed at encouraging a purchase. Today, however, marketers recognize sales promotion as an integral part of the overall marketing plan, and the focus has shifted from short-term goals to long-term objectives of building brand equity, maintaining continuing purchases, and establishing loyalty. For example, a frequent-flyer program enables an airline to build a base of loyal customers and a frequent-stay program allows a hotel chain to attract regular guests.

Both retailers and manufacturers use sales promotions to offer consumers extra incentives to buy. These promotions are likely to emphasize price advantages, giveaways, or special offerings. The general objectives of sales promotion are to speed up the sales process and increase sales volume.

Sales promotions often produce their best results when combined with other marketing activities. Ads create awareness, while sales promotions lead to trial or purchase. After a presentation, a salesperson may offer a potential customer a discount coupon for the good or service. Promotions encourage immediate action because they impose limited time frames. Discount coupons and rebates usually have expiration dates. In addition, sales promotions produce measurable results, making it relatively easy for marketers to evaluate their effectiveness. If more people buy shoes during a buy-one-pair-get-one-free promotion at a shoe store, its owners know the promotion was successful.

It is important to understand what sales promotions can and cannot do. They can encourage interest in both new and mature products, encourage

**sales promotion** marketing activities other than personal selling, advertising, and publicity designed to enhance consumer purchasing and dealer effectiveness

**EXHIBIT 18.5**    Forms of Consumer-Oriented Sales Promotion

**Consumer-Oriented Sales Promotions**

| Forms of Sales Promotion | Description | Examples |
|---|---|---|
| **Coupons** | Consumer is offered discounts on the purchase price of goods and services and redeem coupons at retail outlets. | Philadelphia Cream Cheese distributing coupons by mail, magazine, newspaper, package insert, or via mobile phone. |
| **Rebates** | Consumers are offered cash back for sending in proof of purchase such as the receipt or Universal Product Code (UPC) from the product. | LG offering a $100 rebate when a buyer provides proof of purchase for a new LG television. |
| **Sampling** | Free distribution of a product in an attempt to obtain future sales. | Costco offering free samples to customers of various food items in the store. |
| **Contests and Sweepstakes** | Contests may require entrants to complete a task—such as uploading a picture—while anyone can enter a sweepstakes with an opportunity to win the advertised prize. | HGTV sponsoring a Dream Home Giveaway where viewers can register for a chance to win a luxury home. |
| **Specialty Advertising** | An advertiser's message or logo is placed on useful articles that are distributed to target consumers. | Pepsi giving away t-shirts with their logo at a sporting event. |

**coupons** when consumer is offered discounts on the purchase price of goods and services at retail outlets

**rebates** when the consumer is offered cash back for sending in proof of purchase

**sampling** free distribution of a product in an attempt to obtain future sales

**contests** when entrants must complete a specific task to be eligible to win a prize

**sweepstakes** when any consumer can enter to be eligible for a prize

**specialty advertising** when an advertiser's message or logo is placed on useful articles that are distributed to target consumers

**consumer-oriented sales promotions** encourage repurchases by rewarding current users, boosting sales of complementary products, and increasing impulse purchases

**trade promotion** sales promotion that appeals to distribution intermediaries rather than final consumers

trial and repeat purchases, increase usage rates, neutralize competition, and reinforce advertising and personal selling efforts. On the other hand, sales promotions cannot overcome poor brand images, product deficiencies, or poor training for salespeople. While sales promotions increase volume in the short term, they may not lead to sales and profit growth in the long run if those promotions are removed.

Sales promotion techniques are classified as consumer-oriented or trade-oriented. **Consumer-oriented sales promotions** encourage repurchases by rewarding current users, boosting sales of complementary products, and increasing impulse purchases. These promotions also attract consumer attention in the midst of advertising clutter. Exhibit 18.5 summarizes the various forms of consumer promotion.

**Trade promotion** is sales promotion that appeals to distribution intermediaries rather than final consumers. Marketers use trade promotions to encourage resellers to stock new products, continue to carry existing ones, and promote both effectively to consumers. The typical firm spends about half of its promotional budget on trade promotion—as much money as it spends on advertising and consumer-oriented sales promotions combined. Successful trade promotions offer financial incentives for reseller performance. Exhibit 18.6 summarizes the various forms of trade promotion.

EXHIBIT 18.6 **Forms of Trade-Oriented Promotion**

| Trade-Oriented Promotions | | |
| --- | --- | --- |
| **Forms of Sales Promotion** | **Description** | **Examples** |
| **Trade Allowances** | Financial incentive offered to wholesalers and retailers that purchase or promote specific products. | A beverage company offering a retailer one free case of product for every 10 ordered. |
| **Point-of-Purchase Advertising** | Display or other promotion placed near the site of the actual buying decision. | A prominently placed cardboard display for Vitamin Water at the end of the aisle in the grocery store. |
| **Trade Shows** | Product exhibitions organized by industry trade associations to showcase goods and services. | Caterpillar participating in the MinExpo trade fair in order to interact with firms in the mining industry. |
| **Dealer Incentives, Contests, and Training Programs** | Manufacturers may offer incentive programs and contests to reward retailers and their salespeople who increase sales and promote specific products. | A clothing manufacturer running a sales contest among associates at retail stores who carry their goods. |

**trade allowances** financial incentives offered to wholesalers and retailers that purchase or promote specific products

**point-of-purchase advertising** display or other promotion placed near the site of the actual buying decision

**trade shows** product exhibitions organized by industry trade associations to showcase goods and services

## 18-6b
## CLOSING EXAMPLE

Paisley Lane Soaps offers lotions, lip balm, bar soap, and shampoos made with all natural ingredients and appealing to consumers wishing to eliminate the use of chemicals in their personal care products. The company might benefit most from coupons and rebates offered to consumers who purchase their products. In addition, they might try limited sampling within stores to encourage customers to try the product. They could also reward retailers and distributors for promoting their products by offering trade allowances and free point-of-purchase displays that will gain attention and drive sales.

# 18-7  EFFECTIVE PROMOTIONAL TACTICS

### OPENING EXAMPLE

Hormel Foods strives to innovate and deliver products that meet consumer needs. In the year 2000, the company set a goal to reach $1 billion in sales from new products by 2009. The company met the goal and now is poised to generate $3 billion in sales from new products this year.[10] As Hormel continually seeks

**LO 18.7** Given an example of market conditions and promotional objectives, identify the most effective promotional tactic.

to launch new products into both consumer and business markets, they must simultaneously consider how to best leverage their promotional mix to be most effective and efficient.

## 18-7a

## LEARNING IT: EFFECTIVE PROMOTIONAL TACTICS

Marketers have a variety of tools and techniques available to promote their products. Most likely, they will utilize a combination of elements, which work cohesively to gain consumer awareness and stimulate demand. As discussed in this chapter, certain circumstances favor personal selling over advertising; and if personal selling is selected, marketers can use one or more sales channels to effectively distribute their products. Sales promotion techniques targeted to the consumer or trade are also useful to achieve certain sales objectives and increase revenues. The choice of which elements to use depends upon the situation, marketing objectives, and budget.

If Hormel had a new meat product they wanted to sell to hotels, they would consider this a specific business market with a limited number of customers. It's also a short channel, since Hormel sells directly to customers using sales reps. In this case, personal selling would be the highest priority component of their promotional mix, perhaps coupled with trade promotion. Advertising is not favored in this situation and consumer-oriented sales promotion does not apply here.

Alternatively, if Hormel is introducing a new high-protein snack to be sold in grocery stores nationwide, they would likely stimulate consumer demand by utilizing advertising and consumer-oriented sales promotions such as coupons or in-store sampling. The number of customers is quite large and geographically dispersed. The price is relatively low, and since the item is available in grocery stores, the channel is longer. To encourage resellers to carry the product, they might also utilize personal selling and trade promotion.

Hormel also targets the healthcare market—hospitals, nursing homes, and intermediate care facilities. Suppose it's introducing a new meat entree product that is low in salt, sugar, and fat but contains a higher percentage of protein per ounce. The product is likely more expensive than comparable items and sales representatives would be utilized to present the features and benefits of this new product, including why it's better than competing brands. Advertising would not be effective in this context but Hormel might incorporate trade promotions, such as providing a discount to hospitals that purchase 10 or more pounds of product.

## 18-8 LEARN IT TODAY . . . USE IT TOMORROW

As Hormel continues to innovate, it must make decisions about marketing communications and promotional mix elements that are most effective. Help Hormel determine which promotional tactics to implement.

It's time to get hands-on and apply what you've learned. **See MindTap for an activity related to Hormel's promotional activities**.

# Chapter Summary

**LO 18.1 Contrast the factors that favor use of personal selling versus advertising.**

Both advertising and personal selling represent large expense categories for firms, so it's important to identify factors that may favor greater use of advertising or personal selling.

**LO 18.2 Describe the four sales channels.**

Personal selling occurs through several types of communication channels: over-the-counter selling, field selling, telemarketing, and inside selling.

**LO 18.3 Explain how each step in the sales process relates to the AIDA concept.**

The selling process includes a series of steps which can be aligned with the AIDA concept to be in sync with the consumer's decision process and enable the seller to achieve their sales objectives.

**LO 18.4 Summarize the seven steps of the sales process.**

Professional sales representatives utilize a sequential sales process that typically includes seven steps:

(1) prospecting and qualifying, (2) approach, (3) presentation, (4) demonstration, (5) handling objections, (6) closing, and (7) follow-up.

**LO 18.5 Describe the seven key functions of a sales manager.**

The sales manager performs seven basic managerial functions: (1) recruitment and selection, (2) training, (3) organization, (4) supervision, (5) motivation, (6) compensation, and (7) evaluation and control.

**LO 18.6 Summarize eight types of sales promotion.**

Sales promotion techniques are classified as consumer-oriented or trade-oriented and several forms for each technique are utilized by marketers.

**LO 18.7 Given an example of market conditions and promotional objectives, identify the most effective promotional tactic.**

Determining the most appropriate promotional technique involves analyzing the situation and selecting the option that best achieves the firm's goals in an efficient and cost-effective manner.

# Key Terms

personal selling 378
over-the-counter-selling 381
field selling 382
telemarketing 382
outbound telemarketing 382
inbound telemarketing 382
inside selling 383
prospecting 386
qualifying 386
approach 386
precall planning 386

presentation 387
demonstration 388
objections 388
closing 389
span of control 393
commission 393
salary 393
sales quotas 393
sales promotion 395
coupons 396
rebates 396

sampling 396
contests 396
sweepstakes 396
specialty advertising 396
consumer-oriented sales
   promotions 396
trade promotion 396
trade allowances 397
point-of-purchase
   advertising 397
trade shows 397

Joint life plan, Wakeel, SWOT DSA
price action specification

**APPENDIX** **A**

# DEVELOPING AN EFFECTIVE MARKETING PLAN

**A-1**

# CREATING A MARKETING PLAN

Writing a marketing plan is a key responsibility of a firm's marketers. But the plan must be based on an overall marketing strategy, formulated as discussed in Chapter 2. The basic components of a plan align with the planning process, which involves determining objectives, assessing the firm and the market, then formulating specific strategies and tactics (see Exhibit A.1).

A firm may use a number of tools in marketing planning, several of which are described in Chapter 2. These include business portfolio analysis using the BCG matrix (or another method), SWOT analysis, and study of Porter's Five Forces within its industry.

Once general strategies are determined, marketers begin to flesh out the details of the plan. These include identifying target markets and creating a

**EXHIBIT A.1** The Marketing Planning Process and Basic Components of a Marketing Plan

| | |
|---|---|
| **Executive Summary** | A short overview of the entire marketing plan which provides key information from the major sections of the plan |
| **Environmental & SWOT Analysis** | Details the current external and internal environmental factors affecting the business as well as the company's competitive and unique capabilities |
| **Marketing Objectives** | Details specific objectives to be achieved by the organization |
| **Marketing Strategies** | Longer-term courses of action to achieve objectives |
| **Marketing Tactics (Implementation)** | Shorter term actions to achieve marketing strategies |
| **Key Performance Indicators** | Quantifiable outcome measures to provide objective data |

**EXHIBIT A.2**     Planning Process for Each Area of the Marketing Mix (Product, Price, Place, and Promotion)

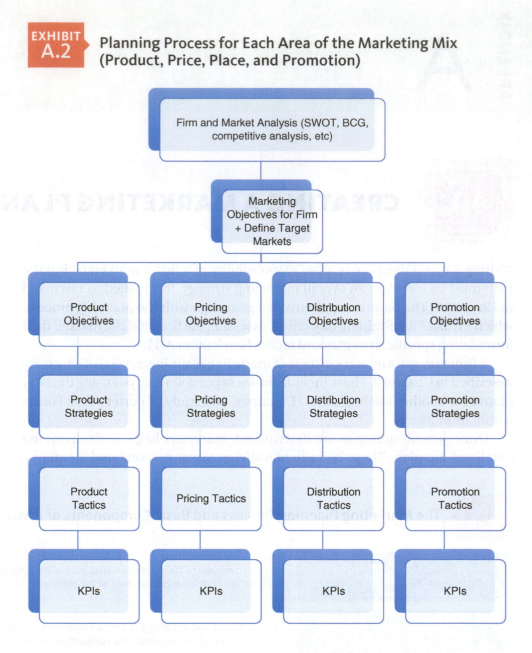

marketing mix to reach those customers. In order to create the optimal plan, the firm will typically use the organization's overall marketing objectives as a foundation for creating objectives, strategies, and tactics specific to each area of the marketing mix. Exhibit A.2 shows a more detailed look at the components of the marketing plan.

Putting it all together, the firm will utilize the analysis and strategies formulated during the planning process to create a written marketing plan. While the format of marketing plans varies from firm to firm, the actual outline for a plan will look similar to the one given in Exhibit A.3.

Keep in mind that a marketing plan should be created in conjunction with other elements of a firm's business plan. A marketing plan often draws from the business plan, restating parts of the executive summary, company description, and competitive analysis to give its readers an overall view of the firm.

**EXHIBIT A.3**    Marketing Plan Outline

1. Executive Summary
2. Company Description (*also called Company Analysis*)
3. Situation and Competitive Analysis (*also called Market Analysis*)
4. Company Objectives
5. Target Market Description
6. Product Strategy
7. Pricing Strategy
8. Distribution Strategy
9. Promotion Strategy
10. Budget, Schedule, and Monitoring

# A-2 SAMPLE MARKETING PLAN

The sample marketing plan for Blue Sky Clothing provides additional insight into what you should consider before crafting a plan of your own. Keep in mind that the plan for Blue Sky is a single example; no one format is used by all companies. Also, the Blue Sky plan has been somewhat condensed to make it easier to annotate and illustrate the most vital features. The important point to remember is that the marketing plan is a document designed to present concise, cohesive information about a company's marketing objectives to managers, lending institutions, and others involved in creating and carrying out the firm's overall business strategy.

## A-2a
## EXECUTIVE SUMMARY

This five-year marketing plan for Blue Sky Clothing was created by its two founders to secure additional funding for growth and to inform employees of the company's current status and direction. Although Blue Sky was launched only three years ago, the firm has experienced greater-than-anticipated demand for its products, and research has shown that the target market of sports-minded consumers and sports retailers would like to buy more casual clothing than Blue Sky currently offers. As a result, Blue Sky wants to extend its current product line as well as add new product lines. In addition, the firm plans to explore opportunities for online sales. The marketing environment has been very receptive to the firm's high-quality goods—casual clothing in trendy colors with logos and slogans that reflect the interests of outdoor enthusiasts around the country. Over the next five years, Blue Sky can increase its distribution, offer new products, and win new customers.

> The executive summary outlines the *who*, *what*, *where*, *when*, *how*, and *why* of the marketing plan. Blue Sky is only three years old and is successful enough that it now needs a formal marketing plan to obtain additional financing from a bank or private investors for expansion and the launch of new products.

## A-2b
## COMPANY ANALYSIS

Blue Sky Clothing was founded three years ago by entrepreneurs Lucy Neuman and Nick Russell. Neuman has an undergraduate degree in marketing and worked for several years in the retail clothing industry. Russell operated Go West!—an adventure business that arranged group trips to locations in Wyoming, Montana, and Idaho—which he sold to a partner. Neuman and Russell, who have been friends since college, decided to develop and market a line of clothing with a unique yet universal appeal to outdoor enthusiasts like themselves.

Reflecting the passion of its founders, the company's mission is to be a leading producer and marketer of personalized, casual clothing for consumers who love the outdoors. Blue Sky wants to inspire people to get outdoors more often and enjoy family and friends while doing so. In addition, Blue Sky strives to design programs for preserving the natural environment.

The company's original cotton T-shirts, baseball caps, and fleece jackets bear logos of different sports, such as kayaking, mountain climbing, bicycling, skating, surfing, and horseback riding. But every item shows off the company's slogan: "Go Play Outside." Blue Sky sells clothing for both men and women, in the hottest colors with the coolest names—sunrise pink, sunset red, twilight purple, desert rose, cactus green, ocean blue, mountaintop white, and river rock gray.

Already Blue Sky has developed core competencies in (1) offering a high-quality, branded product whose image is recognizable among consumers; (2) creating a sense of community among consumers who purchase the products; and (3) developing a reputation among retailers as a reliable manufacturer that delivers orders on schedule. By forming strong relationships with consumers, retailers, and suppliers of fabric and other goods and services, Blue Sky believes it can create a sustainable competitive advantage over its rivals.

Blue Sky attire is currently carried by small retail stores that specialize in outdoor clothing and gear. Most of these stores are concentrated in northern New England, California, the Northwest, and the South. The high quality, trendy colors, and unique message of the clothing have gained Blue Sky a following among consumers between ages 18 and 39. Sales have tripled in the last year alone, and Blue Sky is currently working to expand its manufacturing capabilities.

Blue Sky is also committed to giving back to the community by contributing to local conservation programs. Ultimately, the company would like to develop and fund its own environmental programs. This plan will outline how Blue Sky intends to introduce new products, expand its distribution, enter new markets, and give back to the community.

## A-2c
## SITUATION ANALYSIS

The marketing environment for Blue Sky represents overwhelming opportunities. It also contains some challenges the firm believes it can meet successfully. Exhibit A.4 illustrates a SWOT analysis of the company conducted by its marketers to highlight Blue Sky's strengths, weaknesses, opportunities, and threats.

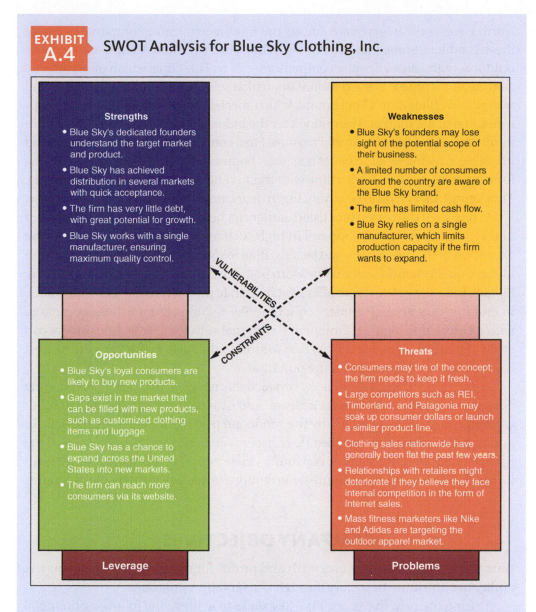

**EXHIBIT A.4** SWOT Analysis for Blue Sky Clothing, Inc.

**Strengths**
- Blue Sky's dedicated founders understand the target market and product.
- Blue Sky has achieved distribution in several markets with quick acceptance.
- The firm has very little debt, with great potential for growth.
- Blue Sky works with a single manufacturer, ensuring maximum quality control.

**Weaknesses**
- Blue Sky's founders may lose sight of the potential scope of their business.
- A limited number of consumers around the country are aware of the Blue Sky brand.
- The firm has limited cash flow.
- Blue Sky relies on a single manufacturer, which limits production capacity if the firm wants to expand.

VULNERABILITIES

CONSTRAINTS

**Opportunities**
- Blue Sky's loyal consumers are likely to buy new products.
- Gaps exist in the market that can be filled with new products, such as customized clothing items and luggage.
- Blue Sky has a chance to expand across the United States into new markets.
- The firm can reach more consumers via its website.

**Threats**
- Consumers may tire of the concept; the firm needs to keep it fresh.
- Large competitors such as REI, Timberland, and Patagonia may soak up consumer dollars or launch a similar product line.
- Clothing sales nationwide have generally been flat the past few years.
- Relationships with retailers might deteriorate if they believe they face internal competition in the form of Internet sales.
- Mass fitness marketers like Nike and Adidas are targeting the outdoor apparel market.

**Leverage**

**Problems**

The SWOT analysis presents a thumbnail sketch of the company's position in the marketplace. In just three years, Blue Sky has built some impressive strengths while looking forward to new opportunities. Its dedicated founders, the growing number of brand-loyal customers, and sound financial management place the company in a good position to grow. However, as Blue Sky considers expansion of its product line and entry into new markets, the firm will have to guard against marketing myopia (the failure to recognize the scope of its business) and quality slippage. As the company finalizes plans for new products and expanded Internet sales, its management will also have to guard against competitors who attempt to duplicate the products. However, building strong relationships with consumers, retailers, and suppliers should help thwart competitors.

## COMPETITORS IN THE OUTDOOR CLOTHING MARKET

The outdoor retail sales industry sells about $4 billion worth of goods annually, ranging from clothing to equipment. The outdoor apparel market has many entries. L.L. Bean, Dick's Sporting Goods, REI, Timberland, Bass Pro Shops, Cabela's, The

North Face, and Patagonia are among the most recognizable companies offering these products. Some mass fitness wear firms, like Nike and Adidas, are targeting outdoors enthusiasts. Smaller competitors such as Title Nine, which offers athletic clothing for women, Ragged Mountain, which sells fleece clothing for skiers and hikers, and Lululemon's Trail Bound, which specializes in hiking apparel, also capture some of the market. The outlook for the industry in general—and Blue Sky in particular—is positive for several reasons. First, consumers are participating in and investing in recreational activities near their homes. Second, consumers are looking for ways to enjoy their leisure time with friends and family without overspending. Third, consumers tend to be advancing in their careers and are able to spend more.

While all of the companies listed earlier can be considered competitors, most of them sell performance apparel in high-tech manufactured fabrics. With the exception of the fleece vests and jackets, Blue Sky's clothing is made strictly of the highest-quality cotton, so it may be worn both on the hiking trail and around town. Finally, Blue Sky products are offered at moderate prices, making them affordable in multiple quantities. For instance, a Blue Sky T-shirt sells for $15.99, compared with a competing high-performance T-shirt that sells for $29.99. Consumers can easily replace a set of shirts from one season to the next, picking up the newest colors, without agonizing over the purchase.

A survey conducted by Blue Sky revealed that a high percentage of responding consumers prefer to replace their casual and active wear more often than other clothing, so they are attracted by the moderate pricing of Blue Sky products. In addition, as the trend toward health-conscious activities and concerns about the natural environment continue, consumers increasingly relate to the Blue Sky philosophy as well as the firm's future contributions to socially responsible programs.

## A-2d
# COMPANY OBJECTIVES

> It is important to state a firm's objectives—what it aims to achieve—both financially and in terms of marketing activities.

Blue Sky's objectives include growth and profits for the company as well as the ability to contribute to society through conservation programs.

During the next five years, Blue Sky seeks to achieve the following financial and nonfinancial objectives:

### Financial Objectives

1. Obtain financing to expand manufacturing capabilities, increase distribution, and introduce two new product lines
2. Increase revenues by at least 50% each year
3. Donate at least $25,000 a year to conservation organizations

### Nonfinancial Objectives

4. Introduce two new product lines: customized logo clothing and lightweight luggage
5. Enter new geographic markets, including Southwest and Mid-Atlantic regions
6. Develop a successful Internet site, while maintaining strong relationships with retailers
7. Develop its own conservation program aimed at helping communities raise money to purchase open space

## A-2e
# THE TARGET MARKET

The target market for Blue Sky products is active consumers between ages 18 and 39—people who like hiking, rock climbing, bicycling, surfing, figure skating, in-line skating, horseback riding, snowboarding, skiing, kayaking, and other such activities. In short, they like to "Go Play Outside." They might not be experts at the sports they engage in, but they enjoy themselves outdoors.

These active consumers represent a demographic group of well-educated and successful individuals; they are single or married and raising families. Household incomes generally range between $80,000 and $150,000 annually. Despite their comfortable incomes, these consumers are price conscious and consistently seek value in their purchases. Regardless of their age (whether they fall at the upper or lower end of the target range), they lead active lifestyles. They are somewhat status oriented but not overly so. They like to be associated with high-quality products but are not willing to pay a premium price for a certain brand. Current Blue Sky customers tend to live in northern New England, the South, California, and the Northwest. However, one future goal is to target consumers in the Mid-Atlantic states and Southwest as well.

## A-2f
# THE MARKETING MIX

The following discussion outlines some of the details of the proposed marketing mix for Blue Sky products.

## PRODUCT STRATEGY

Blue Sky currently offers a line of high-quality outdoor apparel items, including cotton T-shirts, caps, and fleece vests and jackets. All bear the company logo and slogan, "Go Play Outside." The firm has researched the most popular colors for its items and given them names that consumers enjoy—sunset red, sunrise pink, cactus green, desert rose, and river rock gray, among others. Over the next five years, Blue Sky plans to expand the product line to include customized clothing items. Customers may select a logo that represents their sport—say, rock climbing. Then they can add a slogan to match the logo, such as "Get Over It." A cap with a bicyclist might bear the slogan, "Take a Ride." At the beginning, there would be ten new logos and five new slogans; more would be added later. Eventually, some slogans and logos would be retired and new ones introduced. This strategy will keep the concept fresh and prevent it from becoming diluted with too many variations.

The second way in which Blue Sky plans to expand its product line is to offer lightweight luggage—two sizes of duffel bags, two sizes of tote bags, and a daypack. These items would also come in trendy and basic colors, with a choice of logos and slogans. In addition, every product would bear the Blue Sky logo.

## PRICING STRATEGY

As discussed earlier in this plan, Blue Sky products are priced with the competition in mind. The firm is not concerned with setting high prices to signal luxury or prestige, nor is it attempting to achieve the goals of offsetting low prices by

---

*Blue Sky has identified its customers as active people between ages 18 and 39. However, that doesn't mean someone who is older or prefers to read about the outdoors isn't a potential customer as well. By pinpointing where existing customers live, Blue Sky can plan for growth into new outlets.*

*The strongest part of the marketing mix for Blue Sky involves sales promotions, public relations, and non-traditional marketing strategies, including attending outdoor events and organizing activities such as day hikes and bike rides.*

selling large quantities of products. Instead, value pricing is practiced so customers feel comfortable purchasing new clothing to replace the old, even if it is just because they like the new colors. The pricing strategy also makes Blue Sky products good gifts—for birthdays, graduations, or "just because." The customized clothing will sell for $2 to $4 more than the regular Blue Sky logo clothing. The luggage will be priced competitively.

## DISTRIBUTION STRATEGY

Currently, Blue Sky is marketed through regional and local specialty shops scattered along the California coast, into the Northwest, across the South, and in northern New England. So far, Blue Sky has not been distributed through national sporting goods and apparel chains. Climate and season tend to dictate the sales at specialty shops, which sell more T-shirts and caps during warm weather and more fleece vests and jackets during colder months. Blue Sky obtains much of its information about overall industry trends in different geographic areas and at different types of retail outlets from its trade organization, Outdoor Industry Association.

Over the next three years, Blue Sky seeks to expand distribution to retail specialty shops throughout the nation, focusing next on the Southwest and Mid-Atlantic regions. The firm has not yet determined whether it would be beneficial to sell through a major national chain, as these outlets could be considered competitors.

In addition, Blue Sky plans to expand online sales by offering the customized product line via the Internet only, thus distinguishing between Internet offerings and specialty shop offerings. Eventually, the firm may be able to place Internet kiosks at some of the more profitable store outlets so consumers could order customized products from the stores. Regardless of its expansion plans, Blue Sky fully intends to monitor and maintain strong relationships with distribution channel members.

## PROMOTION STRATEGY

Blue Sky communicates with consumers and retailers about its products in various ways. Information about Blue Sky—the company as well as its products—is available via the Internet, through social media and direct mailings, and in person. The firm's promotional efforts also seek to differentiate its products from those of its competitors.

The company relies on personal contact with retailers to establish the products in their stores. This contact, whether in person or by phone, helps convey the Blue Sky message, demonstrate the products' unique qualities, and build relationships. Blue Sky sales representatives visit each store two or three times a year and offer in-store training on product features for new retailers or for those who want a refresher session. As distribution expands, Blue Sky will adjust to meet greater demand by increasing sales staff to make sure its stores are visited more frequently.

Sales promotions and public relations currently make up the bulk of Blue Sky's promotional strategy. Blue Sky staff works with retailers to offer short-term sales promotions tied to events and contests that are communicated via social media sites such as Twitter and Facebook. In addition, Nick Russell is currently working with several trip outfitters to offer Blue Sky items on a promotional basis. Because Blue Sky also engages in cause marketing through its contribution to environmental programs, good public relations have followed.

Non-traditional marketing methods that require little cash and a lot of creativity also lend themselves perfectly to Blue Sky. Because Blue Sky is a small, flexible organization, the firm can easily implement ideas, such as distributing free water, stickers, and discount coupons at outdoor sporting events. During the next year, the company plans to engage in the following marketing efforts:

- Create a Blue Sky Tour, in which several employees take turns driving around the country to campgrounds to distribute promotional items, such as Blue Sky stickers and discount coupons.

- Attend canoe and kayak races, bicycling events, and rock-climbing competitions with the Blue Sky truck to distribute free water, stickers, and discount coupons for Blue Sky shirts or hats.

- Organize Blue Sky hikes departing from participating retailers.

- Hold a Blue Sky design contest on Facebook, selecting a winning slogan and logo to be added to the customized line.

## A-2g
# BUDGET, SCHEDULE, AND MONITORING

Though its history is short, Blue Sky has enjoyed a steady increase in sales since its introduction three years ago. Exhibit A.5 shows these three years, plus projected sales for the next three years, including the introduction of the two new product lines. Additional financial data are included in the overall business plan for the company.

> An actual plan will include more specific financial details, which will be folded into the overall business plan. For more information, see Appendix B, "Financial Analysis in Marketing." In addition, Blue Sky states that, at this stage, it does not have plans to exit the market by merging with another firm or making a public stock offering.

**EXHIBIT A.5** Annual Sales for Blue Sky Clothing 2015-2020

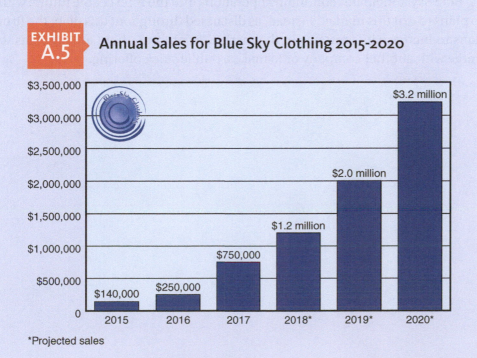

*Projected sales

**EXHIBIT A.6**   Timeline for First Three Years of Marketing Plan

**YEAR 1**

New outlets added: 20
Customized items: 5 slogans/10 logos
Luggage items: 0

**YEAR 2**

New outlets added: 50
Customized items: 10 slogans/10 logos
Luggage items: 2 (duffels and totes)

**YEAR 3**

New outlets added: 100
Customized items: 5 slogans/5 logos
Luggage items: 1 (backpack)

The timeline for expansion of outlets and introduction of the two new product lines is shown in Exhibit A.6. The implementation of each of these tasks will be monitored closely and evaluated for its performance.

Blue Sky anticipates continuing operations into the foreseeable future, with no plans to exit this market. Instead, as discussed throughout this plan, the firm plans to increase its presence in the market. At present, there are no plans to merge with another company or to make a public stock offering.

# APPENDIX B

# FINANCIAL ANALYSIS IN MARKETING

A number of principles from accounting and finance offer valuable tools to marketers. Understanding these concepts can improve the quality of marketing decisions and help marketers justify these decisions using quantitative data. In this appendix, we describe the major accounting and finance concepts that can help managers make informed marketing decisions.

## B-1 FINANCIAL STATEMENTS

Companies prepare a set of financial statements on a regular basis. Two of the most important financial statements are the income statement and balance sheet. The analogy of photography is often used to describe an **income statement**, because it presents an overall picture of a financial record of a company's revenues, expenses, and profits *over a period of time*, such as a month, quarter, or year. By contrast, the **balance sheet** is a *snapshot* of what a company owns (called assets) and what it owes (called liabilities) *at a point in time*, such as at the end of the month, quarter, or year. The difference between assets and liabilities is referred to as owners', partners', *or* shareholders' equity—the amount of funds the firm's owners have invested in its formation and continued operations.

Of the two financial statements, the income statement contains more marketing-related information. A sample income statement for Worthy Composites is shown in Exhibit B.1. Headquartered in Baltimore, Maryland, Worthy Composites is a B2B producer and marketer. The firm designs and manufactures various composite components for manufacturers of consumer, industrial, and government products. Total sales revenues for 2018 amounted to $675 million. Total expenses, including taxes, for the year were $583.1 million. The year 2018 proved profitable for Worthy Composites—the firm reported a profit, referred to as net income, of $91.9 million. While total revenue is a fairly straightforward number, several of the expenses shown on the income statement require additional explanation.

For any company that makes its own products (a manufacturer) or simply markets items produced by others (an importer, retailer, or wholesaler), the largest single expense usually is a category called *cost of goods sold*. This reflects the cost, to the firm, of the goods it markets to customers. In the case of Worthy Composites, the cost of goods sold represents the cost of raw materials and labor for manufacturing the composite panels.

**income statement** an overall picture of a financial record of a company's revenues, expenses, and profits *over a period of time*

**balance sheet** a *snapshot* of what a company owns (called assets) and what it owes (called liabilities) *at a point in time*

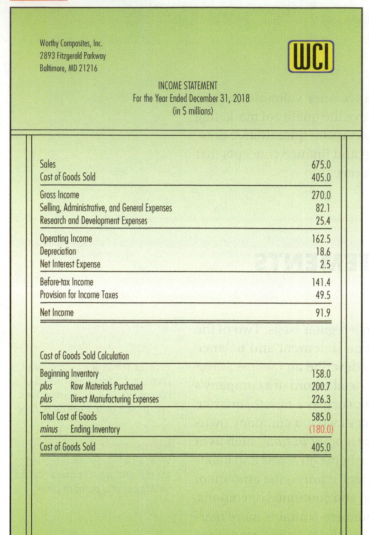

EXHIBIT B.1 **Worthy Composites 2018 Income Statement**

The income statement illustrates how cost of goods sold is calculated. The calculation uses the value of the firm's inventory at the beginning of 2017. Inventory is the value of raw materials, partially completed products, and finished products held by the firm at the end of some period—say, the end of the year. The cost of materials Worthy Composites purchased during the year and the direct cost of manufacturing the finished products are then added to the beginning inventory figure. The result is the cost of goods the firm has available for sale during the year. Once the firm's accountants subtract the value of inventory held at the end of 2018, they know the cost of goods sold. By simply subtracting cost of goods sold from total sales revenues generated during the year, they determine that Worthy achieved gross income of $270 million in 2018.

*Operating expenses* are another significant cost for most firms. This broad category includes marketing outlays such as sales compensation and expenses, advertising and other promotions, and the expenses involved in implementing marketing plans. Accountants typically combine these financial outlays into a single category with the label *Selling, Administrative, and General Expenses*. Other expense items included in the operating expenses section of the income statement are administrative salaries, utilities, and insurance.

Another significant expense for Worthy Composites is research and development (R&D). This category includes the cost of developing new products and modifying existing ones. Firms such as pharmaceutical, biotechnology, and computer companies spend significant amounts of money each year on R&D. Subtracting R&D, selling, administrative, and general expenses from the gross profit equals the firm's operating income. For 2018, Worthy had operating income of $162.5 million.

*Depreciation* represents the systematic reduction over time in the value of certain company assets, such as production machinery or office furniture. Depreciation is an unusual expense, because it does not involve an actual cash expense in the current period—as that cash was already spent when purchasing the assets. However, it does reflect the reality that equipment owned by the company is physically wearing out over time from use or from technological obsolescence. Also, charging a portion of the total cost of these long-lived items to each of the years in which they are used results in a more accurate determination of the total costs involved in the firm's operation each year.

*Net interest expense* is the difference between what a firm paid in interest on various loans and what it collected in interest on investments it might have made during the time period involved. Subtracting depreciation and net interest expense from the firm's operating profit reveals the firm's taxable income. Worthy had depreciation of $18.6 million and a net interest expense of $2.5 million for the year, so its 2018 taxable income was $141.4 million.

Profit-seeking firms pay federal, and sometimes state, income taxes calculated as a percentage of their taxable income. Worthy paid $49.5 million in taxes in 2018. Subtracting taxes from taxable income gives us the firm's *net income*, $91.9 million.

# B-2 PERFORMANCE RATIOS

Managers often compute various financial ratios to assess the performance of their firm. These ratios are calculated using data found on both the income statement and the balance sheet. Ratios are then compared with industry standards and with data from previous years. Several ratios are of particular interest to marketers.

A number of commonly used financial ratios focus on *profitability measures*. They are used to assess the firm's ability to generate revenues in excess of expenses and earn an adequate rate of return. Profitability measures include gross profit margin, net profit margin, and return on investment (or sales).

## B-2a
### GROSS PROFIT MARGIN

The gross profit margin equals the firm's gross profit divided by its sales revenues. In 2018, Worthy had a gross profit margin of:

$$\frac{\text{Gross profit}}{\text{Sales}} = \frac{\$270 \text{ million}}{\$675 \text{ million}} = 40\%$$

The gross profit margin is the percentage of each sales dollar that can be used to pay other expenses and meet the firm's profit objectives. Ideally, businesses would like to see gross profit margins equal to or higher than those of other firms in their industry. A declining gross profit margin may indicate the firm is under some competitive price pressure.

## B-2b
### NET PROFIT MARGIN

The net profit margin equals net income divided by sales. For 2018, Worthy had a net profit margin of:

$$\frac{\text{Net income}}{\text{Sales}} = \frac{\$91.9 \text{ million}}{\$675 \text{ million}} = 13.6\%$$

The net profit margin is the percentage of each sales dollar the firm earns in profit or keeps *after all expenses have been paid*. Companies generally want to see rising, or at least stable, net profit margins.

## B-2c
# RETURN ON ASSETS (ROA)

A third profitability ratio—return on assets—measures the firm's efficiency in generating sales and profits from the total amount invested in the company. For 2018, Worthy's ROA is calculated as follows:

$$\frac{\text{Sales}}{\text{Average assets}} \times \frac{\text{Net income}}{\text{Sales}} = \frac{\text{Net income}}{\text{Average assets}}$$

$$\frac{\$675 \text{ million}}{\$595 \text{ million}} \times \frac{\$91.9 \text{ million}}{\$675 \text{ million}} = 1.13 \times 13.6\% = 15.4\%$$

The ROA ratio actually consists of two components. The first component, *asset turnover*, is the amount of sales generated for each dollar invested. The second component is *net profit margin*. Data for total assets are found on the firm's balance sheet.

Assume Worthy began the year with $560 million in assets and ended the year with $630 million in assets. Its average assets for the year would be $595 million. As in the other profitability ratios, Worthy's ROA should be compared with other firms in the industry and with its own previous performance to be meaningful.

## B-2d
# INVENTORY TURNOVER

Inventory turnover typically is categorized as an activity ratio, because it evaluates the effectiveness of the firm's resource use. Specifically, it measures the number of times a firm "turns" its inventory each year. The ratio can help answer the question of whether the firm has the appropriate level of inventory. Inventory turnover equals sales divided by average inventory. From the income statement, we see Worthy Composites began 2018 with $158 million in inventory and ended the year with $180 million in inventory. Therefore, the firm's average inventory was $169 million. The firm's inventory turnover ratio equals:

$$\frac{\text{Sales}}{\text{Average inventory}} = \frac{\$675 \text{ million}}{\$169 \text{ million}} = 3.99$$

For 2018, Worthy Composites turned its inventory almost four times a year. While a faster inventory turn is usually a sign of greater efficiency, to be really meaningful, the inventory turnover ratio must be compared with historical data and appropriate peer firm averages. Different organizations can have very different inventory turnover ratios, depending on the types of products they sell. For instance, a supermarket might turn its inventory every three weeks for an annual rate of roughly 17 times per year. By contrast, a large furniture retailer is likely to average only about two turns per year. Again, the determination of a "good" or "inadequate" inventory turnover rate depends on typical rates in the industry and the firm's performance in previous years.

## B-2e
# ACCOUNTS RECEIVABLE TURNOVER

Another activity ratio that may be of interest to marketers is accounts receivable turnover. This ratio measures the number of times per year a company turns its receivables. Dividing accounts receivable turnover into 365 gives us the average age of the company's receivables.

Companies make sales on the basis of either cash or credit. Credit sales allow the buyer to obtain a product now and pay for it at a specified later date. In essence, the seller is providing credit to the buyer. Credit sales are common in B2B transactions. It should be noted that sales to buyers using credit cards such as MasterCard and Visa are counted as cash sales, because the issuer of the credit card, rather than the seller, is providing credit to the buyer. Consequently, most B2C sales are counted as cash sales.

Receivables are uncollected credit sales. Measuring accounts receivable turnover and the average age of receivables are important for firms in which credit sales make up a high proportion of total sales. Accounts receivable turnover is defined as follows:

$$\text{Accounts receivable turnover} = \frac{\text{Credit Sales}}{\text{Average accounts receivable}}$$

Assume all of Worthy Composites's sales are credit sales. Also, assume the firm began 2018 with $50 million in receivables and ended the year with $60 million in receivables (both numbers can be found on the balance sheet). Therefore, it had an average of $55 million in receivables. The firm's receivables turnover and average age equal:

$$\frac{\$675 \text{ million}}{\$55 \text{ million}} = 12.3 \text{ times}$$

$$\frac{365}{12.3} = 29.7 \text{ days}$$

Worthy turned its receivables slightly more than 12 times per year. The average age of its receivables was slightly less than 30 days. Because Worthy expects its customers to pay outstanding invoices within 30 days, these numbers appear appropriate. As with other ratios, however, receivables turnover and average age of receivables should also be compared with peer firms and historical data.

## ▶ Key Terms

income statement  **B-1**              balance sheet  **B-1**

# NOTES

## CHAPTER 1

1. http://smallbusiness.chron.com/starbucks-target-audience-10553.html
2. http://fortune.com/2016/12/07/starbucks-millennials-reserve-roastery/
3. http://adage.com/article/news/tide-pods-winning-7-billion-detergent-wars-redefining/238779/
4. http://money.cnn.com/2015/07/06/news/companies/starbucks-price-hike/
5. http://www.forbes.com/forbes/welcome/?toURL=http://www.forbes.com/sites/greatspeculations/2016/09/19/lets-look-at-starbucks-growth-strategy/&refURL=http://www.google.com/url?url=http://www.forbes.com/sites/greatspeculations/2016/09/19/lets-look-at-starbucks-growth-strategy/&rct=j&frm=1&q=&esrc=s&sa=U&ved=oahUKEwjlm5zJleDRAhWph-VQKHTdqD_oQFggcMAI&sig2=DWlswMkTDQhi2Rqho1sQfw&usg=AFQjCNHRWkupiPdXNBvQYXQsqB-kKsvbZ2w&referrer=http://www.google.com/url?url=http://www.forbes.com/sites/greatspeculations/2016/09/19/lets-look-at-starbucks-growth-strategy/&rct=j&frm=1&q=&esrc=s&sa=U&ved=oahUKEwjlm5zJleDRAhWph-VQKHTdqD_oQFggcMAI&sig2=DWlswMkTDQhi2Rqho1sQfw&usg=AFQjCNHRWkupiPdXNBvQYXQsqB-kKsvbZ2w
6. "Bucking the Trend—High-Income Shoppers Visiting Dollar Stores, Reports Mintel," *PR Newswire*, accessed January 5, 2014, www.printthis.clickability.com; Phil Wahba, "Abercrombie & Fitch Same-Store Sales Plummet, Outlook Weak," *Reuters*, accessed January 5, 2014, www.reuters.com; Amy Merrick, 'The End of Saks As We Knew It," *New Yorker*, accessed January 5, 2014, www.newyorker.com.
7. http://www.wsj.com/articles/amazon-conducts-first-commercial-drone-delivery-1481725956
8. Company website, www.kohls.com, accessed January 6, 2014; Rebecka Schumann, "National Coffee Day 2013: Starbucks, Dunkin' Donuts, and 4 Other Places Where You Can Get a Free Cup of Joe," *International Business Times*, accessed January 6, 2014, www.ibtimes.com.
9. Brian Patrick Eha, "Why Steve Case Is Betting Millions on Lolly Wolly Doodle," *Entrepreneur*, accessed January 3, 2014, www.entrepreneur.com; company website, www.lollywollydoodle.com, accessed January 3, 2014.
10. Company website, "FordSocial," www.social.ford.com, accessed January 3, 2014; Andrew Gothelf, "5 Social Media Lessons to Learn from Ford," *Saleforce Blog*, accessed January 3, 2014, http://blogs.salesforce.com; Ric Dragon, "The Big Brand Theory: Ford Motor Company, Parts I and II," *Social Media Today*, accessed January 3, 2014, www.socialmediatoday.com.
11. Company website, www.weather.com, accessed January 3, 2014; Katherine Rosman, "Weather Channel Now Also Forecasts What You'll Buy," *The Wall Street Journal*, accessed January 3, 2014, http://online.wsj.com; Doug Henschen, "Big Data Reshapes Weather Channel Predictions," *Information Week*, accessed January 3, 2014, www.informationweek.com; Brian Stelter, "Weather Channel's Parent Company Is Renamed," *The New York Times*, accessed January 3, 2014, www.nytimes.com; Katie Leslie, "Sandy Gives Weather Channel a Chance to Shine," *Denver Post*, accessed January 3, 2014, www.denverpost.com; Amir Efrati, "Today's Weather Channel Forecast: A Chance of Tweets," *The Wall Street Journal*, accessed January 3, 2014, http://blogs.wsj.com.
12. http://www.economist.com/node/21552590

## CHAPTER 2

1. Company website, https://www.bls.gov/bdm/entrepreneurship/entrepreneurship.htm. Accessed February 18, 2017.
2. Hempel, Jessi (2016), "The Inside Story of Uber's Radical Rebranding," *Wired*, https://www.wired.com/2016/02/the-inside-story-behind-ubers-colorful-redesign/, accessed February 14, 2017.
3. Hempel, Jessi (2016), "The Inside Story of Uber's Radical Rebranding," *Wired*, https://www.wired.com/2016/02/the-inside-story-behind-ubers-colorful-redesign/, accessed February 14, 2017.
4. Company website, http://www.cat.com/en_US/by-industry.html. Accessed February 26, 2017.
5. Simon, Bernard (2008), "Caterpillar to quit US engine market," *Financial Times*, June 13, 2008. http://www.ft.com/cms/s/0/502275c8-38e2-11dd-8aed-0000779fd2ac.html?ft_site=falcon&desktop=true#axzz4ZnqSKojD. Accessed February 25, 2017.
6. Roberts, Jack (2011), "Caterpillar unveils CT660 vocational truck," *Commercial Carrier Journal*, March 20, 2011. http://www.ccjdigital.com/caterpillar-unveils-ct660-vocational-truck/#. Accessed February 26, 2017.
7. Company website. https://www.dieselnet.com/standards/us/hd.php. Accessed February 25, 2017.
8. Simon, Bernard (2008), "Caterpillar to quit US engine market," *Financial Times*, June 13, 2008. http://www.ft.com/cms/s/0/502275c8-38e2-11dd-8aed-0000779fd2ac.html?ft_site=falcon&desktop=true#axzz4ZnqSKojD. Accessed February 25, 2017.
9. Grayson, Wayne (2016), "Caterpillar discontinues on-highway vocational truck line, will exit business immediately," *Equipment World*, February 26, 2016. http://www.equipmentworld.com/caterpillar-discontinues-on-highway-vocational-truck-line-exits-business-immediately/. Accesssed February 25, 2017.
10. Muller, Joann (2013), "Navistars Turnaround Chances Look Worse Says S&P," *Forbes*, June 14, 2013. https://www.forbes.com/sites/joannmuller/2013/06/14/navistars-turnaround-chances-look-worse-says-sp/#22d6717f7534. Accessed February 26, 2017.
11. Muller, Joann (2013), "Navistars Turnaround Chances Look Worse

Says S&P," *Forbes*, June 14, 2013. https://www.forbes.com/sites/joannmuller/2013/06/14/navistars-turnaround-chances-look-worse-says-sp/#22d6717f7534. Accessed February 26, 2017.

12. Shoup, Mary Ellen (2017), "The energy drink market is maturing - and so should brands' marketing strategies, says XYIENCE," http://www.beveragedaily.com/Trends/Functional-Beverages/XYIENCE-Energy-drinks-market-is-maturing-brands-marketing-strategy, accessed February 15, 2017.

13. Roberts, Daniel (2015), "Walmart tells suppliers to slash prices," *Fortune*, April 1, 2015, http://fortune.com/2015/04/01/walmart-suppliers-slash-prices/, accessed February 15, 2017.

14. Roberto A. Ferdman, "McDonald's Is Taking Its Coffee War with Starbucks Straight to Your Kitchen," *Quartz.com*, accessed January 6, 2014, http://qz.com.

15. Company website, http://www.patagonia.com/blog/worn-wear/repair-is-a-radical-act/, accessed February 15, 2017.

16. Miller, Jared T. (2016), *Newsweek*, http://www.newsweek.com/2016/09/09/old-clothes-fashion-waste-crisis-494824.html, accessed February 15, 2017.

17. *Forbes* (2014), "Frito-Lay Dominates U.S. Salty Snacks, but Rising Cracker Sales Could Stall Growth, http://www.forbes.com/sites/greatspeculations/2014/06/27/frito-lay-dominates-u-s-salty-snacks-but-rising-cracker-sales-could-stall-growth/#5775df25274a, accessed February 15, 2017.

18. Company website, "Apple Reports Fourth Quarter Results," press release, www.apple.com, accessed January 6, 2014.

19. Matt Smith, "Meet Microsoft, the World's Best Kept R&D Secret," *TechHive*, accessed January 6, 2014, www.techhive.com.

20. John Carney, "The Student Loan Bubble Is Starting to Burst," *CNBC.com*, accessed January 7, 2014, www.cnbc.com.

21. Company website, www.blaircandy.com, accessed January 6, 2014.

22. *Forbes* (2014), "Frito-Lay Dominates U.S. Salty Snacks, but Rising Cracker Sales Could Stall Growth, http://www.forbes.com/sites/greatspeculations/2014/06/27/frito-lay-dominates-u-s-salty-snacks-but-rising-cracker-sales-could-stall-growth/#5775df25274a, accessed February 15, 2017.

23. Foster, Tom (2016), *Inc.* Magazine, February 2016, http://www.inc.com/magazine/201602/tom-foster/kevin-plank-under-armour-spending-1-billion-to-beat-nike.html, accessed February 18, 2017.

24. Company website, http://about.mapmyfitness.com/2013/11/underarmour/, accessed February 18, 2017.

25. Germano, Sara (2015), *Wall Street Journal*, February 4, 2015. Company website, https://www.wsj.com/articles/under-armour-to-acquire-myfitnesspal-for-475-million-1423086478, accessed February 18, 2017.

26. De la Merced, Michael J. (2015), *New York Times*, February 4, 2015. Company website, https://dealbook.nytimes.com/2015/02/04/under-armour-buys-2-fitness-apps-including-myfitnesspal-for-560-million/?_r=0, accessed February 18, 2017.

27. Foster, Tom (2016), *Inc.* Magazine, February 2016, http://www.inc.com/magazine/201602/tom-foster/kevin-plank-under-armour-spending-1-billion-to-beat-nike.html, accessed February 18, 2017.

28. Company website, http://about.mapmyfitness.com/2013/11/underarmour/, accessed February 18, 2017.

29. Gaudiosi, John (2016), "Under Armour Makes Biggest Push Yet into Fitness Tech," *Fortune*, January 6, 2016, http://fortune.com/2016/01/06/under-armour-fitness-gear/, accessed February 18, 2017.

## CHAPTER 3

1. Company website, Ethisphere Institute names Progressive as a 2013 World's Most Ethical Company, accessed February 16, 2017. https://www.progressive.com/newsroom/article/2013/april/ethisphere-2013/.

2. McNew, B. McDonald's Is Competing Directly With Starbucks. accessed February 15, 2017. https://www.fool.com/investing/2016/10/05/mcdonalds-is-competing-directly-with-starbucks.aspx

3. Fair, L. "FTC Challenges Gerber baby formula claims in court." accessed February 15, 2017. https://www.ftc.gov/news-events/blogs/business-blog/2014/10/ftc-challenges-gerber-baby-formula-claims-court.

4. Organization website, accessed January 14, 2014. www.aarp.org.

5. Association website, accessed January 14, 2014. www.the-dma.org,

6. Tassin, P. "Gerber Class Action Says Good Start Formula Can't Prevent Allergies." accessed February 15, 2017. https://topclassactions.com/lawsuit-settlements/lawsuit-news/385256-gerber-class-action-says-good-start-formula-cant-prevent-allergies/.

7. Zmuda, N. "Five Brands Doing It Right, Doing It Wrong." Advertising Age. accessed February 13, 2017. http://adage.com/article/news/marketing-a-recession-brands-wrong/135780/.

8. Company website. 2008 Operating and Financial Review. accessed February 16, 2017. http://www.debeersgroup.com/en/reports/library.html.

9. Ylan Q. Mui, "Economy Expands 2.8 Percent in Third Quarter, but Consumer Spending Slows," The Washington Post, accessed January 15, 2014, www.washingtonpost.com.

10. Barnes, B. "At Disney Parks, a Bracelet Meant to Build Loyalty (and Sales)." The New York Times. accessed January 15, 2014. http://www.nytimes.com/2013/01/07/business/media/at-disney-parks-a-bracelet-meant-to-build-loyalty-and-sales.html.

11. "A Fresh View of Hispanic Consumers." April 15, 2014. http://www.nielsen.com/us/en/insights/news/2014/a-fresh-view-of-hispanic-consumers.html

12. Alex Konrad, "Food Fight," *Forbes*, November 2, 2015, page 96. Print.

13. Murphy, W. "AG: JFK Airport Hotel penalized for price gouging during storm." February 13, 2017. http://www.newsday.com/news/new-york/ag-jfk-airport-hotel-penalized-for-price-gouging-during-storm-1.13114772.

14. Company website, "Responsibility at IBM," www.ibm.com, accessed February 15, 2017.

## CHAPTER 4

1. Internet World Stats, accessed February 2, 2017, www.internetworldstats.com

2. "VOD Options for Independent Films and Series," *Douglashorn.com*, accessed February 12, 2014, http://douglashorn.com.

3. Justin Thorpe, "11 Examples of Online Personalization You Will Love," https://www.addthis.com/blog/2015/01/20/

examples-of-personalization/#.
WJeZmvkrKUk, January 20, 2015,
accessed February 5, 2017.

4. Lauren Johnson, "McDonald's is Creating
5,000 Pieces of Marketing Content This
Year. Here's Why," *Adweek*, September
26, 2016, http://www.adweek.com/
digital/why-mcdonalds-will-create-
5000-pieces-marketing-content-
year-173711/, accessed February 5, 2017.

5. Paul DeMerry, "B2B e-Commerce Sales
Will Top $1.13 Trillion by 2020," *B2B
e-Commerce*, accessed February 9,
2017, https://www.internetretailer.
com/2015/04/02/new-report-predicts-
1-trillion-market-us-b2b-e-commerce.

6. "SAP Customer Success Story: Royal
Dutch/Shell Group," accessed
February 14, 2014, www.sap.com.

7. https://www.internetretailer.com/
2016/01/29/online-sales-will-reach-
523-billion-2020-us

8. http://www.pewresearch.org/fact-tank/
2017/01/12/evolution-of-technology/

9. Company website, www.westernunion
.com, accessed February 14, 2014;
company website, www.paypal.com,
accessed February 14, 2014.

10. Anne Flaherty, "Study Finds Online
Privacy Concerns on the Rise," *Yahoo
News*, accessed February 10, 2014,
http://news.yahoo.com; government
website, www.ftc.org, accessed
February 10, 2014.

11. Anthony Wing Kosner, "Actually Two
Attacks in One, Target Breach Affected
70 to 110 Million Customers," *Forbes*,
accessed August 15, 2014, www.forbes
.com.

12. Government website, www.ic3.gov,
accessed February 14, 2014.

13. Mark Brohan, "Big Design Changes
Drive Growth Online at Under Armour,"
*Internet Retailer*, accessed February 10,
2014, www.internetretailer.com.

14. https://academic.oup.com/iwc/article/
23/5/473/660020/UX-Curve-A-method-
for-evaluating-long-term-user, accessed
February 28, 2017

15. https://baymard.com/lists/cart-
abandonment-rate, accessed February 28,
2017

16. https://hbr.org/2015/07/the-logic-
behind-amazons-prime-day

17. https://www.similarweb.com/website/
target.com - accessed February 27, 2017

18. https://www.similarweb.com/website/
homedepot.com#overview - accessed
February 27th, 2017.

19. https://www.similarweb.com/website/
macys.com - accessed February 27, 2017

20. https://www.similarweb.com/website/
lowes.com - accessed February 27, 2017

21. Kevin Gold, "What Is the Average
Conversion Rate? A 2013 Update," *Search
Marketing Standard*, accessed February
14, 2014, www.searchmarketingstandard.
com; Meghan Peters, "How To: Get
Started with Google Analytics," *Mashable
Business*, accessed February 14, 2014,
http://mashable.com.

22. https://www.similarweb.com/website/
target.com - accessed February 27,
2017.

23. https://www.similarweb.com/website/
homedepot.com#overview - accessed
February 27, 2017.

## CHAPTER 5

1. https://investors.linkedin.com/
results-and-financials/annual-reports/
default.aspx

2. https://press.linkedin.com/
about-linkedin?

3. *Merriam-Webster Online Dictionary*,
accessed January 17, 2014, www.
merriam-webster.com.

4. http://www.pewinternet.org/fact-
sheet/social-media/ - accessed
March 3, 2017

5. Steve Olenski, "Are Brands Wielding
More Influence in Social Media Than We
Thought?" *Forbes*, accessed January 20,
2014, www.forbes.com.

6. http://fortune.com/2016/12/05/
social-media-ad-spending-newspapers-
zenith-2020/

7. Company website, http://www2.
orabrush.com, accessed January 19,
2014; https://twitter.com/Orabrush,
accessed January 19, 2014.

8. https://www.orabrush.com/story/

9. http://www.nydailynews.com/life-style/
starbucks-pumpkin-spice-latte-social-
media-master-article-1.2357491

10. Emeric Ernoult, "How to Run a
Facebook Timeline Promotion: 6 Tips
for Success," *Social Media Examiner*,
accessed January 18, 2014, www.
socialmediaexaminer.com; "Five
Ways to Get Banned from Facebook,"
*NewsCore*, accessed January 18, 2014,
www.myfoxtwincities.com.

11. Organization website, www.relayforlife.
org, accessed February 6, 2014.

12. Sam Laird, "Pinsanity: How Sports
Teams Are Winning on Pinterest,"
*Mashable*, accessed January 17, 2014,
http://mashable.com.

13. https://wordpress.com/about/ -
accessed March 3, 2017

14. https://wordpress.com/activity/ -
accessed March 3, 2017

15. https://www.tumblr.com/about -
accessed March 3, 2017

16. Albert Costill, "Top 21 Brands Getting
the Most Out of Tumblr," *Search Engine
Journal*, accessed January 19, 2014, www
.searchenginejournal.com.

17. Cotton Delo, "Twitter Teams with
Viacom to Sell Its Ads to VMA
Sponsors," *Advertising Age*, accessed
January 19, 2014, www.adage.com.

18. http://twittercounter.com/pages/100 -
accessed March 3, 2017

19. http://www.nydailynews.com/life-style/
starbucks-pumpkin-spice-latte-social-
media-master-article-1.2357491

20. http://www.businessinsider.com/
how-pumpkin-spice-took-over-
fall-2016-10

21. Matthew Peneycad, "Unignorable Facts
about How Social Media Influences
Purchase Behaviour," *Social Media Today*,
accessed January 20, 2014, http://
socialmediatoday.com.

22. http://www.thedrum.com/news/
2015/04/24/facebook-influences-
over-half-shoppers-says-digitaslbi-s-
connected-commerce-report

23. https://www2.deloitte.com/content/
dam/Deloitte/us/Documents/consumer-
business/us-cb-navigating-the-new-
digital-divide-051315.pdf

24. Company website, "The Virtuous Circle:
The Role of Search and Social Media
in the Purchase Pathway," http://
groupmnext.com, accessed January 21,
2014.

25. "24 Outstanding Statistics & Figures
on How Social Media Has Impacted
the Health Care Industry," *Med City
News*, accessed January 21, 2014,
http://medcitynews.com; Miranda
Miller, "33% of U.S. Consumers Use
Social Media for Health Care Info,"
*Search Engine Watch*, accessed
January 21, 2014, http://
searchenginewatch.com.

26. Matthew Peneycad, "Influencing
Purchase Decisions with Online Reviews
and How to Get More of Them," *Social
Media Today*, accessed January 21, 2014,
http://socialmediatoday.com.

27. Caroline Scott-Thomas, "Social Media
Has Changed How Americans Eat,
Says Hartman Report," *Food Navigator*,
accessed January 21, 2014, www.
foodnavigator-usa.com.

28. "The World's Most Powerful
Celebrities," *Forbes*, accessed
January 22, 2014, www.forbes.com.

29. Adeyeri, Eb (August 27, 2014). "Ice bucket challenge: what are the lessons for marketers?". *The Guardian*.

30. http://www.cio.com/article/3062615/social-networking/10-top-social-media-marketing-success-stories.html

31. Organization website, http://visitlouisianacoast.com, accessed February 6, 2014; "WSI Uses Social Media to Help Louisiana Tourism Coastal Coalition (LTCC) Increase Tourism after BP Oil Spill Disaster," press release, accessed February 6, 2014, http://www.wsidigitalmarketing.com.

32. http://tim.blog/podcast/ - accessed March 3, 2017

33. Issie Lapowsky, "Turning 'Likes' into Loot with Facebook Promotions," Inc., accessed January 24, 2014 www.*inc*.com.

34. http://marketingland.com/exciting-development-weight-watchers-top-marketer-oprah-course-190073

35. https://www.wsj.com/articles/best-and-worst-ads-of-2016-the-things-we-cant-unsee-1482920942

36. Jenna Dobkin, "3 Top Influencer Marketing Campaigns of 2013 and Lessons Every Marketer Can Learn from Them," *Social Media Today*, accessed January 24, 2014, http://socialmediatoday.com; "Sprout It—Backyard Takeover Contest," *Chris Loves Julia*, blog, accessed January 25, 2014, www.chrislovesjulia.com; Dan Eaton, "Sprout It Gardening App Debuts in Partnership with Scotts," *Columbus Biz Insider*, accessed January 25, 2014, http://www.bizjournals.com.

37. http://nypost.com/2016/08/04/weight-watchers-banks-on-oprah-to-improve-companys-figures/#.

38. Saroj Kar, "PSN Breach amid the Largest of Past Years," *Silicon Angle*, accessed January 26, 2014, http://siliconangle.com; Lisa Vaas, "Sony to Pay £250,000 Fine for Play Network Breach," *Naked Security*, accessed January 25, 2014, http://nakedsecurity.com.

39. https://www.wsj.com/articles/best-and-worst-ads-of-2016-the-things-we-cant-unsee-1482920942

40. https://www.nytimes.com/2015/09/21/business/media/retailers-use-of-their-fans-photos-draws-scrutiny.html

## CHAPTER 6

1. Company website. http://www.fmi.org/research-resources/supermarket-facts. Accessed March 5, 2017.

2. Press release (2016), "Aldi Strengthens Senior Management Team as Fast-paced US Expansion Continues," https://corporate.aldi.us/fileadmin/fm-dam/news_and_awards/Press_Release_2016/Laubaugh_Promotion_03.08.16_FINAL.pdf. Accessed March 5, 2017.

3. Press release (2017), "Aldi Customers Find Ways to Say Hello to Healthy in the New Year," https://corporate.aldi.us/fileadmin/fm-dam/news_and_awards/Press_Release_2017/HL_2017_Press_Release_1.9.17_FINAL.pdf. Accessed March 5, 2017.

4. Company website. http://cookieandkate.com/press/. Accessed March 5, 2017.

5. Berr, Jonathan (2016), "How Aldi is beating Walmart in the grocery aisle," *Moneywatch*, March 29, 2016. http://www.cbsnews.com/news/how-aldi-is-beating-walmart-in-the-grocery-aisle/. March 5, 2017.

6. Company website. https://media.ford.com/content/fordmedia/fna/us/en/news/2014/12/30/ford-starts-most-comprehensive-truck-marketing-campaign.html. Accessed March 5, 2017.

7. Company website. https://media.ford.com/content/fordmedia/fna/us/en/news/2014/12/30/ford-starts-most-comprehensive-truck-marketing-campaign.html. Accessed March 5, 2017.

8. Company website. http://www.caranddriver.com/best-pickup-trucks. Accessed March 5, 2017.

9. Company website. https://cars.usnews.com/cars-trucks/compare/?trims=13333-387896_13263-383634_13279-384189. Accessed March 5, 2017.

10. Artun, Omer and Michelle Kelly (2016), "What Lilly Pulitzer Learned About Marketing to Millennials," *Harvard Business Review*, March 31, 2016. https://hbr.org/2016/03/what-lilly-pulitzer-learned-about-marketing-to-millennials. Accessed March 7, 2017.

11. Entis, Laura (2016), "How Lilly Pulitzer, an Almost 60-year-old Brand Became a Social Media Darling," *Fortune*, August 10, 2016. http://fortune.com/2016/08/10/lilly-pulitzer-social-media-darling/. Accessed March 7, 2017.

12. Silverstein, Frank (2013), "Pizza Patrōn founder reveals the secret to capturing the Latino market," http://nbclatino.com/2013/05/08/pizza-patron-founder-reveals-the-secret-to-capturing-the-latino-market/. Accessed March 6, 2017.

13. Peterson, Hayley (2016), "This is what the average Walmart shopper looks like," *Business Insider*, October 7, 2016. http://www.businessinsider.com/walmart-shopper-demographics-2016-10. Accessed March 7, 2017.

14. David Koeppel, "Supermarket Bromance: More Men Are Shopping," Money, accessed February 18, 2014, http://money.msn.com.

15. "Kids Spending and Influencing Power: $1.2 Trillion Says Leading Ad Firm," Center for Digital Democracy, accessed February 18, 2014, www.democraticmedia.org.

16. Artun, Omer and Michelle Kelly (2016), "What Lilly Pulitzer Learned About Marketing to Millennials," *Harvard Business Review*, March 31, 2016. https://hbr.org/2016/03/what-lilly-pulitzer-learned-about-marketing-to-millennials. Accessed March 7, 2017.

17. Entis, Laura (2016), "How Lilly Pulitzer, an Almost 60-year-old Brand Became a Social Media Darling," *Fortune*, August 10, 2016. http://fortune.com/2016/08/10/lilly-pulitzer-social-media-darling/. Accessed March 7, 2017.

18. Company website. https://www.crossfit.com/what-is-crossfit. Accessed March 8, 2017.

19. Brandt, Ari (2015), "Sensory Marketing is the Next Frontier in Mobile Advertising," *AdAge*, January 21, 2015. http://adage.com/article/digitalnext/sensory-marketing-frontier-mobile-advertising/296655/. Accessed March 7, 2017.

20. Company website. https://www.mauijim.com/en/about-us. Accessed March 7, 2017.

21. *PRNewswire* (2017), "Maui Jim Continues to Grow Relationship with Men's Fashion Brand, Grungy Gentleman," http://www.prnewswire.com/news-releases/maui-jim-continues-to-grow-relationship-with-mens-fashion-brand-grungy-gentleman-300416183.html. Accessed March 7, 2017.

22. Company website. https://www.mauijim.com/en/about-us. Accessed March 7, 2017.

23. Pinsker, Joe (2014), "The Psychology Behind Costco's Free Samples," *The Atlantic*, October 1, 2014. https://www.theatlantic.com/business/archive/2014/10/the-psychology-behind-costcos-free-samples/380969/. Accessed March 7, 2017.

24. Company website, www.shinola.com, accessed February 18, 2014; Joann Muller, "In Bankrupt Detroit, Shinola Puts Its Faith in American Manufacturing," *Forbes*, accessed February 18, 2014, www.forbes.com.

## CHAPTER 7

1. https://ww2.frost.com/news/press-releases/global-b2b-e-commerce-market-will-reach-67-trillion-usd-2020-finds-frost-sullivan/
2. https://solvers.ups.com/b2b-ecommerce-trends-shifting-toward-digital/
3. Company website, www.accobrands.com, accessed February 14, 2014.
4. http://www.fikesproducts.com/
5. https://gov.georgia.gov/press-releases/2013-10-21/kings-hawaiian-expansion-create-more-400-new-jobs-hall-county
6. https://www.toysmith.com/

## CHAPTER 8

1. Bureau of Labor Statistics, "Employment by Major Industry Sector," accessed March 8, 2017, www.bls.gov; Central Intelligence Agency, *World Factbook*, accessed February 18, 2014, www.cia.gov.
2. Fox, Susannah, "51 percent of U.S. Adults Bank Online," *Pew Internet*, accessed March 8, 2017, www.pewinternet.org.
3. Varinsky, Dana, "Here's what 5 of your favorite products would cost if they were made in the US," *Business Insider*, accessed March 13, 2017, www.businessinsider.com.
4. Organization website, "World's Richest Countries," accessed February 19, 2014, www.worldsrichestcountries.com.
5. World Trade Organization website, www.wto.org, accessed February 15, 2014.
6. Ibid.
7. Eurostat, "Population on 1 January," http://ec.europa.eu/eurostat/tgm/table.do?tab=table&language=en&pcode=tps00001&tableSelection=1&footnotes=yes&labeling=labels&plugin=1, accessed March 7, 2017.
8. Organization website, "North Americans Are Better Off after 15 Years of NAFTA," www.naftanow.org, accessed March 6, 2014.
9. "Brexit may equal billions in losses for automakers," *Autoweek*, accessed March 13, 2017, www.autoweek.com.
10. Organization website, "United States Wins Trade Enforcement Case for American Farmers, Proves Export-Blocking Chinese Duties Unjustified Under WTO Rules," Office of the United States Trade Representative, accessed March 13, 2017, https://ustr.gov.
11. Company website, "Annual Report and Accounts 2016," accessed March 9, 2017, www.unilever.com; Boyle, Matthew, "In Emerging Markets, Unilever Finds a Passport to Profit," *Bloomberg*, January 3, 2013, www.bloomberg.com.
12. Mahajan, Vijay, "How Unilever Reaches Rural Consumers in Emerging Markets," *Harvard Business Review*, December 14, 2016, www.hbr.org.
13. James, Geoffrey, "20 Epic Fails in Global Branding," www.inc.com, accessed March 6, 2017.
14. Yangpeng, Zheng, "China's internet users grew in 2016 by the size of Ukraine's population to 731 million," *South China Morning Post*, accessed March 7, 2017. http://www.scmp.com/tech/china-tech/article/2064396/chinas-internet-users-grew-2016-size-ukraines-population-731-million.
15. Gan, Nectar, "Is Google another step closer to being unblocked in China?" *CNBC*, accessed March 14, 2017, www.cnbc.com.
16. Goel, Vindu. "Foxconn Audit Finds a Workweek Still Too Long," *The New York Times*, accessed February 20,2014, www.nytimes.com.
17. "Internet Usage Statistics," *Internet World Stats*, accessed March 7, 2017.
18. Organization website, "The Continuing Rise of Cross-Border Ecommerce: The 2016 Pitney Bowes Global Online Shopping Study," accessed March 8, 2017, http://blogs.pb.com/ecommerce/2016/11/16/2016-global-online-shopping-study/.
19. Booton, Jennifer, "Move over China, Yum Brands Setting Its Sights on India," *FOX Business*, accessed February 20,2014, www.foxbusiness.com.
20. Company website, "Enhancing livelihoods through Project Shakti," accessed March 9, 2017, www.hul.co.in.
21. Mahajan, Vijay, "How Unilever Reaches Rural Consumers in Emerging Markets," *Harvard Business Review*, December 14, 2016, www.hbr.org.
22. Company website, www.ikea.com, accessed February 20, 2014.
23. Company website, "Polo Ralph Lauren Enters Into Global Licensing Agreement With Apparel Ventures To Manufacture and Distribute Women's and Girls' Swimwear," accessed March 18, 2017, investor.ralphlauren.com.
24. Max Nisen, "How Nike Solved Its Sweatshop Problem," *Business Insider*, accessed March 18, 2017, www.businessinsider.com; Organization website, www.fairlabor.org, accessed March 18, 2017.
25. https://corporate.ford.com/microsites/sustainability-report-2014-15/people-employees.html
26. "Meidu Holding Co Ltd to Acquire Woodbine Acquisition LLC," *Reuters*, accessed February 18, 2014, www.reuters.com.
27. Berfield, Susan. "Can All-American Gap Succeed in India?" *Bloomberg Businessweek*, accessed September 14, 2014, www.businessweek.com.
28. Mark Rechtin, "Jaguar Land Rover targets 1 million sales in long term," *Automotive News*, accessed March 18, 2017, www.autonews.com.
29. Beer, Jeff. "Marketing to China: Oreo's Chinese twist," *Canadian Business*, accessed March 10, 2017, www.canadianbusiness.com.
30. Smith, Robert. "Rethinking the Oreo For Chinese Consumers," *NPR*, accessed March 10, 2017. www.npr.org.
31. Koellmann, Benjamin. "Smart cookie," *Business Today, India*, accessed March 10, 2017, www.businesstoday.in.

## CHAPTER 9

1. Schultz, E. J. (2017), "PepsiCo's Super Bowl Plans are Decidedly Zero-Calorie." http://adage.com/article/special-report-super-bowl/pepsico-s-super-bowl-plans-decidedly-calorie/307673/. Accessed March 18, 2017.
2. Company website, "Fifth Annual 'What Women Want' Survey Results," www.gingerminneapolis.com, accessed March 12, 2014; "What Women Want: Insights into $7 Trillion Women's Purchasing Power," *PR Newswire*, accessed March 12, 2014, www.prnewswire.com.
3. Ibid.
4. http://timesofindia.indiatimes.com/auto/miscellaneous/53700-vehicles-registered-across-country-every-day/articleshow/53747821.cms
5. Company website, www.harley-davidson.com, accessed March 12, 2014; Rick Barrett, "In Quest to Expand Market, Harley-Davidson Reaches Out to Women," Milwaukee Journal Sentinel, accessed March 12, 2014, www.jsonline.com.
6. Company website, "Fifth Annual 'What Women Want' Survey Results," www.gingerminneapolis.com, accessed March 12, 2014; "What Women Want: Insights into $7 Trillion Women's Purchasing Power," *PR Newswire*, accessed March 12, 2014, www.prnewswire.com.

7. Company website, "Fifth Annual 'What Women Want' Survey Results," www.gingerminneapolis.com, accessed March 12, 2014; "What Women Want: Insights into $7 Trillion Women's Purchasing Power," *PR Newswire*, accessed March 12, 2014, www.prnewswire.com.

8. Company website, www.designbasics.com, accessed March 12, 2014; Mary Umberger, "Designing with Her Outlook," *Chicago Tribune*, accessed March 12, 2014, http://articles.chicagotribune.com.

9. Company website. http://www.cnbc.com/2017/03/16/dollar-general-is-starting-to-look-a-lot-like-wal-mart.html. Accessed March 19, 2017.

10. http://www.teausa.org/teausa/images/2012/02/ppdem01.pdf.

11. Karen Fernau, "Coffee Grinds Fuel for Nation," *USA Today*, accessed March 12, 2014, www.usatoday.com; organization website, "2013 National Coffee Drinking Trends," accessed March 12, 2014, www.ncausa.org; Lyz Pfister, "Coffee Culture in America: Top 4 Cities for a Cup of Joe," *Nerd Wallet*, accessed March 12, 2014, www.nerdwallet.com.

12. Company website. http://news.walgreens.com/fact-sheets/store-count-by-state.htm. Accessed March 19, 2017.

13. Company website. http://news.walgreens.com/fact-sheets/about-walgreens/. Accessed March 19, 2017.

14. Company website. http://www.csnews.com/product-categories/other-merchandise-services/walgreens-plans-purge-product-offering. Accessed March 19, 2017.

15. Company website. https://www2.deloitte.com/global/en/pages/technology-media-and-telecommunications/articles/tmt-pred16-media-mobile-games-leading-less-lucrative.html. Accessed March 19, 2017.

16. Company website. https://hbr.org/2009/09/the-female-economy. Accessed March 19, 2017.

17. Company website. http://www.dove.com/uk/stories/campaigns/real-beauty-sketches.html. Accessed March 19, 2017.

18. Company website. http://adage.com/article/cmo-strategy/spot-target-pint-size-back-school/305015/. Accessed March 19, 2017.

19. Jack Neff, "Why New Clorox CEO Won't Mimic Alma Mater P&G's Marketing Cuts," *Advertising Age*, accessed September 25, 2014," http://adage.com; Michelle Saettler, "General Mills,

Clorox Target Hispanic Mobile Shoppers via Bilingual Promotions App," *Mobile Marketer*, accessed September 25, 2014, www.mobilemarketer.com; Kristen Cloud, "Clorox Identifies Four Mega Trends for Hispanic Consumers," *The Shelby Report*, accessed March 13, 2014, www.theshelbyreport.com; "Content Marketing: How P&G, Clorox and Tampico Engage Hispanic Audiences," *Portada*, accessed March 13, 2014, www.portada-online.com; Tiffany Hsu, "Clorox Launches New Products, Campaign on Latino Cleaning Habits," *Los Angeles Times*, accessed March 13, 2014, http://articles.latimes.com; "Nielsen: Hispanic Consumers' Buying Power to Grow 50% by 2015" *Drug Store News*, accessed March 8, 2014, www.drugstorenews.com; Laurel Wentz, "Clorox Fragancia Launch Targets U.S. Hispanic Consumers," *Advertising Age Hispanic*, accessed March 8, 2014, http://adage.com; Alaric Dearment, "Growing Hispanic Consumer Power Increases Need for Outreach from Retailers, Suppliers," *Drug Store News*, accessed March 8, 2014, www.drugstorenews.com; Allison Cerra, "Clorox, NAHN Introduce Hispanic Nurses Network," *Drug Store News*, accessed March 8, 2014, www.drugstorenews.com; Michael D. Hernandez, "Big Brands Target Hispanic Consumers," *USA Today*, March 8, 2014, www.usatoday.com.

20. Company website. http://www.pewinternet.org/2015/12/15/gaming-and-gamers/. Accessed March 19, 2017.

21. Company website. https://www.esrb.org/ratings/. Accessed March 19, 2017.

22. Company website. https://www.wired.com/2014/03/animal-crossing-director/. March 19, 2017.

23. Company website. http://adage.com/article/news/tv-ad-pricing-chart/305899/. Accessed March 26, 2017.

24. Company website. http://www.pewinternet.org/2016/09/01/book-reading-2016/. Accessed March 26, 2017.

25. https://segmentationsolutions.nielsen.com/mybestsegments/Default.jsp?ID=100&menuOption=learnmore

26. Company website. http://variety.com/2016/tv/news/tv-ad-prices-football-walking-dead-empire-advertising-1201890660/. Accessed March 20, 2017.

27. Company website. http://adage.com/article/media/h/306459/. Accessed March 19, 2017.

28. Wells, Tom and Michael Link (2017), "Facebook User Research Using a Probability-Based Sample and Behavioral Data," *Journal of Computer-Mediated Communication*, 19, 1042–1052. http://onlinelibrary.wiley.com/doi/10.1111/jcc4.12058/pdf. Accessed March 19, 2017.

29. Company website. https://www.colorado.gov/pacific/sites/default/files/DC_CD_fact-sheet_Sugary-drink-consumption_Aug-2016.pdf. Accessed March 19, 2017.

30. Company website. http://www.bevindustry.com/articles/88300-lance-collins-dr-luke-launch-core-natural-water. Accessed March 19, 2017.

31. https://www.forbes.com/sites/michaelskok/2013/06/14/4-steps-to-building-a-compelling-value-proposition/#57585e5b4695

32. https://duckduckgo.com/about

33. Ibid.

## CHAPTER 10

1. http://www.cnbc.com/2016/10/17/netflixs-6-billion-content-budget-in-2017-makes-it-one-of-the-top-spenders.html

2. http://www.usatoday.com/story/tech/news/2017/01/18/netflix-shares-up-q4-subscriber-additions/96710172/

3. Jessica Derschowitz, "Adam Sandler to Make Four Movies for Netflix," *CBS News*, accessed October 3, 2014, www.cbsnews.com; Lacey Rose, "Netflix's Original Content VP on Development Plans, Pilots, Late-Night and Rival HBO," *The Hollywood Reporter*, accessed October 3, 2014, www.hollywoodreporter.com; Dawn C. Chmielewski, "Netflix Executive Upends Hollywood," *Los Angeles Times*, accessed March 12, 2014, www.latimes.com; Rob Toledo, "Tech Tuesday: Netflix and Big Data," *The Best of Netflix*, accessed March 12, 2014, http://thebestofnetflix.com; "8 Marketers Doing Big Data Right," *Mashable*, accessed March 12, 2014, http://mashable.com; Kosha Gada, "Netflix and the Culture of Creation," *Forbes*, accessed March 12, 2014, www.forbes.com; David Carr, "Giving Viewers What They Want," *The New York Times*, accessed March 12, 2014, www.nytimes.com; Andrew Leonard, "How Netflix Is Turning Viewers into Puppets," *Salon*, accessed March 12, 2014, www.salon.com; Alexis Madrigal, "Netflix Built Its Microgenres by Staring into the American Soul," *NPR*, accessed March 12, 2014, www.npr.org.

4. Adrienne LaFrance, "How to Play Like a Girl," *The Atlantic*, accessed March 16, 2017, www.theatlantic.com.
5. Mikkel Rasmussen, "Lego's Serious Play," Strategy+Business blog, accessed March 16, 2017, www.strategy-business.com/blog.
6. Adrienne LaFrance, "How to Play Like a Girl," *The Atlantic*, accessed March 16, 2017, www.theatlantic.com.
7. Bradford Wieners, "Lego Is for Girls," *Bloomberg*, accessed March 17, 2017, www.bloomberg.com/businessweek.
8. Adrienne LaFrance, "How to Play Like a Girl," *The Atlantic*, accessed March 16, 2017, www.theatlantic.com; Jonathan Chew, "How Lego Finally Found Success With Girls," *Fortune*, accessed March 17, 2017, www.fortune.com.
9. http://www.ihrsa.org/industry-research/
10. Jodi A. Mindell, L. Telofski, B. Wiegand, and E. Kurtz, "A Nightly Bedtime Routine: Impact on Sleep in Young Children and Maternal Mood," accessed March 20, 2017, www.ncbi.nlm.nih.gov.
11. Company website, www.johnsonsbaby.com, accessed March 20, 2017.
12. ibid
13. Nataha Singer, "At Estée Lauder, a Brand Is Developed Just for China," *CNBC*, accessed March 21, 2017, www.cnbc.com.
14. Ibid
15. Organization website, www.cdc.gov, accessed March 17, 2017.
16. Charles Duhigg, "How Companies Learn Your Secrets," *The New York Times Magazine*, accessed March 15, 2017, www.nytimes.com.
17. Company website, www.datamonitor.com, accessed March 12, 2014.
18. Company website, "What Is Big Data?" www-01.ibm.com, accessed March 16, 2017.
19. Charles Duhigg, "How Companies Learn Your Secrets," *The New York Times Magazine*, accessed March 15, 2017, www.nytimes.com.
20. ibid
21. Annual financials for Target Corp., accessed March 21, 2017, www.marketwatch.com.
22. Charles Duhigg, "How Companies Learn Your Secrets," *The New York Times Magazine*, accessed March 15, 2017, www.nytimes.com.

## CHAPTER 11

1. http://a1constructionrentals.com/
2. http://oxfordroad.com/
3. Company website, www.cargill.com, accessed March 14, 2014.
4. http://usat.ly/1NCVEJa
5. https://www.forbes.com/powerful-brands/list/#tab:rank - accessed March 31, 2017
6. Company website, "About Y&R," www.yr.com, accessed March 22, 2014; company website, http://bavconsulting.com, accessed March 22, 2014.
7. https://www.marketingweek.com/2015/06/03/data-shows-that-nike-is-the-most-damaged-brand-from-fifa-scandal/
8. http://www.businesswire.com/news/home/20170331005742/en/
9. http://www.philips.com/global
10. http://www.usa.philips.com/a-w/innovationandyou/article/full-video-story/infant-mortality-uganda.html
11. http://www.anibrands.com
12. http://www.prweb.com/releases/2013/8/prweb11020831.htm
13. Ibid.
14. https://corporate.hasbro.com/en-us/community-relations
15. "Food Allergies: Understanding Food Labels," Mayo Clinic website, accessed March 23, 2014, www.mayoclinic.com.
16. Company website "Innovation in Packaging," www.heinz.com, accessed March 21, 2014; Pat Reynolds, "Dip & Squeeze Boasts Dual Functionality," *Packaging World*, accessed March 21, 2014, www.packworld.com; Elaine Watson, "Quote/Unquote: Heinz on Rocking the Boat..." *Food Navigator*, accessed March 21, 2014, www.foodnavigator-usa.com; Emily Bryson York, "More Foods Going to Pouch Packaging," *Chicago Tribune*, accessed March 21, 2014, http://articles.chicagotribune.com; Sarah Nassauer, "Old Ketchup Packet Heads for Trash," *The Wall Street Journal*, accessed March 21, 2014, http://onlinewsj.com.
17. https://www.marketingweek.com/2016/05/04/how-under-armour-plans-to-become-the-worlds-biggest-sports-brand/

## CHAPTER 12

1. Company website, www.asianfoodmarkets.com, accessed March 23, 2014.
2. http://www.latimes.com/business/hollywood/la-fi-ct-mpaa-box-office-20170322-story.html
3. Lee Neikirk, "Samsung's Curved 4K TV Is Fit to Rule," *USA Today*, accessed March 23, 2014, www.usatoday.com; Ty Pendlebury, "What Is 4K UHD? Next-Generation Resolution Explained," *CNET*, accessed March 23, 2014, http://reviews.cnet.com.
4. Amy Kazmin, "India Pressures Pepsi to Reduce Sugar in Drinks and Snacks," *Financial Times*, accessed October 16, 2014, www.ft.com.
5. http://vintagevalueinvesting.com/harley-davidson-motorcycles-economic-moats-qualitative-analysis/
6. Company website, "A New Global Hair Research Center," www.lorealusa.com, accessed March 23, 2014.
7. http://www.cosmeticsdesign-europe.com/Business-Financial/L-Oreal-and-Nestle-end-Inneov-venture
8. Company website, www.bose.com, accessed March 23, 2014.
9. Everett Rogers, *Diffusion of Innovations* (New York: Free Press, 1983), 247-51.
10. Jakki Mohr, *Marketing of High-Technology Products and Innovations* (Upper Saddle River, NJ: Prentice Hall, 2001).
11. Geoffrey Moore, *Crossing the Chasm: Marketing and Selling High-Tech Products to Mainstream Customers* (New York: HarperBusiness, 1999)
12. http://time.com/3921019/streaming-dvds/
13. https://www.nytimes.com/2016/08/17/business/ford-promises-fleets-of-driverless-cars-within-five-years.html?_r=0
14. http://money.cnn.com/2015/04/28/technology/lg-g4-smartphone-camera/
15. http://fortune.com/2016/01/08/blu-ray-struggles-in-the-streaming-age/
16. http://www.businessinsider.com/netflix-lowers-dvd-sales-research-2017-1
17. http://www.postbulletin.com/life/food/holly-ebel-thinking-on-the-back-side-of-the-box/article_5af8e7b8-31d9-51de-9ccb-826a2ea1f084.html
18. Company website, www.armandhammer.com, accessed March 14, 2014.
19. Company website, www.jnj.com, accessed March 14, 2014; company website, www.lifescan.com, accessed March 14, 2014; company website, www.depuy.com, accessed March 14, 2014.
20. Company website, www.geox.com, accessed March 14, 2014; "Geox Sees EMEA, Americas Stabilizing in 2014, Growing in 2015," *Reuters*, accessed March 14, 2014, www.reuters.com.

21. http://www.restaurantnews.com/cheesecake-factory-is-consumers-favorite-casual-dining-restaurant-market-force-study-finds/

22. Organization website, "ISO 9001:2008," www.iso.org, accessed March 14, 2014; organization website, www.nist.gov, March 14, 2014.

23. Barry Glassman, What Zappos Taught Us about Creating the Ultimate Client Experience," *Forbes*, accessed March 14, 2014, www.forbes.com.

24. Zack Whittaker, "Amazon Web Services Suffers Outage, Takes Down Vine, Instagram, Others with It," *ZDNet*, accessed March 14, 2014, www.zdnet.com.

25. https://www.fastcompany.com/3006371/tech-forecast/how-two-tech-companies-are-making-cheesecake-factory-better-customer-experience

## CHAPTER 13

1. Company website. https://www.washingtonpost.com/news/to-your-health/wp/2015/01/20/we-eat-100-acres-of-pizza-a-day-in-the-u-s/?utm_term=.5b527e93541a. Accessed April 5, 2017.

2. Company website. http://www.pmq.com/December-2015/The-2016-Pizza-Power-Report-A-state-of-the-industry-analysis/. Accessed April 5, 2017.

3. Company website. https://www.wired.com/2017/02/verizons-unlimited-data-plan-back-heres-compares-carriers/. Accessed April 4, 2017.

4. Company website. http://www.pcmag.com/article/345123/fastest-mobile-networks-2016/34. Accessed April 14, 2017.

5. Company website. http://www.pcmag.com/article/345123/fastest-mobile-networks-2016/34. Accessed April 14, 2017.

6. Company website. http://www.businessinsider.com/taco-bells-dollar-menu-strategy-2017-1. Accessed April 4, 2017.

7. Company website, "Who We Are," www.caldrea.com, accessed April 5, 2014; company website, "Our Story," www.mrsmeyers.com, accessed April 5, 2014; Michael Burke, "SCJ to Bring Caldrea Operations to Racine," *Journal Times*, accessed April 5, 2014, http://journaltimes.com; "Mrs. Meyers Clean Day," Bubblews, accessed April 5, 2014, www.bubblews.com.

8. Company website. https://corporate.ford.com/content/dam/corporate/en/investors/investor-events/Sales%20Calls/2017/March-Sales-2017.pdf. Accessed April 4, 2017.

9. Trefis Team, "P&G Speeds Up Price Cuts to Munch More Market Share," *Forbes*, accessed March 25, 2014, www.forbes.com.

10. Company website, www.traderjoes.com, accessed October 28, 2014.

11. Company website. http://www.pmq.com/December-2015/The-2016-Pizza-Power-Report-A-state-of-the-industry-analysis/. Accessed 4-6-17.

## CHAPTER 14

1. http://files.shareholder.com/downloads/DOLLAR/4276667855x0x937247/EDA4C123-7935-41B9-A0BF-7F9CB28BD800/Dollar_General_2016_Annual_Report.pdf

2. http://smallbusiness.com/product-development/best-u-s-cities-to-test-market-a-national-product/

3. http://blog.ecornell.com/price-positioning-strategies/

4. Sebastian Blanco, "2014 Nissan Leaf Price Climbs $180 to $28,980, Ghosn Predicts Sales Doubling," *Green Auto Blog*, accessed April 24, 2014, http://green.autoblog.com; Mark Rogowsky, "Will Chevy's $5,000 Price Cut Charge Up Volt Sales?" *Forbes*, accessed April 24, 2014, www.forbes.com; Jason Mick, "As Sales Level in the U.S., Tesla Model S Charges Ahead in Europe, China," *Daily Tech*, accessed April 24, 2014, www.dailytech.com; Luke Sargeant, "Tesla Motors to Reduce Tags over the Next 3 Years," *Liberty Voice*, accessed April 24, 2014, http://guardianlv.com.

5. Saritha Rai, "Its 'World's Cheapest Car Tag' Made the Nano Undesirable in India," *Forbes*, accessed October 30, 2014, www.forbes.com; Kirk Seaman, "The 10 Cheapest New Cars Sold in America for 2014," *Car and Driver*, accessed October 30, 2014, http://blog.caranddriver.com.

6. Brad Tuttle, "Attention JC Penney Shoppers, Look Out for the Return of Sales Galore," *Time*, April 16, 2013.

7. Catherine Rampell, "Turkey Economics, Annotated," *The New York Times*, accessed April 15, 2014, http://economix.blogs.nytimes.com.

8. http://www.caltech.edu/news/wine-study-shows-price-influences-perception-1374

9. http://danariely.com/2009/08/10/the-nuances-of-the-free-experiment/

10. https://www.law360.com/articles/648562/clorox-can-t-ice-retailer-s-price-discrimination-suit

11. Neal Karlinsky and Bonnie McLean, "StubHub, Revolutionizing the Modern-Day Ticket Scalper," *ABC News*, accessed March 27, 2014, http://abcnews.go.com.

## CHAPTER 15

1. https://www.ascotchang.com/en/home, accessed April 14, 2017.

2. http://www.williamfioravanti.com/, accessed April 14, 2017

3. http://www.pginvestor.com/PG-at-a-Glance/Index?KeyGenPage=1073748355, accessed April 10, 2017

4. http://www.unifiedgrocers.com/EN/ProductUniverse/UnifiedBrands/Pages/Unified%20Brands.aspx, accessed April 10, 2017

5. www.keenfootwear.com/americanbuilt, accessed April 11, 2017

6. http://www.nasdaq.com/article/pier-1-imports-inc-q4-earnings-advance-49-20170412-01063, accessed April 12, 2017

7. http://www.star-telegram.com/news/business/article144269469.html, accessed April 12, 2017

8. http://lenkabar.com, accessed April 13, 2017

9. https://about.usps.com/who-we-are/leadership/officers/sup-mgt-vp.htm, accessed April 14, 2017

10. http://www.trucking.org/article/ATA-Releases-2016-Edition-of-American-Trucking-Trends, accessed April 18, 2017

11. U.S. Department of Transportation, Office of Pipeline Safety, "Pipeline Basics," PHMSA Stakeholder Communications, http://primis.phmsa.dot.gov, accessed March 26, 2014.

12. https://www.wsj.com/articles/u-s-postal-service-loss-widens-as-higher-costs-offset-revenue-growth-1479234087, accessed April 14, 2017

## CHAPTER 16

1. Nicholas Rossolillo, "What We Learned From the 2016 Retail Sales Number," *The Motley Fool*, accessed April 5, 2017, www.fool.com; National Retail Federation, "Retail's Impact," accessed April 5, 2017, www.nrf.com.

2. National Retail Federation, "Retail's Impact," accessed April 5, 2017, www.nrf.com.

3. Madeline Farber, "Consumers Are Now Doing Most of Their Shopping Online," *Fortune*, accessed April 10, 2017, www.fortune.com.

4. Arthur Zaczkiewicz, "Amazon, Wal-Mart Lead Top 25 E-commerce Retail List," *Women's Wear Daily*, accessed April 10, 2017, www.wwd.com.

5. Matt McGee, "Walmart reports 29% growth in US e-commerce," *Marketing Land*, accessed April 10, 2017, www.marketingland.com; Krystina Gustafson, "Wal-Mart reiterates guidance, plans to slow store openings to invest in digital," CNBC, accessed April 10, 2017, www.cnbc.com.

6. Company website, "2016 Annual Report," accessed April 12, 2017, www.irtractorsupply.com.

7. Kathryn Dill, "Grass Appeal," *Forbes*, print April 2016.

8. Dan Alaimo, "Tractor Supply revamps e-commerce platform," *FierceRetail*, accessed April 12, 2017, www.fierceretail.com.

9. Madeline Farber, "Consumers Are Now Doing Most of Their Shopping Online," *Fortune*, accessed April 12, 2017, www.fortune.com.

10. Kim Shasin, "Can America's Biggest Beauty Retailer Take On Sephora?" *Bloomberg*, accessed April 10, 2017, www.bloomberg.com.

11. Walter Loeb, "Ulta Beauty: Macy's and Sephora Better Watch Out For This Fast-Growing Beauty Retailer," *Forbes*, accessed April 10, 2017, www.forbes.com; Abigail Stevenson, "Ulta Beauty CEO wants to double market share," *CNBC*, accessed April 10, 2017, www.cnbc.com.

12. Phil Wahba, "How Ulta and Mary Dillon Are Winning the Beauty Battle," *Fortune*, accessed April 5, 2017, www.fortune.com.

13. Jennifer Braunschweiger, "Lessons In Beauty," *Fast Company*, print April 2017.

14. Ulta Beauty, Form 10-K, accessed April 6, 2017, ir.ulta.com.

15. David P. Schulz, "Hot 100 Retailers 2016," *National Retail Federation*, accessed April 10, 2017, www.nrf.com.

16. Company website, 2016 Quarterly Results, accessed April 10, 2017, ir.ulta.com.

17. Tim Feran, "Demise of hhgregg offers rivals market share, maybe new locations," *The Columbus Dispatch*, accessed April 13, 2017, www.dispatch.com.

18. Walter Loeb, "Best Buy Focuses On Shop-In-Shop Sales And makes Changes For Growth," *Forbes*, accessed April 13, 2017, www.forbes.com.

19. Jeffrey Van Camp, "Best Buy To Close 50 Stores, Open 100 Mobile-Only Stores," *Digital Trends*, accessed April 15, 2017, www.digitaltrends.com.

20. Company website, "Renew Blue: Best Buy Analyst and Investor Day," accessed April 16, 2017, www.corporate.bestbuy.com/wp-content/uploads/bestbuy_web_final.pdf.

21. Ibid.

22. Mike Snider, "Best Buy shares surge on Q3 earnings, revenue," *USA Today*, accessed April 16, 2017, www.usatoday.com.

23. Company website, accessed March 26, 2014, www.gloriajeans.com.

24. Ginger Conlon, "2016 Will Be a Growth Year in Marketing Spending," *Direct Marketing News*, accessed April 24, 2017, www.dmnews.com; "Statistical Fact Book 2016," *Data & Marketing Association*, accessed April 24, 2017, www.thedma.org.

25. "Vending Machine Operators in the U.S.: Market Research Report," IBIS World, accessed March 26, 2014, www.ibisworld.com.

26. Kate Taylor, "High-Tech Vending Machines That Serve Healthy Snacks See Rapid Growth," Entrepreneur, accessed March 26, 2014, www.entrepreneur.com.

27. Adam Lashinsky, "How Dollar Shave Club got started," *Fortune*, accessed April 16, 2017, www.fortune.com.

28. Adam Lashinsky, "How Dollar Shave Club got started," *Fortune*, accessed April 16, 2017, www.fortune.com; Mike Isaac and Michael J. de la Merced, "Dollar Shave Club Sells to Unilever for $1 Billion," *The New York Times*, accessed April 16, 2017, www.nytimes.com.

## CHAPTER 17

1. Ana Livia Coelho, "ESPN's X Games Announces Sponsors for X Games Aspen 2014," press release, *ESPN Media Zone*, accessed April 2, 2014, http://espnmediazone.com.

2. https://www.emarketer.com/Report/US-Ad-Spending-eMarketer-Forecast-2017/2001998

3. https://www.emarketer.com/Article/US-Digital-Ad-Spending-Surpass-TV-this-Year/1014469

4. Brad Slager, "'Lego Movie's Success Portends New Product Placement Possibilities," *Breitbart.com*, accessed March 22, 2014, www.breitbart.com.

5. http://www.mercurynews.com/2016/12/08/los-angeles-county-to-sell-naming-rights-for-rail-lines-train-stations/

6. http://neworleanscitypark.com/celebration-in-the-oaks/sponsors

7. https://www.bls.gov/oes/current/oes410000.htm

8. Gerhard Gschwandtner, "How Many Salespeople Will Be Left by 2020?" *Selling Power*, accessed October 23, 2014, www.sellingpower.com; Paul Davidson, "Bosses Lament: Sales Jobs Hard to Fill," *USA Today*, accessed March 19, 2014, www.usatoday.com.

9. http://college.usatoday.com/2014/01/15/20-campus-rep-programs-that-are-available-right-now/

10. "Case Study: Real Beauty Shines Through: Dove Wins Titanium Grand Prix, 163 Million Views on YouTube," *Think newsletter*, accessed October 23, 2014, www.thinkwithgoogle.com; "How Dove's 'Real Beauty Sketches' Becomes the Most Viral Video Ad of All Time," *Business Insider*, accessed March 19, 2014, www.businessinsider.com.

11. Aaron Perlut, "Allstate Bringing Mayhem to Twitter," *Forbes*, accessed March 19, 2014, www.forbes.com.

12. http://www.campaignlive.com/article/last-years-super-bowl-advertisers-tried-hard-funny-failed-study-says/1420644

13. Ben Leibowitz, "LeBron James, Kobe Bryant Top Forbes' List of 2013 NBA Endorsement Deal Earners," *Bleacher Report*, accessed March 27, 2014, http://bleacherreport.com; Sean Highkin, "Magic Johnson Thinks LeBron Doesn't Have Enough Endorsements," *USA Today*, accessed March 27, 2014, www.usatoday.com.

14. https://www.theatlantic.com/entertainment/archive/2016/11/election-celebrities-trump-clinton-endorsements-beyonce-springsteen-david-jackson-bowling-green/507383/

15. https://morningconsult.com/2016/01/25/whats-up-with-those-wireless-attack-ads/

16. https://www.mediapost.com/publications/article/290281/agencies-forecast-moderate-ad-growth-digital-to-s.html

17. https://xappmedia.com/edison-research-internet-radio-weekly-listeners-half-us-population/

18. https://www.statista.com/statistics/272411/newspaper-advertising-spending-in-the-us/
19. http://www.journalism.org/2016/06/15/state-of-the-news-media-2016/feed/plain/
20. https://mrmagazine.wordpress.com/2017/01/09/aarp-the-magazine-relevant-vibrant-still-the-largest-circulation-magazine-in-the-country-with-more-than-23-million-readers-the-mr-magazine-interview-with-shelagh-daly-mille/
21. http://www.dmnews.com/marketing-strategy/2016-will-be-a-growth-year-in-marketing-spending/article/469545/
22. https://www.statista.com/statistics/272415/outdoor-advertising-spending-in-the-us/
23. https://www.statista.com/statistics/266249/advertising-revenue-of-google/
24. http://www.journalism.org/2016/06/15/digital-news-revenue-fact-sheet/
25. Katherine Rosman, "Augmented Reality Finally Starts to Gain Traction," *The Wall Street Journal*, accessed March 31, 2014, http://online.wsj.com.

26. http://www.finn.be/blogs/should-your-ceo-be-face-your-company-and-if-so-how-when-and-why
27. http://www.alistdaily.com/strategy/augmented-reality-shifts-car-marketing-new-gears/
28. http://ftw.usatoday.com/2016/02/how-much-does-super-bowl-ad-cost

## CHAPTER 18

1. U.S. Bureau of Labor Statistics, Employment by Detailed Occupation, https://www.bls.gov/oes/current/oes410000.htm. Accessed May 7, 2017.
2. U.S. Bureau of Labor Statistics, Occupational Outlook Handbook, accessed April 25, 2017. https://www.bls.gov/ooh/sales/home.htm.
3. Company Website. http://beta.fortune.com/worlds-most-admired-companies. Accessed April 25, 2017.
4. Company website. http://invest.grainger.com/phoenix.zhtml?c=76754&p=i-rol-irfactbook. Accessed April 25, 2017.

5. Company website. http://invest.grainger.com/phoenix.zhtml?c=76754&p=irol-irfactbook. Accessed April 25, 2017.
6. "How to Eliminate Annoying Robocalls," Consumer Reports, accessed March 31, 2014, www.consumerreports.com.
7. Lesley Fair, "Ringing in the New Year," Bureau of Consumer Protection, Business Center Blog, accessed March 31, 2014, http://business.ftc.gov.
8. Company website. https://jobs.grainger.com/job/De-Pere-Inside-Sales-Account-Advisor-WI-54115/390170700/. Accessed April 25, 2017.
9. U.S. Bureau of Labor Statistics, "Sales Managers," Occupational Employment and Wages, May 2016, accessed May 6, 2017, www.bls.gov.
10. Company website. http://www.foodbusinessnews.net/articles/news_home/Business_News/2016/06/Hormel_continues_to_innovate_a.aspx?ID=%7B70411471-539F-49EB-A4B2-BAA66oDC7B8C%7D&cck=1. Accessed April 26, 2017.

# GLOSSARY

## A

**accessory equipment** products such as power tools, computers, and office furniture that typically cost less and last for shorter periods than installations

**adoption process** a series of stages from first learning about the new product to trying it and deciding whether to purchase.

**advertising campaign** a series of different but related ads that use a single theme and appear in different media within a specified time period

**advertising** paid, nonpersonal communication through various mass media channels

**AIDA concept** the steps consumers take in reaching a purchase decision

**antitrust** laws help maintain a competitive business environment by preventing the concentration of industry power in the hands of a small number of competitors

**approach** the initial contact with the prospective customer

**atmospherics** the physical characteristics and amenities that attract customers and satisfy their shopping needs

**attitudes** a person's enduring favorable or unfavorable evaluations, emotions, or tendencies toward some object or idea

## B

**behavior segmentation** groups individuals who exhibit similar behaviors, such as benefits sought, usage rates, and level of brand loyalty

**benchmarking** a method of measuring quality by comparing performance against industry standards

**big data** the data that originates in unprecedented volume and at unprecedented speed from the world around us

**blogs** sites that regularly post articles and other content

**bookmarking sites** gives users a place to save, organize, and manage links to websites and other resources on the Internet

**Boston consulting group (BCG) matrix** a portfolio analysis framework that enables managers to plot the relative position of each business unit, brand, or product on the basis of industry growth rate and relative market share

**brand** a name, term, sign, symbol, design, or some combination that identifies the products of one firm while differentiating these products from competitors

**brand equity** the added value the brand gives to a product in the marketplace

**brand extension** implies attaching a popular brand name to a new product in an unrelated product category

**brand insistence** when consumers refuse alternatives and search extensively for the desired product

**brand manager (product manager)** marketer responsible for a single brand or product

**brand mark** is a symbol or pictorial design that distinguishes a product

**brand name** the part of a brand that can be spoken and distinguishes a firm's offerings from those of its competitors

**brand preference** when buyers choose a product over a competitor based on experience

**brand recognition** consumer awareness and identification of a brand

**breakeven analysis** the method for determining the amount of product that must be sold at a given price to generate sufficient revenue to cover total costs—both fixed and variable

**business-to-business (B2B)** transactions that happen between organizations

**business-to-consumer (B2C)** business conducted directly between a business and a consumer

**business products** products purchased for use either directly or indirectly in the production of other goods and services for resale

**business services** intangible products firms buy to facilitate their production and operations

**buyers** people who have the formal authority to select a supplier and begin securing the good or service

**buyer's market** when there are more products than people willing to buy them

**buying center** encompasses everyone involved in any aspect of a company's buying activity

## C

**category management** product management system in which a manager oversees a number of product lines and brands within a single category

**cause marketing** identification and marketing of a social issue, cause, or idea to selected target markets

**channel** the medium for delivering a message, such as a salesperson, a PR outlet, a website, or an advertising medium

**channel conflicts** conflicts between producers, wholesalers, and retailers

**click-through rate (CTR)** the percentage of users who click on an ad

**closing** the point at which the salesperson asks the prospect for an order

**commercialization** when a new product idea is ready for full-scale manufacturing and marketing

**commercial market** individuals and firms that acquire products to support, directly or indirectly, production of other goods and services

**commission** a payment tied directly to the sales or profits a salesperson achieves

**comparative advertising** an approach that emphasizes advertising messages with direct or indirect comparisons to dominant brands in the industry

**competition objectives** pricing practices intended to maintain pricing parity or emphasize overall product value to avoid direct price comparison

**competitive environment** where marketers of directly competitive products and marketers of substitute products compete for consumer purchases

**competitive pricing** pricing strategy designed to reduce emphasis on price as a competitive variable by matching competitors' prices and focusing on other ways to differentiate products

**competitive strategy** an effective strategy for dealing with the competitive environment

**component parts and materials** finished business products of one producer that become part of the final products of another producer

**concentrated marketing (niche marketing)** selecting a single market segment and concentrating efforts on profitably satisfying that segment

**consumer-oriented sales promotions** encourage repurchases by rewarding current users, boosting sales of complementary products, and increasing impulse purchases

**consumer behavior** the process through which the ultimate buyer or household consumer makes purchase decisions

**consumerism** a social force within the environment that aids and protects the consumer by exerting legal, moral, and economic pressures on business and government

**consumer orientation** where the focus is on satisfying the needs and wants of consumers rather than simply producing and selling products

**consumer products** products bought by ultimate consumers for personal use

**containerization** the process of combining several unitized loads into a single, well-protected load

**content marketing** creating and distributing relevant and targeted material to attract and engage an audience, with the goal of driving them to a desired action

**contests** when entrants must complete a specific task to be eligible to win a prize

**convenience products** goods and services consumers want to purchase frequently, immediately, and with minimal effort

**convenience retailers** stores that appeal to customers by having accessible locations, extended store hours, rapid checkout service, and adequate parking

**conversion cost** the total cost of each sale

**conversion rate** the percentage of visitors to a website who make a purchase

**cost-based pricing** using the product cost plus a target markup percentage to calculate the sales price

**cost-volume-profit (CVP)** the relationship between prices, demand, and overall profitability

**coupons** when consumer is offered discounts on the purchase price of goods and services at retail outlets

**cross-promotion** when marketing partners share the cost of a promotional campaign that meets their mutual needs

**culture** the values, beliefs, preferences, and tastes handed down from one generation to the next

**customer-based segmentation** grouping customers by type or industry

## D

**data mining** a technique in which a user employs special software to search through computerized data files to detect patterns

**deciders** people who actually select a good or service

**decline stage** final stage of the product lifecycle, in which innovations or shifts in consumer preferences bring about a steady decline in industry sales

**decoding** the receiver's interpretation of the message

**Delphi technique** qualitative forecasting method that gathers several rounds of feedback from experts inside and outside the firm

**demand** the amounts of a product that consumers will purchase at different prices during a specified time period

**demographic segmentation** defines consumer groups according to demographic variables such as gender, age, ethnic group, family life cycle stage and household type, and income

**demonstration** when the buyer has the opportunity to try out or otherwise see how a product works before purchasing

**department store** a series of specialty stores under one roof

**differentiated marketing** targeting several different market segments using a different marketing mix for each segment

**diffusion process** the process by which new products are accepted into the marketplace

**digital marketing** the process of marketing goods and services over the Internet by utilizing digital tools

**direct channel** carries goods directly from a producer to the ultimate user

**direct marketing** the use of direct communications to generate a response in the form of an order, a request for further communication, or a visit to a place of business

**direct selling** a marketing tactic in which a producer establishes direct sales contact with its product's final users

**discretionary income** the amount of money people have to spend after buying necessities such as food, clothing, and housing

**distribution channels** the individuals and organizations who manage the flow of product from producers to consumers

**distribution** decision involving modes of transportation, warehousing, inventory control, order processing, and selection of marketing channels

**distribution intensity** the number or percentage of intermediaries (usually retailers) through which a manufacturer distributes its goods in a particular market

**downstream management** the management of finished product storage, outbound logistics, marketing and sales, and customer service

**dual distribution** the movement of products through two or more channels to reach the firm's target market

## E

**e-business** using the Internet to provide services to customers and communicate with employees and business partners

**e-commerce** the buying and selling of products online

**early adopters** people who are quick to purchase the latest product once it is somewhat established

**economic environment** consists of factors that influence consumer buying power and marketing strategies

**elasticity** the measure of the responsiveness of purchasers and suppliers to price changes

**elasticity of demand** the percentage change in the quantity of a product demanded divided by the percentage change in its price

**encoding** translating a message into understandable terms and transmitting it through a communications channel

**encryption** the process of encoding data for security purposes

**end-use application** segmenting the business market based on the ultimate way in which a buyer uses a product

**engagement** how much time users spend on the site and which pages they visit

**enterprise resource planning (ERP) system** an integrated software package that consolidates data from among the firm's units

**environmental factors** economic, political, regulatory, competitive, and technological considerations

**European Union (EU)** 28 countries make up the EU, which works to remove trade restrictions, permit the free flow of goods and workers throughout member nations, and promote human rights

**event marketing** marketing of sporting, cultural, and charitable activities to selected target markets

**evoked set** the collection of alternatives a consumer considers when making a decision

**exchange rate** the price of one nation's currency in terms of another country's currency

**exclusive distribution** when a producer sells to only a small number of retailers or grants exclusive rights to a wholesaler or retailer to sell its products in a specific geographic region

**exploratory research** seeks to discover the cause of a specific problem by discussing the problem with informed sources both inside and outside the firm, and by examining data from other information sources

**exporting** the marketing of domestically produced goods and services abroad

**extended problem solving** the most complex decision style and occurs for high-involvement products where financial and/or social risk is high

**extranets** secure networks used for e-business and accessible through the firm's website by external customers, suppliers, or other authorized users

## F

**feedback** the receiver's response to a message

**field selling** sales calls made at the prospective customer's location on a face-to-face basis

**fixed costs** costs that remain stable at any production level within a certain range

**focus group** a small group of individuals in one location to discuss a subject of interest

**foreign licensing** grants foreign marketers the right to distribute a firm's merchandise or to use its trademark, patent, or process in a specified geographic area

**franchise** is a contractual arrangement where the franchisee agrees to meet the operating requirements of a manufacturer or a franchiser

**free-trade area** where participating nations agree to the free trade of goods among themselves, abolishing tariffs and trade restrictions

## G

**gatekeepers** people who control the information that all buying center members ultimately review

**general merchandise retailers** stores that carry a wide variety of product lines stocked in some depth and distinguish themselves from specialty retailers by the large number of product lines they carry

**generic products** products sold without any efforts at branding

**geographic segmentation** dividing an overall market into homogeneous groups based on their locations

**goods** tangible products that customers can see, hear, smell, taste, and/or touch

**gross domestic product (GDP)** the sum of all goods and services produced by a nation in a year

**growth stage** second stage of the product lifecycle that begins when a firm starts to realize substantial profits from its investment

**guerrilla marketing** using unconventional, innovative, and low-cost techniques to attract consumers' attention

## H

**horizontal conflict** disagreements among channel members at the same level, such as two or more wholesalers or retailers

**hypothesis** a testable statement about the relationship among variables

## I

**importing** the purchasing of foreign goods and services

**impulse goods and services** products purchased on the spur of the moment

**inbound telemarketing** sales method in which prospects call a seller to obtain information, make reservations, or purchase products

**inflation** rising prices caused by some combination of excess demand and the increasing cost of raw materials, labor, and/or other factors of production

**influencers** people who affect the buying decision by supplying information to guide the evaluation of alternatives, or by establishing buying specifications

**infrastructure** the underlying foundation for modern life that includes transportation, communications, banking, utilities, and public services

**innovators** people who are first to make trial purchases

**inside selling** the process of inbound sales management utilizing phone, mail, and the Internet

**installations** major capital investments in the B2B market

**integrated marketing communications (IMC)** the coordination of all promotional activities to produce a unified, customer-focused promotional message

**intensive distribution** seeks to distribute a product through all available retailers in a trade area

**interactive marketing** delivering more relevant marketing messages to customers based on event triggers

**intermodal operations** utilizing a combination of transport modes to improve customer service and achieve cost advantages

**international direct investment** financial investment in foreign firms or facilities

**interpretive research** a method in which a researcher observes a customer or group of customers in their natural setting and interprets their behavior based on an understanding of the social and cultural characteristics of that setting

**intranets** secure internal networks that help companies share information among employees, no matter the number or location

**introductory stage** first stage of the product lifecycle, in which a firm works to stimulate sales of a new product

**involvement** the degree of interest an individual has in the product, as well as how important that product is to them

## J

**joint ventures** when companies share the risks, costs, and management of the foreign operation with one or more partners

**jury of executive opinion** qualitative forecasting method that assesses the sales expectations of various executives

## L

**label** a branding component that carries an item's brand name or symbol, the name and address of the manufacturer or distributor, information about the product's composition and size, and recommended uses

**learning** immediate or expected changes in consumer behavior as a result of experience

**limited problem solving** behavior that occurs for purchases that consumers make less frequently and when their knowledge or experience is limited

**line extension** the development and implementation of new sizes, styles, or related product offerings

**loss leaders** pricing tactic where goods are priced below cost to attract customers to stores in hopes they will buy other merchandise at regular prices

## M

**manufacturer brands** a brand name owned by a manufacturer or other producer

**margin** the portion of sales revenue left over after paying product costs

**market** a group of people with sufficient purchasing power, authority, and willingness to buy

**market density** the number of residents within a specific geographic area, such as a square mile

**market development strategy** concentrates on finding new markets for existing products

**marketing** is the process for creating, communicating, and delivering value to customers

**marketing ethics** the marketer's standards of conduct and values

**marketing intermediary** an organization that operates between producers and consumers to help bring the product to market

**marketing mix** product, price, distribution, and promotion

**marketing plan** a written plan that outlines the strategic marketing goals of an organization

**marketing planning** the process devoted specifically to achieving marketing objectives

**marketing research** the process of collecting and using information for marketing and decision making

**market penetration strategy** seeks to increase sales of existing products in existing markets

**market segmentation** the division of the total market into smaller, relatively homogeneous groups

**market size** the number of individuals residing in a particular geographic market area

**markup** the cost multiplied by one plus the target markup percentage

**maturity stage** third stage of product lifecycle, in which industry sales reach a plateau

**media selection** choosing a form of media for advertising

**message** a communication of information

**mobile marketing** marketing messages sent to wireless devices, such as phones and tablets

**motives** inner states that direct a person toward the goal of satisfying a need

## N

**need** is an imbalance between the consumer's actual and desired states

**noise** forms of interference with the transmission of a message that reduce its effectiveness

**North American Free Trade Agreement (NAFTA)** an agreement between the United States, Canada, and Mexico that removes trade restrictions among the three nations

## O

**objections** expressions of resistance by the prospect

**operational planning** where managers develop specific programs to meet goals in their area of responsibility

**opinion leaders** are trendsetters who purchase new products before others in a group, and then influence others in their purchases

**organization marketing** marketing efforts of mutual-benefit organizations, service organizations, and government organizations that seek to influence others to accept their goals, receive their services, or contribute to them in some way

**outbound telemarketing** sales method in which sales personnel contact potential buyers by phone

**over-the-counter selling** selling in retail or wholesale locations in which customers come to the seller's place of business

## P

**penetration pricing strategy** setting a lower price than competitive offerings in order to stimulate demand and market acceptance

**perception** the meaning a person attributes to incoming stimuli gathered through the five senses—sight, hearing, touch, taste, and smell

**personal selling** person-to-person promotional presentation to a buyer

**person marketing** efforts designed to cultivate the attention and preference of a target market toward a person

**phishing** a high-tech scam that uses e-mail or pop-up messages that claim to be from familiar businesses or even government agencies

**place marketing** efforts designed to attract visitors to a particular area; improve consumer images of a city, state, or nation; and/or attract new business

**planned shopping centers** a group of retail stores designed, coordinated, and marketed to shoppers in a geographic trade area

**planning** the overall process of anticipating conditions and determining the best way to achieve organizational objectives

**point-of-purchase advertising** display or other promotion placed near the site of the actual buying decision

**political-legal environment** the component of the marketing environment consisting of laws and regulations to maintain competitive conditions and protect consumer rights

**political risk assessment (PRA)** when a company or business unit evaluates the political risks of the marketplaces in which they operate

**Porter's five forces** five competitive forces that influence planning strategies

**positioning** seeks to put a product in a certain position, or place, in the minds of prospective buyers

**positioning map** a graphical illustration of consumers' perceptions of competing products within an industry

**precall planning** the process of conducting research and gathering information before a sales call

**predictive analytics** the use of marketing intelligence data and model scenarios to create forecasts

**presentation** describing a product's benefits and relating them to the customer's problems or needs

**prestige pricing** establishing a relatively high price to develop and maintain an image of quality and exclusiveness

**price discrimination** when a supplier offers the same product to two buyers at two different prices

**price** the amount of funds required to purchase a product

**price strategy** is the method of setting profitable and justifiable prices

**primary data** information collected for the first time specifically for a marketing research study

**primary demand** seeks to build demand for a product category, not for a particular brand within that category

**private brands** brands offered by wholesalers and retailers

**private exchange** a secure website where a company and its suppliers share all types of data, from product design through order delivery

**product-line pricing** pricing tactic where the firm sets a limited number of prices for a selection of merchandise

**product development** the introduction of new products into established markets

**product diversification strategy** focuses on developing entirely new products for new markets

**production orientation** manufacturers stressed production of quality products and then looked for people to purchase them

**product lifecycle** the progression of a product through four basic stages: introduction, growth, maturity, and decline

**product line** a group of related products sold under the same brand

**product line depth** the number of variations in each product line

**product marketing** involves efforts designed to communicate the benefits of a good or service

**product mix** an assortment of product lines and individual product offerings

**product mix breadth** the number of different product lines a firm offers

**product** refers to a good, service, or idea

**promotion** is broadly defined as communication to a firm's buyers about their products

**promotional mix** advertising, personal selling, sales promotion, direct marketing, and public relations

**promotional pricing** pricing tactic in which a lower-than-normal price is used as a *temporary* ingredient in a firm's marketing strategy

**prospecting** the process of identifying potential customers

**psychographic segmentation** differentiating population groups according to values and lifestyle factors which are common to the group

**psychological factors** are factors internal to the individual

**psychological pricing** pricing tactic based on the belief that certain prices or price ranges make products more appealing to buyers

**publicity** an aspect of public relations where marketers seek unpaid placement of news about the company or a product in mass media or on social media

**public relations** a firm's communications and relationships with its various stakeholders, including customers, suppliers, stockholders, employees, the government, and the general public

## Q

**qualifying** determining whether the prospect meets certain criteria for making a purchase

**qualitative forecasting** techniques that rely on subjective data that reports opinions rather than using statistical data

**quantitative forecasting** techniques that rely on statistical data, such as past sales or results from small tests

## R

**radio frequency identification (RFID)** a tiny chip with identification information that can be read by a radio frequency scanner from a distance, making tracking easier

**raw materials** natural resources that become part of a final product

**rebates** when the consumer is offered cash back for sending in proof of purchase

**reference groups** people or institutions whose opinions are valued and to whom a person looks for guidance in his or her own behavior, values, and conduct

**relationship marketing** refers to the development, growth, and maintenance of long-term, cost-effective relationships with individual customers, suppliers, employees, and other partners for mutual benefit

**research design** a master plan for conducting marketing research

**resellers** a business market comprised of retailers and wholesalers

**retailing** the activities involved in selling merchandise to consumers

**revenue maximization** website strategies designed to increase the size of each customer transaction and encourage repeat visits by the customer

**reverse channels** channels designed to return goods to their producers

**Robinson-Patman Act** a Depression-era law that prohibits price discrimination when selling the same product in the same amount to two different customers

**routinized response behavior** behavior that occurs for low-involvement products that consumers purchase on a frequent basis

## S

**salary** a fixed payment made periodically to an employee

**sales agent** a third-party person or company who represents the producer to wholesalers and retailers

**sales force composite** qualitative forecasting method based on the combined sales estimates of the firm's salespeople

**sales orientation** a belief that creative advertising and personal selling will persuade consumers to buy

**sales promotion** marketing activities other than personal selling, advertising, and publicity designed to enhance consumer purchasing and dealer effectiveness

**sales quotas** specified sales or profit targets that the firm expects salespeople to achieve

**sampling** free distribution of a product in an attempt to obtain future sales

**secondary data** information from previously published or compiled sources

**selective demand** demand for a specific brand based on attributes important to potential purchasers

**selective distribution** when a firm chooses only a limited number of retailers in a market area to handle its line

**self-concept** a person's view of themselves

**seller's market** when there are more buyers for fewer products

**sender** source of the message communicated to the receiver

**service encounter** the point at which the customer and service provider interact

**service quality** the perceived level of service a customer receives

**services** intangible products

**shopping products** products more expensive than convenience items and ones where the shopper lacks complete information prior to the buying process

**showrooming** when a customer examines and compares products at a store, then buys the product through an online retailer

**situational factors** external factors related to the particular circumstances under which a purchase is made

**skimming pricing strategies** intentionally setting a relatively high price compared with the prices of competing products

**social class** based upon an individual's occupation, education, income, wealth, and possessions

**social-cultural environment** the relationship between marketing, society, and culture

**social factors** external influences such as culture, social class, reference groups, family, and opinion leaders

**social marketing** the use of online social media as a communications channel for marketing messages

**social media** different forms of online communication through which users can create communities to exchange information, ideas, messages, and other content

**social media marketing (SMM)** is developing a conversation with current and potential customers on social media platforms

**social media platforms** the home base for an online community

**social networking sites** websites or apps that provide virtual communities for people to share daily activities, send messages, post opinions, increase their circle of online friends, and more

**social responsibility** accepting an obligation to give equal weight to profits, consumer satisfaction, and social well-being in evaluating a firm's performance

**span of control** the number of sales representatives who report to first-level sales managers

**specialty advertising** when an advertiser's message or logo is placed on useful articles that are distributed to target consumers

**specialty products** higher-end products offering unique characteristics that compel buyers to purchase particular brands

**specialty retailers** stores that combine carefully defined product lines, services, and reputations in attempts to persuade consumers to expend considerable effort to shop at their stores

**staples** convenience products that consumers frequently purchase to maintain a ready inventory

**strategic business units (SBUs)** key business units within diversified firms

**strategic planning** the process of determining an organization's long-term primary objectives and adopting courses of action that will achieve these objectives

**subcontracting** when the production of goods or services is assigned to local companies

**subcultures** are groups with their own distinct modes of behavior

**supermarkets** stores that sell mainly groceries, but also a wide selection of items in other categories

**supplies** the regular products a firm uses in daily operations

**supply** the amounts of a product that will be offered for sale at different prices during a specified period

**supply chain** the complete sequence of suppliers and activities that contribute to the creation and delivery of goods and services

**survey of buyer intentions** qualitative forecasting method that samples opinions among groups of current and potential customers concerning purchasing plans

**sweepstakes** when any consumer can enter to be eligible for a prize

**SWOT analysis** an important strategic planning tool that helps managers analyze the internal and external environment to assess strengths, weaknesses, opportunities, and threats

## T

**tactical planning** defines how activities specified in the strategic plan will be implemented

**target market** the segment of consumers most likely to purchase a particular item

**tariffs** taxes levied against imported goods

**technological environment** the application of knowledge based on discoveries in science, inventions, and innovations

**telemarketing** when the selling process is conducted by phone

**test marketing** a marketing research technique that involves introducing a new product in a specific geographic area and then observing its degree of success

**trade allowances** financial incentives offered to wholesalers and retailers that purchase or promote specific products

**trade dress** the visual cues used in branding that create an overall look differentiating a brand or product from competitors

**trademark** a brand for which the owner claims exclusive legal protection

**trade promotion** sales promotion that appeals to distribution intermediaries rather than final consumers

**trade shows** product exhibitions organized by industry trade associations to showcase goods and services

**transaction-based marketing** traditional view of marketing as a simple exchange process

**trend analysis** quantitative forecasting method that estimates future sales through statistical analysis of historical sales patterns

## U

**undifferentiated marketing (mass marketing)** when all customers are targeted using a single marketing mix

**unemployment** the proportion of people in the economy who are actively seeking work but do not have jobs

**unfair-trade laws** laws which require sellers to maintain minimum prices for comparable merchandise

**unique visitors** the number of individuals who visit a website

**unitizing** or palletizing, combining as many packages as possible into each load that moves within or outside a facility

**upstream management** the management of raw materials, inbound logistics, and warehouse and storage facilities

**user experience (UX)** the overall experience customers have when visiting a website

**users** people who actually use a good or service

**utility** the power of a good or service to satisfy the wants of consumers

## V

**value proposition** an explanation of how consumers will benefit from the product and why the company is uniquely qualified to provide those benefits

**variable costs** costs that change with the level of production

**vertical conflict** disagreements among channel members at different levels

**vertical integration** when a producer assumes control over functions that were previously handled by an intermediary

**volume or sales objectives** pricing practices aimed at achieving a particular sales volume or market share

## W

**wholesalers** marketing intermediary who takes title to the goods, stores them in warehouses, and distributes them to retailers, other distributors, and sometimes end consumers

**World Trade Organization (WTO)** a 164-member organization that oversees trade agreements among its members, serves as a forum for trade negotiations, mediates trade disputes, monitors national trade policies, and works to reduce trade barriers throughout the world

# NAME & COMPANY INDEX

# SUBJECT INDEX

## A

accessory equipment, **224**
accounts receivable turnover, **B-5**
adoption process, **249**, 251–252
adoption/rejection stage, 249
advertising, **354**. *See also* marketing; strategy
  billboards, 369
  celebrity sponsorship, 354, 364–365
  celebrity testimonials, 364–365
  clutter, 364
  comparative, **365**
  digital media, 369–370
  direct mail, 368
  fear-based appeals, 363–364
  humorous appeals, 363
  magazines, 368
  media selection, **366**–370
  message, **357**
  mobile, 370
  newspapers, 368
  outdoor, 369
  persuasive, **361**
  product lifecycle and, 256
  radio, 367
  retail, 188–189
  sex-based appeals, 364
  soft drink, 373
  specialty, **396**
  sponsorship *vs.*, **355**
  television, 367
  truth in, 59
advertising campaign, **363**
advocates, 12
Africa
  ethnicity, African American, 181
  global trade, 151
  Internet usage, 65, 158
  political conditions, 158
age
  baby boomers, 180
  Children's Online Privacy Protection Act, 48
  empty nesters, 181
  family purchasing, 120

Generation X, 180
  marketing to children, 181
  seniors, 180
  tweens/teens, 180
  underage drinking, 59
AIDA concept, **357**–359, 384–385
air freight, 327
Airline Deregulation Act, 48
Albania, 155
allowances, trade, 397
American Association of Retired Persons (AARP), 50
Anti-cybersquatting Consumer Protection Act, 48
antitrust, **47**
antitrust regulations, 47
approach, **386**
Argentina
  Internet usage, 65
Asia
  acquisitions, firms, 163
  Asian food markets, 244
  Asiatic pennywort, 206
  cultural influences, 118
  ethnicity, Asian Americans, 181
  global trade, 151
  international market research, 205
  international technological environment, 158
  Internet usage, 158
  market development strategy, 244
  marketing planning, 23
  markets, 207
  subcontracting, 162
Asia-Pacific market, 205
atmospherics, **337**
attention, interest, desire, action (AIDA) concept, **357**–359, 384–385
attitude, **123**
  in consumer behavior, 123
  favorable/unfavorable, 123
Austin
  pork products, 378
Australia
  Internet usage, 65

Austria
  energy drink market, 28
  members of the EU, 155
auto industry, penetration pricing, 296–297
awareness stage, of adoption process, **249**

## B

B2B. *See* business-to-business (B2B) marketing
B2C. *See* business-to-consumer (B2C) marketing
baby boomers, 180
balance sheet, **B-1**
Bangladesh
  international competitive environment, 159
  outsourcing threat, 154
BCG matrix. *See* Boston Consulting Group (BCG) matrix
behavior segmentation, **185**–186
Belgium, 155
belongingness needs, 122
benchmarking, **261**
big data, **209**–210
billboards, 369
  micro-, 90–91
blogging forum, **90**–91
blogging site, **90**–91
blogs, **90**–91
board of directors, 23
bookmarking site, **90**
Boston Consulting Group (BCG) matrix, **34**–35
  and SWOT analysis, 36–39
brand(s), **226**. *See also* product identification
  equity, **228**–229
  extension, **233**
  identity, 229–231
  loyalty, 227–228
  manager, **234**
  manufacturer's, **233**
  preferences, 228
  private, **233**